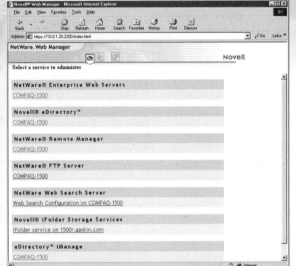

Web Manager

A handy starting point for many NetWare management tasks, Web Manager gathers in one handy place the critical server-specific management tools as well as some eDirectory utilities. Web Server and FTP Server control links are here also. *See Appendix A.*

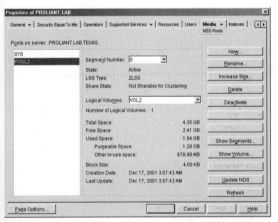

Storage pools

Storage pools add more flexibility and another level of abstraction above the hardware details for NetWare 6 and NSS 3.0. Pools contain volumes and can be stretched by adding open disk space at any time. *See Chapter 14.*

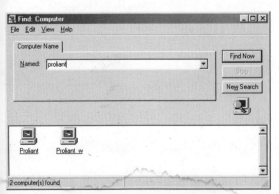

File Access Packs

NetWare 6 eliminates the need for Client32 software in many situations (but Client32 provides more management and security). Have Windows, Macintosh, or Unix clients who need occasional Net-Ware access? File Access Packs turn NetWare storage into universal storage. See Windows find the NetWare ProLiant server and SMB-flavored ProLiant_W (for Windows clients). *See Chapter 13.*

Mastering™
NetWare 6

Mastering™
NetWare® 6

James E. Gaskin

SYBEX® San Francisco London

Associate Publisher: Neil Edde

Acquisitions and Developmental Editor: Heather O'Connor

Editors: Marilyn Smith, Pete Gaughan

Production Editors: Jennifer Campbell, Kelly Winquist

Technical Editor: Robert Abuhoff

Graphic Illustrator: Tony Jonick

Electronic Publishing Specialist: Maureen Forys, Happenstance Type-O-Rama

Proofreaders: Nancy Riddiough, Laurie O'Connell, Dave Nash, Emily Hsuan, Rich Ganis, Yariv Rabinovitch

Indexer: Nancy Guenther

Book Designer: Maureen Forys, Happenstance Type-O-Rama

Cover Designer: Design Site

Cover Illustrator: Sergie Loobkoff

Library of Congress Card Number: 2001096988

ISBN: 0-7821-4023-8

Software License Agreement: Terms and Conditions

As always, this is for Wendy, Alex, and Laura.

Acknowledgments

EVERY BOOK OF THIS SIZE includes a large, unseen, yet valuable team to transform ideas into reality. My name as author may be on the front of the book, but their work behind the scenes made it all possible.

I'd like to thank Heather O'Connor for starting this project with me. The editor, Marilyn Smith, once again provided a light yet experienced touch to maintain consistency and make me appear to be a better writer than I may actually be. She changed no jokes; groaners must be blamed on me, not Marilyn. Jennifer Campbell and Kelly Winquist, production editors, with help from Teresa Trego, kept polite (but firm) pressure to keep the words flowing. Technical editing by Robert Abuhoff served as a strong safety net for catching missteps and technical details.

And lastly, I'd like to mention the proofreaders, Nancy Riddiough, Laurie O'Connell, Dave Nash, Rich Ganis, Yariv Rabinovitch, and Emily Hsuan, and the indexer, Nancy Guenther. Their expertise helps to ensure a quality product comes to you, the reader.

Contents at a Glance

Contents

Introduction

NETWARE 6 IS THE LATEST VERSION of the world's most popular network operating system, developed by the world's most successful networking company. With NetWare 4 and intraNetWare 4.11, Novell engineers took the file and print services that had defined networking for the previous decade and added new components: directory services, messaging, routing, security, and management. They then took the best of the Internet (Web server, Web client, and TCP/IP communications software) and rolled it into the NetWare 6 package.

NetWare 6 builds on exciting new features recently introduced by Novell: native TCP/IP support, the NetWare Enterprise Web Server, distributed print services, multiprocessor support, application preemption, memory protection, virtual memory, Domain Name System (DNS) support, Dynamic Host Configuration Protocol (DHCP) server support, a new tape backup system, a robust and scalable development environment supporting Common Object Request Broker Architecture (CORBA), JavaBeans, JavaScript, Perl scripting, and public-key cryptography. These services are what will define networking as we roll deeper into the new millennium.

More than the above, Novell added the Apache Web Server to the mix to support browser-based administration tools. And, in a radical step sure to surprise and delight users everywhere, Novell now allows NetWare connections without running the NetWare client software. Any computer anywhere on the Internet can now use NetWare resources in some fashion (all things being configured properly at the server end, of course).

Gee, this all sounds pretty fancy. What does it mean to you? If you're new to NetWare, it means that NetWare 6 is the best network for companies small and large. If you're a current NetWare user, it means that NetWare 6 builds on the solid NetWare foundation you're familiar with and adds features necessary for the continued growth of your network.

Just as there are some new features in NetWare, there are some new features in this book. I've worked hard to present this huge wad of information in digestible chunks, ready when you need specific information.

Who Should Read This Book?

If you're a NetWare user already, this book builds on what you know from earlier versions of NetWare and adds the new features in steps. A new management architecture, NetWare Management Portal, was introduced with NetWare 5.1. NetWare 6 builds on this first step by providing many management utilities inside a friendly, easy browser format. Now named NetWare Remote Manager, it complements ConsoleOne, the interface that provides a common environment for Novell and other developers to build management tools. For seasoned NetWare administrators, one change that will not come as a surprise is that the DOS utilities used for server and network administration (such as PCONSOLE, NETADMIN, and PARTMGR) have finally been retired. All these utilities' functions are now included in NetWare Administrator, NetWare Remote Manager, or ConsoleOne.

I've been working with NetWare for more than 16 years, and I believe I have a good understanding of its "feel." I place these new features in perspective so that you, experienced in NetWare but new to version 6, will understand where these features came from and how they fit into the current version of NetWare.

NetWare neophytes will find "ground-up" explanations for NetWare 6 features and utilities. As a networking consultant working with a variety of customer networks, I have learned to explain networking logically and clearly to people who don't have a background in NetWare. I regularly work with people new to networks and NetWare, and can relay networking concepts to users familiar only with their PCs. I have also learned that most people don't care a whit about the networking technology we provide. The users don't care what we go through, they just want their lives to be easier. These guidelines have served me well over the years.

Advanced users, especially those who are performing some network administration for their departments, will find quite a bit of interest here. I recommend recruiting subadministrators and point out the many areas where they are useful. If you fall into the power user or subadministrator category, you will like this book.

Those of you managing small networks will find clear directions on installing and configuring NetWare 6 for your company. Novell answered one criticism of earlier NetWare versions by adding a new, simple-to-use, Java-based graphical installation program. This streamlined installation-and-configuration process makes NetWare 6 as easy to install as pointing and clicking. For us old-timers, using a mouse and working with a graphical user interface at the server console may seem odd at times, but these methods do work.

Those of you managing large networks will find many details about the advantages NetWare 6 offers administrators. This book includes all you need to know about managing users by large groups, both when you're importing them into NetWare 6 and when you're controlling them afterward. Options for NetWare eDirectory suitable for large companies are provided with illustrations and recommendations.

The "real" side of networking, dealing with users and bosses, appears regularly in these pages. Your network clients aren't computers and printers—they are people. Forget that at your peril. Remember that people have jobs to do. Build the network to help them do those jobs and your career will be fine.

How This Book Is Organized

To help you find the information you need, this book is divided into five major sections:

Part I: Setting Up the Network, Chapters 1 through 3   The chapters in this part cover what you need to know about installing your network. The first three chapters walk you through planning your installation and the nitty-gritty of the installation itself. Chapter 2 is devoted to planning and expanding Novell Directory Services (NDS). This part takes you through connecting workstations to the network.

Part II: Managing the Network, Chapters 4 through 10   The first two chapters in this part are about those who are using the network: your users. The next chapter deals with a service those users take advantage of frequently (much too frequently, in my opinion), network printing. Security, an important topic for many networks, is the subject of Chapter 7. Chapter 8 is a complete guide to network management and the NetWare 6 utilities that make those tasks easier than ever. Chapters 9 and 10 cover two basic user needs: applications and network training.

Part III: NetWare, TCP/IP, and the Internet, Chapters 11 and 12   This part teaches you how to take advantage of NetWare's now-default native IP support and to use NetWare 6 in a TCP/IP world. Chapter 11 introduces IP networking and shows you how to plan and administer a TCP/IP network with NetWare. Chapter 12 shows you how to manage IP addresses with the new DNS and DHCP utilities integrated with NDS. We can no longer think of TCP/IP and Internet tools as some "new parts" of NetWare; these technologies now weave through the core of NetWare and are just as integral as file and print services.

Part IV: Taking Advantage of Special Network Features, Chapters 13 through 15   In this part, you'll find coverage of Novell's remote-access capabilities and NetWare 6 enhancements, which include the advancements in the NetWare product other than NDS eDirectory features. The final chapter is where you turn when you (I'm sorry to say, inevitably) have a problem with your network (or a network user or your boss).

Part V: Appendices and Glossary   Appendix A details Web services, both new ones and even newer ones. Appendix B covers upgrading servers and installing NetWare client software. Appendix C contains some of the useful NetWare 6 server SET commands, for those of you who would prefer the command-line route to setting server parameters. Finally, at the back of the book is a glossary of the terms used in this book. When you're not sure what I mean by a particular word, turn to the glossary for a quick definition.

I don't expect you to read this book straight through, cover to cover. (In fact, if you did, I might worry about you a little bit.) You are expected to skip around and dip in and out of the book regularly.

Special Features in This Book

Throughout the book, you will find several interesting features. For your reading convenience, you'll find a topics list at the beginning of each chapter that summarizes the subjects featured within.

"Essential Skills" offers a quick reference for the functions used most often by NetWare administrators. The quick-hit, graphical format should help you get up to speed and prepare you for the coverage of more detailed management tasks in the book.

The "In a Hurry" instructions supply the basic steps of a procedure without the embellishments. They appear throughout the chapters, just under the section heading and before the discussion of that task. These steps are provided for quick-and-easy reference. If the "In a Hurry" instructions give you everything you need, that's great. If you need more information about how or why to do the procedure (or maybe you're just interested), read the following text for the details. And, for extra convenience, all of the "In a Hurry" instructions are gathered in a printable, quick reference available from the Sybex Web site (see the next section).

Another bonus you get with this book is extra networking wisdom, in the form of sidebars. Scattered throughout the book, you'll find special sections with advice about the politics of networking, some historical background on the topic at hand, and any other information I thought you might find interesting or helpful (or both).

And, as you may have grown used to if you read a lot of computer books, you'll see tips, warnings, and notes in the appropriate spots.

INTRODUCTION

The Companion Web Pages

To provide you with useful extras and updated information, Sybex and I have created companion Web pages to go along with *Mastering NetWare 6*. Visit www.sybex.com, click Catalog, and search for this book to find its companion pages. There you'll find:

◆ The In a Hurry Quick Reference in .PDF format. We've gathered together all of the book's "In a Hurry" sections, which show you the basic steps of all important procedures described in the book, into a quick reference for your convenience. You can easily view and print these pages in Acrobat Reader. If you don't have Acrobat Reader, you can also download it from this Web site.

◆ Links to sites where you'll find useful information on NetWare, hardware, software, training, and more.

◆ Links to MasteringNetWare.com, run by the author (or go there directly).

◆ Links to Gaskin.com, also run by the author (also a direct option at www.gaskin.com).

What's on the CD?

Bundled with Mastering NetWare 6 is Novell NetWare 6: a fully functioning, five-user version of the NetWare 6 software, which can be used for 90 days. This CD includes new features such as iFolder, iPrint, Novell Storage Services 3.0, Novell Cluster Services 1.6, Native Access File Protocols, NetWare Web Access, Browser-based management, and Novell eDirectory. This evaluation version of NetWare 6 is multiprocessor enabled. It fully supports up to 32 processors!

To review the online documentation for this CD, visit http://www.novell.com/documentation/lg/nw6p/index.html. To download the Novell Client software, go to http://www.novell.com/download.

Brought to you by Novell and Sybex in your pursuit of "Mastering NetWare 6."

Hardware and Software Used for This Book

Many companies provided hardware or software to help me with this book. The generosity of these companies goes past just the equipment; many provided help and information above and beyond the call of duty. Without their help, this book would have been nearly impossible.

Hardware

Here's a list of the equipment I used creating the examples for this book. This extensive list is a testament to the robust design of NetWare 6 and its ability to run on practically any PC.

◆ Compaq ProLiant 3000 tower server, including:

  ◆ Dual 600MHz Intel Pentium III XEON processors

  ◆ 128MB RAM

  ◆ Three 9.1MB hot-swappable disk drives

- ◆ 24x CD-ROM drive
- ◆ Compaq Net100 Fast Ethernet Adapter
- ◆ Compaq ProLiant ML330 tower server, including:
    - ◆ Pentium III processor running at 1GHz
    - ◆ 512MB RAM
    - ◆ One 9.1GB Ultra2 SCSI hard disk
    - ◆ 32x CD-ROM drive
- ◆ Compaq ProLiant Cluster Server for NetWare, including:
    - ◆ Four PL6400R/550MHz servers, each with four 2MB Pentium III XEON processors (four quad-processor servers)
    - ◆ One RA41000 Storage Enclosure (storage area network)
    - ◆ Twenty 9.1GB Ultra2 drives (two drives per server and one populated array)
    - ◆ Four 64-bit/66MHz StorageWorks Fibre Channel (FC) Host Bus Adapter Kits (Persian)
    - ◆ One seven-port FC hub
    - ◆ One seven-port FC hub mounting kit
    - ◆ One 22U rack (9122)
    - ◆ One six-port KMM switch box
- ◆ Compaq ProLiant 360 Cluster Servers, including:
    - ◆ Dual Pentium III processors running at 1GHz
    - ◆ 1GB of RAM
    - ◆ Compaq StorageWorks SAN Switch 16 (Fibre Channel)
    - ◆ StorageWorks 4100 RAID array with six 9.1GB SCSI hard drives

NOTE *For testing, we configured two servers and three of the RAID disks into storage area network clusters, leaving us with four servers in two clusters, each cluster sharing three of the six RAID disks.*

- ◆ Compaq TaskSmart 1500-R
    - ◆ Pentium II processor running at 450MHz
    - ◆ 512MB RAM
    - ◆ 2 9.1GB Ultra2 drives
    - ◆ 24x CD-ROM and 1.44MB drives

- NetWinder OfficeServer (named Rebel) from now-defunct Rebel.com, including:
  - 275MHz StrongArm processor
  - 64MB of RAM
  - 6GB hard drive
  - Linux operating system
  - Complete office software package, including Web, e-mail, and DHCP servers
- NetWinder OfficeServer (named NetWinder) from Rebel.com, including:
  - 533MHz Transmeta Crusoe CPU
  - 128MB RAM
  - 10GB hard disk
- Two Gateway2000 P5-120s, each with the following:
  - 120MHz Pentium processor
  - 128MB RAM
  - 1.6GB hard disk
  - 8x CD-ROM drive
  - 3Com 3C509 10BaseT Ethernet network adapter

NOTE *The Gateway2000 systems were used in all versions of this book. They have run various beta versions of all sorts of strange software products. None of the three systems have as much as hiccupped.*

- A variety of home-built Pentium and Pentium II machines with a variety of internal hardware:
  - Up to 128MB RAM
  - 1.6GB hard disks to 4.3GB IDE hard disks
  - 3Com 3C509 10BaseT Ethernet network adapter
- Macintosh Performa 6400, with the following:
  - 96MB RAM
  - 1.4MB hard disk
  - 8x CD-ROM
  - Internal 10BaseT Ethernet network adapter
- Other hardware:
  - LinkSys 24-port managed wiring concentrator from LinkSys Corporation
  - Avocent DS 1800 network-based KVM controller

Software

The software I used includes the following packages:

- ◆ NetWare 6 from Novell, Inc.

- ◆ NetWare 5.1 from Novell, Inc.

- ◆ Netscape Navigator and Netscape Communicator for testing Web server connectivity and directory services access via LDAP

- ◆ FullShot99 screen capture software from Inbit Inc.

- ◆ Windows 2000, Windows 98, Windows 95, and Windows NT from Microsoft

- ◆ Word 97 from Microsoft (used for writing the book)

How to Contact the Author

Use this address to reach me electronically:

`james@gaskin.com`

Relax and have fun with NetWare and this book. This isn't a Harry Potter movie or book, and you aren't an orphaned wizard. But sometimes, if you work hard and threaten your servers with a big enough troll club, magic happens.

Mastering™
NetWare 6

Essential Skills

In this section you will learn how to:

- ◆ Monitor server health
- ◆ Check volume status
- ◆ Monitor network traffic statistics
- ◆ Create, filter, and delete objects
- ◆ Manage NetWare Loadable Modules
- ◆ Use C-Worthy utilities, such as MONITOR
- ◆ Monitor multiple servers
- ◆ Salvage accidentally deleted files
- ◆ Stop runaway printers

The Essential Skills for NetWare 6

Welcome to the *Mastering NetWare 6* "Essential Skills" section. This visual section introduces a baker's dozen of the NetWare management operations you'll perform on a regular basis. The section uses a minimum of text and a maximum of easy-to-follow screens, with the important spots highlighted. Think of this as manager-friendly NetWare administration.

This "Essential Skills" section will help you perform the 20 percent of operations that consume 80 percent of management time. The faster and easier you handle the "simple" chores, the more time you'll have to deal with the complicated chores (meaning people).

There are two main administration utilities for NetWare: ConsoleOne and the NetWare Web Manager. But NetWare Web Manager really acts as a portal to a variety of other browser-based utilities, so we have three main administration utilities. Take a look at the NetWare Web Manager screen. This management portal makes life easier than ever. Between this screen and Console One, you can handle almost everything your network, and your network users, need.

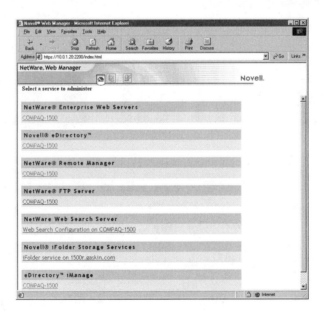

Those with NetWare experience will remember a few DOS-style screens run on the server console, named the C-Worthy utilities (based on the fact that the C-Worthy development toolkit provided the DOS interface). These utilities will be considered the fourth administrative utility, although we're cheating slightly by bundling several different utilities under the name of the interface, rather than listing each utility separately.

MONITORING SERVER HEALTH WITH REMOTE MANAGER

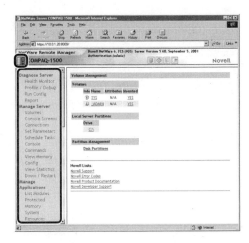

You need to know how your servers are doing before the telephone rings. Novell provides several monitoring options. NetWare Remote Manager's menu options, down the left side, are grouped by function. The red stoplight image beside the server name tells us something is wrong.

Click the first menu item, Health Monitor, or click the second icon from the left in the toolbar.

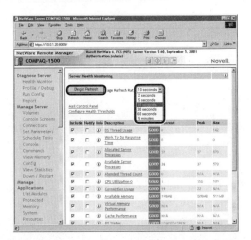

Many critical server health items are gathered on this page for your convenience. To refresh the screen, click the Begin Refresh command button. Notice the range of refresh rates allowed.

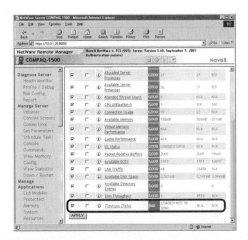

Here, at the bottom of the Health Monitor list, is the problem: Timesync Status is "BAD." Click the highlighted link for more information. To resolve this, dig into Novell Directory Services (NDS) or wait to see if inter-server timing fixes itself.

CHECKING VOLUME STATUS WITH REMOTE MANAGER

Knowing your server chugs merrily away covers only half the troubleshooting territory. Another administrative chore is to make sure that volumes remain available. Yes, the server can be up while the volumes are down or inaccessible. Yes, your users will alert you, repeatedly, until the volumes are available once again.

When you start NetWare Remote Manager, the volume settings appear immediately. Every volume can be examined, including the C:\ disk partition supporting your DOS boot sequence and NetWare program-loading steps.

If you are in another management section of NetWare Remote Manager, simply click the first icon from the left in the toolbar to return to this screen, Volume Management. To see the good stuff, click the Disk Partition link.

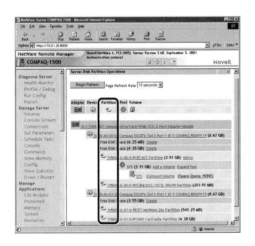

This display, new with NetWare 6, shows almost more than you want to see at one glance. Scan down the page, lining up the icons at the top of the page with the indented entries. Here, you can see how the four partitions align under the Partition heading.

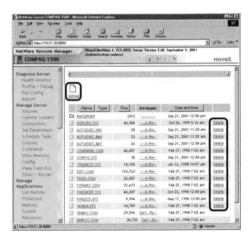

Another volume available for easy access is the C:\ drive of the server. When installing NetWare, a 200MB DOS partition remains to boot the server and hold utilities. If you want to add files here, just click the Upload button. To remove files, click the Delete link.

GETTING QUICK TRAFFIC STATISTICS WITH REMOTE MANAGER

You can't recognize when your server has a problem unless you know what your server's parameters look like when it's working properly. NetWare Remote Manager offers several quick windows into the depths of your network, or at least the statistics of your network (and statistics can be deep).

Many network administrators keep Remote Manager up all day, tuned to one set of statistics or the other. You may find that helpful as well. Few details show the health of your network in the way that it is reflected by the amount of network traffic.

The Server Statistical Information page leads to two quick update areas of particular interest. This screen appears when you click View Statistics from Remote Manager's left menu panel. Click the LSL Statistical Information menu item.

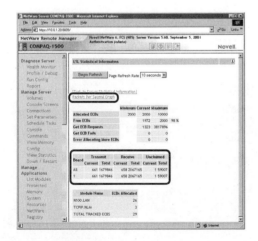

There is a lot of information on this screen, but the critical statistics, especially for servers with multiple network adapters, are the Board totals. Keep your eye on those to make sure a board isn't failing. After you peruse the statistics, click the Packets Per Second link near the top of the page.

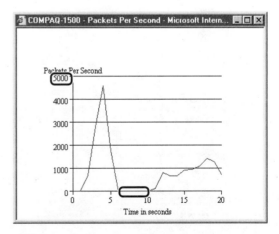

There's nothing like a graph to get a manager's attention. Look at the packets per second rating (one client doing a directory on one server). Notice the flat spot. Those indicators can mean trouble if they continue.

CREATING A USER WITH CONSOLEONE

The most important network object, the user, justifies the network. Without users, NetWare administrators don't have jobs.

The easiest way to set up users in NetWare 6 is with ConsoleOne. This utility supports a wide range of management activities, including:

- Create objects, including users, groups, and Organizational Units
- Modify or delete objects
- Assign rights to files and directories

Creating a User object in ConsoleOne requires a minimum of two screens and a maximum of three. The difference depends on the amount of personal information you want to provide for that user.

As the Admin user or equivalent, open ConsoleOne at a workstation or on the server console. (This instruction covers all ConsoleOne functions: Be the Admin or equivalent, and load the ConsoleOne software to a powerful workstation.)

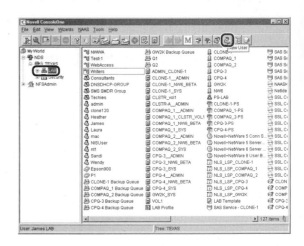

Click the container (Organization or Organizational Unit) to hold the new user. (If the single user and group icons in the ConsoleOne toolbar remain gray, you cannot create a user in that container.) Click the single user icon on the toolbar (or right-click the container and choose New ➤ User).

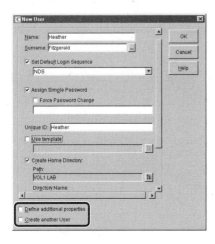

The New User dialog box requires only a name. The two check boxes at the bottom are optional. Check Define Additional Properties and click OK to open another dialog box describing user properties. Check Create Another User to save the current user and display the New User dialog box again.

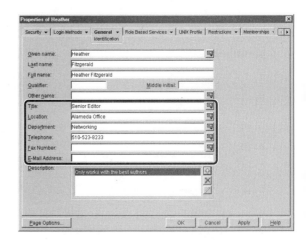

If you check the Define Additional Properties check box in the New User dialog box, a set of tabbed property pages appears. The Title, Location, Department, Telephone, Fax Number, and E-Mail Address fields are particularly useful.

CREATING AN ORGANIZATIONAL UNIT WITH CONSOLEONE

NetWare 6 has dozens of different types of objects for use on your network, some real and some virtual. All objects are created in more or less the same way. A very useful object is the Organizational Unit. Any container object, including another Organizational Unit, can contain an Organizational Unit.

To create an Organizational Unit, start as the Admin user or equivalent and open ConsoleOne from either a workstation or server console.

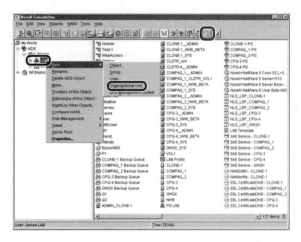

Highlight the Organization to hold the Organizational Unit, right-click the Organization, and choose New ➤ Organizational Unit (or click the Organizational Unit icon on the far end of the ConsoleOne toolbar).

Provide a legal NDS name for the Organizational Unit. The check box you can't see is Create Another Organizational Unit, which saves the Organizational Unit and displays a fresh New Organizational Unit dialog box. Check the Define Additional Properties check box and click OK.

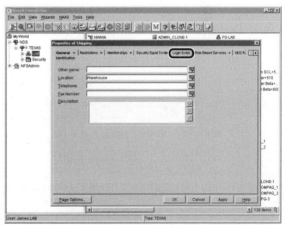

There are fewer properties for an Organizational Unit than there are for a user. Fill in the (physical) location, if that applies. Notice that each Organizational Unit can have its own login script (this also applies to Organizations).

DELETING AN OBJECT WITH CONSOLEONE

Not all things created are destroyed quickly, but some are. Deleting objects inside ConsoleOne isn't difficult, but there are precautions to take. There is no "undo" key for most of the delete actions.

Once again, start ConsoleOne on a server or workstation (preferably a workstation) while logged in as the Admin user or equivalent.

Keep the parent container (in this example, the Organization LAB) on the left side, and double-click that to display its contents. Highlight the object to be deleted and press the Delete key.

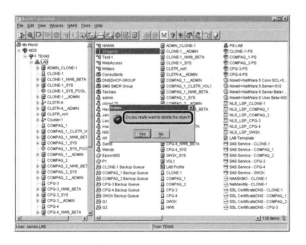

A simple dialog box named Delete asks the important question: "Do you really want to delete the object?" Make sure that you have chosen the correct object, or prepare to wail in pain.

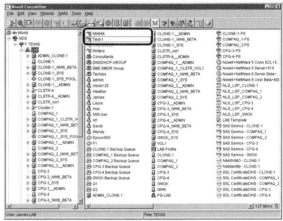

No muss, no fuss, but no other chance to change your mind. If you have objects inside a container of any kind, you may (or may not) get a warning about the consequences. Notice the Shipping Organizational Unit has disappeared without a trace.

FILTERING FOR OBJECTS IN CONSOLEONE

As you can see in the illustrations with the full ConsoleOne screen open, finding just a few objects in the middle of scores, hundreds, thousands, or even millions (Novell regularly demonstrates NDS eDirectory with more than a billion objects) can be difficult. One way to reduce the clutter is to use ConsoleOne's filtering feature.

Once again, start ConsoleOne on a server or workstation (preferably a workstation) while logged in as the Admin user or equivalent.

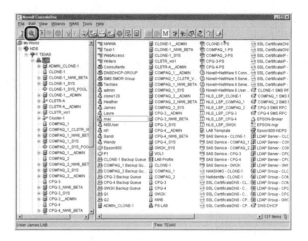

Click the magnifying glass icon on the toolbar, second icon from the left (or choose Edit ➤ Find).

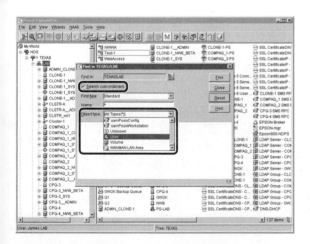

Notice that the Object Type field defaults to All Types, meaning that everything in the current context will display. The drop-down list shows all installed NDS objects. Also notice the Search Sub-containers check box. The default for this option is *not* checked. To display all users, check the box, so that ConsoleOne searches everywhere downstream.

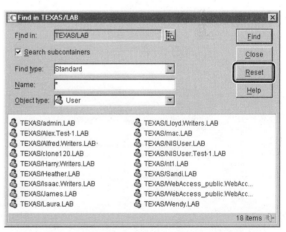

Notice that all users, even in subcontainers, are arranged alphabetically. This is not a bad arrangement, but it would help if the container name came after the object name. Click the Reset button to start another search.

MANAGING NLMS WITH REMOTE MANAGER

NetWare Loadable Modules (NLMs), for all intents and purposes, *are* NetWare. Novell suffers complaints from developers whining that it isn't as easy to write for NetWare as it is for Windows servers. Seeing the reliability difference between NetWare and Windows, perhaps standards are a good thing in this case.

You'll want to monitor the NLMs on your system. Look for memory usage, modules that need updating, and modules that are not being used.

Start the NetWare Remote Manager program as the Admin user or equivalent, or at least use an appropriate name to authenticate into NDS for management purposes.

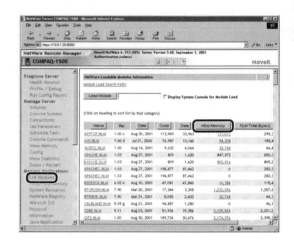

Reach this screen by clicking the List Modules option in the left menu panel. To sort by memory used in the server, click the Alloc Memory button (column heading).

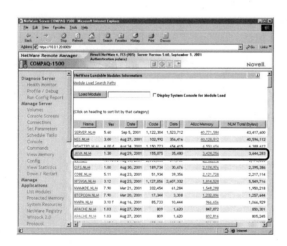

Rarely, some NLM will take off and start gobbling memory. If you suspect one is doing so, click the name to see more details. In this example, the JAVA.NLM looks suspect.

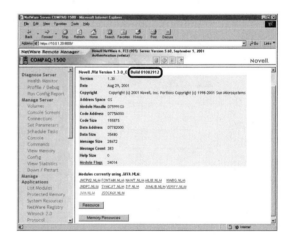

You might think these details are more than you wanted to see, but this information can be useful. For example, the Build identifier will help with updates. NLMs without other modules using them (see the long list using JAVA.NLM) have an Unload command button at the bottom of the screen.

FINDING THE OLD (FASHIONED) CONSOLE SCREENS

The older DOS-style NetWare utility screens are called C-Worthy screens. New NetWare administrators may feel as if they have traveled back in time, but older (experienced) administrators feel as if they have come home.

From NetWare Remote Manager, logged in as Admin or equivalent, click the Console Screens option in the left menu panel. Under HTML Based Screen Pages, click the console screen you want to see in snapshot (non-interactive) format.

The only console screen you really need is accessed from the same Remote Manager screen that lists the open console screens. Click the top option, labeled Console Screens.

This console screen transmits the real, interactive screens. (Here, this screen is reversed to better show the text.) In case the console locks up, the Emergency Console button may come to the rescue.

USING MONITOR

MONITOR, one of the C-Worthy DOS-style utilities, may be old-fashioned, but it has some of the best NetWare information gathered in one place. Run MONITOR by typing that name at the colon prompt on the NetWare console screen, either directly on the physical server or through RConsoleJ, as we do here.

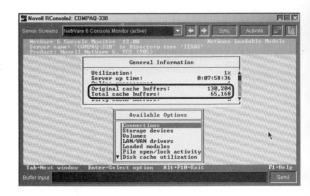

Shown here (reversed to better show the information) is the opening MONITOR screen. RConsoleJ, NetWare's remote-access tool that runs over a pure TCP/IP network, does a great job of reproducing the console screen. Notice the numbers for Original Cache Buffers and Total Cache Buffers. The more Total Cache Buffers on your server, the better.

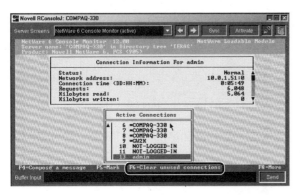

Novell licensing confuses many people, but no matter which license method you use, there will be times when you need to know how many people are logged in to any one server. When connection licenses get tight, choose the Connections options from the MONITOR Available Options menu. From the Connection Information screen, press F6 to clear unused connections.

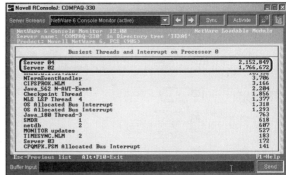

Track threads now and then so you'll know which are the busiest normally. Then you'll know when you see one thread consume more system resources than expected. Server threads, one through four on most single-user systems, will take the most resources. Drill down to this screen from the opening MONITOR screen by choosing Kernel ➤ Busiest Threads.

MONITORING MULTIPLE SERVERS

Few companies have a single server today. This means you, the network manager, must watch every server with the same attention you would normally watch one server. NetWare Remote Manager lets you assemble servers in groups and monitor them together.

In NetWare Remote Manager, click the Build Group option in the left menu panel. Check the servers you want to monitor on one screen, or click the Select All button. Then click the Build Server Group button.

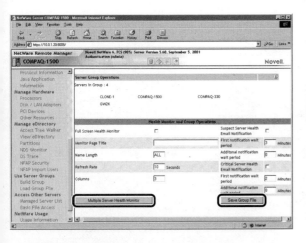

Change any defaults you wish, and then click the Multiple Server Health Monitor button. If you want to build different groups of monitored servers, click the Save Group File button to save specific servers in a group for later recall.

Green lights are good; red lights are bad. Both CLONE-1 and COMPAQ-330 need attention. Notice the different light icon next to GW2K? That server still runs NetWare 5.1.

SALVAGING DELETED FILES

Managers who haven't worked in the user-support trenches may believe that backup procedures prepare for disaster. Network administrators in the trenches know that most recovery exercises are spurred by user mistakes, not disaster.

What can you do when a user deletes a file or two hundred on a server? Open the old standby, NetWare Administrator (NWADMN32.EXE).

After starting NWADMN32.EXE as the Admin user or equivalent, highlight the volume to work on, and then click the Tools menu. The Salvage option sits at the top of the menu.

The Salvage Files dialog box offers multiple ways to display files. The Include option default is *.*, a good choice for most situations. Click the List button when you're ready.

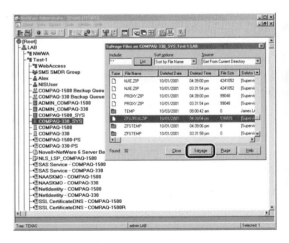

Highlight the file or directory that needs to be salvaged and click the Salvage button. You can also purge files (*purge* means to delete—so the files are no longer salvageable—and release the disk space) from this dialog box by clicking the Purge button after you select them. Click Close to finish.

STOPPING RUNAWAY PRINT JOBS

Printing causes many headaches until it works correctly. Then printing creates more headaches.

Stopping a series of print jobs saves paper and
endears you to the user who made the mistake—if
you can catch the print problem quickly enough, of
course. NetWare Administrator is the utility that
lets you manage print jobs.

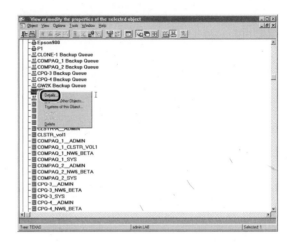

Open NetWare Administrator and highlight the
print queue serving the offending printer. Right-
click and choose Details.

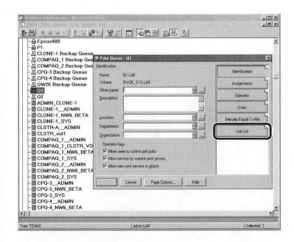

The dialog box that appears shows the Identification page by default, but you need the Job List
page, so click that command button.

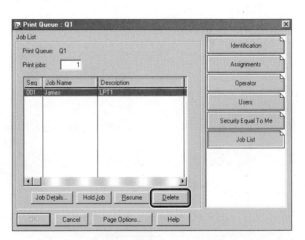

Highlight the job, and then click the Delete button. Then move all these queue-based printers to
iPrint—NetWare 6's new print management tool—
so users can communicate directly with the printer
themselves. (See Chapter 6 for details on iPrint.)

Part I

Setting Up
the Network

Chapter 1

Installing NetWare 6

INSTALLING NETWARE FOR THE first time may give you pause. If you have never installed Net-Ware before, your anxiety about a new procedure is compounded by all your questions about NetWare particulars. If you have installed NetWare before, you may be concerned because Net-Ware 6 doesn't look much like NetWare 4.*x* or any other earlier version.

Although it may give you little comfort now, NetWare 6 is the easiest version of NetWare to install in the history of the product. It's shipped on a nice, shiny set of CD-ROMs. The older versions of NetWare took a bushel basket of floppy disks and constant attention to feed those same disks in mind-numbing repetition. Mistype or forget something with earlier NetWare? Start all over, and feed those flippin' floppies in one after another.

The new GUI (graphical user interface) installation screens are pretty but not necessarily faster or better than the earlier text screens. If you're used to NetWare 4.*x* or 3.*x*, be forewarned that you *need* a mouse for NetWare 6 installation.

The automated installation process has been improved over NetWare 4.*x*, especially if you're using a server equipped with Plug-and-Play capabilities. The installation routines more often understand the drivers for disks and network adapters, meaning that the installer (that's you) doesn't need to reenter driver information and parameters.

Do you have a dual-processor server? When Novell introduced SMP (Symmetrical Multi-Processor) support, the modified NetWare operating systems were licensed to the manufacturers. This allowed vendors to make minor modifications to support their particular hardware. Net-Ware 6 incorporates these improvements, so the software detects multiple processors during installation and adds the proper code.

You'll see the other improvements in NetWare 6 described in the appropriate places here and there throughout the book. However, in many cases, what went for version 5.*x* will also apply to version 6.

This chapter will cover the following topics:

- ◆ Preparing your server machine
- ◆ Preparing for installation
- ◆ Running the installation program
- ◆ Removing NDS

Preparing Your Server Machine

Before you jump into installing NetWare 6 on your server, you need to get that machine ready. You don't want to start the installation process, only to find that you don't have enough hard disk space or RAM. We'll cover the server requirements and components, but first, let's look at an essential part of server preparation: protecting your server.

Protecting Your Server

Personal computers today are built to run in an office environment. No special air-conditioning, raised floors, or expensive fire-dampening foam is needed. Even if you buy a superserver cluster of servers all crammed into a 19-inch rack, an office environment is fine. So why should we make a big deal out of the physical space for your server?

The biggest reason to lock up your server is security. The first part of any security program is to limit accessibility to what you are protecting. What people can't see, they don't try to steal or vandalize. Why do you think the police always tell you to lock packages in your car trunk, rather than leaving them in the back seat? Out of sight—out of their hands.

Mischief is possible from the file server. From a worst-case angle, a malcontent with access to your server could reformat the server hard disk. Even if the malcontent happened to forget a DOS bootable disk, he or she could still cause trouble, because the tools to format and partition the PC hard disk are included with the NetWare installation utilities. The NetWare partition on the disk can be erased even more quickly, which does just as much damage to your network. Either way, you have a long day ahead of you, and your tape backup procedures will be severely tested.

Separate from actual harmful intent to your server, accidents happen more often to equipment out in the open. If your server is on a table, the table will get knocked over. Someone will "borrow" the monitor or the keyboard. Someone will spill coffee directly into the chassis air holes. If bad things do happen, let them happen to someone else's computer; keep your server safe.

NOTE *One customer had five servers sitting together, and they went down every evening. No diagnostics cleared up this mystery until someone spent the night in the office. The cleaning crew unplugged one server for the vacuum cleaner (from the UPS), and the noise on the UPS sent the other servers into terminal weirdness from the electrical interference.*

PROTECTING YOUR SERVER FROM STATIC BUILDUP

Controlled environments are easier to make static-proof and generally safer for sensitive electronic equipment. Yes, this is contrary to the idea that the computers on every desk are safe, but they're really not. In the owner's manual of every computer is a warning about static electricity and how to avoid it. We all ignore that warning, with little consequence. However, since your file server may support dozens to hundreds of excitable people, crashing the server because of static buildup in the carpet will bring all those excitable people to an even higher level of agitation. Better to keep the server in a locked room with a tile floor than risk that one-in-a-million, server-killing, static discharge from the carpet and your wool sweater.

All PC repair manuals go into detail about wearing static wrist-straps while working on a computer. They will give directions for ways to slowly bleed static away from your server (ground equipment through a one mega-ohm resistor). They also remind us to never open the chassis on a system with the power turned on. You wouldn't do anything so stupid, would you? Well, I did, once, by accident. Take it from me, unplugging an Ethernet board from a powered PC will fry that mother…board.

PROTECTING YOUR SERVER FROM POWER PROBLEMS

While you have the server in a locked room with tile floors, run dedicated power lines to that room. It's safest to run every network device from these dedicated lines, but that may not be possible. Propose a dedicated line for every network printer, server, and wiring device to scare your boss into providing a dedicated circuit, at least for your server.

Ground the server (or all these dedicated circuits) to an earth ground if at all possible. Weird things happen with a "floating ground," multiple grounds, and circuits that get cross-wired somehow. If your systems get flaky for no reason, an electrician may be a good person to call.

Always, always, always put the server on a UPS (uninterruptible power supply). There is no excuse for not doing so. UPS systems are cheap today, and many are smart enough to gently shut down your server. Few sites need to worry about power dropping out for more than a few seconds. Many sites do need to worry about power that has malformed signals and constant fluctuations. A good UPS will take care of these problems as well.

The UPS system works like this: A cable from the UPS connects to a server serial port. When a power blackout or brownout activates the UPS, the server software will communicate with the UPS over the connecting cable. When the UPS battery is in danger of being discharged completely, leaving the server without power, the monitoring software will take down the server so all files are closed properly.

All powered network devices, such as wiring concentrators, modems, communication servers, bridges, routers, and tape backup systems, should be on a UPS. Remember to plug the server console monitor into the UPS as well, unless you have memorized all the proper shutdown keystrokes. Figure 1.1 shows the setup for a properly protected server.

Repeat: There is no excuse for having a server without a UPS. None.

FIGURE 1.1

The properly protected server

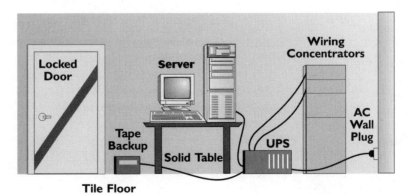

Requirements for NetWare Servers

NetWare 6 operates on a wider range of server hardware and network peripherals than most other network operating systems. According to Novell, your server must meet these minimum requirements:

- A PC or PC-compatible with a Pentium II or better processor
- 256MB of RAM
- 512MB of RAM for servers running application servers such as WebSphere, NetWare Enterprise Web Server, or Apache Web Server
- 2.2GB hard disk space free (and unpartitioned)
- One (or more) network board(s) connected to a functioning network cabling system
- A 200MB DOS partition
- A CD-ROM drive that can read ISO 9660 formatted CD-ROMs (if you're installing from the CD-ROM and not from another server)
- A 3.5-inch disk drive
- A VGA monitor and video board (SVGA recommended)
- A keyboard
- A serial, PS/2, or USB mouse (optional, but *highly* desirable)

Technically, these elements will make a server. Practically, this server will be worthless for most networks. Your choice for server components should read like Table 1.1.

TABLE 1.1: OPTIMUM SERVER COMPONENTS

OPTION	RECOMMENDATION
CPU	Intel Pentium III or XEON (Pentium III 700MHz and up for multiprocessor machines)
RAM	512MB recommended; more is much better
Hard disk	4GB minimum, but more is better; in all but the smallest environments, start with at least a 20GB hard disk
DOS partition	200MB minimum, plus an amount of disk space equal to the machine's amount of RAM, for a possible core dump. A 512MB system would need 712MB (200MB+512MB) to follow this recommendation from Novell.
NIC	PCI bus-mastering 100BaseT
CD-ROM drive	24x speed
Monitor and video card	SVGA
Keyboard	Just about any cheap keyboard will do, since you'll use it rarely (if ever) after installation
Mouse	Serial, P/S2, or USB; it's nearly impossible to run ConsoleOne and other GUI utilities without a mouse

Each item in Table 1.1 is necessary, but choosing some items may demand critical decision-making skills. The items requiring some soul-searching depend on your needs for this server. Our goal in this section is to discern which options best fit your situation for each server you will install.

If your company is like most companies, there is a constant struggle between what is wanted and what is affordable. Every network administrator would love to have nothing but superservers with more RAM and hard disk space than the company's mainframe. However, budget constraints exist in every situation. You may be able to talk your boss into a superserver, but you must justify that expenditure.

The only way to justify expenditures for most bosses is to give clear pictures of the options, with the good and bad points of each option. Normally, the equation is simple: Here are the good points, and here are the bad points (usually price tags or required resources). Then you and your boss argue about the list of good and bad points for each portion of the server until some compromise is reached.

A question for you and your boss: What are the three most important functions for your planned server? The answers from you and your boss may be different. If so, problems will be your constant companion. Only when you and your boss are in agreement regarding the network will you both be happy with the choices you must make.

LIVING WITH YOUR NETWORKING DECISIONS

The question "What are the three most important functions of *x*?" will reappear in various places through-out this book. If you are uncomfortable making decisions, I have one bit of advice: Get over it. Business management, and especially networking, is nothing but decisions regarding the conflict between goals and constraints.

Let me help take the fear out of decisions: Every single one you make will be wrong next year. By this, I mean that technology will change, and better options will appear. If you make the same decision next year as you made yesterday, you will be overlooking better options. Better equipment will be available, prices will be lower, or both, but things will change.

Don't beat yourself up over decisions made in the past that didn't work out as well as you hoped. No one can blame you if you had the right priorities at the time you made that decision. The only action you can be blamed for is not revisiting poor decisions as time makes more options available.

Choosing the Hard Disk (Buy a Bigger One)

No one complains about too much storage space, whether we speak of closets, car trunks, or server hard disks. My friend David Strom has this recommendation for beginning NetWare administrators: Buy twice as much disk space as you think you'll ever need. Better yet, buy three times as much.

Today, three types of disk interfaces are suggested for servers: IDE, IDE Ultra DMA, and SCSI. Let's talk about IDE and SCSI, along with RAID systems.

NOTE *The big change in hard drive drivers is the end of support for* .DSK*-type drivers. NetWare 4 introduced the Net-Ware Peripheral Architecture (NPA or sometimes NWPA) but allowed both NPA-type and* .DSK*-type drivers. Beginning with NetWare 5.x, only NPA-type drivers are supported. Be careful when upgrading to ensure that your controller cards have NPA drivers available.*

IDE DISK CONTROLLERS AND DRIVES

If you buy a PC with an installed hard disk, chances are it will be an IDE system. IDE controllers are usually located directly on the motherboard. Early versions of IDE controllers were limited to 525MB, but now drives up to many gigabytes are supported.

NetWare 6 support of IDE controllers is strong. The standard `IDEATA.HAM` driver included in the installation process works with almost all brands of IDE controllers. With the larger capacity available today, IDE drives are decent choices for servers. PCI (Peripheral Component Interconnect) IDE controllers now support 32-bit access, making disk performance even better. Novell also includes `.CDM` files for IDE hard drives (`IDEHD.CDM`) and CD-ROMs (`IDECD.CDM`).

SCSI DISK INTERFACES AND DRIVES

Another technology "borrowed" from the world of Unix hardware, SCSI adapters and drives are the choice for serious servers and large server disks. Technically, SCSI (pronounced "scuzzy") is an ANSI standard that details an I/O bus capable of supporting as many as seven devices.

The old-style SCSI adapters use a short, 50-pin connecting cable. The newer, faster SCSIs use a high-density 68-pin cable. IDE drives, in comparison, use a 40-pin cable. Since SCSI devices are "chained" together, a terminator must be used on the last device to anchor the chain. SCSI is a popular adapter for CD-ROM drive connections. This popularity helps make SCSI devices more affordable.

The high-performance needs of Unix workstations and servers are advancing the performance of SCSI devices every day. SCSI-2, Fast SCSI, Wide SCSI, Fast and Wide SCSI, and Ultra2 SCSI-3 are improvements being advanced by various parties. The world of SCSI is also being pushed to support longer cable lengths to make disk clusters more convenient.

SCSI works better for servers than IDE because SCSI drives have more flexibility and more throughput, and SCSI taxes the CPU much less than IDE.

RAID DISK SYSTEMS

Coming into popularity in the 1990s, *RAID* (redundant array of inexpensive disks, although some references now say *independent* rather than *inexpensive*) uses several disks to replace the storage capacity of a single disk. The advantage of RAID is fault tolerance. This means that one disk can die, but because the information is spread across all disks, no data is lost. How the data is spread determines the RAID level of a disk system. The levels range from 1 to 5, but RAID levels 1, 4, and 5 are generally used for servers, with RAID levels 1 and 5 the most popular.

The best RAID systems allow bad disks to be replaced without downing the server, thus maintaining server uptime for users despite what is ordinarily a catastrophic failure. This technology is called *hot swapping*. Some vendors build cabinets with multiple power supplies and cooling fans to emphasize the fault-tolerant nature of RAID.

However, two warning notes are attached to this rosy scenario:

- ◆ RAID systems do not, in any way, make a tape backup obsolete. Although a RAID disk system will continue if one drive goes bad, catastrophic (multiple disk) failures can occur. More important, tape backup is most often used to replace files accidentally deleted. If you delete a file on a RAID disk system, the system will happily delete the file, no matter how many disks hold part of that file.

◆ Reconstruction of a RAID system is not transparent. As the new disk in the system is populated to take the place of the failed drive, your server will be involved. The performance for clients will drop drastically.

Despite the warnings, RAID systems perform better in critical systems than any single drive available. No system is perfect, but RAID is a step in the right direction. These systems will become more commonplace as prices settle and companies realize the value of the data on their server disks.

Choosing the Server's NIC

Whether your network runs Ethernet, Token Ring, or something else, the NIC (network interface card) in your server must carry the largest load. Each client talks to one system: the server. The NIC for the server is no place to save money.

Get the fastest PCI network board you can. PCI now supports 64-bit data paths at 133MHz. Unless your network supports few people, get a 100BaseT interface board for every server and your tape backup system. Gigabit Ethernet price drops make this technology affordable, especially for a backbone connecting server to server.

Early advice was to add several NICs in each server to handle higher network traffic loads. Now that switched Ethernet and Token Ring are available, my advice is to avoid multiple NICs. When you add the second network adapter in the server, the operating system turns on the software necessary to route traffic between the two (or more) network segments. This means that each and every packet coming to each network adapter must be examined and routed to either the server itself or to another network adapter. This overhead actually tends to slow server processing of packets in heavy network traffic situations. If at all possible, do not use your server as a local router for your network segments. Figure 1.2 shows the possible and preferred setups.

To paraphrase the old adage, put all your eggs in one basket, and then really watch that basket. Put a stout network adapter in your server, and make sure it has been certified by Novell. Make doubly sure the card has the proper driver not just for NetWare, but for NetWare servers.

The NetWare operating system supports about 50 LAN drivers right out of the box. You can add drivers for any other interface card during installation by using the vendor's configuration diskette.

One more suggestion: Check your NIC vendor for new server drivers now and then. You can improve your server's performance by upgrading your drivers, and vendors regularly supply new driver files.

Choosing the Server's CD-ROM Drive

What's important about your CD-ROM drive is not the drive itself, but the controller card that sits in the server. Since SCSI is an accepted standard, a NetWare-supported card in the server can easily run any new CD-ROM drive. So NetWare doesn't care about the drive, just the controller.

More than 20 drivers for various SCSI adapters are included in the NetWare installation program. Vendors can supply their own Novell-certified drivers with their own SCSI cards. Because NetWare servers are big business, most SCSI board manufacturers provide Novell drivers.

IDE CD-ROM support started in NetWare 5. However, the performance isn't better than with SCSI drives, so there's little reason to go out of your way to get an IDE drive and controller if you are already using SCSI. On the other hand, if you are using IDE, there is nothing wrong with using an IDE CD-ROM.

FIGURE 1.2

Handling high network traffic levels

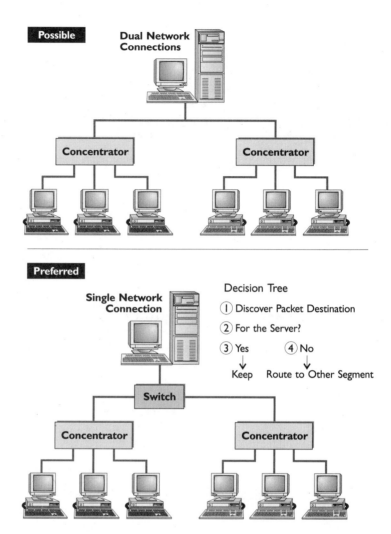

If you plan to use your CD-ROM drive as a NetWare volume after the server is installed, get at least a 24x drive. If you're not going to use the CD-ROM drive as a volume, its speed makes little difference. Here's one place you can save some money, though the installation will take longer. Just make sure that the interface card for the CD-ROM drive doesn't interfere with the network adapter and disk controller.

WARNING   *There have been problems with some SCSI adapters when running both the hard disk and the CD-ROM drive from the same adapter. During installation, the adapter may become unstable and lock up the console keyboard. If that happens, take all the SCSI references out of your* **CONFIG.SYS** *file that boots your server under DOS before restarting the installation process. Then load the proper SCSI driver supplied by NetWare to load the CD-ROM as a NetWare volume, and use that volume as the installation files' source.*

Choosing the Server's Monitor

This used to be another easy choice—any VGA video board and low-end monitor would work fine on your server. Now that NetWare uses a GUI on the server, the video card and monitor are more important. Choose one that is on Novell's approved list, or at least a name-brand card.

Once installation is complete, server console operations are done infrequently. All normal console operations can be performed across the network using the RCONSOLE.EXE, ConsoleOne program, or NetWare Remote Manager (browser-based and cool).

Preparing for NetWare 6 Installation

Now that you've prepared the hardware, it's time to prepare for the actual installation. After you've finished this chapter, you'll have your server installed (or at least you will have read about installing it). Plan to spend about an hour or so for the installation. That's the bad news. The good news is that most of that time will be spent copying files to your server, requiring no intervention or effort on your part.

Of course, the "few-minute install" works best when you take the approach of the cooking shows on TV. You should have all the necessary ingredients (information) at hand. You should have a working oven (server) all preheated and ready to go (properly configured with the correct disk drives and NICs). And you should know the recipe, which means that you should read over the entire installation process once or twice to understand where you're heading with each step.

Your first step is to get a pad and pencil. Write down every ID number, IP address, or any other identifying nomenclature on worksheets. Whatever you don't write down, you'll need in a panic later. Protect yourself and write everything down now.

Also, keep a pad and pencil beside the server during installation. Every time you must make a choice and every time the installation program provides a randomly generated number for you, write it down. Save that paper, because you will forget the information. With luck, you won't need to refer to this information, or at least you won't lose the paper.

Booting Your Server from the Hard Disk

With a brand-new server PC, there may be nothing on the hard disk. Novell and I *strongly* recommend that you create a DOS partition of 200MB or so and boot the server from the hard disk.

If there are files on the hard disk (as is often the case with systems bought from retail outlets eager to add "value" by adding strange software of all types), all those files will be erased. When you run FDISK (and rework your DOS partition), everything on your hard disk will be deleted. Has this PC been backed up? If not, do a backup now if there is the smallest chance you or someone else will one day want any of the files.

To boot your server from the hard disk, there must be a DOS partition. Novell recommends 200MB for the partition. This allows enough room for all DOS files, the NWSERVER directory for the NetWare files, and a little space for other server utilities.

NOTE *Upgraders from previous versions please note: It is no longer possible to boot from a floppy drive. You must boot from the hard drive now.*

On a clean system, you may want to try booting from the CD-ROM and letting NetWare handle all the DOS partition setup. It works pretty well now, and all new servers support booting from the CD-ROM drive. (Check the system BIOS setup parameters to make sure that booting from the CD-ROM drive is enabled.) If this doesn't work, or you prefer using a floppy, keep reading.

With a configured and working PC, you will need to use FDISK.EXE to make the adjustments to your disk partitions. It's painful to press the Y key to say, "Yes, completely wipe the disk contents, never to be seen again," even when you know there is nothing valuable on the disk. I suppose you need to accidentally erase a disk or two before you become paranoid about partitioning a disk. If you haven't wiped away valuable files, you haven't been playing with computers long enough.

Follow these steps to prepare the hard disk of your future server:

1. Boot the system from a DR-DOS or MS-DOS 3.3 or later floppy disk or your server installation license diskette (better). *Do not* use DOS from a Windows system; NetWare depends on the included Caldera DOS.

2. Run FDISK.EXE.

3. Delete the existing DOS partition and any others you may find.

4. Create a DOS partition using 200MB or more of disk space.

5. Set the new partition as the active partition.

6. Exit FDISK.EXE by pressing Esc.

7. Format the small DOS partition (type **FORMAT C: /S**) from the server installation floppy.

8. Create the CONFIG.SYS file on the new hard drive with the following two lines. (You can, if you prefer, simply copy the server installation floppy to the hard drive, but be sure to place these two statements on the hard drive's version of the file.)

   ```
   FILES=50
   BUFFERS=30
   ```

9. Reboot the system and boot from the hard disk to verify the previous steps.

10. If the CD-ROM drive will be used for installation, copy and verify that CD-ROM drivers initialize the drive. If a network connection is needed for installation, copy and verify that NIC drivers connect to the network. If you have an existing network, ensure that you can see and connect to a server.

Before you begin installation, make sure that you know the settings for all the NICs in your machine, as well as the necessary names and passwords. Also, if you are installing into an existing NetWare 4.*x* or 5.*x* system, you should know the design of your NDS eDirectory tree. Knowing the administrator password goes without saying, right?

TIP   I prefer letting the installation program modify the AUTOEXEC.BAT program so that the NetWare server starts every time the system is booted. If something happens to stop the server, such as a power failure, it's nice that the server can restart without someone typing a command or two. You'll see where you can choose this option a bit later in this chapter, when we get to running the INSTALL batch file program.

Use the CD-ROM driver files you saved from the hard disk and placed on the installation boot floppy before you wiped the server hard disk. If your CD-ROM drive supports bootable CDs, life will be slightly easier during the NetWare installation process.

If a network connection is necessary for installation, copy the minimum client files needed from a working network client. You don't need a full-featured client. You can probably use a DOS Shell (NETX) client if you have one; you can definitely use the DOS Requester (VLM) or Client 32 for DOS client. (See Novell's Web site for more information about DOS-based clients.)

Setting Up Your Installation Files

If you are installing your first NetWare server, you have no choice about where your server installation files are located. They must be loaded into a CD-ROM drive on your server.

If you are installing your second or seventeenth NetWare server, your installation files can come from the CD-ROM drive on the server or from a remote server across the network. Installing from a remote server requires an existing network and a server with space for the installation files or the NetWare 6 CD mounted as a NetWare volume.

There is little difference in the actual installation between loading your network operating system from a CD-ROM drive in the server or from another server three floors away. Most of the installation time is spent watching a seemingly endless list of filenames zoom by. After answering a few questions at the beginning and in the middle, you have little to do during the installation of NetWare 6.

Preparing the Network with *NWDEPLOY.EXE*

If your network contains more than three other NetWare servers, particularly if those servers haven't had all the NDS patches applied regularly, use the `NWDEPLOY.EXE` program found on the NetWare 6 operating system CD before starting the server installation. `NWDEPLOY.EXE` updates NDS and a few other little details. If you don't do it, you may catch yourself chasing hard-to-catch weird problems. Go ahead and run the utility, unless you have a completely up-to-date network.

NOTE *You don't want to run a mixed network of NetWare 6, 5.x, and 3.x or 4.1x servers if you can help it, although this is fully supported (with NDS eDirectory). See the online documentation for mixed network operating system issues and procedures.*

Installing from a Server-Based CD-ROM

IN A HURRY 1.1: INSTALL NETWARE FROM AN INTERNAL CD-ROM DRIVE

1. Install and configure a CD-ROM drive on the target server.
2. Boot the server-to-be, loading only DOS and the CD-ROM drivers.
3. Make the CD-ROM drive, with the NetWare 6 operating system CD loaded, your current drive.
4. Type **INSTALL** in the root directory (unless your bootable CD-ROM drive takes care of this for you).
5. Skip to the section about running INSTALL ("Running the Installation Program").

The server-to-be machine must be functioning properly as a DOS system before it can be a server. Test the CD-ROM drive initialization files by rebooting the system, loading only DOS and the CD-ROM startup drivers. These files are all you need for your server installation boot disk. If all is well, you can make your CD-ROM drive (normally drive D:) your active directory and scan the CD just as you can your hard disk. Now you can start the NetWare 6 installation process with confidence.

NetWare 6 does a good job of configuring the CD-ROM drive and starting the process automatically. With any luck and a fairly new server, you can let the CD-ROM boot process take care of all these details. Save yourself some trouble. Unless you're installing a bunch of servers, use the internal CD-ROM method started by booting from the CD-ROM.

After you switch to your CD-ROM drive, you will see the batch file INSTALL.BAT. You now can skip ahead to the "Running the Installation Program" section of this chapter.

Installing from a Remote Server across the Network

The fastest way to install NetWare may be to use a remote NetWare server as your installation source. You can install from a NetWare volume (the fastest choice here) or from a remote CD mounted as a NetWare volume. Even if this is the first NetWare 6 server you are installing, a remote server can be the source of all the installation files, saving you time and aggravation, if you have another NetWare 3 or 4 server available.

HOW CAN A NETWORK BE FASTER THAN A CD-ROM?

If you're new to networking in general or NetWare in particular, you may wonder why transferring files from another PC over the network is faster than reading an internal CD-ROM drive. How can you send information through a bunch of network cabling, involve two different servers, and worry about other network traffic during your file transfer, yet still believe it's faster than an internal CD-ROM drive?

PCI bus-master network cards running at 100Mbps move buckets o' bits quickly. Internal CD-ROM drives, although getting faster, are almost always based on IDE hard drive controller chips. They are just not as fast as network cards.

The next boost of performance comes with the file caching that NetWare does. Even when reading a fast CD-ROM drive, NetWare reads file blocks beyond the information needed to fill the current request. The file stays in the cache of the source NetWare server, so many of the file requests by the target server will be serviced by server RAM rather than by the server CD-ROM drive. If you have copied the installation CD onto the server hard drive, the performance boost by file caching is even more pronounced. Server hard drives are much faster than the fastest CD-ROM drive.

The moral of this story is simple: Install from a remote server if practical. If not, you may have a chance to read three magazine articles rather than two during the installation.

INSTALLING FROM A NETWARE VOLUME

This is probably the first NetWare 6 server you are installing into your network. I base that assumption on your attention to the installation chapter. Since you're reading this section about running the installation process across the network, I assume that you already have a NetWare server or servers available. NetWare 6 is actually fairly simple to install, so as a good NetWare administrator, you probably won't need instructions more than the first time or two.

Copying the Installation Files from the CD-ROM

The easy way to get the installation files from the CD-ROM drive to the NetWare server is by copying everything from a workstation with a CD-ROM drive. There are more than 4000 files and directories that collectively use almost all the space on the operating system CD, so make sure that you have room on your target server before you start. If you add the clients and documentation CDs, the totals balloon to more than 9500 files and about 975MB of space. The copying process will take quite a while, so start at lunchtime or the end of the day.

Here are the requirements for making a copy of the NetWare 6 operating system CD on a different NetWare server:

◆ An existing NetWare server with appropriate disk space available

◆ The target server configured as a NetWare workstation, with at least 2.2GB of free, unpartitioned space available

◆ A workstation with a CD-ROM drive that can read ISO 9660-formatted CDs (almost all CD-ROM drives can read this format)

◆ A functioning network supporting all three machines

Follow these steps to make the copy:

1. Log in to the host server with proper rights to create a subdirectory.

2. Change to the root directory of the NetWare volume (not SYS:, unless you will have plenty of disk space available after copying the CD to the server).

3. Type **MD NETWARE6** (or give it a more descriptive name, such as **NW6OPSYS**).

4. Type **CD NETWARE6** (or whatever you named the directory).

5. Type **NCOPY D: /S /E /V** (assuming D: is the CD-ROM drive).

NOTE   The switch options on the NCOPY command are /S for subdirectory, /E for empty directories, and /V to verify. Use NCOPY rather than XCOPY so that all the NetWare attributes on the files are copied properly.

Setting Up the Target Server as a Workstation

Once the files from the CD-ROM drive are copied on your host server, you can begin installation. The target server must load the files necessary to log in to the host server. This requires loading the NetWare client software appropriate for the workstation.

Log in to the host server as SUPERVISOR (for NetWare 3), as Admin (if it's a NetWare 4 server or above) or as another user with all rights. Map a drive from your workstation—er, server-to-be—to the directory on the host server containing the NetWare 6 files. Change to that drive and type **INSTALL**. You can now skip ahead to the "Running the Installation Program" section of this chapter.

INSTALLING FROM A REMOTE CD-ROM

For those of you with existing NetWare servers already containing CD-ROM drives, your job is simple. Place the NetWare 6 operating system CD in the drive and mount the new volume; any Net-Ware client can now reference that volume.

Once again, the server-to-be must be configured as a workstation. Log in from the target server as SUPERVISOR (for NetWare 3), Admin (for NetWare 4), or any other account that has rights to the CD volume, and make a connection (in other words, map a drive) to the CD volume. Follow these steps to mount the NetWare 6 operating system CD on a remote server:

1. Dismount the current CD (if any) by typing either **DISMOUNT** *volume-name* if you are using Net-Ware 6 or **CD DISMOUNT** *volume-name* if you are using NetWare 3 or 4. Then remove the disk.

2. Place the NetWare 6 operating system CD in the drive.

3. Type **CD MOUNT NW6** if you are using NetWare 3 or 4, or load the **CDINST.NLM** module and then type **MOUNT NW6** if you are using NetWare 5.*x*.

4. From the workstation/server-to-be, log in to the host server as SUPERVISOR (for NetWare 3), Admin (for NetWare 4 or 5), or another user with rights to the volume.

5. Map a drive letter to the CD volume by typing **MAP N:= *host_server*\NW6**. (Note that you can use any drive letter; I just like to use N: to remind myself it is the NetWare CD.)

6. Type **INSTALL**.

This procedure brings you to the same point in the installation process as if the CD were inside the target server's CD-ROM drive. You can now continue to the next section.

Running the Installation Program

Many things in life force a choice—you can make it powerful or you can make it easy, but not both. NetWare changed the rules starting with version 5. You now have an industrial-strength, enterprise operating system with a relatively easy-to-use GUI to guide you through installation. NetWare 6 installation provides some big advantages, including the following:

◆ With the CD-ROM, you spend only a few minutes at the computer—the installation program automatically does the rest.

◆ You can easily correct all installation mistakes.

◆ You can easily make any changes you think of during or immediately after installation.

◆ The installation program is GUI-based, so you have point-and-click access to most options.

Let's take each item and squelch any remaining nervousness on your part. Since there are no floppies to feed during installation, you can actually install a new server with only a few minutes of your time spent at the keyboard. It will probably take you longer, at least the first time, because you will read all the help screens and peruse every word on each screen. If you're a typical NetWare administrator, you also won't collect all the necessary data beforehand, so you'll need to look up some information. That will take additional time.

Later installations will take less time because you will know the answers to the questions that appear during installation. Let me also offer hope for those of you installing from slow (less than 8x) CD-ROMs: You can easily install the second (and third, fourth, and so on) NetWare 6 server in your network by copying information from the first server. If you have a slow CD-ROM, you will need it only twice: once to install the first system, and the second time to load all the installation files onto the server hard disk for easy future installations.

Any time you make a mistake during installation, you can correct that mistake with little trouble. With the new graphical NetWare administration tools, you can easily correct common installation mistakes, such as typos (there is no spelling checker in the installation program). The installation program offers you several chances to stop and start all over. You have opportunities at every section to go back and redo any piece of that section. You can also run a separate installation program in text mode (NWCONFIG.NLM) at any time to fix any mistake or installation confusion.

Starting the Installation

Start the installation process by putting the NetWare 6 operating system CD into the CD-ROM drive and rebooting the system. The installation program will start automatically. If that doesn't work, go through these extra steps:

1. Boot DOS on the PC (without memory managers or other resident programs).

2. Load the CD-ROM drive or network client drivers (as needed).

3. Type **INSTALL** to start the batch file.

It may seem odd, but your PC technically becomes a server the minute the SERVER.EXE program starts. This program is the NetWare kernel. Of course, loading the SERVER.EXE program without any of the disk drivers and LAN connection software makes a useless server. As it sits now, the server can't communicate with anyone or anything else across the network or even with its own internal hard drives. These details are configured during the installation process. If you are loading the system from a remote server, the installation program will know which LAN drivers are being used. You will have the option to verify the drivers and accept them for the new server.

The First Choices

The first screen you see (after a possible question about whether you have an IDE or SCSI CD-ROM drive) is a fairly standard license screen. After you have read it, press F10 to move on. (No arguing about licensing is allowed here, so just accept it.)

NOTE *If you leave the computer idle on some screens for more than a few minutes, NetWare may automatically blank the screen for you. Don't be alarmed. Just press the Shift key to get it back.*

If your server contains a valid boot partition and/or NetWare partitions, you may see a screen asking if you wish to keep the boot partition or wipe the disk and start over. On a clean system, let NetWare wipe the disk and organize things to suit itself. NetWare will try to maintain your other partitions and files if you decide to keep them, but never, ever, ever start an installation procedure without backing up the target system twice and verifying both backups.

While the questions are backwards in Figure 1.3, they're both important. Choose between Express or Custom installation to trust NetWare or make some decisions yourself, respectively. Select Express and then Continue. (I picked Custom to go through all the installation screens). You'll see the details on the next screen. If you don't like what you read about Express installation, go back and choose Custom.

FIGURE 1.3

The first fork in the installation road

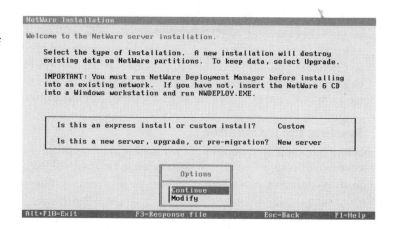

The second question is easy to answer—new, upgrade, or soon to be upgraded (pre-migration)? For now, select the New Server choice. (See Appendix A for information about upgrading options.)

Notice the important message in the second paragraph. With NetWare 6, Novell provides a Deployment Manager to get NDS up to spec before installing a new server in the network. I mentioned this earlier (in the "Preparing the Network with NWDEPLOY.EXE" section), but you probably skipped over it in your hurry to start installing the new server.

TIP   If you have set up Windows computers in the past, you may have heard of the MSBATCH.INF file (for 95/98) or unattended installation files (for NT/2000). These allow you to set some or all of the options needed for an installation, so no user input is needed when the operating system is installed. NetWare 6 offers the same capability. For large installations, you can simply create the response file and let relatively untrained people set up servers at other locations without knowing the intricacies of server installations, NDS, and so on. If this sounds like something you could use, refer to the online documentation.

You may not see many of the next screens discussed if you picked the Express option. Just skip ahead to the section about the screen you have on your computer. You're not missing anything exciting, just the option to change server and NetWare details.

Server Settings

The Server Settings screen, shown in Figure 1.4, used to be an Advanced Settings dialog box, which you needed to press a function key to access. With NetWare 6, it appears as part of the normal Custom installation routine. Isn't it good that screens can work hard and get promoted?

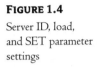

FIGURE 1.4

Server ID, load, and SET parameter settings

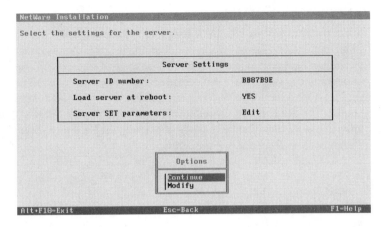

The server ID number makes no difference unless you're in a highly structured environment, where routers pass data only from listed addresses or a descriptive numbering scheme is used. If you do not require a special number, let NetWare generate the semi-random number for the server ID. In rare cases, you may need this number, so write it down. You're supposed to have a pad and pencil beside the server during installation, remember? You will have no chance to change this number after the installation concludes.

The second question on this screen has been the topic of much discussion over the years. Novell has changed the default on this from Yes to No and back with almost every version. I set it to Yes. The server should automatically restart after a power failure, a critical error, or whatever, without me (or potentially an end user) needing to get involved. Anyway, the default is now Yes, Automatically Start NetWare with Each Reboot. The choice is yours; start the debate.

The final setting is Server Set Parameters. The purpose of this option is to allow you to enter any SET parameters needed for the server to boot properly. (SET parameters are covered in Chapter 8 and Appendix B.) These parameters will then be stored in STARTUP.NCF, which is similar in purpose to a PC's CONFIG.SYS file, in that specific server parameters can be set when the server first boots. You will not normally need to enter SET parameters here, but if you do, be sure to spell them correctly. If you don't, NetWare will not recognize them and will ignore them, negating the setting you were trying to make.

Regional Settings

The next screen presents regional settings with defaults that you will probably be using. You can use this screen to set your country code. See your DOS manual (you still have a DOS manual, don't you? Oh well ...), under the heading COUNTRY.SYS for more information about this setting.

In addition, you can modify the code page you will be using. For more information on code pages, see DOS Help under MODE.

The last setting on this screen allows you to change your keyboard type for many countries. If you are installing in the United States in English, simply choose Continue to move on.

Mouse Type and Video Mode

After you choose your regional settings, you can select your video and mouse settings. Now that NetWare 6 has a GUI-based installation (coming up after the file-copy process), it only makes sense to have mouse support as well. You don't need to have a mouse for the installation, but it makes the process much easier. (Have you ever used Windows without a mouse?)

NetWare 6 supports the PS/2-style mouse, the serial mouse on COM1 or COM2, and the USB mouse. I believe that you absolutely must have a mouse on the server, if only for the installation. You may choose to leave it there if you will be using the GUI on the server for additional administrative tasks after installation. Leave the setting on Auto.

NetWare's video support is simple: Super VGA Plug and Play, Super VGA 800 × 600, or Super VGA 640 × 480. Most basic video cards will work, and you can change GUI settings in the GUI.

File Copy (First of Many)

Fetch coffee during the first file-copy break. Several times, the installation process waits for files to be shuttled between the CD and the DOS partition (this time) or the temporary installation directories and the actual NetWare file structure (later on).

You can sit and watch the NetWare installation pre-copy process if you wish. The scrolling filenames give you a better idea of what's going on than the GUI file-copy screens later.

Device Drivers

Without drivers, NetWare can't speak to any hardware component. Because the NetWare software is a server, there are two main types of drivers that need to be loaded: disk and network. Novell has split driver selection between these two broad categories, with some other options on both screens. Let's begin by looking at storage drivers.

PSM, HotPlug, and Storage Adapters

The next screen takes a few minutes to appear, as many driver files are copied. It allows you to choose a Platform Support Module (PSM), a PCI HotPlug Support Module, and the storage adapters that you will be using. This screen is shown in Figure 1.5.

FIGURE 1.5

PSM, HotPlug, and storage adapter options

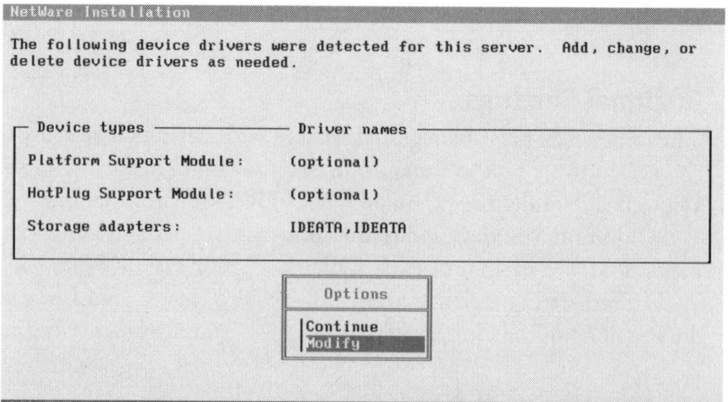

```
 NetWare Installation
  The following device drivers were detected for this server.  Add, change, or
  delete device drivers as needed.


     ┌─ Device types ─────────── Driver names ──────────────────────────────┐
     │                                                                        │
     │  Platform Support Module:    (optional)                               │
     │                                                                        │
     │  HotPlug Support Module:     (optional)                               │
     │                                                                        │
     │  Storage adapters:           IDEATA,IDEATA                            │
     └────────────────────────────────────────────────────────────────────┘


                              ┌─ Options ──────────┐
                              │ Continue           │
                              │ Modify             │
                              └────────────────────┘


 Alt+F10=Exit  Esc=Back                                               F1=Help
```

NetWare has gotten quite good at discovering all the hardware inside your server. Let NetWare try first, and add the details yourself only if you have disks with special drivers supplied by your hardware vendor.

PSM

A *PSM* is a hardware abstraction layer used when you have certain hardware installed. The system will check the hardware settings to detect which PSM is needed, if any. If you have a server with certain proprietary hardware installed (such as Compaq, Dell, or IBM), the drivers will certainly be there when you need them. A name-brand server will often include special CDs with special drivers. If your computer came with CDs like this, keep them handy during installation.

HotPlug Support Module

The second item on this screen is the HotPlug Support Module. Here, you can choose (if NetWare doesn't detect it for you automatically) the module you need to load to support HotPlug. *HotPlug* technology allows you to unplug storage and NICs while the server continues running and replace them as needed. This great benefit keeps the server up when a card needs to be replaced. Rather than shut down the entire server, you can simply remove the card and put in the new one.

Storage Adapters

The third item that NetWare will attempt to detect and display for your approval or modification is the choice of storage adapters. NetWare needs to know what type of disk and disk controller are in the server. A large number of controller definitions come with NetWare. New drivers certified by Novell are available through technical support channels, such as Novell's Web site or your dealer.

Vendors that add NetWare support for disk controllers include the proper drivers on a disk or their Web site. The installation program allows you to add vendor drivers to your system. To modify the list, choose Modify, select Storage Adapters, and press Enter. In the dialog box that appears, shown in Figure 1.6, you can use a standard NetWare convention: Press the Insert key to add something or open a pick list (a list of options available at that point). In this case, pressing the Insert key will display a list of drivers that ship with the product. Press Insert a second time to open a window that asks the source drive of the new driver. Place the disk in the server's floppy drive, and the installation program will pick up the driver and save it on the server.

FIGURE 1.6

Add, edit, or delete storage drivers as needed.

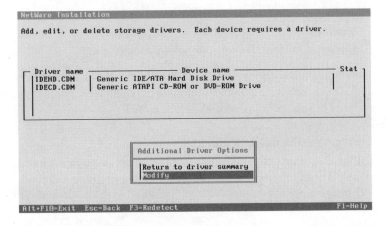

You can modify the properties of a driver by selecting it and pressing Enter. If NetWare incorrectly detects a driver, simply select it and press Delete. When you're finished making changes, choose Return to Driver Summary.

Mandatory starting in NetWare 5.*x* are NWPA (NetWare Peripheral Architecture) drivers. They replace the drivers with the .DSK extension used in previous versions. The DSK drivers were *monolithic* drivers, which meant that a single driver controlled the disk controller and all devices attached to that disk controller.

NWPA drivers continue with Novell's move toward modularity in the operating system. Rather than a single driver that controls all devices, NWPA drivers are in two parts: HAMs and CDMs. HAM (Host Adapter Module) drivers control the interaction between the NetWare operating system and the physical host adapter plugged into the server bus. These drivers use the extension .HAM. There will be one HAM driver for each adapter. CDM (Custom Device Module) drivers control the devices connected to the host adapters. There may be multiple CDM drivers for a single host adapter, since each device connected to the host adapter must have a specific driver. Table 1.2 shows the details. NWPA uses the Media Manager as the storage management layer of the NetWare 6 operating system, providing a storage management interface between applications and storage device drivers.

TABLE 1.2: NWPA DISK DRIVERS, HAMS, AND CDMS

SERVER ARCHITECTURE	CONTROLLER	HAM TO LOAD	CDM TO LOAD
ISA, EISA	AT, IDE (ATA)	IDEATA.HAM	IDEHD.CDM (for hard disk) or IDECD.CDM (for CD-ROMs)
SCSI	Adaptec 1540 and others	AHA154x.HAM	SCSIHD.CDM (hard disk), SCSICD.CDM (CD-ROM), or others depending on the device

New drivers will show up first with the devices they control. Remember to use the Insert key to redirect the installation program to look for new driver files in the floppy drive.

After selecting the adapter driver, you have the chance to verify the parameters for that driver. Any changes to adapter settings should be made here. Once the parameters are set, you can repeat the process for any number of additional drivers.

WARNING *Beware of problems upgrading old disk drivers. The DSK drivers are not supported. You will need to find equivalent HAM drivers for your devices before you upgrade.*

When you continue past the storage adapter screen, you will be presented with a screen on which you can confirm the NetWare storage devices and network cards that were found. (The storage device drivers are the .CDM files I just discussed.)

NICS, STORAGE DEVICES, AND NLMS

Like disk controllers, NICs need a driver. Network adapter drivers have .LAN as their filename extension. The next step in the installation process is choosing and configuring this LAN driver, as well as setting storage devices and NLMs (NetWare Loadable Modules). Figure 1.7 shows this screen.

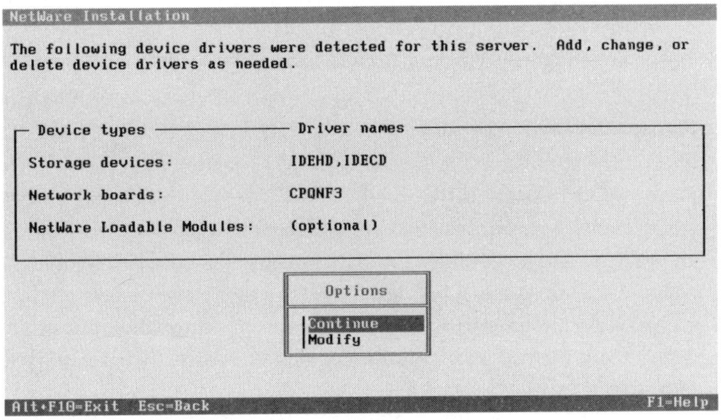

FIGURE 1.7

Storage device, net-
work board, and
NLM selections

```
NetWare Installation
The following device drivers were detected for this server.  Add, change, or
delete device drivers as needed.

  ┌ Device types ──────────── Driver names ──────────────────────────┐
  │                                                                    │
  │  Storage devices:          IDEHD,IDECD                             │
  │                                                                    │
  │  Network boards:           CPQNF3                                  │
  │                                                                    │
  │  NetWare Loadable Modules:  (optional)                            │
  │                                                                    │
  └────────────────────────────────────────────────────────────────┘
                              ┌ Options ─────────┐
                              │ Continue         │
                              │ Modify           │
                              └──────────────────┘

Alt+F10=Exit  Esc=Back                                        F1=Help
```

Network Boards

You must have at least one network adapter in the server for it to communicate with network clients and other servers. You may have multiple LAN adapters in a server. They may all be the same type of adapter, such as Ethernet, or you may have four different topologies represented. It's possible to have Ethernet, Token Ring, FDDI, and WAN connectors in one server (possible, but not likely or practical). NetWare 6 updated the TCP/IP stack to allow two network cards to share the same subnet and gateway.

NetWare commands great respect among network adapter vendors because of the large market share. Novell supplies many drivers as part of the installation process. One interface card will probably have different drivers for use in a NetWare client or a NetWare server. Make sure that you verify that your NIC vendor provides a driver for more than just "NetWare." If it goes into the server, the vendor must provide a server (LAN) driver.

Once again, you can load drivers not detected or supplied with NetWare by choosing Modify, selecting Network Boards, and pressing Enter. In the dialog box that appears, you can select any card, press Enter, and modify that card's properties. You should do this for all of your cards to ensure that NetWare is using the proper settings to interface with each card.

You need to verify, or change if necessary, the following attributes:

Is the card an ISA card?   Set this to Yes if it is a legacy (in other words not Plug and Play) ISA card; otherwise, choose No. You're not installing NetWare 6 on a server so old it needs an ISA network card, are you? Shame.

Interrupt number   Verify (and change if necessary) the number (IRQ) to make sure that the actual settings on the card match those here.

Port value   Verify (and change if necessary) the port used to access the card. Again, it must match those set on the card.

NOTE   *The IRQ and port parameters are usually supplied in hexadecimal. Be sure that you enter the parameter in the correct format and that you know the values for these two settings in both hexadecimal and decimal.*

When you have finished, choose Return to Driver List, and then repeat this process for all remaining NICs. When you have finished reviewing all of the interface cards, choose Return to Driver Summary.

Storage Devices

Back at the summary screen, you'll notice the Storage Devices choice. A reasonable question at this point is, "What's the difference between a storage device and a storage driver?" Recall from our discussion in the previous section (and Table 1.2) that there are now two components you need to load: an .HAM file and a .CDM file. You have already chosen the .HAM file on the previous screen. Here is where you choose the .CDM file. Remember that these drivers are for the various devices (hard drives, CD-ROMs, and so forth) that you have attached to your storage adapter. NetWare will usually detect them for you and have this list filled in correctly here, but you could modify these drivers if necessary.

NLMs

The last thing that you can specify here is any NLMs that are needed for the server to boot. Typically, none are needed, but if you have special hardware, the drivers for it can be loaded here.

When you have finished with the settings on this screen, choose Continue.

SYS: Volume and Partition Properties

Now that you have loaded the disk drivers, you can configure the SYS: volume. The rest of the partitions and volumes will be created later in the process. You can select the device you are interested in, change the size of the NetWare partition and SYS: volume, and so forth. As you can see in Figure 1.8, Novell presents a lot of information in a simple, well-designed manner, with defaults that greatly simplify the installation process.

The only thing that you need to know to create the SYS: volume is that it must be at least 2GB, and preferably 4GB or more. The smallest size the installation program will allow you to choose is 2006MB, because NetWare took half the disk for a 2GB SYS: volume (the minimum size Novell will happily tolerate for SYS: is 2GB). (It's a good thing disks keep getting cheaper.) My recommendation: 4GB for SYS: and put everything else on other volumes.

FIGURE 1.8

Configure the SYS: Volume and Partition

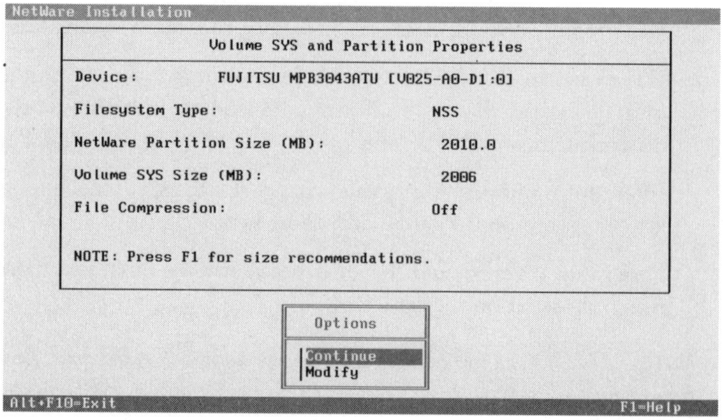

To repeat, for those of you who have multiple disks or desire multiple volumes, these choices are made later in the installation process. Here, we are just getting the SYS: volume set up.

NetWare 6 decided the SYS: volume will be an NSS volume, which wasn't even possible earlier, but is now the default.

NSS, THE NEW FILESYSTEM

The biggest change in the filesystem in NetWare 5 and 6 is the addition of NSS (Novell Storage Services), a 64-bit filesystem with many advantages over the traditional 32-bit filesystem. Table 1.3 summarizes the differences between the two filesystems. More details about NSS are in Chapter 14 (well worth reading).

TABLE 1.3: THE TRADITIONAL FILESYSTEM VERSUS NSS

FEATURE	TRADITIONAL	NSS
Character format	ASCII double-byte	Unicode (the international standard)
Time to mount a volume	Up to several minutes (depending on volume size)	Typically, only seconds
Utility used to repair damaged volumes	VREPAIR	Ongoing JOURNALING filesystem controls
Ability to access DOS partitions on the NetWare server	N/A	Accessible; treated as a standard NSS volume (load DOSFAT.NSS)
Time to repair a volume	Up to several hours (depending on volume size)	From a few seconds to a few minutes (depending on volume size)
Memory required	Increases with volume size	1MB or less for any size volume
Maximum file size	4GB	8TB (8192GB)
Maximum number of files per volume	16 million (with one namespace), 8 million (with two namespaces), 4 million (with three namespaces), etc.	8 trillion files per volume, with any number of namespaces
Volume limitations	64 volumes, 32 segments per volume, 1TB total volume size	Unlimited volumes, no limit on segments per volume, 8TB (8192GB) total volume size
Open files per server	100,000	1,000,000

NetWare 6 now allows the SYS: volume to be an NSS volume. Earlier limitations have been removed from NSS volumes, so go along with NetWare's recommendation and create SYS: on an NSS volume.

Remote Server Login

If you are installing from a local CD-ROM drive, you can skip right to the "NetWare File-Copy Process" section. If you are installing NetWare from a remote server, you'll be prompted to log in once again.

During the installation of network drivers, the connection to the remote server is broken. Reestablishing the connection takes just your login name (on the host server, not the server you are installing) and the password. This step is a necessary security precaution. Under no circumstances do you want someone to be able to connect to and take files from your system without going through security.

NetWare File-Copy Process

Now it's time for the installation program to copy NetWare files. Notice the information in the main window. If you are installing from an internal CD-ROM drive, the source may be drive D: rather than the name of a remote server and volume.

This process will take a while, so be patient. The installation program will copy many, many files to your SYS: volume, and several times during the process it will tell you that control has been passed to another NLM. It expands compressed files just copied from the CD. Also, at this point, the installation program copies the files needed to set up the GUI for the GUI installation portion of the installation process.

When the process is almost finished, it will tell you that it is "Launching NetWare 6 Installation Wizard!" You are now entering the world of the GUI installation. Welcome, I think.

The Age of the GUI Has Arrived

From now until you finish the installation, you will be using the GUI to answer all the questions needed to set up your server. You probably can figure out how to get around in this new environment.

You can, of course, use the mouse if you have one. This is the preferred (and simplest) method. However, the GUI allows you to use the standard keyboard-navigation techniques. (You will die of boredom, so get a mouse.) You can use the Tab key to move between fields, the spacebar to check or uncheck boxes, and the Enter key to perform the highlighted action (for the buttons on the bottom of the screen). Choose Next to move to the next dialog box, Back to go to the previous dialog box, Cancel to end the installation process, or Help for information about the current dialog box.

Server Naming

The first question you will be asked in the GUI, as you can see in Figure 1.9, is what you would like to name your server. It's generally recommended that you choose a short, easily typed name.

With NetWare 6, there are few places a user will need to type the server name. In almost all Windows utilities, the names of all available servers are shown in a pick list. Choosing a server entails either moving the highlight bar or clicking. There is rarely typing involved.

NOTE *In earlier versions of NetWare, the default name was FS1. This resulted in thousands of servers named FS1.*

You can change the name of the server later, but that may create a bit of work if you have referenced the server's SYS: volume (or any other volume, for that matter) in login scripts. Rather than go to that trouble, you can just provide an alias for the volume or reference certain directories with a simple directory map name. We'll get to aliases, directory maps, and login scripts later (in Chapters 5 and 9). I mention them now just to let you know that naming a server is less restrictive than it used to be. That said, choose carefully to save yourself many headaches later.

FIGURE 1.9

The age of the GUI has arrived, and it begins with the prompt for a server name.

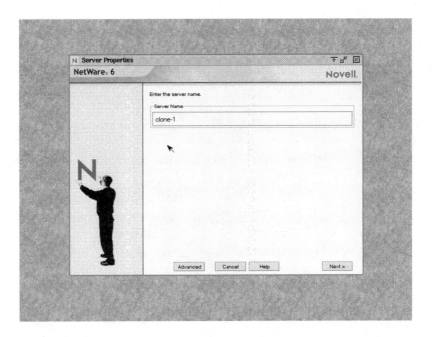

The official naming instructions are 2 to 47 alphanumeric characters, plus the hyphen and underscore. No spaces are allowed; use the underscore or hyphen instead. And go with the urge to use meaningful names for your servers. It's tough to tell your CEO his main server is BETTY_BOOP. Choose a name that means something to your users, like SALES1, 4_FLOOR, or EMAIL1. Most users do not interact with the file server but with the volumes on that server, as in SALES1_SYS or EMAIL1_GROUPWISE.

Filesystem Configuration

In the Configure File System dialog box, you can set up the filesystem any way you like. As shown in Figure 1.10, you will see all the partitions you created, including their types and sizes, the SYS: volume, and any free or unpartitioned space you have on any drives. You can delete existing partitions, create new partitions and volumes, and edit the settings of your SYS: volume (in a limited way) and all the other volumes you choose to create at this point.

Although you can create and modify volumes here, I much prefer to wait. Later on (in Chapter 8), we'll delve deeply into NSS volumes, storage pools, partitions, and other fun disk stuff.

I recommend that you accept the SYS: volume details as decided by the installation program and continue to get your new server up and running. Configuring disks can wait for a while.

Protocol Selection

The next task at hand is to select the protocol or protocols that you want to use in your network, as shown in Figure 1.11. You can choose IP, IPX, or both. New networks will likely use just TCP/IP. If that's the case on your network, don't choose IPX. If you have existing NetWare servers and clients still using IPX, obviously you need to check that protocol as well.

FIGURE 1.10

Checking the
filesystem

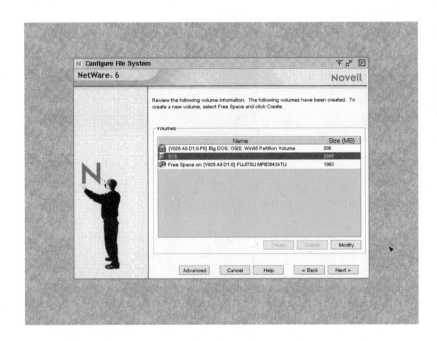

FIGURE 1.11

The Protocols dia-
log box with a NIC
selected

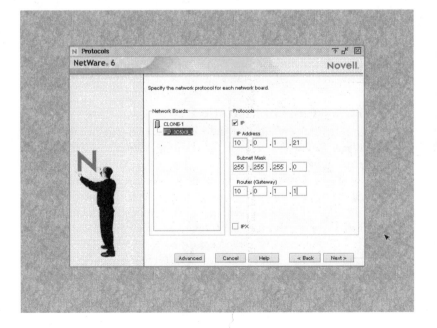

When you choose IP, you will need to fill in the IP Address, Subnet Mask, and Router (Gateway) settings for this node. The Router setting is optional, but you will need to fill it in unless there are no routers in your network. If you are not sure what these are, *do not make up an address* and type it in. If you do, you will have many problems, because wrong addresses will likely play havoc with your network. You can add IP support later. You'll find more information about TCP/IP in Chapter 11.

If you want to use IPX, NetWare will automatically detect the IPX frame type(s) on your network. If it can't detect any, it will default to installing support for the Ethernet_802.2 frame type (as all versions of NetWare since 3.12 have done). If you don't want all these frame types to be bound, at the end of the installation you will be given a chance (when you choose Customize on the Summary screen) to choose the ones you want and/or to set the addresses of each. Or do it now with the Advanced button in the Protocols dialog box.

After you click Next, the installation will take a few seconds to check for duplicate server names and IP addresses. Remember, these names must be unique network-wide. If there is a duplicate, you will get an error message and will need to choose another name.

Domain Name Service Setup

Earlier versions of NetWare, including 5.1, didn't ask about DNS (Domain Name System) until later. But Internet access has become so commonplace, and Novell has made NetWare 6 such a powerful Internet application server, that DNS configuration is now a critical part of the installation process.

Figure 1.12 shows the information for a test server. Only one name server is listed, but at least two are recommended for redundancy. Unfortunately, my ISP lists multiple name servers on the same subnet, so broken links kill my DNS, no matter how many name servers I list.

FIGURE 1.12

DNS details

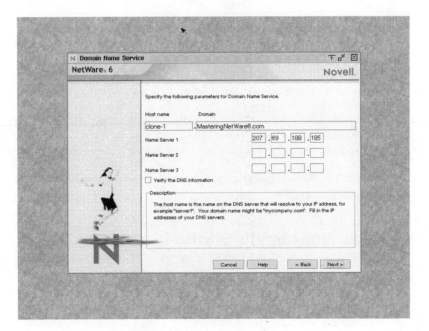

Don't ask to verify the DNS information right now, or your server will start looking for the DNS servers during installation. Set this later to make sure that the NetWare server can find the name server and check for listed entries.

Time Zone Selection

The next installation task is to choose a time zone for the server site. Figure 1.13 shows the dialog box that will appear. You can choose from 54 time zone settings, covering 29 time zones (some are in half-hour increments).

FIGURE 1.13

Choosing your time zone

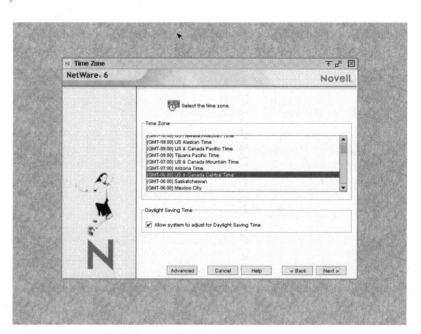

NetWare engineers made a Daylight Saving Time (DST) adjustment automatic in NetWare several versions ago. Check this box if DST applies to your location. Novell made defaults for each time zone. If most places in your time zone support it, it's checked; if not, it isn't checked.

NOTE   *When DST comes and goes, the local time will be affected, but the time that NetWare uses internally will remain the same.*

NDS eDirectory Installation

The next question you will be asked is if you want to use an existing NDS (Novell Directory Services) eDirectory tree or create a new tree. Figure 1.14 shows the dialog box where you must make this important choice. I'll assume that you are creating the first server in the tree; hence, you will need to choose New Independent NDS Tree. If you already have a tree (or trees), you can skip to the "Installing a Server in an Existing NetWare 6 Network" section. Notice that Novell now prefers the name *eDirectory* to *NDS*, although they tend to mash them together (as I did in this paragraph).

FIGURE 1.14

A very important fork in the installation process—create a new tree or use an existing one?

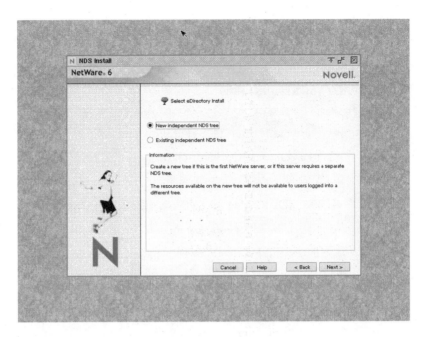

Before continuing with creating your NDS tree, there are some things you need to know about NDS. This installation isn't difficult. However, your choices here will shape what your NDS tree will look like. Read through this section before you install NDS, and if you have further questions, refer to Chapter 2 before you continue.

Before you begin, scan these brief definitions of the NDS terms you'll be seeing:

Tree The hierarchical organization of the network. Like a directory structure for a hard disk, an NDS eDirectory tree has a single root with multiple branches (directories) containing other directories and/or files (other branches and/or leaf nodes).

Container An object that can hold or contain other objects. The Tree (a special container), Country, Organization, and Organizational Unit objects are containers.

Organization A high-level container just below the Country level (if used) or the [Root] of the Tree and just above the Organizational Unit. There must be at least one Organization object in every NDS eDirectory tree.

Organizational Unit The smallest container, below Organization. This container is not required, but it's often used for better management of workgroups, departments, or project teams.

Context A way to describe the position of an object within containers in an NDS eDirectory tree. The context is a position reference point, similar to a user's home directory being a reference point in a filesystem tree.

Admin A User object created during NetWare 6 installation, similar to the SUPERVISOR in NetWare 3.x. Admin has the rights to create and manage all objects in the newly installed NDS eDirectory tree.

Leaf objects   Objects that don't contain any other objects. Leaf objects include users, printers, servers, server volumes, and the like. Leaf objects are effectively the bindery contents from NetWare 3.*x*.

WHAT YOU NEED TO KNOW

To install NDS on a NetWare 6 server, you need to know the following:

◆   The name of your NDS eDirectory tree

◆   Your company (Organization) name

◆   Any company divisions (Organizational Units) (optional)

◆   The NDS location for the server (the default Organization or Organizational Unit)

◆   The password for your Admin user (or provide the password for new installations)

You'll need this information whether you are creating a brand-new NetWare 6 network or plugging this server into an existing NDS tree. The process is remarkably similar in either case.

When you're installing your first NetWare 6 server, you must create an NDS tree and the context for the server being installed. For your subsequent servers, you must decide where in the existing NDS tree they should live.

When you're installing a new server in an existing NDS network, you can still create new NDS trees, Organizations, and Organizational Units during installation. The installation process will offer you the choice of installing the server into an existing context or creating a new context.

Although the best time to fix a mistake is immediately, if you make a mistake during server installation, it's not going to cause you any long-term trouble. If you later decide you don't like the name for a particular Organization or Organizational Unit, you can change it—no big deal.

Figure 1.15 shows four NDS tree arrangements. Each Organization or Organizational Unit is a context. The first illustration, with only a single Organization containing leaf objects, re-creates a classic NetWare 3 network. During NDS installation, you can create as many Organizations and Organizational Units as you desire.

NDS TREE NAMING

Since this is your first NetWare 6 server, you need to give your NDS tree a name and create it. Figure 1.16 shows the dialog box where NDS is configured, including where the tree name is entered. Here are the NDS tree-naming rules:

◆   Must be unique across all connected networks

◆   May use letters A–Z

◆   May use numbers 0–9

◆   May use a hyphen (-)

◆   May use an underscore (_)

◆   May be any length, as long as the complete context name does not exceed 255 characters

FIGURE 1.15
NDS tree examples, from simple to less simple

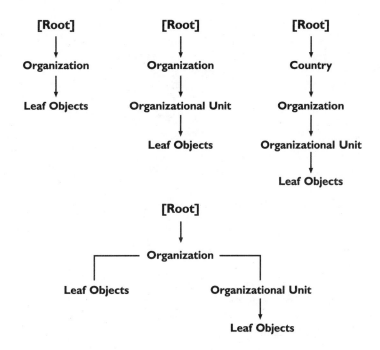

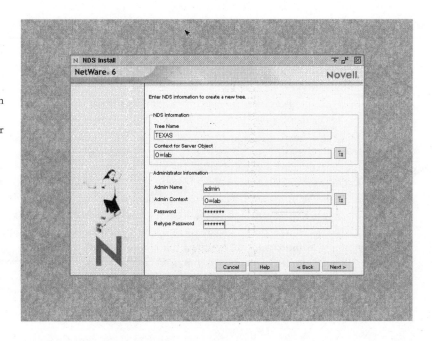

FIGURE 1.16
Entering your tree name, the context for your server and Admin user, the name of your Admin user, and the initial password for that user

There's no reason to give a long, descriptive name to the tree, because the Tree and [Root] objects are always implied (not shown) when listing contexts. This is not a problem, since Novell recommends only a single NDS tree per organization, and the client usually uses only one tree at a time.

NDS trees aren't easily renamed. Trees can be merged, but this is a more advanced topic. Pick a unique name.

THE SERVER'S CONTEXT

You must tell the server its location in the NDS tree. Every server is installed into a context, so the first server must define its own context. The server can change contexts later, but go ahead and get it right the first time.

As you can see in Figure 1.16, we have chosen a name for our new NDS tree, Texas, and set the server's context to O=Lab. The only default user for this new NDS tree is Admin (although the name can be changed at this point), the manager of the entire newly created tree. Notice also that the Admin user account's context is the same as the server context; this also represents a change from the past, where the Admin account was installed near the top of the tree. One more thing to notice in Figure 1.16: Any time a context is needed, the Browse buttons to the right of the text boxes allow you to graphically choose (and/or create) the desired context.

ORGANIZATION AND ORGANIZATIONAL UNIT NAMING

To finish the installation, you need at least one Organization name. Organizational Unit names are optional, both during installation and when your network is up and running. The NDS dialog box displays the Context for Server Object text box and the location in the tree. Next to the text box is a Browse button, where you can graphically create the structure of your tree. Click it and then select Add to create a new container.

You can choose only a Country or Organization as your top-level container. (For a discussion on container types, see Chapter 2.) Typically, you will begin with an Organization.

The Organization name can be the same as the name you gave the NDS tree itself, but that might be confusing to some users later. That's why the lab network tree has the name Texas and the Organization is named Lab (with the Organization reflecting a department). You could also give both the tree and Organization the company name without duplicating the name exactly by using a common naming standard: *TopLevelOrganization*_Tree. For example, if this is the Acme Company's network, you might want to call the tree Acme_Tree and the top-level Organization Acme.

The Organization name you type in and save will appear in the Context for Server Object field.

As you install your first server, keep in mind that this information pertains to more than just this particular server; you are creating a basic NDS framework. Maybe only one server is involved right now, but your network may contain many more servers over time.

Each field can contain a maximum of 64 characters. Legal characters in this section are A–Z and a–z (uppercase and lowercase), along with 0–9 and the underscore (_) character. The limit for the total server context name is 255 characters.

THE ADMIN PASSWORD

Passwords are an art in themselves, and your company may have guidelines set already. If not, and you need to make up a password here, try to follow these guidelines:

- ◆ It should contain at least five characters.

- ◆ It should include both letters and numbers.

- ◆ It is not case sensitive.

- ◆ It is not the name of a loved one or your birthday.

- ◆ Do not tape the password to your monitor, desk, or any other place near the computer. (Yes, people still do that.)

Select the Password field, type your password, select Retype Password, and retype the password for verification. Remember, someone logging in as Admin has full run of your network. Please use a decent password. Notice that the password appears on the display as all asterisks, so type carefully.

One final note before we move on: Once you click Next, you're committed. The installation program will create the NDS structure you have chosen, and there is no going back (although changes can be made after the installation is complete).

FOR YOUR INFORMATION: ALL THE DETAILS IN ONE SCREEN

After you click Next, the installation program will verify that the tree name is unique, and then it will create the structure you just set up in the previous dialog box. The tendency of network administrators to be distracted during installation and forget vital information is well known at Novell. Remember the pad and pencil you're supposed to have beside you during the installation process? Well, go find it, because you do need to write down the information shown in the summary screen. All this information is easy to forget while NetWare 6 is still new.

The only information you don't have on-screen that you will need is the password for Admin. Jot that down now while you're thinking of it (but please don't leave it next to the server).

You can now skip ahead to the section concerning the NetWare License information.

Server Installation in an Existing NetWare 6 Network

There are some differences between installing the first server and adding a second, third, fourth, and so on server into an existing NetWare 6 network. Some of the differences are obvious, but others are not. For example, when installing a second or third server, you may want to add another container for that server by creating another Organizational Unit. These added pieces require a few more decisions during installation, but nothing serious.

As soon as you begin the NDS installation, you must decide whether to include the new server in an existing NDS tree or to create a new tree. To install it into an existing tree, simply choose Existing Independent NDS Tree and click Next.

In the next dialog box, you need to fill in a username and password with the appropriate rights to install this new server in the tree (specifically, the Create right to the selected context, as explained in Chapter 7). This is another security feature—you wouldn't want just anybody to be able to install a server and replicate data or NDS information anywhere.

To choose your tree, click the Browse button to the right of the text box that prompts you for your tree name. NetWare will then compile a list of all known trees and ask you to select one. You can select an existing tree or choose Not Listed (the other buttons allow you to add, delete, or edit the context for your server). Choosing Not Listed displays another dialog box that asks you to enter the tree name and the target server's TCP/IP address or its server ID.

Once you choose your tree, you can then set the server's context, as described in the previous section. When you're finished, a dialog box with summary information appears. You'll notice that it is a little bit different from the one that appears when you create a new tree; this one shows only the tree name and context.

NOTE   *Each NDS tree has its own database of objects that is not visible from another tree. If you're using the Client32 software, multiple trees are not a problem. As you'll learn in Chapter 10, Network Neighborhood in Windows 95/98 and My Network Places in Windows Me/NT/2000/XP, after being enhanced by Client32, can see multiple trees. But this doesn't mean that your users won't get confused, so don't go tree crazy. One tree remains best.*

When the NDS Summary screen appears, it will remind you to write down the Admin user's password, the NDS tree name, and the server context. Remember that notepad you're supposed to have?

The NetWare License Software

One of the disks included with your software is labeled as the license disk. It will also have a user count, such as 5 User, 100 User, and so on. The installation program will ask you to insert that disk. Notice in Figure 1.17 that you can choose another location, for example from a hard drive or a server. This is not usually done, but it can be good backup policy to protect the license disk's contents in case the disk itself gets damaged. You can also check the box Install Without Licenses if you want to do this later or are installing the two-user version to practice with at home.

FIGURE 1.17

Entering the location of the license

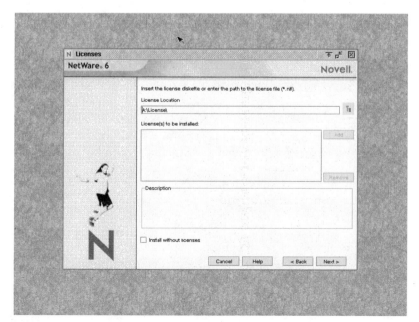

Novell has rejected some of the onerous copy-protection schemes other vendors use. If the license file from another operating system is used, error messages will appear on the servers and workstations.

None of the license schemes around work perfectly all the time. I've had trouble with NetWare releases on occasion, but less trouble with them than almost any other software. The distributed NDS eDirectory database really helps keep the licensing on track.

License management doesn't take very much time but does require care. Leaving licensing until later works for an existing network, since you'll want to put the license files in your regular spot. For new networks, however, go ahead and feed in the disk when requested.

WARNING   *Software piracy is a multibillion-dollar criminal market. Every piece of stolen software used takes money from the developer of the software that could be used to improve the product. Besides that, using software that you didn't purchase is no different from using an automobile that you didn't buy—it's theft.*

Optional Product Installation

There is one last major set of choices to make. These are optional products that can be installed at this point (go ahead and install them). Check out more detailed descriptions later in the book. You have the following choices:

- iPrint/NDPS
- NetWare Enterprise Web Server
- NetWare FTP Server
- NetWare Web Search
- Novell DNS/DHCP Services
- WAN Traffic Manager Services
- Novell Native File Access
- Novell Advanced Audit Service
- NetWare Web Access
- eDirectory iManage Service
- Novell Internet Access Server
- Novell iFolder Storage Services

A dialog box similar to that shown in Figure 1.18 allows you to make your optional product choices. To choose a product or a service, simply check the box in front of the selection (or uncheck a box if you don't want to install that component). When you have made all your selections, choose Next. Many of the components will bring up additional dialog boxes where they can be individually configured.

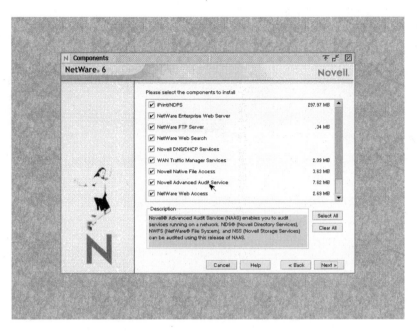

FIGURE 1.18

Choosing your optional components

A short description in the aptly named Description box explains about each product. Some of the products in NetWare 5.1 that were optional are now included in the standard NetWare 6 installation package or grouped with other products. You can always add some or all of these at a later time, or delete them if you wish.

Certificate Security—Your Papers, Please

Not exactly an optional product, the Novell Certificate Server must be installed to enable secure data transmissions, and it is required for the NetWare Enterprise Web Server. Put it in, whether you plan to use certificates or not, because some connections you may not think need certificates will use them, such as the Web servers installed to help manage NetWare 6.

The first server in the tree will create and physically store the Security container object and the Organizational CA (Certificate Authority) object for the entire eDirectory tree. If the tree has another functioning CA, the new server will located and reference the existing server, and create an object for itself.

Figure 1.19 shows a server fitting into an existing eDirectory tree with a functional CA. Otherwise, this server would create the CA in the root of the new tree.

Web Access Setup

The following screen, Figure 1.20, shows how to access the WebAccess object for configuration purposes after the server is up and running. Notice that the screen assumes you have a full internal DNS system up and running, because the reference is to `http://<web-server_name>:2211/webaccess`. If this is your first Internet server, or your DNS servers haven't been updated to hold the new server, you can use the IP address in place of the web server name. Of course, you can do that always, but the name format is easier to remember than 12 digits of IP address.

FIGURE 1.19

Getting your papers (certificates) in order

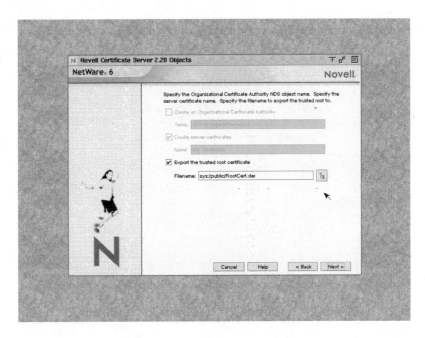

FIGURE 1.20

NetWare Web Access Setup screen

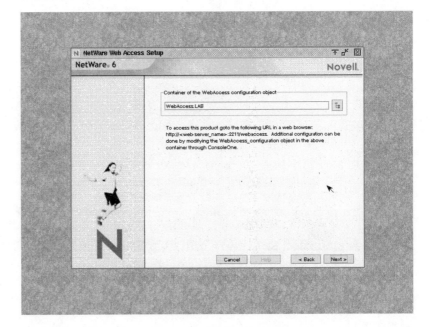

Next appears a follow-up screen asking about the Mail Gadget, iPrint Gadget, and MyFiles Gadget locations. The default checked box for "Setup … later" should be kept. You don't know where any of these things will live yet, so don't worry about it.

iFolder Server Options

Here you are, not at all sure what iFolder is, and you need to set an IP address for it. Didn't you just set an IP address for the server itself? Yes, but we have another software server that needs another IP address. Bump the server IP address up one, as shown in Figure 1.21, to keep things simple.

iFolder, a new utility that synchronizes every client system you have (desktop, home, and traveling laptop for instance) with the files stored in a private server area, runs on the Apache Web Server software. The new IP address makes it easier to control Apache and requires fewer holes in your firewall to support port numbers for connections.

FIGURE 1.21

iFolder configuration details

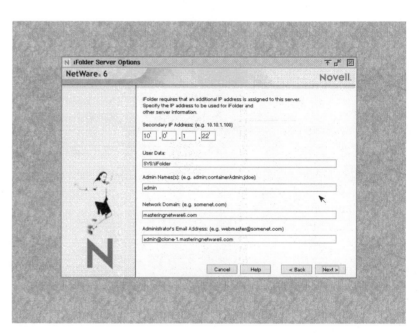

Notice the assumptions made by NetWare: it creates a folder for the iFolder information (SYS:\iFolder), it tags the administrator, it sets the domain name, and it sets the administrator's e-mail address. The e-mail address will be wrong, of course, but the figure shows the default. Feel free to change the e-mail address to one that works on your network.

Installation Summary and Customize Option

Time for the big file-copy blowout, and you get one more chance to go through and change any of the settings you've made so far. Believe it or not, everything you've checked and configured can be reached by clicking the Customize button, which is where the arrow cursor is resting in Figure 1.22.

FIGURE 1.22

Summary and last
configuration chance
(pre-installation)

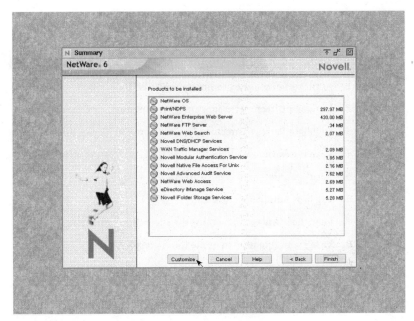

Why doesn't Novell just put this screen up and forget all the rest? Because it's easier to march
through consecutive steps than confront a ton of configuration steps on one screen.

Click the Finish button. Many files get copied—nearly 2GB worth. These include not only the
files you can see in Figure 1.22, but also the operating system files, which take about 1GB. So go to
lunch. The installation will finish before you get back, but you have a good excuse for a break.

Finishing the Installation

Congratulations, you have just installed a NetWare 6 server! Okay, you need to reboot first to get
everything working, but you're really close to finished. That wasn't so hard, was it? While you are
watching the file-copy progress, notice all the information that Novell provides. It looks a lot more
like a Windows product installation than a server installation.

As is typical of almost all Windows programs you install today, there is a progress indicator
toward the bottom of the screen. It will (slowly) move to 100 percent. Along the way, you will see
ads for various new features and capabilities in the background, another feature common to most
modern Windows programs.

The copying process will take quite a long time, depending on the options you have chosen, the
speed of your CD-ROM drive, and so on. Sooner or later, you will see the final dialog box, which
contains a quick summary and informs you of any errors. You should review this file when you are
finished. You are also told that you should restart the computer now, so that all of the selected
options and configuration options may take effect. If you like, you may also read the readme file
now. No, really, that's not a joke. You should read it. I'm serious.

Removing Novell eDirectory

IN A HURRY 1.2: REMOVING EDIRECTORY FROM A SERVER

1. At the server console prompt, type **NWCONFIG**.

2. Highlight Directory Options and press Enter.

3. Highlight Remove Directory Services from This Server and press Enter.

4. Read the warnings.

5. Verify your intent to delete Directory Services.

6. Log in as Admin or equivalent.

7. Read the warnings concerning the single NDS eDirectory tree.

8. Verify your intention to delete the eDirectory.

9. Read the messages about further actions.

Paranoia about planning your NDS tree was rampant when NetWare 4 first hit the streets, because it was new. The tools to recover from mistakes were incomplete, and some customers deleted NDS rather than try to fix it.

That's no longer true, even for the most paranoid of administrators. But if you do want to remove NDS, right at installation is a good time to do so. Play with it a couple of days, if you have this in a test environment, and screw it up good. Installation is so quick with NetWare 6 that it actually may be faster to reload NDS than to rework a mangled tree, especially in a single-server network.

From the server console screen (the one with the prompt), type **NWCONFIG**. Highlight Directory Options and press Enter to see the Directory Services Options menu. Highlight Remove Directory Services from This Server and press Enter. Depending on the situation in your network, you will see various warning messages.

Warning, Warning

NDS removal is a big deal and should be done only under the *rarest* of circumstances after the server has been put in use. However, during initial installation, you may want to play with different NDS arrangements. If one plan doesn't work well, it's little trouble to delete a basically empty NDS tree and reinstall. These instructions are only for situations in which NetWare 6 is in a pilot network test mode, no valuable information is contained on the server, and no users are going to be stranded.

However, and this is serious, *deleting a working NDS eDirectory tree erases all users, objects, printers, print queues, and groups.* This is an important point. When you remove the eDirectory, you perform a lobotomy on your server. This is the same as erasing the bindery files on a NetWare 3.*x* server. No, it's actually worse than erasing bindery files. Bindery files concern only one server at a time. If you erase a bindery, only one server's users are inconvenienced. With NetWare 6, hundreds of users may suffer some aggravation.

Directories that are part of a large network may be referenced in scores or hundreds of object descriptions. Some users may not discover the loss of the eDirectory information for that one server for weeks or months, but that just amplifies the hassle when they do realize it's gone.

Be careful about removing NDS from an existing network. Try *everything* else before you dump the eDirectory (assuming you're not just playing and are redoing NDS for learning purposes). Production systems shouldn't need an NDS replacement. Figure 1.23 shows NetWare's warning.

FIGURE 1.23

Warning! Warning!

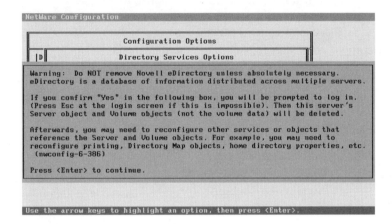

You cannot delete the eDirectory without proving you have the authority to do so. This would be a big security hole if just anyone could trash your server. NDS will demand the administrator's full NetWare name and password before proceeding. Then you'll need to wade through several more screens threatening dire things before you can actually do any deleting.

Installation Is Good, But It Will Get Better

When Novell first included a Simple Installation option in NetWare 4, some network resellers were unhappy. How can you charge a customer for installation when the customer knows the installation process is a snap? With the addition of the GUI for the installation program (beginning in NetWare 5), the procedure can even be considered "user-friendly." NetWare 6 installation is practically a breeze.

Customers, of course, are happy with these new installation features. Installing NDS (eDirectory) is simple, and any eDirectory tree mistakes can be easily corrected. What could be wrong?

What if this is too easy? What if customers figure, "no pain, no gain?" After all, NetWare is now almost as easy to install as DOS. It's much easier to configure than Windows of any version. How can this product be any good?

But only those with experience might take the "too-easy" view. Most people today *expect* things to be easier. You and I are in the computer business, and we know how much easier things are today than five years ago. People in the "real" world just see how computers are still more difficult to use than they should be.

Amazingly, the most difficult areas are those that home computer users most want. Have you installed a sound board and CD-ROM drive lately? Not simple. Modems are still killers, especially if they're cheap (and even worse if the cheap bundled software isn't configured for that particular modem). The result of these problems is that people think computers are getting harder to understand, not easier. They may be right.

I'm waiting for the installation procedure that listens to the network and configures itself. The first disk that loads the SERVER.EXE program would start a network monitor, listen for the NDS information, and fill out several proposed configurations. You then choose your favorite and get another cup of coffee. That's the kind of installation routine I want. It would also make books like this shorter.

Chapter 2

Novell Directory Services: eDirectory Overview, Planning, and Expansion

SOME PEOPLE BELIEVE, MISTAKENLY, that NDS (Novell Directory Services) eDirectory is the only improvement that NetWare 4.*x*, 5.*x*, and now 6.*x* have over the famously popular and reliable NetWare 3.*x*. Many people may also believe, mistakenly, that NDS is some terribly complicated technology that bears no relationship to earlier NetWare software, or is something like Microsoft's Active Directory.

Put your fears to rest. NDS is the next step in network organization and administration, grouping servers the way NetWare 3.*x* grouped users. NetWare 6 provides user access and simplified management to a single department, as well as to an enterprise containing thousands of servers spread across continents.

In fact, notice the name evolution of the directory service: *Novell* Directory Services. The name used to be *NetWare* Directory Services, but it was changed to reflect that NDS runs not only on NetWare, but also on other platforms such as multiple flavors of Unix, Linux, and Windows NT/2000. With these versions of NDS for other platforms becoming popular, Novell started referring to NDS as *eDirectory*, leaving the NDS name for the earlier versions, which ran only on NetWare. When you see eDirectory now, it effectively means Novell Directory Services on any platform.

We'll cover the following topics in this chapter:

- The global network view

- Advantages of NDS eDirectory

- Objects are everywhere

- Hierarchical tree structure and schema

- [Root]: The base of your eDirectory tree

◆ Planning your eDirectory tree

◆ eDirectory context control and management

◆ Bindery Services

◆ New features of NDS eDirectory 8.6

◆ Directory designs and discussions

The Global Network View

Officially, NDS eDirectory is a relational database distributed across your entire network. All servers in the network can take part in supporting eDirectory, making all network resources available to NetWare clients. eDirectory provides global access to all network resources (users, groups, printers, disk volumes, and so on), regardless of where they are physically located. Users log in to a multiserver network and view the entire network as a single information system.

Fancy official words boil down to this: Every client can see everything in the network from a graphical program provided by NetWare 6 (assuming they have the assigned rights to do so, of course). More exciting for you as the administrator is that this single network view works for management as well. You can view, change, add, or delete network resources anywhere in the network (assuming appropriate rights), without logging in to each server where the resource is located.

You've heard about how the old phones worked: You picked up the handset, an operator asked the name of the person you wanted to connect to, and then the operator took care of the rest. NDS eDirectory works in a similar manner. Instead of picking up the phone, you browse Network Neighborhood (in Windows 95/98) or My Network Places (Windows Me/NT/2000/XP), or click the "file open" icon in an application. Instead of asking for a person by name, you highlight the network resource name with a mouse, then click, and you're connected.

Many users already think things are almost this easy, which is testimony to all your hard work managing your network. The reality is, of course, that NetWare 3.x and earlier focused on each server in the network. We call this the *server-centric* view of networking. The NetWare 6 network focuses on the entire network, thus creating what is known as the *network-centric* view. eDirectory is the database, and associated programs help track all the pieces of the entire network.

NOTE   *Some procedural notes before our foray into NDS eDirectory. References to the* Directory *(uppercase D) assume the NDS eDirectory structure;* directory *(lowercase d) references a file directory on a disk or volume. The word* tree *refers to the NDS eDirectory tree (I won't be talking about the oak, willow, or pecan type). And, while you might think Novell Directory Services is plural and should be referred to in that manner, we've decided that it's a singular object and should be referred to in that manner. I will say "NDS is" rather than "NDS are." Although made of many pieces, NDS is a single logical item. (Do you say, "the six pack are cold" or "the six pack is cold"?)*

Advantages of NDS eDirectory

Stretching the earlier phone example a bit further, NDS eDirectory looks like a giant network switchboard. Everything that happens in your network goes through the central authority of eDirectory, although, like the phone company, facilities are distributed.

Another analogy (in case you're collecting them) is that of a card catalog in a library. Each object in the library is listed on a card in the card catalog. If you want a library resource—such as a book, a map, a picture, a tape, a reference book, or a meeting room—the card catalog is the place to start. To make a stronger analogy, the card catalog should be used as the inventory-tracking database as well. eDirectory tracks the location and disposition of all network resources.

NDS eDirectory is a fundamental network service. A client (such as a user, an application, or a server) requests network information, services, or access. NDS finds the resource information and provides information, network services, or resource access based on the information contained in the eDirectory.

NDS eDirectory provides the following:

♦ A global database providing access to, and management of, network information, resources, and services

♦ A standard method of managing, viewing, and accessing network information, resources, and services

♦ A logical organization of network resources that is independent of the physical characteristics or layout of the network

♦ Dynamic (on-demand) mapping between an object and the physical resource to which it refers

The "global" aspect of the database will help you, even if your network doesn't span continents. This ensures that eDirectory is available to every client and every server and that it tracks every network resource.

Let's clarify two of the earlier points. The way that NDS handles network requests and activity is not much different from the way they were handled by the bindery, but some people insist on making things more difficult than they really are. The bindery is just as important in earlier versions of NetWare as eDirectory is in NetWare 6, but eDirectory has a larger scope.

eDirectory does have the ability to handle resources that are physically distant from the file server where you are connected. Since earlier NetWare versions were completely server-centric, the idea of separating the logical object location from the physical object location never came up. With NetWare 6, the server-centric network has been replaced by network-centric eDirectory. Therefore, the physical location of a particular object in relation to a particular server is handled by eDirectory.

All these benefits come from having a single login name/password concept. This is the advantage of having all the servers work through NDS rather than individually. Before, you needed to connect to each server to use the resources controlled there. Now, you log in to the *network*, and all the NetWare 6 servers work together to provide services.

Objects Are Everywhere, and All Things Are Objects

I've mentioned objects many times. If you're wondering what objects are and why they matter, you're not alone. In the world of computing, and especially in networking, things are gradually becoming objectified. (Yeah, we made it a word because it's more fun than "object-oriented.")

An *object* is a distinct, separate entity, in programming or in networking. NetWare uses objects in the NDS structure to store information about a network resource, such as a user, group, printer, file server, or volume.

QUICK SUMMARY OF NDS EDIRECTORY

All network requests go through NDS eDirectory. Looking for a printer? Sending mail to another user? Looking for a file? Any client wanting information about or access to any (that means *any*) network resource must use eDirectory.

NDS eDirectory contains logical resource information about network resources. eDirectory contains information about each object connected to the network. The location of each object within the eDirectory tree may be different than the physical location would indicate. eDirectory is a logical, not a physical, concept.

Here's how it works with the common network task of printing:

1. **Client requests resource.** You need to print. You request a printer by its NDS eDirectory object name.

2. **A NetWare server responds.** A NetWare server, participating in NDS eDirectory as they all do, looks for the Printer object with that name in the eDirectory.

3. **NDS locates object in eDirectory.** The particular Printer object is located in the eDirectory database.

4. **Resource location is identified.** Based on the property values found for the object, eDirectory discovers the physical location of the printer.

5. **Client validity and authority are checked.** Your username and rights are checked and referenced against the list of those eligible to use that particular printer.

6. **Client is connected to resource.** You are connected to the requested printer.

Everything that happens in NetWare 6 goes through NDS eDirectory. Every network resource is tracked by NDS, and every network client uses NDS to find those resources.

---

eDirectory objects are data structures that store information, not the entity they represent. Each object consists of properties. A *property* is a category of information that you can store about an object. Some properties are required to make an object unique; those are mandatory when you create the object. The name of an object is a required property; for example, a User object name property might be "James."

The name of an eDirectory object can be a maximum of 64 characters, but there is a limit of 256 characters for any complete eDirectory name. This should not be a problem, unless you give very long names or have way too many levels in your NDS eDirectory tree.

Other properties are available in the object but not mandatory. There are many, many properties for each object, and different types of objects have different properties. For instance, the description property for James can contain "author," or it can be blank.

The information within the property is called a *value*. In the example just given, the description property value for object James is author. Some properties may have multiple values. If the property is telephone number, for instance, both office and home numbers can be listed.

Objects, properties, and their values are stored in the eDirectory database. Some objects represent physical objects, such as the User object James. Some objects represent logical, not physical, entities, such as the Marketing group. See Figure 2.1 for a graphical representation.

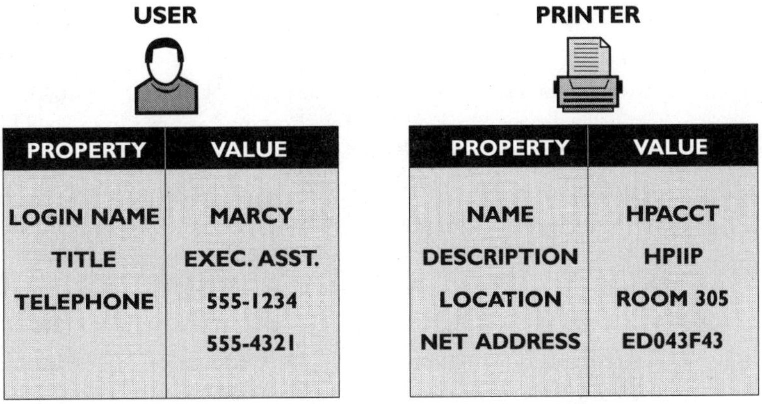

FIGURE 2.1

Examples of objects, properties, and values

USER

PROPERTY	VALUE
LOGIN NAME	MARCY
TITLE	EXEC. ASST.
TELEPHONE	555-1234
	555-4321

PRINTER

PROPERTY	VALUE
NAME	HPACCT
DESCRIPTION	HPIIP
LOCATION	ROOM 305
NET ADDRESS	ED043F43

Whether the object represents a physical or logical entity, remember that the *object* we speak of is itself only a structure for storing information. There are no objects you can touch and manipulate physically in this definition.

The object for a device is not the device. That's easy to remember when speaking of printers, but it can become confusing when speaking of logical items such as groups. The object describes the device, but it is not the device.

The category of an object is important. There are three categories, although one is slightly cheating. The *leaf* category of objects represents the actual network resources represented by the bindery in earlier versions of NetWare. Examples are users, printers, servers, and volumes. Leaf objects cannot contain any other objects. They are similar to files in the filesystem. They are the reason that everything else exists, and you can't place a file inside a file as you could place a file inside a directory.

The *container* category of objects performs that job. Container objects hold, or contain, other objects. Examples of container objects are the Organization and Organizational Unit objects. Container objects are called *parent* objects if there are actually objects inside the container. One container object is mandatory per tree. They are similar to directories in the filesystem. They are useless in and of themselves, but they are crucial for the organization they give to files.

Finally, there is the *[Root]* category, a "super" container category at the very top of your eDirectory tree. This category is created during installation, is mandatory, and slightly stretches the category metaphor. There can be only one [Root]. Each tree must have at least one Organization object. Remember naming your Organization during installation? That's when at least one mandatory Organization is created. You can create other Organizations (and other container objects) during installation or later.

Here's a quick review of the NDS eDirectory terms related to objects:

Object A unit of information about a resource; for example, a user.

Property The information category stored about an object; for example, first name.

Value The specific information within the property; for example, Ashley.

Hierarchical Tree Structure and Schema

Official stuff here: NDS eDirectory is consistent with the international standard, X.500. This specification, drawn by the CCITT (Consultative Committee for International Telegraphy and Telephony, now officially the International Telecommunications Union, or ITU; it is part of the United Nations) and the ISO (International Organization for Standardization), provides a global standard for organizing eDirectory information. The X.500 specification describes a global "telephone book" that can be used with the e-mail specifications detailed in X.400.

The eDirectory *schema* are the rules defining how the eDirectory tree is built. The schema define specific types of information that dictate the way data is stored in the eDirectory database. The following information is defined:

Attribute Information   The type of additional information an object can or must have associated with it. Attribute types are defined within the schema by specific constraints and a specific syntax for their values.

Inheritance   Determines which properties will flow down the tree to objects below the current object.

Naming   Determines the structure of the eDirectory tree.

Subordination   Determines the location of objects in the eDirectory tree.

These are all technical terms for how the standard objects, such as servers, users, and print queues, are technically defined by NDS eDirectory. The NDS schema can be modified to suit your network, which is exactly what we'll be covering soon.

[Root]: The Base—and Top—of Your eDirectory Tree

It sounds backwards to call the top of a hierarchical structure *root*, but that's what we do. A statement such as "[Root] is automatically placed at the top of the eDirectory tree during installation" is true, but sounds weird. So what is this [Root], anyway?

The [Root] object contains everything, which is why the icon for [Root] is a globe. The name of the tree, the only property of the [Root] object, is entered during installation.

The [Root] object is the very first object in the eDirectory tree and cannot be deleted, although it can be renamed. All other objects, including Country and Organization objects, are contained within the [Root] object. Characteristics of [Root] include the following:

- Mandatory
- One per Directory
- Forms the top of the eDirectory tree
- Holds only Country, Organization, and Alias objects (of Country and Organization objects only)
- Created only during installation of NDS when creating a new tree
- Cannot be moved or deleted
- Has only one property, which is the name of the tree

Analogies are fully stocked in our inventory room. In fact, that's a good analogy right there. The storeroom is [Root], the shelves are containers, and things on the shelves are leaf objects. You may have one wall for canned goods (an Organization) and two shelves named Peas and Lima Beans (Organizational Units, or OUs) on that wall.

Or your conglomerate's entire global network is [Root], with each individual subsidiary an Organization (container). Departments are Organizational Units (containers) made of file servers, file server volumes, users, printers, and all your other leaf objects.

NOTE *Do not confuse [Root] with the root directory of a filesystem. When you see [Root] with the brackets and the capital letter, it refers to the top level of your eDirectory tree. The root directory is the first directory of a volume or other hard disk and has no relationship to the [Root] object.*

For nature lovers, the tree trunk is [Root], branches are containers (with many containers from [Root]), and leaves are, well, leaf nodes. A single tree supports multiple branches, which support multiple leaf objects. Similarly, a single [Root] can support multiple Organizations and Organizational Units, which can, in turn, support multiple leaf objects.

Objects with rights to the [Root] object have those same rights all the way down the eDirectory tree. Unless blocked, a trustee of [Root] can have authority over the entire network. The Admin user, created at the same time as [Root] during installation, has a trustee assignment including Supervisor rights to the [Root] object. This allows Admin all rights to all objects in the eDirectory tree. This roughly equates to the SUPERVISOR user created during installation of earlier NetWare versions. Admin, as SUPERVISOR before, uses those rights to set up the network and create the framework for all users and other network resources.

WARNING *If you make any other user or group a trustee of [Root], that user or group may have the same rights as the Admin user. I recommend adding another user or group (besides Admin) as a trustee of [Root]. This is useful in case the Admin object becomes damaged or deleted. During NetWare 6 installation, the Public object is granted the Browse object right at the [Root] object of the eDirectory tree. This setting allows all users to see the entire eDirectory tree.*

Container Objects Go in the [Root] Object

Since [Root] contains everything, the next question is, "What is everything?" Everything, in terms of NDS eDirectory, is containers, more containers, and leaf objects. Here's a summary:

- The [Root] object can hold Country and Organization objects.
- The Country objects can hold Organization and Locality objects.
- The Organization objects can hold Organizational Units, Localities, and leaf nodes.
- The Organizational Units can hold other Organizational Units, Localities, and leaf nodes.
- The Locality objects can hold Organizations, Organizational Units, and other localities.
- Leaf nodes are not containers and cannot contain any other object.

In Figure 2.2, you see a simple NDS eDirectory design. Everything in the figure is a container except for the user and printer objects.

FIGURE 2.2

Focusing on the top
of an eDirectory tree

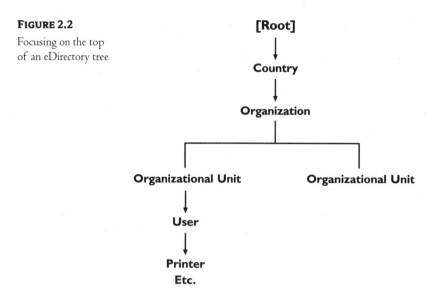

The "official" suggestion is to keep container names short. There are times when users must type a full path (called a *distinguished name*) to an eDirectory object. The location of an object in the tree is called its *context*, much as we call a file's place in the eDirectory tree its path. In Figure 2.2, the name for the user would be typed like this:

```
.USER.ORGANIZATIONAL UNIT.ORGANIZATION.COUNTRY
```

The [Root] name is always assumed to be included, since there can be only one [Root] per eDirectory tree. Country is rarely used, as you'll see.

Although the example for the user in Figure 2.2 looks like a lot of typing, it's rare for a user to type that much. There are programs for all Windows GUIs that allow a user to move around the eDirectory tree without lifting a finger from the mouse or cursor keys.

For the few times a user must type a distinguished name, keep the names of the Organizations and Organizational Units fairly short. Don't, however, sacrifice clarity for a few keystrokes. Use the common abbreviations employed elsewhere in your company, such as Eng for Engineering. Don't truncate Marketing to Mg; use Mktg.

THE COUNTRY (C) CONTAINER

Characteristics of the Country container include the following:

◆ Optional for most networks

◆ Designates the country for your network

◆ Organizes all eDirectory objects within the country

◆ Must use a two-character country abbreviation

◆ Can exist only in [Root]

◆ Holds Organization, Locality, and Alias objects only (plus a few special leaf objects described later)

NetWare 6 is a global network operating system, and the inclusion of a Country object makes that distinction clear. But the Country container is optional, even for those networks that do cross international lines. Country objects are included mainly for compatibility with X.500.

If you can avoid using the Country object, do so. Using it when you don't need to will only complicate things for your users and administrators. How often do all of one department's functions fit solely in one country, while another department's work is only in another country? Novell's recommendation is to use Organizations, Organizational Units, and Localities instead.

If you do use a Country object, it can contain only Organization, Locality, and Aliases of those objects. The only leaf objects allowed are the special leaf objects LAN Area, SLP Directory Agent, and SLP Scope Unit.

If you're in doubt about needing the Country object, you don't. Remember that even multinational networks don't require (and rarely use) the Country object to function. In fact, even in those rare situations where a Country object is desirable, an Organization object is used instead. Why? With an Organization object (or Organizational Unit or Locality), the name of the country can be spelled out, instead of using an obscure two-character code.

THE ORGANIZATION (O) CONTAINER

An Organization container has these characteristics:

◆ Mandatory (at least one per tree)

◆ Created under [Root], Country, or Locality only

◆ Typically represents a company, university, or department

◆ First level that can support leaf objects

◆ Can contain Organizational Unit, Locality, leaf, and Alias objects

◆ Named during installation, but subsequent Organizations can be created during installation or later

The next mandatory object after [Root] is the Organization container, indicated by the O abbreviation. There must be one Organization object per eDirectory tree. Novell recommends one Organization per tree if possible, but more may be created if each Organization object represents a completely separate and distinct business unit. Smaller networks get along perfectly well with a single Organization object, using Organizational Units to separate workgroups or divisions. You may give the Organization the same name as your tree, but it's much clearer during network use if you don't. For example, you might name the tree GCS_Tree and give the Organization the name GCS. This pattern avoids confusion the few times you or a user may need to type the entire tree name and context of an object.

The Organization object is the first container that can hold leaf objects. It can also hold Organizational Unit, Locality, and Alias objects. You could create an eDirectory tree with a single Organization object, place all network resources in that single container, and have a flat network design modeled on NetWare 3.*x* layouts. The big advantage that this design has over a NetWare 3.*x* network is the ability to support multiple servers and their resources for all users with a single login. In fact, this design is common in small networks and works quite well.

Multiple Organization objects can exist in [Root], and each can contain as many Organizational Unit or leaf objects as you wish. However, users must be able to search the container without being overwhelmed.

Organization objects usually contain either Organizational Unit or leaf objects, with networks tending to lean toward one or the other. If your network is large, you may have several Organization objects, each containing multiple Organizational Units, each containing leaf objects. If your network is small, you may have many of your leaf objects in the Organization object, with few or no Organizational Units. Neither way is better than the other, and the choice is usually determined by company organization rather than philosophy.

The Template object is a convenient object for providing similar services for groups of users. This object holds information you can apply to new User objects as they are created. Common details for groups of users, such as file restrictions, language used, and the like, are put in the Template object. More information on this will follow in the section on leaf objects.

The first Organization must be named during the installation of the first NDS server in the tree. Later servers can be installed into the existing Organization or in a new one created for them. Organizations may also be created in the various administrator utilities.

THE ORGANIZATIONAL UNIT (OU) CONTAINER

The following are characteristics of the Organizational Unit container:

- ◆ Optional

- ◆ Created in Organization, Locality, or other Organizational Unit objects

- ◆ Typically represents a division, department, workgroup, or project team

- ◆ Can contain Organizational Unit, Locality, leaf, and Alias objects

- ◆ Created during installation or later

The Organizational Unit (OU) object is optional but helpful in grouping leaf objects. If you have a single Organization in your network but many users and resources, the Organizational Unit objects will be valuable in organizing which resources belong closest to which users. If you have multiple Organization objects, your user base is large enough to subdivide each Organization into multiple Organizational Unit objects.

Organizational Unit objects are created within Organization objects or within other Organizational Unit objects. Organizational Unit objects can hold other Organizational Unit objects, Locality objects, leaf objects, and Alias objects.

Organizational Unit objects can be created during installation or later through normal administration utilities. They are also useful as anchors for user login scripts.

NOTE   *One early approach of shortsighted administrators was to create an OU for every NetWare 4 file server. They felt more comfortable pushing NDS into the same role as NetWare 3's bindery. But they lost many timesaving advantages and didn't let their users benefit from NDS's single view of the network. That's why I called them shortsighted.*

THE LOCALITY (L OR S) CONTAINER

The following are characteristics of the Locality container:

- Optional

- Created in Country, Organization, Locality, or Organizational Unit objects

- Typically represents a physical location or geographic area

- Can contain Organization, Organizational Unit, other Locality, and Alias objects (plus a few special leaf objects described later)

- Created during installation or later

The final container, Locality, is optional but helpful in grouping geographic areas. When you create a Locality object, it may take on two forms: the generic Locality (L) or the State or Province (S). This container was new in NetWare 5. Previous versions mentioned this object in the documentation, but it was never implemented until version 5.

If you have a single site, you will probably never use Locality objects. If you have multiple sites, you may choose to use Locality objects to represent geographic regions, states, counties, and so on, or individual sites. However, many administrators (including myself) prefer to use the Organizational Unit instead, because it can also hold leaf objects, such as servers, directory maps, and other useful objects.

Locality objects are created within Organization, Country, Locality, or Organizational Unit objects. Locality objects can hold other Locality objects, Organization objects, Organizational Unit objects, and Alias objects.

Locality objects can also be created during installation, like most of the foregoing objects, or later through administration utilities.

THE LICENSED PRODUCT (LP) CONTAINER

The Licensed Product (LP) container is for tracking licenses to various products, including the operating system itself. The licenses you purchase for a product appear as License Certificate leaf objects under this container. This container type and its associated leaf objects have a special purpose; it is not for general use.

CONTAINER RULES

Each container has rules defining where it must reside and which objects it can contain. Table 2.1 summarizes these rules.

TABLE 2.1: RULES OF CONTAINMENT FOR NDS EDIRECTORY OBJECTS

OBJECT	CAN EXIST IN	CAN CONTAIN	SAMPLE NAMES
Country	[Root]	Organization, Locality, Alias objects	US, FR
Organization	[Root], Country, Locality	Organizational Unit, Locality, Alias, leaf objects	GCS, UTDallas
Organizational Unit	Organization, Organizational Unit, Locality	Organizational Unit, Locality, Alias, leaf objects	Marketing, Integration, South Central Region, Dallas
Locality	Country, Locality, Organization, Organizational Unit	Organization, Organizational Unit, Locality, Alias objects	South Central Region, Dallas

Figure 2.3 shows four examples of eDirectory trees that illustrate the rules of containment. The first example shows the simplest tree possible. All the other examples could have multiple Organization objects, spreading the network horizontally (remember, however, that Novell recommends only one Organization per tree). There's no practical limit on the number of Organization objects that [Root] can hold, but there are reasons to keep the network from spreading too far. I'll cover many of those reasons when we look at NDS replication and how to take advantage of the fault-tolerant nature of the NetWare 6 (in Chapter 8).

FIGURE 2.3

Some sample
structures

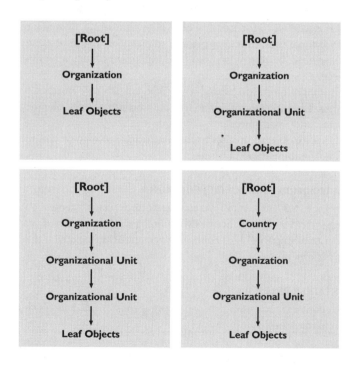

Container objects hold (contain, get it?) other eDirectory objects. A container object that holds other objects, regardless of level, is officially called a *parent* object.

Leaf Objects

Now we've come to the point of all the new objects and containers and global eDirectory trees: *leaf objects*. These are the network resources that make networking worthwhile. Yes, these are all the bindery components (and more!) that you learned to love in earlier versions of NetWare.

Figure 2.4 is an image from early in the development process of my lab network. The line divides the new NDS eDirectory containers from the older bindery-type elements familiar to NetWare 3.*x* users.

FIGURE 2.4

Old and new demarcation point between container and leaf objects

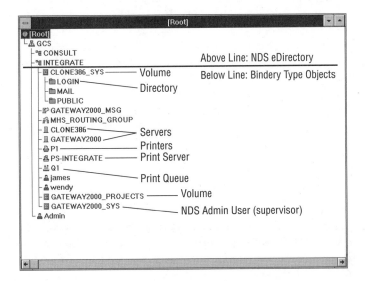

In Figure 2.4, you can see the [Root] object, with a globe icon, highlighted. Below [Root] is the Organization object named GCS. Two Organizational Unit objects are contained in GCS. The first, CONSULT, is not expanded. The second, INTEGRATE, is the main context for this early version of the lab network.

Labeled for you are a few of the leaf objects that directly correspond to earlier NetWare versions. You can see NetWare volumes, NetWare servers, users, and some standard NetWare system directories (such as LOGIN and PUBLIC).

Later, you will see many pictures of the lab network as it grows and changes and transmogrifies to illustrate the flexibility of NetWare 6. But now, let's see what new spin NetWare 6 has put on our old friends such as users and groups. We'll also look at some new items that didn't exist until NetWare 4 or later.

The name of a leaf object can contain a maximum of 64 characters, but be aware of your limits and your users. The distinguished name of an object cannot exceed 256 characters. Painfully long names for leaf objects will aggravate your users.

NOTE *Remember that each item discussed here is represented by an icon for the object, not the device itself. That's the trick with object-oriented systems, you know. You always speak of the object representing some physical or logical item, not necessarily the item itself.*

USER

The entire reason for the network is users. The icons of the User objects represent the people who log in to the network and use the network resources.

There are many User object properties that you can set, such as login restrictions, login scripts, password and password restrictions, and security equivalencies. In fact, there are 18 pages of properties that you can set, and more may be added depending on what other services (such as e-mail) you add to the network.

When you create a User object, you may create a home directory, just as in earlier NetWare versions. You can create User objects anywhere in the eDirectory tree, but your users typically must know that location in order to log in. However, with the new Catalog Services, the system can locate the User objects that match the user's login name and display a list of possible contexts. This having been said, it's best to create them in the context in which they will spend most of their time. It is only a matter of clicking one context or another in the ConsoleOne, Remote Manager, or NetWare Administrator programs.

GROUP

Just as in earlier NetWare versions, a *group* is a collection of users with common network requirements. The Group object is a list of User objects that can be located anywhere in the eDirectory tree. There is no requirement to limit Group object members to a particular context.

Group objects act as management shorthand. Rather than make many similar trustee assignments to individual User objects, applying these same trustee assignments to a Group object does the job for each User object listed in the Group object. Many of these same statements can be made for members of the same container too. If you prefer groups, you can include members of different containers. Groups are most useful for subsets or supersets of a container.

NOTE *Remember that the Group object is a leaf object, not a container object, in much the same way that you may be a member of an auto club, but the auto club doesn't contain you in any way.*

NETWARE SERVER

Also called NCP (NetWare Core Protocol) Server objects, the NetWare Server object represents some machine running NDS eDirectory on your network. The server can be a NetWare, Unix, or NT server, or any other operating system that has NDS eDirectory ported to it. The Server object is created automatically when the NetWare Server software is installed.

The NetWare Server object is used as a reference point for several other objects, such as NetWare volumes. The Server object's properties hold a great deal of information, such as that particular server's physical location, services provided, and the error log.

NOTE   A bindery-based server (as in a NetWare 3.x server) must have a Server object created for the server in order to access the server's volumes in ConsoleOne or NetWare Administrator. The bindery server must be up and running when this happens, so the Add New Object routine in ConsoleOne or NetWare Administrator has a server to use for verification and reading during the installation process. Or you can use the Novell Upgrade Wizard and upgrade your 3.x servers, as Novell is pushing you to do (don't fall for it; replace those servers with new hardware).

NETWARE VOLUME

Volume   The Volume object represents a physical NetWare volume on the network, automatically created during the NetWare 6 server installation. You may, however, need to create the Volume object inside ConsoleOne to display the volume's icon. Double-clicking the Volume icon in ConsoleOne displays the volume's filesystem. The Volume object's properties include information such as the name of the host server, volume location, space limits for users, and available disk space, among many other details.

You can create multiple Volume objects that refer to a single physical volume, for example, to refer to it easily in other contexts. You can also create Volume objects to refer to volumes on NetWare 2.x or 3.x servers, as eDirectory reaches back to include volumes from these earlier versions.

PRINT OBJECTS

NetWare 5 introduced a new method for printing, called Novell Distributed Print Services (NDPS), but NetWare 6 still supports the old queue-based system for backward compatibility. There are separate objects for both types.

NDPS Printing

The following objects are used in NDPS:

NDPS Broker   **NDPS Broker**   Represents an NDPS Broker, which is used to enable the advertising of printer services, handle printer events, and deal with resource issues (such as printer drivers for clients). NDPS creates one Broker object by default.

NDPS Manager   **NDPS Manager**   Represents an NDPS Manager, which is used to create and maintain NDPS Printer Agents. NDPS Manager objects are central to the entire NDPS scheme.

NDPS Printer   **NDPS Printer**   Represents a printer in the NDPS system. NDPS printers come in two types: public access and controlled access. Public-access printers are available to anyone on the network and are not represented by NDPS printer icons in the tree. A controlled-access printer can be limited and is associated with NDPS printers in the eDirectory. You can search through the list of controlled-access printers for a printer with certain characteristics. They have a broad range of security, event notification, and status notification options.

Queue-Based Printing

The NetWare print objects for queue-based printing include the following:

P1   **Printer (non-NDPS)**   Represents a physical network printing device. One Printer object is required for each printer in the network.

PS-LAB   **Print Server (non-NDPS)**   Represents a network print server, whether located on a NetWare server or another machine. One Print Server object is required for every network print server.

Q1   **Print Queue**   Represents a network print queue. A Print Queue object is required for every network print queue.

You create the print objects using the NetWare Administrator utility program. Some third-party print server devices may create the Printer object for you, but you should verify this before trusting that it is done correctly with eDirectory.

NOTE   *All of the above leaf objects (except for the NDPS printing objects) existed in the old bindery (a.k.a. NetWare 2.x and 3.x) days. The rest of the objects in this section are unique to NDS. Most of them have existed since NetWare 4 days, but a few were new in NetWare 5.*

DIRECTORY MAP

Directory Map   The Directory Map object points to a particular directory on a volume. This works like the MAP command by representing what could be a long pathname as an easily remembered label. Directory Map objects help you manage your login scripts. In the login script, use a Directory Map object to refer to a particular directory. Then, if the pathname changes, you won't need to update each and every login script that includes the directory.

A common example is a product upgrade. Say you use Visual Kumquat Designer version 2.2. As is their wont, the software makers release a new version, 2.401, which is not compatible with version 2.2. If you have a Directory Map object pointing to the directory holding Visual Kumquat Designer, you can place the new software in a newly created VKD_2401 directory. Then make a single change in the Directory Map object. That's all it takes to point all Directory Map requests from the old VKD_24 directory to the new VKD_2401 directory. You won't need to change a single login script; all users will automatically access the VKD_2401 directory.

ORGANIZATIONAL ROLE

Organizational Role   Perhaps my favorite eDirectory object, the Organizational Role object represents a position or role within the company organization. It is typically used for jobs that have well-defined requirements but that are performed by a rotating group of individuals rather than a single person.

For instance, team leader may be a position that needs some access rights above and beyond those of the rest of the workgroup. Granting those rights to the Organizational Role rather than to individuals makes it easy to track which person has these extra rights at any one time. When the team leader changes, the next person can be assigned the Organizational Role. That user will immediately inherit all the team leader rights. You may even have multiple users assigned to the role, for example, in the case of co-team leaders. The big difference between Group and Organizational Role objects is that Groups have members but Organizational Roles have occupants.

PROFILE

Profile   The Profile object contains a Profile login script, a special login script used by individuals with common needs but little else in common. If the Profile object is listed as one of a User object's properties, the Profile object's login script is executed when that User object logs in.

The Profile object provides a way for users who don't belong to the same context, such as accounting payroll clerks from multiple divisions, to share common login script commands. For example, the Profile login script may provide these users with access to particular directories or special printers. This process also works for a subset of users in the same container. The biggest caveat here is that each User object may be assigned a maximum of *one* profile.

COMPUTER

A Computer object represents any computer on the network that is not a server, such as a workstation, a router, an e-mail gateway, or the like. Use the Computer object properties to store information about the system, such as network address, configuration, serial number, the person it's assigned to, and so on. The Computer object is informational only; it has no effect on network operations. Because it is for documentation purposes only, it is rarely used. When was the last time you had time to document your server configuration, much less that of all your workstations? If you have done it, when was it last updated? I thought so.

ALIAS

The Alias object points to another object in the eDirectory tree in a different context. When you use the Alias object, objects appear to be in places they really aren't. Using an Alias object is an easy way to allow users to access an object in another context.

This is fun: The Alias object is a representation of a representation of an entity. In other words, the Alias object takes the form of another object and makes it appear that the second object is in a place it's not really in.

When an object is moved or renamed, you have the option of leaving an Alias object in its place. This keeps resources in the (seemingly) same place for the users who rely on those resources, even after the resource has been moved. If you delete or rename an Alias object, the Alias itself is affected, not the object to which it's pointing.

WARNING *Be careful when modifying an Alias object or an object that has an Alias. The Alias object takes the shape of the object it replaces or points to, so changes made to either affect both. Look for the small Halloween mask beside the Alias object.*

If you want to access the Alias object and the properties of the object it refers to, you need the Read right to the Alias name and the Read right to the properties of the object it refers to. You can set these options in ConsoleOne or NetWare Administrator.

BINDERY AND BINDERY QUEUE OBJECTS

The Bindery object represents an object placed in the eDirectory tree by an upgrade or a migration utility (such as the Novell Upgrade Wizard).

The Bindery Queue object is exactly what you might expect: a print queue from a NetWare 3.*x* server placed in the eDirectory tree by an upgrade or a migration utility.

Both of these objects are used by NDS eDirectory to provide compatibility with bindery-based utilities. Some third-party print servers still expect the bindery and its capabilities and require it to function. You'll find more on bindery emulation at the end of this chapter.

UNKNOWN

The Unknown object is an eDirectory object that has been invalidated or corrupted. The eDirectory tree does not recognize the object. These Unknown objects appear when changes are made to eDirectory, such as when a NetWare server is deleted and the administrator forgets to delete the volumes for that server. The volumes will then appear as Unknown objects.

During large-scale changes to the eDirectory, some objects may briefly appear to be "unknown." This is caused by changes being made faster than eDirectory can synchronize. If you make changes and see Unknown objects, wait awhile. However, the best action is to delete Unknown objects that persist. You can also try the maintenance utilities discussed in Chapter 8 to see if they fix the problem. In the case of orphaned volumes, re-create them if they belong to a server that has been re-created or modified.

TEMPLATE

The Template object is used to create users with common properties. This is a very powerful object, because you can modify all the users based on the template at once.

For example, let's say that your accounting department is moving from an outpost in Houston to corporate headquarters in Dallas. Do you want to edit the location property for 100 accountants? Me neither. All that you need to do is select the template in ConsoleOne, change the location in its property page, click OK, and *voilà*, they are all updated. A template also helps when you have many properties that are the same for a bunch of users (like a department), users who need the same restrictions placed on them, and so on. Try it—you'll like it.

MISCELLANEOUS OBJECTS

You will see some other objects as you use NetWare 6. Some of the objects are standard, and some will show up when you install optional components, upgrades, and so on. I'll discuss those that appear when you install optional components later, as they come up. The other standard objects provide advanced functionality:

- The SLP (Service Location Protocol) Directory Agent object and SLP Scope Unit object are used for the new Service Location Protocol (the replacement for SAP when using TCP/IP).

- The Key Material object is used for cryptography services.

- The NDSCat: Master Catalog object and NDSCat: Slave Catalog object are the NDS entries that make up Catalog Services, which allow contextless login, among many other things.

- The LAN Area object is used like the Groups object, but for servers rather than users, in that all servers that belong to this object have a common WAN policy applied to them.

Planning Your eDirectory Tree

NetWare 6 uses building blocks in network design that were not available until NDS version 2. These include the NDS eDirectory tree, Organizations, and Organizational Units. Only when we speak of the leaf nodes, such as users, printers, servers, and volumes, do we overlap the pieces used by NetWare 3.x and earlier versions.

Although some administrators new to NetWare 6 fear these building blocks, many others understand the advantages that the eDirectory tree offers to network architects. How many NetWare customers have a single server to handle every job? A few, but the normal sequence is to get one server, then have an application or two grow beyond that one server. Suddenly, the workgroup that started with one server has four servers.

With pre-NDS versions of NetWare, the management overhead quadrupled (and more) as the new servers arrived. With NetWare 6, however, each server is just another object in the eDirectory tree. More important, each disk volume is just another object, and any one user can easily reference a dozen volumes with a single network login.

Some Goals for Your eDirectory Tree Design

Plan your large eDirectory tree to meet the following goals:

- Fault-tolerance for the Directory database
- Decreased traffic on the network, especially over WAN links
- Easy lookup of information and resources for users
- Simplified network administration and maintenance

There is no one, perfect way to plan your eDirectory tree. The design that works for your network may not work for another network. The design for one division of your network may not work for another division. How your tree begins may not be how it ends. There are tools to modify the NDS structure, and I'll discuss them in due course. Expect your network to change; expect to change NDS as a result.

NOTE Every new network and installation must have a complete, detailed plan describing every particular. One customer once told me, "We plan monthly and revise daily." Although he said it as a joke, a lot of networking truth is in that statement. Since a network is a collection of people, things will change because people change. That's a guarantee. But even though things will change, you need a plan to provide a network framework. Once you have a plan, you can deviate from the plan. If you don't have a plan, you will wander about, getting more lost every day.

Before I get into specific planning and installation ideas, remember that adding NetWare 6 will be an adjustment for both you and your users, especially if coming from NetWare 3.x or even NetWare 4. The more comfortable the users feel, the easier the transition to the new network. Here are some tips for improving your rollout process:

- Run NetWare 6 in a lab environment.
- Demonstrate NetWare 6 to your power users before the upgrade.

◆ Train users before the upgrade (but not too long before or they'll forget).

◆ Draw NDS designs until everyone's priorities are covered.

◆ Coordinate with all other network administrators during the planning process.

Work with all other network administrators to develop an eDirectory tree that everyone can accept. No network design suits everyone perfectly, but you need to cover the priorities. This will require input from the other network administrators and representative users during the NDS design stage. The more closely everyone works together, the more successful your network will be.

When Novell implemented NDS on its global corporate network, managers met and talked (argued) about the design for months. Those wanting a purely geographical design disagreed with those wanting a design modeled strictly along job function lines. Finally, a hybrid network was designed and built. If the people at Novell themselves don't have a "magic" design that suits everyone, why should you?

When we speak of planning NDS design, we get into some gray areas, since each company and network is different. The process differs considerably depending on whether you will be doing all the setup and management or whether you are one of many network administrators. If you do it all, your plans can be less detailed, because you will be the one making all the decisions as new questions arise. If you're working with a group of administrators, planning is the most important part of the process. You and all other administrators must be in agreement about NDS before starting.

The goal is supporting your users in the most efficient manner (for them) possible. Making resources easy for your users to find will speed their workday and, more selfishly, keep them from bothering you all the time. A good network design can save hours of network training.

Semantics can cause arguments in this section. Is a "bottom-up" design the same as a "logical" design? Is "top-down" the same as "managed" or "preplanned"? Who cares? The important part is making the network fit your situation.

The focus here is on designing networks based on user function or user location. These roughly correspond to the top-down and bottom-up labels. As you might guess, a large network, or one that covers several geographic areas, will use a combination of both methods.

Setting Up a Pilot System

It will save you time and aggravation to have a pilot NetWare 6 server up and running before you begin the rollout, particularly if coming from NetWare 2.11 or earlier. It will also help immensely if you can have representative samples of your clients set up as well. Include the different architectures, models, brands, and so on of computers and the operating system(s) that you plan to run on them. I know this sounds like a lot of work, but it will save you a lot of time and grief later on (not to mention embarrassment when something doesn't work right in front of the user). Even if the pilot server is running for only a week or two, the experience will be invaluable.

Build some sample users with different rights and let people experiment. User 1 may have the run of the server, while Users 2 and 3 can use only specific areas. Place instructions in the test area so that users can log in and tour the network under each username already created for them.

Be sure to make the pilot system available to the power users in your organization. You know the users I'm speaking of: those who read all the computer magazines, haunt the Internet, and informally help all the users in their area. They will be interested in the workgroup management facilities, since that kind of authority will verify what they've been doing unofficially for quite a while.

NDS Design Phases

Each network design, regardless of the architecture, has two phases: logical and physical. The *logical phase* focuses on the eDirectory structure and the process for implementing that structure. There are three main steps in the logical design sequence:

1. Determine the eDirectory tree structure.

2. Identify the naming conventions for your network.

3. Plan your implementation method.

The *physical phase* focuses on how users access the eDirectory during their workday. This phase also considers how information is stored on the servers and how it is coordinated to provide accurate eDirectory and time information. The physical design sequence also has three main steps:

1. Determine security considerations.

2. Set up eDirectory replication.

3. Synchronize eDirectory time.

The departmental design that served so well with earlier versions of NetWare also works fine with NetWare 6. But NetWare 6 gives you many more options than the basic "one department, one server" design strategy. Even better, you can take the departmental strategy and fold it into a bigger, more client-friendly framework.

DESIGNING FOR USERS: WHO WORKS WITH WHOM, AND FOR HOW LONG?

Don't get timid when designing your new company network. You must have the courage to ask questions. Some people you must question don't normally get involved in the network. You must, if no one else in your company ever has, make some sense of which people really work on which projects with which other people.

This may sound easy, but if it is easy, you haven't dug down deep enough. You may have set up your existing network to mirror groups of people sitting close together in departments all in one building. That worked well with the limitations forced on large companies by departmental, server-centric networking. Although you can still set up your network in this manner, you are no longer limited to a departmental design.

Are you familiar with the futurists (and network designers) and their new definitions of work? According to sources as varied as Alvin Toffler and developers of workgroup software such as GroupWise and Lotus Notes, people regularly shift and change their internal work partners. A project begins; a team is gathered. A project ends; the team members go in various directions.

This is cleaner than what usually happens, of course. Theories, no matter how outlandish, pale beside the mess we people make of plans. If your life as a network administrator is typical, you are a member of ten ad hoc groups. You have meetings to choose new software, to review current vendors, and to get authorization for a new server or two, in addition to managing personnel, marketing support, remote computing, and network security. If you ever dream of pieces of yourself being pulled apart and flying in all directions, save the psychological counseling fees. You're just dreaming about your normal workday.

E-mail and groupware help us deal with the mess we've worked ourselves into, but they can't do it all. Your network design for NetWare 6 will go a long way in helping improve the ease of user interaction. The easier it is for users to share information, the better the resulting project.

Design versus Implementation

Your network *design* is planning the NDS structure. Your network *implementation* is creating the NDS structure. You might think that the "design" component always comes before the "implementation" component. That's not true. The best designs always consider the problems of implementation and maintenance. The key here is simple: The more time you spend *planning* your eDirectory tree, the less time you will spend *re-creating* your tree later (which can be very time-consuming).

Are you upgrading from an earlier version of NetWare? If so, some of the design choices will be made for you. The users, tied to a particular server throughout their NetWare experience, may want to remain tied to that server. Create a comfortable environment for them by intelligent NDS design, and their transition will be smoother.

If you are upgrading, are you upgrading all servers at once? With a small network, it's possible to upgrade all servers in one pass, usually over a weekend. The user leaves an office with one network design and returns to the same office with a different network design. If you aren't upgrading all the servers at once, you may wind up creating multiple eDirectory trees and merging those trees later, although this is not usually recommended.

Are you "seeding" the network with one NetWare 6 division and gradually expanding the NDS eDirectory reach through the rest of the company? This method offers more time for training users and coordinating departments, but it isn't magic. You must provide Bindery Services for those users caught between two departments that upgrade at different times.

If you create multiple eDirectory trees, a consistent naming convention must be agreed upon before the rollout begins. If a single eDirectory tree is created and expanded when each part of the company is connected, the naming consistency is just as important but a bit easier. The only advantage is that you will know about name conflicts as they arise during each department's installation, rather than all at once during the upgrade procedure. More work will be necessary to combine multiple trees into one tree than to create one tree and add to it.

Developing Naming Standards

With earlier NetWare versions, a "naming standard" generally meant using the last name and first initial, or the first name and last initial, for user login. Large companies focused on the last name; small companies and departments favored the first name.

With NetWare 6 and the global eDirectory database, you must develop a more complete naming standard. Names are needed for User, Printer, Server, Volume, Group, Organizational Role, Directory Map, and Distribution List objects, to name a few. A lot of names will be needed before all is said and done.

Naming standards provide a framework for naming all network users and resources. These standards work best with consistency and a goal of making users comfortable while navigating a large network full of resources. The new search capabilities, as well as Catalog Services, in NetWare 6 eDirectory work best when simple wildcard searching is possible. If all servers are named SRV*something*, a search with SRV* provides usable results. The same is true with printers: Name all laser printers LAS*something*, and searching for a printer becomes simple.

Name length for any object is the same: 64 characters. The caveat is that the total length for the distinguished NDS name of an object cannot exceed 256 characters including periods, equal signs, and name type designators. Long names or deep eDirectory trees will cause users to work unnecessarily hard and may bump against your name-length limit. Short but descriptive names have these characteristics:

- Make names easier to remember
- Simplify logins
- Use capitalization to increase readability
- Use hyphens rather than spaces
- Reduce NDS eDirectory traffic across the network

If you are using Bindery Services, keep in mind the naming restrictions of NetWare 3.*x*. Keep names particularly short to fit all systems the user will be encountering.

If you are migrating some NetWare 2.*x* or 3.*x* users, there may be some renaming necessary. If you have been planning to redo your naming standards, the transition to NetWare 6 is a good time to make your move. Even if it's not technically true, everyone will believe you when you tell them they must change names because of the new network.

Table 2.2 shows some naming standards and the rationale behind them, along with some suggestions.

TABLE 2.2: SOME SUGGESTIONS FOR NAMING STANDARDS

OBJECT	NAMING STANDARD	EXAMPLES
User	You might want to limit names to 8 characters. Shorter names make good home directories, and some applications still choke on longer names. Using middle initials will reduce the number of duplicate names in your tree. Decide now how to handle duplicate names if they still occur. Choose names that work with both the network and your e-mail package.	James E. Gaskin becomes JEGASKIN; Raquel Ethyl Baker becomes REBAKER.
Server	Server names must be unique on the network. Use a set of 3- or 4-letter codes for the location, department, and server. Airline city codes are good location designators (DFW for Dallas Ft. Worth; LAX for Los Angeles) because they are unique, but they can be difficult for nontravelers to recognize. (Do you know that YYZ is Toronto, Ontario?)	SRV-LAX-ACCT-001
Group	Base group names on the group function.	GP-ACCT for the accounting group
Printer	Use city codes as for servers, along with building location codes and printer type. Preface the name with P for queue-based printers or NDPS for NDPS-based printers to distinguish them.	NDPS-DFW-HP-LJ4SI
Print Queue and Print Server	Start with PQ or PS. Include the host server name and the numeric ID of each.	PS-GATEWAY2000-1

continues on next page

TABLE 2.2: SOME SUGGESTIONS FOR NAMING STANDARDS *(continued)*

OBJECT	NAMING STANDARD	EXAMPLES
Organization and Organizational Unit	Use your company's internal abbreviations if possible. Reference a short version of the company name for the Organization object.	OU=SALES.OU= WEST.O=ACME
Organizational Role	Base the name on the job function. Always grant administrative rights to the Organizational Role rather than to particular users for ease of control when job descriptions or people change.	OR-ACCT_MGR
Profile	Base the name on the job function.	PR-PTRS-Y
Directory Map	Base the name on the application being mapped.	DM-WP, DM-EMAIL

Some may complain about the extra characters needed for the "type" designator at the beginning of each name, such as DM-EMAIL. This is not a requirement, of course, just a suggestion from Novell. If your company wants to rely on the icons under Windows to provides those clues, that's fine. But be consistent. For example, don't label some groups GP-EMAIL and other groups just ACCT. Your users may be more aggravated by the confusion than they are about typing the extra characters.

Organizing by User Location (Bottom-Up)

This tree organization is often labeled the *departmental* or *workgroup* method, but the terms *bottom-up* or *user-location* method work just as well. The key point is that this is an independent group that will later be part of a larger group.

Some references assume this bottom-up plan can be done only by creating separate eDirectory trees for each department and joining them later. That method will work and may make sense when the eDirectory trees that the department will later join are geographically dispersed. Instead, you can make the department a self-sufficient Organizational Unit inside an existing eDirectory tree. The important consideration in the user-location method is to set the department as a distinct entity from the rest of the corporate network, whether it is NetWare 3, 4, 5, or 6. A group of users who share a location and a set of resources fits this profile, regardless of whether these users have their own tree or just their own Organizational Unit.

DEPARTMENTAL DESIGN

Focusing on the department when designing your eDirectory tree makes sense under several circumstances. Especially with the new NDS eDirectory utilities offered with NetWare 6, there is no longer an administrative penalty to pay for developing a network design that must be changed later.

When the departments will stay isolated from one another, the bottom-up (figuring the department is the bottom of the organization chart) design works well. This design also works well if there is no strong, central administration group dictating standards. Even if there is a central group, it may not yet be prepared with a comprehensive plan that supports all departments. It wouldn't be the first time the people doing all the work are inconvenienced by the HQ folks trying to figure out what they're doing, would it?

There are benefits of the departmental design, whether each group is a completely separate tree or just containers that don't interact. Each department can maintain the names used in earlier NetWare versions for ease of learning and minimal disruption. Although duplicate names in the same context are not allowed when the trees are merged, separate trees spread the learning curve out a bit. However, if you do your job right, this shouldn't be much of a problem. Forcing users to learn NetWare 6 at the same time as renaming all their network resources (again, if you do your job right, this will be, at most, their username) is a lot to handle all at once, but it may make sense. Why have them learn three or four transitional schemes? Plan up front and get all the pain out of the way at once.

NetWare 6 users running Client32 software will be able to see multiple trees at one time. If each department is its own container, some sharing can be introduced gradually. This situation is perfect for Alias objects, which allow you to refer to other container resources. You don't need to teach the users all about contexts and the NDS hierarchy until they're ready to learn, if ever. If you do your job well, most users will never know about contexts, NDS, and so forth anyway.

If you set up separate trees before a central plan is established, you'll need to combine trees. Remember that servers must have a unique name across the entire tree. Some minimal guidelines must be available for server names before you can integrate each department into the larger network. To help ease context issues after you merge, consider having a common Organization under the [Root] and placing all your other objects under it. When you merge the trees, simply rename one of the Organizations and merge the trees; there are no context issues.

PHYSICAL AND LOGICAL VIEWS

Network diagrams are handy, at least until they're outdated (which happens constantly). With NetWare 6, two types of network diagrams can become obsolete: physical and logical views of your network.

The physical view of your eDirectory tree shows the branches clearly, with all network resources of that branch grouped together. Once the department tree is merged into the larger network, the current administrator may well continue to be the container administrator. The authority of the container administrator is similar to that of a full administrator, except that this authority is over only a specific container or branch of the tree.

Figure 2.5 is a physical diagram of a departmental design network in its own tree. Both servers and volumes are represented, as are users, printers, and the like.

NOTE *The physical diagrams are not what you are used to. They are not the ones that show the wire and all users, servers, and printers attached to that wire. You may have one diagram for each floor of your building or just one large diagram for everything. Those are* wiring *diagrams, which prove useful when expanding and troubleshooting your physical network. What we mean by a* physical view *here is the icons strung together.*

The physical diagram is less important in small networks than in larger ones. However, if you have no naming designators (as is the case for the items in Figure 2.5), the icons help clarify which name refers to a Group, a Directory Map, or an Alias object.

FIGURE 2.5

A departmental
eDirectory tree,
physical view

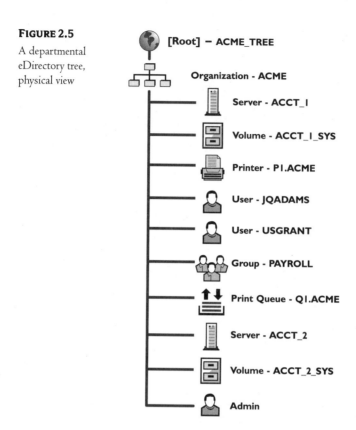

Figure 2.6 shows the same information as Figure 2.5, but uses block diagrams and NDS abbreviations rather than icons, for a logical view. Admittedly, there is not a lot of difference when showing small networks. Notice that the naming designators would help clarify some details in the logical view that didn't really need clarification in the physical view. Quick, without looking back at Figure 2.5, what is PAYROLL? Is it a group, a volume, or a directory map?

Organizing by User Function (Top-Down)

The top-down design model works well when a central MIS (Management Information Services) or LAN control group is in charge of the network. If your HQ folks know their business, this is the model you will likely use. If you are the MIS department, as often happens in smaller companies, this is a good option.

It's a delicate balancing act to design by user function. If the network is geographically wide, your WAN connections may be too slow to provide good service if half your network traverses the WAN for normal business. If the network is physically in one place but contains too many servers to upgrade all at once, it may be difficult to use this model as well. However, this is a great design for networks that are mostly local and have clearly defined job descriptions that stretch across internal departments.

FIGURE 2.6

A departmental
eDirectory tree, logi-
cal view

[Root]

O=ACME

ACCT_1

ACCT_2

ACCT_1_SYS

ACCT_2_SYS

P1.ACME

Q1.ACME

JQADAMS

USGRANT

PAYROLL

ORGANIZATIONAL DESIGN

During the past few years, the trend in business has been to place support functions (such as account-ing, sales, design, engineering, human resources, and the like) directly in the departments they support. Earlier, the model was to always group like job functions, as in the bottom-up design method previously described. With the business pendulum swinging, however, your company may well decide to disperse these functions.

Figure 2.7 shows our mythical Acme Corporation built around a top-down model, grouping the various functions in separate Organizational Units. This design requires that you know and make sense of your company's organization.

FIGURE 2.7

An organizational
view of Acme
Corporation

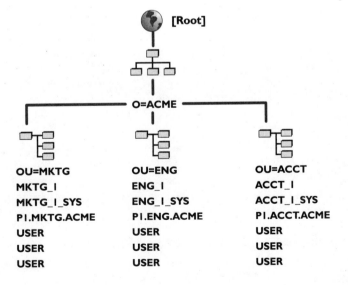

OU=MKTG	OU=ENG	OU=ACCT
MKTG_1	ENG_1	ACCT_1
MKTG_1_SYS	ENG_1_SYS	ACCT_1_SYS
P1.MKTG.ACME	P1.ENG.ACME	P1.ACCT.ACME
USER	USER	USER
USER	USER	USER
USER	USER	USER

This illustration makes good sense for central planners, who don't need to worry about which user sits in which cubicle. If you are responsible for maintaining the connection of user Guy H. Davis in cubicle 4-E-2, you may need an additional map, like the one shown in Figure 2.8.

FIGURE 2.8

A cubicle view of the organizational design

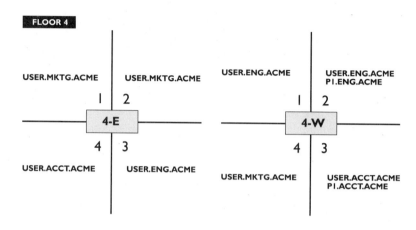

The cable contractor who installed your network cabling was supposed to leave an "as-built" map showing each connection in each physical location. You probably can't find that now, so get the cubicle layout from the human resources space-planning department. On copies of the floor plan, label each user and his or her context in the eDirectory tree. This type of planning and forethought is rewarded during emergencies but is difficult to maintain. Make an effort to start and maintain such a map for the feeling of self-satisfaction if nothing else. Again, this idea is wonderful on paper and in theory, but don't beat yourself up if you don't have the time to document all aspects of your network. If you have done what was suggested earlier in the process and have a good naming standard, you simply ask the user in cube 4-E-2 what his or her name is (if you don't already know that his name is Guy H. Davis), then search for GHDAVIS in the tree.

Notice that engineers are sitting next to marketing people, who are next to accounting people. This is slightly fictionalized, to enhance the contrast. If this were real life, translators would be needed between each cubicle.

The printers for two of the groups are in the west cubicle. Printers can be physically located anywhere on the network, either by connecting them to workstations or by using print servers that attach directly to the network cabling. By the way, I highly prefer the latter approach, which will make your life much simpler.

Even if your company begins the year by placing each group in the same physical location, normal business chaos will mangle that plan before long. People get promoted, people change jobs, the accounting department runs out of room so the managers place a few people in the marketing area, and so on—things just change. The type of map shown in Figure 2.8 helps monitor that change. Can you track each cubicle user to their spot on the map in Figure 2.7? See, context names do help, don't they?

Distributed Organization Chart with a WAN (Mixed)

Let's say Acme Corporation has grown beyond its founders' wildest dreams. Hey, when marketing people and engineers learn to communicate, great things happen.

The new layout for Acme will probably be a mix of departmental and user-function designs. WAN considerations particularly push this mixed design, since small, remote offices often don't have enough personnel to keep job functions separate. But the slow WAN connections limit the practicality of using a top-down design.

Figure 2.9 shows the expanded Acme Corporation spreading across the country. The designers have chosen not to use the Country level, even though the company has grown from the United States into both Canada and Mexico. The design is clearly discernible without needing the extra layer of name contexts that the Country object introduces. Notice the lack of planning in designing the naming standard for locations. There is Corp (a business unit located where?), Mexico (a country), and Toronto and San_Jose (cities). Doesn't make much sense, does it?

FIGURE 2.9

A global corporate/division/ department/ workgroup design

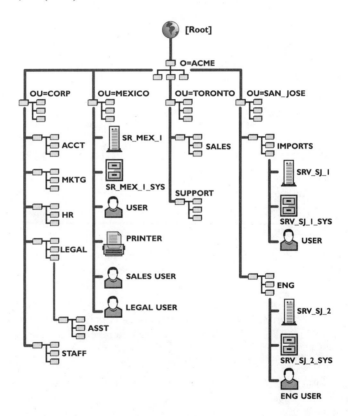

You should notice that OU=CORP is the largest and is not labeled by location. Each department has clearly defined groups, since more people in the corporate office tend to have specific job functions.

The other cities are labeled geographically, since that made the most sense during the design phase. In Mexico, the small office has no departmental subgroups or OUs within the OU. Toronto, a larger office, contains an OU for both Sales and Support. San Jose includes two OUs, labeled Imports and Eng. Although there are defined groups in San Jose, the file servers are named incrementally by the location. Does this all make sense? Probably not, but it's a common situation. In fact, it is one of the most common designs for a network.

This tree follows Novell's recommendations, namely designing the top of the tree (the first two to three layers) to reflect your WAN topology and the bottom of the tree (all the rest) to cover departments and other corporate organizational structures. And the lesson to learn from this is twofold:

◆ NDS is flexible enough to cover your crazy company.

◆ No NDS design is inherently better than another.

Some consultants and authors devote many chapters in NetWare books, and entire books, to NDS. True, NDS is complicated. Even more true, these consultants have spent a long time learning the arcane details of NDS and want to show off that knowledge for you. Luckily for you, I don't have that much knowledge, and I don't want to devote a ton of time to studying NDS.

Why not? Isn't NDS important? Absolutely, but it should be an infrastructure issue, supporting network design and user goals, not an end in itself. NDS is a great and complicated tool, but just a tool nonetheless. Ray Noorda, the CEO of Novell from the early 1980s through the NetWare glory years into the 1990s, used to say he wanted NetWare Everywhere. He even joked about NetWare UnderWear. That's exactly what I think NDS eDirectory should be: NetWare UnderWare.

NDS Context Control and Management

As you may recall, *context* refers to the location of an object within the eDirectory tree. Not the physical location, but the logical position.

In the example in Figure 2.9, the context of the first file server in San Jose (SRV_SJ_1) is:

IMPORTS.SAN_JOSE.ACME

The context here is given in *typeless* format. In this format, no container abbreviations are used. The translation of the above typeless name is "Organizational Unit Imports in the Organizational Unit San_Jose in the Organization Acme."

The other format for context is called *typeful*. It includes abbreviations for all containers and leaf objects (if appropriate). The abbreviations for container object types were listed earlier in the section on containers. The typeful method of referring to the above context is:

OU=IMPORTS.OU=SAN_JOSE.O=ACME

All leaf objects are referred to as CN, which stands for the Common Name of the object. The typeful, distinguished name of that server would be written as:

CN=SRV_SJ_1.OU=IMPORTS.OU=SAN_JOSE.O=ACME

Personally, I prefer the typeless names and am glad they are available. With typeless names, the trick to remember is that, typically, the Organization is to the far right, and the object is at the far left. Anything in the middle is usually an Organizational Unit.

See Table 2.1, earlier in this chapter, for the complete, official list of the rules of containment. For a shorthand and simplified list, remember that [Root] contains Organizations, and Organizations hold Organizational Units, which can hold other Organizational Units but not Organizations. Remember that most leaf objects go in Organizations or Organizational Units.

Why Current Context Is Important

Knowing where you are is important in every endeavor, especially when we're speaking of something like NDS eDirectory, with the capacity for a global network. Think of your current context as the map with a red arrow saying, "You are here."

Current context and knowing how to change your context are just as important in the eDirectory tree as in a filesystem's directory tree. The biggest difference is that with NetWare 6, you can have many drives mapped to different points in the filesystem tree but only one active point in the eDirectory tree.

Let's break this into components. First, the far-left name is the common name, with the abbreviation of CN. The common name denotes a leaf object, such as a user, printer, server, or volume.

In Figure 2.10, PAT is the username for both users. Although PAT by itself doesn't help us differentiate the two users, the rest of the object's distinguished name (that is, its context) will always let us know which PAT is which. (Of course, using PATD or PJONES instead works without confusion.)

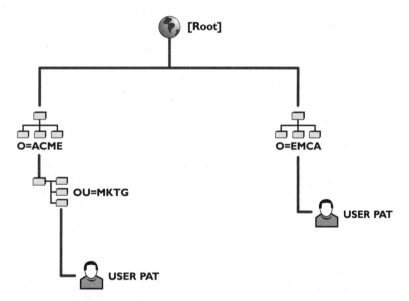

FIGURE 2.10

Find and describe PAT in as many ways as possible.

Since we don't know anything about PAT or even if it's Ms. PAT or Mr. PAT, we need a better way to describe this PAT object. Hence, we have *distinguished names*, another label for the complete context of an object.

Current context works similarly to the current directory context in a filesystem. The context acts as the CD (Change Directory) DOS command might work, by referencing where an object is located. People don't use this function of the CD command often, but just typing CD by itself will list your current directory. The Unix command pwd (for Print Working Directory) does the same thing. If you are in the same directory as the file you're looking for, just the filename is enough to reference the file. If you are in another directory, you must give the path to the file.

The distinguished name for the PAT on the right is PAT.EMCA; the PAT on the left has the distinguished name PAT.MKTG.ACME. However, if you are currently in the EMCA Organization with PAT, you can merely reference the name PAT without any of the extra identifiers for context.

What if PAT.EMCA wants to send a message to the other PAT? How should that be addressed? The distinguished name is PAT.MKTG.ACME. A subset of this is the *relative distinguished name*. Are you comfortable using the CD command to move up one directory level, then going down from there? If so, using a relative distinguished name should be comfortable for you as well.

When a network administrator with a context of O=ACME needs to refer to PAT.MKTG.ACME, there is a shortcut. Use either CN=PAT.OU=MKTG or just PAT.MKTG, since both refer to the same object. If the administrator is already in the MKTG container, the reference would be either CN=PAT or just PAT.

A beginning period in a name tells the system that the following name is complete and referenced from the [Root] of the current eDirectory tree. This is, in fact, the definition of a distinguished name. The period works the same as a leading backslash in DOS pathnames for file designations.

The last trick is the trailing period in object naming. A name with a trailing period tells the system to start the partial naming one level up from the current context. This method is rarely used, although those familiar with the command prompt and bad typists use it more frequently. You are effectively removing one object name from the *left* side of the current context. Note that this works only for relative distinguished names. For example, if your current context is

```
OU=MKTG.O=ACME
```

and you enter the relative distinguished name

```
CN=Admin.
```

NDS will remove the OU=MKTG object from the current context and prepend the relative distinguished name to the remainder:

```
.CN=Admin.O=ACME
```

Of course, looking at Figure 2.10, you will see that NDS will not be able to locate that object, and you will get an error.

USING CX TO CHANGE YOUR CONTEXT

Changing contexts is as easy as changing directories from the DOS command line. The CX command stands for Change conteXt just like CD stands for Change Directory (but the acronym is more of a stretch).

Typing CX on the DOS command line will display your current context. In our example, if PAT on the left types CX, the result will be:

```
mktg.acme
```

Somewhat underwhelming, but often helpful.

The CX command with no options is used more than the CD command with no options, because there is no "Context" prompt like the DOS prompt that automatically shows your filesystem location.

The easiest way to use CX is to always type the following:

```
CX distinguished_name (.MKTG.ACME)
```

Replace *distinguished_name* with your desired context name, of course, although relative distinguished names are permissible.

For ease of use when logging in to a server, the CX.EXE command is included in the LOGIN directory. If you connect to any NetWare server in the desired tree, you can then change your context before logging in to the system.

How to Use Contexts to Your Advantage

Current context is most important when a user logs in to the system. As we have just been discussing, several people may have the same name. When PAT wants to log in, how will the system know which PAT is being referred to? Context helps here. NDS looks for objects in the following order:

1. The user's distinguished name or relative distinguished name plus current context

2. During login only, the context of whatever server the user is currently attached to

There is no "search path" as in DOS and NetWare. If the user who wants to access any object doesn't provide the necessary context, the object will remain unfound. The exception is with the LOGIN program: If you start to log in from the wrong context, NDS will search the container of the server you are communicating with. If that context is not correct and you don't have Catalog Services, you'll get the error message "User not found." You must try again. With Catalog Services, however, a list of users with the specified name will appear, and the user can choose the right one.

Let's take that login problem PAT had just a moment ago. Some suggestions require you to type the full distinguished name every time a user logs in, looks for a printer, or references a network resource. But that's a lot of typing, and you are likely to meet a lot of resistance and anger from users who must now type 150 characters to log in, instead of the old eight. However, if everyone is in the same container, including all the various file servers for that department, full distinguished names aren't necessary. When PAT logs in, NDS searches the current context. *Voilà!* The file server holding PAT's object is in that current context, and login continues without a hitch.

The advantages of grouping similar users in Organizations or Organizational Units together with their file servers and other network resources make NetWare 6 feel more comfortable. Users of earlier NetWare versions don't need to make a drastic leap of faith to take advantage of many of NetWare 6's strong points.

SETTING A USER'S "HOME," OR DEFAULT, CONTEXT

Part of the reason some advisors make a big deal of using the shortest container names possible is to avoid having users enter many characters when typing their distinguished name. Since NetWare allows a user to log in from any machine on the network (very handy for network administrators, this ability to gain your full rights from any desktop), worrywarts and concerned users will get confused if they need to type a long distinguished name.

This is a problem for few networks today, because most users log in on their own computer almost all the time. When networks started, it was more common for companies to have several users share a computer. Today, almost every employee has full access to his or her own computer or two, or they feel slighted.

The advantage of this situation is the ability to place user-specific commands in the Client fields of the NetWare Client Properties on the client PC workstation, if the user is running Windows. In PAT's case, the following will show up in the Client Configuration screen:

```
Preferred server: (leave blank)
```

```
Preferred tree: ACME
Name context: MKTG
First network drive: F
```

The preferred tree line is only necessary if your company has multiple eDirectory trees active on the network. That's fairly rare.

When the client is loaded, the client preferences (or the NET.CFG file under Windows 3.1 if you're still stuck with some of these) will set the default context. NDS won't need to search for PAT's user object, since the system will assume PAT belongs in MKTG.ACME before the LOGIN command appears.

If and when PAT does wander to another desk, there's still not much to remember to log in to the proper context. Have PAT type this:

```
LOGIN PAT.MKTG.ACME
```

Then she needs to give the proper password when asked. PAT will be connected in the proper context without any problems.

Using Bindery Services to Emulate the Old Bindery

NDS supports Bindery Services to allow users still using the NETX client shells to connect to NDS and to support third-party products, such as older (and now obsolete) tape backup programs and print servers. As NDS permeated third-party products, some bindery emulation was necessary. That day has passed, but you still may be stuck with some network peripherals that demand a bindery.

If you have slipped into a comfortable mode with NDS during this chapter, give that up and remember what it used to be like. Bindery Services provides only some access to leaf objects on a server-centric basis within NDS. The global, distributed NDS eDirectory database pretends to be a flat, limited structure for server resources and users. Only the leaf objects in specified containers can be seen under Bindery Services.

How Bindery Services Works

The *bindery context* refers to the container object where the Bindery Services feature is set. The bindery context is normally set during server installation, but only the first three servers automatically receive a replica of the NDS partition during installation. Without the replica, the server can't support Net-Ware 6's Bindery Services feature. When you upgrade a NetWare 3 server to NetWare 6, its bindery context is automatically set, and the server will automatically receive a replica of the container it is in.

You may add replicas to any NetWare 6 server you wish in order to support Bindery Services. Check Chapter 8 for details on using the NDS Manager program to add replicas.

Once the server in question is ready, you can set as many as 16 bindery contexts for a single Net-Ware 6 server. The contexts are then added together, in the order they were listed in, to form one large, emulated bindery. This is done by using the Monitor utility at the server console or by directly modifying the AUTOEXEC.NCF file. The activation of Bindery Services is limited to the specific server modified.

Once active, Bindery Services responds to NETX requests (or NetWare 6 clients using VLM files with the /B switch at the end of their LOGIN command, Client32 users with the Bindery Connection box checked, or Windows 95/98 Microsoft Client for NetWare clients without their

NDS services installed) from clients or applications. Leaf objects—and only leaf objects that meet the bindery's naming conventions—are presented by Bindery Services as if they were a standard NetWare 3.x bindery. Containers are not presented under Bindery Services.

Information contained in NDS but not in the bindery is not visible under Bindery Services. The invisible items include e-mail names, phone numbers, aliases, profiles, NDS (though not bindery) login scripts, and directory maps.

Why Bindery Emulation May Be Necessary

Even the most gung-ho NDS advocate may be forced to use Bindery Services sometimes. During the transition to NetWare 6, some NetWare 3.x or NetWare 2.x servers may not be upgraded immediately. Some computers may not have the prerequisite hardware to upgrade, or you may not have time to reach them all at once to upgrade the client connection software to be NDS-aware.

Print servers from some third-party vendors use Bindery Services to verify user access to the printers. Although most companies are moving (or have already moved) to support NDS, it takes time.

Make no mistake: There's no advantage for a NetWare 6 server to run Bindery Services except under the circumstances listed above. NDS has far too many advantages to emulate a server-centric bindery system.

Installing Bindery Services

If you are upgrading a NetWare 3.x server, or it's one of the first three NetWare 6 servers, Bindery Services will be installed automatically. The appropriate lines, such as

```
SET BINDERY CONTEXT=MKTG.ACME
```

will be written into the AUTOEXEC.NCF file during installation.

You may later add Bindery Services by typing the SET command at the server console and listing the server's context in the command. To engage Bindery Services each time the server is restarted, you must add the SET command to the AUTOEXEC.NCF file manually (or choose to save the change in Monitor). Remember that an NDS replica must be stored on this server to support Bindery Services.

The other option for adding Bindery Services is through the Monitor console utility. At the console, follow these steps:

1. Type **MONITOR**.

2. Choose Server Parameter in the Available Options window.

3. Choose Directory Services in the Select a Parameter category.

4. Scroll down to Bindery Context.

5. Press Enter to modify the bindery context setting.

6. Enter as many as 16 valid bindery context listings (remember that you must have replicas on this server for each context listed), separated by semicolons.

7. Press Esc three times, and then save the changes to your SYS:\SYSTEM\ AUTOEXEC.NCF file.

8. Exit Monitor.

9. Verify that the context was set correctly by typing **CONFIG** at the console prompt; it should match.

The single-container eDirectory tree makes sense for the first NetWare 6 server in a network, especially as a way to roll out a pilot server. With this setup, clients can test the new NDS features while keeping the server resources available to all the bindery clients.

Bindery clients can see only the eDirectory leaf objects that are covered by a bindery context. What if there are two Organizational Units in a company, and one of them is running Bindery Services? What can bindery clients see? Figure 2.11 illustrates this example.

FIGURE 2.11

A bindery context that covers a portion of the eDirectory tree

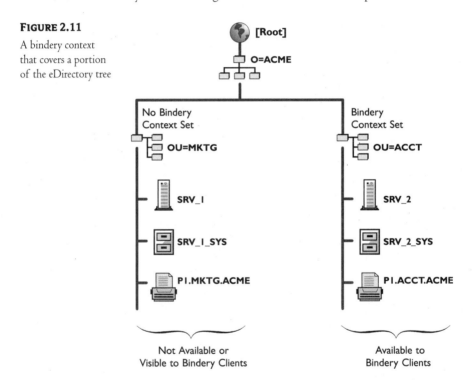

As you might guess, leaf objects that do not exist in a container running Bindery Services are invisible to bindery clients. If Joe Bindery wants to connect to the Acme eDirectory tree, the only part he will see is the container OU=ACCT.O=ACME.

New Features of NDS eDirectory 8.6

Novell is putting much of their brainpower behind eDirectory, since directory services remains one area where they have a substantial lead over Microsoft (Active Directory is about NDS version 2 or 3).

New or Improved Tools

Management tools increasingly do a better job with eDirectory with each new version. NetWare Administrator (NWADMIN), the only graphical tool available earlier on, is fading away. The DOS-style C-Worthy Interface screens (blue screens with yellow borders) now stay out of the mix most of, but not all, the time.

ConsoleOne, while not exactly zippy, now shucks the "ConSlowOne" tag, which so aptly described its performance early on. Not all management duties can be done through ConsoleOne, as you'll see, but more can be done with each version. Soon, maybe by the mid-release upgrade, Novell will give ConsoleOne the strength to do everything.

But that would mean giving up the newer, more powerful NetWare Remote Manager and companion NDS iMonitor browser-based utilities. Given my druthers, I'd druther do Remote Manager than ConsoleOne. Maybe the mid-release upgrade will make that wish come true.

SLP (Service Location Protocol), an Internet standard that enables client applications to discover network services over TCP/IP, now ships inside eDirectory. So far, only the NetWare-based eDirectory versions support SLP and their User, Service, and Directory agents.

SBCON.NLM provides a way to back up and restore NDS eDirectory. I always tell people to ignore NDS backups and use intelligent replication schemes, but some people feel the need for tape backups. Single-server implementations certainly need a backup option, so check out SBCON.NLM if you fall in that boat, because not all third-party backup software understands NDS.

NMAS (Novell Modular Authentication Services), an optional NDS add-on, provides real security and management improvements. NDS forms the foundation for the NMAS add-on.

Other new utilities, such as the Novell Certificate Server and Advanced Audit Service, also require NDS. Effectively, everything in NetWare 6 involves NDS in some way.

NDS Data Structure

Novell hides all the NDS control and index files, which is smart. Even smarter was the upgrade with NDS 8 (NetWare 5.1) that allows unlimited numbers of NDS items to remain under control.

Think you have a large network? Novell has claimed for some time that they could store the Internet inside NDS. During NDS 8 rollout, they demonstrated an NDS structure managing over a billion (yes, that's a *b*) objects.

With NDS 8, Novell moved from using their long-time Transaction Tracking System (TTS) for transaction control to a new journaling filesystem. This new indexed database uses log files to back out of transactions that can't be fully performed because of a system failure of any type, so the transactions can be completely performed when the system is right again. Let's look at these files briefly:

◆ NDS.DB is a control file, which also contains the rollback log.

◆ NDS*.LOG tracks transactions until completed, storing information until interrupted transactions can be completed.

◆ The NDS.01, NDS.02, and so on files contain all records and indexes found on the server. The file size limit is 2GB. When NDS.01 gets that big, NDS.02 is created for new data, followed by NDS.03, and continuing as far as necessary.

◆ Stream files have .NDS extensions and hold such information as login scripts and print job configurations.

Indexes in the NDS.01 file (and siblings) include substring indexes for many of the most important object properties. Attribute indexes for strings beginning with the CN (Common Name), uniqueID, Given Name, and Surname fields make locating people faster. Separate indexes for just the CN and uniqueID fields help find any network object. LDAP connections have their own indexes to improve LDAP coordination and performance.

Do you need to worry about these files? Not at all. You should avoid them unless directed by Novell support technicians to use them. But these details are listed here so you better understand how Novell has upgraded NDS to handle billions and billions of network objects.

Directory Designs and Discussions

"Are we there yet?" If you've ever taken children on a car trip, you've heard those words too often.

In NetWare 6, the eDirectory answers those questions. Are we there yet? Yes, we are. NetWare 4.x wasn't quite there, and NetWare 5.x was better, and now we are there.

Where is there? That's the important network question. Where is there? What's there? Where is anything? Where is everything?

It's all around the network, that's where. Everything now has a place, and there's a place for everything, just as your mother told you.

The beauty now is that we can safely ignore much of NDS management overhead, because eDirectory has reached the golden (and critical) point of keeping NDS undercover, not front and center. NDS should be network plumbing, and it's starting to disappear into the woodwork.

Yeah, yeah, Novell engineers get all hot and bothered discussing how much better NDS eDirectory is over Active Directory. They're technically correct, but I don't care. I don't want to mess with the Directory; I want to manage the network. NDS eDirectory should, and pretty well does, stay out of my way and let me manage the network while it takes care of many of the details.

NDS schema management is improved for both the network manager and any third parties making NDS-enabled products. Some have criticized Novell's deliberate rollout and control of third-party NDS products, but this control has been critical to NDS's success. Anyone here feel that Microsoft's Windows Registry database, with all the extensions available to any third party with no control or structure, is anywhere close to reliable? Didn't think so. And Active Directory will suffer several embarrassing meltdown problems until Microsoft puts out some patches. NDS has avoided these problems and will continue to be the safest place for network object information.

Will users like this? Sure, if the tools that make NDS simple for users are in place for them. Will all the users like this? No. All users never like all things. You will have some users complaining because of the change just because it is a change. Can't help those folks.

The trick is that complaining users will need to use the new network, whether they like it or not. Over time, they will all start complaining about something else and will deny they complained about the network at all.

Change is constant, and so are complainers. Don't let a few ruin your work for the many. Go forth and set NDS loose upon your users. Realize that the complainers will complain, but they are few and the eDirectory advancements are many.

Chapter 3

Connecting PC Clients to Your Network

IT's EASY TO FORGET that the word *server* originated from *service*. In our situation, a server is something that is of use, available, and convenient. The person being served in a network is the client, or user.

NetWare provided a client/server system long before the term became a buzzword. In the early days, the only things a client needed were file and printer services. Today, much of a server's time is still spent providing controlled and shared access to files and printers. But the client of today needs more than just access to files and printers. There are seven services that the modern client requires. In addition to file and print services, the client needs directory, management, routing, messaging, and security services.

NetWare 6 supports DOS, Windows of every type, Macintosh, Linux, and Unix clients. The majority of NetWare clients are PCs with Intel microprocessors running some version of Windows. All these various clients can be connected to the same server at the same time and share all the server resources.

Using Client32 software for Windows 32-bit client operating systems (Windows 95, 98, NT, 2000, or XP) changes the rules quite a bit from the struggles of the past, as you'll see in this chapter. Client installations are easier than ever, and for many new NetWare users, no client software is necessary at all with NetWare 6.

In this chapter, we'll cover the following topics:

◆ Installing and configuring Client32

◆ Configuring Windows clients

Installing and Configuring Client32

You can download software from the Novell Web site (`www.novell.com`) if you would like to get started with Client32 before upgrading to NetWare 6. If you copy the files, just run the `SETUP.EXE` file from the local or network hard drive that holds the Client32 files.

NOTE *If you're still stuck with DOS and/or Windows 3.1 clients, you have my sincerest condolences. That said, download the latest DOS and Windows 3.1 clients from the Novell Web site (they aren't on the NetWare 6 client CD-ROM) and follow their directions. An even easier solution is to leave the clients on those old systems alone, since if they connected to NetWare 5.1 (or even NetWare 4) they'll connect to NetWare 6.*

To run NetWare's Client32 software, a PC must meet the following requirements:

◆   Be IBM PC-compatible

◆   Have one of these types of processors: Intel 8088, 80286, 80386, 80486, Pentium, Pentium II, Pentium III, or Pentium 4 (or equivalent)

◆   Have a 1.44MB disk drive (a CD-ROM drive is handy, but not mandatory; a 1.2MB floppy will work, but only after much pain)

◆   Have a network interface card and suitable network cabling

THE STORY BEHIND NOVELL'S 32-BIT WINDOWS CLIENTS

Microsoft's move to real 32-bit client operating systems (Windows 95, 98, NT, 2000, and now XP) meant that Novell needed to make some major changes in the Windows client software. Of course, Microsoft developers made their own 32-bit NetWare clients, hoping to freeze Novell out of the loop. Microsoft's lack of a decent directory service caused the designers to ignore NDS in their original Windows 95 client, implying that directory services aren't really all that important.

Well, NDS turned out to be important to NetWare users, and folks were upset. Their aggravation was aimed in equal parts at Microsoft for making such an underpowered 32-bit client and at Novell for being so slow in bringing out its own client for Windows 95.

With the continued update of Novell's Client32 software, excellent clients for Windows are available with NetWare 6. If you haven't upgraded to NetWare 6 yet, you may want to download the new client files from Novell's Web site.

In the licensing terms for the new client, you'll notice that you may freely use these client files *only* when connected to a Novell operating system. If that seems strange, you must have missed Microsoft's File and Print Services for NetWare product running under Windows NT. To encourage the use of Windows NT servers as replacements for NetWare servers, Microsoft copied the basic NetWare 3.1 file and print services, but running under Windows NT. The idea was that users could use their own NetWare client files to connect to the Windows NT server—the same files they used for connecting to the NetWare server.

I have the dubious honor of being the person who pointed out (in a review in *Information Week*) that Microsoft, a stout defender of their own product licensing, was unusually sleazy in encouraging the misuse of Novell client software. It turns out Novell's lawyers thought the same thing, and Microsoft was forced to release their own pseudo-NetWare client software for their own pseudo-NetWare server clone. Don't you love legal retribution?

Client32 for Windows 95/98

Yes, Microsoft includes NetWare client files with Windows 95/98 systems, but I bet you'll be happier with the Novell client files. After all, if you're installing NetWare 6 clients, you probably want the best NDS support possible, plus tools for NDPS (Novell Distributed Print Service) and extra management control. All these work better with the Novell client software. Some details are missing completely from the Microsoft Windows 95/98 client software, such as tight integration with NDS, which is another good reason to stick with the Novell software.

For now, let's assume that you're installing your first Windows 95/98 client from the Novell Client CD or upgrading in the same way. This is a good idea, even if you plan to use one of the automated methods later (see the "Automated Client Installations" section later in this chapter and Appendix A for details on automating Windows client installations). There are several differences between the NetWare 6 and NetWare 5 installation routines, and you'll need to see the NetWare 6 choices at least once.

What's the first exciting new development? It's a browser-based installation routine. Take a gander at Figure 3.1 for the new look of NetWare client installations.

FIGURE 3.1

Browsers take over client installation tasks

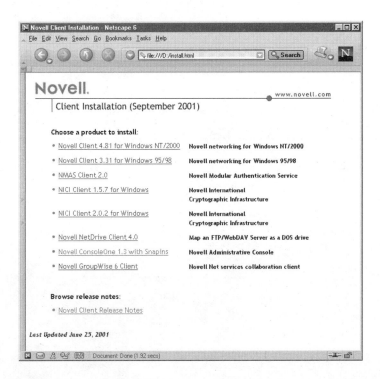

The INSTALL.HTML file awaits in the root of the NetWare Client CD, which replaces the ZENworks CD for NetWare 5, which replaced the NetWare 4 Client CD. We've made a circle, but the HTML file adds a new twist to the story. If you prefer, you may go down to the \WIN95\IBM_ENU directory on the Novell Client CD and run the SETUP.EXE program from there, but there's not much advantage to that.

Oops, if your Windows 95 client doesn't have Service Pack 1 installed, you will have no joy. My copy of Windows 95 didn't, so I downloaded the file from Microsoft and installed it. Windows 98 machines don't have this problem, although Microsoft did release a Service Pack pretty quickly after the official release, so be ready for your own Service Pack download for whatever Windows client you're cursing lately.

Standard screens go by, beginning with the license agreement (say Yes or get dumped from the installation program). When you get to the Typical or Custom installation screen, choose Typical for your first installation to see what you get.

Figure 3.2 shows the first of the Custom installation options (pretty much the same for all Windows 32-bit systems). First, choose your protocol (IP and IPX for this station, since I use it for RCONSOLE to a NetWare 5.1 server, but I only use IP to the NetWare 6 servers).

FIGURE 3.2

Start your protocols

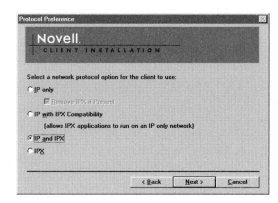

The next choice offers an option to include NetWare bindery server (NetWare 3.x and before). Shame on you if you have any NetWare 3.x servers still in use. This isn't too interesting, so I won't put a picture here.

Now come the fun choices for the Custom installation. The choices checked are the default for the Typical installation. The two choices you can't see in Figure 3.3 are for Novell Remote Access Dialer and Novell NDS Provider-ADSI.

FIGURE 3.3

Client configuration choices

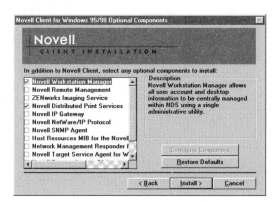

As you can see in Figure 3.3, highlighting each choice provides a brief description in the cleverly named Description area of the dialog box. The Configure Component command button works for the following choices:

◆ Novell NetWare/IP Protocol (less used today, and not necessary with NetWare 6)

◆ Novell SNMP Agent (used for large network management platforms)

◆ Host Resources MIB for the Novell Client (part of SNMP)

◆ Novell Target Service Agent (backs up local drives to a server)

Then watch the scary part: removing the existing client. That always makes me nervous. Even Novell smart guys, like my friend Henry Sprafkin, get nervous when doing this for customers to demonstrate new products.

The next screens update you on the processes of removing the existing client, copying files, and building driver information databases for Windows. You can't do anything here except watch.

Have your Windows 95/98 CD-ROM close at hand, or better yet, have the appropriate directories from those CDs loaded onto a convenient server. Just when you think the installation is about done, a request will appear for some Windows file. If you have your CD ready, you may not need it. If your CD is hiding behind a filing cabinet, you'll definitely need it.

Next comes the reboot, and cross your fingers as the machine comes back with—we all hope— the new Novell client software properly installed and configured.

TIP   *One of the best ways to upgrade multiple Windows 95/98 machines to Novell's Client32 at the same time is to use the server-based Windows 95/98 installation routine (ACU.EXE for Automatic Client Update). See Appendix B for details.*

There's one more important point about the Windows 95/98 client that must be mentioned: Client32 software adds a network file cache, speeding access to and from network resources by using part of your workstation RAM. If some software turns out to be touchy about the local cache, set it to 0 (zero) to disable the local cache. (Some third-party software will not work with file caching; you may want to check with your software vendor to avoid problems.)

Some reports have come from disgruntled users who have seen huge amounts of memory gobbled up by their Client32 software. These reports have slowed after the early versions of Client32 software, but you need to understand that the goal here is local caching of network information. The more RAM dedicated to local caching, the better most network interactions.

Balance this RAM gobbling depending on the user's needs, especially on workstations without enough RAM (and who really has enough RAM?). The way to curtail RAM grabbing by Client32 software is one level deeper in the Network Control Panel below the properties of the NetWare client. The File Cache Level setting is on the Advanced Settings tab of the Novell Client Configuration dialog box, as shown in Figure 3.4. The default, as shown, sets the level at 3.

Setting the number to 0 (zero) eliminates the RAM file cache completely. Raising the number to 4 guarantees that no application will have enough memory. Okay, that's a slight joke, but never underestimate an application's desire for RAM. Can you say "office application code bloat"? Of course, if your workstations have 256MB of RAM, the default level of 3 works quite well.

FIGURE 3.4

Slowing the
RAM grab

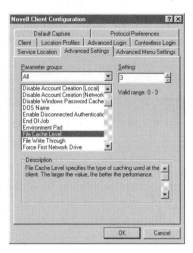

Client32 for Windows NT/2000/XP

Microsoft used to put forth the (now obvious) untruth that much of Windows 95/98 and Windows NT shared a common code base. Regardless of semantics about the number of lines of code in one version or another overlapping, the physical communication details in Windows 95/98 are vastly different from those in NT. Windows 2000 was supposedly rewritten from scratch (as is probably the case for Windows XP). Most critically, applications can't communicate directly with the hardware in NT, 2000, and XP; all access is under the control of the operating system. This means the network client guts must be different.

The differences in the code don't mean that the user interface of the network clients must vary wildly. Novell has done a good job making the Windows 95/98 and NT/2000/XP clients look and feel much the same. In fact, some of this chapter may feel like *deja vu* all over again, as we see the NT/2000/XP client so soon after the Windows 95/98 client.

Follow the directions from the previous section: put the CD in the NT/2000/XP workstation or server destined to be a Novell client, and let auto-run do its stuff. You have other alternatives. You could direct your network pointer to the server directories holding the NetWare files for an across-the-wire client upgrade. You could also set the /ACU (Automatic Client Upgrade) command in the login scripts that the NT/2000/XP workstations will use, letting the system interrogate the client and upgrade any files necessary, but that's covered in the next section. For now, let's put a CD in the drive for consistency.

Choose your language, then choose your option. Since the heading above here says "Windows NT/2000," I suppose that's the choice for now (include XP under the 2000 heading), so click the Windows NT Client option on this screen. Choose this option for both NT Workstation and NT Server machines used as workstations. Then click Install Novell Client to finally start something.

Your first choice is whether this is a Typical or Custom installation. Next is your choice of protocols. The default is typically IP only. However, if the installation routine discovers that you are already running IPX (which you may be if you're performing any automatic or other type of network installation), then the default is both IP and IPX. If you choose IP only, you may also choose to delete IPX (this seems rather drastic to Novell old-timers, but those are your options).

NDS or Bindery? NDS, of course, so choose that on the next screen. Then read that you have finished the custom portion of the installation, and click the Finish button to continue.

Hear disks churn and see the progress bar inch left to right as filenames zoom by too fast to read. Notice how many are forced into \WINNT\SYSTEM32 or \WINNT\SYSTEM, and you see one of the main problems with Microsoft's method of cramming so much into one directory.

More information dialog boxes stream past your screen, then you should notice bindings being set and configured. Then, as always, choose to reboot.

Novell has so much experience now with these automated client installation routines that you have a great chance of success. When your NT station finally reboots, you'll see the new Novell Client login screen, shown in Figure 3.5.

FIGURE 3.5

New login, new security, but same old control

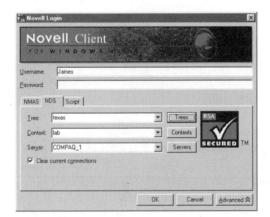

Clicking any of the buttons to the immediate right of the Tree, Context, or Server text fields opens a browser window (how handy). You may scroll around to your heart's content to find your context, tree, or server.

Automated Client Installations

Novell employees really learned to "eat their own cooking" during the development of NetWare 5 and 5.1. There was more time spent testing NetWare 5 and pushing it to a higher level of quality before release than has been the case for any other NetWare product release I can remember (and I've been watching for nearly 17 years). NetWare 6 is no different, although the move from version 4.11 to 5 was bigger than the move from version 5 to 6 in terms of network changes (but not user interfaces).

A minimum of 5000 client updates were made per week in Novell headquarters, with 1500 to 3000 clients at once upgraded an average of twice a week, for several months before the release of NetWare 5 and later NetWare 6. Some of the upgrades were optional; some were forced. Some were NetWare client upgrades only; some included GroupWise updates as well.

The method used by Novell, and one you should consider before using any other group installation option, is the ACU, or Automatic Client Update. This option assumes that you have some level of client-to-server communications already, such as a NetWare 4.11 server that you're upgrading.

ZENworks helps quite a bit with this whole business, if you have it, and all the files you need are on the Client CD. Here's the skinny on ACU: A single command in the login script (/ACU with very few options) can handle the upgrade process for you.

Here are the four steps to automated client installation:

1. Copy the Novell client files from the Client CD and the Windows installation files to the same directory on a NetWare server.

2. Create a group named **ACU** (no changes allowed) and give all members Read and Scan rights to that folder.

3. Edit the NWSETUP.INI file in the directory, along with the SETUP.EXE file for Windows. Directions can be long and involved and subject to change, so check Novell documentation for the latest details.

4. Add the following command to the login scripts that the workstations will use:

   @\\SERVER\VOLUME\PUBLIC\WIN95\SETUP/ACU

There, you've done it. Novell recommends that you warn your users before you set this up the first time, so you don't get a call from every single user as each of their workstations takes off during the login process and starts copying files without their permission. Or you can schedule this for a day you're out of the office, and let the fun begin (that's a joke—don't even think about it!).

NCIMAN.EXE and Installation Parameters

New with NetWare 6, the Novell Client Install Manager (NCIMAN.EXE) allows NetWare 6 administrators to re-create all of the configuration details that used to be part of the NWSETUP.INI file, which set the parameters from the old NETWARE.INI file. Since most of your client installations and/or upgrades will be on the same network, many of the same details work for all the workstations. Setting those details, now done with NCIMAN.EXE and various text files, is illustrated in Figure 3.6. The NCIMAN.EXE file sits in the \WIN95\IBM_language\Admin directory for Windows 95/98, and the \WINNT\ i386\Admin directory for Windows NT. Windows 2000 and XP hide this in the C:\DOCUMENTS AND SETTINGS\USER_NAME\LOCAL SETTINGS\TEMP\NOVELL\ENGLISH\ WINNT\I386\ADMIN directory.

FIGURE 3.6

Configuring clients for automated installations

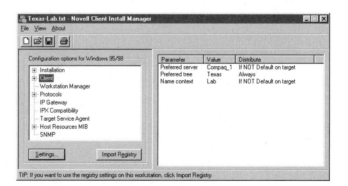

Every value found in the Novell Client Properties screens can be preset using NCIMAN. Of course, the defaults work fine in most cases, but Novell can't know your tree name or context. That's why Figure 3.6 shows the NCIMAN application setting every client to the Texas tree and Lab context. For this example, they all log in to server COMPAQ_1.

Underneath the Client heading (highlighted in Figure 3.6) sit all nine tabs for setting all manner of client settings. Want to set File Cache Level down to 2 rather than the default 3? Click Advanced Settings, then Performance, then Cache, and set the File Cache Level value you prefer. Clicking the OK button then creates the record for the configuration file. Make these settings as simple or as involved as you wish, but remember to give the files names that make sense, such as WIN98-NEW.TXT, so you can reference the filename correctly using the ACU.EXE [UNATTENDFILE] *file = configuration file path* setting during installations.

Configuring Windows Clients

There are more configuration options available with the new NetWare Client32 software for Windows clients than ever before. Luckily, you need to check just a few to get the clients up and running just as well as ever. In fact, you will rarely need to change any configuration options, because the defaults for NetWare 6's client software give just about everything you need.

Novell Client Options

If you right-click the red *N* in the system tray, you will see many options. Some duplicate Windows offerings, such as Network Neighborhood or My Network Places (which have their own semi-useful icon on the Desktop) and options to map and disconnect network drives. These few options are available under Windows Explorer's Tools menu, but the Novell options here are easier to find and seem to work slightly faster.

Some of the options in the pop-up menu are old Novell utilities still rattling around inside the product, such as the Send Message option. Plop a message onto the center of your friends' screens using the Novell instant one-way messaging option. Plop enough messages, and you won't have any friends left (hint).

New options on the menu include NetWare Connections, which is a pop-up window, not the magazine. Click this menu item, and a box labeled NetWare Connections appears, showing the resources you are authorized to see and use. Other information includes your username, the connection number, the authentication method (usually NDS), the tree holding the resources, the transport protocol used, and the NetWare address. This information is helpful for troubleshooting, but the average user won't spend much time perusing it.

Printer port capturing and configuring are also available from the Novell pop-up menu, although these options are still available through Windows Explorer as well. You may also start the login process again, which is handy for workstations alternating between administrative use and standard client operation.

Novell Client Properties

The last Novell pop-up menu option, Novell Client Properties, is a shortcut to drilling down through the Control Panel, Network, and Novell Client Configuration dialog box. Figure 3.7 shows the default view when you choose this option.

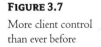

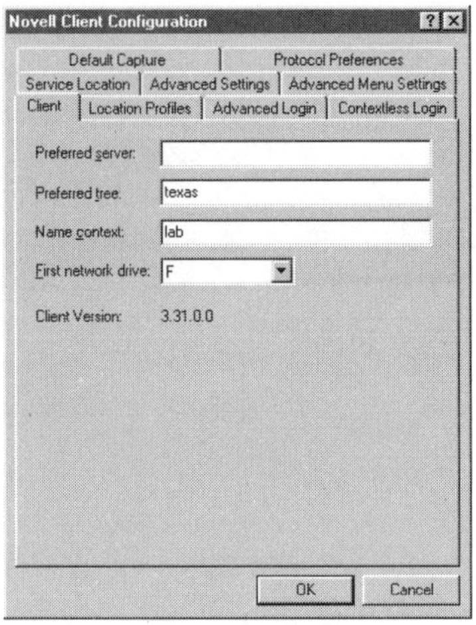

FIGURE 3.7

More client control
than ever before

You have seen some of this before, of course, in earlier login screens. Until Novell Client32-equipped clients could see multiple trees, there was no reason to make room to show more than one tree at a time. Now there is.

Little functional difference can be found between the Windows 95/98 and NT/2000/XP versions of the Novell client properties. The NT client has some extra options in the Advanced Login page, but these only give you a chance to change the welcome screen and caption. There is no File Cache Level setting for Windows NT/2000, as there is for Windows 95/98 clients. Many other Advanced Settings options differ between the two clients, but few (if any) administrators will ever need to mess with any of these, so don't worry too much about them.

The Default Capture options help set the stage for each client's use of the printer, but this is not a good place to put those details. Unless it's impossible, you should put printing details into the default printer configuration on the print server. As you know, individual client changes are to be avoided whenever possible.

Other options, such as mapping NetWare drives, are handy at the client for power users but become nightmares for less-experienced users. Rather, they become nightmares for you trying to manage those newbies gleefully changing every setting they can find in their Novell menus, and never understanding why you aren't excited by their constant voyages of discovery. If only a real voyage were an option for about two users out of every hundred, life would be much, much better.

Too Many Client Options, Too Little Time

When I have a problem with my car, I pull up the hood and look for a button that's labeled, "Push this and all will work again." Unfortunately, there isn't one of those, at least not on any of the cars I've owned.

When I have a problem with a computer or a network, I want to open the manual and see a heading that says, "James, here is the answer to your question." Unfortunately, there isn't one of those, either.

NetWare clients used to require almost as much compiling (yes, compiling) as the NetWare server itself. Those weren't happy days.

Now you'll see better networking and easier client configurations with NetWare 6 than ever before. Of course, you still need to be careful. The added client complexities of Windows 95/98 and NT/2000/XP add a new layer of confusion and potential disaster, especially with the Microsoft habit of hiding everything inside the Registry. But the automated client installations have become much better, and NetWare 6 makes these installations almost foolproof.

Speaking of Microsoft, you may be wondering why I haven't said anything about Microsoft's clients in this chapter. After all, Microsoft went to all that trouble to put these clients inside its operating systems, so I should describe how to use them. Well, not necessarily. If you want to use Microsoft's mediocre, bindery-based, NDS-unaware clients for your network, I can't stop you, but I can try to talk you out of it.

Use Novell clients for NetWare networks. You can keep the Microsoft clients for Microsoft networks, although you'll find that the Novell client for NT/2000 works better by itself than the Microsoft NetWare and Microsoft network clients do. Who knows the most about high-speed, highly reliable network clients? Novell, that's who. Don't accept the pale imitation of Microsoft clients when there are NetWare servers involved.

Part II

Managing the Network

Chapter 4

Creating and Managing User Objects

IN NETWORK SUPPORT DEPARTMENTS, this is the first joke that rookies learn: *User* is a four-letter word. If your boss hears you, explain that this joke mines the same humor vein as college professors who love teaching but hate students, salespeople who love selling but hate customers, and editors who love books but hate authors. The things we know best, we both love and hate, depending on the stress of the moment.

For those few moments when the stress overwhelms you and user *does* become a four-letter word, just remember that users require administration, which requires you. When users are a pain, it's often because they are untrained and ill-equipped for their job as network clients.

The smart network user needn't like computers, but smart network administrators like both the business they're in and networking. Since users won't come to you until it's too late or something is broken, you must go to them. Learn their job function goals and provide them the proper tools to reach those goals, and your users will be happy and productive.

But first, before they can be a pain in the neck, users must be created on your new file server. With some management help, users will pain you less (except for that one user who drives everybody crazy—there's one on every network).

In this chapter, we'll explore two main topics:

◆ Creating User objects with ConsoleOne

◆ Creating User objects with NetWare Administrator

Users and NetWare 6

The User object in NetWare 6 is the fundamental object in NDS eDirectory. It contains information about the person it represents, and as the system administrator, you can set or control every aspect of the User object's interface to the network. The following are the only requirements for the User object:

- A username that is unique within the container
- A completed Last Name field (not empty)

That's it. Everything else for a User object is optional, but much is recommended. Each physical user on the network should have a unique User object, but that's not mandatory either.

If you are coming to NetWare 6 from NetWare 5 or even 4.x, you will be familiar with the User object properties. Users of earlier versions of NetWare will still be familiar with many of these properties. User object details are as follows:

Group Membership   When added to a group, the User object inherits the rights assigned to that group.

Home Directories   The home directory serves as the user's personal disk space on the server. It's best if the directory is placed under an umbrella directory and uses the person's name for the directory name, as in SYS:\USERS\CORI.

Security Equivalences   This is a quick way to assign the same rights to one User object as the rights held by another. This makes administration slightly more difficult, however, so verify the string of equivalent rights all the way through for each User object. If you assign Riley the same rights as Katie, Riley suddenly has access to everything Katie controls. Be sure that's what you want before granting this equivalence.

User Login Scripts   Login scripts are configurable network batch files that customize the User object's network environment by setting environment variables, mapping drives, attaching printers, and the like.

User Account Restrictions   Security restrictions limit a person's access to the network or limit the use of certain network resources. For example, you can place limits on disk space used, connection times, and network computers from which to connect. You can make passwords mandatory and force the user to change them at specified intervals.

User Trustee Rights   Trustee rights allow the user to access other NDS objects. These rights must be granted by the Admin user, the equivalent, or a user with the necessary rights.

Print Job Configurations   You can set up specific print job details for each User object, or put print job configurations in a container for all the User objects within that container.

Account Manager   The configuration of one User object with the necessary rights (usually Supervisor right) to other objects allows the supervised object's rights to be modified. This way, one object can be granted rights to other objects to fulfill certain functions, such as modifying phone numbers for each User object.

If you are the first user connecting to a NetWare 6 server, you will see only one configured user: Admin. The Admin User object is the NDS counterpart to the user SUPERVISOR from the bindery (NetWare 3.*x* and earlier versions). Everyone else must be created using either ConsoleOne, NetWare Administrator (NWADMN32), or, with less control, under iManage or Web Manager. (The DOS-based NETADMIN utility was not included with NetWare 6.) In this chapter, I will discuss how to use ConsoleOne, Novell's Java-based utility of the future, and NWADMN32, Net-Ware Administrator for 32-bit Microsoft desktops, the utility of the past.

For new installations, you must log in as the Admin User object to have the proper rights to create new users. Later, subadministrators can be allowed to create User objects in parts of your network. Workgroup administrators granted Admin equivalence can also create any NDS object.

You can create and manage users with either of the NetWare administration programs, and you can modify any user information you enter during setup of the User object in the same manner.

This is not a linear chapter: the majority of the time will be spent with ConsoleOne, since that's Novell's stated direction. But if you prefer NetWare Administrator, skip ahead to that section. The processes are remarkably similar in both utilities.

NOTE   *You can now use the iManage and Web Manager programs, running in a browser, to create a NetWare user. But all you can do with them so far is just create the User object, not modify properties or anything else really useful. This does give a hint that soon all functions will be available in both ConsoleOne and through WebAccess.*

WHY A NEW ADMINISTRATION UTILITY?

Since the beginning of NetWare, the server console has not been a pretty picture for network administrators. In the early days, nobody knew any different. Everything was DOS-based—ugly, but functional. But somewhere along the line, mainly influenced by Windows, the world turned GUI. Everybody and everything went graphical, except the NetWare server console and other utilities.

Why the resistance? Well, issues such as server performance and the ability to use existing hardware have long been big selling points for NetWare. The Novell model with NDS and NWADMN32 has been to distribute network administration to a separate workstation. A GUI at the server might entice the administrator to spend more time doing work at the server console, affecting server performance. Unlike Microsoft, Novell doesn't help administrators dilute their server's power by forcing the server to support a massive GUI for every little change.

I won't pretend to know what goes into Novell product direction, but I would bet that ConsoleOne was created to appease the clamor coming from "eye-candy" addicts—not a bad tactic in the perception war. But I'm personally for substance over style, and there is no doubt that NetWare has provided, and continues to provide, substance to the networking industry.

Technically, NetWare Administrator simply ran out of gas. The memory limitations of a Windows workstation didn't allow NetWare Administrator users to load large directories into memory. Too many objects choked NetWare Administrator, because of memory architecture limitations.

ConsoleOne, using Java, has no such memory constraint. When Novell engineers demonstrate a billion-user network at conventions, only ConsoleOne can handle the job.

Creating User Objects with ConsoleOne

ConsoleOne is a Java-based program with which you can browse and organize network resources, set up users and group accounts, control access to network resources, and configure and monitor the network for optimum efficiency. Because it is Java-based, ConsoleOne can be run from any system with Java Virtual Machine (JVM) software, including the NetWare server console.

Being Java, ConsoleOne can be used on the NetWare 6 server or from a workstation. ConsoleOne doesn't yet duplicate completely everything in NWADMIN32, but soon it will push the Windows program out the door. Let's go through the details of creating User objects with ConsoleOne from the server console, or highlight areas where ConsoleOne includes more features than NWADMIN32.

Setting Up User Objects with ConsoleOne

IN A HURRY 4.1: CREATE A USER OBJECT WITH CONSOLEONE

1. Start ConsoleOne.

2. Expand Entire Network and browse to the tree you want to access.

3. Click the tree and log in as Admin.

4. Expand the organization and highlight the container where you want to create the user.

5. Click the Create User icon in the toolbar or choose File ➢ New ➢ User.

6. Provide the Name and press Tab.

7. Provide the Surname and press Enter.

8. At the Set Password screen, enter a password for the user and click OK.

The best place to run ConsoleOne is on a high-powered workstation with plenty of RAM and a fast network connection. Use the Client Installation CD-ROM and choose Novell ConsoleOne with Snap-ins to load the software on your workstation.

If you prefer, you can open ConsoleOne on the server console by navigating to NetWare's GUI screen—the server lists "current screens" when you press Ctrl+Esc. It's referred to as X Server—Graphical Console. Click the Novell icon at the bottom-left corner of the screen and choose ConsoleOne from the pop-up menu.

Everything about ConsoleOne looks exactly the same, no matter whether you run the program on the server console or your workstation. Well, there is one minor detail: The icon to expand a directory or open a container is different. On a workstation, the icon appears as a plus, just like a typical Windows Explorer program. On the server console, the icon looks exactly like a toilet flush handle. Click a handle, I mean icon, when it's pointing to the right, and the object opens and the handle turns down. All we need now are sound effects to complete the illusion and introduce a bit of scatological humor into network management.

With ConsoleOne open, expand Entire Network by clicking the little round icon (a globe, I believe) next to the My World icon. Repeat to expand the Trees object.

Notice that when you select the tree you want to work in, you must first authenticate to NDS. A Login dialog box appears, prompting you for a username, context, and password. You will want to log in as Admin or as another user with rights to add users to a container.

Once you've authenticated to the tree, the tree expands, showing the container objects. Browse through the tree until you find the container where you want the new User object to exist.

Non-NetWare 5.x or 4.1x users (those using NetWare 3.x or earlier NETX shells on their workstations) must be created in the containers where Bindery Services is enabled. Their context is not important when they log in, because those users log in through Bindery Services. They log in directly to their target NetWare 6 server (which must be running Bindery Services).

The ConsoleOne toolbar changes depending on what is highlighted in the left pane. With a container highlighted, four icons appear on the toolbar: New Group, New User, New Organizational Unit, and New Object (a cube).

To add a user, you can either click the New User icon (represented by the single individual) on the ConsoleOne toolbar or choose File ≻ New ≻ User. The New User dialog box that appears should look familiar if you're used to NetWare Administrator. Notice the Unique ID field—new in the improved ConsoleOne. The two mandatory properties, Name and Surname, are required before the Create button is activated. You can also choose to define additional properties or create another user (one or the other), as shown in Figure 4.1.

NOTE *In Figure 4.1, I have moved the New User dialog box to the right so that it does not cover the NDS eDirectory tree. For many of the illustrations in this book, I moved the windows for clarity. So don't be alarmed when your screen doesn't look exactly like the one shown in the picture.*

FIGURE 4.1

Adding Sandi

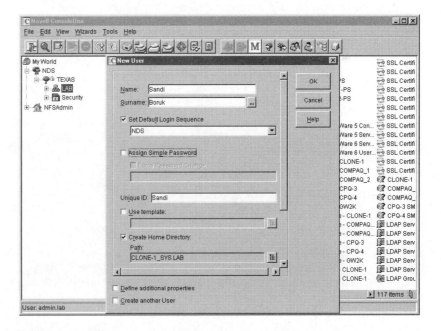

The NDS conventions that applied to objects created in earlier NDS versions still apply here. The username, though not case-sensitive, will appear as it is typed. If you type it in all uppercase letters, that is how it will appear in ConsoleOne. The requirements for login names are simply that they must be fewer than 64 characters and must be unique within the container.

If your NetWare 6 server must support non-NDS clients or work with earlier NetWare server versions, you need to be mindful of the restrictions placed on login names by the bindery:

◆ Names longer than 47 characters are truncated.

◆ Spaces are shown as underscores.

◆ The following characters can't be seen by non-NDS clients: slash (/), backslash (\), colon (:), comma (,), asterisk (*), and question mark (?).

The special characters above are legal within NDS but not within bindery systems. These characters also have problems in DOS names. The path of least trouble is to develop a naming standard for users that allows only alpha and numeric characters. If e-mail is important to your company, verify names with that system before assigning them inside NDS. You want to use names that work across all applications and systems.

The Surname field has no restrictions except making the name fit into the field. My example, Sandi Boruk, is my oldest niece, and I'll give her this tiny bit of fame, although she seems to be doing quite well on her own.

Once you've filled in the Name and the Surname fields, you can click Create to create the object. Or you can click Define Additional Properties before creating the object. If you want to define the properties after you create the object, simply right-click the User object and select Properties. You'll see the same property page that would appear if you had checked the Define Additional Properties check box.

Adding User Property Information

If you click the Define Additional Properties check box in the New User dialog box, you'll have the option to include a lot of information for this User object. Don't be overwhelmed; none of this information is mandatory, but some is helpful.

Figure 4.2 shows a property page for user Sandi. The NDS Rights tab is active and is displaying the Trustees of This Object option. I probably shouldn't let Sandi edit her own login script—a good security option change for everyone. You can see in Figure 4.2 that the Write check box remains checked but Write is highlighted (there is a box around the word). One more click, and I don't need to worry about Sandi changing her login script. This feature becomes more important for proactive management when you realize all users have the option of changing their own login script by right-clicking the red N icon in their Taskbar.

Let's take a quick look around the property pages. The ConsoleOne property screens look different from the ones in NetWare Administrator, but as we go through the tabs, you will see that you have access to the same object properties. ConsoleOne groups the properties into the following tabs:

◆ Security includes controls for Login Sequences (NDS or LDAP) and Certificates.

◆ Login Methods offers NDS Password (default and recommended) or Simple Password options.

FIGURE 4.2

Properties for
user Sandi

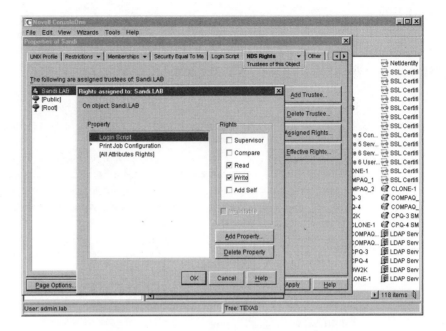

- ◆ General includes Identification, Postal Address, Environment, and See Also fields.

- ◆ Role Based Services includes Owned Roles (attached to that specific object) or Assigned Roles.

- ◆ Unix Profile contains the Unix User ID, Group, Login Shell, and Home Directory for cross-connected users.

- ◆ Restrictions includes Password Restrictions, Login Restrictions, Time Restrictions, Address Restrictions, Intruder Lockout, and Account Balance.

- ◆ Memberships includes Group Membership and Security Equal To.

- ◆ Security Equal to Me lets you set security equivalence grants. This used to be located under Memberships in earlier versions, but NetWare 6 moves it to its own tab.

- ◆ Login Script includes the Login Script property page.

- ◆ NDS Rights includes Trustees of This Object, Inherited Rights Filter, and Effective Rights.

- ◆ Other contains "Leftover attributes that are not handled by custom pages," according to Novell.

- ◆ Rights to Files and Folders lets you give individual users rights to files and directories (a new feature in ConsoleOne).

When you select a tab, it becomes active and moves to the foreground on your screen. Under the tab title is the name of the property page you are viewing. If additional property pages exist on that tab, you'll see a down arrow to the right of the tab title. To display the other available property pages, click and hold the down arrow. Continue to hold down the left mouse button and drag the mouse to highlight the page you want to display. Release the mouse button, and you're taken to the new property page.

Adding General Information

Let's look at the General tab first. The options here are Identification, Environment, Postal Address, and See Also.

ENTERING IDENTIFICATION INFORMATION

When you open the Identification property page in ConsoleOne, the only information filled in is the Last Name field. (NetWare Administrator includes the Login Name with full context, but ConsoleOne just puts the object name in the title of the property page and assumes you know the context.) The WHOAMI command-line utility presents the information in the Other Name, Title, and Description fields if they are not blank.

The fields in the Identification page contain plenty of information that can be useful when searching for particular people or locations on the network. Here's the obligatory list:

Given Name   User's first name

Last Name   User's last name (filled in automatically)

Full Name   User's complete name

Qualifier   Jr., Sr., II, III, and so on

Middle Initial   User's middle initial

Other Name   Nickname, job function name, or other identification information (60 characters maximum per entry; duplicates are not allowed)

Title   Position or function of user (60 characters maximum)

Location   Physical location, such as floor, wing, or mail stop

Department   User's department, division, or workgroup

Telephone   User's telephone numbers

Fax Number   User's fax numbers or those available to the user

E-Mail Address   Finally, the e-mail address appears on this page

Description   Function the user performs (30 lines of 37 characters each maximum)

Why should you enter all these things? Seems like a lot of extra work, doesn't it? Well, what if your boss asks for all the network users on the third floor? How many network users are senior editors? How many network users will use the new fax modem when we replace the fax machine with the number 214-555-2599? These answers are easy to find if the database information is available. The More buttons at the end of many text boxes allow multiple values to be entered.

Notice the last field: E-Mail Address. Finally! The address in Figure 4.3 isn't legal, but it expresses my feelings. And my feelings continue in the Description box.

FIGURE 4.3

Identification
information

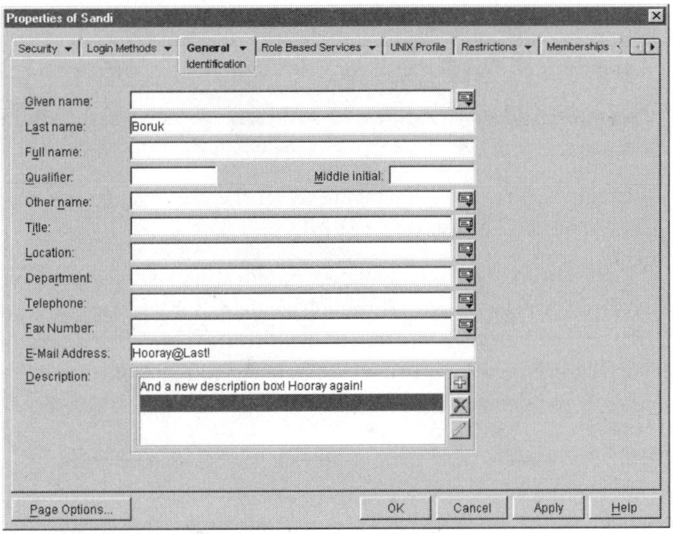

> **NOTE** *I must say entering information directly into NDS on a user's record seems wrong to me. NDS won't be as successful as I believe it can be until it becomes invisible. Technically, it's invisible here, but I much prefer a user Address Book type utility rather than using the user's NDS records. Which is why I like the new WebAccess portal and the Address Book utility that ship with NetWare 6.*

ENTERING ENVIRONMENT INFORMATION

The Environment page, shown in Figure 4.4, used to be strictly informative but became fully functional with NetWare 5.1. This functionality continues in NetWare 6.

FIGURE 4.4

Environment
information

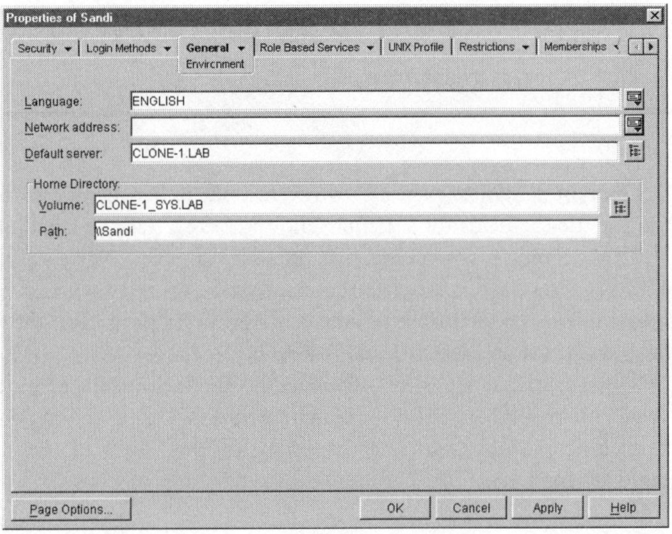

The Environment page includes the following fields:

Language From the SET command, shows the language for system messages.

Network Address Address or addresses of the workstation this user is currently using to connect to the network. This will change when the user connects from a different station.

Default Server The NetWare server the user tries to connect to when logging in, provided by the network administrator, not NDS.

Home Directory The volume and directory of the user's home directory. You can add or change a home directory through this field, but you cannot create a home directory from here. You can point the object to a home directory, but if the directory doesn't exist in the filesystem, you'll need to create it using NetWare Administrator or some other way. ConsoleOne still doesn't allow you to create the directory—an oversight in NetWare 5.1 yet to be fixed in NetWare 6.

NOTE *Notice that the More buttons to the right of the fields are somewhat different from those in NetWare Administrator, which uses an ellipsis, or three little dots, in the button to indicate that there is more information. ConsoleOne employs a drop-down menu icon that expands as necessary for the contained items.*

SPECIFYING THE USER'S POSTAL ADDRESS

IN A HURRY 4.2: SET POSTAL ADDRESS INFORMATION

1. Open ConsoleOne and locate the User object in the eDirectory tree.

2. Open the user's property page by right-clicking the User object name and selecting Properties.

3. Select the General tab.

4. Click the down arrow and select Postal Address.

5. Fill in the fields in the top half of the window.

6. To copy the information to the Mailing Label Information, click the Copy to Label button.

7. Click OK to save the information.

The Postal Address page allows you to track either the home or the business address for each user. You can use the fields for searching and to create a mailing label format.

After opening ConsoleOne, find the user you want to give a physical address listing. To open the user's property page, right-click that name and choose Properties, or you can highlight the user and choose File ➤ Properties. From the user's property page, click the General tab. Then click and hold the down arrow and select Postal Address.

No particular secrets here—there are no Browse buttons or pick lists. The only concern is if you plan to use this information for searching your NDS eDirectory database later. Only the top half of the dialog box will be searched, the result showing Mailing Labels. Figure 4.5 shows the fun and games for snail mail.

FIGURE 4.5

Snail mail support

For some reason, the last name doesn't get copied directly to the mailing label. Perhaps the Given Name text on the Identification page means the complete name. But since I'll never use mailing labels generated through NDS, who cares?

These fields accept all international postal codes. If you have international addresses, just supply the appropriate codes and countries in the Zip Code field.

ADDING REFERENCE INFORMATION

IN A HURRY 4.3: TRACK RELATED OBJECTS FOR A USER

1. Open ConsoleOne and locate the User object in the eDirectory tree.

2. Open the user's property page by right-clicking the User object name.

3. Select the General tab.

4. Click the down arrow and select See Also.

5. Click the Add button to list more objects related to the user.

6. Choose the related objects from the Select Objects dialog box.

7. Click OK to move the selected objects to the See Also page.

8. Click OK to save the information.

The See Also page is strictly informational. It does not affect any network configurations. This page is a handy place to put items you may need for reference, such as the Computer object type used by Sandi.

You cannot enter text in the See Also page. You can choose multiple objects in the Select Objects dialog box. Just hold down the Ctrl key as you click the left mouse button on each object you want to select.

Configuring User Object Security with ConsoleOne

So far, many of the user configuration options we've covered have been informational. The rest of the properties involve security.

I'll get into more serious security discussions in later chapters. Now, however, let's focus on the particular security information that is necessary to set up and manage individual User objects through ConsoleOne.

THE MEMBERSHIPS TAB

You use the Memberships tab to add a user to a particular group and to set the user's security rights equal to that of another object. Let's look at each of these options individually.

Setting Up Group Membership

IN A HURRY 4.4: ADD OR DELETE USER OBJECTS FROM A GROUP

1. Open ConsoleOne and locate the User object in the eDirectory tree.

2. Open the user's property page by right-clicking the User object name and selecting Properties.

3. Select the Memberships tab.

4. Click the down arrow and select Group Membership.

5. To add a user, click the Add button, choose a group or groups in the Select Objects dialog box, and click OK.

6. To delete a user, highlight the group name and click Delete.

7. Click OK to save your changes.

Groups are a marvelous tool when administering networks. Instead of dealing with each user, you can maintain a list of similar users and deal with the Group object. User objects inherit all the properties of their Group objects.

Be careful—a Group object is *not* a container. A Group object merely keeps a list of User objects. When some action is taken with that Group object, the same action is taken with each User object listed as part of the group. Think of this as a macro for a group of users with similar needs.

After opening ConsoleOne and selecting the User object to be added to a group, right-click the User object and select Properties. Click the Memberships tab on the user's property page. Click and hold the down arrow, and select Group Membership if it isn't already selected. The Group Membership page will open, showing all the groups of which this particular user is a member. There is no practical limit to the number of groups to which one user can belong.

If this particular user is not a member of any groups, click the Add button to open the Select Objects dialog box, as shown in Figure 4.6. By clicking the down arrow in the Look In box, you can see what context the user is in, or you can browse to a different context to find the group to which you want to add the user. In the example, you can see that the context is currently Consultants.LAB, and the only groups contained in this context currently are Consultants. In the Objects pick list, Consultants is highlighted. Clicking OK will pop the group name into the Memberships listing in the Group Membership page.

FIGURE 4.6

Adding Sandi to the Consultants group

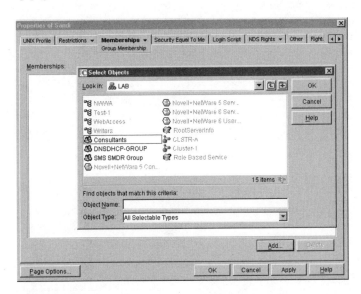

The Delete button works as you would expect. After highlighting a group name, clicking Delete erases the User object's name from the Memberships list. This screen is not where you delete the Group object itself; it just takes this particular User object out of the Group object.

Setting Security Equal To

IN A HURRY 4.5: SET SECURITY EQUIVALENCE

1. Open ConsoleOne and locate the User object in the eDirectory tree.

2. Open the user's property page by right-clicking the User object name and selecting Properties.

3. Select the Memberships tab.

4. Click the down arrow and select Security Equal To.

5. To add security equivalence, click the Add button, choose objects in the Select Objects dialog box, and click OK.

6. To delete security equivalence, highlight the Security Equivalent object and click Delete.

7. Click OK to save your settings.

Security equivalence grants one User object the same rights as another object. This is the same idea as Group objects, where the members of the group all have the rights of the group itself. However, granting security equivalence of a User object to another User object is more dangerous than putting users into groups. We'll cover security equivalence and other security-related topics in Chapter 7.

Open ConsoleOne and choose the User object to make equivalent to another object. In the user's property page under the Memberships tab, select the Security Equal To page. Click the Add button to open the Select Objects dialog box, as shown in Figure 4.7. Notice that, in our example, Sandi already has security equal to the group Consultants. That's the result of our last operation, when we added a User object to a Group object.

FIGURE 4.7

Modifying a User object's Security Equal To setting

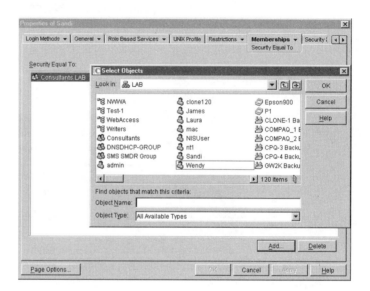

As an example, I have changed the context to LAB and am now able to make Sandi equivalent to file servers or volumes as well as to other User objects. This inappropriate type of assignment would be dangerous, since Sandi could suddenly have rights and access privileges of a server such as COM-PAQ-330, a Compaq workgroup server.

Deleting equivalence is simply a matter of highlighting the equivalent object in the Security Equal To box and clicking Delete.

SETTING SECURITY EQUAL TO ME

The Security Equal to Me option allows you to specify the users who are security-equivalent to this object. This is the opposite of the Security Equal To option described above, which allows you to specify this object as security-equivalent to other objects.

You can follow the same steps you took in Setting Security Equal To, except instead of the Membership tab, you select the Security Equal to Me tab. The rest of the steps are identical. You can view which objects have security equivalence to this object, or you can grant or remove security equivalence by using the Add or Delete buttons, as illustrated in Figure 4.7.

THE NDS RIGHTS TAB

The NDS Rights tab presents three security-related options:

◆   Trustees of This Object

◆   Inherited Rights Filters

◆   Effective Rights

Chapter 7 covers these options in detail. For our purposes here, I'll explain how you can set these items from ConsoleOne.

Trustees of This Object

IN A HURRY 4.6: VIEW OR CHANGE TRUSTEES

1. Open ConsoleOne and locate the User object in the eDirectory tree.

2. Open the user's property page by right-clicking the User object name and selecting Properties.

3. Select the NDS Rights tab.

4. Click the down arrow and select Trustees of This Object.

5. To add a trustee, click the Add Trustee button to choose the new trustee from the Select Objects dialog box.

6. To delete a trustee, highlight the trustee and click the Delete button.

7. To modify rights, highlight each trustee, click Assigned Rights, and toggle the appropriate check boxes.

8. Click OK to save the settings.

The Trustees of This Object page allows you to view or change the list of trustees for this object. This property page gives you several options. You can add a trustee, delete a trustee, assign or change the rights of a trustee, and view the effective rights of a trustee, as shown in Figure 4.8.

To add a trustee, simply click the Add Trustee button and select a new trustee object. Use the Select Objects dialog box to browse the tree until you find the object you want to add as a trustee (I left it open in Figure 4.8 for illustrative purposes). Highlight the user and click the OK button. The first object will now appear as a trustee of the selected object.

Delete a trustee by highlighting the trustee and clicking the Delete Trustee button.

To assign rights or view previously assigned rights for a trustee, highlight the trustee and click the Assigned Rights button. You'll know how to get around this screen. It should look familiar to you.

Remember that just because you delete a trustee or remove rights doesn't necessarily mean that object doesn't still have rights to this object. The trustee may have rights granted through security equivalence. By clicking the Effective Rights button, you will be able to see what effective rights a trustee has to this object. This screen should also look familiar to you. You can use the browse function to view the effective rights of other objects as well.

FIGURE 4.8

The Trustees of This
Object page

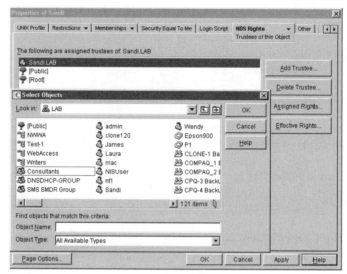

NOTE *When you finish making changes on this page or any other page, you must click the OK button or the Apply button for the changes to take effect.*

Inherited Rights Filters

> **IN A HURRY 4.7: VIEW OR SET INHERITED RIGHTS FILTERS**
>
> 1. Open ConsoleOne and locate the User object in the eDirectory tree.
> 2. Open the user's property page by right-clicking the User object name and selecting Properties.
> 3. Select the NDS Rights tab.
> 4. Click the down arrow and select Inherited Rights Filters.
> 5. View or set inherited rights filters (IRFs) for this object.

You can use the Inherited Rights Filters page, shown in Figure 4.9, to view or set inherited rights filters (IRFs) on this object.

Here some things to remember about IRFs:

◆ IRFs don't give rights to anyone and then take rights away. If a user is granted rights at a certain level of the directory or container structure, the only way to keep those rights from flowing down through the subdirectories and subcontainers is by setting up an IRF or by reassigning that user rights at lower directories.

- IRFs can block only inherited rights, or those rights that are flowing down because of granted rights somewhere up the line. Rights that are granted at the current level by explicit assignment cannot be blocked.

- When you set an IRF for an object, it applies to all trustees.

FIGURE 4.9

Setting an inherited rights filter to Sandi

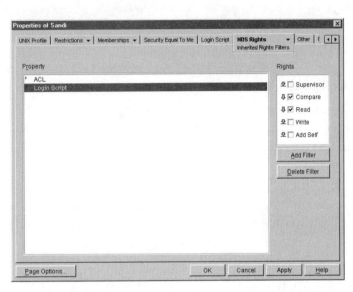

The Inherited Rights window for Sandi shows the target resource that the IRFs shown on this page are affecting, which is Sandi's login script in this example. You cannot browse and view IRFs for another object without closing the property page and opening the properties for another object.

The Rights section allows you to view or set the IRF that blocks object rights from being inherited by the current object. It is easy to block an object right. You can block five rights: Supervisor, Compare, Read, Write, and Add Self.

Figure 4.9 shows that when the box next to the object right is checked, the flow down arrow is large. But when the box is unchecked, the large arrow is replaced with a stumpy arrow with a line underneath, signifying the object right has been restricted or filtered to this object. So, to block an object right, uncheck the corresponding check box.

The Property section allows you to view or set the IRF that blocks property rights from being inherited by the current object. Again, you can block the property rights by unchecking the box next to the specific right. You will get the same stumpy arrow and line, indicating that right has been filtered.

Again, with property rights, you have the option to set the IRF for all properties or for selected properties. To block the property rights to all properties, click the top menu option for [All Attributes Rights] and uncheck the box next to the right you want to restrict. Notice that I took away Sandi's right to modify her own login script, to counteract my earlier mistake where I forgot to block Sandi's right to do that.

To block the property rights to individual properties, click the Add Filter button to open the menu, highlight a property, and uncheck the box next to the right you want to restrict. You can't do multiple properties at once anymore, for some reason, so you'll need to make a new filter for every property. Maybe this gives you more granularity, or maybe some Novell engineer blew it. You decide.

Effective Rights

IN A HURRY 4.8: VIEW EFFECTIVE RIGHTS

1. Open ConsoleOne and locate the User object in the eDirectory tree.

2. Open the user's property page by right-clicking the User object name and selecting Properties.

3. Select the NDS Rights tab.

4. Click the down arrow and select Effective Rights.

5. View the trustee's effective rights to this object.

The Effective Rights page is an informational page that allows you to view a trustee's effective rights to this object. You cannot make any changes here, but it's a good way to get a report on the effective rights of a trustee to any given object. Figure 4.10 provides a view of this page.

FIGURE 4.10

Trustee James' effective rights to Sandi

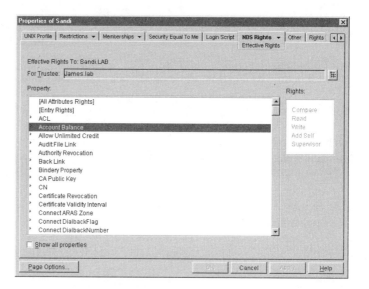

The Effective Rights To field shows the distinguished name of the target resource, in this case Sandi.LAB.Texas. Sandi is the object to which the trustee has effective rights. You cannot edit this field. If you want to see the effective rights trustees have to another object, you must open that object's Effective Rights property page.

The For Trustee field shows the distinguished name of the trustee whose effective rights are displayed on this page. In this case, the trustee is James.LAB. Notice the Browse button to the right of the field. You can browse for another trustee and view its effective rights to the target resource.

In this case, James has all applicable object rights to Sandi (as the James user, I am an Admin equivalent). Notice that if the trustee has those rights, they appear on the right in the Rights box. Also notice that the Create right does not appear. The reason for this is that you cannot create an object within a User object, so that right is not applicable here.

The Property list shows James' effective property rights to Sandi's Account Balance setting. These rights include Compare, Read, Write, Add Self, and Supervisor. Admin (and an equivalent) has all these rights, but another trustee would have fewer property rights.

In the Property Rights field in the corresponding screen in NetWare Administrator, you have the option to view Admin's effective rights to All Properties or to Selected Properties. All Properties is the default. Here in ConsoleOne, the question changes to a check box asking whether you want to show all properties of this object class to help greatly expand the pick list that appears. To view a trustee's effective rights to a single property, click that property in the Property pick list, and the listing of the effective rights in the Rights box will change accordingly.

THE RESTRICTIONS TAB

The Restrictions tab contains all the property pages that you can use to limit or restrict users' access to certain parts of the network. Remember, you are making the same changes to objects whether you use NetWare Administrator or ConsoleOne. Here is the official list of options for the Restrictions tab in ConsoleOne:

◆ Password Restrictions

◆ Login Restrictions

◆ Time Restrictions

◆ Address Restrictions

◆ Intruder Lockout

◆ Account Balance

Password Restrictions

IN A HURRY 4.9: SET PASSWORD RESTRICTIONS

1. Open ConsoleOne and locate the User object in the eDirectory tree.

2. Open the user's property page by right-clicking the User object name and selecting Properties.

3. Select the Restrictions tab.

4. Click the down arrow and select Password Restrictions.

5. Set the desired password restrictions.

6. Click OK to save the settings.

The single most important user security tool is a good password system. If security is important to your company, password restrictions will be important as well.

Select the Password Restrictions page from the Restrictions tab of the user's property page to see the screen in Figure 4.11. Notice the new, easy-choose calendar included in ConsoleOne to help you pick a date.

Providing passwords for users usually isn't a good idea. Users like to feel that their password is known to only them. Even though you have access to all their data files as the administrator, users still feel more secure if they set their own passwords. A good compromise is to allow users to make their own passwords within certain restrictions.

FIGURE 4.11

Tightening password parameters

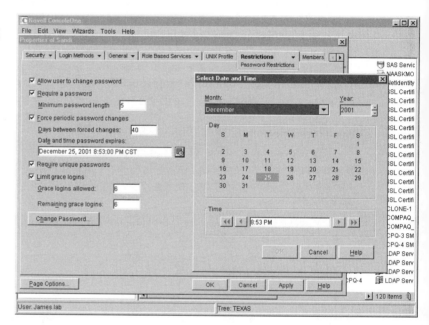

Here, for the sake of our example, we have poor Sandi restricted every which way. This looks like an enormous amount of extra work for the network administrator, and it may be. However, tight security takes time. Few networks use all these options. Most network administrators prefer to train users and teach them why security is important. Let's take a look at each option and see what choices we have. Then, later, apply them to all users rather than just one.

Allow User to Change Password   If your security is extremely tight, you may not allow the user to change his or her own password. This idea is both good and bad. It's good because the passwords you choose will be better than the ones most users will choose. You won't choose the user's wife's name; users often choose a family name as the password. It's bad, however, because users will not easily remember the passwords you choose. This leads to passwords written on calendars or desk blotters, which is not secure either. There's no good way to cover both these contingencies.

Require a Password   If this box is unchecked, everything else in this dialog box turns gray to show that it's unavailable. Checking this box allows you to set the minimum password length and choose whether to force periodic changes. The password minimum length can be between 1 and 999 characters, although setting this field larger than 11 characters makes it impossible for Macintosh clients to log in. Most security experts recommend a password of at least five characters. The longer the password, the harder it is to remember.

TIP   Although NetWare doesn't demand that you mix alpha and numeric characters, some Unix systems do. Following the Unix example and requiring a minimum of five characters including at least two numeric characters makes passwords much more difficult to guess. It also cuts down on using family names, unless someone on your network is related to 007. John007 is still more secure than Marsha.

Force Periodic Password Changes   When this box is checked, the user is forced to change his or her password at the interval you specify. The default for days between forced changes is 40 days (and 40 nights). The date the password will expire is listed on the screen for you. Changing that date does not change the Days Between Forced Changes field. ConsoleOne with NetWare 6 pops open a real calendar dialog box rather than forcing you to push the up or down arrows to slide the date. I think this is a nice improvement.

Require Unique Passwords   When password changes are forced, the option to require unique passwords becomes available. If you choose not to have unique passwords, users can simply alternate between their son's name and their daughter's name for passwords. If you require passwords to be unique, NetWare tracks each user's last 20 passwords and does not allow duplication.

Limit Grace Logins   If you force password changes, NetWare allows each user a few grace logins. In other words, even though the password is expired, NetWare will allow that password for a certain number of times. The default is six, and this dialog box displays how many grace logins are left. This is a friendly thing to do when forcing users to change passwords. If users must make up their own new passwords, they may not feel creative the morning their old password expires. The grace logins allow them to carefully consider their next password. If you or your department parcels out passwords, the user will need time to contact you to obtain a new one.

Change Password   If you do want to change users' passwords for them, here's the place. Click this button, and a smaller dialog box pops open with two fields. With NetWare 5.1, if you logged in as an Admin-equivalent user, you needed to type the old password, then the new password, and then the new password again for verification. With NetWare 6, an Admin-equivalent user doesn't need to enter the old password. You will see only asterisks for each letter you type. This feature also works when a user forgets a password; you can assign a new one here.

Login Restrictions

IN A HURRY 4.10: SET THE LOGIN RESTRICTIONS FOR A USER

1.   Open ConsoleOne and locate the User object in the eDirectory tree.

2.   Open the user's property page by right-clicking the User object name and selecting Properties.

continued on next page

IN A HURRY 4.10: SET THE LOGIN RESTRICTIONS FOR A USER *(continued)*

3. Select the Restrictions tab.

4. Click the down arrow and select Login Restrictions.

5. Check the boxes to disable the account, set the account expiration date, or limit concurrent connections.

6. Read the last login time and date (if applicable).

7. Click OK to save your settings.

Login restriction setup is one situation in which NetWare 6 focuses on the individual user. Normally, any configuration that can be done to a particular user can be done better working with a group. Restrictions on a particular user are useful at times, however, and this is where you set some of those restrictions.

Login restriction sounds like a way to stop someone from connecting to the network. That's only part of the value of the restrictions here. Maintaining tight network security often means limiting network access for users and tracking the resources used by each user.

After starting ConsoleOne, choose the User object to be restricted and open the user's property page. Select the Restrictions tab, click the down arrow, and select Login Restrictions. You will see a screen similar to the one in Figure 4.12, which shows three action boxes and one piece of information. And I left the Select Date and Time box open because it's cool.

FIGURE 4.12

Setting account limits

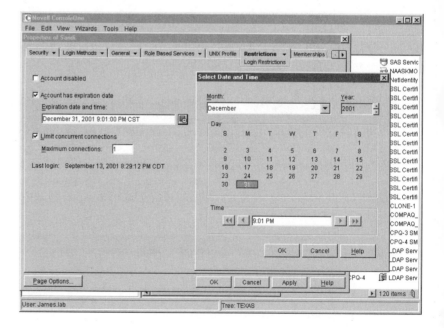

Since users tend to share passwords and login names even when the manager begs them not to, security heads south. Login restrictions provide one way to slow this trend. This page includes the following fields:

Account Disabled   This check box is an excellent security tool when dealing with a shifting user base. This stops anyone from using this account but does not erase the applicable login scripts, change passwords, or delete data. When a user goes on vacation, check this box. It will prevent co-workers from borrowing this account while the user is gone. This method also works well for temporary users. Let's say you bring in accounting help at the end of every month. Do you want to create and delete these users each month? No way. Create some generic accounting users, such as ACCT_1 and ACCT_2, and use the Account Disabled check box. When the temporary workers are gone, no one will be able to log in with the ACCT_1 or ACCT_2 names. When they come back, one click of the mouse sets everything back into place for them.

Account Has Expiration Date   This option works similarly to Account Disabled. Once the expiration date is reached, the account disappears as far as any login attempts are concerned. The date can always be extended by changing it here. Do you have a group of visitors who need network access during their two-week stay? Set their usernames with an expiration date, and you won't need to worry about other users getting access to their information after they're gone. Again, this option offers a nicer calendar dialog box than provided with earlier versions.

Limit Concurrent Connections   This option controls one of the features developed in the early days of NetWare: the ability to log in from two or more places on the network but have the exact same rights and access for each login. Novell had this feature before any of its competitors. If security is important in your network, however, this field should always be set to only one concurrent connection per user. Limiting concurrent access is a good way to slow down the sharing of passwords among the users. If a second person tries to access the account of a person already connected, that user will get an error message. When the users complain, remind them that sharing passwords breaks several security rules.

Last Login   This field displays the last time this user connected to the network. Only one historical connection is listed here.

There are other places to limit connections, and I'll cover them later in the book (in Chapter 7). If your default is to allow multiple connections, you can use the Login Restrictions page to limit particular users to a set number of connections.

Time Restrictions

IN A HURRY 4.11: SET THE TIME RESTRICTIONS FOR A USER

1. Open ConsoleOne and locate the User object in the eDirectory tree.
2. Open the user's property page by right-clicking the User object name and selecting Properties.
3. Select the Restrictions tab.

continued on next page

IN A HURRY 4.11: SET THE TIME RESTRICTIONS FOR A USER *(continued)*

4. Click the down arrow and select Time Restrictions.

5. On the grid, indicate the times to lock out the User object.

6. Click OK to save the restrictions.

You may want to restrict access to your network for several reasons. First, and most common, is to allow tape backup systems to work properly. Most backup systems skip open files. If users are logged in and still have applications open, the files in use will likely be skipped. Closing all connections before the backup starts eliminates that problem.

Security is another reason to restrict access. If no one in your company works the night shift, any user on your network at 2:12 A.M. is probably up to no good. Locking out all the users during the night and early morning limits your exposure to network tampering.

If you use login scripts to inform users of upcoming events with an MOTD (Message of the Day), you want them to log in to see it. If they stay connected overnight, the login script can't call the MOTD and display the same. So set the login time restrictions to force users to disconnect from the server during the night.

Open ConsoleOne, choose the User object for your restriction operation, select the Restrictions tab, click and hold the down arrow, and select Time Restrictions. This is one utility that really takes advantage of the graphical interface, as you can see in Figure 4.13.

Each block on the time grid represents a half-hour. White blocks allow connection; dark blocks restrict. Clicking each block toggles its state. Click a white block and it turns dark. Click a dark block and it turns white. The time displayed under the grid shows the block touched by the cursor.

FIGURE 4.13

Blocking Sandi out during backups

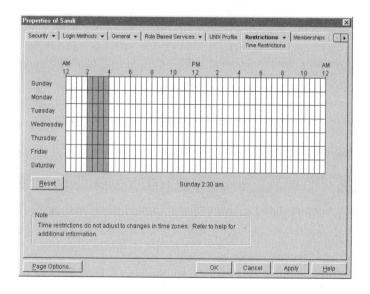

Clicking each half-hour block is cumbersome, so you can use a shortcut. Click the first block of time to restrict, hold down the left mouse button, and drag the rectangle to the last time to restrict. When you release the mouse button, all the blocks within the rectangle will change state.

Address Restrictions

IN A HURRY 4.12: SET THE ADDRESS RESTRICTIONS FOR A USER

1. Open ConsoleOne and locate the User object in the eDirectory tree.

2. Open the user's property page by right-clicking the User object name and selecting Properties.

3. Select the Restrictions tab.

4. Click the down arrow and select Address Restrictions.

5. Click the Add button.

6. Choose the protocol the User object uses for connection to the network from the NetAddress Type field.

7. Provide the protocol address for the allowable workstation.

8. Click OK to save the settings.

As you saw earlier (in Figure 4.12), the Login Restrictions page for a user has a Limit Concurrent Connections check box. The second step in restricting the number of concurrent logins users can have is to restrict the workstations from which they can connect to the network. This action is drastic and makes more work for the network administrator, but it is possible.

There is one good way to use this option to improve security without inconveniencing your users: Make the restriction for your tape backup system. If your tape backup system runs from a network node, as most do, tie the backup User object to the address of the machine with the tape backup attached.

The User object for backup (usually called BACKUP or something equally creative and inviting to hackers and snoopers) has full rights over the network filesystems, which could be a serious security breach if a person got hold of the backup user's username and password. If that happens, but you have restricted the address for the backup User object, the thieving user must gain access to that physical workstation for mischief.

After opening ConsoleOne, choose the User object to restrict, open the user's property page, and select the Restrictions tab. Click and hold the down arrow and select Address Restrictions to open the Address Restriction page.

To add a restriction, click the Add button to open the Create Network Address dialog box. In the NetAddress Type field, click the down arrow to select the protocol for that user, as you see in Figure 4.14. In the NetAddress field, enter the specific address of that particular machine. Each protocol has different address requirements.

FIGURE 4.14

List of protocols for tying a user to a particular network address

Figure 4.14 shows a TCP/IP address, which also allows a particular port designation for tighter security. If you choose IP, the Port option isn't offered. Novell's proprietary protocol, IPX, requires a long NetAddress broken into three parts. The figure shows TCP/IP because that's the transport protocol of choice for Novell now.

Intruder Lockout

IN A HURRY 4.13: RESET INTRUDER LOCKOUT

1. Open ConsoleOne and locate the User object in the eDirectory tree.

2. Open the user's property page by right-clicking the User object name and selecting Properties.

3. Select the Restrictions tab.

4. Click and hold the down arrow and select Intruder Lockout.

5. Click the Account Locked check box to reopen the account.

6. Click OK to save the settings.

The intruder lockout function is a "gotcha" from NetWare, special delivery to hackers, or at least users trying to remember their own passwords or guess those of co-workers. If the intruder-detection feature is active, you will always know when someone connects to your network while guessing a password. Of course, you will also know when users forget their password, possibly even before they come crying for help.

Intruder detection must be set for the container (see Chapter 8) before this dialog box becomes active for the User object. You may have detection active on some containers but not on others.

Once again, start ConsoleOne and open the Intruder Lockout property page found under the Restrictions tab of the user whose account has been locked. The page you'll see is shown in Figure 4.15.

There is nothing to do here except clear the workstation by clicking the Account Locked check box. You can't lock the account by clicking this check box. You lock accounts using the Account Disabled check box in the Login Restrictions tab (Figure 4.12), as explained earlier in this chapter.

FIGURE 4.15

Intruder lockout
activated by using
the wrong password

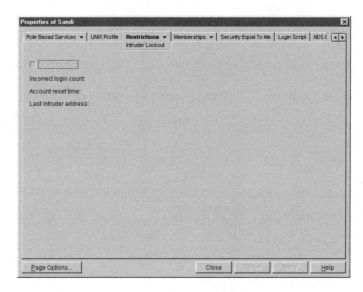

Yeah, this boring screen looks worthless. But it will be exciting when a user comes crying about a lost password. And you'll know about the blunder before the user has the nerve to call or drop by.

Account Balance

IN A HURRY 4.14: SET THE ACCOUNT BALANCE FOR A USER

1. Open ConsoleOne and locate the User object in the eDirectory tree.

2. Open the user's property page by right-clicking the User object name and selecting Properties.

3. Select the Restrictions tab.

4. Click and hold the down arrow and select Account Balance.

5. Set the current Account Balance and the Low Balance Limit.

6. Click OK to save your settings.

NetWare was the first network operating system to allow accounting. By tracking such details as connect time, disk space used, and service requests to a file server, NetWare accounting moved away from a PC LAN level toward mainframe-type control. Some network administrators use accounting to charge company departments, and others use accounting to track when resources are being used more heavily than in the past.

If accounting is enabled on a server, the users of that server can be assigned a value for each server operation. The screen in Figure 4.16 shows you how simple it is to track the server resources consumed by a user.

FIGURE 4.16

Accounting for user
Sandi

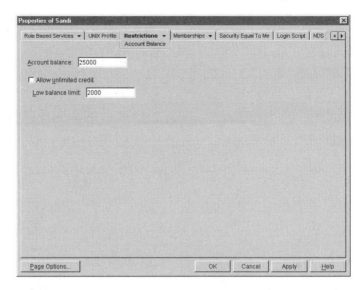

The Account Balance field shows the credits available for this user. The credits are set on the network resource itself, not here (see Chapter 8 for details). The Low Balance Limit field shows the credit level at which to warn the user before the account is disabled.

If you want to track the accounting information for charge-back or overhead calculations but don't want to prevent users from reaching their network resources after they've used up their allotted credit, click the Allow Unlimited Credit box. This field will track the information needed for the accounting reports but never lock out users.

NOTE   If a user's credits drop to the level of the Low Balance Limit field and the user gets locked out of the system, nothing happens to the user's information. The user will be back in business as soon as an administrator increases the Account Balance value.

THE LOGIN SCRIPT TAB

IN A HURRY 4.15: ADD A LOGIN SCRIPT

1. Open ConsoleOne and locate the User object in the eDirectory tree.

2. Open the user's property page by right-clicking the User object name and selecting Properties.

3. Select the Login Script tab.

4. Enter the login script commands.

5. Click OK to save the login script.

The Login Script tab has only one available option, which is to add a user login script. The login script was the single place to manage user configuration in the earliest NetWare versions. Later, more control was available in the system login script, but there could be only one system login script per server. That limited what could be done for any particular user or groups of users (or you ended up with a huge and unwieldy system script).

With NetWare 6, four scripts work together to control the network configuration of any one user. The user login script, once the most important, has now become the least important.

The user login script executes last and overrides all previous settings. This is the same relationship as with NetWare 3.*x*'s system and user login scripts. But the extra scripts available in NetWare 6 make the user login script necessary only for unique needs of that particular user. We'll discuss the various types of login scripts in the next chapter, but if you do need individual user login scripts, the User property page's Login Script tab is the one to click. But only click this as a last resort.

After starting ConsoleOne and selecting the User object to examine, display the user's properties by right-clicking that User object. Select the Login Script tab, as shown in Figure 4.17.

FIGURE 4.17

Adding a test login script for User Sandi

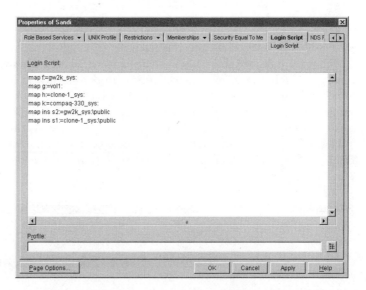

NOTE *See the Profile field toward the bottom of the dialog box in Figure 4.17? That will become important soon. Since we haven't created a profile login script yet, we can't include it in the user login script here.*

In the Login Script page, enter the login script commands. See the next chapter for information about login script commands and syntax, because we deal there with groups of users, not individuals. That should be a strong hint about your management approach.

THE RIGHTS TO FILES AND FOLDERS TAB

IN A HURRY 4.16: SETTING RIGHTS TO FILES AND FOLDERS

1. Open ConsoleOne and locate the User object in the eDirectory tree.

2. Open the user's property page by right-clicking the User object name and selecting Properties.

3. Select the Rights to Files and Folders tab.

4. Click Show and select the appropriate volume, directory, or file.

5. Click Add beside the Files and Folders box to choose the object(s) to be modified.

6. Check the appropriate rights, then click Apply.

7. To verify rights, click the Effective Rights command button.

One note: Don't make a habit of giving individual users rights to files and directories. Address this problem as shown in the next chapter, where we handle groups of users, not individuals.

That said, there are times when individual users need more control over some volumes or directories than the other users. Power users, acting as workgroup managers, can really help with little problems by taking care of special areas. Users who create and manage material, such as all the reports or final documents for the marketing department, will need more rights than their co-workers.

Open ConsoleOne and tag the user of choice, such as Sandi once again. The Rights to Files and Folders may be the last tab on the right, so you'll need to use the navigation arrows at end of the tab display to find it. The only menu item is Trustee File System Rights, so the page shown in Figure 4.18 is the display you'll get.

FIGURE 4.18

Standard user rights to a volume

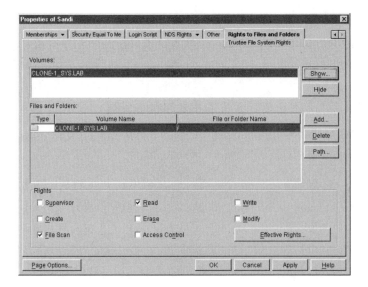

When you click the Show button, the Select Objects dialog box opens. Drill down the Organization and Organizational Units as necessary to find your desired volume. (Maybe *desire* is too strong a word for a volume—pick the one the user desires ... hmm, not much better.) If you want to change rights for a user, you can just skip the Volumes section and go straight to the Add command button to the right of the Files and Folders section.

Figure 4.18 displays the rights Sandi has to the full SYS: volume of CLONE-1. The Rights check boxes at the bottom of the page fill automatically, waiting for you to change them. These rights are the default rights, allowing users to read files and get full directory listings, but nothing else.

Since Sandi is a responsible young woman (she's my first niece, and I know she's responsible even if a dicey driver), she gets the job of controlling all the files in the Documents directory on the SYS: volume of COMPAQ-330. She must have full rights to make all file changes, including creating new subdirectories or granting rights to other users, as she sees fit.

Using the Show button in Volumes, I drilled down to the Test-1 Organizational Unit to find the workgroup server COMPAQ-330 (a clever name for a Compaq 330 server, don't you think?). Then, using the Add button in Files and Folders, I drilled down to the Documents directory. Here sit all the final versions of documents for the imaginary department Sandi works for (and she gets an imaginary check, too).

Since Sandi will be the final authority for all the files in this directory, I gave her every right possible. Figure 4.19 shows all the details, including all the checked boxes in the Rights area.

FIGURE 4.19

Sandi controls the Documents directory

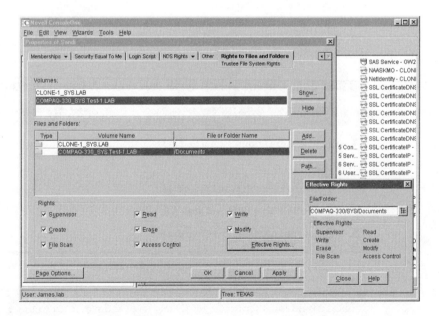

You can see the Effective Rights display box in the corner of Figure 4.19. This may seem to be redundant checking, but it's better to take a few more mouse clicks now than to discover I missed a check box when Sandi complains she can't control all the files in the Documents directory. The Effective Rights feature is a good way to verify that the correct rights have been assigned.

Remembering NetWare Administrator

I call this "remembering" NetWare Administrator because this utility is almost, but not quite, gone. Everything we've covered so far in this chapter can be done with ConsoleOne. Novell engineers want you to move to ConsoleOne and away from NetWare Administrator, but some functions have yet to be transferred. But all the user functions have been transferred, and sometimes upgraded, in ConsoleOne rather than NetWare Administrator. We're forced to use NetWare Administrator for some printing functions in a couple of chapters, but not for individual users or groups.

We'll touch only briefly on NetWare Administrator for NetWare 6. You won't get all the details here, because I would be doing you a disservice teaching you a lame-duck utility. If you already know and love NetWare Administrator from earlier NetWare versions (or just know it yet feel indifferent), you don't need hand-holding.

Once you are connected to the network and have the proper client programs loaded for your workstation, you can run the NetWare Administrator program, NWADMN32. Most NetWare 6 administrators will use a Windows system. So, when I reference NetWare Administrator, I'm speaking of the version specific for 32-bit Windows platforms. You must use it in conjunction with Novell's Client32. Run the program with the `SYS:\PUBLIC\WIN32\NWADMN32.EXE` command.

NOTE *To avoid all the browsing in the future, map a drive to the WIN32 subdirectory, and/or create a shortcut on the Windows Desktop.*

Upon initial login on a new system, the Admin user has access to the root of the SYS: volume, to SYS:SYSTEM, and to SYS:PUBLIC, just as in earlier NetWare versions. The LOGIN command for Admin assumes the Admin object was placed in the main Organization container.

Basic User Object Setup with NetWare Administrator

IN A HURRY 4.17: CREATE A BASIC USER OBJECT IN NWADMN32

1. Open NetWare Administrator and move to the context for the new User object.

2. Press Insert to open the New Object list box or click the User icon on the toolbar.

3. Choose the User object and press Enter.

4. Provide the Login Name and press Tab.

5. Provide the Last Name and press Enter.

When I say basic, I mean basic. The bare-bones User object created using the minimum configuration has no login script and no rights except those granted to the [Public] trustee object.

The first thing to do, as when performing any administrative task while in Windows, is to load the NetWare Administrator program. When the program opens, you will see the [Root] object with the globe icon. Each container you open displays the objects contained inside, both container and leaf objects. You can open a container by double-clicking the container object or by choosing View ➤ Expand. (If you ask me, double-clicking is easier.) You can also press Alt+V+X if you don't want to use the mouse.

Before you can create the User object, you must reach the context in which it will reside. Technically, you can create a User object in any context you wish, and the user will have access to the NDS eDirectory tree. The trick is that the individual user must know his or her context when logging in, or the context must be placed in the Login prompt. Practically, it's easiest to create each user in the same context as that user's primary server.

Once all the containers are open, or at least the container in which you plan to create a new User object, highlight the Organization or Organizational Unit name. To create a new object, you have several choices to start the process:

◆ Press the Insert key.

◆ Right-click the container name, and then left-click the Create button.

◆ Press Alt+O or click Object on the main menu, then highlight Create and press Enter.

◆ Click the Create User Object icon on the toolbar.

Old NetWare hands will no doubt press the Insert key, since that's the time-honored NetWare tradition. No matter which method you choose to start the Create process (unless you click the Create User icon), you wind up with what's shown in Figure 4.20.

FIGURE 4.20

Beginning the process of creating a User object

The NetWare Administrator program runs as a multiple-document interface (MDI) application. The main, full-screen NetWare Administrator window becomes the background for multiple secondary windows.

In typical Windows fashion, you can click the scroll bar to the right of the window until User comes into view, as it is in the screen in Figure 4.20. In typical NetWare fashion, you can also press the first letters of your choice until that choice appears under the highlight bar. In Figure 4.20, pressing U was all that was necessary to highlight User.

Then finish with NetWare Administrator exactly the way described earlier with ConsoleOne. They really are that similar now.

Adding User Identification Information

If you click the Define Additional Properties check box in the Create User dialog box, you will find tons of things to fill out about this particular User object. Don't be overwhelmed; none of this information is mandatory. However, many items are helpful, and you are probably already familiar with such things as the Login Script properties from earlier NetWare versions.

Figure 4.21 shows the main user Identification page, identified in two ways. First, the page name appears in the upper-left corner, just under the main title bar. Second, the Identification button on the right side is pressed and has black borders.

Doesn't this look like Figure 4.3? But where's the e-mail address text box? Not in NetWare Administrator, that's where.

FIGURE 4.21

Sandi's info, but no e-mail address

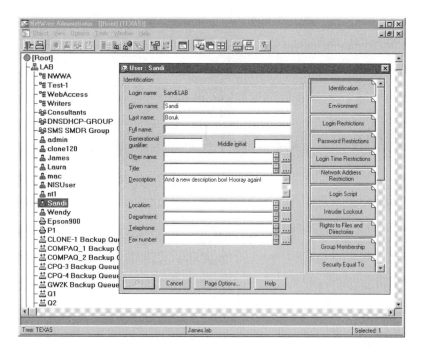

So don't waste much time with NetWare Administrator. Use Remote Manager via your browser to monitor your network from your workstation, or use ConsoleOne to make changes.

The Users and You

As stated at the beginning of the chapter, *user* is a four-letter word. So is *work.* The two are closely related.

Think of how the users on your network see you. If your company charges an internal budget for network hardware, software, and personnel, you're seen as an overpriced leech. If your company considers you overhead, you're seen as part of the group that sucks profits out of the profit-sharing plan, and hence out of the user's very own pocket. None of this is flattering, is it? Do you want to change this perception?

First, realize that you can't change everyone's mind. Some people won't like you or your job because they don't like computers. You'll never convert them, so be friendly but realistic.

Second, let users know that the internal prices for services are competitive or better than services purchased on the "outside." If they aren't competitive, figure out why not and fix the problem. If corporate management has set some outrageously high figure for labor or markup, you have a problem. It won't be easy to convince that same management to lower the internal rates; but if you don't, you'll never look good compared with the outside world.

Finally, let the users do some of your work for you. Believe it or not, they will love the opportunity.

This works especially well with vocal users and non-computer management. Most people believe their own job is rougher than anyone else's. If you offer them a chance to apply their business experience to your "deficiencies," they will quickly discover the problems you face every day. Let some of those bean-counters (excuse me, those esteemed accountants) debate the need between more server hard disk space, a new laser printer, a better tape backup system, or training for the new guy in the tech department. Maybe then they will appreciate your position a bit more. You might even offer to help them out a bit or volunteer to handle your own payroll. It can't hurt to ask.

Seriously, the bottom line is this: The users are your job; the network is not. The network is a business tool for the users, supported by you. The activities of the users matter more than you and your network.

Is this terrible? Not if you adopt the proper viewpoint. Mechanics love cars, veterinarians love animals, and you love computers and networking. The first two groups need customers to support their favored occupation. So do you.

Chapter 5

Handling More Than One User at a Time

IN THE OLD DAYS, it was easy to manage each user individually. Early NetWare systems often had a dozen or fewer attached workstations. The big network started at about 25 workstations. PCs were new; only a few people in each company had access to a PC full time. No applications required more complexity than file and record sharing. The network stopped at the department; at the most, it went to the walls of the building.

Today, a large network starts at 500 users supported by 10 servers (according to the guidelines for the Express Installation option used by Novell in NetWare 6). Most people connected to the network have full-time access to a computer, whether it's a PC running Windows or Linux, or a Macintosh or Unix system. Applications are mutating and replicating across the company, often with tools and technologies not yet fully developed. A logical workgroup may now include several continents.

You, the network manager, still have only 24 hours in your workday. Luckily, improvements in technology make it possible for one lonely administrator to keep up with more users in more places than ever before. Early NetWare had a single group function to gather users. NetWare 6 has a variety of ways to organize and manage network users and resources.

In this chapter, we will explore the following:

- ◆ Using NetWare 6 tools to manage users and resources
- ◆ Creating and managing Group objects
- ◆ Saving time with the template
- ◆ Using login scripts
- ◆ Creating and managing login scripts

NetWare 6 Tools for Managing Users and Resources

NetWare 6 provides several ways to organize and manage network users and resources:

Organization object   The Organization object is the largest grouping option. Your company may have one or several Organizations defined in an NDS eDirectory tree. You can assign trustee rights, login scripts, and user defaults to all the User objects in the Organization object.

Organizational Unit object   The Organizational Unit is the second-largest grouping option and the subunit for an Organization. A network will typically have many more Organizational Units than Organizations. Once again, you can assign trustee rights, login scripts, and user defaults to all the User objects in the Organizational Unit object.

Group object   A Group object is similar to the earlier NetWare idea of groups, meaning a list of users sharing common items such as directory access rights. Objects in the same group may be from any part of the eDirectory tree. The Security Equal To property in the User object lists the groups connected to the User object.

Profile object   Depending on your NDS design, you can place many users requiring similar work environments in different containers. The Profile object login script can be executed just before the User object login script. Each User object can belong to only one profile; hence, each User object can have only one Profile login script.

Organizational Role object   An Organizational Role is a leaf object that defines a specific operational role, such as operations manager or team leader. The expectation is that the person or persons filling this role will change regularly, but the responsibilities and rights needed for the position will not change. The difference between a Group object and an Organizational Role object is that a Group object usually has many members and an Organizational Role object usually has only one or two.

Role Based Services   New with NetWare 6, Role Based Services (henceforth RBS) upgrades the Organizational Role object by building specific object rights a user granted RBS tasks can perform. Any user can be granted any RBS rights, such as being able to add, modify, or delete user passwords, but those rights and tasks must be defined in advance. You'll learn more about RBS in Chapter 8.

User Template   Technically a limited User object, the User Template functions as a list of properties that can be applied to newly created leaf objects. You can place common information—such as a fax number, login time restrictions, addresses, password restrictions, and language—in the User Template for easy replication. When a User Template is created, you can take information from the parent container's User Template (if one exists).

NOTE   *The NDS eDirectory tree itself is not considered a grouping resource for our examples. Resources cannot be used across trees, and users can't be NDS clients in multiple trees at one time, unless you're running Client32 software.*

Before you can manage more than one user, you need to have a group of users. Although there are alternative options to the old NetWare implementation of a group, let's start with the Group object for old times' sake.

Creating and Managing Group Objects

Technically, the Group object is a leaf object, like a User object or a Printer object. The Group object, unlike Organization and Organizational Unit objects, is not a container (seems like it should be, but the joke is on us).

Many of the group functions performed in earlier NetWare versions are more easily managed using rights and login scripts assigned to containers. The Group object is still, however, an efficient way to manage only one object (the Group object) instead of many individual User objects.

Practically, the Group object will do most of what is necessary in the area of granting file and printer rights to users listed as group members. After all, the group idea came from earlier versions of NetWare, in which there were no object and NDS rights to worry about. The Group object in Net-Ware 6 carries the idea of a group of users into the new operating system format by focusing on the filesystem and printer-access rights afforded to Group object members.

Plenty of third-party products make extensive use of groups, especially the ability of groups to contain members from multiple containers. Services such as e-mail, fax-servers, modem pools, and host-access gateways need groups. The applications generally build the groups themselves, but be prepared to help now and then.

Just as you can use ConsoleOne or the NetWare Administrator program from Windows to create and manage User objects, you can use these administration utilities to work with Group objects. If you still prefer to work with NetWare Administrator, we'll touch on that after we handle group chores in ConsoleOne.

NOTE *The assumption during this chapter is that the person managing network users is either the Admin or an Admin-equivalent user. NetWare 6 allows more flexibility than early NetWare versions. A User object may be granted rights to create objects but not be able to access the information contained in the object. For that capability, the Supervisor right must be given to that person, or property rights must be granted along with the object rights. These new rights and how they relate to earlier NetWare versions and to each other will be explained in detail in Chapter 7. For now, do the work as the Admin user or equivalent, and there will be no surprises.*

Creating Group Objects with ConsoleOne

You can use ConsoleOne to create and modify Group objects from the server console or from a workstation running a variety of different operating systems (Windows, Linux, Unix, or Tru64 Unix). Windows workstations running ConsoleOne must also be running the Client32 software.

Creating new objects of any kind in ConsoleOne can be done a variety of ways. So as not to bore you any more than necessary in the "In a Hurry" boxes, let's agree to mention only one or two options there. What we'll leave out most of the time are the options to create a new object (group in this case) by right-clicking the container to hold the new object, then choosing Object or Group from the pop-up menu. If you're an experienced NetWare administrator (old guy like me), you may hit the Insert key out of habit from early NetWare days. That works too, but it pops open the New Object dialog box. From there, you pick the class of object you want (such as Group) and continue.

SETTING UP GROUP OBJECTS WITH CONSOLEONE

IN A HURRY 5.1: CREATE A GROUP OBJECT WITH CONSOLEONE

1. Start ConsoleOne.

2. Expand Entire Network and browse to the tree you want to access.

3. Click the tree and log in as Admin.

4. Expand the organization and highlight the container where you want the group created.

5. Select the New Group icon in the toolbar or choose File ➢ New ➢ Group.

6. Provide the group name and press Enter.

With ConsoleOne open, expand Entire Network by clicking the little round tab next to the Entire Network icon. Do the same thing to expand the Trees object.

When you select the tree you want to work in, you must first authenticate to NDS. A Login dialog box appears, prompting you for a username, context, and password. You will want to log in as Admin or another user with rights to add groups to a container.

Once you've authenticated to the tree, the tree expands, showing the container objects. Browse through the tree until you find the container where you want the new Group object to exist.

When you first highlighted a container within a tree, did you notice that the toolbar changed? It added three icons that represent the three objects that you are most likely to add to the tree using ConsoleOne—Group, Organizational Unit, and User. The New Object icon, a block, appeared at the end of the toolbar when you first highlighted a tree.

To add a group, you can either click the new Group icon, represented by the multiple individuals on the ConsoleOne toolbar, or you can choose File ➢ New ➢ Group.

There is no difference between the New Group dialog box that appears in ConsoleOne and the Create Group dialog box in NetWare Administrator. They are identical and accomplish the same tasks. The only mandatory property for groups, Name, is required before the OK button is activated. You can also choose to define additional properties or to create another group (one or the other), as shown in Figure 5.1. Well, you probably can't see the Create Another Group option (the second check box), because it turns gray when the Define Additional Properties box is checked. Just to be fair, the reverse is also true.

The naming rules for the Group object are the same as those for the User object (and all other leaf objects for that matter). The same rules apply in ConsoleOne as in NetWare Administrator. Here is a short recap of the naming rules:

◆ Names must be fewer than 64 characters. Names longer than 47 characters are truncated for non-NDS clients.

◆ Names must be unique within the container.

◆ Names are not case-sensitive but will be displayed as they were typed in the Name field of the New Group dialog box. For example, SalesSupport will display that way, but NDS regards it as identical to salessupport and SALESSUPPORT.

♦ Spaces can be used and will be displayed as spaces within NDS. Spaces are shown as underscores for non-NDS clients.

♦ The following characters can't be seen by non-NDS clients: slash (/), backslash (\), colon (:), comma (,), asterisk (*), and question mark (?).

FIGURE 5.1

Creating the Techies group

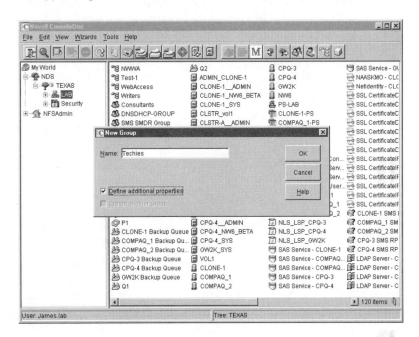

Once you've filled in the group name, you can click OK to create the object. Or you can select Define Additional Properties before creating the object. If you create the object and then want to define the properties, simply right-click the Group object and select Properties. You will see the same property page that you would if you had checked the Define Additional Properties check box.

The property page in ConsoleOne, as you probably have gathered by now, differs drastically from the Group dialog box in NetWare Administrator you probably used for previous NetWare versions. For this reason, it warrants some attention.

ADDING GROUP IDENTIFICATION INFORMATION

IN A HURRY 5.2: IDENTIFY A GROUP OBJECT

1. Open ConsoleOne, right-click the Group object to modify, and select Properties.

2. Fill in the optional information for the Other Name, Owner, Location, Department, Organization, and Description fields.

3. Click OK to save the information and exit the property page.

Identification for a Group object is not required, but it is helpful when searching a large NDS system. All the fields in the Group property page can be searched.

If you're not currently running ConsoleOne, start it from either the server console or a workstation. Once the program is running and the main browser screen is open, expand the Entire Network icon, the Trees icon, and the specific tree in which you want to work. Double-click the tree, and you will be prompted to authenticate by entering your username, context, and password. Be sure to log in as either Admin or another user who has rights to modify the Group object.

Once you are authenticated, the tree expands to display the objects contained within it. Navigate to and right-click the Group object to modify. Select Properties to open the group's property page. Select the General tab, click and hold the down arrow, and select Identification. Figure 5.2 shows the Identification property page for the Techies group.

FIGURE 5.2

Providing searchable
information for the
Techies group

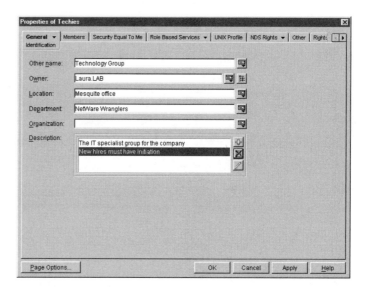

NOTE *Notice the Role Based Services tab in the Group property page. I added it by choosing Tools ➤ Install in ConsoleOne. Chapter 8 describes how to use this new NetWare 6 tool.*

The information here is optional, as is the corresponding information for User objects. As in the property pages for User objects, the More buttons at the end of the fields allow multiple entries in those fields. Clicking the More button once pops up a dialog box for the other field entries. You can fill in the fields as follows:

Other Name Provides space for more descriptive or alternative names for the Group object. Multiple entries are allowed, and you can display them by clicking the More button at the end of the field. Each name can be up to 64 characters. Each entry in this field can be searched.

Owner Provides space to list owners or administrators for this group. NetWare 6 allows multiple subadministrators, a feature that will save you time once each subadministrator understands what he or she can and can't do. You must supply the full name for the Group object, even if the current context is set to the container for the Group object and User object to be labeled as Owner. Click the Browse button, and then locate the User object you want to make an owner of the group, or type the owner's name directly into the text box. Multiple owners display in the same text box. To delete an owner, click the More button beside the text box, highlight the name to be deleted, and press Delete.

Location   Provides space to indicate the physical location of this Group object. Multiple entries are allowed. This field allows any information (maximum of 128 characters) and can be searched. With dispersed companies, this field is helpful when looking for all group members in a particular place, such as a building, a wing, or a state.

Department   Shows the company department to which this group reports. Multiple entries are allowed. Unlike Location, this field has a 64-character limit.

Organization   Shows the organization to which this group reports. Multiple entries are allowed, but each is limited to 64 characters.

Description   Holds free-form text, with a maximum of 30 lines of 1024 characters of any text you find helpful concerning this Group object. Long descriptions are scrollable. Unfortunately, the search program does not parse each word, so only a complete match of the Description field contents will result in a successful search. The scroll arrows are provided to help you if the text goes beyond the limits of the small field.

The OK and Cancel buttons at the bottom apply to all the pages of the property page. Don't click OK when you finish modifying the first page if you plan to modify more pages. There is no penalty if you do, but you will need to go through the steps necessary to return to the property page, wasting a bit of time and increasing your frustration level because you forgot, once again, that you shouldn't click OK until you've finished all your work here.

ADDING SEE ALSO INFORMATION

IN A HURRY 5.3: TRACK RELATED OBJECTS FOR A GROUP

1. Open ConsoleOne, right-click the Group object to modify, and select Properties.

2. Select the General tab.

3. Click the down arrow and select See Also.

4. Click the Add button. Browse and select objects related to the group by highlighting the object and clicking OK.

5. The object appears in the main See Also property page. Click OK to save the information and exit the property page.

Purely informational, the See Also page is a place to make references for your group to other network resources. Which printer is the primary printer for the group? Which server? Place those names here. You can place other related resources here, too, but not by typing their names. You must choose each object through the Select Objects dialog box, as shown in Figure 5.3.

FIGURE 5.3

Relating other
objects to Techies

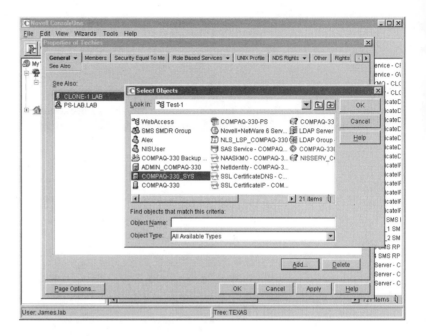

After opening ConsoleOne, browsing, and choosing the Group object's property page, select the General tab, click the down arrow, and select See Also. Click the Add button to open the Select Objects dialog box. To select multiple items, hold down the Ctrl key while clicking.

You can see in Figure 5.3 that the Compaq-330 server object has been selected for inclusion in the Selected Objects box in the immediate background. It will join the Clone-1 server object and the print server PS-LAB already in the See Also list. Yes, we pulled things from two Organizational Units, which is perfectly legal.

To delete an object from the See Also page, simply click the object and click the Delete button.

NOTE   *These sections concerning group setup look amazingly like those for user setup. If you read the user information in the previous chapter, you will be able to perform the same procedures with groups as you do with users. If you did not read the user information first, excuse this note (but shame on you).*

ADDING MEMBERS TO A GROUP

IN A HURRY 5.4: ADD MEMBERS TO A GROUP

1.   Open ConsoleOne, right-click the Group object to modify, and select Properties.

2.   Select the Members tab.

3.   To add objects as members of the group, click the Add button.

4.   Browse and select an object to be added to the group by highlighting the object and clicking OK.

5.   The object appears in the Members property page. Click OK to save the information and exit the property page.

The Members tab contains only one option. Therefore, when you select the tab, you go directly to the Members property page.

Adding members to a group works identically to adding objects to the See Also page. When an object is added as a new member, it receives all rights assigned to the Group object. (Once again demonstrating that NetWare can be simplified if you learn to manage groups instead of individual users.)

To add a new member to the group, click Add, browse, select the object by clicking it, and then click OK. The object now appears in the Members property page. Figure 5.4 shows the Techies group getting a second member, again from another Organizational Unit than the current member.

FIGURE 5.4

Adding members to a group

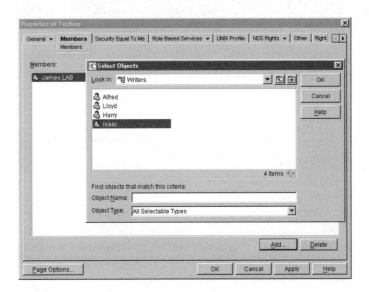

JOB DESCRIPTION FOR ASSISTANT NETWORK ADMINISTRATORS

Adding members to, or subtracting them from, a group is a good job for assistant administrators. In fact, this is one area where the idea of workgroup administrator that first appeared in NetWare 3.x makes great sense. NetWare 6 takes this idea further, allowing added security constraints for the main Admin user to truly separate a container from the rest of the NDS eDirectory tree.

The assistant administrator, charged with responsibility for this group, can add and subtract members as necessary for the needs of the department. This can be done without bothering the main network administrator.

Positive benefits happen two ways: The primary network administrator goes about his or her business, while the people in the department feel they have much more control over their own network destiny.

This job is also one that doesn't take constant administration and worry time. People tend to stay in particular groups for a long time. When a user leaves and you delete that user, the name is deleted from the User object list of members. When someone transfers, that user often keeps some of the old job's responsibilities, meaning the user will stay in the old group and become a member of an additional group as well.

Remember that even though you add the user to the property page, that user is not yet a member of the group. You must always click the OK button or the Apply button to save your changes. ConsoleOne will remind if you forget, just as I'm reminding you now.

To delete an object from group membership, highlight the object and click the Delete button. That doesn't delete the object itself; it just removes the connection to that group.

VIEWING EFFECTIVE RIGHTS INFORMATION

IN A HURRY 5.5: VIEW EFFECTIVE RIGHTS

1. Open ConsoleOne and locate the Group object in the eDirectory tree.

2. Open the group's property page by right-clicking the Group object name and selecting Properties.

3. Select the NDS Rights tab.

4. Click the down arrow and select Effective Rights.

5. View the trustee's effective rights to this object.

The Effective Rights page is an informational page that allows you to view a trustee's effective rights to this object. You can't make any changes here, but it's a good way to get a report on the effective rights of a trustee to any given object. Figure 5.5 provides a good view of this page.

FIGURE 5.5

The trustee James' effective rights to Techies

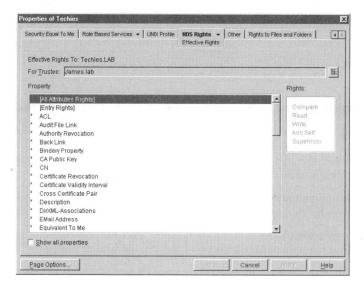

The Effective Rights To field shows the distinguished name of the target resource, in this case Techies.LAB. Techies is the object to which the trustee has effective rights. You cannot edit this field. To see the effective rights that trustees have to another object, open that object's Effective Rights property page.

The For Trustee field shows the distinguished name of the trustee whose effective rights are displayed on this page. In this case, the trustee is james.LAB. Notice the Browse button to the right of the field. You can browse for another trustee and view its effective rights to the target resource.

The Rights display box shows the trustee's effective object rights to the target resource. These rights include the following:

- Compare

- Read

- Write

- Add Self

- Supervisor

- Create

- Delete

- Rename

In this case, user james (that's me) has all applicable object rights to Techies. The Create right doesn't apply, because you cannot create an object within a Group object. It would apply if we were looking at a volume, for instance, because then we could create files and directories.

The Rights field shows user james' effective property rights to Techies. These rights include the following:

- Compare

- Read

- Write

- Add Self

- Supervisor

I have all these rights because of Admin equivalence, but another trustee would have fewer property rights.

On this page, you have the option to view a user's effective rights, the default, or check the Show All Properties box, which you don't want to do unless you wish to be impressed by the complexity of NDS eDirectory.

ADDING NDS TRUSTEES TO A GROUP OBJECT

IN A HURRY 5.6: VIEW OR CHANGE THE NDS TRUSTEES FOR THE GROUP OBJECT

1. Open ConsoleOne, and locate and choose the Group object to modify.

2. Open the group's property page by right-clicking the Group object name and selecting Properties.

3. Select the NDS Rights tab.

4. Click the down arrow and select Trustees of This Object.

5. To add a trustee, click the Add Trustee button to choose the new trustee from the Select Objects dialog box.

6. To delete a trustee, highlight the trustee and click the Delete button.

7. To modify rights, highlight each trustee, click Assigned Rights, and toggle the appropriate check boxes.

8. Click OK to save the settings.

Groups have trustees, and Techies is no exception. Trustees are those network users or resources that have some control over the group. For more information about trustee rights and what they involve, see Chapter 7.

After opening ConsoleOne, highlight the Group object whose trustee list you want to modify, and right-click. The same Trustees of This Object page can be summoned by using the NDS Rights tab's menu.

If you must add a trustee or two, you will once again use our friend the Select Objects dialog box. Scroll through the dialog box to find the user (most likely) or other resource to make a trustee of the Techies group. Figure 5.6 shows user Heather gaining control over the Techies group.

FIGURE 5.6

Heather controls Techies

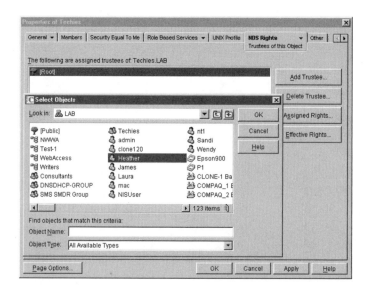

Of course, once you give Heather control over the Techies (and hope the power doesn't go to her head), you must solidify that power by granting appropriate rights. No sense giving Heather some power if she can't wield same, right?

Figure 5.7 shows the rights granted to Heather as trustee over the Techies group. After choosing Heather as trustee, the Rights Assigned to *selected object* dialog box opens, offering the list of check boxes in the Rights area.

FIGURE 5.7

Heather's specific rights over the poor Techies

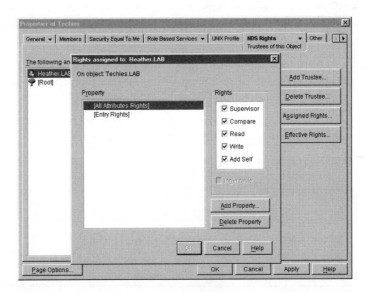

Give yourself a pat on the back if you realize this looks startlingly close to the same process used to add trustees to users, volumes, servers, and so on. Consistency may be the realm of small minded-ness, but it certainly cuts the learning curve for network managers.

WARNING   *Be careful in deleting trustees from a resource or group, because the users may have some procedures that require access to a resource for which they no longer have trustee rights. This can cause some aggravation later, so think hard before granting or deleting individual trustee rights.*

Heed the warning note, because the process just described works for modifying and deleting trustee rights. A click of the Delete Trustee button rather than the Add Trustee button, and we strip the power from one. Ah, the administrator giveth, and the administrator taketh away.

SETTING INHERITED RIGHTS FILTERS

IN A HURRY 5.7: VIEW OR SET INHERITED RIGHTS FILTERS

1. Open ConsoleOne and locate the Group object in the eDirectory tree.

2. Open the group's property page by right-clicking the Group object name and selecting Properties.

continued on next page

IN A HURRY 5.7: VIEW OR SET INHERITED RIGHTS FILTERS *(continued)*

3. Select the NDS Rights tab.

4. Click the down arrow and select Inherited Rights Filters.

5. View or set Inherited Rights Filters (IRFs) for this object.

6. Click OK to save the settings.

You can use the Inherited Rights Filters page, shown in Figure 5.8, to view or set Inherited Rights Filters (IRFs) on this object. Here are some things to remember about IRFs:

◆ IRFs don't give rights to anyone; they take rights away. If a group is granted rights at a certain level of the directory or container structure, the only way to keep those rights from flowing down through the subdirectories and subcontainers is to set up an IRF.

◆ IRFs can block only inherited rights, or those rights that are flowing down because of granted rights somewhere up the line. Rights that are granted at the current level by explicit assignment cannot be blocked.

◆ When you set an IRF for an object, it applies to all trustees.

If you need to brush up on IRFs, see Chapter 7.

FIGURE 5.8

Setting an Inherited
Rights Filter to
Techies

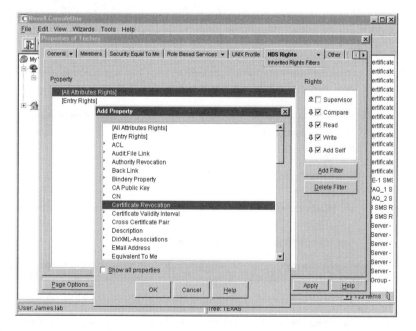

The Inherited Rights Filters page (see active tab) shows the distinguished name of the target resource in the upper-left corner, in this case Techies.LAB.TEXAS, that the IRFs shown on this page are affecting. You cannot browse and view IRFs for other objects without closing the property page and viewing the properties for another object in the tree.

The Rights section allows you to view or set the IRF that blocks object or property rights from being inherited by the current object.

It is easy to block an object right. The rights that can be blocked are Supervisor, Compare, Delete, Browse, Rename, Read, Write, Add Self, and Create, depending on the property highlighted. Figure 5.8 shows that when the box next to the object right is checked, the flow down arrow is large. But when the box is unchecked, the large arrow is replaced with a stumpy arrow that has a line underneath, signifying that the object right has been restricted or filtered to this object. So to block an object right, uncheck the corresponding check box.

To block the property rights to individual properties, highlight a property or multiple properties (hold down the Ctrl key to select more than one property) in the Add Property dialog box, and uncheck the box next to the right you want to restrict. You will see the same stumpy arrow and line, indicating that right has been filtered. The property rights are Supervisor, Compare, Read, Write, and Add Self. You can set the IRF for all properties or for selected properties. We allowed the Techies all rights to the Entry Rights, but blocked their Supervisor right to All Attributes Rights. Techies shouldn't be omnipotent, even though they sometimes think they are.

NOTE   *When you finish making changes on this page or any other pages, you must click the Apply button for the changes to take effect.*

SETTING SECURITY EQUAL TO ME FOR GROUP OBJECTS

IN A HURRY 5.8: ADD OR DELETE OBJECTS ON THE SECURITY EQUAL TO ME PAGE

1. Open ConsoleOne, and locate and choose the Group object to modify.

2. Open the group's property page by right-clicking the Group object name and selecting Properties.

3. Click the Security Equal to Me tab.

3. To add an object, click the Add button, select the object from the Select Objects dialog box, and click OK.

4. To delete an object, click the object in the list, click the Delete button, and click OK.

The Security Equal to Me page displays a list of users with security equivalent to that particular object. You can add or delete users from here.

Just as users can use the Security Equal to Me tab to display all the objects to which they are security equivalent (as mentioned in Chapter 4), the Security Equal to Me page for Group objects looks at the same information from the object's point of view. It displays all objects that are security equivalent to the object.

To add a user to the list, click the Add button. The familiar Select Objects dialog box appears, as shown in Figure 5.9. We should all be experts in using this by now. Remember that you browse on the right and select on the left. Highlight one or multiple users in the left box.

FIGURE 5.9

Adding user Harry to the Security Equal to Me page for Techies

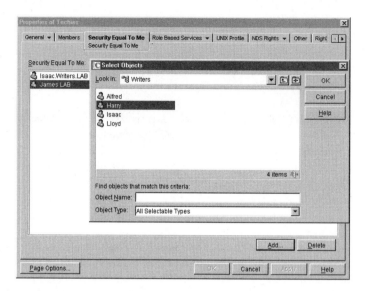

Click OK to add the object or objects to the Security Equal to Me page. You'll notice that when you add a user to the list, the full name of the user appears.

To delete a user from the list, highlight the user and click the Delete button.

SETTING UP RIGHTS TO FILES AND FOLDERS

IN A HURRY 5.9: MANAGE FILE AND DIRECTORY ACCESS FOR THE GROUP OBJECT

1. Open ConsoleOne, and locate and choose the Group object to modify.

2. Open the group's property page by right-clicking the Group object name and selecting Properties.

3. Click the Rights to Files and Folders page tab (you may need to click the right arrow at the top right of the box to see the tab).

4. To view assigned rights, click the Show button, and then highlight each volume or directory you want to view.

5. To add a volume, click the Add button to open the Select Objects dialog box and choose the new volume.

6. To delete access, highlight the volume and click the Delete button.

7. To grant access, click the Add button to open the Select Objects dialog box and choose the volume or directory.

8. To grant rights, highlight the object in the Files and Folders box and toggle the check boxes in the Rights box. To modify rights, toggle the check boxes for each volume or directory.

9. Click OK to save your settings.

This section is exactly like the corresponding section for the User object we worked with back in Chapter 4. Here, we are granting access to a single group, but the group includes many users. Although we modify only a single object, we affect anywhere from a few to hundreds of users, all at once.

Once ConsoleOne is running and the main browser screen is open, you must expand the container to see all the objects inside. Navigate to and right-click the Group object to modify. Select Properties to open the group's property page, and then click the Rights to Files and Folder tab.

First, you will want to check which rights the Group object has before granting any more rights. Find this information by clicking the Add button once. Select the volume and click OK. Highlight each directory, and the Rights box just below the Files and Folders box will reflect the group's rights to that file or directory.

To delete all trustee assignments from a particular volume, highlight the volume or directory and click the Delete button. To modify rights to a particular directory or file, check the appropriate boxes in the Rights box. All the check boxes are toggles, so if one is blank, checking it grants that right to that object.

The Effective Rights button displays the actual rights for the highlighted directory or volume object. When you click this button, a small dialog box pops up, listing the actual directory under examination. It also has a Browse button to help you search more areas of the network.

After setting the rights for the Techies to play Doom2 (stress testing systems, of course), I clicked the Path button. The full path appears in the small foreground window in Figure 5.10.

FIGURE 5.10

Checking rights to the Doom2 directory

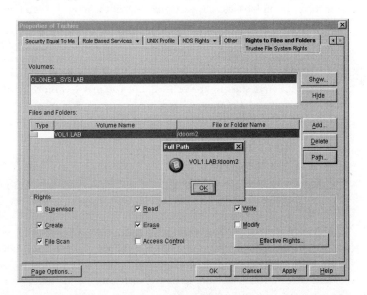

You can select multiple directories by holding down the Ctrl key while clicking the file or directory (okay, folder) name. After you choose your file, folders, or directories, grant the appropriate rights. Then, good luck getting the techs to finish all their work before starting their Doom tournaments.

Any single user that belongs to the Techies group inherits all the rights of the group. The rights will become available to all the members almost immediately upon clicking the OK button, or at least as soon as the NDS eDirectory changes propagate.

Creating and Modifying Group Objects with NetWare Administrator

IN A HURRY 5.10: CREATE A GROUP OBJECT

1. Open NetWare Administrator, highlight the Organization or Organizational Unit container that will hold the new Group object, and press the Insert key.

2. Choose the Group object from the list, provide the Group object name, and press Enter.

3. Click OK to create the new Group object.

Before you can place users in a Group object, you must create a Group object. This process is remarkably similar to that of creating a User object, as we did in the last chapter. The similarity is planned. Both groups and users are leaf objects, so the process should be almost identical. The differences appear as we configure the objects for their different roles.

Log in again to your server using the Client32 software, and double-click the NetWare Administrator icon. If you look closely, you will see that the icon shows a figure before a wall map of an NDS eDirectory tree.

Once NetWare Administrator is started, I prefer to double-click each container to open each of the Organizational Units. This allows me to see all the objects in each container, making it easier to avoid duplications. NetWare does not require you to open the container that will contain the new Group object before starting the process, but you may feel more comfortable if you can see everything in the container before you begin.

While the container name is highlighted, you can do one of three things to begin the creation of a new object:

◆ Press the Insert key.

◆ Click the right mouse button, and then click Create in the menu that appears.

◆ Choose Object ➤ Create.

NetWare veterans will be comfortable with pressing the Insert key, a common function in earlier NetWare versions. If you are new to NetWare, pressing the Insert key whenever you're not sure of the next step can't hurt; in fact, it will often help.

Hard-core mousers will appreciate the increasing use of the right mouse button in NetWare 6. The NetWare Administrator program is even more mouse-friendly than it appears in the listing above. If you hold the left mouse button while sliding the highlight bar down the menu items, releasing the button while highlighting Create opens the New Object dialog box.

Hard-core keyboard users will appreciate the Alt-key functions that speed menu operations. Most of the menu shortcuts available in earlier NetWare versions are still available in NetWare 6. If you have some keystroke combinations memorized, try them. The keystrokes may work.

The result of any of the three options mentioned above is to open the New Object dialog box, as shown in Figure 5.11. From there, you can choose any of the new object classes listed. Since we want to create a Group object, highlight the Group entry by using the cursor keys, using the mouse, or pressing the G key.

FIGURE 5.11

Preparing to create a new Group object in NetWare Administrator

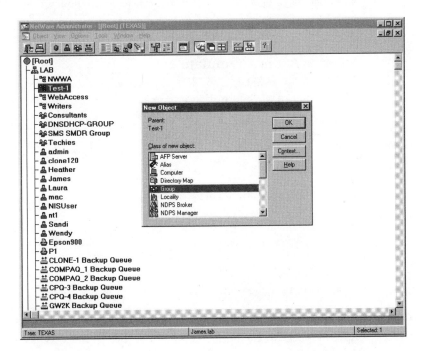

Once you begin to create your new Group object, a two-step process starts. First, you create the basic object, and then you set its properties.

The creation of the Group object takes little time and requires almost no detail. If you remember creating a User object, the process will be familiar. When creating new User objects, the only information needed is the login name and the last name of the user. Since Group objects don't have last names, the only information required before creating the Group object is the name of that Group object.

From here, the steps for setting properties using NetWare Administrator and ConsoleOne line up pretty well. The main difference is that NetWare Administrator uses pages called by command buttons down the side of their dialog boxes, while ConsoleOne uses tabbed pages arranged across the top. Is one display technique better than the other? Flip a coin.

Saving Time with the Template

Now that you've gone through and created both User and Group objects by hand, so to speak, you're probably ready for some shortcuts. The first one to explore is the *template*. The name clearly indicates the purpose and function of this object, which is to provide a template of information for use when creating users.

NOTE   *A Template object is a leaf object that provides a basic set of properties and setup procedures to apply to new, but not existing, users. In NetWare 4.10, these were called* user templates. *In NetWare 5, the name was shortened to* template, *and it remains so for NetWare 6.*

What to Put in a Template

Technically, the template is an NDS object holding default information common to many users. Here is some of the information you might include in a template:

◆ Login time restrictions

◆ Password restrictions

◆ Language

◆ Phone, location, and department information

◆ Print job configuration details

◆ Login scripts

◆ Group memberships

◆ Security equivalence settings

◆ Account balance information

Remember that a template is meant to be used to create users who work in a similar environment. All properties set in the template should be common to all users. For example, if you put information about the template in the Description field or a specific phone number in that field of the Identification page, that information will be carried over to each user created using that template. That will require you to go in to each user and change the information. Suddenly, you are doing the work you had hoped to avoid by using the template.

You can create a template in any Organization or Organizational Unit objects. If a template exists in the container above, you can copy information from that template. In our example, if there were a template in LAB, the template created in LAB.Texas could include all the parent information as a starting point.

The template information is passed to a new User object if you check the Use Template option when you create the User object. The information in the template may change later, but that change will not be reflected in the User object information. There is no live link between the template and the User object; there is just a one-time copy process from the template to the user. Rights may not be granted via a template.

No one may log in as the template, but it appears to be a normal User object during setup and modification. This anomaly is a helpful utility, not a security hole.

Creating a Template

IN A HURRY 5.11: CREATE A TEMPLATE WITH CONSOLEONE

1. Open ConsoleOne and locate the container to hold the template in the eDirectory tree.

2. Right-click the container object name and select New.

3. Select Template to open the Create Template dialog box.

4. Check Use Template or User if you want to use another template or user as a baseline. Browse for the template or user.

5. Check the Define Additional Properties check box.

6. Provide information as you would for a User object.

7. Click OK to save the template.

When you're creating a template, a small dialog box opens, asking for the name of the template. Type in a name. The next option is Use Template or User. This allows you to use another template or user as a baseline for the new template, rather than starting from scratch. Next, you can choose whether to create another template or define additional properties. When you indicate (by checking the proper check box) that you want to define additional properties, the property page opens, presenting the standard information for new objects.

Fill in the various property pages as you would for any other User object. Fill out the Template Members fields just as you would to add members to a Group object. In Figure 5.12, notice some new tabs we haven't seen before:

New Object NDS Rights   Sets the rights to other objects, the IRF, and trustees of the object being created via the template.

New Object FS Rights   Sets the NetWare file access and control rights granted to users created via the template. The home directory, with all rights, is set by default.

Volume Space Restrictions   Sets space restrictions for all objects created via the template on any or all volumes.

When the information is complete, click OK to save it.

When you check the Use Template check box next time you create a user or group, you can then browse for a template to use. Once you select a template and click Create, the user is created with all the template information added to the appropriate account properties.

Using Login Scripts

Login scripts are files that contain instructions to configure the networking environment for users. These scripts are read and executed when a user logs in to the network. A login script is similar to an AUTOEXEC.BAT file for an IBM-compatible PC. Login scripts are properties of objects.

FIGURE 5.12

Template
configuration

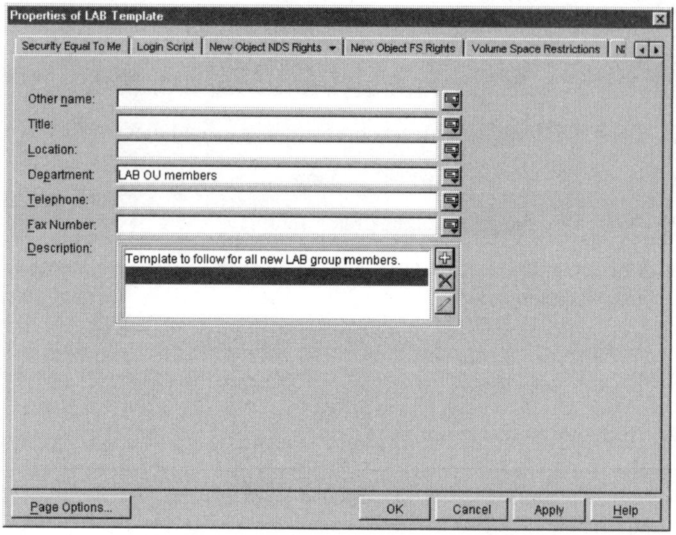

Login scripts are excellent tools for shielding computer-phobic users from the network. With a well-designed login script, a user may never need to know any details concerning application locations and data file directories.

The primary use of the login script is to set different drive letters to provide users with an easy way to reach their applications. It is true that the entire network is open to users, and they can use any resource to which they have been granted trustee rights. It is also true that most users do not know how to navigate even a small network. Our job is to make network applications and other resources available to users with as little work on their part as possible. Login scripts go a long way toward making the network easy for users to navigate.

USERS, LOGIN SCRIPTS, AND YOU

The effectiveness of login scripts is evident when you speak to most users and ask them where any of their application directories are. Word processing is on drive G:, and the database is on drive M:. Does this answer tell you anything of value? No. It tells you that the user doesn't understand how NetWare handles drive redirection and has no clue about the network environment.

You can take this two ways. You can regard the user as stupid and computer-phobic, since he or she is unaware of fundamental network processes. This guarantees you will burn out and become bitter toward the users before much longer. You can also regard this as a successful network setup on your part, since the user is able to function perfectly well without worrying about network technical details. This mental approach will make you much happier in your work.

Perhaps the second method is the best way to approach network support in general and login scripts in particular. Your job is to provide a network foundation that supports the users' primary jobs without drawing attention to the underpinnings. Login scripts are your most direct tool to make the network an invisible connection between people and the resources they need.

Types of Login Scripts

There are four types of login scripts: container, profile, user (can be inherited from a template), and default. As with earlier NetWare versions, the last login script to execute has the last word, meaning it can change any and all information from previous scripts.

With four scripts available, you may wonder how to keep them all straight. It's not difficult, and you will see how each type of login script makes sense. Besides, all login scripts are optional.

The order of execution for these four login scripts is:

◆ Login begins

◆ Container object login script

   Exists = Execute and continue

   Does not exist = Continue

◆ Profile object login script

   Exists = Execute and continue

   Does not exist = Continue

◆ User object login script

   Exists = Execute and stop

   Does not exist = Continue

◆ Default login script

   Executes if there is no User object login script

The user login script and the default login script are an either/or situation. If you have a user login script, the default script will not run. If you don't have a user login script, the default login script will run. There are two exceptions to this rule:

◆ When a user has a NO_DEFAULT line in a container or profile login script, which prevents the default login script from executing

◆ When an EXIT statement exists in the container or profile login script, causing the user to exit that script

Since the login scripts execute in the same order each time, there are some guidelines for each script's role. Container login scripts should focus on access to resources used by most network users, such as volumes and printers. Specific group needs can be addressed by the profile login script. Individual requirements belong in the user login script. You cannot configure the default login script.

THE CONTAINER LOGIN SCRIPT

The container login script has the following characteristics:

◆ It is a property of an Organization or an Organizational Unit.

- Each user can execute only the container login script.

- The user will execute the login script for the container to which his or her User object belongs.

The container login script is executed first. This replaces the system login script from earlier NetWare versions. The system login script was server-based; the container login script is a property of the user's container. Whether the container is an Organization or Organizational Unit makes no difference. If the parent container for a User object does not have a login script, no other container login script will be available for that user.

Use container login scripts to do the following:

- Establish network drive mappings to horizontal application directories.

- Establish a link to the user's home directory.

- Connect each user to the PUBLIC directory for NetWare utilities.

- Connect a default printer for the entire container.

- Activate menus or applications used by all members of the container.

- Send login messages to all container users.

You can use conditional IF statements based on login times, group membership, or other variables to make your container login scripts more versatile.

THE PROFILE LOGIN SCRIPT

The profile login script has the following characteristics:

- It is a property of a Profile object.

- A person can belong to only one profile and, hence, can have only a single profile login script.

- Many users can execute the same profile login script.

The profile login script works differently from an IF MEMBER OF statement referencing a group in a login script. (Using the IF MEMBER OF statement in login scripts is covered a little later in the chapter.) One important difference is that a User object can belong to many groups but can have only one profile login script. The profile login script executes after the container login script.

Use profile login scripts to do the following:

- Establish drive mappings to special data and/or application directories.

- Set specific search mappings for application directories.

- Connect to special-purpose printers (such as color or high-speed printers) unique to a group.

- Send login messages to a specific group.

THE USER LOGIN SCRIPT

The user login script is a property of the User object. The user login script executes after both the container and profile login scripts. It is normally used for specific network details for one user only. There can be only one user login script per User object.

Use user login scripts to do the following:

- Establish drive mappings to specific user directories.

- Send user-specific login messages.

- Activate menus or applications for each particular user.

THE DEFAULT LOGIN SCRIPT

The default login script has the following characteristics:

- It is contained in the LOGIN.EXE program.

- It cannot be edited.

- It executes in the absence of the user login script.

- It provides minimal functionality.

The default login script executes last, but only if there is no user login script. There is only one default login script for the network.

The default login script does not exist as a text file to be edited. It is contained within the LOGIN.EXE program and cannot be changed. Since so little happens in this login script, few (if any) networks use only the default login script.

There are three ways to avoid using the default login script:

- Exit from an earlier login script.

- Have a user login script.

- Use the NO_DEFAULT command in a container login script.

As an introduction to login scripts in general and some sample commands used, the following are the lines in the default login script, along with a quick explanation for each one:

`MAP DISPLAY OFF`	MAP redirects a local drive letter to a network resource, either a regular drive or a search drive (similar to the DOS PATH command). MAP DISPLAY OFF prevents MAP commands from displaying on the screen, similar to the DOS command ECHO OFF.
`MAP ERRORS OFF`	Prevents mapping errors and the resulting messages from displaying on the screen.
`MAP *1:=SYS:`	Maps the first drive to volume SYS:. The *1 indicates a wildcard symbol for mapping the first non-local drive letter. This avoids possible problems in mapping particular drive letters (F: or G:) that may not be available for all clients.

`MAP *1:=VOL1:USERS\%LOGIN NAME`	Maps the first drive to the user's home directory, if LOGIN_NAME is the same as the user's home directory. If the user has no home directory, the first drive is still mapped to SYS:. %LOGIN_NAME is an identifier variable and will be interpreted differently for each person who logs in. The value given by the user as the login name will be captured by the login process and passed to this variable.
`IF %1=Admin THEN MAP *1:=SYS:SYSTEM`	If the login name is Admin, the first drive is mapped to SYS:SYSTEM instead of to the user's home directory. This is an example of the IF THEN statement.
`MAP P:=SYS:PUBLIC`	For OS/2 workstation clients only (have any left?). With OS/2, drive P: is mapped to SYS:PUBLIC. If the user is not using an OS/2 workstation, this drive mapping is ignored during execution of the default login script.
`MAP INS S1:=SYS:PUBLIC; MAP INS S2:=SYS:PUBLIC\%MACHINE\%OS\ %OS_VERSION`	INS stands for insert, which places S1 (first search drive) into the DOS PATH statement in a way that does not overwrite any of the existing PATH commands. If the user is using a DOS or a Windows workstation, the first search drive is mapped to SYS:PUBLIC. The second search drive is mapped to the directory where DOS is stored. The two MAP commands are joined by a semicolon. If the user logs in from an OS/2 workstation, these drive mappings are ignored.
`MAP DISPLAY ON`	Allows MAP commands to display.
`MAP`	When the MAP command is used alone from the DOS command line or inside a login script, it displays a list of all drive mappings on the user's screen.

Common Login Script Commands

You know the old story: 80 percent of the work is done by 20 percent of the blank. Fill in the blank with people, tools, circus elephants, or login script commands.

The complete list is located with the other commands in the online documentation. There are more login script commands than any one company will ever use. As you look over the list, you may think some commands seem strange. But remember that each command solves a problem for some customers. Every command has a use, no matter how specialized.

Most of your login scripts will use the following few commands over and over. These descriptions show the command, the explanation, and a usage example.

WARNING   Always place a final carriage return at the end of each login script. The cursor should be on a line by itself, beyond the final login script command line, before saving the script. This will save you much troubleshooting, because unless you do this properly, the last line may not execute.

THE ATTACH COMMAND

The ATTACH command connects to bindery-based NetWare servers (NetWare 2.*x* or NetWare 3.*x*). This command can be used with NetWare 6 servers to bypass NDS. This external `ATTACH.EXE` no longer works from the command line. It has been replaced by the LOGIN/NS command. Do not confuse the ATTACH command native to `LOGIN.EXE` with the external executable program. ATTACH works only from a login script. An example is:

```
ATTACH 312_NW/JAMES
```

THE # COMMAND

The # command indicates an external program that will execute and return control to the login script. The example here is the most common, setting the print redirection from a local printer port to a network system printer using the CAPTURE command:

```
#CAPTURE Q=LASER_Q1 NB NFF TI=9
```

THE EXIT COMMAND

EXIT stops execution of the LOGIN utility and executes an external program. This command doesn't apply to OS/2 workstations. An EXIT command placed in any login script stops any subsequent login scripts from running. Here is an example:

```
EXIT "NMENU ACCOUNTING"
```

THE FIRE PHASERS COMMAND

The FIRE PHASERS command emits an electronic space gun sound that may fire as many as nine times. Two is the tasteful limit:

```
FIRE PHASERS 2 TIMES
```

This command was helpful to signal login messages or the conclusion of a login process, but with all the chirps and sound clips from Windows versions lately, its value has diminished.

THE IF THEN COMMAND

IF THEN is a conditional statement used to perform an action only under certain conditions. Earlier NetWare versions with a single system login script often used IF THEN statements to check the user for group membership before mapping certain drive connections. Although it is still useful, some conditions requiring IF THEN statements in the past can now be done with a combination of the container and profile login scripts.

The following example specifies that members of the group WIN95 will have the next available search drive (S16 tells the system to start with the highest possible search drive number, 16, and count down until it finds the next open search drive letter) mapped to the \APPS\WIN95 directory. The interior part is indented for clarity, as is commonly done in IF THEN statements.

```
IF MEMBER OF "WIN95" THEN
  MAP INS S16:=SYS:\APPS\WIN95
END
```

THE MAP COMMAND

The most popular way to use login scripts is to map a drive to a particular network directory. The MAP command maps drives and search drives to network directories and NDS objects. Here are two examples:

```
MAP G:=TODDNW5_SYS:\REPORTS
MAP INS S16:=SYS:\APPS\WIN95
```

THE PAUSE COMMAND

PAUSE stops the execution of the login script until a key is pressed. It provides a handy way to force a user to look at the screen, since FIRE PHASERS tends to be ignored after the novelty wears off.

THE SET COMMAND

The SET command sets a DOS or OS/2 environment variable. For OS/2 workstations, SET commands affect the environment only while the login script is running. Values must be enclosed in quotation marks, as in this example:

```
SET PROMPT="$P$G"
```

$P sets the drive letter, and $G sets the symbol >.

THE WRITE COMMAND

WRITE displays messages on the workstation screen while the login script is running. It's best to put these commands at the end of the login script so that they stay on the screen or to use them in conjunction with the PAUSE command.

All values, including special characters, must be in quotation marks. The following special characters help you control text strings:

\r	Inserts a carriage return
\n	Starts a new line
\	Displays quotation mark
\7	Beeps the internal speaker

Here is an example:

```
WRITE "Welcome to the Corporate Network \7"
```

Common Login Script Identifier Variables

Identifiers personalize login scripts. They work by using variables known to the NetWare client programs as information to fill in the blank of the identifier variable. For example, the user gives a login name as part of the login process. This name identifies that user to the system. After checking NDS for authentication, the system asks for that user's password. With the proper password, the user gains access to the network.

By the time a user gets access to the network, the network knows everything about that user. Since this happens before the login script is started, the information about every user is available to personalize the login script using a common set of variables. The most familiar to many people is the greeting often used by network administrators. As you prepare for work in the morning, it's nice to see:

```
Good morning, Mackenzie!
```

More important, it's easy for the administrator to make this happen.

Table 5.1 describes the most commonly used login script identifier variables. When you use an identifier variable in a WRITE statement, it must be within quotation marks, typed in all capital letters, and preceded by a percent sign (%). In NetWare 3.x, the identifier variable didn't need to be within the WRITE statement's quotation marks, but this is a requirement in NetWare 6.

NOTE *The requirement for identifier variables to be in uppercase letters suggests that you should always use capital letters in all your login scripts. This looks a bit garish, especially to people with a Unix background. Using all capitals is, however, the easiest way to avoid potential problems with your login scripts.*

TABLE 5.1: COMMON LOGIN SCRIPT IDENTIFIER VARIABLES

IDENTIFIER VARIABLE	FUNCTION	EXAMPLE
%GREETING_TIME	Uses the workstation clock to determine morning, afternoon, or evening time frame. Supplies the proper term for the time of the day upon login.	WRITE "Good %GREETING_TIME"
%LOGIN_NAME	The variable for the client's unique login name.	MAP F:=GATEWAY2000_ SYS:USERS\%LOGIN_NAME
%MACHINE	Determines and displays the type of non-OS/2 computer used by the client.	WRITE "Your computer is: %MACHINE"
%OS	Determines and displays the operating system used by your system, such as MS-DOS.	WRITE "Your %MACHINE is running %OS"
%OS_VERSION	Determines and displays the version of DOS, such as 6.0 or 6.2.	WRITE "You are using version %OS_VERSION of %OS"
%STATION	Determines and displays your workstation connection number.	WRITE "You are connection number %STATION"

TIP   *The %LOGIN_NAME identifier variable works well when first names are used for login names, less well if the naming system uses initials or name combinations. Being greeted by "Hello, CWB" is not particularly warm or friendly. However, this variable is great for mapping a drive to the user's home directory. Since the home directory name is the same as the login name, this variable will reliably map each user to that user's particular directory.*

Creating Login Scripts

IN A HURRY 5.12: CREATE OR EDIT A LOGIN SCRIPT IN CONSOLEONE

1. Open ConsoleOne, and locate and choose the container, profile, or user that has the login script to modify.
2. Open the object's property page by right-clicking the object name and selecting Properties.
3. Click the Login Script tab.
4. Create or edit the login script.
5. Click OK to save the script.

Now that you know what login scripts are and the commands that are available, let's get scripting. You must have the trustee rights to create and modify the login scripts for each object. The easiest way to be sure of this capability is to be the Admin or equivalent.

The login script is an object property. Not all objects have login scripts, just User, Profile, and container objects. There are no mandatory login scripts or even mandatory login script commands for containers, profiles, or User objects. The profile script is stored in Organizations or Organizational Units as an NDS leaf object. Container scripts are stored in their respective containers. The User object login script is stored as a property of each User object. See Figure 5.13 for a graphical look at these storage locations.

FIGURE 5.13

Scattered scripts

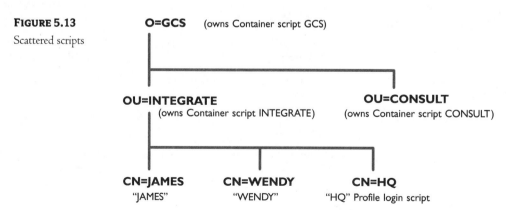

As Figure 5.13 illustrates, you must go to the particular object that owns the login script you want to create or modify. No central database exists for login scripts.

In the ConsoleOne program, you can create or edit login scripts for containers and users. Browse down your eDirectory tree to find the object of your scripting endeavors. Once you've found it, open its property page and click the Logon Script tab. If you do not find such a tab, the object does not support the Login Script property. Printers and NetWare volumes, for instance, don't have login scripts.

When you click the Login Script tab, the page is dominated by a text box. Type your login script, or edit the existing one, using the standard Windows text-editing commands and keystrokes. To copy a login script from one user to another, use Windows Cut and Paste commands.

CREATING OR EDITING A CONTAINER LOGIN SCRIPT

Once you locate the container needing a login script inside the ConsoleOne program, open the property page by right-clicking the container, then choosing Properties. Then click the Login Script tab to open the Login Script page. From there, you can create a new container login script or modify one that already exists.

Let's look at a sample container login script, shown in Figure 5.14.

FIGURE 5.14

A sample container login script

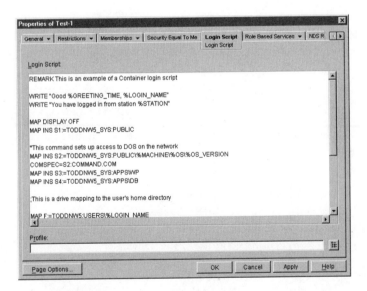

Since the login script is longer than the text box (not unusual for container login scripts), let me expand on it. Each line is followed by comments and clarifications.

```
REMARK This is an example of a Container login script
```

REMARK allows you to add comments that are not executed. Four commands (REMARK, REM, ;, and *) perform this same function.

```
WRITE "Good %GREETING_TIME, %LOGIN_NAME"
```

The WRITE command displays the information inside the quotation marks. The resulting line will look something like this:

```
Good morning, Riley
```

Variables must be within quotation marks and in all uppercase letters. You're limited to four identifier variables per script.

```
WRITE "You have logged in from station %STATION"
```

This WRITE command displays the connection number for this login.

```
MAP DISPLAY OFF
```

This command turns off the information display to avoid multiple MAP statements clogging the screen. A later profile or user login script will provide the MAP DISPLAY ON command.

```
MAP INS S1:=TODDNW5_SYS:PUBLIC
```

This MAP INS command inserts the first network search drive into the DOS path statement, allowing the NetWare utilities in the PUBLIC directory to be available to the user from anywhere on the system.

```
*This command sets up access to DOS on the network
```

This line shows a different way to exclude lines from executing with the login script. Comments such as this are helpful to other administrators who work on the network. They are also helpful to you a year later when you have no idea what you were thinking when you set up this system.

```
MAP INS S2:=TODDNW5_SYS:PUBLIC\%MACHINE\%OS\%OS_VERSION
```

This command inserts the second network search drive into the DOS path statement. This drive uses variables to point to the particular machine type and DOS version necessary for each user.

```
COMSPEC=S2:COMMAND.COM
```

The COMSPEC command sets the DOS pointer to the correct `COMMAND.COM` file on the network. This command must follow the network mapping to DOS in the login script, but it doesn't need to be the next command. It can also be set locally. This command is rarely used anymore, because Windows systems demand control over this value.

```
MAP INS S3:=TODDNW5_SYS:APPS\WP
```

This inserts the third network search drive into the DOS path and gives access to the WP directory.

```
MAP INS S4:=TODDNW5_SYS:APPS\DB
```

This inserts the fourth network search drive and points to the DB directory.

```
;This is a drive mapping to the user's home directory
```

Beginning a line with a semicolon is another way to add a comment line that doesn't execute.

```
MAP F:=TODDNW5:USERS\%LOGIN_NAME
```

This MAP command sets drive F: to the user's home directory. However, if another MAP command later uses drive F:, this entry will be overwritten. Since Windows setup demands constant drive letters, using a variable such as *1 for this mapping may not work.

```
REM This sets up printing for users in this container
```

The last, and most popular, line-exclusion command, REM works just as it does in a DOS `AUTOEXEC.BAT` file.

```
#CAPTURE P=LJ4SI NB NT NFF TI=9
```

The crosshatch or number sign (#) starts execution of a .COM or an .EXE file. Once the program is finished, control returns to the login script. Larger programs may not work, since the login script remains in memory during this procedure, taking about 70KB of RAM. This command did more good in the past than with NetWare 6. Using iPrint, or at the least default container printers, saves much more time than using the DOS-oriented CAPTURE program. But you may need it, so here it is. Just keep in mind that you shouldn't use it if you can avoid it.

```
#COMMAND /C CLS
```

This executes the external command to clear the screen and then returns to the login script.

```
;This command displays a DOS text file the administrator
;creates for daily messages
FDISPLAY TODDNW5:Admin\MESSAGE.TXT
```

FDISPLAY can handle word processing files. In this example, it displays the file MESSAGE.TXT during the login process. (DISPLAY works only with text files.)

```
PAUSE
```

This command stops the login script until a key is pressed. It is identical to the DOS PAUSE command.

```
SET PROMPT="$P$G"
```

This SET command works the same as the DOS SET statement, but the variable must be enclosed in quotation marks.

```
IF MEMBER OF
```

This command allows you to adds conditional statements based on group memberships, as in this example:

```
IF MEMBER OF DEVELOPERS THEN MAP P:=TODDNW5:\APPS\SRC_CODE
```

You can see the ways in which this script is tailored to a large group of users: It sets the default printer, sends messages to the group, and maps drives to the users' home directories and the most generic applications.

CREATING OR EDITING A PROFILE LOGIN SCRIPT

The profile login script executes after the container login script but before the user login script. This type of script is still general, but more narrowly targeted to a smaller group of users within a larger container. Open ConsoleOne and find the Profile object. Since this is not a container, double-clicking will open the property page, as will pressing the Enter key. Then click the Login Script tab to open the Login Script page. From there, you can create a new profile login script or modify one that already exists.

If you haven't already assigned a user to the profile, you can do this by following either of the two processes below:

♦ Right-click the User object, choose Properties, and then click the Login Script tab. Type the name of the Profile object in the Profile field or use the browse option to find the Profile object, located below the login script box. Click OK to save the settings.

♦ Right-click the Profile object (located by browsing through the main ConsoleOne window), choose Trustees of This Object, and then click Add Trustee. Select the user or users, and assign the appropriate object and property rights. Click OK to save the settings.

Some coordination must happen between the container and profile login scripts. If you include user login scripts as well in your network, you must coordinate all three. Figure 5.15 shows a sample profile login script.

FIGURE 5.15

Profile login script details

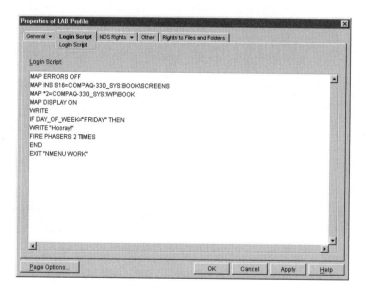

Let's take a line-by-line look at this profile login script.

```
MAP ERRORS OFF
```

If any drive-mapping errors occur, they won't show on the screen. Even if MAP DISPLAY OFF is set, errors will still display unless you specifically exclude them with this command.

```
MAP INS S16:=COMPAQ-330_SYS:BOOK\SCREENS
```

This MAP command uses the highest search drive number, rather than relying on a specific drive letter designation.

```
MAP *2:= COMPAQ-330_SYS:WP\BOOK
```

This MAP command uses a wildcard to set the actual drive letter, although we are assuming there is only one other mapped so far.

```
MAP DISPLAY ON
```

Remember that the container login script turned MAP DISPLAY OFF but never turned it back on? Here it is.

```
MAP
```

Executing the MAP command by itself lists all configured drives for this user.

```
WRITE
```

With no text, the WRITE command inserts a blank line on the screen. This is generally used to separate information.

```
IF DAY_OF_WEEK="FRIDAY" THEN
```

This is a simple example of the IF THEN statement, using a date variable picked up by the Net-Ware client software from the workstation.

```
WRITE "Hooray!!"
```

What's to explain?

```
FIRE PHASERS 2 TIMES
```

This makes some noise for Friday, but only IF it is Friday, or THEN goes to the END statement.

```
END
```

This marks the end of the IF THEN structure.

```
EXIT "NMENU WORK"
```

This EXIT command stops the login script execution and runs the specified program if there is one. This example goes from the login script straight to a menu, bypassing any lower login scripts, including the user (or default) login script.

CREATING OR EDITING A USER LOGIN SCRIPT

Once the most-used login script, the user login script has become less important in NetWare 6. It is still useful, however, and some situations can be handled only by a user login script. The main problem with individual login scripts is the time it takes to manage them in any kind of a dynamic network environment.

Open the ConsoleOne program and browse until you find the User object to get the login script. Open the property page by right-clicking the User object and click Properties. You will probably need to scroll across the tabs to see the Login Script tab. When you find it, click it to open the Login Script page, and then create or modify the user login script.

The sample user login script in Figure 5.16 works well with the previous container login script. Take a look at it in graphic format in the figure, and then read the following explanations.

```
REM This is an example of a User login script.
; Type the login script commands in UPPERCASE;
*it is not necessary but will save some debugging time.
```

FIGURE 5.16

A user login script with conditional commands

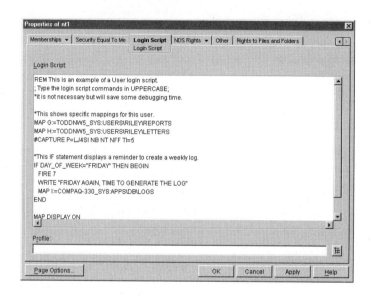

The beginning of each line shows the different ways to exclude comment lines from the login script. The line about using capital letters states a good idea. The commands themselves don't need to be in uppercase, but identifier variables must be. By getting in the habit of putting everything in uppercase except comments, you avoid a potential problem.

```
*This shows specific mappings for this user.
```

This is another comment line, describing the first section of the login script.

```
MAP G:=TODDNW5_SYS:USERS\RILEY\REPORTS
MAP H:=TODDNW5_SYS:USERS\RILEY\LETTERS
```

These two MAP commands map specific drive letters to specific directories.
```
#CAPTURE P=LJ4SI NB NT NFF TI=5
```

A CAPTURE command that redirects all printing to the LJ4SI printer.

```
*This IF statement displays a reminder to create a weekly log.
IF DAY_OF_WEEK="FRIDAY" THEN BEGIN
 FIRE 7
 WRITE "FRIDAY AGAIN, TIME TO GENERATE THE LOG"
 MAP I:=TODDNW5_SYS:APPS\DB\LOGS
END
```

This use of the IF THEN structure is based on a variable, Friday. When DAY_OF_WEEK does equal Friday, too many phasers are fired (FIRE and FIRE PHASERS are the same command to the system), and a new drive mapping is set. On Friday, drive I: becomes available to the user in order to write the necessary log.

```
MAP DISPLAY ON
```

Again, this turns on the map information display. If it's on already, there's no problem.

```
MAP
```

Finally, the MAP command lists all the drive mappings in place for this user.

Swear Off Single Users

Let's get this title right: swear *off*, not swear *at*, single users. This slogan tells you to never make changes to a single User object on your network (unless forced). This has nothing to do with marital status, but everything to do with maximum management. Anything done for a single User object will be repeated in the future. Why? If one user needs some part of his or her network fixed, another user will need the same thing done. Maybe not today, maybe not this week, but sometime. You can bank on that.

So, if you bend this rule and make a change to user Alex today, you will do something similar for user Laura in the future. After a time, you'll discover you've done the same thing for users Nicholas, Natalie, and Bradley.

One day, the fix you put in quickly "for one user" will blow up. A directory will be moved, an application will be upgraded, a printer will move to another print server, or something equally as innocent will happen. Then Alex, Laura, Nicholas, Natalie, and Bradley will all come to visit you in your office, loudly proclaiming, "Our network is broken."

So you'll scramble around for a while looking for the problem. After a time, you'll remember you did something special to Alex's login script. Then you'll realize you did it to everyone's login script. Then you'll need to fix each individual login script. Then you'll swear not to do the same thing again.

Go ahead and swear that today, and avoid the trouble.

Chapter 6

Network and Internet Printing

PRINTING ON PAPER HAS been a wonderful technology for centuries. In fact, you're holding some of that technology at this moment. Books have been excellent knowledge-transfer agents for 500 years.

Today, however, newer technologies highlight the disadvantages of printing on paper as the primary way to transmit information. Change is nearly impossible on paper; the content of this book can be changed only with great difficulty, and no changes will be reflected in existing copies of the book. It's likely that some of the data in the report you received yesterday has already changed, but the printed copy of the report has remained the same. Business assumptions you make tomorrow based on that report could be mistaken. Even worse, when you check your paper files, you'll probably find several copies of the same report, each with slightly different information. Which copy is correct? Does this copy match the report your co-workers are using for their assumptions?

Even when you receive accurate printed information, the printed paper format makes it difficult to use that information. Active data links in applications today, or hyperlinks to Web pages pulling real-time data from multiple sources, make it possible to view a memo that contains graphs that change based on the current information. When you print that memo and graph, however, the information is locked and won't ever be accurate again.

Some people object more to paper printing because of the waste. Companies today discard tons of used paper every month, and paper consumption goes up 40 percent when a new e-mail system hits a company. The idea of leveling a forest to turn trees into quickly discarded paper seems ridiculous, yet paper consumption is higher today than ever.

Your users will complain more about printing than any other single network component (although they may call the help desk more for password help). Why? Many people don't consider what's inside the computer "real" until it appears on paper. If you are new to the network administration game, you will soon hate paper because of the hassles printing causes you.

Whatever your personal reasons, controlling printing will save your company time and money. In the dynamic swirl of information, paper has been left behind. The less your company relies on paper to transfer knowledge, the more dependable that knowledge will become.

However, since we're stuck with all this printing, we might as well do it right. NetWare 6 offers several advantages over earlier NetWare versions in the setup and control of the printing process, but also retains compatibility with older network printing methods. First, let's all agree on how the network printing process works in general; then we'll get to setting up and managing NetWare 6 printing in particular. This chapter covers the print objects and properties. The client side of printing is covered in Chapter 10, "Teaching Your Clients to Use the Network." The following topics are covered in this chapter:

- NetWare printing system overview
- Understanding the Novell Distributed Print Services (NDPS) architecture
- Migrating to NDPS
- Setting up and managing NDPS
- Configuring NDPS objects
- iPrint printing
- Replacing traditional queue-based printing

NetWare Printing System Overview

Early PCs printed to an attached printer containing little or no intelligence. The printer was often a small Epson dot-matrix unit, connected to the PC by a 10-foot cable. A diagram of this relationship is simple and uncluttered. Figure 6.1 re-creates the scene on many corporate desks in the 1980s. Millions of home computers and attached printers are still configured this way today.

FIGURE 6.1

Printing the old way

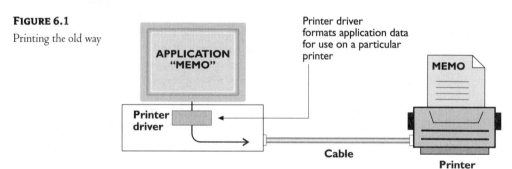

The components of this process are straightforward:

1. An application sends data (the print stream) through the print driver to the designated printer.
2. The PC directs the print stream to the printer port.
3. A printer cable carries the print stream (now formatted by the driver) to the printer.
4. The printer puts characters on paper and responds to the PC, indicating when the print stream can continue.

5. The printer cable carries the acknowledgment and request for more data to the PC.

6. The PC directs the request to the application.

7. The process repeats.

This process can look overly complicated for a single PC connected to a single printer, but even simple processes often require complicated underpinnings. Some details that cannot be clear in the diagram and text also impact the user sitting at this PC. For instance, notice that there is a direct connection between the printer and the application. The application sends data through the printer driver and must wait for the printer to request more data. Printer cache buffers were tiny in the old days, so the application would patiently wait for each request for more data until the entire print stream had been delivered to the printer. Unfortunately, the user was staring at a screen that flashed "Wait Wait Wait" or "Printing Printing Printing." Both meant the same thing.

Several things happened over the space of two or three years. First, people forgot how much time the PC saved them and grew impatient with the slow printing process. The printers were slow, the applications were slow, and the PC was useless until the print process was finished.

This problem was solved with stand-alone print spoolers—little devices that contained memory (sometimes as much as 256KB!) that sat between the PC and the printer. The application would send the print stream, and the print buffer would accept it all quickly and tell the PC application everything was printed. The buffer would then wait for the slow printer to finish printing, but the user could go back to work.

Print buffers helped, but each person still had his or her own printer, which was expensive. Worse, the printers were often dot-matrix printers, which produced crude characters and a lot of noise. The loud BZZZZZZ of tiny pins hitting paper still sends chills up my spine.

Then laser printers appeared and changed the world of printing forever. The quality was a thousand-fold better than the dot-matrix printers, but laser printers were expensive. Companies couldn't justify spending many thousands of dollars per PC to add laser printers for everyone.

The push to share laser printers probably had more to do with the growth of Novell than any other single factor. Thousands and thousands of networks were cost-justified by sharing one or two laser printers among the members of a workgroup.

Novell's Queue-Based Printing System

NetWare has traditionally used a queue system to route print jobs through the network. Figure 6.2 shows our previous application's print stream reaching the printer through the network.

THE WORKSTATION SIDE

The components of the process in Figure 6.2 are a bit more involved. First, at the workstation:

1. The application generates print output "Memo" to the print driver.

2. The CAPTURE.EXE or Windows spooler program checks the destination: local or network printer?

3. If the destination is local, CAPTURE ignores the print stream, and it goes to the local printer, or the Windows spooler directs the job to be printed on the local printer.

FIGURE 6.2

Printing the Net-Ware way (the queue system)

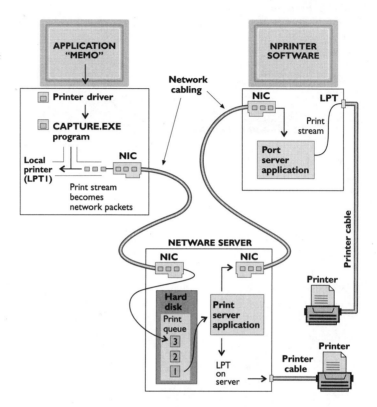

4. If the destination is the network printer, CAPTURE or the Windows spooler converts the print stream into packets that the network understands.

5. The network interface card addresses the packets and transfers them to the network cabling system.

6. If an existing file is being printed with NPRINT, the CAPTURE or the Windows spooler program is bypassed, and NPRINT feeds the print stream to the network card.

NOTE   *The DOS utility CAPTURE is almost obsolete today since the vast majority of network workstations now use Windows. Windows programs send their print jobs to a program called the spooler, which makes the decision about which printer should service a print job. Novell still offers a choice to "capture" a printer port (when you click the N on the Taskbar). If you still support DOS stations, read about CAPTURE in the NetWare documentation.*

Most applications are network-savvy and print directly to the network client software, especially through Windows of some flavor. A few applications may still have a default of printing to a locally attached printer. For these packages, the NetWare client software program CAPTURE redirects the print stream from the local printer port to the network. Windows clients can set the default printer to a network printer using the Windows spooler instead of using the CAPTURE program, but the effect is the same: The application doesn't know about the network printer; only the network client software does.

The DOS CAPTURE utility works by intercepting the print stream for particular printer ports and converting that print stream into packets that can travel over the network. These packets are sent to the network interface card, which addresses them to the server running the print server software.

If the printer port addressed by the application is still a local port, not controlled by CAPTURE, the NetWare software stays out of the way. It's possible to reference two printers in many applications and in Windows. Making one printer local and one printer available through the network is no problem. Multiple network printers are even allowed.

The network cabling transports the print stream (now converted into data packets) across the wire to the file server running the print server software. The specific print server is referenced when the CAPTURE program is started or the Windows printer is chosen. There is no practical limit on how many clients can feed print jobs to a print server. The number of clients is not limited to the number of concurrent licenses allowed by the file server software. Any NetWare client can send a print job to any NetWare print server, attached to a server or linked via network cabling.

THE SERVER SIDE

Once the print stream (now split into data packets) leaves the workstation, the following occur:

1. The packets travel across the network cabling to the addressed file server hosting the print queue.

2. The server strips the addressing information from each packet and saves the print stream as a file on the server hard disk.

3. When the last packet of the print stream is received, the application and the user running it are able to go back to work.

4. The file is closed, and the filename (assigned by NetWare) is fed into the queue with any other waiting print jobs.

5. The print server polls the queue for the next available job. When other jobs in the queue have printed (or sooner if the priority level for this print job is higher than the priority of the other waiting jobs), the file is transferred to the control of the print server.

6. If the specified printer is locally attached to the file server, the print server software and the printer negotiate concerning forms and availability, and printing starts.

7. If the specified printer is attached to a remote print server or to a workstation running the NPTWIN95 or NPRINTER software, the print server passes the print job to the network card.

8. The network card splits the print stream into packets, addresses them, and sends the packets on their way.

THE PRINTER SIDE

When the print stream (once again split into data packets) reaches the remote workstation supporting the remote printer, the following occur:

1. The network card strips the address information from the packets and passes them to the NPTWIN95 or NPRINTER software.

2. The port server software included in NPTWIN95 or NPRINTER reassembles the print stream from the packets and initializes the printer port.

3. NPTWIN95 or NPRINTER negotiates with the locally attached printer. If it is printing in the background, time slicing is used to avoid disturbing the primary application (at least in theory).

This process sounds much more convoluted than it seems to the users if everything is working properly. The users neither know nor care what happens underneath the surface. All they want is for their printouts to appear more quickly.

Be careful, because the Novell manuals often include remote links and routers in their printing diagrams to emphasize NetWare's global reach. Nothing stops your printing setup from looking like that, of course. But no company today can get away with forcing users to traverse a great distance when looking for their printouts. In the old days, mainframe users often went from one building to another in search of their paper. Huge printouts were stacked by the operations staff in cubbyholes waiting for the departmental wheelbarrow (okay, cart) to come and fetch paper by the dozens of pounds.

Today, an employee forced to walk more then five cubicles away for a printout might file a labor grievance. Users want fast printers close by. People will walk the length of the building for the fax machine without complaining, but they've been spoiled by personal printers. Most network users prefer a laser printer beside their desk and will put up with a walk to the next cubicle for the color laser printer.

Physical Printer Connections

You can physically connect a printer to the network in four ways:

◆ Plug a network-attached printer into the network cabling system directly.

◆ Plug a printer into a network-attached print server (some printers have internal print servers).

◆ Connect a server-attached printer by serial or parallel port to a file server.

◆ Connect a workstation-attached printer by serial or parallel port to a workstation.

There is nothing new in these physical methods of connecting printers. However, larger networks and smarter printers make the choice of a network-attached printer more practical for more networks today than ever before. Printers with their own network connection provide, by far, the best performance, because Ethernet runs faster than a printer port.

Network-Attached Printers and Print Servers

Many companies are working to make printing faster and easier. The client software for Windows workstations takes advantage of Microsoft's pseudo-multitasking for quicker printing. Third-party vendors make print server boxes that attach directly to the network cabling and eliminate the need for a PC running the NPTWIN95 software (nope, Novell hasn't changed the name to NPTWIN98 or NPTWINXP yet). These print servers cost less than a PC and speed up printing. Some print servers plug directly into the printer, and some need a printer cable to connect the printer and the network.

As early as 1989, I started seeing devices that allowed a network printer to be attached directly to an Ethernet or a Token Ring network. These devices had print server software that connected them to a NetWare server and allowed them to service a NetWare print queue, generally speeding up the printing process quite a bit. They also removed the restriction that printers be physically close to a workstation or file server. You could get around this, of course, with serial or parallel port extenders, but I had terrible luck with those.

Hewlett-Packard (HP) led the market when the company released JetDirect printer interfaces that plug directly into the network. Most HP printers, starting with the HP LaserJet II, have ports that allow you to plug the JetDirect devices into the printer. These JetDirect devices have separate management programs that are used to configure the JetDirect print server software.

Even some NAS (Network Attached Storage) boxes include print servers. LinkSys (`www.linksys.com`) released its Instant GigaDrive 20 in late 1999, combining a 20GB hard drive with one of its print server modules. It doesn't emulate NetWare, like the Snap! Server does (albeit only NetWare 3.*x*), but it uses Windows networking to connect PCs and Macintoshes to the 20GB drive. Any TCP/IP or Windows-enabled printer software can send print jobs through the network to the GigaDrive via its built-in 10/100 Base-T connection. Linux controls the box, with administration through a browser interface. It's very slick and fast.

Even though things are better than they were, printing will still be your largest network hassle. As you can tell from Figure 6.2, plenty of software and hardware pieces must mesh for printing to work properly. Any slip in any part of the journey can send your print job to the print job burial ground.

Novell Distributed Print Services (NDPS)

Novell started developing *Novell Distributed Print Services* (NDPS) as an add-on product for NetWare 4.11 and has bundled NDPS with each version of NetWare since. When I first looked at the specifications for NDPS, I was impressed and suspected that this was the way network printing would be handled in the future. Now I'm not so sure. The problems are that few manufacturers have jumped onto the NDPS bandwagon, the code takes 184.32MB to install on existing servers, and third-party gateways for printers other than HP and Xerox models remain dicey.

NDPS remains the party line, and we'll respect that. Don't be surprised, however, if some nice, smart Internet-driven printing facility comes along and replaces or hides NDPS. Oops, that's what iPrint does. But since iPrint is built upon NDPS, we'll keep going.

NDPS ADVANTAGES

Developed jointly with Xerox and HP, NDPS streamlines NetWare printer management. Some of the advantages of NDPS include the following:

- Bi-directional communication with newer printers allows proactive management of printers by letting printer administrators to receive messages and errors related to events such as paper jams, low toner, out of paper, and so on. Administrators can be notified of as many events as the printers are capable of reporting; for some printer types, there are more than 100 events. Administrators can obtain printer status information in real time.

- Interoperability with queue-based printing makes upgrading go fairly smoothly.

- Networked printers can be centrally administered through a single management interface, the NetWare Administrator program. This includes managing functions formerly built into utilities such as HP JetAdmin, ConsoleOne, and NetWare Administrator.

- NDPS printers are easier to set up than the queue/printer/print server model used by NetWare 4. Newer HP printers can also be set up automatically when you first plug them into the network.

- Vendors can develop plug-in applications for NDPS to further extend the management capabilities of their own printers.

- Printer device drivers can be automatically downloaded if a user selects a printer, even if the user has never used that printer before. This feature alone can save network administrators hundreds of hours of configuration time. This is supported for Windows clients that had the NDPS software installed when the NetWare 6 client software was installed.

- Printers can be filtered based on capabilities, location, or type.

- Banner pages are customizable.

- NDPS supports ISO (International Organization for Standardization) 10175 Document Printing Architecture and SNMP (Simple Network Management Protocol) MIB (Management Information Base) RFC 1759.

- Job scheduling is customizable.

- Print jobs can be easily moved from one printer to an alternate printer.

- Drag-and-drop printing is supported for ASCII text and PostScript files, without launching the application that created the file.

MANAGEMENT UTILITY MISHMASH

Novell remains conflicted about management utilities. NetWare Administrator used to be the king, then ConsoleOne took the crown in the hearts of Novell executives (but not in real life among NetWare users). Now iManage makes a bid for leadership. When Novell executives ask people about utility preferences, they probably get the same answer I get: People like browser-based utilities like iManage, followed by the familiar NetWare Administrator. ConsoleOne comes way down the popularity list, usually below the console-based C-Worthy DOS-style utilities.

Nowhere does this utility confusion get more pronounced than with the printing area. NetWare Administrator does NDPS better (fewer screens, more logical, more direct), than iManage. Yet iPrint doesn't appear anywhere in NetWare Administrator (at least that I can find)—it's only in iManage. And ConsoleOne runs a slow third in the print utility race.

COMPARING NDPS AND QUEUE-BASED PRINTING

Sometimes, sharing printers on a network can be inconvenient. If the printer you select has run out of paper, you discover that only when you make the trip to pick up your nonexistent print job. Then you load the paper and wait for the printer to finish jobs that were sent earlier to that print queue. If you need to print in a hurry, your best bet is to call someone sitting near a printer or to make a trip to see if the printer is available.

NDPS allows users to discover the current condition of a printer through software. In other words, without leaving your desk, you can get information such as whether a particular printer is out of paper or low on toner, if a print job is complete, or the location of a color printer on the system that is not busy at a particular time. NDPS printers can be connected to the network through third-party gateway products, such as HP's print servers. NDPS printers can also be connected as remote printers using LPR (for Unix or TCP/IP printers), attached to the file server, or attached to local ports on network workstations.

Novell's traditional queue-based system requires that administrators create and manage three objects—a Print Server, a Print Queue, and a Printer—for each printer device on the network. An appropriate printer driver is needed on each client computer for a particular type of printer so that the user can print. Novell's CAPTURE utility or the Windows spooler redirects a client application's print job to a queue stored on the file server, which will hold it until the printer assigned to that queue is available to print it.

With the advent of NDPS, all those functions have been built into one Printer Agent object. The DOS-based `PCONSOLE.EXE` utility has been discontinued, and the NLM program loaded at the file server, PSERVER, has been replaced by NDPSM.

Understanding the NDPS Architecture

If you have been working with versions of NetWare prior to NetWare 4, you are familiar with the process of "unlearning." After working with numerous Advanced NetWare through NetWare 2.*x* networks, I found NetWare 3 a bit of a shock (in a good way). I had to learn a lot of new features and capabilities in order to properly design and maintain NetWare 3 networks. I had eagerly anticipated NetWare 4 with NDS, but it was a shock to me also. For NetWare 4, I had to "unlearn" my notions of managing bindery-based NetWare servers, since NDS used an entirely different management approach.

The same can be said for NDPS. Although they are supported for backward compatibility, you must "unlearn" the concepts of print queues, printers, and print servers in order to grasp some of the new NDPS concepts such as agents, brokers, and managers. Okay, Novell people have moved on, but let's admit queue-based printing isn't all that bad, especially with the quick setup options inside NetWare Administrator. Even so, take a deep breath and dive right into the wonderful world of NDPS. You'll be glad you did, especially when you move onto iPrint (described later in this chapter), which builds on NDPS.

Printer Agents and Printer Types

Printer Agents are at the center of NDPS. Printer Agents represent the printers on the network, and there is one agent for each device. The agent combines the functions of the print server, queue, printer, and spooler. It provides information to users regarding features and status of the printers and their print jobs, and it sends data directly to the printer. The Printer Agent can be software or firmware embedded in the printing device, or it can be software running on a print server that connects the printer to the network.

Printer Agents provide access to the two types of printers available in the NDPS environment:

Controlled-access printers   Printers specified as NDS objects, with rights defined for certain users or groups, and can provide bi-directional feedback to users.

Public-access printers   Printers that are available to anyone on the network, but lack the extra functionality of NDPS. A public-access printer would appear on the network, for example, if an HP printer were installed and set to automatically configure itself.

Users can find it easier to access public-access printers on their own, but they need an administrator to set them up to use controlled-access printers. Table 6.1 describes the differences between public-access printers and controlled-access printers.

TABLE 6.1: PUBLIC-ACCESS PRINTERS VERSUS CONTROLLED-ACCESS PRINTERS

CONTROLLED-ACCESS PRINTERS	PUBLIC-ACCESS PRINTERS
Have an NDS printer object associated with them.	Do not have an NDS printer object associated with them.
Rights can be assigned and usage can be restricted.	Anyone can use a public-access printer.
Security can be administered through NDS.	No security is associated with public-access printers.
Must be configured through the NetWare Administrator program.	Printers that support automatic configuration can automatically configure themselves as public-access printers.
Event notification through e-mail, pager, event logging, or pop-up messages.	Event notification only for job-related events.

The NDPS Broker

The *NDPS Broker,* BROKER.NLM, supervises three services that run on the NetWare file server:

The Service Registry Service (SRS)   Stores information about public-access printers on the network, including type, manufacturer, and model.

The Event Notification Service (ENS)   Can send customizable messages about printer events and status to managers or users if, for example, a printer is out of paper or is low on toner. These messages can be in the form of pop-up messages, e-mail, or log files.

The Resource Management Service (RMS)   Centralizes storage of printer resources such as drivers, fonts, banner pages, and printer definition files (NPD), facilitating client installations.

BROKER.NLM runs on a server on the network, storing information on a specified volume and supervising printing activities anywhere on the system. When a file server is first installed, an NDPS Broker can be created automatically. NDPS requires that at least one broker be active on the system. If you have a larger NetWare network, you should plan to have at least one NDPS Broker per subnet.

Other NDPS Components

Along with Printer Agents and NDPS Brokers, NDPS has the following components:

NDPS Managers (NDPSM.NLM**)**   Entities that communicate with the modules running on the file server. They can supervise any number of printer devices attached to a network. At least one

NDPS Manager must be present on the network, but there can be only one NDPS Manager per server. NDPS Managers also manage the Printer Agents.

Gateways   Software modules (such as HPGATE) that manage communications between NDPS and a printer device. These are provided either by the printer manufacturer (for example, HP or Xerox) or by Novell. Novell's gateway employs the *Printer Device Subsystem* (PDS), which accesses the printer through a port handler that you specify when you set up the Agent object. You use the Novell gateway to communicate with printers attached to parallel and serial ports, as well as remote printers such as those connected via `NPRINTER.EXE` or `NPTWIN95.EXE`.

NDPS embedded printers   Printing devices that the NDPS Printer Agent software built directly into the printer's firmware. Administrators and users can communicate directly with printers that have this software embedded in them. Many printer manufacturers are working to incorporate NDPS technology in their next generation of printers. If you want NDPS to work correctly, spend the money to get real NDPS-enabled printers.

NDPS-enabled client   A Windows client that has had the NetWare 6 client software installed with the Novell Distributed Print Services option checked during custom installation (see Figure 6.3). If the NDPS client software is not installed, the client will be able to print only to iPrint or queue-based printers.

FIGURE 6.3

The Novell Distributed Print Services client installation option

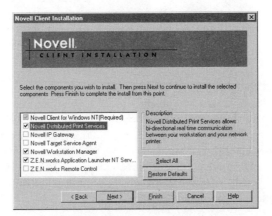

NDPS Configurations

Figure 6.4 shows the three ways that an NDPS printer can be attached and configured on the network and how an NDPS client can access that printer:

- ◆ In the first configuration, the client communicates directly with a printer in which the NDPS software is embedded.

- ◆ In the second configuration, the printer is attached directly to the server (through the parallel or serial port), and the Printer Agent redirects the job through the Novell PDS, which is one of the components of the Novell gateway.

◆ In the third configuration, the printer communicates through a gateway product such as HP's or Xerox's printer gateway.

FIGURE 6.4

How NDPS printers can be attached to the network

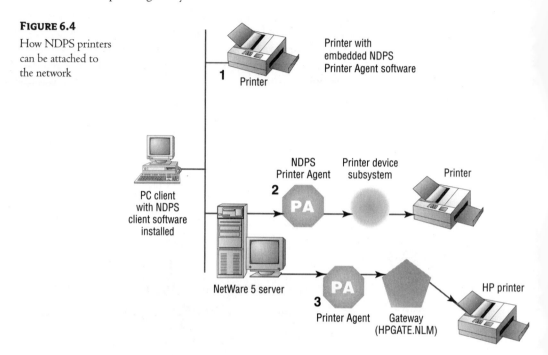

In planning your printing environment, use a diagram to indicate where individuals and printers are physically located. You can determine access by matching the following: job function, particular needs (large volume, duplex, color, and forms), location, and printer characteristics. Other important variables include whether you are supporting NetWare 4.1 or older servers; DOS, OS/2, and Macintosh clients; and older printers, which will require queues. Which network protocols are in place—IPX, TCP/IP, or both? In a mixed environment, you can assign queues to an NDPS printer, or you can reserve specific printers to handle queues.

Migrating to NDPS from Your Existing System

When you start planning your move to NetWare 6, you need to make sure you include printers in your migration plan. There is no single "best" way to migrate from your existing older printing system to NDPS. The only thing I can tell you for sure is that NDPS is Novell's recommended path for network printing, although NetWare 6 still supports the traditional queue/printer/print server system.

Your migration path is going to depend on a number of factors, and you need to answer the following questions:

◆ How many printers need to be migrated?

◆ How many clients will need to have their software upgraded to the NetWare 6 client software?

- Which network protocols will you be using: TCP/IP, IPX/SPX, or both?

- What is your current network operating system version?

Novell offers an Upgrade Wizard on its Web site (`www.novell.com`), which upgrades a queue system to NDPS. Or, you can install NDPS and manually reconfigure clients and printers as needed. You must convert your queue-based printers to NDPS to support iPrint. At the end of this chapter, I'll take you quickly through the steps for a "quick-and-dirty" NDPS setup to replace queue-based printing.

Should I Migrate Immediately?

Before I start talking about interoperability between the queues and NDPS, let me first jump into the line of fire and make some firm recommendations:

- If you have fewer than 25 queues and all of your clients will be upgraded to NDPS client software, plan to upgrade immediately. I don't have hard-core data to support that 25—it's just a manageable number of print queues to migrate simultaneously.

- If you have fewer than 200 workstations and can easily deploy the NetWare 6 client software (including the NDPS option), go ahead and migrate to NDPS.

- If you are currently using NetWare 3.x, you will need to convert from the NetWare 3 printing model anyway. For fewer than 25 print queues, start over from scratch. For more than 25, use the NetWare 6 Upgrade Wizard that ships with NetWare 6 to upgrade your NetWare 3.x printing objects "across the wire."

NOTE *Again, there is nothing magical about the 25 number; for me, that is a manageable number of print queues. You'll need to select your own realistic and manageable number.*

- If you are migrating from another operating system such as Windows NT Server or Unix, you will need to redo your printing architecture anyway. Go ahead and get the printers configured using NDPS so you can support iPrint.

If you have decided that it is necessary to use both NDPS and the traditional NetWare queue-based printer system, you need to be aware of the interoperability that is provided between NDPS printers and NetWare 6 queues. NetWare 6 Queue, Printer, and Print Server objects can coexist on the same server as NDPS Broker, Agent, and Manager objects.

Of course, if you don't have many printers, and they're all working fine, you can postpone NDPS installation. There's no law that says you must change your printer arrangement. If this task falls way down on your priority list, so be it. But if you will benefit from NDPS, let's get going. Plus, read about the advantages of iPrint before you decide against NDPS.

Designing Your New NDPS System

As part of your upgrade or network design process, Novell says you should have written records of the following (no, this isn't a joke):

- All printer types and physical locations

♦ How each printer connects to the network (through a network printer interface card, work station, print server, NetWare server, or some other type of server such as Unix or Windows NT/2000)

♦ Restrictions that need to be placed on any specific printers (for example, the Marketing department folks may not want the Sales department using their snazzy new color laser printer)

♦ Management responsibilities for each of the printers—does the help desk manage all the printers, or is there a person in each department or area who should be given that task?

As you start planning your NDPS system, remember that at least one server should be an NDPS Manager. On multiple-segment or multiple-location networks, I suggest a server with an NDPS Manager in each segment or location. Because the Printer Agents communicate with the NDPS Managers, you want the NDPS Managers to be near their Printer Agents. You will create one Printer Agent for each printing device on your network. Each Printer Agent is assigned to an NDPS Manager.

An important design issue concerns which network protocols will be used. NDPS uses IPX/SPX and TCP/IP—you can use either protocol or both. The NCP (NetWare Core Protocol) requests on a NetWare 6 network that is based on TCP/IP are transported natively in IP packets. Earlier versions of NetWare supported TCP/IP clients, but the NCP data were transported across the TCP/IP network as encapsulated IPX frames in an IP datagram. NetWare 6 has full native TCP/IP support, and you should use only TCP/IP unless you have many legacy IPX devices around.

Maintaining Interoperability with NetWare Queues

As stated earlier, no single "correct" way exists to migrate from a queue-based printing system to an NDPS system. Let me offer one path for a large system with many network printers.

Your clients must run the NetWare 6 version of the client software before you can move from a queue-based system to an NDPS system. Until you have upgraded these clients, you must maintain your queues, and your clients will continue to print as they have in the past (see Figure 6.5). You can continue to operate your printers in this manner indefinitely if you decide that you don't want to move to NDPS.

FIGURE 6.5

A non-NDPS client printing to a Net-Ware queue that is serviced by a print server

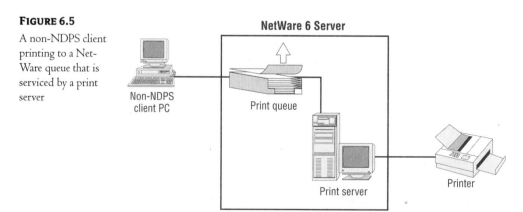

Next, create NDPS Managers and NDPS Brokers on the servers near the printing devices, and create NDPS Printer Agents for each printer on the network. Then you can test your newly created Printer Agents before putting them into production. Now, both the queue system and the NDPS Printer Agent send jobs to the same printing device.

Reassign printing responsibility for your queues; instead of having the print server managing print jobs from the queue, assign the Printer Agent to manage print jobs. Figure 6.6 shows non-NDPS clients using the traditional queue, NDPS clients using the Printer Agent, and all print jobs being delivered to the same print device. For details, see the section "Assigning an NDPS Printer Agent to Service a NetWare Print Queue," later in this chapter.

FIGURE 6.6

NDPS and non-NDPS clients both going through the same Printer Agent

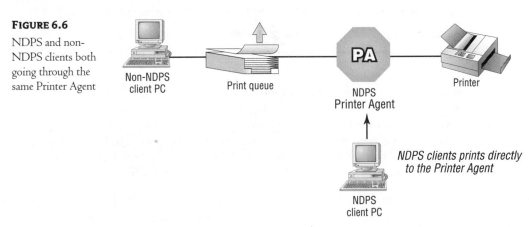

Now you're almost there! All printers are configured with Printer Agents, so you can start upgrading clients slowly. Once all clients that depend on using queues are upgraded, delete the NetWare queues. Delete your queues only a few at a time. There could possibly still be users on your network who are printing to queues rather than to NDPS printers. If you delete them all at the same time, your phone calls will only be drowned out by irate users yelling and cursing at you.

TIP See the "Replacing Queue-based Printing: A Quick-and-Dirty NDPS Setup" section at the end of this chapter for a step-by-step approach to quickly re-create a queue-based printer using a server-attached NDPS printer.

Setting Up NDPS

In a typical scenario, you need one NDPS Broker, one or more NDPS Managers, and as many Printer Agents as there are actual printers attached to the network. You must create a manager for each file server attached to a printer. You might also create multiple managers if you are assigning operator rights to specific departments.

All the tasks required for creating and managing NDPS used to be exclusively in NetWare Administrator, but now you can do everything in the new browser-based iManage utility. We'll start with iManage, but cover some NetWare Administrator functions as well.

Creating the NDPS Broker

1. Open iManage and log in if necessary.

2. Expand iPrint Management in the menu listing on the left and click Create Broker.

3. Choose NDPS Broker.

4. Fill in the Broker name.

5. Browse to designate a volume in which to store the NDPS Resource database.

6. Click Create to exit and create the NDPS Broker object.

If you chose the Express installation option when you set up NetWare 6, an NDPS Broker should have been created for you. You can optionally choose to create or add new brokers later. If you chose the Custom installation option, you may have decided not to copy the NDPS Resource database, which saved over 60MB of storage space on your server. To add this service later, you need to run the GUI on the server console (using STARTX), click Novell, choose the Install option, and then follow the directions to install the appropriate files for NDPS.

NOTE   *In NetWare 5.1, ConsoleOne is the utility of choice for creating an NDPS Broker object. But NetWare 6 changed those rules, pushing the printer controls over to the new browser-based utility, iManage, even though all the pieces aren't quite ready yet. And that's fine, because iManage is new and cool.*

Ogle Figure 6.7 for the new way to handle printing. No doubt, a patch or two will fix some of the NDPS printing problems we're about to discuss.

At the very minimum, you need to supply a broker name, useful for future memory jogging. You can also specify whether to enable the Service Registry Service (SRS), the Event Notification Service (ENS), and the Resource Management Service (RMS). Yes, you should have all three services enabled. In addition, you can provide the volume name and path that contain the RMS data. If you don't provide data for these fields, the defaults apply.

Notice the name of the volume I chose? Do I need to remember the fully qualified name for this volume and type it in myself, ham-fingers and all? No, I can just click the magnifying glass to browse available volumes inside this container. The brand-new eDirectory Object Selector appears on you screen, just as in Figure 6.8.

Is that cool, or what? I bet you can't wait to find out what other things are possible through these new browser utilities. Maybe you'll see some more iManage features as we finish this section.

After picking the appropriate volume from the fancy new pick list, click the OK command button at the bottom of the iManage Create Broker screen (Figure 6.7). In Figure 6.8, the ProLiant system awaits on the second page, requiring a click of the Next command button. The selection approval result seriously lacks pizzazz—it shows another page saying, "The Create Broker request succeeded." Maybe some sparkle will sneak in with the first service pack.

FIGURE 6.7

Creating an NDPS Broker in iManage

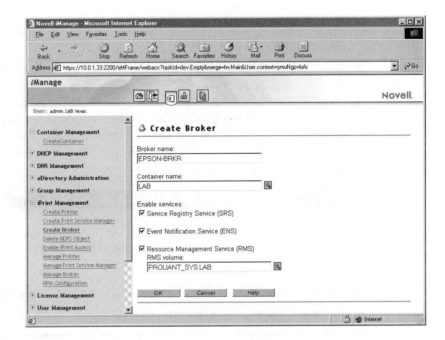

FIGURE 6.8

The new Search facility in iManage

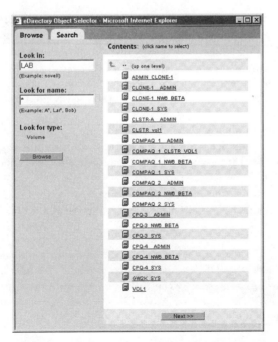

Activate the NDPS Broker modules at the server by typing the following at the system console:

```
LOAD BROKER EPSON-BRKR.LAB
```

Then add this line to the `AUTOEXEC.NCF` to load the broker automatically when the server is restarted (this line is automatically inserted if NDPS was installed on the server during initial installation). The NDPS Broker is called EPSON-BRKR and is located in the LAB context. This command loads the `BROKER.NLM` and initializes a screen at the server console. From this screen, you can view broker events and disable the Service Registry, Event Notification, and Resource Management Services.

Creating the NDPS Manager

IN A HURRY 6.2: CREATE AN NDPS MANAGER

1. Open iManage and log in if necessary.

2. Expand iPrint Management in the menu listing on the left and click Create Print Service Manager.

3. Fill in the Print Services Manager name.

4. Browse to designate a volume in which to store the NDPS Print Service Manager database.

5. Click Create to exit and create the NDPS Manager object.

Next, we need to create an NDPS Manager that will interact with the services running at the server. From iManage, follow the on-screen directions that politely request that you choose a menu item on the left. For our current purposes, click iPrint Management to expand the menu, then click Create Print Service Manager.

Type the name (appropriate NDS-style name, of course), and then choose the container and the volume holding the database. Figure 6.9 should strongly remind you of the previous operation for creating a broker.

At the very least, you need to supply a useful name for the NDPS Manager. You should also choose a resident server that will store the database of driver files and configurations, and you should choose a volume on that server. Servers that have shared printers attached directly to their local ports must run an NDPS Manager.

It makes sense to put the manager on the same server as the broker created earlier. In fact, if you're working up to a printer physically attached to the server, all the NDPS components must reside on that same server.

NOTE *NetWare 5.1 restricted NDPS printers to the SYS: volume almost by accident. NDPS uses the TTS (Transaction Tracking System) to run the NDPS database, and earlier versions of NSS didn't support TTS. Hence the SYS: volume, which needed to have TTS for several reasons in NetWare 5.1, became the almost mandatory NDPS volume of choice. That restriction (TTS on NSS) disappeared with NSS version 3.0, which ships with NetWare 6, so NDPS databases can go on NSS volumes now.*

FIGURE 6.9

NDPS Manager creation time

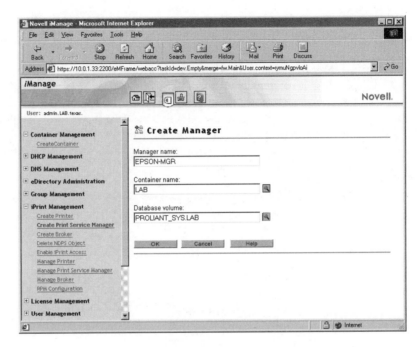

Return to the server console screen to start the NDPS Print Service Manager module by typing, in my case, **LOAD NDPSM EPSON-MGR.LAB** at the colon prompt. If this doesn't work as you expect (an error appears instead of success), try putting a period at the beginning of the print manager name (**.EPSON-MGR.LAB**). If you have spaces in the name (which makes me wince), you must surround the command with quotation marks. Unfortunately, NDPS isn't yet smart enough to add this command, and the previous one, into **AUTOEXEC.NCF** for you automatically. Do it manually, and hope the next upgrade in iManage adds at least the option of an automatic line insertion. They don't expect network administrators to spend all day typing commands, do they?

WARNING   *You can use iManage or ConsoleOne to delete NDPS Manager objects, but if you do, NetWare will also delete any Printer objects associated with that NDPS Manager object.*

Creating Printer Agents

IN A HURRY 6.3: CREATE A PRINTER AGENT

1.   Open iManage and log in if necessary.

2.   Expand iPrint Management in the menu listing on the left and click Create Printer.

3.   Fill in the printer name.

4.   Browse to find the NDPS Print Services Manager.

5.   Click Create to exit and create the NDPS Printer Agent object.

Printer Agents represent the actual printers on the network. You can create and manage them at the file server console with the NDPS Manager (`NDPSM.NLM`) or at a workstation with ConsoleOne or iManage. Be sure you've created the NDPS Print Manager first (just like cookie-cutter pop groups, the manager comes before the performing object). It would have been nice of Novell developers to put these items in order of creation on the menu, to make mistakes less common, but they didn't. Just remember that you must create the NDPS Manager prior to creating Printer Agents.

Either type the name of the NDPS Print Manager, or, to avoid typos and memory slips, click the search button to find the correct manager. The Novell IPP (Internet Printing Protocol) gateway appears as the default, and should stay that way unless you're linking a Unix or Linux printer. Figure 6.10 shows the now-familiar iManage screen.

FIGURE 6.10

Creating an NDPS printer

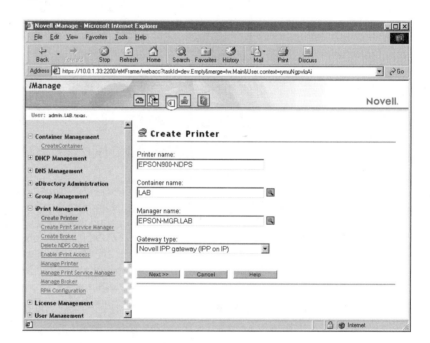

The next screen asks for the printer URL (IP address or URL of the server). This tells the IPP gateway how to find the printer.

If you forgot to load the NDPS Manager, a screen appears to remind you. Load the NDPS Manager at the server console and click OK (if you see this screen).

Next comes a long file-update listing showing a ton of available print drivers for various Windows versions. You must choose the appropriate one for each client type so the users (remember them, the ones who demanded a new printer?) will get the proper printer driver downloaded when they use NDPS. Figure 6.11 shows some of the printer drivers.

After picking the drivers, click the Next command button at the bottom of the screen. A terse but affirmative message appears to tell you the printer has been created as expected.

FIGURE 6.11

Picking printer
drivers

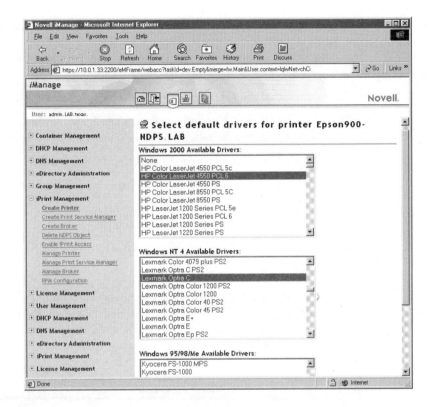

ADDING PRINTER DRIVERS

Since printer models appear faster than cockroaches in cheap motels, you will probably need to add a printer driver or three to the list. Cross your fingers, because this routine appears rough in the first shipping version.

One stupid restriction appears: You must be running iManage on the same operating system for which you add the driver. You won't be able to add a printer driver if it is for an operating system that is different from the operating system running on the client doing the Web browsing. This probably has something weird to do with the way the Windows GUI handles print drivers and is beyond Novell's control. At least it's beyond my control. Also, you must use Microsoft Internet Explorer (IE). Here are some of the fun and games I had while adding new printer drivers:

◆ IE hung trying to load the iManage screen on Windows 2000.

◆ IE hung trying to add the printer driver on Windows 98.

◆ IE ran happily along, copying driver files here and yon, until a dialog box appeared, declaring "WinSock 10049 Address Not Available" on Windows 2000.

◆ Much cursing and threatening chassis harm to servers until things finally worked.

This should make you feel better when you play with the printing. If it works slick as a greased doorknob, you should be happy. If it crawls like a line at the DMV, you know it's not your fault. At least I don't think so, because I'm not taking the blame for the problems I had.

To add a new printer driver, take this nonobvious route:

1. Start iManage and choose Manage Broker ➤ Search for Broker ➤ Choose Broker.

2. Click the Resource Management Service tab. Ignore any message saying the NDPS Broker NLM isn't loaded, because the message appears occasionally when the NLM is running.

3. Choose the correct operating system driver family and click the Add button.

4. Search for and select the printer INF file. Help find the auxiliary files if the installation routine gets lost. Cross your fingers.

5. See the HTTP 500 - Internal server error dialog box.

6. Do it all again (and maybe again and again).

7. Whew, finally enjoy your new driver.

Try everything you can think of to make this work, if you don't breeze through the first time. Reboot your client. Stop iFolder on the server. Restart iFolder. Reload Netscape and/or Apache or both if both are running. Reload all the NDPS server components. Something—no telling what—will finally work. I rebooted everything, including the server and client twice, and studied magic chicken entrails, until I finally saw the screen in Figure 6.12.

FIGURE 6.12

A new printer driver (finally)

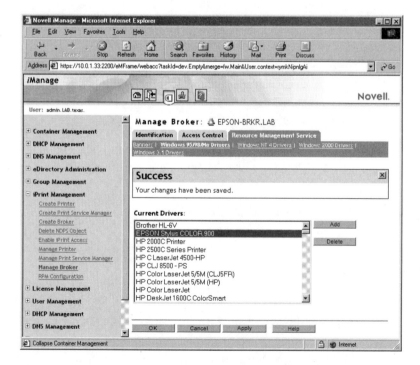

After the printer driver finally crawls up to the server, remember to click the Apply command button. Hate to waste all that work just to redo it tomorrow, wouldn't you?

In case you're wondering, you can't install drivers from multiple floppy diskettes. I always copy the driver's directories onto a file server from the printer vendor's CD-ROM to keep things handy for every client computer. Others I know burn a CD-ROM master printer driver disk to carry along with them for nonnetworked clients. But if it's not networked, can it be called a client? This seems odd; no doubt some vice-president ordered the setup.

Configuring Remote Printer Management

IN A HURRY 6.4: CONTROL PRINTERS THROUGH REMOTE PRINTER MANAGEMENT (RPM)

1. Open iManage and log in if necessary.

2. Expand iPrint Management in the menu listing on the left and click RPM Configuration.

3. Select the object (such as the user, group, or container) to receive printer instructions and downloads.

4. Configure the NDPS Printer object for your situation.

5. Click Apply to configure RPM.

Let's subtitle this section "Forcing NDPS Printers on Your Users." Yes, you can do that technically, if not practically. Since many companies spread printers around the office like cold germs, any user who wants a printer often gets one. Just in case your situation requires more control, here's how you force users to stick with certain printers.

Even if you can't force users to use only particular printers, you can force them to load a particular printer. Do you have a special form printer? NDPS and Remote Printer Management (RPM, a highly overused acronym) can help. You can force a certain printer to start as the default Windows printer, but users can change that manually.

Figure 6.13 shows the primary RPM screen. Notice you have choices for using printers to subjugate users:

Do Not Update Workstations   There is no change to users.

Allow Only Specified Printer to Reside on Workstations   This is full subjugation mode.

Show the Results Window on Workstations   Although this is informational, some users may freak if you set it.

Notice that you may remove printers from workstation configurations. This is a cool trick when you update printers for certain groups and wish to cut down on support calls when users force formatting for one printer through another printer.

Once you have set the printer straightjacket to your liking, click the Apply command button. A "Success" banner will appear, if all works correctly. (This part isn't particularly dicey, so you should be okay.)

FIGURE 6.13

Controlling users'
printer options

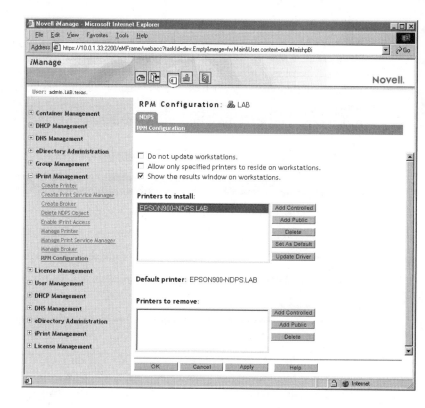

Managing NDPS

Printing support lags in iManage and ConsoleOne. Be ready to switch back to NetWare Administrator for management tasks, as we must do now.

To view the NDPS Printer Control property page, using NetWare Administrator, browse the NDS eDirectory and locate the printer you want to control. Highlight the printer, right-click, and choose Details to open the Printer Control property page of the NDPS printer. At this point, you are ready to use the bi-directional features of NDPS. (But be aware that not all printer types and printer configurations will support bi-directional printing.)

Click the various buttons to familiarize yourself with the Printer Control property page. The Printer Control property page shown in Figure 6.14 describes the Epson Stylus 900N (*N* for Network) printer I struggled to install drivers for earlier.

NOTE *Epson developers didn't help design the NDPS components, as did Xerox and HP. However, they added their own gateway for NDPS support for their own printers, including the fast and high-resolution Stylus 900N they sent me for testing.*

FIGURE 6.14

The Novell Printer Control properties

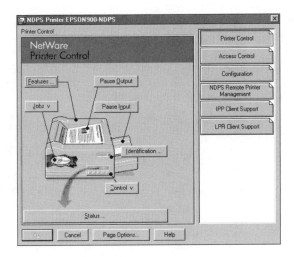

The Printer Control property page has seven buttons:

Features   Contains information about the printer, including document formats (PostScript or PCL), speed, memory installed, duplex capabilities, resolution, and mechanism type (for example, laser).

Jobs   Leads to two submenus. The first displays current print jobs (Job List). You can view details of the spooled jobs there. The second, Spooling Configuration, controls spooling details such as the volume to use for spooling, setting spooling disk space limits, and the spooling output priorities. (First In, First Out is the default, but you can also arrange jobs to suit loaded media, minimize form changes, or print the smallest spooled job first.) For some odd reason, this menu also includes the list of NetWare queues supported by this NDPS printer.

Pause Output   Toggles printer output on or off.

Pause Input   Toggles printer input on or off.

Identification   Includes the NDPS Manager and Printer Agent names, as well as optional information that can be helpful to you as the administrator, including Description and Location boxes, as well as the server's IP address.

Control   Opens a submenu with four options: Reset to reset the printer; Form Feed to push a blank page through; Mount Media to change paper (okay, media) type; and Statistics to show printer history, including total jobs, total pages, and time spent waiting for attention (tattletale).

Status   Displays the printer's current status, such as Active, Paused, Disabled, Idle, and a few others.

Your printer details will differ, depending on the printer manufacturer and model. Figure 6.15 shows a similar screen with just about the same information, but from HP rather than Epson.

FIGURE 6.15

Printer controls from
another viewpoint

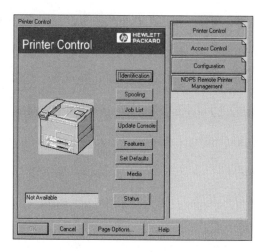

On the HP Printer Control property page, the Set Defaults option allows you to add customized banners, select printer drivers, and set up pauses and hold jobs (with a fair amount of control). This is also where the Notification options are located. Click the objects to notify a user when a print job has been completed. The Spooling option for the HP printer allows you to direct the location of the spool files on your server and restrict their size if you have constraints. You can also change the order of the print jobs—the default is first in, first out. Another item allows you to direct printer queues to this device.

How about one more? The EpsonNet NDPS Gateway special control panel included with this third-party gateway is too pretty to leave out, I think. Take a look at Figure 6.16.

FIGURE 6.16

Epson's flashy
NDPS gateway

The six command buttons down the far-right side of the screen look and function in the same way as they do for other NDPS printer property pages. The seven command buttons inside the Epson frame, however, offer some new and interesting features. Most interesting, at least to those who manage inkjet printers, is the Consumable command button. Clicking that button shows the percentage remaining of both the blank ink and color ink cartridges. This is good forewarning, since one or both always run out at the wrong time. The Advanced button opens up to seven submenus full of information about this particular printer. A Features submenu item/sales job (420 sheets per hour and maximum resolution of 1829 dpi) tells you to be happy with your printer purchase. The Medium submenu describes the two dozen types and sizes of paper supported by the printer.

Other nice touches include the traffic signal display, now showing green (well, gray in this book). The information window under the printer picture disagrees with the green light, but that's because I opened the printer to see what error message would appear. I closed it, and it's ready to go, but it still wants to tell me there was a problem.

Setting NDPS Printer Agent Access Control

A really nice feature in NetWare printing is the ability to set different levels of access to a network printer. NDPS printers are no exception. To set access to a particular printer, highlight the printer in NetWare Administrator, choose Object ➤ Details, and select the Access Control command button. You'll see a screen similar to Figure 6.17.

FIGURE 6.17

Printer access control entries

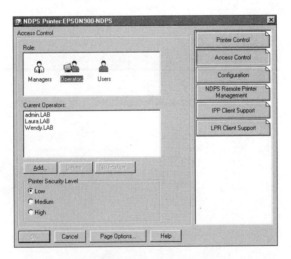

In the Role box at the top of the page, you see that users and groups can be assigned three roles:

Managers   Can perform any function required on the printer such as printing, managing others' print jobs, and changing device drivers. The person who created the printer is automatically a manager.

Operators   Can print to the printer as well as manage other people's print jobs and pause the printer. The person who created the printer is automatically an operator.

Users Can send print jobs to the printer and delete their own print jobs from the printer. By default, when a new printer is created in an NDS container, the container is given User permissions to that printer. This means that all users located in that NDS container will have the User permission. The person who created the printer is automatically a user.

In Figure 6.17, notice that there are three operators listed under Current Operators (three who have the authority to manage other people's printing, not three doing it at this moment). When you highlight the Managers icon in the Role box, the second box changes labels, and the same happens when you highlight the Users icon.

Configuring Print Jobs

If you were an administrator of any earlier version of NetWare, you may have needed to create a print job configuration using the old DOS utility PRINTCON. You can also assign print jobs to NDPS Printer Agents using NetWare Administrator, and I think you will find this setup much easier than the DOS counterpart.

NDPS just calls these *configurations*. Configurations are properties assigned to NDPS Printer Agents that will control the default behavior of all print jobs or specific print jobs. To create a configuration for a Printer Agent, highlight the printer in NetWare Administrator, choose Object ➤ Details, and click the Configuration button to open the Configuration dialog box. Figure 6.18 shows a list of printer configurations for the NDPS printer Epson900-NDPS. From this page, you can create new printer configurations, modify and/or rename existing printer configurations, or delete printer configurations you no longer need.

FIGURE 6.18

Printer configuration entries

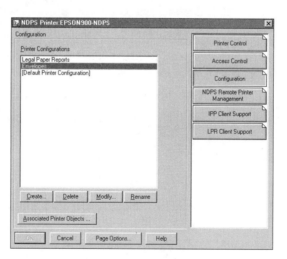

This may be a good place to mention IPP Client Support, a command button on the right side of the screen in this figure and the two figures previously. IPP Client Support, activated by clicking this tab and enabling the Enable IPP Access to this Printer check box, adds the software necessary to convince the printer to accept IPP data streams and print jobs.

To modify an existing configuration, highlight the configuration you want to modify and click the Modify button. To create a new printer configuration, click the Create button. Clicking either Create or Modify opens the Printer Configuration dialog box, shown in Figure 6.19.

FIGURE 6.19

Printer configuration options

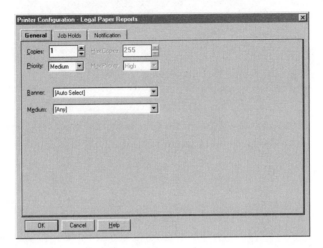

This dialog box has three tabs: General, Job Holds, and Notification. Let's see what each tab has to offer.

GENERAL CONFIGURATION OPTIONS

On the General tab (see Figure 6.19), you can set the number of copies, maximum number of copies, job priority, maximum priority, banner type, and the medium (form) on which jobs can print. Specifying a medium that is different from the current form mounted on the printer will pause the printer.

JOB HOLD OPTIONS

On the Job Holds tab, shown in Figure 6.20, you can specify the following options (all of which are optional):

Operator Hold Specifies that print jobs that use this configuration do not print until the operator releases them.

User Hold Specifies that print jobs that use this configuration do not print until the user who printed them releases the job.

Pause Printer on Job Start Causes the printer to pause before the print job starts. Only a printer operator or manager can restart the printer. The printer will remain paused for 15 minutes by default. You can also specify a notification message you want to see when the job causes the printer to pause.

Pause Printer on Job End Much the same as Pause Printer on Job Start, except occurs when the job is completed. Both options might be useful when a particular form is required.

Retain Job For   Causes the print job to be retained after it is printed. You can control the length of time that the job is retained.

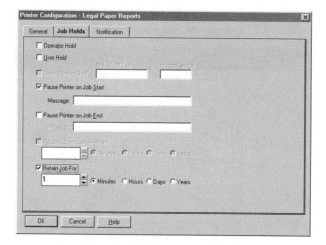

FIGURE 6.20

The Job Holds tab

Some choices displayed in Figure 6.20 are available only when working with individual print job properties. These grayed-out choices include Delay Printing Until and Retain Job No Longer Than.

NOTIFICATION OPTIONS

The events on the Notification tab, shown in Figure 6.21, work in conjunction with the Event Notification Service to notify users or operators of specific events that can occur on the printer—low toner, out of paper, paper jams, and so on.

FIGURE 6.21

The Notification tab

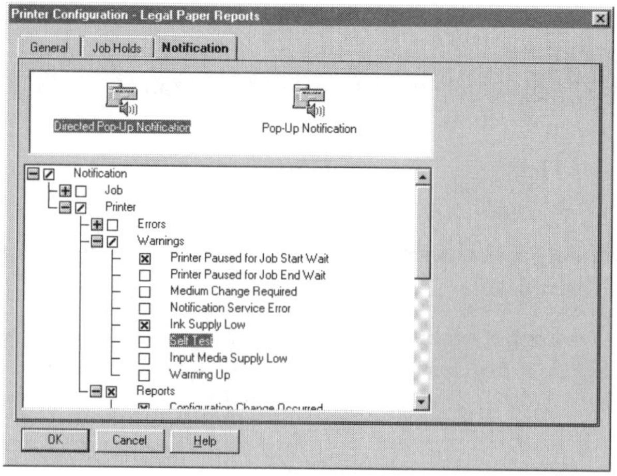

The Event Notification Service uses three types of delivery mechanisms: pop-up messages, e-mail, and log files. The NDPS system provides an open architecture for vendors to develop other notification systems. How would you like to be paged every time a printer runs out of toner or gets a paper jam? The way I look at it, if my job is fixing paper jams, I am going to hear about it whether the printer beeps me or the user calls me. I would rather be on top of things and on my way to fix the problem when the user calls.

NOTE   *Are some of these specific notifications overkill? Yes, for most users, but not all. If you manage a slew of printers, you might really enjoy knowing some details about an error message on a printer three floors away. The Epson NDPS gateway provides detailed error reporting to the point that you'll know whether to bring paper or toner to the offending printer.*

Assigning an NDPS Printer Agent to Service a NetWare Print Queue

If you are making a phased migration from traditional NetWare queue-based printing to NDPS Printer Agents, one feature you should be aware of is the ability to assign a Printer Agent to service NetWare print queues. This is done in NetWare Administrator from the Spooling Configuration dialog box, shown in Figure 6.22, which is easy to miss if you don't know exactly where to look for it. Here's how to get to this dialog box:

1. In the NDS eDirectory tree, select the Printer Agent, and display the Printer Agent's details.

2. Click the Printer Control button.

3. Locate your printer's spooling option. This is easy for an HP printer, which has the Spooling button on the front page. For an Epson printer, however, you need to go through the Jobs submenu (choose Jobs ➢ Spooling Configuration). Look carefully, and choose the appropriate option to open the Spooling Configuration dialog box.

4. In the Service Jobs from NetWare Queues section, click the Add button and select the NetWare print queue that you want this Printer Agent to service.

FIGURE 6.22

NDPS supporting queues

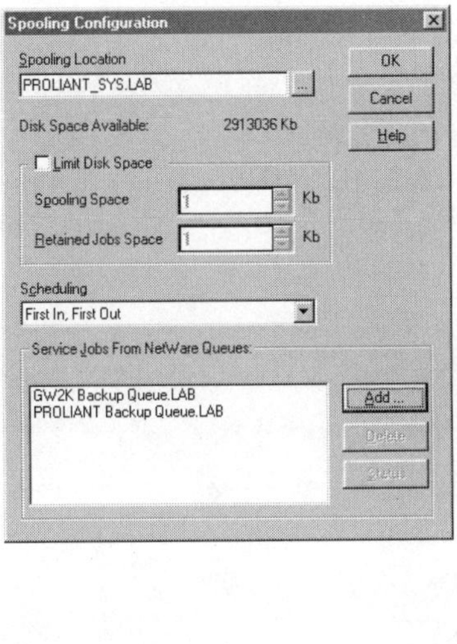

From the Spooling Configuration dialog box, you can also set the maximum amount of disk space that the Printer Agent will use for spooling and the scheduling priority of jobs. The Scheduling drop-down list gives you three options: Print Smallest Job First, Minimize Media Changes, and First In, First Out.

Administering the NDPS Broker and Manager

You can perform a few tasks at the server console. The two NDPS NLMs that run at the server are the NDPS Broker (BROKER.NLM) and the NDPS Manager (NDPSM.NLM). Both have a console screen.

MANAGING THE NDPS MANAGER AT THE CONSOLE

Figure 6.23 shows the NDPS Manager console with its Available Options menu.

FIGURE 6.23

The NDPS Manager console main menu

You have two options:

Printer Agent List   Displays a list of agents that have been assigned to this NDPS Manager. You can also create additional Printer Agents from this screen.

NDPS Manager Status And Control   Displays the NDPS Manager Status and Control menu, shown below. You can see how long the NDPS Manager has been up and running, as well as the number of Printer Agents assigned to this NDPS Manager. The Status and Database Options items are described in the next sections.

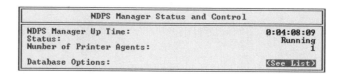

Unload Options

If you choose Status from the NDPS Manager Status and Control menu, you have four options:

Cancel Unload   Cancels a previously requested unload request.

Unload Immediately   Shuts down the NDPS Manager even if print jobs are currently printing.

Unload After Active Print Jobs   Stops the NDPS Manager after the currently active print jobs have completed. No new print jobs will be started.

Unload After All Print Jobs   Stops the NDPS Manager when no more print jobs are waiting to be printed.

Database Options

Finally, you can choose Database Options to open the NDPS Manager Database Options menu. This is a rarely used but sometimes helpful menu, as shown here.

From this menu, you have eight choices.

Examine Database   Allows you to view the database statistics and the number of objects within each object class.

Backup Database Options   Allows to you specify how often the database is backed up. The default is to back up the database daily at 1:00 A.M.

Backup Database Files   Backs up the current database.

Restore Database   Restores the database from the most recent backup.

Resynchronize Database Files   Rebuilds the database index file using the current database file.

View Log File   Displays the log file from the resynchronize operations. The log file is stored in SYS:SYSTEM\DPREPAIR.LOG.

Delete Log File   Deletes the SYS:SYSTEM\DPREPAIR.LOG file.

Uninstall Database   Removes the NDPS Manager database and supporting directories.

MANAGING BROKERS FROM THE CONSOLE

The BROKER.NLM also has a console screen. It doesn't contain many options, but I didn't want it to feel left out. Take a look at Figure 6.24 for the short list.

FIGURE 6.24

The NDPS Broker console screen

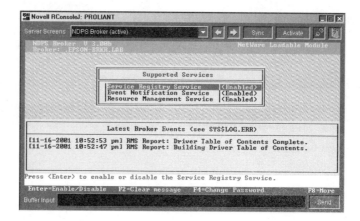

You can use the Supported Services menu to enable or disable the three services that a broker provides: Service Registry Service, Event Notification Service, and Resource Management Service.

WARNING   *Don't disable services unless you know exactly what results to expect.*

Also notice the Latest Broker Events field in Figure 6.24. This field contains error and warning messages for the five most recent events that were reported to the NDPS Broker. These events will also appear in the SYS:SYS$LOG.ERR file. To clear events from this screen, press F2.

iPrint Makes Printing Almost iDiot-proof

What do users want? Easy computing. Ask them, and their answers wander all over the place, depending on their individual needs, but a good summation? Users want computers to work more easily.

Enter iPrint. The headline says it's "almost idiot-proof" so we don't run afoul of the old joke. You know, "every time we make something idiot-proof, they make a better idiot." Let's not tempt fate and call iPrint idiot proof. Let's just call it a serious advance toward simple printing for the users.

Printing problems rank number one or two at most help desks, jockeying for position with "I forgot my password." No matter which ranks number one at your site, printing problems make for support headaches. Using iPrint will cut down your Ibuprofen consumption by half, meaning you can buy the 250-count bottle rather than the 500 next time you're at the store.

Built on the IPP standard and the strong NDPS architecture, iPrint does a good job of hiding printing complexity from the users. What do users like to use for everything possible today? They like to use their Web browser. How do they like to install software today? Click a link inside their Web browser. Novell's iPrint does all this, and more, making your users happier and thereby retaining your grip on sanity a bit longer.

NDPS Support for IPP and iPrint

All the NDPS fun and games earlier provide the foundation for iPrint. After all, your handy Web browser diagrams must have some way to feed print drivers and printer information to and from the iPrint browser software, and NDPS provides the plumbing to make all that happen.

Although relatively successful, NDPS did not set the printer world on fire. Many companies built NDPS support for their printer line, as is the case with the Epson Stylus 900N I've used for demonstration. But many more companies and printer models ignored NDPS, waiting for a "real" standard to appear.

RFC 2911 came out in September 2000, and it solidified IPP with version 1.1. Critical decisions included using HTTP for IPP transport, rather than developing some type of printing-specific protocol for communication. Since HTTP support comes in everything from computers to PDAs to wristwatches to refrigerators (really), this decision makes IPP much more practical to implement. With the guidance in RFC 2911, printer manufacturers can build and implement IPP support across their product lines, knowing other IPP components will fit together. Sometimes, the pieces fit together easily, and sometimes they don't, but at least manufacturers have a way to coordinate products and eliminate problems with RFC 2911.

Enabling IPP in your NDPS setup becomes a critical point in linking NDPS and IPP to make iPrint. Enabling all your NDPS printers to support IPP greases the skids for iPrint, leading to easier user printing and fewer printing support calls. If you still have queue-based printers, you must go back to the NDPS section and convert them to NDPS printers to make iPrint work.

The first time a browser hits the iPrint server, the client gets checked for the iPrint client. If the user refuses to download and install the client, the iPrint software kicks out the browser (clever, right?).

NIPP.EXE, the 2.5MB iPrint client software, may be downloaded and run on the local hard disk, or installed directly from inside the Web browser. We'll see all this in the client section, but first, let's build an iPrint system for clients to use.

Setting Up Servers for iPrint

Configuring NDPS becomes the first task for iPrint setup. If you skipped the first section of this chapter hoping to avoid NDPS, you're out of luck. Go back and suffer like the rest of us.

Second, you must install the iPrint components on your server. Although tied into eDirectory for global reach, portions of NDPS and iPrint require specific server support. You should have installed iPrint automatically with the rest of NetWare 6. If you somehow expressly chose not to install iPrint, go back to the console GUI, run Install, and follow the installation drill.

All these pieces must be in place to support iPrint:

- NDPS Broker

- NDPS Print Service Manager

- NDPS Printer Object

- iManage browser-based management utility

Not only must these be in place, they must be functioning. Go back and clean up any NDPS messes you left, hoping you could ignore.

You can make the Print Service Manager more portable by giving it a name and entry in your DNS listings. If you call your manager NDPS-MGR.MyCompany.com, it matters little which server hosts the actual software server. When you migrate to a new server, a current DNS listing will enable you to move the NDPS Manager without needing to relabel all of your iPrint URLs.

At the NetWare 6 server console, use the NDPSM command with this format:

NDPSM *NDPS-Manager-Object-Name* /dnsname=*NDPS-Manager-Object-Name*

In our case, using the Epson Stylus 900N example, type:

NDPSM EPSON-MGR /dnsname=NDPS.MasteringNetWare.com

Verify that NDPS.MasteringNetWare.com correctly sits within the NetWare DNS/DHCP Services. Restart the NDPS Manager on the server console after the DNS listings have been made.

Putting Printers on the iPrint Map

Once users start using a Web browser, what do they want to do in every program? Follow hyperlinks to everything they need, that's what. Some users compulsively click on every underlined word, which is pretty silly when they're spell-checking a Word document. But you understand their hopes, right? See a printer, click the printer, and use the printer—that could be the new iPrint slogan. Of course, you need to make the map and build the references so the printers they see and click are real printers, which download drivers when necessary. With the help of iPrint and NDPS, you're halfway there already.

Your printers must be IPP-enabled. If you have NDPS configured already, just open NetWare Administrator, go to the IPP Client Support page for each printer, and click the Enable IPP Access to This Printer check box, as shown in Figure 6.25. Yes, ConsoleOne should have this option, but it doesn't yet. If you prefer using iManage, highlight the NDPS printer, click Manage Printer, then find the Enable IPP Access check box on the Client Support page of the printer information screens.

FIGURE 6.25

Setting IPP support for a printer

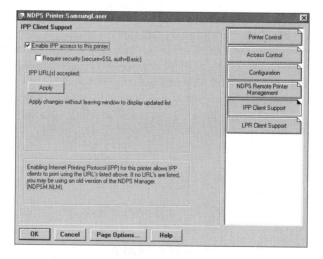

For security, check the Require Security box underneath the Enable IPP Access setting. With security, SSL transactions between a printer and the iPrint server keep the data stream encrypted, making it safe to connect to an iPrint printer over the Internet. The 443 port number, rather than the 631 port number, engages the SSL connection. Realize that SSL links take much more server overhead, so don't require them for internal printers.

Novell included multiple browser-based tools for setting up what they call "location-based" printing. That's just fancy developer talk for a map with printers flashing "you are here" at the appropriate places.

Still behind on the browser curve, NetWare 6 demands Microsoft IE 5.5 or later. Netscape bogs down, and I tried both Communicator 4.7 and 6.2. Oh well, at least they all work for clients, if not for creating the maps themselves.

Working locally, or at least on the same network as the NDPS host server, point your IE 5.5 or higher browser to a drive mapping to the following: SYS:\LOGIN\IPPDOCS\MAPTOOL.HTM. Two maps are included for samples, and I made a quick map using the first included file, OFFICE.GIF. See the results in Figure 6.26. Novell expects you to add in your own architectural drawings, and accepts images in JPEG, GIF, and BMP formats. If you don't have an electronic image already, scan some floor plans and get creative. It could be fun.

FIGURE 6.26

Mapping printers

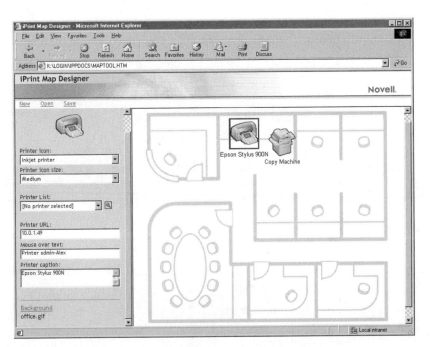

On the left menu frame, the first image is chosen by the menu choice in the Printer Icon dropdown list. The inkjet printer icon appears above the menu and in the map, because I needed to highlight the map icon to force the display of the last three items. But let's go in order through the menus:

Printer Icon Includes five choices: Laser Printer, Copy Machine, Inkjet Printer, Dot Matrix Printer, and Color Printer. You can see the inkjet printer and copy machine icons on the map in Figure 6.26.

Printer Icon Size   Offers five ranges, from smallest to largest, including smaller, medium, and larger between the end points. The icons in Figure 6.26 are medium size.

Printer List   Offers a way to type in official NDPS printer names in a text box that appears at the top of the page. If adding the printer doesn't work, you must go back and enable IPP for that printer.

Printer URL   Displays the URL created when the printer became IPP enabled. You shouldn't need to change this, but you can.

Mouse Over Text   Offers a nice way to include some information about the printer that pops up when a cursor slides over the icon. The default shows the Printer Agent's name, but listing something such as the printer administrator's name or special printer information works better for me.

Printer Caption   Allows you to type in text that appears directly on the printer map. In the example shown in Figure 6.26, I wrote the names of both items under their icons.

Background   Not a text box but a hyperlink, opens a dialog box showing the contents of the SYS:\LOGIN\IPPDOCS\IMAGES\MAPS directory. This directory, the logical location to put your own maps, includes two samples from Novell, and I chose the first sample, OFFICE.GIF. Check out the files hiding inside IPPDOCS and other directories in that area.

TIP   Keep an eye on Novell's download pages for new map tools.

Novell includes plenty of HTML help to design lists of printers rather than maps, a method happily used by about half of Novell's iPrint customers according to feedback. Multiple examples are included in NetWare 6. The browser plug-in API interface using HTML supports the following operations:

- Get client information (client version)
- Install printer
- Remove printer
- Get printer status
- Get printer details
- Pause/resume printer
- List/purge jobs
- Print test page
- Send printer-ready file
- Get job information
- Hold/release/cancel job

There's much more HTML coding in here than I can do, being programming-challenged, but others I know have jumped in and found the developing fine. Try it yourself if you're smarter with HTML coding than I am, or grab one of the Webmasters for an afternoon.

Letting Users Enjoy iPrint

None of this matters if the users don't find iPrint easier to use than anything else they've ever done with a printer. Not only will the users enjoy iPrint, they shouldn't need to make many decisions to install and get the iPrint party going.

There's no need to create fancy maps if you don't want to (or more likely, don't have time). When users attach to the iPrint server via http://*servername_or_address*:631/ipp, a defined list of all the printers will appear. They just need to click the printer they wish to use to install the drivers (if necessary) and start printing.

If the user hasn't downloaded the NetWare iPrint client, that user is once again politely offered the opportunity. NetWare is consistently polite and persistent.

Replacing Queue-based Printing: A Quick-and-Dirty NDPS Setup

Novell makes it nearly impossible to support traditional queue-based printing on NetWare 6. Why? Because iPrint holds so much promise, and it requires NDPS as a foundation. Smarter printers and a move away from departmental servers kept in the department rather than a central server room make NDPS a better choice in almost every instance. Most important, however, all the queue-based printing remains tied closely to IPX, Novell's proprietary protocol, which lost the battle to TCP/IP.

You may be thrilled to see, inside NetWare Administrator, that the Tools menu still includes Print Services Quick Setup (Non-NDPS). Your joy will sour quickly, as mine did, when you realize that queue-based printers demand IPX and your NetWare 6 server runs only IP. The Quick Setup remains on the menu because Novell hasn't upgraded NetWare Administrator, leading us down a blind printing alley.

I fought this for a time, and struggled to add IPX back into the NetWare 6 servers in my lab, but finally gave up. After considering installing a new server from scratch to add IPX during initial installation, I come to the conclusion that was far too much trouble just to support an old printing method. We fought bravely, but Novell won the battle by kicking all the IPX support out from underneath queue-based printing.

Face it, longtime NetWare users, queue-based printing now sits in the junk room, along with the 9-pin dot-matrix printers and your worn-out, original HP LaserJets you can't find parts to repair. Even if I tell you how to struggle and fight against NetWare 6 and setup queue-based printing once again, I won't be doing you any favors.

So take a moment of silence to reflect on the passing of a simple printing method from simpler times. Don't let anyone see you wipe the tear from your eye, or at least claim an allergy if they do. Then follow along with the steps presented here, where we cheat as much as possible to re-create a simpler time for printing.

We don't have much of a loophole, but we do have one. NDPS printers no longer support workstation-attached printers, but they do continue to honor the server-attached printer. Let me show you how to quickly re-create a queue-based printer using a server-attached NDPS printer. I'll even hook up a new, $200 laser printer from Samsung, using no NDPS gateway software or other tricks. Just a printer, a cable, and a server with a printer port can provide quick access to printing for your users.

Let's rip through this quickly, using default values every step of the way. Plenty of screen shots and no detailed explanations, coming right up. And let's skip all the new tools Novell provides. Everything we need is inside NetWare Administrator. ConsoleOne and iManage will be up to speed soon, but while we still have NetWare Administrator, let's take advantage of that and run through this.

Prepare by starting NetWare Administrator and a Remote Console (RConsoleJ, discussed in Chapter 8, "NetWare 6 Administrator Duties and Tools") session and going to the server that will have the printer attached. Figure 6.27 shows NetWare Administrator focused in on Test-1.LAB, where I'll use the Compaq-1500 server for the printer host.

FIGURE 6.27

Starting the speedy NDPS setup course

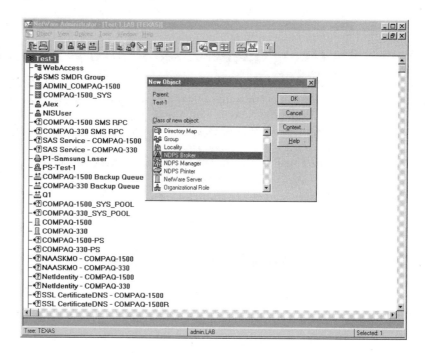

Then follow these steps:

1. Right-click the container to hold the NDPS print components, highlight NDPS Broker, and click OK.

2. Provide the NDPS Broker name (Samsung-Broker). Click the search button and select the volume to hold the NDPS components (COMPAQ-1500_SYS:Test-1.LAB). Do *not* change any of the check boxes from their defaults. Click the Create button to save the broker name.

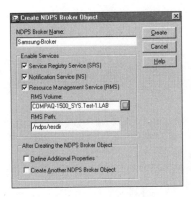

3. Right-click the container to hold the NDPS Manager (the same container as before) and click OK.

4. Provide the NDPS Manager name (Samsung-Mgr). Click the search button and select the Resident Server for the NDPS Manager (COMPAQ-1500). Click the search button and select the Database Volume to hold the NDPS Manager databases (COMPAQ-1500_SYS:Test-1.LAB). Do *not* change either of the check box defaults. Click Create to save the NDPS Manager.

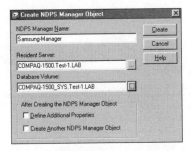

5. At the server console colon prompt, type **BROKER**. Locate the earlier-created broker, highlight the broker, and press Enter.

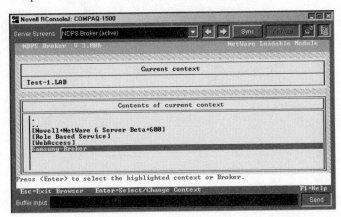

6. Wait and verify that the broker starts correctly. Notice the three entries on the Supported Services menu. They appear automatically, since we accepted the defaults.

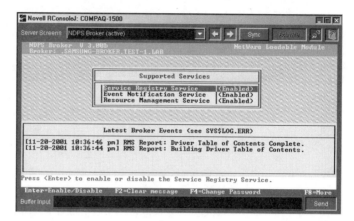

7. At the server console colon prompt, type **NDPSM** (NDPS Manager). Locate the earlier-created manager, highlight the manager, and press Enter.

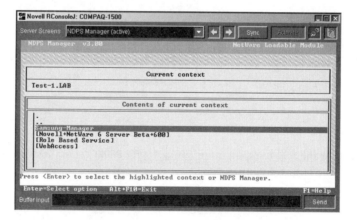

8. Wait and verify that the manager starts correctly. Now we need to create the printer that belongs on this screen.

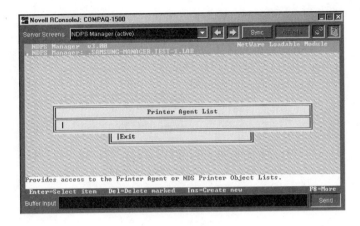

9. Right-click the container to hold the NDPS Printer object (the same container as before) and click OK.

10. Provide the NDPS printer name (Samsung-Laser), verify that the Create a New Printer Agent radio button is chosen (the default), and click Create to save the NDPS Printer object. If a warning comes up about reinstalling every client installation of this printer, click OK. If you don't see this warning, never mind.

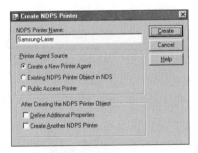

11. When the Create Printer Agent dialog box pops open, verify that the printer name is correct in the Printer Agent (PA) Name field. Click the search button and locate the NDPS Printer Manager name (Samsung-Manager). Highlight the NDPS Manager name and click OK. Inside the Gateway Types box, find and highlight Novell Printer Gateway, and then click OK.

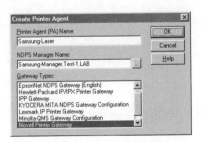

12. Next comes the Configure Novell PDS for Printer Agent dialog box. Inside the Printer Type box, highlight the appropriate printer type. If you can't find it, as I can't find Samsung ML 1210 in my list, highlight Generic PCL or another appropriate generic print controller language. Click OK to save the Printer Agent configuration.

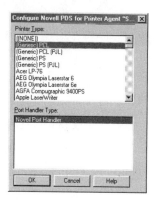

13. Inside the Configure Port Handler for Printer Agent dialog box, choose the proper Connection Type radio button. In my case, I chose Local (physical connection to the server). Choose the proper Port Type for your connection (LPT1 on the server for my system). Click the Next command button.

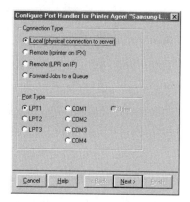

14. Choose the Controller Type (Auto Select, Compatible, or 1284 ECP). The default is Auto Select, which I chose. Choose the Interrupt setting. The default, None (polled mode) remains my choice. Click the Finish command button.

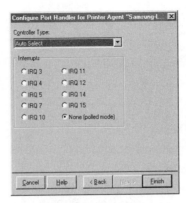

15. Next comes the painful part that I described earlier in the chapter—the printer drivers. Let's skip it. Verify each tab shows None under each Windows GUI type. Click Continue.

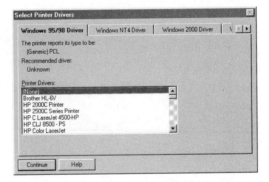

16. Verify the information ignoring all the NDPS help with printer drivers. Click the OK command button.

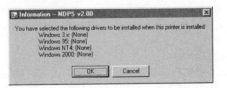

17. Look back at your server console screen, at the NDPS Manager screen. Notice that the printer Samsung-Laser went from blank to Idle while we were refusing to load drivers.

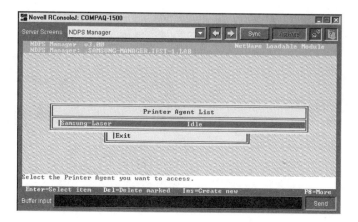

18. Press Enter while highlighting the new printer (Samsung-Laser) on the server console. The NDPS printer controls appear.

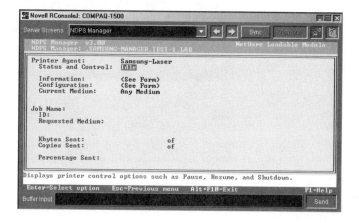

Thus ends the saga of the quick-and-dirty NDPS printer setup. You can add other printers, and you can get a bit fancier with printers (notice back in step 13 you can also have remote printers via IP and the like). Or you can just tell your users to pick the new printer when they need it.

Without the drivers in place for nonsupported printers (like my Samsung ML-2110), users will need to load their own drivers, just as they always did. This will be the case until you fight the battle to provide new drivers. But that's not what we're doing here, right now. We just put a printer together and are happy with our success.

It looks like a lot of steps when you see all the screen shots, but it's not that bad. The only things you need to know are the names you want to give the NDPS Broker, Manager, and Printer Agent, and the locations used to hold them. That sounds quick and dirty to me.

The good part I see in this? NDPS does seem faster than the old queue-based printing. Plus, when you search for printers through Windows Start ➤ Settings ➤ Printer, NDPS printers have their own heading, so you can find the printer you want a bit more quickly.

Potshots on Printing

The prognosticators lied to us all: The paperless office prediction is not only wrong, but more paper is sold today than ever before. You have as much chance of winning the lottery as your office does of going completely paperless in the next three years.

Should we say phooey and buy printers for everyone? No. Despite what people want, the time for information primarily stored on paper is past. You make your children eat vegetables when they don't want to, and you must gently but firmly push your network users into less paper dependency.

Don't be hard on your users when they complain, "My report doesn't look right. The graphic looked great on the screen, but the printed version stinks! Why don't we have color lasers for everybody?"

Why not blow your top the seventeenth time you hear that type of remark in one day? Because to most people, what the computer does is not real. Paper is real. Until information from the computer appears on paper, they are not sure if that information really exists.

Someday, when everyone is carrying their PDA that connects over a wireless network to the company Web server, holding every document in holographic storage cubes rather than paper, users will understand. But some of them will still print things when you're not looking.

NDPS offers some advantages over queue-based printing, but that doesn't matter because Novell made the choice for us. The good part is that NDPS sinks into foundation status, as users will see and use iPrint for most of their printing device interaction. Giving users browsers and hyperlinked printers to click and install will make their day easier and cut down on your support call volume. The best tech support phone is the one that rings the least, because that's the best support department. Making life easy for your users, in this case in their never-ending desire to smear ink on tree products, makes life easier for you.

Chapter 7

Securing Your NetWare 6 Network

SECURITY—WHAT DOES IT MEAN to you? Hackers sneaking in and deleting entire volumes? Illegal software on the system? What does security mean to your boss? Inventory asset tags on all the computers, so you know the location of every piece of hardware? Competitors tapping into your system and stealing the plans for the rollout of your new product line?

Security, like much of life, is a desirable abstract state sought through the use of material items. No two people think of the same thing when they hear the word *security*. Regardless of the situation, some people never feel secure. Other people may feel content and secure when actually their systems are vulnerable. The trick is to develop a sense of appropriate paranoia, without becoming obsessed.

In this chapter, we'll cover the following security issues:

◆ Planning security

◆ Understanding filesystem security

◆ Understanding NDS security

◆ Managing security with ConsoleOne

◆ Protecting your network from viruses

◆ NetWare 6 security improvements

Planning Security

Each company must make a decision about what security means and about the amount of effort that it will expend to reach a comfortable level of security. Securing your network, including all the physical and virtual items, will be expensive. This brings up another management decision point: How much security is enough?

Security: A Definition

How about a definition: "Security is an aspect of networking administration concerned with ensuring that the data, circuits, and equipment on a network are used only by authorized users and in authorized ways." This comes from the *Complete Encyclopedia of Networking* by Werner Feibel, published by Sybex (the folks who bring you this book).

Notice the order of items to be secured: data, circuits, equipment. Management often focuses security measures on physical items, such as computer hardware and telephone connections and modems. But if a computer is stolen, all that's necessary to replace that computer is money. Circuits must be protected from tampering and eavesdropping, and they must be available when needed.

If data is destroyed, years of work, effort, and thought are gone. Unfortunately, work, effort, and thought are not easily replaced.

Mr. Feibel suggests four threat areas to manage for your system security:

Threats to hardware   Theft, tampering, destruction, damage, unauthorized use, and ordinary equipment wear and tear.

Threats to software   Deletion, theft, corruption, and bugs.

Threats to information   Deletion, theft, loss, and corruption.

Threats to network operations   Interruption, interference, and overload.

Can you and your boss agree on these items? Do some of them seem outside the realm of security, such as ordinary equipment wear and tear? What about the threat of overload?

Some network managers think of security from a negative aspect only. Something is stolen or deleted. I don't believe that definition is wide enough to support the network needs of today.

Let's agree that system security means that the system is available to authorized users doing their job. Anything that interferes with this is a security problem. If a file server is stolen, people can't do their work. What if the file server is overloaded or erratic? Isn't the result the same? People can't do their work. What if the file server is safe and running well, but someone deletes (either accidentally or on purpose) some of the system files? The result is the same once again: people can't do their work.

Where Is Your Security Plan?

In 1988, the Internet Worm ran amok, clogging thousands of computers and data circuits for days. The Worm was not destructive but caused disruptions in computer services all across the Internet. Front-page stories were copied by paranoid managers and handed to network technicians with a question: "Where is our security plan?"

One of the responses of the Internet community to the Worm of 1988 was to establish CERT (Computer Emergency Response Team). This group responds to and helps resolve Internet security incidents. Part of the group's job is to help network administrators protect their systems against intruders before an attack is attempted.

The good news is that upgrading security takes surprisingly little work for most systems. Unfortunately, that's also the bad news. CERT estimates that 60 to 75 percent of network problems are caused by the following:

◆ Accounts with no passwords

◆ Poor passwords

◆ Unwatched guest accounts

◆ Poor user security management, especially giving users more rights than necessary

Are the listed problems familiar to you? Do you understand how easy these problems are to fix?

Before doing anything else, check the easy things. Many cars are stolen simply because the keys are left dangling from the ignition switch. Don't make things that easy in your network.

THE SITE SECURITY HANDBOOK

To help you devise your security plan, RFC 1244 was developed in 1991, then updated in 1997 by RFC 2196. Here is the opening:

```
Network Working Group                          B. Fraser
Request for Comments: 2196                        Editor
FYI: 8                                           SEI/CMU
Obsoletes: 1244                          September 1997
Category: Informational


                    Site Security Handbook


Status of this Memo

    This memo provides information for the Internet community. It does
    not specify an Internet standard of any kind. Distribution of this
    memo is unlimited.


Abstract

    This handbook is a guide to developing computer security policies and
    procedures for sites that have systems on the Internet. The purpose
    of this handbook is to provide practical guidance to administrators
    trying to secure their information and services. The subjects
    covered include policy content and formation, a broad range of
    technical system and network security topics, and security incident
    response.
```

continued on next page

THE SITE SECURITY HANDBOOK *(continued)*

As is the norm, the information in this RFC may be freely copied and distributed. I'll quote two small sections, skipping most of the valuable information in this handbook.

```
1.5  Basic Approach

     This guide is written to provide basic guidance in developing a
     security plan for your site. One generally accepted approach to
     follow is suggested by Fites, et. al. [Fites 1989] and includes the
     following steps:

     (1)  Identify what you are trying to protect.
     (2)  Determine what you are trying to protect it from.
     (3)  Determine how likely the threats are.
     (4)  Implement measures which will protect your assets in a cost-
          effective manner.
     (5)  Review the process continuously and make improvements each time
          a weakness is found.

     Most of this document is focused on item 4 above, but the other steps
     cannot be avoided if an effective plan is to be established at your
     site. One old truism in security is that the cost of protecting
     yourself against a threat should be less than the cost of recovering
     if the threat were to strike you. Cost in this context should be
     remembered to include losses expressed in real currency, reputation,
     trustworthiness, and other less obvious measures. Without reasonable
     knowledge of what you are protecting and what the likely threats are,
     following this rule could be difficult.
```

The last two sentences apply to everyone in the computer business but are difficult to quantify at times. You know what you have is valuable, but how valuable? How do you put a price on a database or spreadsheet templates or transaction history? Someone, preferably management, must assign some value to the information stored in your network. Quick estimate: How long will it take you to replace the database? (Multiply that by twice as long, then figure a high rate per hour, and you're on your way to setting a value.) You know what's coming from all this, don't you? Audit—inventory every server, workstation, network component, remote access device, wiring diagram, and each module of application and system software. Your manager will probably ask you to do this in your "spare" time. If you don't have a value assigned to what you're protecting, you don't know when the protection is more expensive than what's protected.

Another set of management decisions is described in this section:

```
2.2  What Makes a Good Security Policy?

     The characteristics of a good security policy are:

     (1)  It must be implementable through system administration
          procedures, publishing of acceptable use guidelines, or other
          appropriate methods.
```

continued on next page

THE SITE SECURITY HANDBOOK *(continued)*

(2) It must be enforcible with security tools, where appropriate, and with sanctions, where actual prevention is not technically feasible.

(3) It must clearly define the areas of responsibility for the users, administrators, and management.

The components of a good security policy include:

(1) Computer Technology Purchasing Guidelines which specify required, or preferred, security features. These should supplement existing purchasing policies and guidelines.

(2) A Privacy Policy which defines reasonable expectations of privacy regarding such issues as monitoring of electronic mail, logging of keystrokes, and access to users' files.

(3) An Access Policy which defines access rights and privileges to protect assets from loss or disclosure by specifying acceptable use guidelines for users, operations staff, and management. It should provide guidelines for external connections, data communications, connecting devices to a network, and adding new software to systems. It should also specify any required notification messages (e.g., connect messages should provide warnings about authorized usage and line monitoring, and not simply say "Welcome").

(4) An Accountability Policy which defines the responsibilities of users, operations staff, and management. It should specify an audit capability, and provide incident handling guidelines (i.e., what to do and who to contact if a possible intrusion is detected).

(5) An Authentication Policy which establishes trust through an effective password policy, and by setting guidelines for remote location authentication and the use of authentication devices (e.g., one-time passwords and the devices that generate them).

(6) An Availability statement which sets users' expectations for the availability of resources. It should address redundancy and recovery issues, as well as specify operating hours and maintenance down-time periods. It should also include contact information for reporting system and network failures.

(7) An Information Technology System & Network Maintenance Policy which describes how both internal and external maintenance people are allowed to handle and access technology. One important topic to be addressed here is whether remote maintenance is allowed and how such access is controlled. Another area for consideration here is outsourcing and how it is managed.

continued on next page

THE SITE SECURITY HANDBOOK *(continued)*

   (8) A Violations Reporting Policy that indicates which types of
        violations (e.g., privacy and security, internal and external)
        must be reported and to whom the reports are made. A non-
        threatening atmosphere and the possibility of anonymous
        reporting will result in a greater probability that a violation
        will be reported if it is detected.

   (9) Supporting Information which provides users, staff, and
        management with contact information for each type of policy
        violation; guidelines on how to handle outside queries about a
        security incident, or information which may be considered
        confidential or proprietary; and cross-references to security
        procedures and related information, such as company policies and
        governmental laws and regulations.

RFC 2196 may be retrieved from many places on the Internet. The source for these quotes, the IETF (Internet Engineering Task Force) archive, can be found at www.ietf.org/rfc.html.

Should I Be Concerned Since My NetWare Network Is Connected to the Internet?

Yes, of course you should worry. Bad things sometimes happen to networks connected to the Internet. But you shouldn't be overly paranoid.

Your boss, however, will be overly paranoid. That's because the nontechnical press latches onto every hacker story like a starving pooch on a pork chop. You and I know these stories are poorly researched and written by journalists who either don't understand computers or don't trust them, so we ignore most of them. Bosses can't ignore them because their bosses read the same articles in the same papers, and misinformed hysteria feeds upon nontechnical misunderstanding, and everyone gets all worked up.

Prepare yourself every time the *Wall Street Journal* or *New York Times* runs a computer hacker or system crash story—your boss will come and ask how nervous you are about the horrible state of Internet security. If you're of a certain type of mind, that is the time to increase your budget considerably under the guise of improving security. Even if you're not of that type of mind regularly, chances like that don't come around often, so you should take a shot and ask for enough money to get a new server, firewall, and/or software upgrade.

The truth is that connecting any part of your network to the Internet requires plenty of extra work, caution, and responsibility. You must keep the bad people out and keep the irresponsible people in.

THE INTERNET AND FIREWALLS

No intelligent network manager will connect to the Internet without some type of firewall in place to provide security. If your company already has an Internet connection and you are adding your own

NetWare network to the list of Internet-aware networks, a firewall is in place already. Talk to the network administrator in charge of your TCP/IP network, and get the details you need to feel good about network security.

Firewall is an unusually descriptive term, even for the term-spewing computer industry. In construction, a firewall stands against disasters by forming an impenetrable shield around the protected area (I got the impenetrable shield slogan from my deodorant). Most disasters in buildings revolve around fires; hence, the term firewall.

The goal of a firewall is simple: to control access to a protected network. Firewall managers use two philosophies during configuration:

◆ Allow everything except designated packets

◆ Block everything except designated packets

Today, the proper attitude is to block everything except designated packets. Novell's products come this way straight from the box. When you enable filtering, everything is blocked, and you must designate what is allowed to pass through the firewall and/or filtering software.

There are four types of firewalls. Table 7.1 shows each type of firewall matched up with where it functions in the OSI seven-layer model.

TABLE 7.1: MATCHING SECURITY FILTERS AND NETWORK LAYERS

OSI MODEL LAYER	INTERNET PROTOCOLS	FIREWALLS
Application	HTTP, FTP, DNS, NFS, Ping, SMTP, Telnet	Application-level gateway, stateful inspection firewall
Presentation		
Session	TCP	Circuit-level gateway
Transport	TCP	
Network	IP	Packet-filtering firewall
Data Link		
Physical		

Let's see what each of these firewalls can do for you:

Packet filters (FILTCFG)   The lowest level, packet filters, was once enough to protect your network, but that is no longer true. IP addresses are used to allow or deny packets, and IP address spoofing (disguised packets) has ruined the idea of this level of protection being enough to protect your network.

Circuit-level gateways   Circuit-level gateways do more to control internal traffic leaving your protected network than to keep outsiders at bay. Rules for users, such as allowable hosts to visit and time limits, are handled at this level.

Application-level gateways   Application-level gateways are specific to network services, such as FTP or e-mail. These are most common today with Web browsers, used by software meant to monitor or block Web access to certain sites.

Stateful inspection firewalls   Finally, the most critical area is the stateful inspection firewall, used by Novell and few others. This software examines incoming packets to match them to appropriate outgoing packets and is able to examine packet contents to maintain control. The more options you have, the better your security, and NetWare gives you plenty of options. Of course, you'll need more time to configure more settings, but NetWare utilities will help with that chore.

PROTECT YOUR CORPORATE NETWORK

If your network is the corporate network, check out Novell's BorderManager software. You aren't familiar with this product? It adds a complete security- and performance-enhancing software server to any NetWare 4, 5, or 6 server.

You can run both the NetWare 6 server and BorderManager on the same hardware. Larger networks will want to separate the BorderManager software on its own server for performance reasons. One BorderManager server protects your entire network when configured correctly. Feel free to look up my *IntranetWare BorderManager* book, also from Sybex, at your local bookstore or favorite online shopping destination.

Keeping Up with Security Threats

Can one person, namely you, keep up with all the network miscreants out there? No, but there are more people on your side than you might imagine.

Enlist the resources of your firewall vendor, whether Novell for BorderManager or another vendor. Keep up-to-date on all bug fixes, patches, and upgrades for your firewall software. Maintain proper security for the physical firewall system (lock it up in the server room or equivalent).

Also, watch the trade magazines and Web sites pertaining to security. Security information is all over the place if you keep your eyes open. Please don't be one of those who become paranoid *after* you get burned. Go ahead and start being paranoid, or at least well informed, before something serious happens to your network.

Here's a regularly repeated warning: *Watch your users carefully.* Some companies are using "internal" firewalls to keep employees out of sensitive areas. A serious security breach, where valuable information is stolen or compromised, almost always includes help from the inside. Every user is a potential thief. Always provide new services with tighter rather than looser security, and then loosen the leash as you and your management feel more comfortable with the security situation on your network. Most data thieves walk out rather than break in.

When the network is new, or a security problem has occurred, everyone is conscientious. After a time, however, human nature takes over and everyone gets sloppy.

Your network changes constantly, and each change is a potential security disaster. Add a new user? Did you take care to match the new user to an existing group with well-defined security and access controls? How about new files created by the users themselves? Do you have a plan for watching the access level of those files? Do users have the ability to allow other users access into a home directory? If so, no private file will be safe. Don't allow file sharing within each person's private directory. Send the file by e-mail or have a common directory in which users can place files to share. Do not allow them more file rights to the \PUBLIC directory, even though some will ask for it.

Watch new applications. Many vendors have modified NetWare rights for files and directories for years, especially during installation. Are these loopholes closed in the new application directories you created just last week? Take the time to check.

Passwords and Login Restrictions

In our discussion of user creation and setup, I spoke at length about the value of login and password security. Much of Chapter 4 concerns these very topics. Rather than repeat all that information here, I'll provide a quick synopsis. For more details, you can thumb back to Chapter 4 and review it with a new understanding of security.

PASSWORDS

Each user must have a password. Here are some tips for your passwords:

♦ The longer the password, the better. Novell's default minimum is five characters; try for six or lucky seven.

♦ Encourage the use of mixed alpha and numeric characters in the password.

♦ Set passwords to expire (the default is 40 days).

♦ Let the system keep track of passwords to force unique ones. The limit is 20.

♦ Limit the grace logins; two is enough.

LOGIN RESTRICTIONS

Using login restrictions, you can limit users' network access and track the resources they use. Here are some tips for setting login restrictions:

♦ Limit concurrent connections for all users.

♦ Set an account expiration date for all temporary workers.

♦ Disable accounts for users away from the office who don't communicate remotely to your network.

THE ADMIN USER, ADMIN RIGHTS, AND THE SUPERVISOR RIGHT

The only user created with NetWare 6 is named Admin, short for Administrator. If you just climbed up the version tree from NetWare 3.1x, don't bother looking for SUPERVISOR, because Admin replaced SUPERVISOR.

Make the mental note that the Admin user is separate from the Admin rights over the network operating system and included objects. As you'll see later, the more advanced management techniques that arrived with object management and the Admin user are a way to block this SUPERVISOR equivalent from managing parts of the network. Oops.

continued on next page

THE ADMIN USER, ADMIN RIGHTS, AND THE SUPERVISOR RIGHT *(continued)*

The Admin user is a supervisor's supervisor, able to control the network completely as the old SUPERVISOR did in earlier NetWare versions. The Supervisor right, however, may be granted to any user for particular NDS eDirectory objects or containers. Being able to set up subadministrators for specific tasks, as I have spoken of before, can be a great help.

This flexibility of supervision is an important feature of NetWare 6—one of the many features that place NetWare ahead of the competition. With global enterprise networking the norm for many companies today, the job of supervision is far beyond the abilities of any one person. NetWare 6 allows the supervision chores to be distributed in whatever method you prefer.

You can have different administrators for different parts of the tree, as well as different volumes, directories, or files. Admin may control the NDS design and overall setup but have no control over the files. Filesystem supervisors in each container will handle those chores. Admin in Chicago may share duties with Admin in Cleveland, with each responsible primarily for his or her own city but able to support the other network across the WAN if necessary.

Understanding Filesystem Security

There are two main security areas for NetWare 6: filesystem and NDS security. If you are familiar with NetWare 3.*x*, you will be familiar with filesystem security. NetWare 4.1*x* added some attributes to support data compression and data migration features and changed a bit of the terminology, but most of the details and the security goals remain the same, even in NetWare 6. The main goal is to provide users access to and control of the proper files and directories.

NetWare files are protected in two ways:

◆ Users must be granted the right to use files and directories.

◆ File and directory attributes provide hidden protection.

What is hidden protection? Suppose that Doug has the right to create and delete files in the \LETTERS directory. If he writes a letter named SLS_GOAL.OCT and decides he doesn't like that file, he can delete it. Files can be deleted from within applications or from the DOS prompt. He can use Windows Explorer.

What if Doug's mouse slips a fraction within Explorer, and he tries to delete the SLS_GOAL.PLN file, the template for all the sales goal letters? Is the file doomed?

Not necessarily. If the network administrator (probably you) has set the attribute to SLS_GOAL.PLN as Read Only or Delete Inhibit, Doug can't delete the file. However, if Doug also has the right to modify the file attributes (a bad idea, knowing Doug), he could change the Read Only or Delete Inhibit designation and delete the file anyway. But he would need to work at deleting the file; he couldn't do it by accident.

When granting Doug rights to use the \LETTERS directory, we call him a *trustee* of the directory, given to him by way of a *trustee assignment*. He has been trusted to use the directory and files properly. The trustee concept works with objects and NDS items, as we'll soon see.

Someone in authority must grant Doug, or a group or container Doug is a member of, the rights to use the file, directory, or object in question. The administrator is the person who places trust in Doug, making him a trustee of the rights of the object. This is referred to as making trustee assignments to a directory, file, or object. The trustee assignments are stored in the object's ACL (Access Control List) property inside NDS eDirectory.

The rights granted to users flow downhill (kind of like *stuff* on a bad day). This means that the rights Doug has in one directory apply to all subdirectories. This idea works well, and the official name is *inheritance*. If your system is set up with \LETTERS as the main directory, and Doug has rights to use that directory, he will automatically have the same rights in the \LETTERS\SALES and \LETTERS\PROSPECT subdirectories. He will inherit the same rights in \LETTERS\SALES as he has in \LETTERS.

One way to stop Doug from having full access to a subdirectory is to use the IRF (Inherited Rights Filter). The IRF filters the rights a user may have in subdirectories and will be covered later in this chapter. The other way is to explicitly make a new trustee assignment to this subdirectory. A new assignment always overrides the inherited settings.

NOTE *NetWare 3.x had Inherited Rights Masks (IRMs). NetWare 4.1 and later have Inherited Rights Filters (IRFs). The name has changed, but the actions are the same.*

[Public] is a special trustee, for use by all the users on the network, and can always be specified as a trustee of a file, directory, or object. Although it sounds similar to the group EVERYONE in earlier NetWare versions, containers act more like the EVERYONE group than [Public] does.

File and Directory Rights

The rights to use directories and files are similar, so we'll take a look at the directory situation first. Users' rights in dealing with files and directories are also similar, making explanations fairly simple.

DIRECTORY RIGHTS FOR USERS AND GROUPS

There are reasons to grant rights to directories rather than files, not the least of which is the timesavings. Even with wildcards available, I would rather set the rights of users to use a directory and all subdirectories than set their rights to the files in each directory.

What are these rights that users can have over a directory? And did that last sentence in the previous paragraph mean subdirectories? Yes it did. The directory rights available to users are summarized in Table 7.2.

TABLE 7.2: DIRECTORY RIGHTS IN NETWARE 6

RIGHT	DESCRIPTION
Supervisor (S)	Grants all rights to the directory, its files, and all subdirectories, overriding any restrictions placed on subdirectories or files with an IRF. Users with this right in a directory can grant other users Supervisor rights to the same directory, its files, and its subdirectories.
Read (R)	Allows the user to open and read the directory. Earlier NetWare versions needed an Open right; Read now includes Open.

continued on next page

TABLE 7.2: DIRECTORY RIGHTS IN NETWARE 6 *(continued)*

Write (W)	Allows the user to open and write files, but existing files are not displayed without Read authorization.
Create (C)	Allows the user to create directories and files. With Create authorization, a user can create a file and write data into the file (authority for Write is included with Create). Read and File Scan authority are not part of the Create right.
Modify (M)	Allows the user to change directory and file attributes, including the right to rename the directory, its files, and its subdirectories. Modify does not refer to the file contents.
File Scan (F)	Allows the user to see filenames in a directory listing. Without this right, the user will be told the directory is empty.
Access Control (A)	Allows the user to change directory trustee assignments and the IRFs for directories. This right should be granted to supervisory personnel only, because users with Access Control rights can grant all rights except Supervisor to another user, including rights the Access Control user doesn't have. The user can also modify file trustee assignments within the directory.

Let's see how these directory rights appear in ConsoleOne. Figure 7.1 shows the group Techies and the file and directory rights the members have. Why use ConsoleOne rather than NetWare Administrator? To get ready for the future, since ConsoleOne gets the Novell developer's attention today, while NetWare Administrator remains static. Like it or not, ConsoleOne is the future.

FIGURE 7.1

An example of the rights a group can have

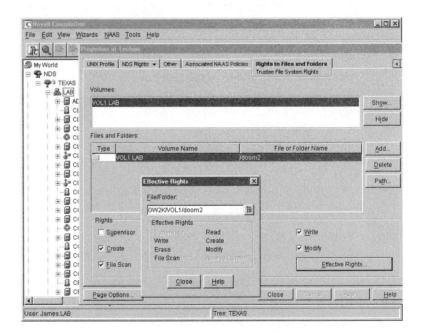

The Effective Rights dialog box in Figure 7.1 appears when you click the Effective Rights command button in the Rights to Files and Folders tab of the Techies property page. The odd arrangement here helps show all the pieces without blocking the parent window. Unlike NetWare Administrator, ConsoleOne requires you to drill down through the volume to the directory in the Select Object dialog box (not shown here).

The Supervisor and Access Control check boxes are clear in the Rights area. This means that the group Techies does not have those two rights. Giving a group of users (especially a group of techs) the Supervisor right could be dangerous. Giving a person or group the Access Control right is equally dangerous. With the Access Control right, the user or group member can change his or her own rights and add more rights without your knowledge or consent.

NOTE   *If you're just moving up from NetWare 3.x, you should be aware of a change to users' home directories rights: The home directories created during the initial user setup now have all rights, including Supervisor.*

These rights apply to the directory where they are granted and to all subdirectories. Rights are inherited from the top directory levels through all the existing subdirectory levels.

The rights are displayed (in DOS with the RIGHTS command) as a string of the initials within brackets: [SRWCEMFA]. If some are missing, a space is put in their place. For instance, the most rights nonadministrative users generally have are [_RWCEMF_]. As you can see, underscores were put in place of the S (Supervisor) and A (Access Control) rights. If the generic user listed previously didn't have the rights to Erase in a particular directory, the listing would appear as [_RWC_MF_].

FILE RIGHTS FOR USERS AND GROUPS

In contrast to directory rights, file rights address only specified files. Sometimes the files are identified individually, and sometimes they are specified by a wildcard group (*.EXE, for example). There are minor differences between how the rights are applied to a directory and to a file. Table 7.3 summarizes the file rights.

TABLE 7.3: FILE RIGHTS IN NETWARE 6

RIGHT	DESCRIPTION
Supervisor (S)	Grants all rights to the file, and users with this right may grant any file right to another user. This right also allows modification of all the rights in the file's IRF.
Read (R)	Allows the user to open and read the file.
Write (W)	Allows the user to open and write to the file.
Create (C)	Allows the user to create new files and salvage a file after it has been deleted. Perhaps the latter should be called the Re-create right.
Erase (E)	Allows the user to delete the file.
Modify (M)	Allows the user to modify the file attributes, including renaming the file. This does not apply to the contents of the file.
File Scan (F)	Allows the user to see the file when viewing the contents of the directory.
Access Control (A)	Allows the user to change the file's trustee assignments and IRF. Users with this right can grant any right (except Supervisor) for this file to any other user, including rights that they themselves have not been granted.

You might notice that the Create right is a bit different, and the Supervisor and Access Control rights apply to individual files. Why do we have the differences between directory and file rights?

THE IRF AND FILE AND DIRECTORY RIGHTS

Let's pretend that your filesystem is set up so that all the accounting data is parceled into subdirectories under the main \DATA directory in the volume ACCOUNTING. Many people on your network will need access to the information in these accounting files. Some will need to use the accounting programs, some will need to gather the information into reports, and others may need to write applications that use those data files.

Since directory rights flow downhill, this will be easy: Give the group ACCOUNTING rights to use the \DATA directory, and the information in \DATA\AR, \DATA\AP, \DATA\GL, and \DATA\PAYROLL is available to everyone. But suddenly your boss realizes that giving everyone rights to see the information in \DATA\PAYROLL is not smart (your boss must be slow, because salary information paranoia runs pretty high in most bosses).

This is what the IRF was made for. The IRF controls the rights passed between a higher-level directory and a lower-level directory. In our example, that would be \DATA to \DATA\PAYROLL. The IRF does not grant rights; it strictly revokes them. The IRF default is to let all rights flow down unless otherwise instructed.

Figure 7.2 shows a simple look at our example. Everyone has access to all directories except for \DATA\PAYROLL. The IRF is blocking the rights for everyone in that directory.

FIGURE 7.2

Keeping prying eyes out of PAYROLL

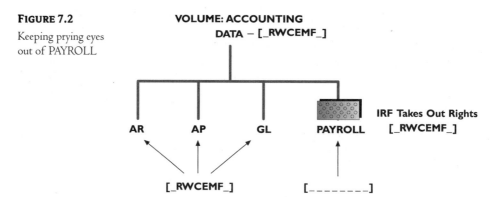

There's a problem here: How does anyone see the \DATA\PAYROLL directory? The network administrator must specifically grant rights to the \DATA\PAYROLL directory for those users who belong there. The IRF filters between the parent directory and subdirectory. It does not dictate the rights assigned specifically to the subdirectory.

When you type RIGHTS from the DOS command line, you see your rights in the current directory listed with an explanation. If you have all rights in a directory, such as your home directory, the RIGHTS command will show something like the display for user Alex in Figure 7.3.

NOTE *Like Figure 7.3's old screenshot using Novell DOS? Yes, they had it for a while until they sold it to Caldera—the Linux people.*

FIGURE 7.3

Results of the
RIGHTS command

```
[Novell DOS] I:\HOME\ALEX>rights
GATEWAY2000\PROJECTS:\HOME\ALEX
Your rights for this directory:  [SRWCEMFA]
   Supervisor rights to directory.         (S)
   Read from a file in a directory.        (R)
   Write to a file in a directory.         (W)
   Create subdirectories and files.        (C)
   Erase directory and files.              (E)
   Modify directory and files.             (M)
   Scan for files and directories.         (F)
   Change access control.                  (A)


[Novell DOS] I:\HOME\ALEX>
```

If you have no rights in a directory, such as if our friend Alex typed the RIGHTS command in the HOME directory above his own, the result would look something like this:

```
GATEWAY2000\PROJECTS:\HOME
Your rights for this directory: [  ]
```

You can approach the IRF in two ways: Ignore it and set up your filesystem so that inheritance is never a problem, or take a minute to figure out how it works. The problem with the first option is that reality always rises up and bites you when you try to ignore problems, such as the previous example with the \DATA\PAYROLL directory. Since inheritance is always going to be with us, and the IRF makes good sense in certain situations, let's look at another view of the IRF.

First, let's add a complication: group rights. Users can be assigned rights directly, or they can get them through group memberships. The individual and group rights are additive. If you have one right granted individually and another granted through group membership, you effectively have both rights.

The IRF works against both the individual and group rights. The results of the individual plus group rights minus those taken away by the IRF are called the effective rights. Figure 7.4 stacks up the individual and group rights, subtracts the IRF, and shows the effective rights.

FIGURE 7.4

Stacking and sub-
tracting rights

Individual Rights	[_RWCE_F_]	[_RWCEMFA]	[_RW_E_F_]
plus Group Rights +	[_____M_A]		[_R___MF_]
minus IRF −		[_____M_A]	[__W_EM__]
Effective Rights	[_RWCEMFA]	[_RWCE_F_]	[_R____F_]

Notice that the Supervisor (S) rights aren't mentioned anywhere. The IRF does not block the Supervisor rights, whether granted to the individual or a group. This is true only of the directory and file rights IRF. Later, you'll see that the object rights are a different story.

DIRECTORY AND FILE SECURITY GUIDELINES

No two networks are alike or use the same security profile. However, some general guidelines are applicable:

♦ Design your network top-down, from tighter security at the higher directories to looser security in the lower directories.

♦ Fight the urge to grant trustee rights to individuals. Always look for groups first, second, and third before you work with the individual user.

◆ Plan for inheritance. Grant Read and File Scan rights high, and Create, Erase, and Modify rights lower in the NDS eDirectory tree.

◆ Avoid granting any destructive rights high in the directory structure.

◆ Remember that the Supervisor right for the filesystem cannot be blocked by the IRF. Grant that right carefully, if at all.

File Attributes as a Security Enhancement

File attributes in NetWare, as in DOS, detail the characteristics of a file or directory. NetWare administrators often call these attributes *flags*. The NetWare DOS command-line utility FLAG.EXE displays and modifies these attributes.

Since we've decided that security includes making sure all network resources are available, the safety of files on the file server is important. Someone besides you deleting or renaming files is a security problem.

File and directory attributes are not a defense for cases of willful destruction and sabotage. They are a defense against mistakes and typos by innocent users. Haven't you ever had a user type DEL *.* in a directory on drive G: instead of drive C:? Having some of the files set as Read Only or Delete Inhibit may lessen the damage from a confused user.

Attributes control what can and can't be done with files and directories. They are also a limited form of virus protection. Since most viruses work by modifying executable files, keeping those executables Ro (Read Only) will stop viruses from trying to rewrite files and save them back with the same name.

WARNING   *Ro flags won't help with the new genre of Word macro viruses or with many of the other multitude of viruses out there. Flagging files Ro is never enough virus protection; it just helps a little.*

FILESYSTEM: DIRECTORY ATTRIBUTES

As is the case with much of NetWare, there are attributes for directories as well as files. Again, this makes sense. Unlike the rights to use an object, most directory rights don't directly affect the files in the directory. The attributes dealing with compression and data migration obviously do impact individual files. Since compression may be set by volume, the Immediate Compress attribute may be used more often than the Don't Compress attribute. Table 7.4 lists the directory attributes with their abbreviations and descriptions.

TABLE 7.4: DIRECTORY ATTRIBUTES IN NETWARE 6

ATTRIBUTE	DESCRIPTION
All (All)	Sets all available directory attributes.
Don't Compress (Dc)	Stops compression on any files in the directory. This overrides the compression setting for the volume.

contnued on next page

TABLE 7.4: DIRECTORY ATTRIBUTES IN NETWARE 6

ATTRIBUTE	DESCRIPTION
Delete Inhibit (Di)	Stops users from erasing the directory, even if the user has the Erase trustee right. This attribute can be reset by a user with the Modify right.
Don't Migrate (Dm)	Stops files within the directory from being migrated to secondary storage.
Hidden (H)	Hides directories from DOS DIR scans. NDIR will display these directories if the user has appropriate File Scan rights.
Immediate Compress (Ic)	Forces the filesystem to compress files as soon as the operating system can handle the action.
Normal (N)	Flags a directory as Read/Write and nonshareable. It removes most other flags. This is the standard setting for user directories on the server handling DOS programs.
Purge (P)	Forces NetWare to completely delete files as the user deletes them, rather than tracking the deletions for the SALVAGE command to use later.
Rename Inhibit (Ri)	Stops users from renaming directories, even those users who have been granted the Modify trustee right. However, if the user has the Modify trustee right, that user can remove this attribute from the directory and then rename the directory.
System (Sy)	Hides directories from DOS DIR scans and prevents them from being deleted or copied. The NDIR program will display these directories if the user has appropriate File Scan rights.

NOTE *The Don't Compress, Immediate Compress, and Don't Migrate attributes for files and directories were added when NetWare 4 introduced compression and advanced storage features.*

Most of these directory attributes are seldom used to protect a directory from confused users. The options you will probably use the most are those that concern the operating system, such as Don't Compress and Immediate Compress. The Normal attribute will be used most often, if your network follows true to form.

FILESYSTEM: FILE ATTRIBUTES

Most flagging happens at the file level and doesn't get changed all that often. After all, once you set the files in a directory the way you want (all the .EXE and .COM files Read Only and Shareable, for instance), few occasions require you to change them.

The time to worry about file attributes is during and immediately after installation of a new software product. Many product vendors today advertise, "Yes, it runs with NetWare," and they normally set the flags for you during installation. However, it's good practice to check newly installed applications, just in case the developers forgot to set a flag or three. The available file attributes are listed in Table 7.5, with their abbreviations and meanings.

TABLE 7.5: FILE ATTRIBUTES IN NETWARE 6

ATTRIBUTE	DESCRIPTION
All (All)	Sets all available file attributes.
Archive Needed (A)	DOS's Archive bit that identifies files modified after the last backup. NetWare assigns this bit automatically.
Copy Inhibit (Ci)	Prevents Macintosh clients from copying the file, even those clients with Read and File Scan trustee rights. This attribute can be changed by users with the Modify right.
Don't Compress (Dc)	Prevents the file from being compressed. This attribute overrides settings for automatic compression of files.
Delete Inhibit (Di)	Prevents clients from deleting the file, even those clients with the Erase trustee right. This attribute can be changed by users with the Modify right.
Don't Migrate (Dm)	Prevents files from being migrated from the server's hard disk to another storage medium.
Hidden (H)	Hides files from the DOS DIR command. The NDIR program will display these files if the user has appropriate File Scan rights.
Immediate Compress (Ic)	Forces files to be compressed as soon as the file is closed.
Normal (N)	Shorthand for Read/Write, since there is no N attribute bit for file attributes. This is the default setting for files.
Purge (P)	Forces NetWare to automatically purge the file after it has been deleted.
Rename Inhibit (Ri)	Prevents the filename from being modified. Users with the Modify trustee right may change this attribute and then rename the file.
Read Only (Ro)	Prevents a file from being modified. This attribute automatically sets Delete Inhibit and Rename Inhibit. It's extremely useful for keeping .COM and .EXE files from being deleted by users, and it helps stop a virus from mutating the file.
Read Write (Rw)	The default attribute for all files. Allows users to read and write to the file.
Shareable (Sh)	Allows more than one user to access a file simultaneously. Normally used with the Read Only attribute so that a file being used by multiple users cannot be modified. All the utility files in the \PUBLIC directory are flagged Sh (and Ro, Di, and Ri).
System File (Sy)	Prevents a file from being deleted or copied and hides it from the DOS DIR command. NetWare's NDIR program will display these directories as System if the user has appropriate File Scan rights.
Transactional (T)	Forces the file to be tracked and protected by the Transaction Tracking System (TTS).

File attributes are normally assigned to the files using a wildcard with the FLAG command, as in this example:

```
FLAG *.EXE RO Sh
```

This command says, "Change the file attributes of all files with the .EXE extension to be readable, but not writable, and to share the file by allowing multiple clients to use the program file concurrently."

TIP   *When a user has a problem with a file, the first two things to check are the user's rights in that directory and the flags set on the problem file. One of these two settings, mismatched in some way, accounts for 80 percent or more of user file problems.*

Let's look at how to type an exploratory FLAG command and examine the results. Figure 7.5 shows the command and result.

FIGURE 7.5

Checking the FLAG setting in the \PUBLIC directory

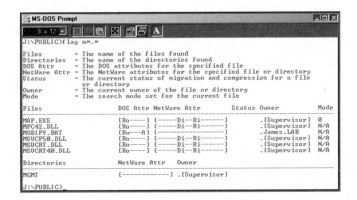

In this example, we can see the file attributes for a few of the NetWare utility files. Most are Ro (Read Only), meaning they also have the NetWare attributes of Di (Delete Inhibit) and Ri (Rename Inhibit) set as well. Looking at the second set of attributes, you see this is true.

The MODIFY.BAT was created by me (James). You can tell because the flag is set to Rw (Read Write) and the Archive attribute is set, meaning the file changed since the last backup. The rest of the files in the example are owned by the Supervisor. The ownership for these files was set during installation.

To check for all the various FLAG command-line switches, from the DOS command line, type:

```
FLAG /? ALL
```

You'll see six screens' worth of information.

NOTE   *Don't think that FLAG is the only way to change file attributes. The FILER, ConsoleOne, and NetWare Administrator utilities allow these same functions, just not as quickly and easily (in my opinion).*

ConsoleOne's new beefy manifestation, like the weakling working out after being embarrassed, impresses me with its progress. Early versions of ConsoleOne couldn't get to the file level, but Novell engineers whipped that problem in NetWare 5.1. See Figure 7.6 for ConsoleOne's new file-control features.

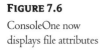

FIGURE 7.6

ConsoleOne now
displays file attributes

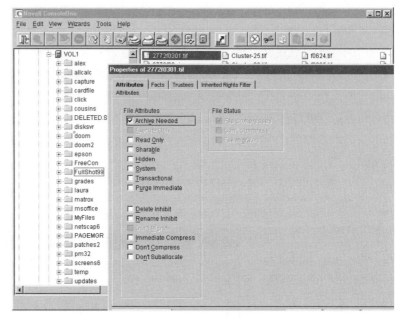

Notice the strange icons on the ConsoleOne toolbar? The red X means delete, the scissors mean cut, the pages mean copy, and the A with a strikeout and the B means rename. Not the best iconography for rename, I grant you, but new and impressive overall.

Understanding NDS Security

Since NDS was new to NetWare 4, the idea of NDS security was new to old NetWare hands at the time, and it may still be new to those just jumping up from good old NetWare 3. NDS security is concerned with the management and protection of the NDS database and its objects.

The SUPERVISOR user in NetWare 3 was concerned about both file security (as we just discussed) and network resources security. The second part of the job included creating and managing users, setting network access privileges for all network users, and creating and managing network resources, such as printers and volumes.

The Admin user has, by default, all the rights and power of the SUPERVISOR user. In NetWare 6, however, the management can easily be split between NDS security and filesystem security. It's entirely possible to have one administrator with no control over file and user trustee rights and another administrator with no control over containers, Organizations, or Organizational Units. You can also set up sub-administrators with complete control over their containers, having both file and property rights.

Let's be quite clear about this: filesystem and NDS security systems are (almost) completely separate from each other (the Supervisor right crosses the line). Just as filesystem security controls which users can control which files, NDS security controls the same functions for the NDS objects. Having the rights to control a container gives you no authority over a file kept on a volume in that container, unless rights are granted to that volume. The two security systems are not in any way related. Let me repeat: Having control over the NDS attributes of an object (let's say a disk volume) does not grant the rights to the files contained in that volume.

The NDS database allows multiple management layers. You can create as many Organizations and Organizational Units as you want, nesting the Organizational Units as many levels as you want. As you'll see when I talk about how the IRF works on object and property rights, it's possible for the Admin of a network to have full control over the Organization and the first Organizational Unit, but no control over the final Organizational Unit. Make sure this is what you have in mind before setting up such a system, however. If you can't trust your Admin with access to everything, you have more problems than can be solved by NetWare.

Object Rights versus Property Rights

There are two types of rights in NDS: object rights and property rights. *Object rights* determine what a trustee (user with the proper rights) can do to an object, such as creating, deleting, or renaming the object. *Property rights* determine whether a trustee can examine, use, or change the values of the various properties of an object.

Only in one case does an object right intrude into the property rights arena: the Supervisor right. A trustee with the Supervisor right to an object also has full rights to all properties of that object. But unlike with file and directory rights, the Supervisor right can be blocked on object and property rights by the IRF.

The opposite of the Supervisor right is the Browse right. This is the default right for users in the network. It allows users to see, but not modify, objects in the NDS eDirectory tree.

Object rights concern the object as a whole in the Browser. Actions taken on an object in the Browser, such as moving a User object from one context to another, exemplify object rights.

Property rights concern the values of all the properties of an object. The User object that was moved in the last paragraph has hundreds of properties. The ability to change a property value, such as Minimum Account Balance or Telephone Number, requires property rights.

Objects have inheritance rights, meaning a trustee of one object has the same rights over a subsidiary object. If a trustee has rights over one container, that trustee has the same rights over any container objects inside the main container.

Let's play "Pick Your Analogy." Object rights are like moving boxes, and the box contents are properties. The movers have authority over the boxes (object rights) but not over the contents of the boxes (property rights). A mover supervisor, however, has the rights to the boxes and to the contents (property rights) of those boxes for management situations.

When you turn your car over to a parking lot attendant, you give that attendant object rights: Your car can be placed anywhere in the parking lot. The attendant has full control over where your car is and if it needs to be moved while you're gone. You probably exclude the Delete right from the attendant, however. The property rights to your car, such as the items in your trunk, glove compartment, and backseat, do not belong to the parking lot attendant. You have granted the attendant some object rights to your car, but no property rights. Do you think armored car drivers have object rights or property rights to the money bags? Which would you prefer if you were a driver? Which if you owned the bag contents?

To keep things consistent, object rights and property rights overlap only in the Supervisor right. The trick is to remember that sometimes a C means Create and sometimes it means Compare. Take a look at the official list of object rights in Table 7.6.

TABLE 7.6: OBJECT RIGHTS IN NETWARE 6

RIGHT	DESCRIPTION
Supervisor (S)	Grants all access privileges, including unrestricted access to all properties. The Supervisor right can be blocked by an IRF, unlike with file and directory rights.
Browse (B)	Grants the right to see this object in the eDirectory tree. The name of the object is returned when a search is made, if the search criteria match the object.
Create (C)	Grants the right to create a new object below this object in the eDirectory tree. No rights are defined for the new object. This right applies only to container objects, because only container objects can have subordinates.
Delete (D)	Grants the right to delete the object from the eDirectory tree. Objects that have subordinates can't be deleted unless the subordinates are deleted first, just like a DOS directory can't be deleted if it still contains files or subdirectories.
Rename (R)	Grants the right to change the name of the object. This officially modifies the Name property of the object, changing the object's complete name.

The object rights tend to be used by managers, not by users. Create, Delete, and Rename rights are not the type of things normally given to users. The Browse object right is granted automatically to [Root], meaning everyone can browse the NDS eDirectory tree. Remember that the Supervisor object right automatically allows full access to all property rights. The property rights are listed in Table 7.7.

TABLE 7.7: PROPERTY RIGHTS IN NETWARE 6

RIGHT	DESCRIPTION
Supervisor (S)	Grants all rights to the property. The Supervisor right can be blocked by an IRF, unlike with file and directory rights.
Compare (C)	Grants the right to compare any value with a value of the property for search purposes. With the Compare right, a search operation can return True or False, but you can't see the value of the property. The Read right includes the Compare right.
Read (R)	Grants the right to read all the values of the property. Compare is a subset of Read. If the Read right is given, Compare operations are also allowed.
Write (W)	Grants the right to add, change, or remove any values of the property. Write also includes the Add or Delete Self right.
Add or Delete Self (A)	Grants a trustee the right to add or remove itself as a value of the property, but no other values of the property may be changed. This right is meaningful only for properties that contain object names as values, such as group membership lists or mailing lists. The Write right includes the Add or Delete Self right.

The Access Control List (ACL)

The ACL is the object property that stores the information about who may access the object. Just as Joe is a value of the Name property, the ACL contains trustee assignments for both object and property rights. The ACL also includes the IRF.

To change the ACL, you must have a property right that allows you to modify that ACL value for that object. Write will allow this, as will the Supervisor object right. Add or Delete Self is for users to add or remove themselves from a Members List property of a Group object.

Do you want to grant object or property rights to another object? You must have the Write, Add or Delete Self, or Supervisor right to the ACL property of the object in question.

Although it sounds as if the ACL is some list somewhere, it's really just one of many properties held by an object. Each object has an ACL. If a user is not listed in the ACL for an object, that user cannot change the properties of that object.

How Rights Inheritance Works

As I said before, rights flow downhill (ask a plumber what else flows downhill). Directory rights pass down to subdirectories, and container rights flow down to subcontainers. The only way to stop rights from flowing to a subcontainer is to use the IRF in the subcontainer. This forces users with rights to the parent container to also get the trustee rights to the subcontainer in a separate operation. That means the network supervisor (probably you) must go back and grant trustee rights to those users who need access to the subcontainer.

The system works well, with one exception: Selected property rights are not inherited. If a user is granted trustee rights to an object for selected property rights only, those rights do not move down to the subcontainer or other objects. Figure 7.7 shows an example of the process of granting a user selected property rights.

FIGURE 7.7

Granting limited rights that cannot be inherited

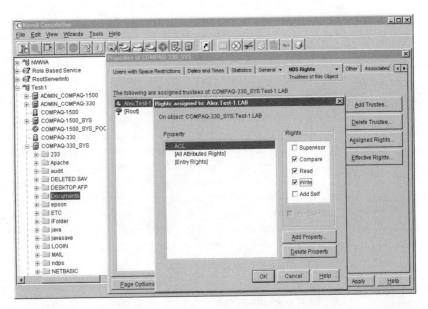

Selected property rights always take precedence over inherited rights. Even without an IRF, setting particular trustee rights in one container puts those rights in effect, no matter which rights are assigned to the container above. ConsoleOne shows these rights assignments in a different way than we're used to, but you can see in Figure 7.7 that we just added property rights to the ACL property for the Documents volume for Alex. I clicked the Add Property button in the foreground dialog box to pop up the long list of rights to choose for Alex.

The IRF and Object and Property Rights

The IRF works the same with object and property rights as it does with file and directory rights. The IRF doesn't give rights to anyone; it only takes rights away.

You, as network manager, set the level of rights users should have to an object. If a particular user has more rights than that, the IRF will filter that particular user to the level of access you set.

The big difference in the IRF when dealing with the NDS object and property rights is the ability to block the Supervisor object right. This gives some departments a warm fuzzy feeling, since no one except their administrator can control their part of the eDirectory tree. But care must be taken in organizing your system.

NetWare helps safeguard against accidentally eliminating all supervision for part of your tree by not allowing you to block the Supervisor object right to an object unless at least one other object has already been granted the Supervisor right to that object. The problem comes if the other Supervisor object is deleted. Deleting the sole Supervisor for part of your NDS eDirectory tree leaves part of the system without management, which is not a good thing.

This is a good reason to never delete the Admin user, even if you have one or two Admin-equivalent users. Over time, something will happen to both equivalent users, and suddenly your network will not have anyone able to perform supervisory functions over the entire tree. Some paranoid people have both Admin-equivalent users and users not set as Admin-equivalent but granted the full set of rights. Why? If Admin is deleted or the properties are garbled, the Admin equivalency may be worthless as well.

So, when you grant someone the Supervisor trustee right to a section of the eDirectory tree, also grant them all other trustee rights. This precaution allows that person to maintain the ability to create, delete, rename, and modify objects, even if the Supervisor right is blocked by the IRF.

NDS Security Guidelines

Security management is not the most exciting stuff in the world, 99 percent of the time. The goal of this section is to help you ensure that the one percent of security management that is exciting—a security breach—happens only in the mildest way possible. Maybe only a bad joke breach.

Realize that few users need to create, delete, or modify objects (users, printers, and so on) during their normal workday. Those users who have occasion to need these trustee rights should be made an official or unofficial helper. The designation of "Power User for Marketing" will help that person feel better about spending extra time helping other users without getting paid for it. At least recognize those power users, since recognized helpers will help keep security strong, not tear it down. The big problems come when someone accidentally gets too many rights, not when the department's power user has defined a new printer.

A CNI (Certified NetWare Instructor) friend of mine offers these guidelines for granting rights:

◆ Start with the default assignments. Defaults are in place to give users access to the resources they need without giving them access to resources or information they do not need.

◆ Avoid assigning rights through the All Properties option. Avoiding All Properties will protect private information about users and other resources on the network.

◆ Use Selected Properties to assign property rights. This will allow you to assign more specific rights and avoid future security problems.

◆ Use caution when assigning the Write property right to the ACL property of any object. This right effectively gives the trustee the ability to grant anyone, including himself or herself, all rights, including the Supervisor right. This is another reason to use extreme care when making rights assignments with All Properties.

◆ Use caution when granting the Supervisor object right to a Server object. This gives Supervisor filesystem rights to all volumes linked to that server. This object rights assignment should be made only after considering the implication of a network administrator having access to all files on all volumes linked to a particular server. Furthermore, granting the Write property right to the ACL property of the Server object will also give Supervisor filesystem rights to all volumes linked to that particular server.

◆ Granting the Supervisor object right implies granting the Supervisor right to all properties. For some container administrators, you might want to grant all object rights except the Supervisor right and then grant property rights through the Selected Properties option.

◆ Use caution when filtering Supervisor rights with an IRF. For example, a container administrator uses an IRF to filter the network administrator's rights to a particular branch of the NDS eDirectory tree. If the network administrator (who has the Supervisor right to the container administrator's User object) deletes the User object of the container administrator, that particular branch of the NDS eDirectory tree can no longer be managed.

Here's my security slogan: Grant to containers or groups; ignore the individuals. The more individual users you administer, the more time and trouble it will take. I've known some NetWare managers to make groups holding only one person. That sounds stupid, but consider the alternative: When a second person comes, and then a third person, you'll find yourself handling each one by hand. If a group is in place, each new person who arrives takes only a few seconds to install and give all the necessary trustee rights and network resource mappings.

Whenever possible, handle security (access to network resources) through the container. If not a container, then a group. If not a group, look harder to make the need fit an existing group or develop a new group. The more adamant you are about securing your network by groups rather than by individual users, the lighter your network management burden. The more you use the container to grant rights, the neater things are.

Managing Security with ConsoleOne

When NDS first installs, there are two objects: Admin and [Public]. By default, the Admin object has Supervisor object rights to [Root], which allows Admin to create and administer all other network objects.

The [Public] object has the following object and property rights by default:

◆ Browse object rights to [Root], which allows all users to see the NDS eDirectory tree and all objects on the tree

♦ Read property right to the Default Server property, which determines the default server for the User object

When you create User objects, each has a certain set of default rights. These rights include what the User object can do to manage itself, such as Read and Write the user's login script and print job configuration. To get around in the eDirectory tree, users are also granted limited rights to [Root] and [Public]. Here's a summary of the default User object trustee, default rights, and what these rights allow a user to do:

♦ Read right to all property rights, which allows the reading of properties stored in the User object.

♦ Read and Write property rights to the user's own Login Script property, which allows users to execute and modify their own login scripts.

♦ Read and Write property rights to the user's own Print Configuration property, which allows users to create print jobs and send them to the printer.

The [Root] object has one default property right: the Read property right to Network Address and Group Membership, which identifies the network address and any group memberships.

As you can see, the default NDS rights are fairly limited. A new user can see the network, change his or her own login script and printer configuration, and wait for help.

If that's too much—perhaps you don't want users to have the ability to change (and mess up) their own login scripts—change it. Merely revoke the User object's Login Script property right. Figure 7.8 shows the User object details, with the Write capability for the Login Script property revoked. The Read capability is necessary so that the user can log in.

FIGURE 7.8

Preventing Laura from changing her login script

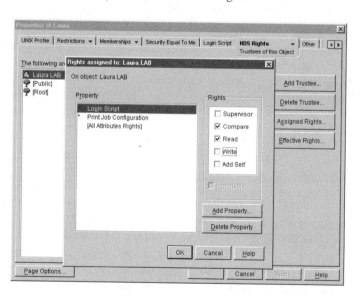

Revoking a Property Right

IN A HURRY 7.1: PREVENT USERS FROM MODIFYING THEIR OWN LOGIN SCRIPTS

1. Open ConsoleOne from some Java Virtual Machine–enabled system.

2. Open the user's property page by right-clicking the User object name and selecting Properties.

3. Click the NDS Rights tab and choose Trustees of This Object.

4. Highlight the User object and click the Assigned Rights button.

5. Click the property to modify (you may need to click the Add Property button).

6. Clear the Write check box while Login Script is highlighted.

7. Click OK to save the information.

Think of this process as a prelude to the other security-management tasks we're going to do in the following sections. First, you must start ConsoleOne from some Java Virtual Machine (JVM)–enabled system and highlight the User object that you want to modify. You must either right-click and choose Properties or use the File ➢ Properties menu choice.

When we get to the property page for the User object (as you can see in Figure 7.8 in the previous section), we want to change the Property Rights setting. It may sound odd, or at least different, but with ConsoleOne, we need to check the Trustees of This Object right under NDS Rights. Drill down to Laura.LAB.TEXAS. Then click the Assigned Rights command button, which opens the Rights Assigned To dialog box. Scroll through the list, find Login Script, highlight it, and review the rights.

The default is to have both Read and Write capabilities. By clicking the Write check box, that right is cleared from our user. The change will become active after the dialog box is saved with the new setting and the NDS database has a second to digest the change.

In Figure 7.8, I also opened the Rights Assigned to: Laura.LAB dialog box by clicking the Effective Rights button from the NDS Rights page. When I highlighted Login Script, the rights for user Laura to her own login script were shown: Compare and Read appeared in the Rights box. So now we know user Laura has the capability to read, and therefore execute, the login script, but not to change it.

TIP The other way to prevent users from playing with their login scripts is to bypass them entirely. Remember the sequence of login script execution? The User object's login script comes last. Just use the EXIT command in the container login script, and the personal login script for everyone in the container will be bypassed. Users can then make all the changes they want in their login scripts, but it won't make a bit of difference.

Setting or Modifying Directory and File Rights

You can allow a user or group of users access to a directory in two ways:

◆ You can go through the user side and use the rights-to-files-and-directories approach.

◆ You can go to the directory to be accessed and use the trustees-of-this-directory angle.

Which method you use depends on whether you're making one directory available to many users or granting trustee rights to one set of users to a lot of other network objects. We'll take a look at both approaches.

FROM THE GROUP OR USER'S POINT OF VIEW

IN A HURRY 7.2: GRANT TRUSTEE RIGHTS TO A VOLUME OR DIRECTORY

1. Open ConsoleOne.

2. Drill down in the left window to the Organizational Unit that contains the Group or User object.

3. Right-click the Group or User object and choose Properties.

4. Click the Rights to Files and Folders tab.

5. Click the Show command button and choose the correct volume in the Select Object dialog box.

6. Click the Add command button, and drill down to the correct directory or file.

7. Check the boxes near the rights you wish to grant.

8. Click the OK command button, or click the Apply button if you have more changes to make.

You can easily grant trustee rights for a single object to multiple volumes, directories, or files. The object gaining the rights should be a group of some kind, such as an Organization, an Organizational Unit, or a Group object, but it works for single User objects as well.

Start ConsoleOne as either the Admin user or another user with the Supervisor right to both the user side and the network resource side of this equation. Drill down until the group appears on the right side of ConsoleOne. We'll work with our Techies group in this example. Right-click that group, choose Properties, click the Rights to Files and Folders tab, and you'll see most of what appears in Figure 7.9.

First, click the Show command button to find and select the correct volume (COMPAQ-330_SYS: in this case). Then click the Add command button, select down to the directory level, and choose the Apache directory. Techs demand access to Web pages and source code, so let them have it.

Notice that all rights are being granted to Techies. If you don't give them all rights, they'll just whine and complain until you change your mind and upgrade their rights. Give them all rights the first time, then let them worry about what happens if they screw up. They're programmers, so if they do screw up, they'll never admit a thing. That's what I'm doing in Figure 7.9—giving them all rights to the Apache directory.

Unlike in NetWare Administrator or other Windows utilities, ConsoleOne won't allow you to select multiple files or directories on the Rights to Files and Folders tab of the group's property page. You could use another utility, but I would rather you take the hint: Don't change one file at a time, but focus on the directory.

The default rights to any new volume, directory, or file are Read and File Scan. Figure 7.10 shows that this is the case for the Techies group's effective rights to the Documents directory.

FIGURE 7.9

Granting Techies access to the Apache directory

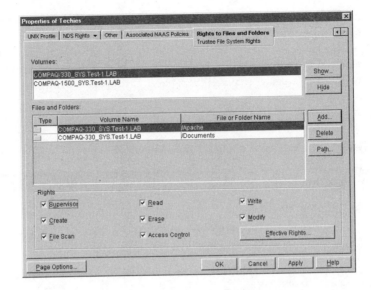

FIGURE 7.10

Granted rights are bold; excluded rights are gray.

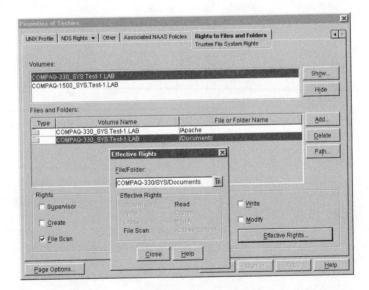

Contrast the limited array of rights (the default rights) in Figure 7.10 to the full platter of rights available in Figure 7.9. While we all agree Techies can make good use of their full access to the Web server directory, giving them access to corporate documents may prove less useful. This is why they have almost no rights to the Documents folder. Trust me, writers hate to let techs attempt to write or edit their work.

Granting rights to a directory in another container is not a problem, but one more step may be needed. If the users want to map a drive to another container in their login script, they can't get there from here. You must create an Alias object for the remote volume and then map the groups and users to the Alias. We'll get to that in the management chapter coming right up (Chapter 8).

You can grant trustee rights to a Volume object rather than to a directory or file. If you do, the object with those rights has complete access to the root directory, meaning the entire volume. If you have enough volumes to parcel them out in that manner, that's great, but many networks grant rights to a directory. That allows plenty of accessibility for the users, since they can build a full directory structure, while still maintaining an easy method of control.

FROM THE DIRECTORY OR FILE'S POINT OF VIEW

IN A HURRY 7.3: GRANT TRUSTEE RIGHTS TO A GROUP OR USER

1. Open ConsoleOne.

2. Drill down to the volume or directory desired.

3. Right-click the directory or file and choose Properties.

4. Click the Trustees tab to check current trustees. Click the Add Trustee command button to add another trustee.

5. Drill down to the object to become a trustee of the directory.

6. Highlight the groups and/or users in the Select Objects dialog box and click OK.

7. To modify the rights, check or clear the check boxes in the Rights section. Repeat as necessary for each group or user.

8. Click OK to save the settings.

Approaching rights from the directory's (or file's) point of view is the best method to use when granting several users or groups trustee rights to the same volume, directory, or file. One screen allows you to choose multiple trustees at once and yet assign different rights to each of them. Although this technique can work with volumes and files, let's use a common scenario: making a group of users trustees to a directory.

Start the ConsoleOne program. Browse through the NDS eDirectory tree as necessary to locate and highlight the object that you want to make available to the new user or users. In our example, the Documents directory is the one to be shared with Sandi and now the Writers Organizational Unit (yes, an OU can have trustee rights, as we discussed earlier).

Once the volume is highlighted in the left pane, the directories will appear in the right pane. Pressing Enter will display the directories in the left pane, leaving the right pane still empty. Right-click the directory name (in either pane you prefer) and choose Properties.

We added Sandi and the Techies earlier, so she and that group appear as trustees of the directory. Click the Add Trustee command button to open the Select Objects dialog box, and then select the Writers OU, as shown in Figure 7.11. Once you've found it, click OK to add the Writers OU to the list of trustees for the Documents directory.

FIGURE 7.11

Adding the Writers OU to the Documents directory's Trustees list

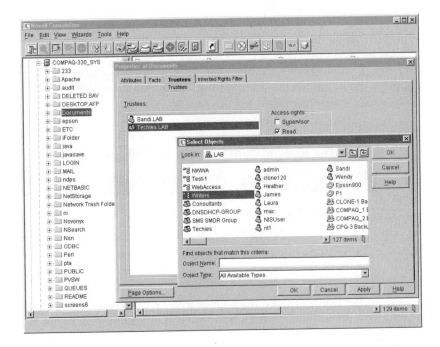

Once the new trustees are copied to the list, checking the Access Rights boxes for each group will set the level of control the group has over the directory. Since few groups should ever have Supervisor rights, leave that box unchecked.

In ConsoleOne, the Access Rights check boxes do an excellent job of showing the Effective Rights. In Figure 7.12, you can see that the Writers OU has all rights, except Supervisor, to the directory.

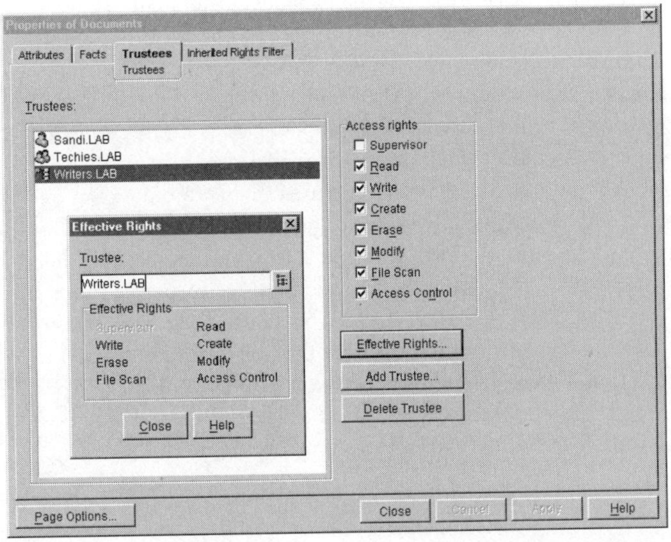

FIGURE 7.12

The effective rights to the Documents directory for the Writers OU

Click OK to save and exit, or just click Close since the rights have already been changed, and then reenter to check that all the rights you planned to grant have in fact been granted. It's easy to skip a mouse-click here and there, so make it a habit to check yourself.

Once again, granting rights to a directory in another container is not a problem, but one more step may be needed. If the users want to map a drive to another container in their login script, they can't get there from here. You must create an Alias object for the remote volume and then map the groups and users to the Alias.

Setting or Modifying Object and Property Rights

IN A HURRY 7.4: GIVE AN OBJECT TRUSTEE RIGHTS TO OTHER OBJECTS

1. Open ConsoleOne.

2. Right-click the object to be given trustee rights to another object and choose Properties.

3. Click the NDS Rights tab and choose Trustees of This Object.

4. Click the Add Trustee command button to open the Select Objects dialog box.

5. To find the object to become an assigned trustee, click the down arrow to open the eDirectory tree listing, or click the folder icon with the up arrow to move up one context level. Move up or down the tree as necessary.

6. Select the object and click OK.

7. Click OK to save the settings.

Sometimes, one network resource must be managed, controlled, or modified by multiple other objects. That's what we did in the previous section. And sometimes, one object must manage or control multiple other objects.

The network administrator does this, of course, for the entire network. But many users need some control over more than just their home directory. Even medium-power users can help by controlling a department printer or volume. Real power users can become de facto subadministrators with the proper cooperation with your department.

Do you want to give an object trustee rights to more than one other object at a time? Here's the place. This procedure allows you to grant trustee rights to multiple objects from one screen.

As the Admin user or equivalent, start ConsoleOne. Highlight the object, such as a user, a group, or a container, that you want to make a trustee of one or more other objects, right-click, and choose Properties. Then click the NDS Rights tab and select Trustees of This Object from its menu.

The first step is to discover what the object already has rights to. This requires our first real search operation. Figure 7.13 shows the Select Objects dialog box open, with the user Laura's NDS Rights property page in the background. The Select Objects dialog box offers two ways to cruise the NDS eDirectory tree, and Figure 7.13 shows one of them.

FIGURE 7.13

Searching for other objects for Laura to control

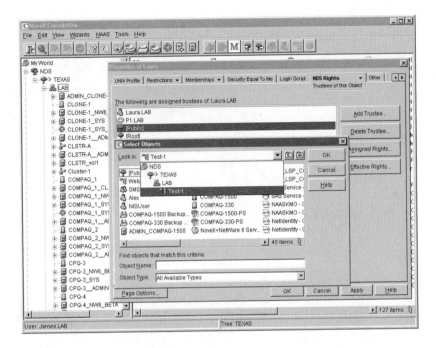

When the dialog box opens, the current context displays. Use the down arrow at the end of the Look In box to display the full eDirectory tree down to your current context. If you need to go up only one context level, you can click the up-arrow icon to the right of the down arrow instead. Drill down, or slide up, the eDirectory tree until you find what you need. Since we're going to let Laura control some servers in a minute, we need to move up to the Test-1 Organization level.

Our goal is to Add Trustee. Browse through the NDS eDirectory tree and highlight the object or objects to gain trustee rights over, as shown in Figure 7.14. In our example, Laura now gains some control over the COMPAQ-1500 and COMPAQ-330 servers.

Notice that we may once again tag several objects in one screen by using either the Ctrl-key-and-multiple-click or the Shift-key-and-inclusive-click technique. We can see the current context of the items we're choosing, not the context of the objects gaining the trustee rights. Click OK to save your choices and move them to the Trustees of This Object property page for final configuration.

Figure 7.15 shows the final step in this process. We can configure both of our chosen objects concurrently. As long as one or more items in the Rights Assigned To list is highlighted, the check boxes will apply to all of the objects. Click the Assigned Rights button, then click the rights you want the object to have over the target object (in our example, the rights of Laura over COMPAQ-1500_SYS and COMPAQ-330_SYS). When you're finished, click OK to save and exit the object's property page.

FIGURE 7.14

Laura selects volumes to control.

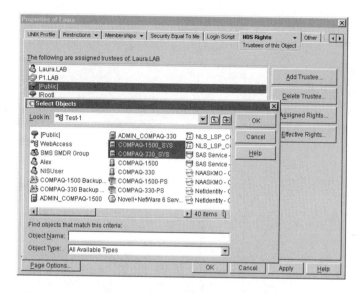

FIGURE 7.15

Granting trustee rights to more than one object at a time

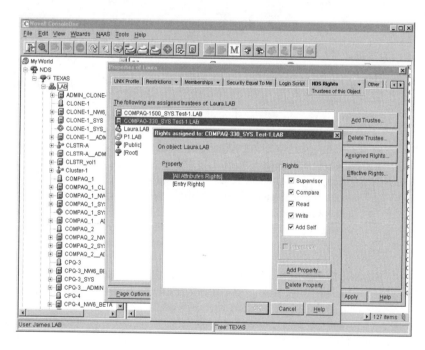

The same process works for modifying existing rights to objects. In that case, making sure you search the entire network for all objects is even more important. If you want to delete the assignment, highlight the previously Assigned Rights and click the Delete Property command button. The rights assignment, not the object itself, will be deleted.

Protecting Your Network from Viruses

Viruses are always a concern, even if they are statistically insignificant. People worrying about viruses waste more time than viruses waste, although the proliferation of operating systems with Swiss cheese security (the initials are Microsoft) makes virus protection more critical than in years past. Knowing that a virus attack is rare doesn't make you feel any better or get your network back to normal any faster if it does happen. Time spent preventing viruses is much more fun than time spent cleaning up after one.

Some Precautions

You can take some precautions without adding optional software to your network or much time to your workday. Mark all .EXE and .COM files as Read Only. Viruses generally function by modifying executable files. If all your executable files are read-only, viruses have a much harder time getting started.

Keep a tight watch on users' access rights to system areas—there shouldn't be any. Only managers, with a proper understanding of virus prevention, should have access to system files.

Do not allow users to bring disks from outside and load them to the network before being tested. Some companies go so far as to lock floppy drives, not so that users can't steal from the company, but so that users can't load infected software. This method is difficult to enforce and not good enough to be your only prevention step. Better to offer a virus-free check station for users to test floppies than try to ban floppies altogether. If you ban them, people will just sneak them into the building. The same goes for CDs, the preferred method of program distribution today.

The days when users regularly downloaded unknown files from bulletin boards and booted their systems with those disks are long gone. That's good. Commercially sponsored download sites now pride themselves on running a clean site. That's good also. But the number of files copied from unknown sources across the Internet is growing tremendously, and that's bad. Unix administrators often don't know which DOS and Windows files are on their systems, and they don't have the time or tools to test them for viruses. That's also bad.

Feel free to restrict or eliminate FTP (File Transfer Protocol) programs from your Internet suite of applications, except for those trustworthy users who understand the need for virus protection. Although you can't always stop users from downloading files with a Web browser such as Netscape, keeping the FTP programs away from the general user population may help a little, even though few "regular" users ever attempt using FTP.

Virus-Protection Software

Special virus-protection software is available for networks, often in conjunction with software metering or network user management. If your company is overly concerned with a virus attack, the software may give some peace of mind. However, antivirus software used inconsistently is worse than none at all. When you have none, people are more careful. When you have antivirus software used poorly, people develop a false sense of protection.

Here are some of the virus-protection features the optional programs provide:

◆ Install and configure easily. NetWare versions are run as NLMs (new Java versions have yet to appear).

- Block unprotected clients from logging in to a protected server.

- Distribute protection to multiple servers and clients.

- Include an administration program for Windows as well as DOS.

- Send alerts to specified users when a questionable event occurs.

- Schedule when and how security sweeps are made.

- Report on status and other statistics.

There are two major camps regarding the primary means of protection against the virus-developer community. One idea is to track the signature of all viruses. The *signature* is a piece of code inside the virus that identifies that virus, usually included by the virus criminal as an ego enhancer. As more viruses are discovered, the signature database must grow. Those systems that scan for known virus signatures should receive regular database updates.

The other option is to register a *CRC* (cyclical redundancy check) of every executable file on the server when the file is installed. The CRC is checked each time the file is read from the server. If the CRC value changes, this means that the file has been tampered with. The alert sounds, and the software shuts down the use of that file.

I lean toward the CRC method, for several reasons. First, a new virus obviously can cause you problems, and this threat is eliminated with a CRC. Second, the overhead of checking a large virus database with every file-read request will only get heavier. As the demands on servers grow, this overhead will become burdensome. Finally, my friend John McCann was one of the first programmers to make quality add-on NetWare utilities, and he says the CRC method is better. Since he knows more about NetWare programming than anyone else I know, I'll take his word for it. (It's especially easy when I agree with his conclusion anyway.)

Do you have a favorite antivirus program? Do I? Not really. Be sure to check several major brands if you don't have virus protection already (and why don't you have protection already?). Those readers with multivendor networks (which usually means some Windows NT or 2000 servers) will find that many of the companies in this market make virus products for both NetWare and NT/2000.

Some people ask about the values of server-based versus client-based virus protection. We could even have separate sections extolling the virtues of both types of protection. But we won't, because I feel strongly that you can't trust users to do your job for you. Yes, the users will suffer if they have a virus attack on their personal system, but they will demand that you fix things for them. So, asking them to protect against virus attacks on the client is asking them to do your job for you. Even if they were willing, they don't have the mental discipline to do a good job. They'll trust a file from a friend, assuming their friend knows the file's history. That's usually a bad move, as recent virus writers have demonstrated by forwarding viruses through every contact in an infected system's Outlook address book (thanks again, Windows).

A critical part of virus protection is regular updates. Server-based products need a single update session to protect hundreds of clients. This is much more efficient (and reliable) than upgrading hundreds of clients individually.

Verify that your virus protection works on the client when the user logs in. Kicking off a check of the client during the login process catches most of the viruses introduced by careless users. You won't catch them all, unfortunately, because if you make the process idiot-proof, your company will hire a better idiot. Just make sure the virus doesn't spread.

TIP   *If your manager is particularly scared of a virus attack, use that fear to your advantage. Clip an article about a virus attack and the resulting damage to the company. Nearly every single report includes a line about how the company had an inadequate backup procedure in place, meaning extra loss. If you've been angling for a bigger tape backup system or an upgrade, play the cards you're dealt, and hit your manager with the tape backup request in one hand while waving the virus attack article in the other hand. Is this dishonest? Not at all. Some people need to be pushed into doing the right thing. You should take care to push your manager when he or she is already staggering. This way, you don't need to push noticeably hard, but you still get what your network needs. Our world will never be virus-free again, so you must keep upgrading your protection systems. Nudge and/or blackmail your management as necessary.*

NetWare 6 Security Improvements

Ever-evolving features required Novell to add some bang to the security section of NetWare 4.1x and NetWare 5. Novell could have done this by adding a few extra security screens everyone ignores, marked the security matrix as "improved," and gone on with their business.

Security became much more prominent than that. Novell hired one of the original developers of the U.S. Government's "Red Book" security project. That developer, and other work done by Novell deep inside the operating system, helped certify NetWare 4.11 as a "C2 Red Book" network. This is a big deal. NetWare 6 must also be certified, but Novell officials declared this rating important and will submit NetWare 6 soon.

WHY IS C2 SECURITY CERTIFICATION A BIG DEAL?

First of all, it's a big deal because Microsoft made so much noise about Windows NT getting C2 security. The Novell folks can't stand for Microsoft to beat them in any purchase order check-off category, and that's what was happening. The fact that Windows NT was only C2 secure in stand-alone mode left the door open for Novell to top Microsoft, at least in the PR war. Not that the government followed their own regulations; departments regularly ignored the security guidelines and bought NT.

Second, it's a big deal for customers who support and use such security systems already, such as the government, the armed forces, and paranoid corporations. It's true that the government has a sizable NetWare installed base, and huge areas of some departments can't run computer equipment rated lower than C2.

Does C2 security do much for you? Probably not. Realistically, C2-level security is a giant hassle, and few companies go to that much trouble. If your company is one of the C2 adherents, you know of what I speak.

I will be amazed if your company increases your NetWare security profile up to the C2 level, unless you work for one of the aforementioned groups such as the military. For one thing, only C2-authorized software can run on a NetWare NTCB (Network Trusted Computing Base). All those NLMs you have? Gone, unless they've been certified.

Are you and the other administrators certified? Gone. Do you have NetWare 3.x networks still running on your corporate network? Gone. Only secure systems can run on a secure network. Do you have your server under lock and key? Gone until that's done. Have you limited access to remote console programs, such as RCON-SOLE? Gone. See what I mean? It's more trouble than it's worth, at least for the majority of corporations.

Adding the JVM will make your NetWare 6 server more popular for all types of utilities for the server, including security. Distributed applications are all the rage today, and security is becoming a consideration in the design phase. This falls under the heading of "a good thing," as Martha Stewart would say.

NetWare 6 includes a certificate authority for added security, but don't confuse that with C2 security certification. Those certificates guarantee that traffic across the Internet came from whom you think it came from and have nothing to do with normal, intracompany network business. We won't go into much depth with the Internet security options, because that topic deserves a book or two or ten devoted to ways to secure Internet traffic.

When Security Stinks, Management Smells the Worst

A "rock and a hard place" describes security. The tougher the security, the more people will hate the network. Looser security makes for happier users but more virus problems and file mishaps.

Remember, here we're speaking about NetWare security, not complete Internet security for all your Web and e-mail servers. That subject has its own bookshelf.

Your company routinely allows access to every room of your building to the lowest paid, and least monitored, employees: cleaning crews. The biggest risk is crews employed by the building management, especially those who use temporary helpers. Do you have any idea what these people are doing? Does your management? Probably not.

This is one of the areas where hard choices must be made, and your management must make them. If your bosses won't do their jobs, push a little. If they still refuse, document the security measures in place, the reasons for those measures, and apply them absolutely. When users complain to their bosses, and their bosses complain to your boss, let your boss modify the procedure. Then get your boss to sign any changes. Accountability is shared; blame is yours alone.

Don't let management overcompensate for lousy security elsewhere by tightening the screws on the network. That's like a bank with a vault full of cash, while the bearer bonds, cashier checks, and negotiable securities are lying out in the open, ready to be picked up and carried away.

Force management to define a consistent security profile. It makes no sense to restrict network users to the bone while leaving the president's file cabinet unlocked. People looking to steal information, both from the inside and outside, will happily take paper or computer disks. While it isn't legal to steal a report off your computer system, it is legal to grab a printout of that same report out of the dumpster.

Inconsistent security control runs both ways. I once had a customer so worried about security that he refused to have a fax server on the network. The owner was afraid of dial-in hackers going through the fax modem into the computer system. We finally convinced the owner that this was impossible.

The flip side was a major oil company in the mid-1980s that had the typical tight security on its mainframe. Terminal and user IDs were tracked, users were monitored, and passwords were everywhere—the whole bit. Then someone noticed it was possible to copy information from the mainframe to a PC connected with an IRMA board (an adapter in the PC that connected via coax to an SNA cluster controller, effectively making the PC a 3270 terminal). A management committee studied the matter and verified that yes, anyone could copy any information from the mainframe to disks and paper. The information could then be dropped in the trash, carried home, or sold to a competitor. All these options obviously violated the company's security guidelines.

What did the managers do? They decided to ignore the problem and placed no security on PCs with IRMA boards beyond what they had on the terminals the PCs replaced. It may be noble to trust the employees, but it was inconsistent security. Those users with PCs deserved security training and a warning about the severity of potential security leaks. They got nothing because corporate management was too lazy to do its job. If a problem developed, who would be blamed? You know— the computer managers who had no control over the decision.

More security concerns will be addressed later when we get to the Web-related portions of Net-Ware. If you thought your managers were paranoid before, wait until they come to you waving copies of the *Wall Street Journal* predicting doom and gloom because hackers stopped another Web site for a few minutes. Is this a realistic threat to your servers? Probably not, especially when running your Web servers on NetWare. Is this a realistic threat to your schedule because of paranoid managers? Probably—your whole day will be wasted chasing nonexistent loopholes and manager security blankets.

Chapter 8

NetWare 6 Administrator Duties and Tools

NOVELL PROVIDES TOO MANY supervisory utilities. That sounds weird, because the better the tools, the easier the management (usually). NetWare 6, unfortunately, suffers from the same problem shown by NetWare 5.1, NetWare 5.0, and on, back since NetWare 3.12 became obsolete: overlapping and conflicting management tools.

What's the easiest way to describe network management? List each tool and what it does, then go on to the next tool and repeat. That's the way the Novell documentation does things and the way certification test books present their information. I, however, don't believe that's the way real people manage real networks.

When you have a problem with a printer, you want to go to a "printer problems solved" chapter in the book. As explained in Chapter 6, "Network and Internet Printing," you can go to iManage or NetWare Administrator to solve printer problems, which can mean confusion. I prefer to describe a problem, and then discuss solution options. When only a single tool handles that problem, I'll describe that single tool. When several tools overlap, such as the way you can create a new user in ConsoleOne, NetWare Administrator, iManage, and Web Server Manager, I'll show you what I believe is the best way to accomplish the task.

Unfortunately, Novell's lack of clear management utility vision means we'll jump around from tool to tool within this chapter, and perhaps within minor topics. I wish I could make things neat and easy for you, but Novell won't let me. Maybe things will get a bit tidier in the next version.

The following topics are covered in this chapter:

- ◆ Daily administration tasks
- ◆ Supervisory functions and rights
- ◆ NetWare's new management utilities
- ◆ Container and leaf object management
- ◆ User and group management
- ◆ Server and network management

- Remote server console access
- Protocol management tools
- Storage management
- NDS eDirectory management
- Novell Licensing Services (NLS) management

Managing Your Network with a Plan

What are administrator duties? The short answer is that if you're the administrator, anything you do on the network is an administrator duty. When you're playing a network game such as Max Payne or Arena Quake, you're not wasting time; no, you're the network administrator using a network-intensive application to test the network's performance under load.

The long answer to the question of administrator duties is to list everything that is expected of you. Take a look at the standard list of administrator duties:

- Plan the network.
  - Design the cabling.
  - Decide on server location and other equipment placement.
  - Devise the NDS eDirectory structure.
  - Create the user list and appropriate access privileges.
  - Define application and data storage requirements.
- Install the network.
  - Perform or oversee the physical cabling installation.
  - Configure server machines.
  - Install NetWare on the servers.
  - Install or upgrade workstation software.
  - Configure Web services running on all NetWare servers.
- Support the network users.
  - Make all network resources available to authorized users.
  - Provide protective, but not restrictive, security.
  - Train the users as necessary.
  - Protect network files and data from mishaps.
  - Maintain a high level of network performance.

◆ Leap tall buildings in a single bound.

◆ Plan for the future.

◆ Understand network growth.

◆ Foresee and avoid network bottlenecks.

◆ Watch new technologies and investigate ones appropriate for your network.

If you're a perfectionist or can't live with chaos, get another job. Likewise, leave if you're sensitive to real or imagined criticism. Do you need constant praise to maintain your self-esteem? Good luck, and tell your therapist "Hello" for me.

NetWare administration is a thankless job about 80 percent of the time; 5 percent of the time, it's worse. However, the rest of the time makes up for everything. When the network hums along and nothing disrupts either the network or your good mood, no job in the world can beat the life of a network jockey. The light that goes on in people's eyes when they start to understand how the network can help them warms your heart.

Now that you've seen the list of what a "good" network manager should be doing, you may feel like taking up a career in something less challenging, like brain surgery or astrophysics or juggling chainsaws. No one can do everything on that list of standard administrator duties, can they?

No, of course not. All you can do is work hard and work smart. I can't help you with the work hard part, but perhaps we can make some progress in the working smarter department.

If the network is new to your company, everyone will be thrilled for a few weeks. No matter how poorly the network is running, it's still a thousandfold better than *no* network. If your company has just moved up to NetWare from some other network, such as a peer-to-peer workgroup solution that was outgrown much too quickly, people will still think this is amazing. Again, even a poor NetWare network is a hundredfold better than the best peer-to-peer system whose capabilities have been surpassed. Most peer-to-peer networks reach the end of their rope at about 8 users, but most companies won't justify the cost of a server and separate operating system like NetWare until at least 20 users are screaming for improvements.

The supervision and plans for stand-alone workstations, or even for a small, underpowered workgroup network, are not sufficient for a NetWare network. If you are new to this, you must upgrade your thinking quite a bit.

Some books go into long, detailed plans on how to manage your network. I've even seen books with timesheets, planning every hour for you. There used to be a trend where company management tried to make the network a "utility," such as that provided by the electric company or telephone company. Flip a switch, and there's the network. Of course, this was before the electrical service started fluctuating widely enough to reset everyone's VCR at home, and a few software problems downed large parts of the national long-distance network.

Management doesn't use the utility example as much anymore, but it's not a bad idea to emulate, with slight provisions. Having electrical and telephone service available at every moment is a fact of modern life we have grown to love. But both these services spent decades as monopolies. There are advantages to monopolies, not the least of which is the ability to mandate the infrastructure and set rules for the users. The disadvantages include the Department of Justice and far too many angry lawyers, but that's another story.

Translate the electrical grid throughout a city into a plan for supporting network connections in every corner of your company. When management complains about building the network for sections of your company that are not yet inhabited, point to the growth trends and economy of wiring as many connections as possible to maximize every labor hour by the cabling contractor. If they're building a new building, are they expecting to see the electrical company executives standing in the street, scratching their heads and wondering how to get power to it? Of course not. Don't let that be the case with your network.

Managing Your Future Network

This may seem like an odd section heading. How do you manage a network you don't have yet? By making sure the network you want is the one you eventually build.

If you're driving from Baltimore, Maryland, to San Francisco, California, how do you get there? By driving west. You may drive north or south for a bit now and then, but most of the time, you keep driving west. When you come to an intersection, you want to go west if at all possible.

You get to your future network the same way. You must decide what your future network will look like and move in the direction of that vision with every network decision. There are choices to make every day when running a large network, and you want to choose the option that will get you closer to your future network.

Decisions about what your network of the future will be must be made with your management. We can always say that tomorrow's networks must be larger and faster, have more disk storage, and be more fault-tolerant than the networks of today, but those guidelines are a little too vague to serve as directions.

What does "larger" mean for your future network? Does it mean more users? Does it mean more locations? Does it mean more types of clients to service? Will you have more types of data to carry across the network? If it means geographically larger, then a method of WAN connections and data distribution may be necessary. More clients, or different types of clients, need support in the physical cabling and network protocol area. Is your boss hot to run video across the LAN? Does she want to teleconference across a campus using desktop-mounted cameras and microphones? Then you must move toward a network transport layer that guarantees support for priority packet types and real-time data streams.

What type of storage will be needed? Do you want more hard disk space, stringing together hundreds of gigabytes? Or does your network information better suit a plan using HSM (Hierarchical Storage Management)? Do you keep some data on server hard disks for immediate access, some other data on magneto-optical jukebox platters with a few seconds of delay, and other data on tape? Or does your company need to move more toward a large disk cluster, with every byte available instantly through any file server? Each option has a learning curve and a foundation that can be laid today.

Does "fault-tolerant" mean absolutely no service interruptions? Or does it mean that you must recover from a hardware failure within a certain number of minutes? How about two hours? How much does it cost your company when the network is completely down? Can you work with your management to set that number? If you don't know how much it costs when your network is broken, how will you know how much you can spend to make sure it doesn't break? Should you plan for an extremely well-protected and fault-tolerant central server cluster, or should you maintain high network availability by distributing network access and replicating the data? These two options are directly opposed to each other and will make a difference in every network plan and hardware purchase over the next few years.

Many of these questions can only be answered after you (and your management) develop a network philosophy. Once everyone agrees on the philosophy of your network and the services that will be provided to your network clients, you have a decision framework.

Perhaps this section could be called "Developing Your Network Philosophy" rather than "Managing Your Future Network." A well-developed network philosophy today helps you make decisions concerning all parts of your network for tomorrow.

A SAMPLER OF MANAGEMENT SLOGANS

If you're currently running a network, you know that "interrupts" happen not only to computer CPUs but also to your day. Every phone call may be a disaster on the other end. Your day is not your own.

Make a mental change, and make it simple: You run your network, not the other way around.

Sure, you say, that's easy for me to say, sitting back in Texas. Nobody's hollering for my head because the laser printer goes offline every time the president sends it a spreadsheet.

Let me give you some network advice as stated by your grandmother. Sayings that are simple, short, and clear, but echo longer and louder than you would expect. Perhaps we can get Granny to stitch these slogans onto some pillows for the office.

"UP IS GOOD, DOWN IS BAD"

Every network resource should be available at all times. That's a "good" thing. Unavailable network resources are "bad" things. This seems amazingly simple, but it needs to be said.

However, sometimes the definition of "up" needs to be slightly reworked. The users will complain that the network is terrible when the only problem is that their favorite network printer is not working properly. Show them the other network printers, and they will rephrase their network complaint. Instead of "not printing," it becomes "print over there." The printing system itself is working, even if their particular printer is not.

"MAXIMIZE UPTIME BY SCHEDULING DOWNTIME"

Maintenance time should be scheduled for your network every day or every week. If your network is smaller, there is probably time every night or early morning for the network downtime.

Downtime need not be serious, with major overhauls of server and hard disk. You may want to reorganize the print servers. You may need to add a new protocol to a network segment. You may need to readjust the physical wiring and add an extra concentrator or two.

This type of network maintenance isn't serious, but it is necessary. Even more necessary is making sure that your management understands that the network is always available when people need the network. If no one is in the office at 5:00 A.M., who cares if the network is down? If you need to shut down a database running on a server to get every system file on a backup tape, shut it down.

Continued on next page

A SAMPLER OF MANAGEMENT SLOGANS *(continued)*

There will always be reasons to take the network offline for maintenance. If you schedule regular downtimes, it never becomes a question or a concern to management. When your network has been running for 86 days and you say it must be taken offline, people will think the reason for the downtime is more serious than it really is. Perhaps we should say this is an example of managing not the network, but your management's expectations.

"PROMOTE CONFIDENCE THROUGH PARANOIA"

To make your users confident in your network, you must be slightly paranoid. You must have a constant, nagging worry in the back of your mind, forcing you to examine every inch of your network for flaws and weaknesses.

Like the old joke says, you're not really paranoid if they really are out to get you. If you run a network, fates are actively conspiring to make it break. So you're not paranoid; you're just doing your job.

Spare parts are a good example of paranoia. Does your boss demand an HA (High Availability) system—not quite fault-tolerant and able to continue in the face of hardware failure, but able to resume operations fairly quickly? Then keep available spare parts for all the servers that must keep running. If your main server's main data lives on a set of 36GB drives, you better have more on the shelf or another server ready to take the backup files and start running immediately.

Do you imagine a server's power supply is making some kind of strange noise, but you're not quite sure? Replace it. That's an example of paranoia that will enhance your network by minimizing downtime.

NetWare 6 makes clustering affordable to everyone except the smallest companies with the most limited budgets. You should gather system pricing to keep shared data systems available through two NetWare 6 servers 99.999 percent (five nines) of the time. When uptime appears on the meeting agenda, present your case. If data paranoia exists, your confidence-building cluster may get approved.

"EVERY USER IS AN HONORED GUEST AND A POTENTIAL CRIMINAL"

The chapter about security (Chapter 7) should make this warning clear, but it's worth restating. Your worst security problems are the people at the end of your network wires. Retail executives will tell you that much more stolen property goes out the back door with employees than out the front door with shoplifters.

While you would like to think your fellow employees will not knowingly harm your network or steal your data, the sad truth is that one or more of them will. The man in the elevator with you yesterday evening may have had an illegal copy of WordPerfect in his briefcase. The woman beside him may have had the marketing plan for the next quarter in her purse.

Many users destroy security through inattention or incompetence. Small comfort, of course, as your hacked servers gasp and wheeze, because security violators care little how they get in. Put procedures in place, such as immediate account locking for those employees who leave, even for vacation, to close one of the biggest loopholes. Build clear password policies through cooperation with management, so management helps put some teeth in the rules.

You must provide network access to all users in order for them to perform their jobs. Any more access than necessary will lead to trouble.

Selling Your Network Plan to Your Boss

One problem with network (or personal) philosophies is that everyone has his or her own. While this makes for a more interesting society at large, it makes it more difficult for you to plan and run your network unless some agreement is reached.

No matter how brilliant your network plan or how comprehensive your network philosophy, all is lost unless your boss agrees. I've met some wonderful network administrators who failed because they and their bosses never agreed on the network. I've also met some very "un-technical" network administrators who built amazing, complicated networks with the full support of their bosses in particular and their company in general.

The key here is for you and your boss to share the same network vision and philosophy. If you have been hired to support an existing network, the boss's philosophy is probably well set, and you must go with that. If you built the network from nothing, your philosophy provided the guidelines. The trick is to get your boss to agree with the work you've already done and to help you continue on the same path.

Just as *you* get pressure from higher up the management chain, so does your immediate manager. So you are now in a situation where you must sell to not only one layer of management, but to another layer or two above that.

Yes, *sell*. Your boss must be sold on the facts that you know what you're doing technically and that your ideas for network growth make sense. Don't assume that your boss will understand the technical parts and agree because your choice of technology is superior to all other options. It's not, and your boss won't.

I prefer to lay out the network choices in such a way as to "lead" people to the conclusion I have already reached. This only works when the facts support my idea, so it helps if, before I present the case to anyone, I verify that I'm on the right track. We can call this method the "Pros-and-Cons Weighing of Technical Alternatives," but in sales, it's called the "Ben Franklin Close." Evidently, old Ben used this trick on the other Founding Fathers to sell them life insurance after the Revolutionary War.

This method works by listing three columns: the decision to be made, the pros, and the cons. In sales, you actually sit with the customers and write down each element of the chart, letting them come up with some of the pros and cons. If you think this won't work with your boss, think again. It works every time, because your boss helps list the pros and cons for the decision with you. If your boss picks the "wrong" decision, you'll know why, because you went over the reasons together. Either you didn't know your facts or your boss feels differently about the situation than you do. Better to find out during a discussion than from a rejected proposal.

Let's say that you feel the need for a software-metering product, but your boss doesn't want to spend the money. Sit down together and draw a line separating a page into two columns labeled Pro and Con. Write the decision to be made across the top of the page, such as Start Software Metering Y/N. Now ask your boss for the primary objection, and write that down. Ask for the next, and the next. You may have a list like this:

- Too expensive.

- Too much management time.

- Current software inventory system works okay.

- Inconveniences the users.

After your boss is finished, you can write down a list similar to the following:

◆ $5 per user.

◆ Installation reads the NetWare user list and automatically builds access tables.

◆ No one knows how many copies of each program have been purchased.

◆ Users are now copying software illegally and trying to install it themselves.

◆ Tracks application use.

◆ Forces all applications onto the server, meaning consistent backup and easier upgrades.

◆ Lists software that users may not know is available, especially between departments.

◆ Demonstrates compliance with software-use laws to auditors.

In case the pros and cons don't line up exactly, draw lines between each. If you're careful with the two lists, your columns will look like this when you're finished:

Con	Pro
Too expensive.	Only $5 per user.
Too much management time.	Installation reads the NetWare user list and automatically builds access tables.
	Demonstrates compliance with software use laws to auditors.
	Forces applications onto the server, meaning consistent backup and easier upgrades.
Current software inventory system works okay.	No one knows how many copies of each program have been purchased.
	Tracks application use.
Inconveniences the users.	Lists software that users may not know is available, especially between departments.
	Users are now copying software illegally and trying to install it themselves.

Every objection from your boss has at least one response. Several of your responses apply to more than one of the objections. For example, to the objection "Too expensive," you can say that the cost of the metering software is a new cost, but it reduces the cost of software purchases, since everyone can share better. It also saves time (money) with better backup and upgrades, and it tells which applications are really used. If you have 20 copies of presentation software that only six people are using, you'll save money when it's time to upgrade by upgrading only six copies.

Will Ben Franklin come to your rescue every time your boss gives you a hard time? No, but the idea of selling your boss rather than arguing will help. Everyone needs to be sold on ideas—and often resold several times. The sooner you understand that selling is a big part of network management, the better off you'll be.

Selling Your Network Plan to Your Users

You're not through with sales when you convince your boss of your positions. You must still convince the users that the way you run the network provides them the best support within the constraints dictated by management.

What constraints? Generally money. The network would run faster if you had a row of super-servers, like those shiny Compaq ProLiant systems, stacked against the wall, and maybe a rack of quad-servers in the computer room. Storage space wouldn't be a problem if you had an extra 200GB of hard disk for every workgroup. User applications would run better if each desktop came equipped with a fast Pentium 4 (heck, let's ask for a 2GHz dual Pentium 4) computer with 512MB of RAM (okay, 1GB of RAM).

The users understand these types of constraints. Each of them wants more desk space in a bigger office, a company car, more vacation time, paid trips to conventions, and a bigger bonus. They're so worried about their dreams and constraints that they haven't given any thought to your problems.

This is where your network philosophy can help clarify exactly what the network can and can't do. If you (and your boss, of course) can condense your network philosophy into a mission statement, your users will better understand what to expect from the network today and tomorrow. The shorter the mission statement, the better. Two paragraphs are too much.

How would your users like this: "Our network will be available a minimum of 20 hours every business day, providing secure access to applications, data, printers, and host access services." This tells the story quickly, but doesn't promise 24-hour satisfaction of every tiny network desire they may have. This also excludes 24/7 systems such as Web servers, but those are generally for outside users.

Unless there is an immediate network problem, unhappy users are expressing a conflict between their expectations and your network reality. Align the users' expectations to the network you can provide, and everyone will be happier.

Daily Administration Tasks

Those readers new to the world of network administration may wonder if their day will be so full of idle time that they will need to follow a daily checklist to keep from falling into a deep sleep caused by their workday boredom. If you are one of those people, take this book to an experienced network administrator and let him or her read the first sentence of this paragraph. Be sure and stand back, because when people laugh hysterically they often drop things, and this book hurts your foot when it lands on it.

Perhaps you detect the wry smile I'm sporting as I write this. The trick is not how to spend your idle moments as a network administrator; it's finding some of them in the first place.

Yes, the workload is too large in most situations. If you're a good administrator, you're more nervous when things are going well than when they aren't, because you know disaster is sneaking up behind you. So, it isn't that checklists aren't needed. There are still a few things that, regardless of how busy you are, you must—repeat, *must*—do on a daily basis. I discuss them in this section.

NOTE *You'll find other, more specific administration topics scattered about the book. For example, check Chapter 6, "Network and Internet Printing," if you have questions about printing. You'll find plenty of information about setting up users and other objects in Chapter 4, "Creating and Managing User Objects." If you don't find your topic here, check the index or the table of contents, and I bet you'll find what you're looking for.*

System Backups (Have a Plan and Follow It)

The title is "system backups," but it could be "data" or "file" backups, because that's what we're discussing here. Files will disappear all too often, and a good backup is your only defense. Certainly, plan for the catastrophic disaster, such as a fire in the computer room that melts all your servers (but that will never happen—well, almost never), but also plan for the daily screw-ups that accompany life.

File security means several things, but right now it means file safety. Your files are secure if they are copied to a reliable backup system a minimum of once per day. Many companies copy critical file sets several times per day, having determined that recovering a crashed or lost file at any expense is cheaper than taking the network down for any reason.

First, you need a plan for rotating backup tapes in order to keep files close at hand, yet safe from localized disaster—you know, like that computer room fire that never happens (until it does). The rotation details in Chapter 14, "Clusters of Enhancements and Special Features," may not be the best ever, but they will work. If you have a better rotation plan, feel free to use it, but use something.

Here's the crux of this section: Back up your critical files every day, or even more often if possible. Do not trust the fact that your server hard drive has a mean-time-between-failure rating of over 125,000 hours and so should last over 14 years. "Mean" time between failures means the average time, and if one drive happens to be good enough to work for 28 years, another drive must quit in three days to balance things out. Unfortunately, drive manufacturers don't label the drive that will fail in three days.

Besides, you will not face a file crisis because a drive fails nearly as often as a user will make a mistake. That's why "user is a four-letter word" to some network administrators. Files *will* be deleted by accident, and they must be recovered. Normally, this means tape, but if you want to push the envelope and copy all critical files to writable CDs (now a fairly cheap option), feel free. Just back up the files to some reliable device every day that any files change. Every day. Period.

Keeping Antivirus Software Up-to-Date

This is critical, and it's also surprisingly easy. The reason to keep your antivirus software up-to-date is simple: More social misfits make more viruses every week. Each virus has a signature-code pattern within the software that identifies it and can be used to identify that particular virus. Adding these virus signatures to your antivirus software's signature table gives you protection against these viruses. It isn't complete protection, but it's a good start.

The highest-quality antivirus software offers free updates, either forever or for a subscription period. These updates normally happen on a scheduled basis across the Internet, which is a good approach.

I recently reviewed Symantec's Norton AntiVirus for Microsoft Exchange Servers. That product may or may not apply to your situation, but the item that illustrates my point is Symantec's Live Update feature. Inside the software is a scheduling program to specify how often the antivirus software itself should go out through an Internet connection and download the most recent virus signature files. Options range from as frequently as once a day to as infrequently as never (not a good choice).

Demand that your antivirus software vendor provide capabilities similar to Symantec's easy updates. Is time short? If your vendor doesn't have an automatic schedule, train an assistant in the technical department or a secretary to download the file regularly. Just make sure that file is downloaded and applied to your antivirus software regularly.

Checking Your System Log Files

There should probably be a separate heading for "Weekly Administration Tasks," but then you might believe a free moment is rarer than an honest politician. Free moments are rare, but not that rare.

Checking log files should be a habit if you have a Web server open to the public, because you want to know who has come to your Web site. Checking log files in NetWare isn't that much fun, but at least you have a fighting chance of seeing some errors develop over time rather than having them sneak up on you. NetWare's log files include SYS$LOG.ERR, BOOT$LOG.ERR, VOL$LOG.ERR, TTS$LOG.ERR, and ABEND.LOG. See Chapter 15, "Troubleshooting Your Network," for descriptions of these files.

Supervisory Functions and the Necessary Rights

In order to perform your administrative tasks, you will need the necessary rights. Let's take a moment to review NetWare rights and trustee assignments. Then I'll explain how you can use workgroup managers to lighten your load.

Rights Overview

When the first NetWare 6 server is installed in a new network, the Admin user is created. Granted the Supervisor right to the [Root] level of the network, Admin controls the entire new network through inheritance.

Let's take a quick look at what rights go where:

Directory rights	Apply only to the directory in the filesystem where they are assigned. Directory rights are part of the filesystem, not of NDS. Unless blocked or redefined, directory rights are inherited by subdirectories and files. A User object may be granted directory rights to any directory on a volume.
File rights	Apply only to the file to which they are assigned. Trustees inherit rights to a file from the directory rights above the file.
Object rights	Apply to NDS objects. Object rights are inherited from higher objects or are assigned directly. Inherited object rights continue to be passed down to lower objects. Assigned object rights do not flow down the NDS eDirectory tree.
Property rights	Apply to the properties of NDS objects. Rights can be assigned to specific properties of a given object. Rights to a specific property do not flow down the tree through inheritance.
All Property rights	Allow the trustee assignment to apply to all rights of the given object with one assignment. The All Property rights trustee assignment, unlike Property rights, *does* flow down the NDS eDirectory tree, through inheritance.

Trustee Assignments

A *trustee* is a user or group granted rights to a directory, file, or object. This user or group is then called a trustee of that directory, file, or object. Although this naming reminds me of bad prison movies, the root of the term *trustee* comes from *trust*. A trustee is trusted to properly use the objects placed in his or her trust.

Trustee assignments grant rights for one object to another object. The trustee rights assignments are kept as part of the object to which they grant access.

The trustee assignments are stored in a trustee list. The trustee list for an object is stored in the ACL (Access Control List) property. Every object in the network has an ACL property.

[Public] is a special trustee and acts somewhat like the group EVERYONE in earlier NetWare versions. Rather than granting EVERYONE rights to a directory in NetWare 6 as you did in NetWare 3, you might instead specify the rights of [Public] in that directory. [Public] may also be a trustee of a file or other object, besides just a directory.

If a user has no specific trustee rights to an object, directory, or file, that user automatically has the same rights as the [Public] trustee. [Public] is assigned the Browse right to the [Root] of the NDS eDirectory tree and so has the ability to read the entire tree. This allows all users to see the available network resources.

More coverage of rights across the network can be found in Chapter 7, "Securing Your NetWare 6 Network." If you've skipped to here and bypassed Chapter 7, skimming back through that information may eliminate any confusion.

Workgroup Managers to the Rescue

Although I'm terrified of granting workgroup administrators complete control with no Admin supervision, I think they are a valuable tool in your network management toolkit. In fact, proper use of workgroup administrators will keep you closer to your end users than a crowded elevator.

Workgroup administrators are closer to the department's problems and hence are quicker with easy solutions than you are. More than that, they serve as your cheerleader in the department. If you make them feel special by sharing information and responsibility, the workgroup administrators can help make the network better. Let's take a look at some ways the workgroup administrators, and by extension the user community, can work with you:

◆ Involve them in pilot projects. Two great benefits come from their involvement. First, they know more about how your end users work than you do and will make sure all the bases are covered. Second, they will spread the word about your new project and generate positive word-of-mouth among the groups that will most likely need to pay for the new service. This makes your job of selling the benefits much easier.

◆ Have them let you know how the users really feel. Your network clients won't tell you the truth. This is not really their fault; it just works that way. Formal questionnaires and focus groups help, but the little things won't get passed along. Your workgroup administrator will know what users are happy about and what they hate.

◆ Let them help you define training goals and courses. Generic application training is always helpful. Specific job-related training on those same applications is invaluable but difficult to identify and develop. Your workgroup administrator will know where your training courses are falling short and how to stretch them back out again.

◆ Ask them to explain the computer decisions made by you (or your department) to the users. No one likes hearing pronouncements handed down from above, and your network users are no exception. Having one of their own able to translate "HQ" talk into "people" talk will soften the resistance to network changes. Of course, if you're involving them in pilot projects, there won't be any surprises.

Are there more ways in which the workgroup administrator can help? Many more methods are available, but they depend on your situation. Remember, power users are your friends.

WARNING   When setting up your network security, do not lock Admin out of parts of your eDirectory tree. If a department has its own administrator and has locked you out, what do those employees do when this person is on vacation or is out sick? What about when that person quits or transfers? If Admin is blocked, you can call the airlines and get the estimated arrival time for the wandering administrator, but you can't retrieve the files until you've got the administrator on the phone. If Admin is not blocked, you can step in and save the day. See Chapter 7 for details on rights and security.

Wake Up and Smell the Java: NetWare's New Management Landscape

Over the years, I've said a fond farewell to a wide variety of NetWare management utilities. Sometimes, I think I should load up an old server with NetWare 386 just to play with SYSCON once again. But time waits for no man or network utility. Novell's direction clearly says NetWare Administrator belongs to the past. ConsoleOne was supposed to win the future, but public sentiment for browser-based utilities may call for another course correction in the search for management nirvana. All I can say today is that NetWare Administrator now is referred to as a "legacy" tool in the NetWare documentation.

Before we go into the details of all the NetWare management actions you will use on a regular basis, let's take the time to meet all the current management utilities. First, we'll take a quick look at all the new browser-based utilities, and then we'll get to ConsoleOne.

NOTE   In this chapter, when there's only one way to do something, I'll show the one tool that does it. When both ConsoleOne and one of the browser-based utilities perform a job, I'll explain how to use both, but put the utility I prefer first (that should give you a clue or two what my thoughts are about management tools). Sometimes, neither of these new avenues—ConsoleOne or the browser-based utilities—will be the right tool for a job. Then we'll go back to NetWare Administrator or the old C-Worthy DOS-style screens on the server console.

Browser-based Utility Overview

NetWare 5.1 included the first browser-based utility, named NetWare Management Portal. Novell engineers rushed this name to market a bit quickly; the Marketing folks later decided the Portal name should be reserved for a new product. Now, NetWare 6 calls the same (but substantially upgraded) utility NetWare Remote Manager. The other browser-based tools you'll find in NetWare 6 include the Welcome page, Web Manager, iManage, Web Server Manager, Web Search Manager, and iFolder Management.

I think several of these tools have the horsepower to take over most or all of the administration duties for NetWare 6, but the browser-utilities are too new. It would be nice if Novell designers decided on a direction and stuck with it, rather than jumping back and forth between ConsoleOne and browser-utilities so fast they can't catch up and convert all the NetWare Administrator and even C-Worthy DOS utilities.

NOTE *The first shipping versions of these utilities, when all running on the same physical server, had a tendency to create problems for each other. Although administrators frequently reboot Windows NT/2000/XP servers for all sorts of problems, needing to reboot a NetWare server to kick-start a management utility seems bizarre. Keep an eye out for upgrades and service patches for these utilities.*

WELCOME TO NETWARE 6

Novell developers finally put a decent Welcome page on their servers in NetWare 6. In the previous version, when you put in the DNS name or IP address of a NetWare 5.1 server, a splash screen for the NetWare Enterprise Web Server appeared. This could be helpful at times, but not particularly welcoming or indicative of threading Web services throughout the NetWare server.

NetWare 6 opens with a Welcome message and quick links to many of the important NetWare services. Built for users more than administrators, the Welcome page provides information about new and revamped services, along with sample screens. In many cases, users can link directly to the services from this Welcome screen, which is a smart method of leading users to useful functions. Figure 8.1 shows the first Welcome screen your browser-based users will probably see.

FIGURE 8.1

Welcome, it says (and seems to mean it)

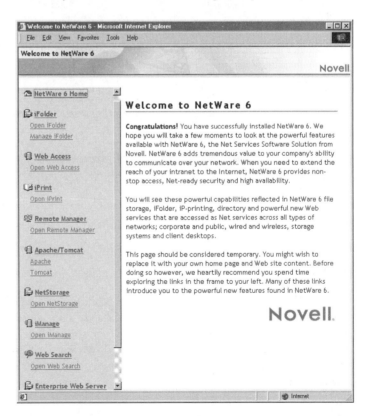

You can leave this screen as a generic Welcome page for users or modify it to reflect your network and servers (see the last paragraph on this screen). You really won't use this page much at all. If you wish to modify the code to reflect your own network, Novell makes it easy to do so.

WEB MANAGER

If you want a page to remain on the screen, this Web Manager page is it. All of the browser-based utilities link from this convenient page (thanks, Novell). When describing specific management tasks, I won't refer to this page often, because I'll start with the appropriate management utility for the job at hand, but you can always start from the screen in Figure 8.2, if you wish.

FIGURE 8.2

NetWare Web Manager, your real management portal

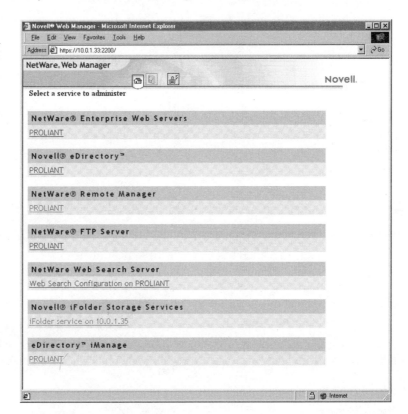

Here's what you can do from this utility:

◆ Set your management portal preferences by clicking the icon on the right end of the toolbar

◆ Use this as a gateway to all browser-based management utilities

◆ Link to novell.com by clicking the red Novell icon on the far right

If you want to set portal preferences, click the desk icon (I'm not sure why that's supposed to represent preferences, but that's what we have) on the right end of the toolbar. You'll see the Network Settings screen, as shown in Figure 8.3.

FIGURE 8.3

Web Manager
housekeeping

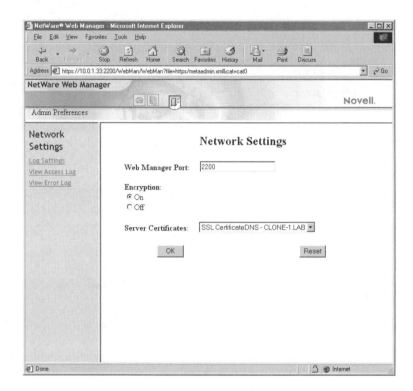

If you can read the address on the screen, you'll notice it says `https://`, indicating the screen uses SSL encryption. Since these utilities may be used from remote locations, encryption is the default. You can change that, if you wish. You can also change the Web Manager port from 2200 to another port, if you don't want to open another hole in your firewall.

The other menu options in the left frame concern log setting and viewing options. The default log locations are as follows:

- The access log is in `SYS:/novonyx/suitespot/admin-serv/logs/access.txt`.

- The error log is in `SYS:/novonyx/suitespot/admin-serv/logs/errors.txt`.

Clicking either the View Access Log or View option pops open the requested log. (You can find the Apache logs, if you're interested, at SYS:\APACHE\LOGS.) This is handy for quick checks, although any real analysis will be done directly on the log files themselves.

IMANAGE

iManage is a brand-new utility that many Novell people didn't expect to actually be finished in time to be in the first release of NetWare 6, but here it is. Lucky for us, because it handles all the new iPrint management, along with taking over the DNS (Domain Name System) and DHCP (Dynamic Host Configuration Protocol) management chores (covered in Chapter 12, "DHCP and DNS Support").

You'll go through a login screen first to get here, but I think you're smart enough to figure out how to put in your password and click Login without a screenshot. (If not, perhaps you better brush up on your NetWare basics before diving into management.) Figure 8.4 shows the opening iManage screen.

FIGURE 8.4

iManage, uManage, weManage from here

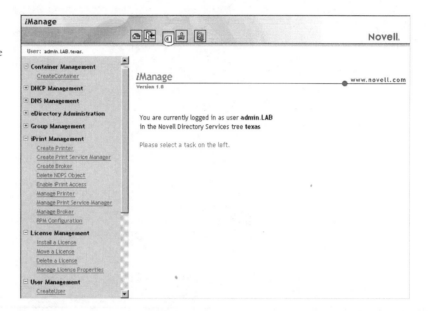

Here's what you can do from this utility:

◆   Set up and manage iPrint

◆   Configure and manage both DHCP and DNS

◆   Manage licenses

TIP   *Bypass various NDS options, such as Create Container, because they're pretty lame inside iManage.*

You will be here quite a bit, as you can guess from the printing details in Chapter 6. You should also remember that many of the printing details were still a bit weak inside iManage. Look for upgrades on the NetWare download site, because the framework inside the server portion of iManage will support much more value than what's on display so far.

REMOTE MANAGER

Here's the server-specific browser utility you'll spend plenty of time playing with, and you should be pretty happy. A direct descendant of the Management Portal from NetWare 5.1, the NetWare Remote Manager drills down to great depths of hardware and server-specific configuration utilities. Figure 8.5 shows the Server Health Monitoring screen in Remote Manager.

FIGURE 8.5

Health monitoring
inside Remote
Manager

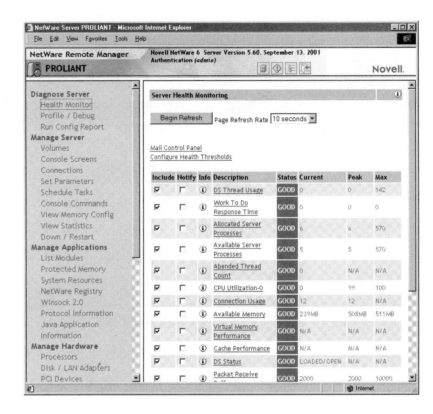

Here's what you can do from this utility:

◆ Monitor 17 critical server functions at one glance

◆ Manage volumes, storage pools, and partitions

◆ Launch remote-console screens

◆ Perform all SET parameter configuration

◆ Set the cron function (scheduled console commands)

◆ View server memory configurations and current allocation

◆ View the server's network and disk activity statistics

◆ Take down and restart the server

◆ List all NLMs and drill down for details

◆ Show every open file on each volume

◆ Check every hardware-specific setting or report necessary

◆ Launch Remote Manager on a prepared list of other servers

◆ Collect NetWare usage information on a single server for easy reporting

The list looks long, but it could have been much longer. There are an amazing number of configuration tools and viewports into the server function inside this one utility. Could Remote Manager be The One utility in the near future? It certainly has a good head start on the others.

WEB SERVER MANAGER

If you do anything with the NetWare Enterprise Web Server, you'll use the utility shown in Figure 8.6. Notice the number of menu options in the left frame. Most of these don't appear in regular NetWare administration.

FIGURE 8.6

Managing the NetWare Web server

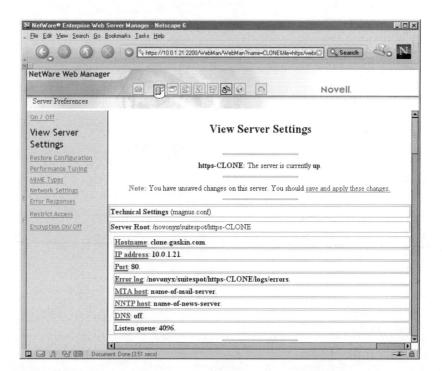

Here's what you can do from this utility:

◆ Turn off the Web server

◆ Completely configure Web servers running on the NetWare Enterprise Web Server

◆ Control access to the Web server

◆ Provide some level of NDS administration

Notice another nice thing about the screen in Figure 8.6: It shows a Netscape browser, rather than Internet Explorer from Microsoft as all the others show. Novell may not have their server administration tools ready to support Netscape 6.2, but at least Netscape does. One should expect that, but affirmation of what makes sense often makes one feel better.

NETWARE WEB SEARCH MANAGER

Have you ever noticed how fast the Search function is at novell.com? That same speed awaits your Web server, with the Web Search Manager utility, shown in Figure 8.7.

FIGURE 8.7

Searching for answers the easy way

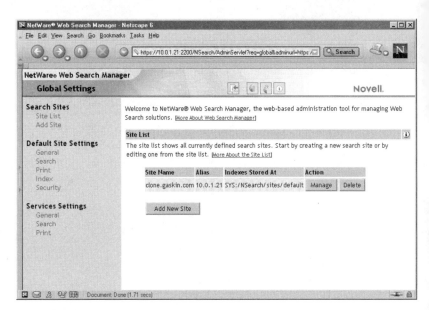

Here's what you can do from this utility:

◆ Specify which sites will be searched

◆ Set default settings for all searched sites

Just because your Web developers don't trust NetWare as a Web server doesn't mean you can't set one up for an intranet server. Let users store a pool of documents on your NetWare server, then set up the Search server. Users will be amazed at the performance, and Web developers will gnash their teeth.

See Appendix A, "NetWare Web Services," for details on using Web Search and building a search site.

IFOLDER MANAGEMENT

One of the best new features of NetWare 6, iFolder, provides a way for users to synchronize their data files with a local or remote NetWare server over the Internet or LAN, all without using Net-Ware Client32 software. Tired of e-mailing files back and forth, and trying to keep straight which file has the latest information? The utility in Figure 8.8 solves all those problems, and more.

Here's what you can do from this utility:

◆ Monitor iFolder server status

◆ Set client policies for types of access and synchronization

◆ Set the amount of disk space available per iFolder client

FIGURE 8.8

Easy configuration for one of NetWare 6's best new features

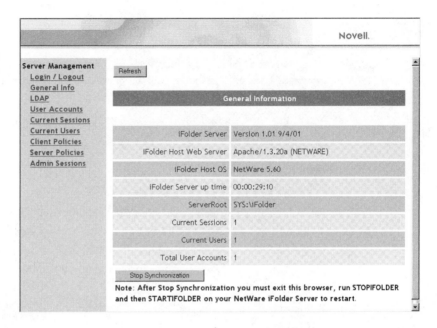

Plenty more information on iFolder awaits in Chapter 13, "Remote File Access with iFolder and NetDrive," along with other new options for accessing NetWare files across the Internet.

ConsoleOne Overview

We'll delve deep into each of the browser-based utilities as we examine various functions they perform. Since there won't be any one time that ConsoleOne gets a solid overview, let's do that now.

CONSOLEONE BENEFITS

First, let's consider why Novell pushed ConsoleOne over NetWare Administrator. The reasons are grouped in decreasing importance, at least the way I see it:

◆ ConsoleOne holds more objects. Improved memory management on the client side (limitations caused by Windows, NetWare Administrator, or both) allows ConsoleOne to load and display thousands more objects than NetWare Administrator.

◆ ConsoleOne runs on multiple platforms. It has the same look (almost exactly) and feel on a NetWare server or a workstation running Windows, Linux, Solaris, or Tru64 Unix (not a big call, but it is Unix).

◆ It lets you manage the latest new object goodies. Obviously, Novell developers could have written support for new objects into NetWare Administrator if they wished, but they didn't. That's what I call a neutral recommendation.

◆ It lets you access content in remote trees without logging in. This might be a useful feature for large networks.

◆ It lets you modify multiple object types at once. NetWare Administrator can only modify groups of User objects (but Novell designers could have upgraded NetWare Administrator to do this, couldn't they?).

◆ You can use it to set up Role Based Services. This is a minor upgrade from Organizational Roles in NetWare Administrator.

CONSOLEONE SHORTCOMINGS

ConsoleOne includes several remaining shortcomings:

◆ Its support for print services is incomplete. As covered in Chapter 6, "incomplete" is a very polite word for the state of print services in ConsoleOne and iManage.

◆ It can't manage some older Novell products. This says more about those products, I think, than about ConsoleOne, but how can you trumpet an administration tool that can't administer everything?

◆ Performance "can be sluggish" on older hardware. Novell's phrasing implies ConsoleOne speeds up on hot hardware. Sorry, but I haven't noticed that nearly as much as Novell would like us to believe.

Being a realist, it doesn't matter what I say about ConsoleOne versus browser-based utilities or NetWare Administrator. I get what Novell gives me. The best third-party NDS and other NetWare tools from Visual Click Software, Inc. (www.visualclick.com) include much more pizzazz and value than ConsoleOne, so you have that option and a very few others. But let's work with what we have.

THE CONSOLEONE INTERFACE

Figure 8.9 shows a view of ConsoleOne with as many icons active as possible. Let's go over the menus first, and then catch up to the icons.

FIGURE 8.9

A crowded ConsoleOne screen

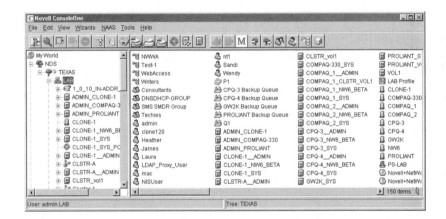

TIP   You can easily change the spacing of the columns in the right display pane of ConsoleOne. Move your cursor slowly over the area between two columns, as if there were a line separating them. When you hit the right spot, your cursor will become a two-headed arrow pointing right and left. Click and adjust the invisible column divider to your liking, and then release the left button. All the columns will reapportion themselves to set the spacing between each column the same distance as you chose for the two columns.

THE FILE MENU

The File menu offers some standard choices and some that might surprise you:

New   Opens a submenu offering the following new objects to create: Cluster, Object, Group, User, and Organizational Unit. Cluster, the first submenu, includes Cluster Resource and Cluster Volume. (The Insert key no longer works as a shortcut for New as it did in older NetWare menus.)

Migration   Migrates NIS (Network Information Services) domain name and IP address information into NDS eDirectory in support of Native File Access for Unix.

Authenticate   Logs in to NDS eDirectory, in case your connection timed out, you connect to the ConsoleOne running on the server, or you cross into another eDirectory tree.

Unauthenticate   Logs out of eDirectory.

Delete NDS Object   Deletes the highlighted object.

Move   Moves selected leaf objects or files to other locations. Destinations are selected in a dialog box that appears.

Rename   Opens a dialog box to rename the selected object. You have the option to keep the old name to maintain existing references to the object.

Trustees of This Object   Shows which other objects have rights to the selected object. This option is also used to set the object's Inherited Rights Filter (IRF).

Extensions of This Object   Shows any defined class extension and offers a command button to Add Extensions to the highlighted object.

Right to Other Objects   Shows which rights the highlighted object has to other objects. You must specify which part of the NDS eDirectory tree you wish to search to gather this information.

Properties of Multiple Objects   Starting with NetWare 4.11 and now continued in NetWare 6, you may choose multiple objects and take some action on all highlighted objects at one time.

Actions   Reserved for future use and upcoming snap-ins.

Properties   Opens the property page for the object highlighted in the left frame.

Exit   Closes the ConsoleOne program.

THE EDIT MENU

The Edit menu contains three helpful options:

Go To Opens a dialog box to jump directly to an object. This is handy for jumping down multiple containers when a large network slows ConsoleOne more than normal.

Find Opens a Search dialog box—the same action as clicking the magnifying glass icon on the toolbar below the Edit menu.

Preferences Sets the display preferences for ConsoleOne, a very dull page with this release.

THE VIEW MENU

The View menu offers options for changing your view in ConsoleOne:

Console View Shows ConsoleOne's view of objects (as in Figure 8.9, shown earlier).

Partition and Replica View Shows ConsoleOne's view of partitions and replicas found inside the highlighted container.

Filter Opens a dialog box offering to filter based on object type. A pick list of every object type imaginable is provided.

Set As Root Makes the container object highlighted in the right pane the top level of the visible eDirectory objects.

Go Up One Level Sets the root of the browser window up one level in the eDirectory hierarchy.

Show My World Reserved for future use.

Show View Title Opens a status bar across the top of the right pane labeled either Console View or Partition View. It takes up space, and the setting is pretty obvious without the status bar stealing screen real estate.

Refresh Queries eDirectory to display any changes since the view inside ConsoleOne had been requested earlier.

Set Context Changes the context shown at the top of the browser window or panel.

THE WIZARDS MENU

The Wizards menu offers two options:

NDS Import/Export Opens a dialog box offering to import or export an LDIF (Lightweight Directory Interchange Format) file in ASCII format to or from eDirectory.

Filtered Replica Configuration Provides help in creating a replica containing only those types of objects and properties you want it to contain.

THE NAAS MENU

NAAS (Novell Advanced Audit Service), an optional snap-in for ConsoleOne, tracks resource and object usage. Its menu has three options:

Filter   Filters NAAS to keep the scope manageable.

Report   Lets you pull programmed reports from the Pervasive SQL database (the new name for Btrieve) included as part of the auditing service.

Query   Queries the Pervasive SQL database created by NAAS.

THE TOOLS MENU

The Tools menu offers access to the following tools:

Disk Management   Opens a submenu with six options: Devices, RAID Devices, Free Space, Partitions, NSS Pools, NSS Logical Volumes, and Traditional Volumes. All are server-specific utilities.

Issue Certificate   Works with Novell security infrastructure by offering a space to paste a Certificate Signing Request (CSR) or browse for a CSR file to be signed.

Install   Opens an Installation Wizard to install additional services onto your server and into the ConsoleOne management framework.

Install Novell-Defined Reports   Pulls from a set of Novell-written reports, if you have installed the Reporting Services Install snap-in.

Schema Manager   Opens a dialog box showing each and every class and attributes inside eDirectory, with the option to create more or delete existing classes and attributes.

WAN Traffic Manager   Opens a submenu offering to Add Wanman Schema (or delete it).

Configure NAAS   Offers a dialog box with radio buttons to install, in order, an NAAS Agent, NAAS server, and NAAS database, and to configure the NAAS framework.

THE HELP MENU

The Help menu provides help in the following ways:

Contents   Pops open a Java Help window utility, but often just uses a browser to link to the NetWare 6 sites.

Novell on the Web   Every beginner's favorite new menu command, offers three choices: Product Documentation, Support, and Novell Home.

About Snapins   Opens a nice Registered ConsoleOne Snapins dialog box, with each installed snap-in given a separate page linked from the dialog box.

About ConsoleOne   Opens the standard Windows About box, popping up a dialog box with the Java version, JDK software kit, copyright, patents, and a hyperlink to ConsoleOne information on the Novell Web site.

CONSOLEONE TOOLBAR ICONS

Most of the ConsoleOne toolbar icons duplicate menu options. Let's start from the left and go all the way to the right.

Icon	Function
Door	Exit ConsoleOne
Magnifying glass	Find
Strange box with arrow	Set As Root
Box with curved line (gray)	Show My World
Circle with dash (gray)	Stop
Small ball with swoosh	Refresh
Paper with question mark	Help Contents
Computer box	Device Disk Management
Box with pie piece	RAID Device Disk Management
Box with no pie piece	Free Space Disk Management
Box with circle and pie piece	Partition Disk Management
Blue diamond	Pool Disk Management
Disk drive with racing stripes	Logical Volume Disk Management
Disk drive by itself	Traditional Volume Disk Management
Pyramid with ball (gray)	New Cluster Resource
Disk drive with ball (gray)	New Cluster Volume
M	Migration
Tree with white arrow	Authenticate
Tree with no leaves	NDS Unauthenticate
Group	New Group
Single user	New User
Organizational Unit	New Organizational Unit
Block	New Object

NOTE *Those of you running a 3D cursor may have trouble with ConsoleOne screen refreshes. Go back to your normal, bland cursor and see if there is a difference.*

DEAD UTILITIES

Here's a direct quote from the NetWare README . TXT file:

"Many DOS utilities have been removed from NetWare 6. The following utilities are still included for your convenience, but they are not supported:

CAPTURE

CX

FILER

LOGIN

LOGOUT

MAP

NCOPY

NDIR

NetWare Administrator

NLIST

NPRINTER

RIGHTS"

See anything on that list that shocks you? The one in uppercase and lowercase, perhaps? Yes, NetWare Administrator now belongs on the junk heap, at least according to the readme file. Do you have any more questions about ConsoleOne and the browser-based utilities taking over?

Container and Leaf Object Management

The move to a graphical utility for management reinforced the object-oriented foundation of Net-Ware 4 when it appeared. Perhaps it's just me, but the ability to open containers and see their containers, which might hold even more containers, helps emphasize the idea of inheritance. Drilling down through your network from the highest [Root] context through an Organization, through one or more Organizational Units, through a Volume object, through a directory, and down to an individual file displays the organization like a giant network x-ray.

NOTE   A distributed database takes time to "ripple out" the changes. Just as the waves from a pebble splash take a moment to reach the bank of the pond, so, too, does NDS eDirectory take a bit of time to synchronize all servers. The control over user information is quick, just as it was with SYSCON or NetWare Administrator. The control over eDirectory takes a bit longer. Try to wait for results twice as long as you think is possible, and you'll be about right.

When you create container and leaf objects, you'll give them a name. Let's take a moment to reiterate the naming rules and guidelines for NDS objects:

◆ Names must be less than 64 characters long. Names longer than 47 characters are truncated for non-NDS clients.

◆ Names must be unique within the container.

◆ Names are not case-sensitive but will be displayed as typed in the Name field. For example, although SalesSupport will display as you see here, NDS regards it as identical to salessupport and SALESSUPPORT.

◆ Spaces can be used and will be displayed as spaces within NDS. Spaces are shown as underscores for non-NDS clients.

◆ The following characters cannot be seen by non-NDS clients: slash (/), backslash (\ ), colon (:), comma (,), asterisk (*), and question mark (?).

Creating Container Objects

IN A HURRY 8.1: CREATE A CONTAINER

1. Log in to the network as the Admin user or equivalent and start ConsoleOne.

2. To create an Organization, highlight the NDS Tree level. To create an Organizational Unit, highlight the Organization or Organizational Unit that will hold the new container.

3. Right-click and choose New ➤ Object.

4. Choose to create an Organization or Organizational Unit.

5. Type the name of the new container.

6. You can check either Define Additional Properties or Create Another Organizational Unit (or Create Another Organization), but not both. Check Define User Defaults if you want the container to inherit the parent container's template.

7. Click Create, then Yes or No for the template if the Define User Defaults box was checked in the previous step.

An Organization can contain anything except another Organization. Only the NDS eDirectory tree (called [Root], with MyWorld above it to hold multiple trees) can contain an Organization. All leaf objects may be contained in an Organization. Single-server networks may easily be a single Organization holding all servers, users, and network resources, mimicking a flat, NetWare 3 network. NetWare 6 Small Business Suite uses this type of design. Even large networks, however, often have only a single Organization.

Used much more often is the *Organizational Unit*. Any container, including another Organizational Unit, can contain an Organizational Unit. Typically, there are multiple Organizational Units per

Organization, and darn few Organization containers. (See Chapter 2, "Novell Directory Services: eDirectory Overview, Planning, and Expansion," for a review of all NDS containers.)

The process of creating either container is the same. The difference is only where you put the container. Here are the results of right-clicking on the LAB Organization container and rolling the cursor through the New entry to pop open the submenu:

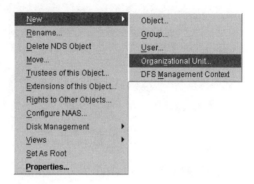

From this submenu, you can scroll down and choose Organizational Unit directly or choose Object and scroll down the search window that appears until you find the Organizational Unit object. If you're really daring, you can just highlight the container and click the Organizational Unit icon on the far end of the ConsoleOne toolbar. (So many choices for a simple process, and we haven't even looked at the other administrative tools yet.)

Menu items from the right-click pop-up menu come and go, depending on the situation. For instance, if I had right-clicked a file server, the only New item that would not be grayed out in the submenu would be Object. Since anything can go in an Organization container, all menu options appear.

After you've chosen what you want to create, you can give it a name. Here is the New Organizational Unit dialog box, with the name Test-2 in the Name field. It's not terribly creative, I know, especially since I already have Test-1.

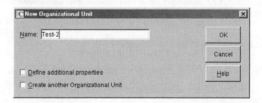

Containers have as many details about themselves as do User and Group objects. In fact, the property page for the Organizational Unit Test-2.LAB has as many tabs as there are in the User and Group object property pages. Check out Figure 8.10 to see what I mean. The screen in this figure should be familiar, since it's the same as for a User object or Group object. The users in Test-2.LAB have rights to files and directories, because their container has rights to those files and directories.

FIGURE 8.10

Showing that a container has access to directories and files, just like a user

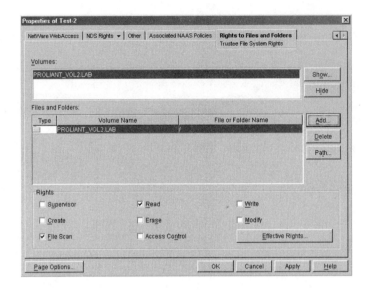

This is an advantage of NetWare 6 over NetWare 3 versions. Using container objects similarly to how you used a group in NetWare 3 allows you to grant trustee rights to files and directories without modifying any of the User object's rights individually. NetWare 6 Group objects do have the advantage of being able to grant trustee rights to User objects from different containers, and so they are still useful.

The only improvement in this screen from the similar screen in NetWare 4.11 came with NetWare 5.0. This is the addition of the Path command button beside the Files and Folders list. When you click this button, a little information box appears to inform you of the full pathname of the volume highlighted in the Files and Folders list.

Creating Leaf Objects

IN A HURRY 8.2: CREATE A LEAF OBJECT

1. Log in to the network as the Admin user or equivalent and start ConsoleOne.

2. Right-click the container for the new leaf object.

3. Choose the leaf object to create from the New Object list.

4. Name the new leaf object. If necessary, provide file or location information.

5. Check a box to either Define Additional Properties or Create Another leaf object.

6. Click Create to save the new object.

The process for creating a leaf object is basically the same for all types of objects. The differences are related to whether the new object depends on a directory or volume path or on some other reference to the NDS eDirectory tree that a User or Group object won't need.

As an example, let's create a Directory Map object. A directory map represents a particular directory in the filesystem. We'll cover details about directory maps and their uses in Chapter 9, "Providing Applications for Your Network Clients."

After right-clicking the container for the object, the New Object list box opens. Choose your object by double-clicking or by highlighting it and clicking OK.

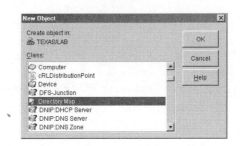

Then the Create *object* dialog box opens. (The dialog box title always indicates which type of object you are creating.) Since a Directory Map object works with the filesystem, the Create Directory Map dialog box has more information than usual. Here, we need to detail the volume used and the path within that volume.

You need a name for the Directory Map object and a link to the directory represented by the Directory Map. Click the Browse button to the immediate right of the Volume and Path fields to open a search box. Drill down until you find the directory needing the Directory Map object, then double-click or highlight and click the OK command button.

If you prefer to type the path, take note of two important details. First, the Path field starts with a backslash, with slashes between the directories. Second, eDirectory doesn't create the directory structure you type in here. If you mistype and tie the Directory Map to a nonexistent directory, the directory map will happily send users to la la land. That's why I always use the search box to drill down to the directory. It avoids typing mistakes and ensures that the directory really exists.

Let's pretend our company has a Unix-based product named 233, which includes documentation. The documentation path makes sense within the overall documentation structure, but the structure does not lend itself to easy location for nontechnical network users. By putting the documentation link within the UnixDocs directory map, users can find what they need more easily without forcing a change in the directory structure. Here's the New Directory Map dialog box for creating the Unix-Docs Directory Map object:

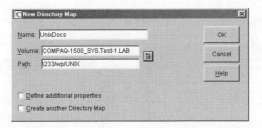

NOTE   *Directory Map objects carry no special NDS rights to the files and directories listed. When users take the directory map shortcut, they still need assigned rights to the target directory and files.*

Modifying Multiple Objects

Adding on to our example from the last section, let's pretend several users outside the documentation department must have access to change the files inside the Directory Map object's directory location. You can click and modify the Rights to Files and Folders for each of the users individually, but that would show you didn't pay attention to my advice back in Chapter 5, "Handling More Than One User at a Time," to swear off single users.

We have two choices for easy ways to add new rights to multiple users: Put them in a group, or manage a group of like objects together. Let's do it the wrong way (at least to my way of thinking) and modify multiple objects rather than put them into a group.

Take a look at some clever mousing around to manage four people's rights at once.

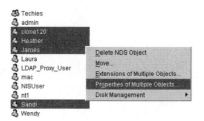

Hold down the Ctrl key as you click each user, just as you do to select multiple items in a Windows application. If all objects are consecutive, you can click the first one, hold down the Shift key, then click the last in the series, and all will be highlighted.

Once the set of multiple objects have been tagged, you can select File ➤ Properties of Multiple Objects. Alternatively, you can right-click one of the highlighted objects, which is what I did, so I could pop open the menu you see above. Yes, those choices are inside the File menu, but that's not as much fun as right-clicking and seeing the items appear close to the action, rather than being listed as active menu options. This is just a personal preference, so you can ignore my choice without repercussion.

The property page that opens can't say the target object name, because there isn't a single target object. So the page is titled Properties of Multiple Objects, which is true. Notice the Add and Remove command buttons just to the right of the main screen in Figure 8.11. When you realize you've clicked one too many objects, as I have with the phantom user clone120.LAB, you want to click Remove to get rid of that item.

The Delete warning sounds ominous: "Do you really want to delete the object?" Of course not, but, yes, I really do. Although unclear, the Delete function applies only to the object's listing as one of the multiple objects. Saying Yes to delete clone120.LAB only takes it out of the list, not out of eDirectory.

Now that you have the list you want, you can use this property page to change most of the normal properties you can change for any of the objects. Yet in one of the aggravating quirks showing the immaturity of ConsoleOne, you can't give the multiple objects rights to files and folders. Notice that in Figure 8.11 the last tab at the top of the dialog box is Associated NAAS Policies. If I had a single user selected, the Rights to Files and Folders tab would be the last tab on the right, sitting in the currently empty space.

FIGURE 8.11

Removing one of multiple objects

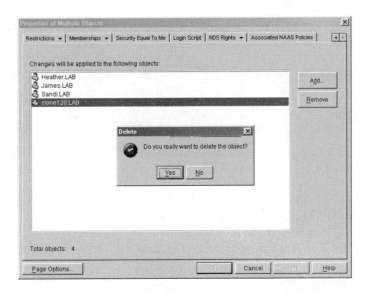

So, back to NetWare Administrator we go, at least if you want to change access for a group of users at once. Figure 8.12 shows the same group as in Figure 8.11, but inside NetWare Administrator. Here you must use the Object menu to choose Details on Multiple Users, since only users can be grouped in this manner.

FIGURE 8.12

Back to NetWare Administrator for granting file access rights

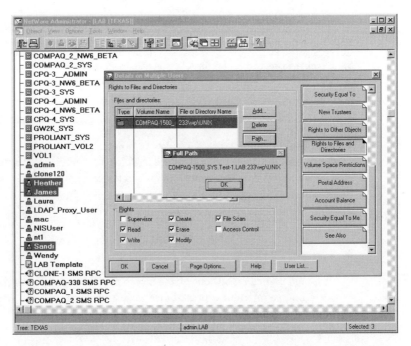

To be fair, ConsoleOne allows you to group many more things than just users, as long as you choose like objects. And ConsoleOne does seem slightly quicker drilling down to the directory in question, making the NetWare Administrator search function feel old-fashioned and slow. But at least the old-fashioned and slow method works for file access, which the spiffy new ConsoleOne doesn't. Consider yourself warned about this hole in ConsoleOne's abilities. If I wanted to change hours of access, or make special login script additions to add the new Directory Map object to each user upon login, I could do that through ConsoleOne. It just so happened we hit the one thing ConsoleOne couldn't do in this case.

A warning dialog box appears when you click the OK button, saying applying changes to multiple objects may take an extended period of time, and giving you a chance to bail out. Modifying three user profiles shouldn't take long, so I clicked OK.

Notice that I'm granting the users rights to Read, Write, Create, Erase, Modify, and File Scan the files in the target directory, but not Supervisor or Access Control. Either of those choices would allow these three users to add more names to the list whenever they wanted, allowing access I wouldn't know about. This is never a good thing. (See Chapter 7 for more on access rights.)

Moving Objects

IN A HURRY 8.3: MOVE AN OBJECT

1. Log in to the network as the Admin user or equivalent and start ConsoleOne.

2. Right-click the object to be moved and choose Move.

3. Click the Browse button to open the Select Object dialog box.

4. Choose the new location and click OK to exit the Select Object dialog box.

5. Check the Create an Alias for All Objects Being Moved option if you want to leave a pointer in the old location.

6. Click OK to save the settings.

When you move a leaf object, all NDS eDirectory references to the moved object are changed. The common name of the object will remain the same, but the full name showing the context will change.

NOTE *Early versions of NetWare 4 allowed the moving of leaf objects only. Now, however, you may move any container object as well, but with some caveats. A container object can be moved only if it is the root of an NDS partition that has no subordinate partitions.*

Dropping user clone120 out of the mix in the earlier section reminded me that perhaps this test user belongs in a different context. Since we just made the Test-2.LAB Organizational Unit earlier, let's move clone120 down there.

Right-click our imaginary user friend and choose Move from the pop-up menu. The Move dialog box appears, and in an "improvement" over NetWare Administrator, ConsoleOne doesn't allow you to type the new location in the Destination field. You must use the Browse button to the right of the field. That's safer anyway, so maybe ConsoleOne is doing us a favor to help avoid typos.

We don't need to drill down too far, just to the Test-2.LAB OU one level below LAB. When you highlight an object that will accept the moved object, the OK command button becomes active. Click that button when you're happy with the location.

Moving objects referenced in other places can cause problems. To avoid those, Novell long ago added a way to leave an Alias object in the old location, pointing to the new location for the object. Check the Create an Alias for All Objects Being Moved box if you wish to leave such a reference point. I leave an alias for every object except a user. All the details are arranged for viewing in Figure 8.13.

FIGURE 8.13

Moving that trouble-maker clone120

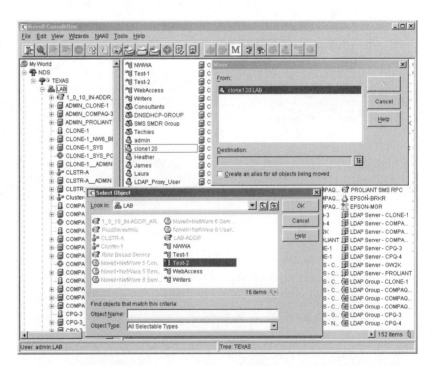

NOTE *NetWare 4.10's NetWare Administrator program introduced the idea of an option to create an Alias object in place of the moved object. That idea disappeared in NetWare 5, perhaps because research told Novell that people didn't use the function or because the designers forgot to upgrade those lines of code. Either way, once you moved an object, the only way to leave an alias in its place was to create one yourself. Funny how times change, and the alias option appears once again in NetWare 6.*

Renaming Objects

1. Log in to the network as the Admin user or equivalent and start ConsoleOne.

2. Right-click the object and choose Rename.

3. Type the new name.

4. Indicate whether to save the old name and whether to create an alias if renaming a container.

5. Click OK to rename the object.

This may come as a shock to you, but things in your network will change. Some brilliant vice president will decide that SLS+MKTG must become MKTG+SLS, and every reference in the company, including the network Organizational Unit, needs to change. Luckily, this is easier and much cheaper than getting new business cards (quicker, too).

To change an object's name, you just highlight the object that needs the name change and pick Rename from the File menu, or right-click it and use the pop-up menu. A small dialog box appears, asking for the new name. Here is a picture of the process of renaming Test-2 to Test-Two (yes, some corporate directives are just that stupid).

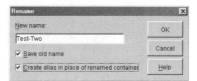

With this step, all references to Test-2 will become Test-Two, throughout the entire eDirectory tree. What about the users who will go looking for Test-2, only to be disappointed? As you can see in the Rename dialog box, there are two ways to make sure the users can find the container:

◆ The first check box asks if you wish to save the old name. This will keep the name as an alias in the NDS database, so searches for the old name will work. The search results will tell the users (or other network administrators) what the new name for the object is.

◆ The second check box creates an Alias object with the name of the original object. The Alias object points to the object with its new name. Users with references to the newly renamed object in their login script will be connected properly.

Finding Objects

As your network and eDirectory database both get larger, finding particular objects will get tough. Your users will be okay, since they spend most of their time in specific containers using a small set of servers and volumes. You, however, must patrol the entire network. ConsoleOne provides several ways to locate objects. We'll also look at one NetWare Administrator technique.

FILTERING OBJECTS

IN A HURRY 8.5: FILTER OBJECTS IN YOUR VIEW

1. Log in to the network as the Admin user or equivalent and start ConsoleOne.

2. Choose View ➢ Filter.

3. Check the box or boxes for object types to display.

4. Enter a name in the top field (optional).

5. Click Preview to see the filter results.

6. Click the OK command button to activate the filter.

ConsoleOne can get crowded and make things tough to find. Even in the small lab network I'm using for these screen shots, plenty of "stuff" can get in the way.

One of the real advantages of ConsoleOne over NetWare Administrator comes in its ability to handle large numbers of objects with much more control and stability than ever before. After all, to filter thousands of objects down to just a few requires plenty of horsepower.

Let's say you want to spend some time working on just the servers in one of your large containers. Even though the right pane of ConsoleOne groups the servers together, finding them in the window can be more aggravation than you want.

To get to the Filter function, open the View menu to find and choose Filter. The Filter dialog box, shown in Figure 8.14, offers a fairly clean method of operation. By default, the filter is always active, but the first item in the Object Type list box is All Types (*), meaning that everything gets through the filter. When you check another box in this list, ConsoleOne deletes the All Types check. Scroll down to find and check the object types you want to display; feel free to mix and match any two or more object types.

Since many "servers" inhabit a single NetWare physical server, the code for what we consider a "NetWare" server is NCP Server. In Figure 8.14, the NCP Server box is checked, and then I clicked the Preview button. With this great tool, I can get a look at what will happen before committing to the filter.

Notice that the servers line up alphabetically, but only the servers in the current context appear. That's the limitation of the Filter feature, but there are other options available to search through all containers, which we'll discuss soon.

When you're finished with the filtered output, remember to reopen the Filter dialog box and click the Reset command button. If you forget, you may give yourself a heart attack when you come back and wonder what happened to your network.

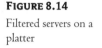

FIGURE 8.14

Filtered servers on a platter

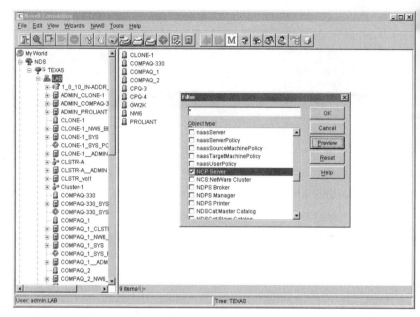

JUMPING TO OBJECTS

IN A HURRY 8.6: JUMP TO OBJECTS

1. Log in to the network as the Admin user or equivalent and start ConsoleOne.

2. In the left pane, highlight the container holding the object targeted for jumping.

3. Click anywhere in the right pane.

4. Start typing the name of the object.

5. Click OK to start the search.

6. Use the search results in their own browser window.

What if you're in a context and just want to find one server? How about if you're tired of scrolling around and just want to find a particular printer?

Rather than filter for all the servers or printers, which you now know how to do, you can just "jump" to an object (I guess "jaunting" wasn't used because no one at Novell is an Alfred Bester fan). When you jump to an object, your feet land on the first object that fits the jump information you provided.

It's not hard to jump to an object. Set the context for your object jump, then click somewhere on the right pane—it doesn't matter where you click or what you highlight. Then, believe it or not, just type. The letters appear as you type in the bottom-right corner of ConsoleOne, as you can see below.

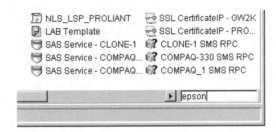

The letter case you use for the jump doesn't matter, so don't sprain your little Shift key fingers. Just type the letters, and when you type enough to clearly identify the object you want to jump to, hit the Enter key.

Nothing startling happens, although the result can save some time. The screen shifts, and suddenly the named object matching the letters you typed is highlighted, awaiting further action. Notice I didn't say the "object you wanted" is highlighted, because you can get fooled. If several objects start with the same letters, such VOL1 and VOL2, the first object that matches the typed letters gets jumped on. If you type **VOL** in this example, you'll jump to VOL1. If you want VOL2, you had better type **VOL2**.

GO TO: JUMPING WITH DRILL DOWN

IN A HURRY 8.7: GO TO OBJECTS

1. Log in to the network as the Admin user or equivalent and start ConsoleOne.

2. Highlight the container in the left pane holding the object targeted for finding.

3. Click anywhere in the left pane.

4. Type the full name of the object you want to go to.

5. Click OK or press Enter to go to the object.

The NetWare 6 documentation calls this "Finding an Object by Distinguished Name." Could that be any duller? Yet the full, dull name does a more technically accurate job than my "Go To: Jumping with Drill Down" (but it doesn't play off the earlier "Jumping" section).

You can take the less-fun way out and open the Edit menu and choose Go To, but starting to type in the left pane pops open the Go To dialog box. The label above the text box says, "Full object name," and it means exactly that. When you don't type the full name in the Go To dialog box, you get an error message, like the one shown here.

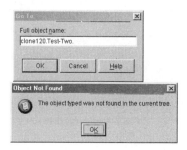

The Object Not Found dialog box appeared because I hit Enter too soon in the Go To dialog box. You probably can't see it in the screen shot, but there's a period at the end of "clone120.Test-Two." I wondered if that would be enough to tell Go To it should look up a level, but no such luck.

When I typed the rest of the name for clone120 (added the *LAB*), the right pane of ConsoleOne changed to show the contents of Organizational Unit Test-Two and highlighted clone120. The left pane changed as well, shifting and highlighting the Test-Two Organizational Unit.

FINDING OBJECTS BY NAME OR TYPE

IN A HURRY 8.8: FIND OBJECTS BY NAME AND/OR OBJECT TYPE

1. Log in to the network as the Admin user or equivalent and start ConsoleOne.

2. Select Edit ➢ Find or click the magnifying glass icon on the toolbar.

3. Check the Search Subcontainers box if desired.

4. Choose Standard in the Find Type box.

5. Type the name to find or leave the wildcard (*) in place.

6. Pick the object type (optional).

7. Click the Find command button.

Now we're getting to some specialized Find functions that are most valuable in large networks. After all, searching a single container may not help if you've got a bucket load of containers to search. Using more advanced Find utilities for better searching will help ease some of your management burden.

Technically, this option works by finding objects by either their name or the object type. When searching by name, the Find feature works better than Go To, because it can search subcontainers. When searching for object types, the same drill-down features make it a winner as well.

Figure 8.15 shows the Find dialog box. In this example, I've searched for servers once again. Notice the difference? The highlighted server resides in a container rather than in the current context.

FIGURE 8.15

More searching flexibility with the Find feature

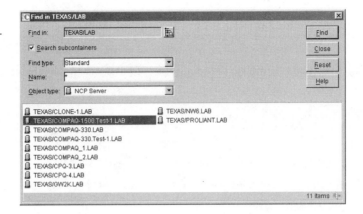

All servers on the network, or at least those in or below the LAB container, appear in the search results window. And only five short steps to such success!

1. Decide which context to start and set that in the Find In text box. Once again you can't type, but the search dialog box that appears when you click the Browse button works fairly quickly.

2. Check the Search Subcontainers box, unless all you care about are the objects visible in the right pane of ConsoleOne. If you just want one container's worth of objects, why not use the filter? To each his or her own, I suppose.

3. The Find Type drop-down list offers two choices: Standard and Advanced. That choice determines whether we're searching by name or object type, or searching for properties matching certain values. The Advanced option will be covered in the next section.

4. If you're looking for particular name or group of letters starting a name, type that into the Name field. If you're going to search by object type, leave the wildcard (*) in this field.

5. If you are going to search by object type, you'll have fun scrolling through the hundred plus object types listed in the Object Type drop-down list. Type the first letter of your desired object type and save yourself some scrolling.

Once the object type is set, the Find fun begins. Pretty quickly, your results will appear in the results box. If you want to adjust the column spacing, move your cursor over the area between two columns until your cursor becomes a two-headed arrow pointing right and left. Drag the invisible column divider to change the spacing, and then release the left button. All the columns will adjust to have the same spacing as you chose for the two columns.

After you've found your object(s), you may highlight them and treat them as you will. Right-click any one or combination and make your choice from the pop-up menu that appears. This menu is exactly the same one as if you had searched manually through your container to find the object.

FINDING OBJECTS BY PROPERTY VALUES

IN A HURRY 8.9: FIND OBJECTS BY NAME AND/OR OBJECT TYPE

1. Log in to the network as the Admin user or equivalent and start ConsoleOne.

2. Select Edit ➢ Find or click the magnifying glass icon on the toolbar.

3. Check the Search subcontainers box if desired.

4. Choose Advanced in the Find Type box.

5. Choose the object type, Boolean operator, and object class.

6. Choose End or New Group for more complicated searches.

7. Click the Find command button.

The most advanced Find option allows you to build complicated Boolean search queries using as many object types and object classes as you wish. Think of this as a "do-it-yourself" search engine.

Start the search by selecting your context (TEXAS/LAB in my example), again via a search dialog box rather than typing it in. I wish the Search Subcontainers box came checked by default, but I understand that large networks mean slower response, so that choice should be made by the administrator.

The outlined box in the middle of the screen displays the search criteria you build using multiple "Object Type Equals/Not Equals Object Class" phrases. If you don't speak Boolean-flavored eDirectory, let me translate: You search by NDS attribute that matches or does not match in some way an NDS object type. See Figure 8.16 for a potentially helpful example.

FIGURE 8.16

Click and choose your way to Boolean phrases

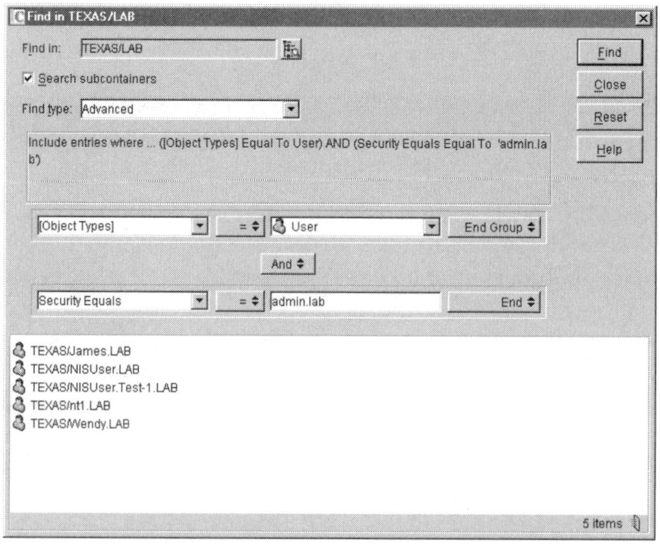

Opening with a single "something equals something" pair of menus, the Advanced Find dialog box only hints at the mind-numbing number of choices you can make. I opted for a simple "Object Type Equals User" for my opening bid. Depending on the object type chosen, your comparison operator (button with the equal sign) can be Equal To, Not Equal To, Less Than or Equal To, or Greater Than or Equal To. The command button at the end of the line offers the choices of And, Or, Insert Row, Delete Row (gray in the first row), New Group, and End (the default).

I took Block 1, "Object Type Equals User," and then chose And to start the second block. Here, I chose Security Equals from the hundred plus NDS attributes available (including VehicleInformation and WorkForceID, telling me that Novell really wants people to use eDirectory as their total person-nel database). Then I typed ADMIN.LAB to search for all users with Admin equivalency. When I clicked the Find button, five names appeared.

One of the most serious security breaches occurs when the wrong person has the ultimate net-work access privileges, and this type of search can tell you if this has happened. (NetWare 6 no longer has the SECURITY.EXE file that NetWare 3 used to list security settings for all users.) So, this search routine bears repeating on a regular basis. Let's just hit the Save command button… oops, this dialog box doesn't have a Save button. Here, we stumble on another ConsoleOne shortcoming. Let's rerun the same function in NetWare Administrator and see what we find.

SEARCHING FOR OBJECTS WITH NETWARE ADMINISTRATOR

IN A HURRY 8.10: SEARCH FOR OBJECTS WITH NETWARE ADMINISTRATOR

1. Log in to the network as the Admin user or equivalent and start NetWare Administrator.

2. Highlight the container from which to start the search (optional).

3. Select Object ➢ Search or click the flashlight icon on the toolbar.

4. Choose your search filters in the dialog box, or open a previously saved search filter.

5. Click OK to start the search.

6. Use the search results in their own browser window.

The Search option on NetWare Administrator's Object menu (you could click the flashlight icon on the toolbar instead of going through the menu) is equivalent to ConsoleOne's Edit ➢ Find command, but it offers one advantage: You can list search requirements based on an enormous num-ber of options and *save* the search query for reuse. Once the search is finished, the results appear in their own browser window, so they are easy to keep in one place and remain available for quick reference.

NOTE *Make sure you run the Search utility as a user with as many trustee rights as possible. The minimum rights required for a search are the Browse rights to objects, so you can see the entire network, and the Read and Compare property rights, so you can match a particular value to the object of your search profile.*

Figure 8.17 shows a search about to start in NetWare Administrator. This is the same search for users with Admin equivalency that we conducted with ConsoleOne in the previous section. Notice two differences: the Save and Open command buttons at the bottom of the dialog box. These are what are lacking in the ConsoleOne Find dialog box.

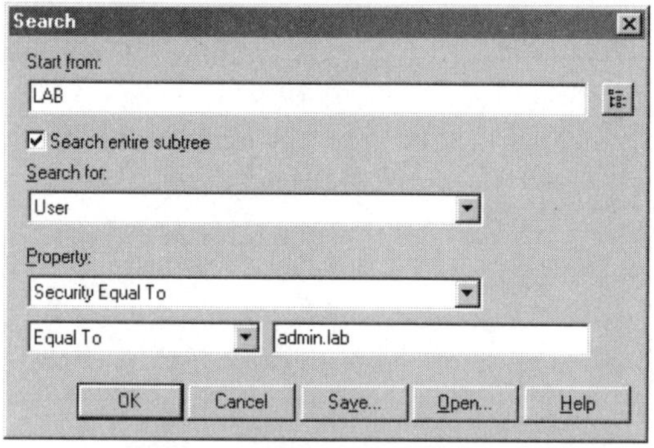

FIGURE 8.17

Searching for users who may be security risks

Setting a Search Filter

There are several steps in setting up a search filter. Here are some suggestions for the Search dialog box fields:

Start From The context you have highlighted when calling the Search dialog box is placed in the Start From field. If you don't wish to start from that point, click the Browse button at the end of the field and move through the NDS eDirectory tree until you find your preferred context.

Search Entire Subtree Checking this option searches the current container and all subordinate containers. When it isn't selected, the Search utility looks only in the current container.

Search For You can search for every leaf object, plus additions such as volume, Organization, and Organizational Unit. The default is User, figuring that some network client will be causing the problem you are searching to resolve.

Property This specifies the property value to search, based on the item in the Search For field. None is the default, somehow meaning all.

The field directly below Property could be called the Boolean field, since the contents tend to be Equal To or Not Equal To, Present or Not Present, Greater Than or Less Than, and the like. If you use this field to indicate a number or text, such as Equal To or Greater Than, enter the value in the text box to the right. In our example in Figure 8.17, "Equal To admin.lab" is specified for the search.

Search results appear in a separate browser window, waiting for you to take some action. You may minimize the window, keeping it available for use but out of your way while you go about your business within NetWare Administrator. Using the defaults of the Search window gathers all users in the container in one tidy spot, as you can see here.

Saving Search Criteria

The search results always inhabit their own browser window entitled Search. There's no way to save the search results for reuse later, but you can save the search criteria.

Notice the command buttons across the bottom of the Search dialog box in Figure 8.17. We expect OK, Cancel, and Help, but Save and Open are a surprise in NetWare Administrator. Once you have the search questions set the way you want them, click Save. A Save As dialog box appears, prompting you to put the saved procedure files in the MyDocuments directory, with an .SCH extension.

If you later click Open, the File Open dialog box arrives, aimed at the subdirectory you used to store the earlier searches. The File Name list box is set for the .SCH extension, so you merely need to double-click the name of the procedure you want to retrieve.

Once summoned, the Search dialog box waits for you, with all the previously configured information in the proper places. You may then click OK and either conduct the same search operation or modify any of the fields' contents before starting the search.

Mark up another hole in ConsoleOne.

User and Group Management

Most of the information about individual user creation and management is back in Chapter 4, "Creating and Managing User Objects." Turn to Chapter 5 for managing users in groups of one type or another, including how to set up menus and login scripts. What may be called the traditional user management information has thus already been covered.

But tradition isn't worth much now that we've burned through the new millennium and the new economy, is it? So we still have a few things worth covering about user management in this chapter. Here, we'll discuss account balances, disk space limitations, intruder detection, and the new Role Based Services.

Setting User Account Balances

1. Log in to the network as the Admin user or equivalent and open ConsoleOne.

2. Right-click the User object and choose Properties.

3. Select the Restrictions tab.

4. Click the down arrow and select Account Balance.

5. Click the Allow Unlimited Credit box to enable accounting for the user without the lockout restrictions.

6. Set the current Account Balance and the Low Balance Limit.

7. Click OK to save and exit.

If accounting is enabled on a server, the users of that server can be assigned a value for each server operation. The screen shown in Figure 8.18 shows how simple it is to track the server resources consumed by a user.

FIGURE 8.18

Accounting for user Wendy

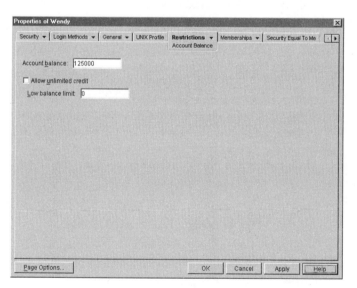

The Account Balance field shows the remaining credits available for this user. The credits are set on the network resource itself, as described in upcoming sections. The Low Balance Limit field shows the credit level that will trigger a warning to the user before the account is disabled. If the Allow Unlimited Credit box is checked, the Account Balance field will allow a negative number. This reflects the amount of resources used by that user since accounting was enabled or since the previous number was cleared.

If you wish to track the accounting information for charge-back or overhead calculations, but you don't wish to prevent users from reaching their network resources, click the Allow Unlimited Credit box. This tracks the information for the accounting reports but never locks out users.

Nothing bad happens to the user's *information* if a user is locked out of the system because of dropping to the level of the Low Balance Limit field. What happens with the *user*, on the other hand, is a matter for concern—obviously for him or her, but also for you. The user will be back in business as soon as an administrator changes the Account Balance field (that means another interruption for you), but that might not happen as quickly as the user will demand. Of course, if the person who runs out of credit occupies a higher position in the company hierarchy than you do, and it happens while you're out of town, you may wish you had never agreed to activate accounting. Before your boss forces accounting on you, make sure that all the possible problems, such as locking users out at the worst possible time, are covered and have an answer waiting.

We can set these limits for users, but not groups. Both ConsoleOne and NetWare Administrator work the same way for this setting, but server accounting can only be turned on using NetWare Administrator.

Limiting User Disk Space

IN A HURRY 8.12: SET THE USER DISK SPACE LIMIT

1. Log in to the network as the Admin user or equivalent and open ConsoleOne.

2. Locate the Volume object in the NDS tree, right-click it, and click Properties.

3. Click the Users with Space Restrictions tab.

4. Click the Add command button to add a user to restrict.

5. Use the Browse button to find the user to restrict.

6. Check the Limit User Space box and provide the maximum storage space for this user.

7. Click OK to save and exit.

Here's where you catch the disk hogs and tie them up if you desire. Setting disk space limits has a much more direct effect than charging back to the department, since the user will personally run out of disk space. The effect of reaching your disk limit is the same as emptying your bank account—there is nothing left. The disk will be full as far as that particular user is concerned.

TIP   *The capabilities of NDS eDirectory will allow watching the disk space for users scattered about the network, but that will take quite a bit more development. Also, NetWare provides no easy way to print this disk space information. I would be surprised if some third-party software developer isn't busy at this moment, working on software to query NDS and put this information into a report. You might want to check Visual Click Software, Inc. (*www.visualclick.com*).*

There are some interesting touches in the example shown in Figure 8.19. First, notice that the restrictions are based on volumes, not total network storage. ConsoleOne retains the handy feature from NetWare Administrator of showing the amount of disk space the user "owns" already. Good thing, since NetWare Administrator no longer includes the capability of setting space restrictions on NSS drives (although you can use NetWare Administrator to set restrictions on traditional NFS volumes). Score one for ConsoleOne.

FIGURE 8.19

Checking (and potentially clamping) a disk hog

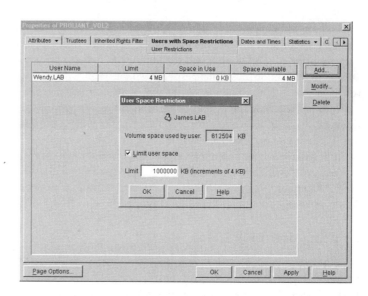

All the disk space numbers are in kilobytes, in 4KB blocks for NSS volumes. The default is to allow all users unlimited disk space, and that works fine for most networks.

In NetWare Administrator, the Space Available column shows the total amount of volume space available for everyone. That's because any *one* person can use that much space, not because *each* person can use that much space. NetWare makes no space restrictions by default; you must make those changes here. If you don't change the settings, the first users to fill the gigabyte that's available will get that gigabyte to themselves, and everyone else will go without. But ConsoleOne doesn't show these totals, so score one for NetWare Administrator.

In larger networks, it's much faster to check one container than to check the current container and all containers below that. However, the query doesn't generate enough traffic to noticeably slow the network, and it's much easier to look at all users of a volume at once.

Setting Intruder Detection

IN A HURRY 8.13: SET INTRUDER DETECTION

1. Log in to the network as the Admin user or equivalent and start ConsoleOne.

2. Highlight the container to modify, or immediately modify a new container with the Define Additional Properties box checked during setup.

3. Open the property page, and then click the General tab.

4. Click the down arrow and select Intruder Detection.

5. Check Detect Intruder and accept or modify the default settings.

6. Check Lock Account After Detection and accept or modify the default settings.

7. Click OK to save and exit.

Every new container deserves some security from the first moment of creation. You should get in the habit of thinking of security every time you create an object. Maybe you should stay ahead of the curve by considering security even *before* you create the object.

If you are setting up a new container, you may wish to select the Define Additional Properties check box in the Create Organizational Unit dialog box. If you are creating several containers at one time, that's not an available option. If you want to set intruder detection for an existing container, open that container object's property page, click the General tab, and choose Intruder Detection from the tab's menu. Adjust the settings from there.

Intruder detection works on the idea that anyone trying the same username with multiple password attempts is up to no good. We've talked about the simple passwords people choose if you let them pick their own, and other employees and crooks know to try the obvious choices first when trying to break into accounts. Figure 8.20 shows the setup screens for Intruder Detection, along with NetWare's much too lenient default settings.

FIGURE 8.20

Stopping the password guessing game

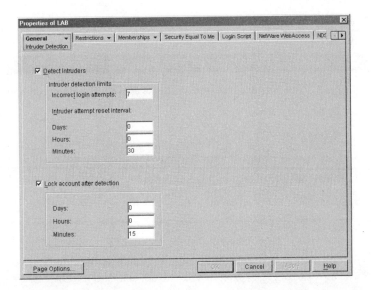

As you can see, the default setting for Incorrect Login Attempts is 7. This is much too high. If an employee coming back after a liquid lunch can't type a password in three tries, send that person home in a cab. The reset interval is 30 minutes, meaning three bad password guesses in 29 minutes will be counted as a possible intrusion. Since someone trying to crack the password will probably try several at a time, 30 minutes is enough for employees. But it isn't enough for outside attackers, who know about these detection settings. Set the time longer, such as one or two days, until someone complains.

The second check box tells the system what to do after the maximum password retry limit is exceeded. When the proper password isn't given in the set number of tries, the server console will beep, and the account will be locked. Again, the default (15 minutes) is far too short. Some recommend that the account be locked for a day or more. What if someone is trying to break the account on Friday evening? Locking it for only one day lets the perpetrator try again on Saturday and Sunday evenings without detection. Since you can reset the locked account easily by clicking the Intruder

Lockout command button for the user, set the lock to last for three days and protect your system through the weekend.

TIP *Keep notes on users who consistently come and ask for help clearing their messed up login attempts. You will have a paper trail of potential intruders, or at least a list of users who need a "password memorization techniques" training session.*

Using Role Based Services (RBS)

Another new feature appearing in NetWare 6, Role Based Services (RBS), expands and improves the Organizational Role from earlier NetWare versions. Now that NetWare covers the gamut from LAN concerns to global Internet integration, many new roles need players on your administrative team.

Many functions and names for these new role players await you inside templates in the RBS setup process. You may, as I did, be happy to learn how many onerous chores you can dump—er, reassign—to role players.

PREPARING FOR RBS

IN A HURRY 8.14: EXTEND THE NDS SCHEMA FOR RBS

1. Log in to the network as the Admin user or equivalent and start ConsoleOne.
2. Highlight the Tree or a container.
3. Choose Tools ➤ Install.
4. Check the Role Based Services box in the Product Name list and click Next.
5. Verify the Tree to hold RBS and click Next.
6. Verify the installation details in the Summary page and click Finish.

RBS installs automatically during NetWare 6 installation, but you also must extend the NDS schema to support new features that are not standard in eDirectory. This extension project should also happen automatically, but if it doesn't, you can take care of it quickly.

Start ConsoleOne while logged in as the Admin or equivalent user (do I still need to mention this for supervisory functions?). Highlight the Tree or any Organization or Organizational Unit in that Tree to coax the Tools menu to offer the Install option. Once there, choose the RBS product to install, as shown in Figure 8.21.

Verify the Tree you want, verify that all the details are configured as desired, and let eDirectory churn briefly to add the extra RBS widgets to NDS. You'll be finished with this in no time.

NOTE *Just about everything in RBS can be done in both ConsoleOne and iManage. If you want to try the iManage route, choose Extend Schema under the Role Based Services Setup menu item. It will tell you if the extensions have already been made.*

FIGURE 8.21

Extending the NDS schema for RBS

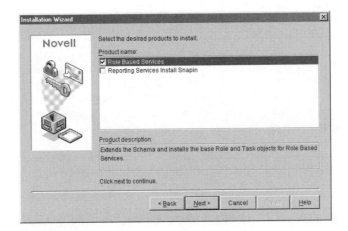

Before you start creating RBS roles, you need a special container to hold the roles and special task objects we'll soon make. Check your Tree for an item called Role Based Services, since it should have been created during installation or when you extended the schema. If it does not exist, create it.

Let's do this in iManage, because that utility keeps you from duplicating the object if it's already there. Of course, there's a small hiccup: You must create the rbsCollection object before iManage will tell you if it's a duplicate.

Click the Create rbsCollection menu item under Role Based Services Setup. The Name field will automatically supply Role Based Services. You only need to pick the container for the object. Higher containers are better than lower ones, as with most administrative objects. Once you've found your container, click OK, and the object will appear. If one is already there and you missed it, iManage will present you with an error message for your trouble.

ASSIGNING EXISTING RBS TEMPLATES TO USERS

IN A HURRY 8.15: ASSIGN RBS ROLES

1. Start iManage and provide the Admin user name or equivalent.

2. Click the Configure icon (the little man at a desk) in the iManage toolbar.

3. Click Modify Role under the Role Management heading on the left.

4. Click the magnifying glass in the Member column for the tasks you wish to assign.

5. Specify an object name (user, group, or container) in the Name column, then click Add.

6. Check the box by your choice, select the scope for the role, and click Add.

7. Click OK to close the window and assign the roles.

You can dive in and start creating new RBS roles, but there may be an easier way. You might be able to take advantage of all the hard work Novell engineers did by creating a set of RBS templates.

Start iManage, providing the appropriate username and password, and then click the Configure icon (the one that looks like a man at a desk) in the toolbar at the top.

NOTE   *If you've worked with NetWare 5.1, you might notice that the Configure icon looks much like the Organizational Role object from that version. It makes a certain sense to use this icon, and besides that, icon development remains an inexact science many people feel requires more skill than programming.*

Once you click the Configure icon, the menus on the left change. Gone are the DNS and DHCP and Licensing options, and in their place are the RBS options. Take a look at Figure 8.22 to see these new options.

FIGURE 8.22

New menus distracting you from the RBS templates

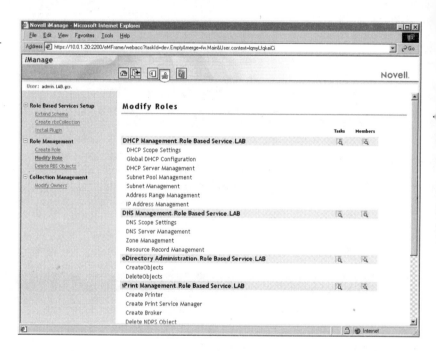

Don't let the menus distract you too terribly, but take a quick look. Notice the Modify Role item in bold and the Delete RBS Objects below it. One controls the main screen display, and one will be necessary to eliminate any RBS mistakes. You figure it out.

See all the nice templates? In particular, the DHCP Management and DNS Management Role Based Service templates make great sense, because DNS and DHCP management are new to NetWare but old hat to network and Unix administrators. If your company has either of the latter two positions, those techs become prime candidates for RBS assignment. Of course, you'll need to figure out how to get them listed in the proper place before they can help.

Let's pretend we chose the DNS Management Role setting on the first page, and clicked the Members icon (the blue magnifying glass in the Members column). This looks straightforward but may fool you. It took me a bit to figure out the weirdness you can see in Figure 8.23.

FIGURE 8.23

Assigning names and scope

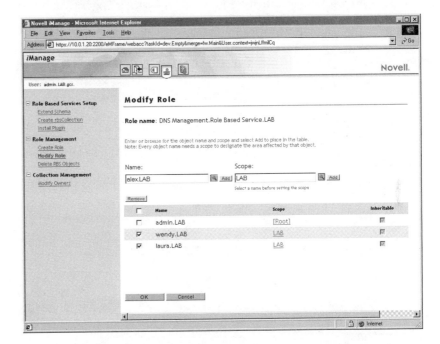

The default user, Admin, appears, as you would expect. To add other names, click the magnifying glass beside the Name column. This opens the search box. Here, unlike many other places, you can choose multiple names, and they will all be carried back to this screen and appear inside the Name field.

You want to go to the Scope setting, and then say OK for everything. But that won't work as you hope. Instead, you need to take a few more steps.

When you get the name(s) picked, click the Add button. Then the objects you chose appear in the list at the bottom of the page under Admin.

Once you have all the names of objects (users, groups, or even containers) chosen, check the boxes by each one to assign the scope. Use the magnifying glass beside the Scope listing to pick your scope of choice. Be aware that the system will allow you to pick worthless scopes, so be careful.

After you pick the scope you want for each checked object, click the Add command button beside the Scope field. That's the way to add the scope to each object. You can't do it (well, maybe you can, but I couldn't) all at once. First pick the object name, and then choose the scope. Click the OK button at the bottom of the page to say, once again, you have made your choice.

Notice the Remove command button above the names. If you want to dump a few users from their roles, check the appropriate box, click Remove, and then click OK.

MODIFYING RBS TASKS

You can change the tasks in the RBS templates, but don't do this until you've gotten some experience with RBS and how the assigned tasks work when scattered about your network.

Click the magnifying glass under the Task heading back in the screen shown in Figure 8.22, and you'll see lists of tasks available and those assigned. Take a look at Figure 8.24 for an example.

FIGURE 8.24

Modifying RBS
task lists

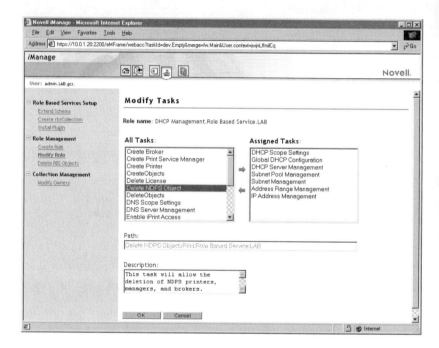

The procedure here could hardly be simpler: Pick a task in the All Tasks list, then click the arrow pointing to the Assigned Tasks list. Conversely, you can pick an assigned task and move it back to the All Tasks list, effectively removing that task from the template. But notice that you see every imaginable task in the All Tasks list, not just tasks that make sense for the task at hand. In Figure 8.24, notice I've highlighted Create NDPS Object. That makes sense for a task, I agree, but not for a task template entitled DHCP Management. Be wary and double-check everything. To paraphrase a carpenter, check twice, click once.

DEFINING RBS ROLES

The RBS templates don't cover every possible role, so you may want to define your own. For example, one template offers an iPrint manager, but suppose you want to create a more restricted NDPS manager. RBS provides many options and many ways to pick and choose among your users, objects, tasks, and scopes.

To define an RBS role, log in to iManage as an appropriate user and click the Configure icon. Choose Create Role under the Role Management heading. The Create a Role screen includes Role

Name, Description, and Collection fields. Figure 8.25 shows the name and description, along with the RBS Collection object to hold our newly defined role for NDPS manager.

FIGURE 8.25

Creating an NDPS Printer Wrangler

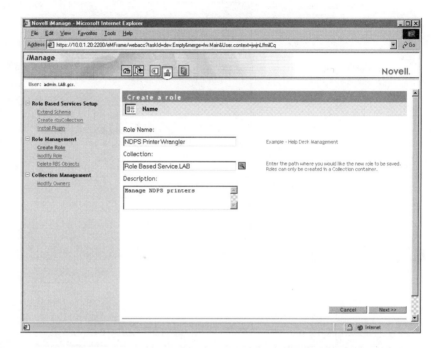

Put a descriptive role name in the first field; spaces are allowed. Use the search box to find the RBS Collection to hold the new role, or type it in directly if you're brave and remember accurately. Then put some type of description in place, so the next NetWare jockey has a fighting chance to figure out what in the world you did here. Click Next to continue your fascinating odyssey.

The next screen, shown in Figure 8.26, shows all the possible tasks in a similar presentation to the Modify Tasks screen (Figure 8.24, shown earlier). Pick the tasks you want, one by one, and move them to the Assigned Tasks list. Here, of course, the software can't have any idea what type of role you're creating, so listing each and every possible task doesn't seem to be a problem.

Choose all the tasks you want, and mix and match to your heart's desire. Do I care if you get all types of tasks all mixed up into one new role? Not at all, but you may, so pay attention. Click Next to move forward when you're ready.

After this, your choices get more intelligent. iManage presents the object name to receive the new role and the scope for that role on two different screens. Again, you can assign your newly created role to a user, a group, or a container. Choose carefully, since inappropriate rights given to a group or container may be hard to track down later if odd things begin to happen. Click Next once more.

Next, assign the scope for the new role. When you click Next after assigning the scope, you'll see a summary of what you've created. The details will appear much like the task lists in Figure 8.22. Click Done, and guess what—you're done.

FIGURE 8.26

Picking tasks for
your new role

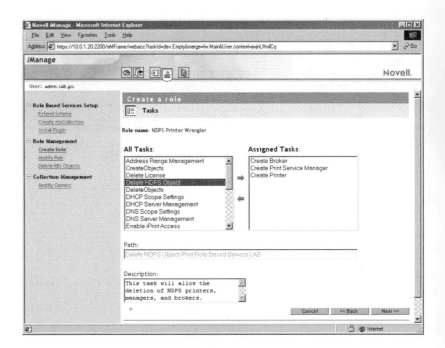

The only other option on the menu on the left that we haven't talked about is Collection Management. One of these versions, no doubt more information will be under this heading. Currently, however, all you can do is change the owner of the RBS object from the Admin to another user. Don't bother, unless you're forced to change it by some weird boss or menacing fortune cookie.

Server and Network Management

NetWare 4 moved from the server-bound approach used in NetWare 3 to a network-wide, global approach. NetWare 6 extends that global outlook even more. But the engines for all this worldliness are still the servers, busily supporting the replicated NDS eDirectory database, managing the disk drives that make up the volumes, and connecting to the clients across the network cabling.

A Hollywood director would move the viewpoint from the server to the enterprise network, like pulling the camera up and away from a single car to show the entire highway. Soon, however, the focus would come back down to the hero, forcing his car ever faster. In our movie, that hero is you, forcing the server ever faster. If the car dies, the traffic backs up, and something bad happens to our hero. Similarly, if the server dies, then the network backs up, and your phone rings with calls from angry users.

Just as the movie hero must check the car gauges, so must you check the gauges of your network. Your primary gauges for the physical server are NetWare Remote Manager and the MONITOR.NLM program. Your toolkit includes DSMERGE.NLM, DSREPAIR.NLM, the DSTRACE function, INSTALL.NLM, and a few other assorted commands.

NetWare 5.0 shipped with a group of immature but promising control programs, all written in Java, that worked, but their lack of speed nearly killed our hero. Luckily, with NetWare 5.1, the Web browser rocketed onto the scene. Now, NetWare 6 includes more browser-based management than ever before, making administrative tasks more intuitive and reachable across the Internet.

Server Management through NetWare Remote Manager

The NetWare Management Portal appeared in NetWare 5.1. Novell developers upgraded the program so drastically they decided to change the name to NetWare Remote Manager (okay, as I mentioned earlier, they actually changed the name for marketing reasons). Name notwithstanding, this utility contains the most options of all the browser-based applications and will be the tool of choice to manage items such as disks and volumes, NLMs, SET parameters, connections, and remote console screens. You can even take down the server from this utility, but you still might need to go to the server to turn it off.

Novell's own literature from before the launch of NetWare 5.1 proclaimed the Remote Manager similar in functionality to all of these utilities:

- NWADMIN

- ConsoleOne

- RConsoleJ (and RCONSOLE)

- NWCONFIG

- SERVMAN

- MONITOR

- FILER

The exuberance continues with the revamped utility shipping in NetWare 6. Many features barely implemented in NetWare 5.1 now spring fully developed into the NetWare 6 release of Remote Manager.

How do many network managers react? They plead on bended knee, saying, "Please, Novell, forget NetWare Administrator, forget ConsoleOne (pretty please), forget RConsoleJ, and move everything under the server's management banner to NetWare Remote Manager." Really, they do. At least some of them do, because they told me.

When you have the NetWare Enterprise Web Server installed on a server, you must use the port number in the address (for example, `http://10.0.1.33:8008`). It won't hurt to give the port address, even if the Enterprise Web Server isn't loaded. If you forget to give the port number on servers with the Web server, you'll pull up the general "Welcome to NetWare 6" screen, with quick links to information about iFolder, Web Access, iPrint, Remote Manager, NetStorage, iManage, and so forth. This screen is informative, but not capable of deep server probing.

An opening screen that provides good information portends great value from the NetWare Remote Manager. From the top of the page down, you know the application (NetWare Remote Manager, says the banner), the server name (PROLIANT), the NetWare version generally (5.60 for some reason, even with NetWare 6), date of code version (September 13, 2001), and the authenticated user (Admin).

Now if Novell asked me (which somehow they always forget to do), I would have told them to put the Health Monitor screen up first as the default start page, rather than Volume Management as you see in Figure 8.27. I look at the Health Monitor screen much more than the Volume Information screen, and you'll soon find out why. (But we will see what the Volume Information screen has to offer later, in the "Monitoring Volumes through Remote Manager" section.)

FIGURE 8.27

Remote Manager: the new face of NetWare management (I hope)

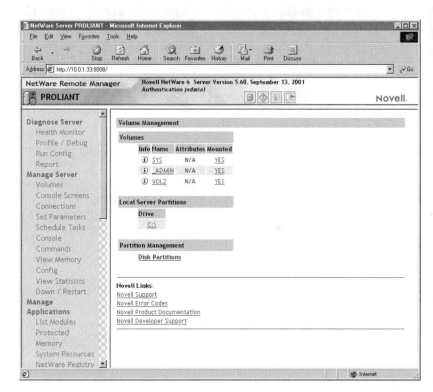

See the traffic light in the upper-left corner next to the server name? This is a recent addition, which is used to great effect later (although the light in this version appears tiny compared to the light that shipped with NetWare 5.1). One glance tells you all is well (green light), something should be checked (yellow light), or something must be fixed (red light).

But first, let me show you what I do with every new server as soon as it's up and running: Disable that darned annoying alert bell.

SETTING ALERT BELL AND OTHER GENERAL PARAMETERS

Remote Manager makes it easy to change the Sound Bell for Alerts parameter setting, along with many other parameter settings. To get to the Miscellaneous settings, which include the Sound Bell for Alerts parameter, choose the Set Parameters option under Manager Server in the left menu pane. You'll see the screen shown in Figure 8.28.

FIGURE 8.28

This bell will not toll for thee.

See this offending parameter in the sixth row from the top of Figure 8.28? You change this toggle setting by clicking the value listed (another hyperlink, of course) and making the setting fit your needs. The default for the danged bell is ON. I turn mine to OFF immediately.

Help screens hide behind the question mark icons at the end of each parameter. Ranges, when appropriate, are shown in both the Help screens and the screen where the values are actually changed.

Yes, I can change the alert bell status through the MONITOR.NLM on the server console, but this is more fun. Also, this section of Remote Manager has much better help and background information than any of the older C-Worthy DOS-style screens.

MANAGING HARDWARE THROUGH REMOTE MANAGER

Since Remote Manager ties directly into an individual server, plenty of hardware details are close at hand. On the Remote Manager home screen, scroll down to the Manager Hardware menu item, and you'll see four submenus: Processors, Disk/LAN Adapters, PCI Devices, and Other Resources.

Processors

The Processors screen provides basic processor details. PROLIANT has a 1GHz Pentium (okay, 993MHz) Pentium III processor. I see from the details that it's from Family 6, Model 8, and Stepping

6, if that helps anyone reading along. If there's a second (or third, fourth, and so on) processor, a command button provides an option to stop the processor or restart it if it's already stopped. Why would you need to stop one processor? I'm not sure, but if you come up with a reason, you can do it here.

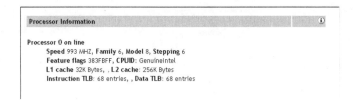

Disk/LAN Adapters

LAN adapters are tied strongly to the network performance of your NetWare server. Luckily, most adapter vendors work closely with Novell engineers to provide correct drivers when necessary. Many adapters require different drivers when used in a server as opposed to connecting a workstation to the network.

While no one will accuse the minimal information provided here inside NetWare Remote Manager with threatening the sales of any real network analysis software, sometimes it's nice to get an idea of how many packets whiz around your network during the day. For packet information, click Disk/LAN Adapters under the Manage Hardware menu heading to open the Hardware Adapters screen.

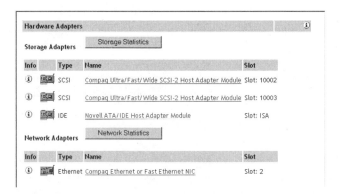

From this screen, click the Network Statistics command button. A fair amount of network information awaits, including total packets transmitted and received by each active network adapter in the server. The hyperlink for Packet Per Second Graph sits just above all the statistics sitting politely in tables. Click it to see a graph showing how active the network adapters for this server are, like the one shown here.

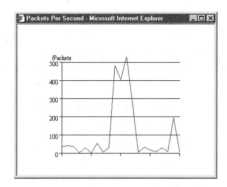

TIP   You can cheat to see this graph. Go to the Health Monitor screen and click the LAN Traffic parameter in the Description column. The graph X axis changes to most closely match the range of packets per second (pps) during your monitoring time. The top line may be 35 pps, then bump to 40 pps, then zoom to 600 pps or higher if someone starts a file transfer.

PCI Devices

You can drill down to great depths of PCI slot minutiae, including the Vendor ID, Device ID, Subsystem Vendor ID, and Subsystem ID. More thrilling information of this type awaits in case you can't sleep one evening.

If you ever need to know which PCI slots remain open on a server, NetWare Remote Manager provides the easiest way to find out. Just click the PCI Devices option under the Manage Hardware menu heading.

Other Resources

This section shows a more descriptive label, Hardware Resource Selections, when clicked. Want to know about interrupts, slots, ports, DMA, or shared memory on your physical server? You'll find those details by choosing Other Resources under the Manage Hardware menu heading.

HEALTH MONITOR: A BIG REMOTE MANAGER PLUS

IN A HURRY 8.16: MONITOR SERVER HEALTH

1. Open NetWare Remote Manager for the server you want to monitor.

2. Click Health Monitor in the menu in the left panel.

3. Modify displayed information or health thresholds if desired.

This heading should be at the top of the Remote Manager home page, because more value hides in here than anywhere else in the Remote Manager utility. Figure 8.29 shows the Server Health Monitoring screen, reached by clicking the Health Monitor submenu under Diagnose Server in the left frame, or by clicking the diamond-shaped icon in the middle of the toolbar at the top of the screen.

FIGURE 8.29

A good, healthy server with explanations

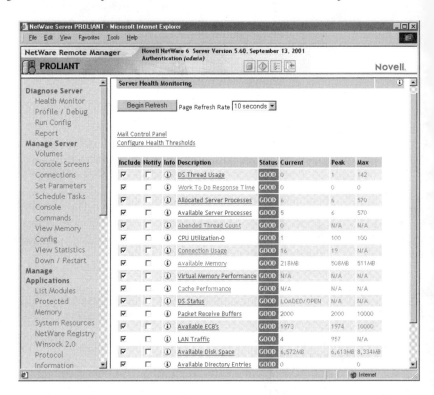

There are two more monitored items you can't see at the bottom of the screen: Disk Throughput and Timesync Status. Both also have the Include, Info, and Notify buttons.

At the top-right side of the screen shown in Figure 8.29, you can see a small circle with the letter *i* inside. Click this Info icon to get information about the entire screen contents. Click the corresponding Info icons beside any health parameter to read help information about that single parameter.

Above the screen Info icon sits the red Novell logo. This name, also a hyperlink, connects you directly to www.novell.com. If you're on any other Remote Manager screen, click the traffic light icon in the top-left corner to jump right back here to the server Health Monitor screen.

Notice the command button labeled Begin Refresh at the top of the screen. Next to the command button is a drop-down list offering refresh rate choices that range between 2 seconds and 5 minutes per refresh. The 10-second default refresh makes me dizzy enough, so I can't imagine a 2-second refresh rate being useful. When I check that speed, the screen refreshes so quickly I can't read any of the numbers. If something went wrong, I wouldn't be able to catch the details.

But details can be caught, and you can decide which details you want to catch, by using the Include check boxes and the Apply command button at the bottom-left side of the screen. Notice that Include has every box checked? The default from Novell sets each health parameter to display on this screen. If you don't want to see one or more parameters, click the box to clear the check box, and the information won't feed into this screen summary.

In Figure 8.30, I scrolled the health parameters upward, to show the Apply command button. I also grabbed this screen shot just as I came out of Refresh mode, and it happened to hit a server LAN traffic trough for a second as it reloaded the screen after my Refresh cancellation. No other packets hit the server at that second, so the Health Monitor correctly turned the Status block from GOOD to BAD for the LAN Traffic parameter.

FIGURE 8.30

A rare red light, and notice the Apply button

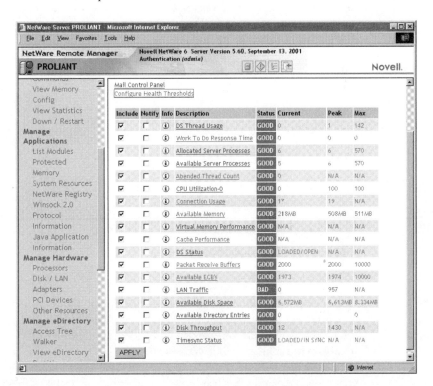

The Status blocks for each of the health parameters generally only turn yellow (for suspect) or red (for bad) when you have the Refresh function active. This is not so for the traffic light; it may flash yellow or red for some transient problem without changing the Status block. If the traffic light stays yellow or red, the Status blocks will clue you in.

But what if you're not sitting and staring at the screen? Perhaps you've been called away to replace another cup holder on a vice president's computer? E-mail to the rescue.

See the check boxes on the left side of each entry? The second column, Notify, tells the software to send an e-mail message to addresses listed on the page behind the Mail Control Panel link at the top of the screen. Up to eight e-mail addresses may be listed, and a secondary mail server may be specified for redundancy. Do you have a pager tied to an e-mail address? That's a perfect solution. Do you get wireless e-mail through a PDA when inside the building? That will provide quick notice of every problem you care to hear about. Only the health parameters you check in the Notify column will generate e-mail messages.

You say you want to get e-mail, but not a message every time some little detail wanders slightly off the parameter footpath? Then click the Configure Health Thresholds link at the top of the screen to set the parameter thresholds where you want, rather than accept Novell's idea of good, suspect, and bad.

Each item comes equipped with a question mark icon at no extra charge. Click that and get information more valuable than usual from an online Help system.

Clicking a hyperlink in the Description column takes you directly to that page or chart. Charts pop up for the following items:

◆ DS Thread Usage

◆ Allocated Server Processes

◆ Available Server Processes

◆ CPU Utilization (one listing for each processor)

◆ Available Memory

◆ Cache Performance

◆ LAN Traffic

◆ Available Disk Space

◆ Available Directory Entries

◆ Disk Throughput

The rest of the options zoom directly to the appropriate page, perhaps one we've already discussed.

This screen does have value for a regular, repeated refresh rate. If something goes from green to yellow or yellow to red, you want to know about it immediately. So don't just hope you have a chance to look at it. Set up an e-mail alert system.

You'll need to reload the HTTPSTK.NLM and PORTAL.NLM (yes, the NLM's name stayed the same, even though the utility has been renamed) after making many of these changes, so plan on restarting both after each change. It's no fun discovering the server you thought chugged away happily slowly ran out of memory or disk space and no one told you because the utility wasn't restarted.

Checking Memory

The eighth entry from the top of the screen in Figure 8.30, Available Memory, may be one of your regular checks (or have Notify checked). You can reach this same screen by choosing the View Memory Config menu item under Manage Server from the left frame menu. NetWare 6 demands more memory than any version of NetWare ever before (256MB minimum, but 1GB is necessary for a decent performance under load). So let's look at Figure 8.31 and see how the memory stacks up.

FIGURE 8.31

Where your memory went

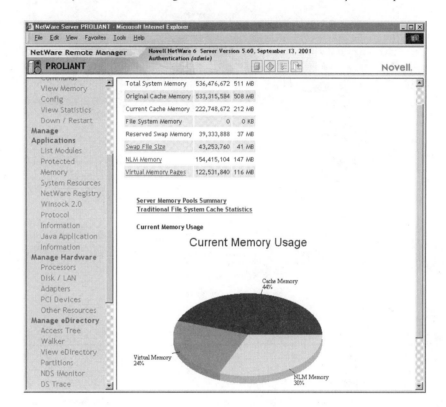

Aha! The NLMs have eaten 30 percent of my memory! No surprise there, with the Web server and other things running. Actually, this percentage compares favorably with the greedier NLMs in NetWare 5.1. In the "Managing Applications through Remote Manager," section coming up shortly, we'll check to see exactly which NLMs are sucking up which memory. For now, let's focus on non-NLM memory usage.

Notice the Server Memory Pools Summary link above the pie chart? How could you miss it, right? Figure 8.32 shows what you'll see if you click it—an excellent breakdown of server memory, where it is, and how it's used.

Again, notice the Begin Refresh button, with the Page Refresh Rate settings ranging from 2 seconds to 5 minutes. Unless your server dynamically handles wide load swings, the refresh option won't show you too much. But it's nice to have, just in case.

Critical information can be seen in the Cache Information details in the lower-right corner. This information shows I'm in good shape, because the ProLiant computer has 512MB of memory. NLMs take up 147MB, but the percentage works well against the 512MB in the server. Only 30 percent of the memory gets sucked up by the NLMs. I told you more memory always helps.

FIGURE 8.32

Concise memory-use summary

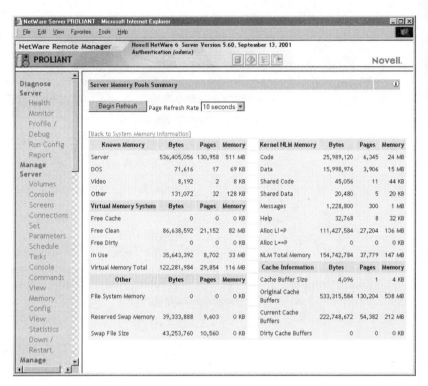

Monitoring Multiple Servers

The Multiple Server Monitor option should be under Server Health Monitoring, but instead, it has its own listing. You'll find it under Use Server Groups toward the bottom of the left frame menu items (Build Server Group). True to the name, the Multiple Server Monitor shows multiple servers' health at one time.

The setup for this fun feature inhabits Figure 8.33. Rather sparse yet useful, the plan for this page is to pick which servers will show up with a traffic light beside them.

This screen shot came when I tested the second wonderful Compaq ProLiant Cluster for Net-Ware, overflowing through the lab. This cluster of four Compaq ProLiant 360 1U servers had been on tour, demonstrating NetWare 6 to dealers and large customers. One rack (huge and heavy) came to visit me for a time for a review for *Network World* magazine and some other business. (See Chapter 14 for details on my testing of this cluster.)

NOTE   *Unfortunately, the Compaq cluster couldn't stay long enough for me to load the official shipping version of Net-Ware 6. That's why the NetWare 6 Beta 3 label appears on the screen. But since Beta 3 was the last public beta, the look, feel, and performance of NetWare Remote Manager came very close to the shipping version. I can't say that about all the Net-Ware Beta 3 code, and I wouldn't embarrass any module by picking them out (iManage and worse Netscape support in the shipping version), but this screen shot looks the same in both the last beta and the product you have.*

FIGURE 8.33

Pick your servers for group display here.

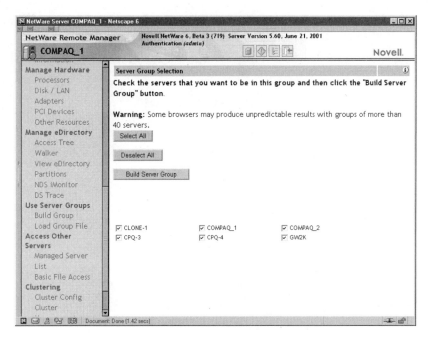

You can tell from the banner that the active server is Compaq_1, and in NetWare 5.1's version of this, the "host" server wouldn't show up in the listing. NetWare 6's Remote Manager fixed this.

Click the Select All command button to save time, unless you plan to pick and choose the displayed servers. That's fine if you want to, but I say pick 'em all. All of them up to 40 or so, if you believe the warning sign.

Next, we see the results of our hard work of building a server group and displaying it: Happy servers showing their green contentment in Figure 8.34. Clone-1 is an Acer system moved from personal system to test system, running NetWare 6 software. Compaq_1 and Compaq_2 are the first two of the four clustered servers, doing their own two-node cluster. CPQ-3 and CPQ-4 are the other two servers, also clustered together. These are four servers and one RAID array (Compaq R4100 if you're keeping track) organized into two, two-node clusters sharing half the RAID array between each two nodes.

Notice which server I left out of the previous paragraph? GW2K is an old machine (Pentium 120, with 128MB of RAM and a 1.6GB hard disk) provided by Gateway2000 several versions of this book ago. It runs NetWare 5.1 as a benchmark to compare NetWare 6 against. Take a good look at the green light for GW2K. See the difference? That's the way all the NetWare 5.1 servers appear in the group health screen.

Improvements over the NetWare 5.1 version of the multiple health monitor include the ability to show the host server, add a title, and define and save a "group file," so you can gather different servers together for different situations.

Click any of the hyperlinked names to go directly to the main Remote Manager page of the server in question. This beta version also did a better job supporting Netscape's browser than the shipping version of NetWare 6 does.

FIGURE 8.34

Good servers glowing green

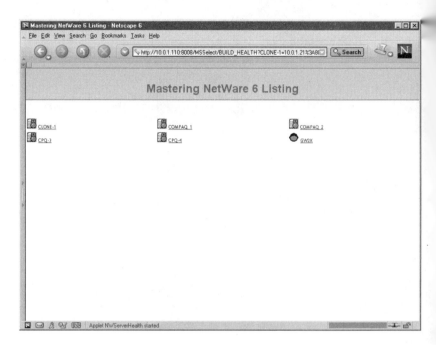

Won't it be wonderful to see a server go red, drill down to the problem, fix it, then wait and laugh at the users calling to report the problem? Well, maybe you shouldn't laugh. But having a clue about the problem before your desktop auditory trouble-reporting tool (a.k.a. telephone) starts ringing will definitely make your life easier.

MANAGING APPLICATIONS THROUGH REMOTE MANAGER

There are now seven headings inside Remote Manager's Manage Applications section, up from four in NetWare 5.1. Let's take a detailed look at one and cover a couple of the others quickly.

Most important is List Modules. Protected Memory concerns only the few programs run in protected memory, but since iFolder now carves out some protected memory, that area needs a quick look. Java Application Information covers new areas, which we'll discuss here (after the NLM check). Protocol Information, also new, provides more protocol information. Both NetWare Registry and Winsock 2.0 go into areas rarely, if ever, visited on standard networks.

Checking NLMs

List Modules shows information about your NLMs. These can be a source of frustration when something goes out of whack. One bad NLM can ruin your whole day, even your whole weekend. The quicker you can find out about a troubled NLM, the better. Check this list when adding a new application to your server, just in case the NLM needs an update or causes problems.

Figure 8.35 shows the first page of 226 loaded NLMs on PROLIANT, organized by allocated memory. As the on-screen instructions say, clicking a heading sorts by that list.

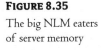

FIGURE 8.35

The big NLM eaters of server memory

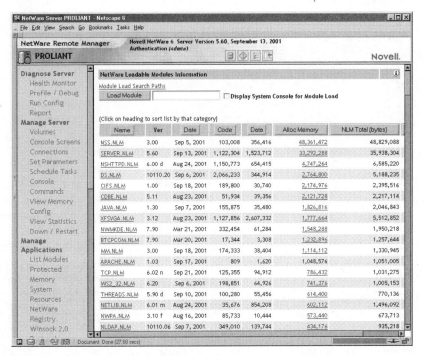

What struck me with NetWare 5.1 was that the DS.NLM, for Directory Services, took much more memory than the server operating system (number four on our memory hit parade last time). I regarded this rating as a sign of Novell's emphasis on directory services.

Yet this time, NSS leads the NLM memory-used listing, with SERVER.NLM second and DS.NLM fourth, but with a memory footprint less than half the size as in NetWare 5.1. Either eDirectory can run in much less memory, NetWare engineers split some of the eDirectory application among other modules, or both. But look at Figure 8.35 for yourself, and see if an NLM resource hog surprises you.

As you can see in Figure 8.35, each listing shows the NLM name (the default listing is alphabetical), followed by the version and date. These details are often critical when troubleshooting a problem, since an old NLM can ruin all your other troubleshooting. The Code and Data columns show how much of your precious server memory gets sucked up the program code versus the data controlled by the NLM. The last column on the right, NLM Total (bytes), just expresses the NLM total in megabytes.

Drilling down by clicking the name of the module pops open a new page full of interesting, if not particularly useful, information. Version number and date are on the first page, where they belong. Copyright, the address space used, and other details fill about a page of information. The only really useful information is a line listing other modules currently using the NLM in question. For NSHTTPD.NLM, the dependent NLMs are WEBDAV.NLM, WEBDAV.NLM, and NHWDIR.NLM. Knowing about dependencies such as these can be helpful, and this is one good place to find out about them.

In case you don't want to check out `AUTOEXEC.NCF` to see the server search paths for NLMs, the details are here on this page. A hyperlink cleverly named Module Load Search Paths occupies the upper-left side of the page, just under the banner (see it there in Figure 8.35?).

Checking the Java Virtual Machine (JVM)

New in the Manage Applications list, the Java Application Information utility shows more details about Java applications running on NetWare 6 than ever before. I don't know if this means Java success on NetWare servers now has critical mass, but if you use your NetWare 6 server for Web applications, this information may prove helpful.

The main Java page lists the Novell JVM version and build date, along with the number of running applications. A scrolling listing labeled Running Java Applications put the Apache Tomcat application service at the top of the list, so I highlighted that entry and clicked the Show Application Details command button. Figure 8.36 shows the second page that appeared.

FIGURE 8.36

Tomcat sings for you.

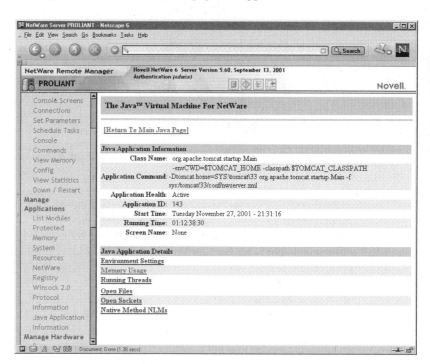

Show this screen to programmers writing for your Web server, and they should appreciate the information about memory usage, threads, open files and sockets, and which NLMs get dragged into the mix. When you click the Memory Usage link, several heap statistics lead the list, indicating that only programmers care about this. But since the page also includes a link labeled Memory Details for Developers, that could be exactly what Novell had in mind. Drill down there if your programmers want to see a list of NLMs showing Location in Code of Return Address, Number of Times Called, and Number of Bytes Allocated. They'll understand, even if normal people don't.

NOTE   *Oh, sure, get all upset because I implied programmers aren't normal people. Fine, I'll admit programmers dying to get their hands on code memory location D608F58E in* SYMCJIT.NLM, *which was called 67 times since starting, are normal—right after supermodels come beg me to leave my wife.*

MONITOR Almost Everything

The MONITOR screen has been my primary place to check the health of servers for years and years. You may only rarely use another server utility, especially when the server runs fine. When checking a new server on a new network, use the MONITOR program before you do anything else. Half the time, it will provide the answers to your questions (and when it doesn't, running it gives you some time to think of what to do next).

Many network supervisors leave MONITOR running all the time. With earlier NetWare versions, a snake appeared as a screensaver, blanking the MONITOR display. The snake is an ASCII-graphic creature made of various red-tinted blocks following a bright red head. Now you must use the SCRSAVER utility. Still, the longer and faster the snake goes, the busier the network.

It's a good idea to check the MONITOR information now and then. Some network managers take screen shots of server-information screens—such as those that show redirected blocks, cache utilization, and processor utilization—to have a benchmark for later reference. You're a busy person; don't believe you can remember your cache utilization statistics from four months ago. Make notes or make screen shots, but keep some record of the health of your network as shown by MONITOR.

VIEWING GENERAL SERVER INFORMATION

IN A HURRY 8.17: VIEW SERVER INFORMATION WITH MONITOR

1. Type MONITOR from the console prompt.

2. Press Tab once or twice to get to the Available Options menu.

3. From the Available Options menu, choose the menu option for the utilization data you want to view: Disk Cache Utilization, Virtual Memory, or System Resources.

The opening screen of MONITOR holds the most useful information. See Figure 8.37 for a look at the screen from PROLIANT running under RConsoleJ.

The PROLIANT server in this example has 512MB of RAM and a 9100MB (9.1GB) hard disk. This equates to 130,204 buffers of 4KB each, of which just over 50,000 are usually available. The number fluctuates as NLMs take and return server RAM for various operations. Running the ConsoleOne program takes quite a few of these, but luckily NetWare allows you to unload the server GUI (unlike Windows NT, 2000, and XP, which suck CPU cycles with the GUI whether you want the GUI or not). The NetWare Enterprise Web Server, and brethren like the FTP Server and News Server, use quite a few resources as well.

FIGURE 8.37

Server secrets
unveiled

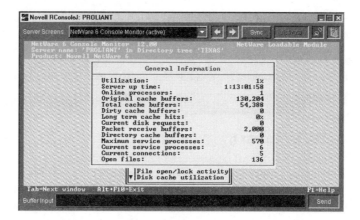

NOTE *The ALTOS486 server used during the first iteration of this book had a 500MB disk with 32MB of RAM. The original cache buffer number there was 7620, with about 5450 available. NetWare 4.10 was slightly more conservative than NetWare 4.11, but not that much. Server CLONE386, the underpowered server with only 8MB of RAM and a 312MB disk that lived out its usefulness just after finishing the 4.10 version of this book, had 1487 original cache buffers, of which only 740 or so were available. (That server was a test to show it can be done, not an attempt to sell an 8MB server to unsuspecting users.)*

Across the top of the MONITOR screen, the version of the NetWare operating system (6) and of the MONITOR program (12.00) are listed, along with the fact that this is an NLM, in the upper right. The server name and tree are also listed at the top. The last line in the top information section gives the server operating system version again, along with the date of manufacture. This information will be important as you upgrade pieces of your server operating system over time and Novell support asks what versions you have.

You expand the General Information window by pressing the Tab key or by just waiting 10 seconds. The window will expand itself, covering some of the Available Options menu. Press Tab again (or Escape) to return it to a smaller size. The fields on the MONITOR General Information screen are described in Table 8.1.

TABLE 8.1: FIELDS ON MONITOR'S GENERAL INFORMATION SCREEN

FIELD	DESCRIPTION
Utilization	Percentage of time the CPU is busy. This normally hovers under 5 percent, unless you have NLMs that do active processing, such as Web servers and databases.
Server Up Time	Days, hours, minutes, and seconds since the server was started.
Online Processors	The number of CPUs in this server that are in use.

Continued on next page

TABLE 8.1: FIELDS ON MONITOR'S GENERAL INFORMATION SCREEN *(continued)*

FIELD	DESCRIPTION
Original Cache Buffers	The number of 4KB buffer blocks contained in your server memory, minus room for the operating system and DOS. This number is rarely high enough.
Total Cache Buffers	The number of buffers available for file caching after loading all the NLM programs and other server housekeeping programs. This number is never high enough.
Dirty Cache Buffers	Buffers waiting to be written to a server disk.
Long Term Cache Hits	Cumulative success percentage of disk block requests served from cache.
Current Disk Requests	Number of disk requests waiting for service.
Packet Receive Buffers	1KB buffers that hold client requests while the server processes them. The default is 10, but the server allocates more as needed. Web service bumps this up to 2000.
Directory Cache Buffers	Buffers dedicated to holding the server directory entries, speeding access to files since the directory need not be read from the disk when a request comes. The server allocates more as needed, and Web service again bumps this up to 2000.
Maximum Service Processes	Largest number of task handlers, or processes, available for servicing client requests. Once the server allocates this maximum number, the number cannot be reclaimed. This number can be lowered using a SET command, freeing memory for cache buffers. When there is no more memory to allocate more processes, performance suffers. Web service bumps this up to 500.
Current Service Processes	Current processes available for servicing client requests.
Current Connections	Total of licensed and unlicensed active connections on this server.
Open Files	Number of files accessed by the server and other clients.

Some of these numbers have a direct impact on server performance. The more memory, the better the performance. How much is enough? Superserver manufacturers are advertising the ability to support 4GB of server RAM. My guess is that should be enough—for a while. The ProLiant Cluster I tested shipped with 1GB of RAM for each of the four 4-processor servers in the box, with the ability to support 4GB. Other Intel servers now support even more RAM.

NOTE *If you're used to earlier versions of MONITOR, you may be looking for the detailed information for Maximum Licensed Connections. It has moved to the Licensing server item inside iManage. Current Licensed Connections has made the same move, as you might expect, leaving those experienced with earlier NetWare versions feeling just a bit lost until they remember the new Licensing menu option in iManage, moved from NetWare Administrator for the last several versions.*

If your total cache buffers number is suffering because of many NLMs, you need more memory. The amount of total cache buffers available is probably the quickest indicator of server health and performance. Plus, you always need more memory, no matter what.

CHECKING DISK CACHE UTILIZATION

Cache use by NetWare is one of the biggest performance advantages of the operating system over its competitors. The cache is a temporary storage area for files read from the disk. Once a file is read from the disk, it stays in the server memory for a time, guessing that you may need that same information again. If you do, then the next request comes from server RAM rather than being read from the disk, saving tremendous amounts of time. It's common to sort a large database from your workstation and have all of the database file stay in the cache, finishing 20 times faster than reading the file from the disk.

The MONITOR Available Options menu option to get to the important cache information is labeled, clearly enough, Disk Cache Utilization (you can see it at the bottom of the screen in Figure 8.37). Highlight it and press Enter, and you will see a screen much like the one shown in Figure 8.38 (if you check a traditional NetWare filesystem volume).

FIGURE 8.38

Checking the cache

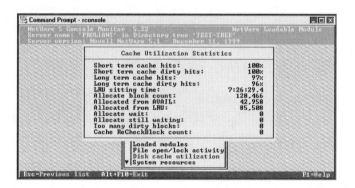

Before NetWare 6, cache always meant RAM. Now, with NetWare 6's virtual memory support, cache means a combination of RAM and disk space. RAM is used first, so more RAM still helps, because writing memory out to disk means slower performance.

The most important indicator for more RAM is the Long Term Cache Hits listing. If this number was below 98 percent in NetWare 4.11, Novell engineers suggested that you should add more RAM. (Of course, Novell engineers suggest that you add more RAM for almost every problem, but statistically they will be right once in a while.) Now, they suggest that you add more RAM if the number falls below 90 percent.

The Long Term Cache Hits number is averaged for every cache request since the server has started. It is the most accurate reflection of cache utilization, much better than the Short Term Cache Hits number here, and even the Total Cache Buffers number from the previous screen. After all, if all the file requests are being handled from cache, whatever amount you have must be enough.

The fields on the Cache Utilization Statistics screen are described in Table 8.2.

TABLE 8.2: FIELDS ON MONITOR'S CACHE UTILIZATION STATISTICS SCREEN

FIELD	DESCRIPTION
Short Term Cache Hits	Percentage of disk block requests serviced by the cache in the last second.
Short Term Cache Dirty Hits	Percentage of disk blocks requested in the last second that were in cache, but changed since being read from the disk.
Long Term Cache Hits	Your trigger to get more memory. Below 90 percent is a failing grade.
Long Term Cache Dirty Hits	Percentage of disk blocks requested since the server started that were in cache but waiting to be written to the disk.
LRU Sitting Time	The age of the block that is the oldest in the LRU (Least Recently Used) list. Higher times are better, indicating that there is plenty of memory to service the clients. Time is in days, hours, minutes, and seconds, including tenths.
Allocate Block Count	Total block requests since the server was started.
Allocated From AVAIL	Number of cache block requests filled by available (i.e., not being used) blocks.
Allocated From LRU	Number of cache block requests filled by blocks from the LRU list of used cache blocks.
Allocate Wait	Number of instances where a cache request waited while a block from the LRU list was made available. If this number increases regularly, you need more RAM.
Allocate Still Waiting	Number of times the operating system was forced to wait for an LRU block in the last 10 minutes. If the number is greater than 7, your blocks are being reused too quickly. Add more RAM.
Too Many Dirty Blocks	Number of block write requests delayed by an overloaded write queue. This can be caused by a busy disk channel. Add more RAM.
Cache ReCheckBlock Count	Number of times a cache request had to try again because the target block was still being used. If this number is steadily increasing, add more RAM.

NSS volumes show cache details differently, hampered a bit by using a large swap file. This gets in the way of good "traditional" statistics, but you can get some information using NetWare Remote Manager, as explained in the "Health Monitor: A Big Remote Manager Plus" section earlier in the chapter.

CHECKING PROCESSOR UTILIZATION

Some people worry constantly about the server CPU. Part of this worry comes from competitors who claim that their multiprocessor versions gives them an advantage over NetWare's single processor (the most popular option in terms of sales). Unfortunately for competitors, this isn't necessarily true, especially when you consider the price and performance of these multiprocessor servers versus a single

CPU server running NetWare. In fact, Novell's internal tests show that NetWare 6 runs faster with one processor than Windows NT/2000/XP Server 4 does with two processors.

To satisfy your curiosity about how hard your processor(s) works, go to the Health Monitor screen in NetWare Remote Manager and look at the CPU Utilization number. For a graph, click the CPU Utilization listing in the description column.

But to keep up in the RFP check box feature war, Novell released SMP (Symmetrical Multi-Processor) support as part of NetWare 4.11. NetWare 6 ships with support for up to 32 symmetrical processors right out of the box, for no extra charge. Part of the move to virtual memory was to support easier engineering for multiple processor support.

Most network bottlenecks happen at the disk channel. The server CPU is rarely loaded, unless you are running NLMs on the server that execute as databases and gateways. Even then, people misunderstand the utilization number. When it reaches 100 percent, it doesn't mean that things are going to blow up; it just means that the CPU is working on all barrels. It isn't uncommon to see utilization spike above 100 percent, because your server processor is probably faster than the benchmark processor used to set the percentages.

VIEWING VIRTUAL MEMORY INFORMATION

Available memory is another performance indicator. NLMs use memory as they load and release it when they unload. However, like Microsoft Windows 3.1*x* (and Windows 95/98, for that matter), occasionally some of the memory never gets released. Unlike Windows, NetWare 4 provided an easy way to reclaim that lost memory. NetWare 6 does away with that need, with the combination of physical and virtual memory allocation and regular collection of "orphaned" memory segments.

When discussing memory, this new technology makes a decision necessary—are you speaking of physical memory (RAM) or virtual memory (RAM plus disk space)? For some extra confusion, Novell adds memory displays under both an Address Spaces option and a Swap Files option, since both are so important now.

Figure 8.39 shows some of the information you may want to check now and then just for personal reassurance. This is the display you'll see when you choose Virtual Memory from the Available Options menu. Some of the details within MONITOR have become so obscure that they don't help, but memory use is always worth watching.

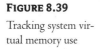

FIGURE 8.39

Tracking system virtual memory use

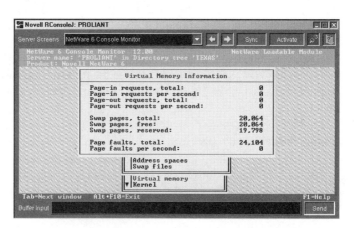

Table 8.3 describes the fields on the Virtual Memory Information screen.

TABLE 8.3: FIELDS ON MONITOR'S VIRTUAL MEMORY INFORMATION SCREEN

FIELD	DESCRIPTION
Page-in Requests, Total	Number of memory moves in from swap files since the server was started.
Page-in Requests Per Second	Number of requests to move one of the 4KB virtual memory pages from the swap files in the last second.
Page-out Requests, Total	Number of memory requests out to swap files since the server was started.
Page-out Requests Per Second	Number of requests to move 4KB virtual memory pages for file swap space.
Swap Pages, Total	Number of 4KB blocks currently used.
Swap Pages, Free	Number of 4KB blocks available for use.
Swap Pages, Reserved	Number of 4KB pages set aside for use by the memory system.
Page Faults, Total	Number of virtual memory retrievals from a swap file since the server came up. (*Fault* doesn't mean error in this situation.)
Page Faults Per Second	Number of times in the last second that information was retrieved from the swap files (meaning the information wasn't in RAM).

It's a whole new world of NetWare memory management, isn't it? Don't worry, because this is actually a more traditional way to handle memory. Unix servers, especially high-performance systems running huge databases and Internet Web servers, have always done memory this way.

GETTING SWAP FILE INFORMATION

If you look just under the foreground window in Figure 8.39, you'll see two menu choices: Address Spaces and Swap Files. Swap Files offers some information that is worth a quick look.

Figure 8.40 shows the Swap File Information screen for the file created during installation on the SYS: volume of server PROLIANT. You may delete the swap volume on SYS: and create it somewhere else using the SWAP command from the colon prompt, but I didn't do that here.

Most of what you see in Figure 8.40 is easy to understand. The penultimate listing, Maximum Swap File Size, is the total space of the volume holding the swap file, in this case SYS:. The last entry, Minimum Free Per Volume, shows the threshold below which NetWare can't go to protect free space on the volume. In other words, this space is kept away from the swap file, no matter how hungry the file becomes.

CHECKING SYSTEM RESOURCE UTILIZATION

When you choose System Resources from MONITOR's Available Options menu, the Server Memory Resource Utilization screen appears. Although this screen looks like more server memory information (the main window titled Server Memory Statistics is a good clue), the memory tracked here is used by NLMs only. The operating system forces NLM programs to use a resource tag when they allocate resources, somewhat like tracking books taken from the library. This way, the system can track which module has which memory page.

FIGURE 8.40

Swap file details

In Figure 8.41, the top window shows the summary of all server memory with the information displayed two ways. First is the number of bytes allocated to the pool, and second is the percentage of total server memory allocated to the pool.

FIGURE 8.41

Server memory resource utilization

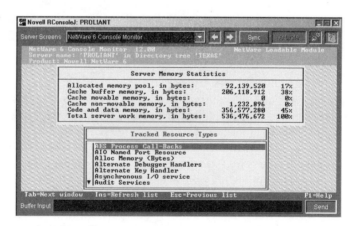

Table 8.4 describes the fields in the Server Memory Statistics window of the System Resources screen.

You can highlight an item in the Tracked Resource Types list at the bottom of the screen and press Enter to see specific details for that resource. Scrolling through these lists is fascinating only if you want to be impressed by the depth and complexity of modern NetWare. Little (if any) of this information will ever be of direct use to network managers, so don't worry about memorizing each list of options.

TABLE 8.4: FIELDS ON MONITOR'S SYSTEM RESOURCES SCREEN

FIELD	DESCRIPTION
Allocated Memory Pool	Memory reserved for NLM programs. The cache buffer pool allocates memory to NLMs (and hence to this allocated memory pool) dynamically. When the NLM is unloaded, the memory is returned to the cache buffer pool. The Memory Utilization option (see Table 8.3) offers a look at the NLM programs and the memory they have allocated.
Cache Buffer Memory	The pool of memory currently being used for file caching. This used to be the largest pool, and if it fell below 50 percent, more RAM was needed ASAP. With the new virtual memory scheme, this goes up and down without a call to buy RAM.
Cache Movable Memory	Memory directly allocated from the cache buffer pool. It returns to that pool when released. The memory manager of the operating system may move the location of these memory blocks to optimize memory usage, unlike the non-movable pool.
Cache Non-Movable Memory	Used when large blocks of memory are needed. Allocated directly from the cache buffer pool and returned there when released.
Code And Data Memory	Memory used by the operating system and other NLM programs to store their executable code and data.
Total Server Work Memory	Sum of the memory pools in RAM, not counting the swap files.

CHECKING CONNECTIONS

IN A HURRY 8.18: CHECK CONNECTIONS WITH MONITOR

1. Type **MONITOR** from the console prompt.
2. Choose Connections from the Available Options menu.
3. From the Active Connections screen, choose the connection to view.

The choices in MONITOR we've covered so far have to do with serious server management. The last few may be the ones you use more often. What do you think will happen more often—tracking the memory usage of one NLM or clearing a connection because a user locked up Windows again?

When a user does lock up a program, or leaves for the day with his or her system still connected, the Connections screen is the place to take care of the problem. There are ways to see which files are still open, to check how long the user has been connected, and to disconnect that user, all from your desk.

When you open MONITOR, the default choice of the Available Options menu is Connections, which is first in the list (this was labeled Connection Information in earlier versions). The list is not alphabetical, so Novell engineers obviously felt this was the option you would use the most often.

After opening the Connection Information screen, you will see a list of the active connections. The number to the left of each entry is the connection number, assigned when each user or resource logs in. The names are kept in alphabetical order. Connections with the asterisk in front of the name are NDS connections, not counted against the server license count. They access the NDS eDirectory database of information on this server, but they don't use the file and print resources specific to the server. The Not-Logged-In connection is a user workstation that has not logged in to this server or has not used a specific resource of this server. Take a look at Figure 8.42 and notice the starred connections versus the normal connection.

FIGURE 8.42

Active connections on PROLIANT

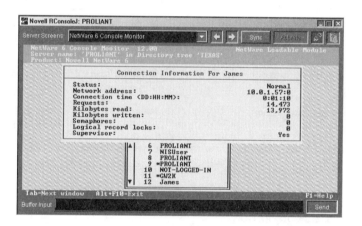

To view details of one of the active connections, highlight the connection and press Enter. To delete a connection, highlight it and press Delete. You can choose multiple connections with the F5 key before pressing the Delete key. Press F6 to clear all the unused connections.

Figure 8.43 shows the information for my workstation. This time I switched back to NetWare Remote Manager to show you that it offers a different view, yet provides most of the same information. Drill down through Connections to the user in question to reach the screen shown in Figure 8.43.

MONITOR may actually show more information. Let's take a look at the same screen in MONITOR in Figure 8.44, so you can compare the two.

The bottom window in Figure 8.44 shows the files currently open for the client. The first file opened winds up at the bottom of the list, since all subsequent files appear from the top of the list. If you choose one of the open files and press Enter, another window opens, showing the physical file lock status. More details on file locking will be explained in the "Seeing File Open/Lock Activity" section, coming up in just a bit.

FIGURE 8.43

Checking on my connection in Remote Manager

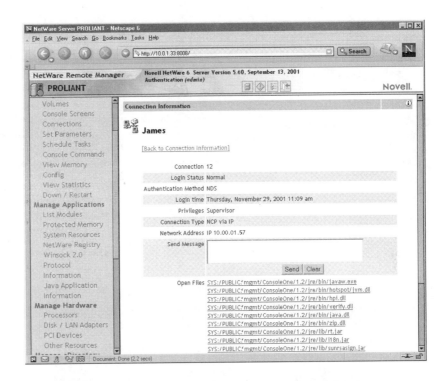

FIGURE 8.44

Old-fashioned MONITOR, yet still ahead in some ways

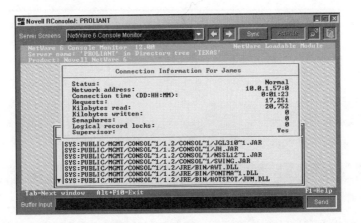

Wonder what some of those files are? The \PUBLIC\MGMT\CONSOLEONE\1.2 directory holds files to support Java management programs and utilities, such as the RConsoleJ.EXE file creating the list.

Table 8.5 describes the fields on MONITOR's Connection Information screen.

TABLE 8.5: FIELDS ON MONITOR'S CONNECTION INFORMATION SCREEN

FIELD	DESCRIPTION
Status	Possibilities are Not Logged In (client is not authenticated and so does not count against the licensed user count), Authenticated (client authorized by NDS but cannot access other resources on the server), Normal (authenticated by NDS and currently using a server resource, so this connection counts against the server license count), Waiting On a Lock (normal connection waiting for a locked resource, generally a file, to become available), Waiting on a Semaphore (normal connection waiting for access to a semaphore-controlled resource).
Network Address	Logical address of the client. The format is *network:node:socket* on the server. The socket number is used to separate server processes or programs in use by each client. The socket number may be the same or different, depending on the client. Clients using TCP/IP will have an IP address in this space.
Connection Time	Days, hours, and minutes the user has been connected to this server. If the user isn't logged in to this server, the number will be zero.
Requests	Service requests sent to the server from the client during this connection.
Kilobytes Read	Number of kilobytes read from all the server disks on all volumes during this connection.
Kilobytes Written	Number of kilobytes written to any of the server disks on any volume during this connection.
Semaphores	Number of semaphores in use by the client. A *semaphore* is an interprocess communication signal used to control access to resources such as multiuser data files. NetWare supervisors never need to worry about semaphores; developers set and control them within programs. NLMs use lots of semaphores.
Logical Record Locks	Locks used by the client to restrict access by other users to a file in use by the client.
Supervisor (or Equivalent)	Yes or No, depending on the client's authorization.

CHECKING STORAGE DEVICES

IN A HURRY 8.19: VIEW DISK INFORMATION IN MONITOR

1. Type **MONITOR** from the console prompt.

2. Choose Storage Devices from the Available Options menu.

3. From the Registered Storage Objects screen, choose the adapter module, partition, or CD-ROM drive to view.

4. Press Tab to expand the Drive Information window.

5. View the information in the Drive Status window. If you can highlight an item, you can press Enter to display further details about it.

When you choose Storage Devices from the Available Options menu, you enter the disk drive information section of MONITOR. There isn't a lot you can change in this section, but it's a great way to check the status of the server drives. We'll get to the best ways to create and manage disk volumes and storage pools later in this chapter, in the "Storage Management" section.

One critical item to review is the number of disk blocks used by the Hot Fix feature because of a failing disk. If this number increases slowly, your disk may be failing. If this number increases drastically, perform a backup immediately and buy another disk today.

When you go into this section, you will see Registered Storage Objects in the bottom window, as shown in Figure 8.45. This new screen shows more information about your hard disk than any previous version of NetWare. Most of this information for the drive was set during installation and has not changed, and you can't change it here. But in this section we're most interested in the status of your Hot Fix drive sections, to make sure things are all right. To check for Hot Fix usage, you must drill down past this screen.

FIGURE 8.45

Hard disk details

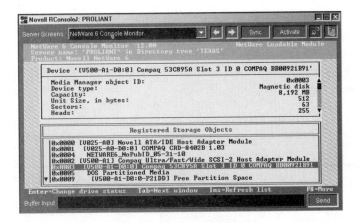

NOTE *If you have installed disk mirroring, check here regularly. You may not know if the disks are mirroring properly unless you look into this section of MONITOR. I've seen systems where one disk died, but no one knew it until someone checked the console MONITOR screen.*

NetWare 6 is kind enough to put this information right into the menu window, rather than forcing you to look around. Hotfixed Partition is the next menu item at the bottom of the window in Figure 8.45, just out of sight. That's what we want, and when I highlight that line and press the Tab key, the screen in Figure 8.46 appears.

The key number is Used Hot Fix Blocks, three up from the bottom of the top window. So far, so good, because no Hot Fix blocks are in use on my server. If that number increases, however, trouble is on the way.

FIGURE 8.46

A Hot Fix check
shows all is well.

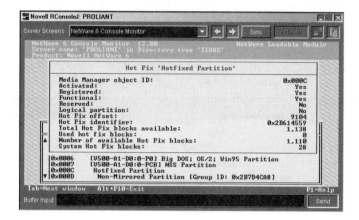

CHECKING VOLUMES

What little disk information that used to be in one area in NetWare 4.11 and earlier versions is now spread over two sections. The next area to check is Volumes, to view all the volume settings in one quick, easy location.

Figure 8.47 shows the volume information for server PROLIANT volume SYS:. I reached this screen by pressing Enter on the Volumes option from the main menu, then expanding this information in the Mounted Volumes listing. I then highlighted my choice and pressed the Tab key.

FIGURE 8.47

Volume details
galore

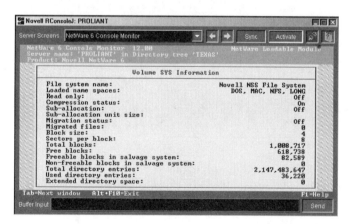

Do you need to know that this volume is not read-only? Probably not, but that's the type of information on display. Those of you with earlier versions of NetWare may be surprised to see the NSS File System label on a SYS: volume. Until NetWare 6, that wasn't possible.

VIEWING LAN/WAN INFORMATION

IN A HURRY 8.20: VIEW LAN/WAN INFORMATION IN MONITOR

1. Type **MONITOR** from the console prompt.

2. Choose LAN/WAN Drivers from the Available Options menu.

3. From the Available LAN Drivers screen, choose the LAN driver to view.

There are three fields to check on each LAN/WAN driver when giving a network the once over. When you choose LAN/WAN Drivers from MONITOR's Available Options menu, you'll see the Available LAN Drivers screen. From there, pick the LAN driver of interest to see details. Figure 8.48 shows the top part of this screen for the Compaq N100 interface card in my PROLIANT server.

FIGURE 8.48

More details about the network board than you can really use

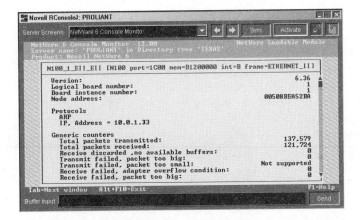

The first fields you want to check are Total Packets Transmitted and Total Packets Received. These give a good clue to your network health. The statistics are kept from the time the server starts or the network adapter is bound to the protocol. When it goes down or is unbound, these numbers are cleared.

The information at the top of the screen shows the version of the driver, the node address of the server, a list of the protocols supported on this board, and the board's network address. Other boards in the server will show similar information, with different addresses. Notice that this board, although it's only one of two logical boards based on one physical 3Com board, shows its address in TCP/IP, which started with NetWare 5.0.

Although this information is overkill for the typical network, you should appreciate the complexity of the information tracked for each network adapter card. Management software for your network and server uses these values to determine network health. For this Compaq N100 board, there are tons of statistics gathered for the Desktop Management standards and Compaq's own hardware monitors. It doesn't bother us to have all these extra details, although I wouldn't want to explain them all right now. Try pressing F1 for the Help screen, and you'll get seven pages that don't really explain the how or why of the protocol statistics.

VIEWING LOADED MODULE INFORMATION

IN A HURRY 8.21: VIEW NLM INFORMATION IN MONITOR

1. Type **MONITOR** from the console prompt.

2. Choose Loaded Modules from the Available Options menu.

3. From the Loaded NLMs screen, choose the NLM program to view.

4. Choose an item from the Resource Tags list to see details.

"System modules" is a fancy name for NLM programs running on the server. The System Module Information option on the Available Options menu shows the list of all loaded NLMs and information about each one. We saw these earlier, with more information, under NetWare Remote Server, but since we're in the neighborhood we may as well drop in.

Figure 8.49 shows the screen several options deep. This screen looks at the memory usage of each NLM, and it allows you to check the resource usage of every NLM.

FIGURE 8.49

Details for every loaded NLM on your system

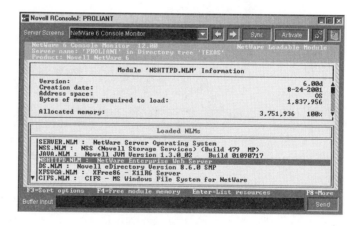

In Figure 8.49, I have chosen NSHTTPD.NLM (Netscape Hypertext Transfer Protocol Daemon), the NetWare Enterprise Web Server NLM (an upgrade to the NetWare Enterprise Server first appearing in NetWare 5.1). *Allocated memory* is that memory set aside by the operating system exclusively for use by this one NLM. If I had pressed the Tab key on this option, the top window would show that of the 100 percent of allocated memory, 96 percent of the bytes were in use, 2 percent were not in use, and 2 percent of the bytes were declared overhead.

Do you have a suspect NLM or two? Do some of your server-based programs go crazy now and then? These screens will give you a chance to track the memory usage of each problem NLM, as well as all the subsidiary NLMs called by the main programs. But don't head to this screen at the first hint of trouble. These things are far down the troubleshooting list. However, they do give you some great ammunition against a vendor saying that its "NLM software is perfect, so all the problems must come from another program."

SEEING FILE OPEN/LOCK ACTIVITY

IN A HURRY 8.22: VIEW FILES OPENED AND LOCKED ACTIVITY IN MONITOR

1. Type **MONITOR** from the console prompt.

2. Choose File Open/Lock Activity from the Available Options menu.

3. Use the Select and Entry list to find the specific file, and then choose that file to view the lock information.

The File Open/Lock Activity option on MONITOR's Available Options menu is a companion to the Connections screen that shows the files in use by each individual user. Here, you can check on a particular file to see the lock status and which connection number is using the file. This used to be more important when cross-locked files caused more grief. That's rare today, but still possible.

Figure 8.50 shows the end of the file hunt, reaching down to a particular file and seeing those particulars. In this case, it's the **NLSMAN32.EXE** file from the PUBLIC/WIN32 directory. Of course, the joke is on me, as you'll see when we reach the "Novell Licensing Services (NLS) Management" section later this chapter, since Licensing now runs under iManage. The fields in the two windows of lock information are described in Table 8.6.

FIGURE 8.50

Checking out who has a file checked out

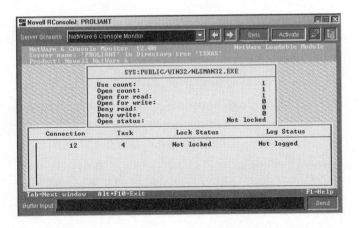

TABLE 8.6: FIELDS ON MONITOR'S FILE OPEN/LOCK ACTIVITY SCREEN

FIELD	DESCRIPTION
Use Count	Number of connections using this file by having it open, locked, or logged.
Open Count	Number of connections with this file open.
Open For Read	Connections reading this file.
Open For Write	Connections using this file with access to write to the file.
Deny Read	Connections that have opened this file and requested that other stations not have the right to open the file for reading.
Deny Write	Connections that have opened this file and requested that other stations not have the right to open the file for writing.
Open Status	Lock status of the file.
Connection	Number of the connection on the Connection Information screen. Use this field to find out who has the file open or locked.
Task	A task number defined by the NLM and of little use.
Lock Status	Shows whether the file is in use and how the file is configured (Shareable, Read-Only, etc.).
Log Status	Whether the file activity is logged.

This information is useful when a particular file is giving you problems and you can't track down the user holding the file open or locked. However, it's more common to track the files a user has open in the Connection Information screen.

Locking the File Server Console

IN A HURRY 8.23: LOCK THE FILE SERVER CONSOLE

1. Type **SCRSAVER** from the console prompt.

2. Set the delay time and enable the lock feature.

3. To unlock the file server console, type the administrator name and password.

Knowing that easy access to the server console can cause damage to your network (the villain can disconnect users or take drives offline, not to mention change all the other server parameters), Novell engineers offer a lock for the MONITOR screen, which is put into effect with a program called SCRSAVER. In a clever bit of programming, even the RCONSOLE and RConsoleJ connections are locked when this option is used.

NOTE   *It used to be that you locked the MONITOR display with MONITOR's Lock File Server Console option. In NetWare 5.0, this moved out of the MONITOR area into the separate SCRSAVER program.*

After typing **SCRSAVER** at the colon prompt, type **SCRSAVER HELP** to see all the new details you must learn. To set the console to start the snake after about two minutes, type the following:

```
SCRSAVER ENABLE; DELAY=120; ENABLE LOCK
```

Here is the password screen used to verify access to the console, whether local or remote:

This option is useful when many people can reach your server. Not everyone has the ideal situation of keeping the servers in a locked room. If the console is in a location where you can see it, or if you are using MONITOR remotely from your workstation, you want to be able to see the information or the snake whenever you look in that direction. Taking the keyboard and monitor away is more secure, but that approach may be inconvenient. Plus, remote access to servers makes it easy for villains to attempt their skullduggery via distant keyboard, so you need a good console-locking routine.

TIP   *Being lazy, I got tired of typing the entire* **SCRSAVER** *command every time. I created a clean text file named* SNAKE.NCF, *which I stored in the SYS:\SYSTEM directory with all the system NCF (NetWare Command File) administrative files stored there. Now, I only need to type* **SNAKE** *at the console and put* SNAKE.NCF *in the* AUTOEXEC.NCF *file for the server.*

Now, you can leave the display running in your cubicle without fear of someone with malicious intentions getting his or her hands on your server, or just someone clumsily pressing the wrong key.

SET Command Overview

The SET commands allow you to change almost every server parameter you can imagine. There are well over 100 SET commands, and most of them have from two to one million options. The number of possible commands at your fingertips is greater than the United States federal deficit, believe it or not. For a discussion of some of these commands, see Appendix C, "NetWare 6 SET Commands."

Great power lives in the SET commands, but it's like a medieval fantasy in which our hero finds a magic sword that can conquer the dragons. Unfortunately, he usually destroys half the town before he learns to manage the power of the sword. Keep that in mind as you look over the SET commands.

Fortunately, the default SET command parameters have been honed over the years to a point where few, if any, changes are needed. Even more fortunate for us, SET commands have migrated from the command line, to the stand-alone SERVMAN utility, to part of MONITOR, to an outstanding utility inside NetWare Remote Manager. All utilities (even the command-line options) will make configurations that are necessary for the SET parameters, as well as for AUTOEXEC.NCF and STARTUP.NCF.

Figure 8.51 shows the SET command categories on the server console. Before the list, the help information for SET is displayed, showing the format used by all the SET commands.

FIGURE 8.51

A set of SET categories

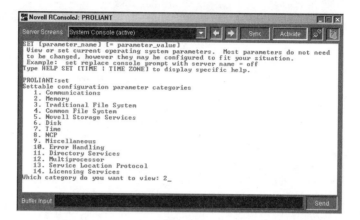

The example given with the Help command is a small detail that wasn't under our control with earlier NetWare versions, but it is now. As you can see, the server name is displayed as part of the server console prompt. The following command overrides the default setting of On.

    SET replace console prompt with server name = off

(SET commands have long names, as this one illustrates.)

The format, as just shown, is as follows:

    SET [parameter_name] [=parameter_value]

Here is a quick summary of each of the categories listed in Figure 8.51.

Communications   Of the twenty communications parameters available, four of them control packet receive buffers, and four control the watchdog packets. *Packet receive buffers* hold data packets in the server's memory while they are being processed. (Use MONITOR to view the number of packet receive buffers allocated.) *Watchdog packets* make sure that stations are connected. If the client doesn't communicate with the server within a certain time (configurable, of course), the server sends a watchdog packet. Over another configurable time (59.3 seconds by default), a default of 10 packets is sent to the station. If the workstation doesn't respond to 10 minutes of requests, the server assumes that the station is disconnected and clears the internal connection for that workstation.

Memory   The Memory section holds six commands that control the dynamic memory pool and work with servers for proper memory registration. The command you are most likely to use is Set the Number of Reserved Buffers Below 16MB. (With NetWare 4, you also used Register RAM Above 16MB, but that is no longer necessary.)

Traditional File System   NSS handles itself quite well, but there are many network managers experienced enough to make some SET modifications to the traditional filesystem.

Common File System   New for NetWare 6, the Common File System works with the Windows NT/2000 mediocre NetBIOS-based networking protocol. NetWare servers can host those files products more securely, more reliably, and faster.

Novell Storage Services   Many of the NSS configuration settings await your perusal and possible modifications. This isn't the best place for these changes, but they can be made here if you wish.

Disk   The three parameters in the disk area control one part of the Hot Fix feature: redirection. Redirection as part of Hot Fix may now occur during a write or read request or during a read-after-write verification.

Time   The 20 parameters concerned with time synchronization help configure the `TIMESYNC.CFG` file. Time zone settings, time synchronization to other servers, and time source references are covered as well.

NCP   These 12 parameters help configure NCP details, such as NCP packet particulars and server packet security levels between the workstation and server. For example, you can set the security option for packet signatures (a NetWare exclusive) to guard against counterfeit stations impersonating authorized stations. The ability to support LIPs (Large Internet Packets) is also set here.

Miscellaneous   This catchall area is composed of 24 parameters. Maximum Service Processes, Allow Unencrypted Passwords, and Automatically Repair Bad Volume illustrate the range of choices in this section.

Error Handling   These 12 options control the log files, the size of the log files, and what happens when the log files reach the configured maximum size. For example, you can set the log file size for the volume log, server log, and TTS log (if TTS is enabled).

Directory Services   This category includes another baker's-dozen options for NDS support. These include setting the bindery context, NDS synchronization intervals and restrictions, and time intervals for maintenance processes. Maintenance items include reclaiming disk space and controlling the NDS trace file. This group of SET parameters is new since NetWare 4.0.

Multiprocessor   This is a relatively new area, because NetWare 5.1 handled multiprocessor systems differently than NetWare 4 did, and NetWare 6 improves multiprocessor support even more. Three parameters handle load-balancing questions, when to start secondary processors, and how to handle certain details when a processor is taken offline.

Service Location Protocol   These parameters are new with NetWare 6, because the need to use a TCP/IP protocol required Novell to locate services without the broadcasts used by IPX. SLP is an Internet standard now, and NetWare 6 is the first large commercial product to use this (as far as I can tell, anyway). But since all the NetWare TCP/IP innards will take care of these details, you shouldn't need to deal with these parameters too much, if at all.

Licensing Services This category is so new that the NetWare 6 documentation still thinks licensing is an entry in the Miscellaneous category. It's not, although with only two entries it certainly could have stayed there without inconveniencing anyone. But with digital certificates ensuring authentication with other companies across the Internet, licensing is important, so Novell engineers evidently decided to set aside a new SET category for licensing.

NOTE *I don't present the SET command descriptions and details in this section for two reasons. One is that the Net-Ware Remote Management and even MONITOR do a better job with Help screens and information than the SET commands on the console. The other is that both options relieve you of the necessity of typing the SET command and parameter at the console prompt. I always make a typo or forget a word when typing the long command, so I prefer the NetWare Remote Manager. Nonetheless, SET commands are discussed in Appendix C.*

The complete list of each parameter and all the options that go with it is in Appendix C. As I've said before, and as the manuals and Help screens say, the SET parameters are not something to play with when you're bored with Solitaire. The Help text options on the server are a little sparse, but the full Help screens and other details in MONITOR and NetWare Remote Manager make those programs the way to go.

Commonly Used Console Commands

This section contains the commands typed at the console most often. The command frequency was determined by pure happenstance: I asked some friends which console commands they used, if any. These came up more than any other, but each network and network administrator is different. The "top five"—DISPLAY SLP SERVICES, DOWN, MODULES, VERSION, and VOLUMES—are described in the following sections. They're listed in alphabetical order, not ranked by importance.

DISPLAYING NETWORK RESOURCES

The DISPLAY NETWORKS command used to list just the known NetWare servers on the network. NetWare 6 changed the command to DISPLAY SLP SERVICES. Not exactly the same thing, but as close as we get now. Figure 8.52 shows an example at the top of the screen.

FIGURE 8.52

The result of the DISPLAY SLP SERVICES command

You can see the various services listing the servers they use, as well as the IP addresses and names for various services. Unlike the old version, we see more than we really want.

SHUTTING DOWN THE SERVER

The DOWN command writes information in the server cache to disk, closes files, updates directory-entry tables and file allocation tables, and shuts down the server in an orderly manner. When you use DOWN, warnings are sent to each connected workstation, after which you'll see a message saying that it's safe to reboot or power off the server.

LISTING NLMs

The MODULES command lists all loaded NLM programs, along with version information. Novell offers you so many ways to look at these modules, you may begin to think they're important for some reason. Figure 8.53 shows an example of the result.

FIGURE 8.53

Using the MODULES command

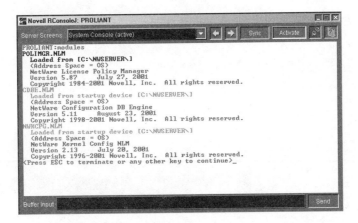

This list takes many pages, and the modules don't seem to appear in any particular order. However, they are listed in the order loaded. When modules are unloaded, they leave a slot open for the next module. If no free slots exist, later modules are appended to the end of the list.

Dates of modules can become critical when chasing stubborn problems. Rest assured, whatever date you have on your system modules, at least two will be out of date already (or at least that will be the problem according to technical support).

There are other places to list these modules, such as within MONITOR or NetWare Remote Manager, that actually give you useful information—like memory usage, which is always critical.

NOTE *Me? I'll never use the console MODULES command again. Not only are there too many modules to scroll through, but they can't be sorted. MONITOR sorts by the default Allocated Memory listing and offers a way (F3=Sort options) to sort by date or name. But personally, my favorite view is from NetWare Remote Manager.*

LISTING VERSION INFORMATION

Use VERSION to list the NetWare operating system license information. This command used to show a decent amount of information, but NetWare 6 cuts down the detail considerably. All you see now is the NetWare version, with the date stamp, which is useful when you're checking for needed upgrades or patches. No longer does this command show the number of licensed connections and serial number of the operating system.

LISTING VOLUME INFORMATION

VOLUMES shows mounted volumes on the server, including CD-ROM volumes. Figure 8.54 shows an example of the result, with VERSION at the top of the screen and VOLUMES at the bottom. Notice the new NSS VOLUMES command, and how the information differs from the original VOLUME command.

FIGURE 8.54

Using VOLUMES to see server volumes (and VERSION at the top)

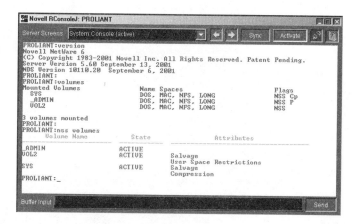

The Name Spaces section shows DOS here, but includes Mac, NFS, and LONG when those namespaces are supported on the volume. Namespaces are set per volume, not per server.

The Flags column shows volume characteristics: Cp means compressed, Sa means block suballocation, and Mg means data migration is enabled (which isn't the case for the volumes shown in Figure 8.54). In the original VOLUMES command output (middle entry), NSS shows up as a flag as well. The P for the _ADMIN "non-volume" could be for Proprietary or Phantom; take your pick.

Remote Server Console Access

Perhaps you think this section seems contradictory. After all, all the browser-based utilities we've discussed, such as iManage and NetWare Remote Manager, work remotely by definition. Not only do you run these programs at the physical server console, with proper Internet security, you can run them from anywhere on the Internet.

Notice we're talking about remote "console" access. While the new browser-based utilities, along with ConsoleOne running across the network, reduce the need for console interaction, there are some tools and commands on the console that still have value. If you've been doing NetWare admin-istration for a long time, you may feel comfortable with some of the console utilities and resist the fancy new utilities just a bit. Besides, experienced managers can attack a server console with flying fingers, type a few commands, and search through some quick utilities—all before the browser-based utilities have loaded onto the desktop and connected to the server in question.

Each of the connection methods we'll discuss work for a single NetWare server console. Multiple server consoles may be connected from one desktop, but by definition, a console command or utility works on a single physical server. Yes, I'm specifically ignoring some of the eDirectory utilities just to make my point.

Remote Console Control with RConsoleJ and RCONSOLE

Unless you enjoy hunkering down in a small computer room, squatting over and around several servers, learn to use at least one of the remote-console utilities: RCONSOLE or RConsoleJ. These are client/server flavored applications that run both on the server and on your local Windows work-station. RConsoleJ, written in Java, does the same remote-connection trick using a Java client applica-tion and TCP/IP for a network transport layer that RCONSOLE did for so many versions over IPX. If you don't run IPX, you must use RConsoleJ for connection. Once connected, the utilities are identical, so we'll talk about RConsoleJ first to help experienced NetWare managers get comfortable.

RConsoleJ

RConsoleJ allows you to perform the following tasks:

- ◆ Execute all console commands remotely

- ◆ Run all console utilities remotely

- ◆ List directories in the NetWare and DOS partitions of the server

- ◆ Edit text files in either the NetWare or DOS partitions of the server

- ◆ Take down and/or reboot the server

- ◆ Install products or upgrade NetWare

Instead of the old C-Worthy interface screen, we get a nice Java login screen, as shown below. If you can't tell at this size, the little icon in the upper-left corner is the official Java coffee-cup logo.

The drop-down list in the upper left of the background box labeled Connection Options also offers Unsecure IP as an option, sending clear text passwords and transmissions. When you activate the Unsecure option, the drop-down list to the right offers a choice of a direct connection or to go through a proxy.

Clicking the little server icon to the left of the Server text field pops open the List of Remote Servers window. Only IP servers appear; RConsoleJ provides no IPX connection (although you can load an IPX RConsoleJ proxy utility on a server running both protocol stacks).

When you start a secured connection (strongly recommended by Novell and me when linking from outside the local network), you'll get a chance to see NetWare's Certificate Authority at work. See it all in Figure 8.55.

FIGURE 8.55

Ensuring a secure connection via RConsoleJ

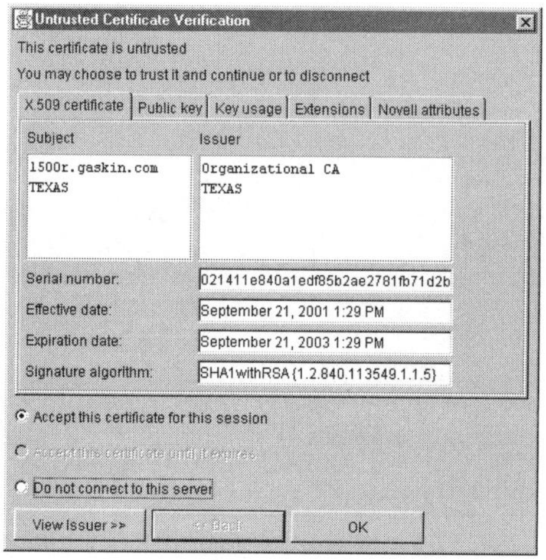

Notice that the default settings I left on my Compaq-1500 server don't allow for a choice to Accept This Certificate Until It Expires. It's probably a good idea to leave this default and force remote connections to verify through as much security as possible for each connection.

Once security controls accept each communication partner as legitimate, the RConsoleJ connect begins. Take a look at Figure 8.56 and tell me if you notice any real differences from the old RCON-SOLE utility?

The Server Screens pull-down menu at the top of the console screen allows you to pick any active server console display except for X-Server. Since the X-Server display spends most of the time running ConsoleOne at the server console, you have many options to run ConsoleOne remotely. Plus, the C-Worthy screen format used originally in RCONSOLE and faithfully reproduced in RConsoleJ can't handle high-resolution screens.

If you prefer, you can click the two large arrows beside the Server Screens pull-down menu to roll through the available console screens. The Sync command button jumps to the Active console screen. It stays down and enforced until you toggle it. The Activate command button allows you to make the current screen the active one on the server console, as well as on your workstation.

FIGURE 8.56

An old look through a new connection

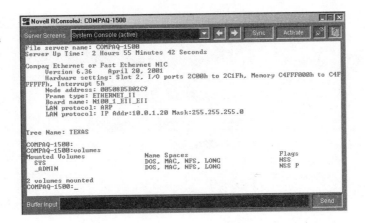

NOTE   *A screen shot of text doesn't do RConsoleJ justice for re-creating the precise look and feel of RCONSOLE (this will be important in a moment) See the MONITOR screens in the "MONITOR Everything" section earlier in this chapter (for example Figures 8.47 and 8.48) for examples of real screens as they appear in RConsoleJ.*

There can be slight hang-ups using RConsoleJ and the Tab key for some functions. When I hit the Tab key and it doesn't seem to work, I click the Activate command button, and then try it again. It almost always works the second time.

Next to the Activate button sits the Disconnect button. It may be hard to see, but the Disconnect icon includes cable connectors a slight bit apart. Nothing tells us if they are getting closer together or farther apart, which means icon development lags behind many other computer skills. Nonetheless, if you click the Disconnect command button rather than the X in the upper-right corner, RConsoleJ retreats back to the opening login screen (like the one shown earlier). The last icon on the toolbar across the top of RConsoleJ is the Help screen call button (the book with a question mark icon).

NOTE   *The Buffer Input text field at the bottom of the screen probably hung around from the remote-console screens built into NetWare Remote Manager. Some remote screens through Remote Manager aren't interactive, so any commands need to be loaded into the buffer and transmitted to the remote server. There, NetWare pretends to type them on the console for server execution. You'll see how remote-control access works in Remote Manager in the "Console Screen Support Inside Remote Manager" section later in this chapter, but you won't like it after RConsoleJ and RCONSOLE.*

RConsoleJ Server Setup

Setting up RConsoleJ on servers isn't quite a no-brainer, but almost. The only aggravation comes when you realize the changes you must make to activate RConsoleJ are exactly the type of changes RConsoleJ works best for. It's nice of NetWare to provide irony lessons when we least expect them.

Inside the `AUTOEXEC.NCF` file, toward the end, awaits a line mentioning `RCONAG6.NLM`. This file prepares the NetWare server to respond to RConsoleJ connection requests. The line in `AUTOEXEC.NCF` defaults to being commented out with a number sign. See this line in Figure 8.57, just about in the middle of the screen.

FIGURE 8.57

Configuring the
server portion of
RConsoleJ

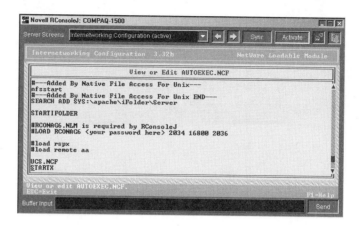

Remember that number signs (#) before commands tell the processing engine to ignore that particular line. To activate RConsoleJ, you need to do only three things:

◆ Remove the # signs.

◆ Create a server password and enter it to replace the "<your password here>" line lamely provided by NetWare. (Yes, replace the < and > as well.)

◆ Go back to the main menu in INETCFG, scroll to the bottom, and choose Reinitialize System.

In about 20 seconds, you'll be ready to roll with your new fancy RConsoleJ connection tool.

RConsoleJ in a Mixed TCP/IP and IPX Environment

RConsoleJ really does a decent job of making me forget RCONSOLE. So I wondered if there was any way to use RConsoleJ on IPX-based servers. Luckily, there is, if you allow some NetWare 6 server to perform as a bridge between the two protocol worlds. TCP/IP bigots may not like having any IPX in their networks anymore, but many people do.

The key is the `RCONPRXY.NLM` program sitting in the SYS:\SYSTEM directory. Run this program from a server with both TCP/IP and IPX support, and it will become a bridge for you between the two protocol worlds.

Port 2035, the default port for the RCONPRXY program, sits between port 2036 (secure IP connection) and port 2034 (insecure, clear-text IP connection). Port 2035 is the link between RConsoleJ in TCP/IP and RCONSOLE in IPX.

RCONSOLE HANGS ON

Just as with RConsoleJ, the server part of RCONSOLE must be started before the client can make a connection. If you have `RCONSOLE.EXE` and supporting files on your local workstation, you are not required to be logged in to NDS to run RCONSOLE.

Configuring the Server for Remote Access

There are two steps in configuring the server for remote access:

- ◆ Start the REMOTE program, with or without a password. A password is preferred, and you have an option of using an encrypted password.

- ◆ Start the `RSPX.NLM` program for access across the network or start `AIOCOMX.NLM` (or other communication port driver, depending on your server hardware), `AIO.NLM`, and `RS232.NLM`.

To start REMOTE, at the server console colon prompt, type **REMOTE <*password*>** and press Enter. Then type **RSPX** and press Enter.

Until you encrypt the password, the password you give at the console is the one you must type when making a remote connection. NetWare 6 no longer allows the Supervisor password to unlock the REMOTE program, so if you want a password, you must specify that password. These commands should be placed at the end of the `AUTOEXEC.NCF` program, so that remote access is configured every time the server starts.

For an encrypted password, you must run the REMOTE program and provide your password, letting the system generate the encrypted password. For the connection, you must then provide the encrypted password result. (The password *good* came out as 0A137773E4AEAFFA3B on my system.) Every time you load REMOTE on that server, you must use the encrypted password. A better idea is to let the system save the command to load the REMOTE program and the encrypted password automatically by placing it in a specially created `SYS:\SYSTEM\LDREMOTE.NCF` file. Then, rather than typing **REMOTE -E 0A137773E4AEAFFA3B**, you can type **LDREMOTE**. (Since LDREMOTE is a batch file-type program, you don't need the LOAD command.)

You must then add the appropriate command to enable LAN or async connections. You can add those commands to the `LDREMOTE.NCF` program, but if you generate another encrypted password, the new file will overwrite your modified file.

To disable remote connections, you can use the following command:

```
REMOTE LOCK OUT
```

This is best done at the physical console, although it does work from a remote connection. Once that remote connection is broken, however, the console remains locked; you can't get back in. To enable remote connections, use this command:

```
REMOTE UNLOCK
```

RCONSOLE from the Client Side

Once the remote connection software is loaded at the server, the client part is fairly simple. From a DOS prompt, type **RCONSOLE** and press Enter. (The `RCONSOLE.EXE` file sits in the search drive SYS:\PUBLIC.) A screen will appear, asking for your choice of connection type: asynchronous or LAN. On LANs, the answer is (surprise) LAN. Next, you'll see a listing of all the servers answering the broadcast request from the RCONSOLE program, as shown below.

Notice that there is no mention of containers or contexts with the server names. RCONSOLE bypasses NDS and speaks directly to the server. You can connect directly to a specific server, skipping the pick list, by giving its name with the command, as in **RCONSOLE PROLIANT**.

Whether you pick from the list or go directly to the server, the next step is to provide the password configured for that server. Type in the password given when you loaded REMOTE on the server, and you will immediately become a remote console.

Here are some keystrokes that you need for your remote console work:

◆ Press Alt+F1 to open the Available Options menu overlay.

◆ Press Alt+F2 to exit RCONSOLE.

◆ Press Alt+F3 to move to the next server console screen.

◆ Press Alt+F4 to move to the previous server console screen.

◆ Press Alt+F5 to show the network address of the RCONSOLE workstation.

The Ctrl+Escape combination on the server that opens the Current Screens menu does not work with RCONSOLE. Neither does the Alt+Escape combination to roll through the screens. However, the up and down arrows to scroll through previously entered commands do work remotely.

Everything you need in RCONSOLE can be done from the Available Options menu called by the Alt+F1 combination. (If you're like me and have trouble remembering which keystrokes work with which program, write Alt+F1 somewhere on your cubicle wall.)

Figure 8.58 shows the Available Options menu, overlaying the Help screen for the REMOTE console command. Move the highlight bar with the cursor keys and press Enter to activate any menu item.

FIGURE 8.58

The RCONSOLE Available Options menu

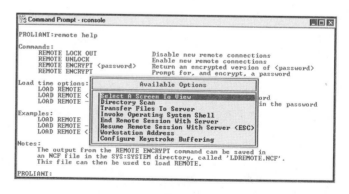

The menu items are fairly straightforward. Let's take a quick look at each option:

Select a Screen to View   Opens a submenu of all active console screens. Move the highlight bar to a screen and press Enter to move immediately to that screen.

Directory Scan   Lists the files and subdirectories in any directory on the server, both the NetWare and DOS partitions. To reference the DOS partition, use C:\<*directory_name*>.

Transfer Files to Server   Copies files from any local or mapped workstation drive to any directory on any server partition. Long files show the progress of the amazingly slow transfer process.

Invoke Operating System Shell   Exits to the DOS shell, but RCONSOLE takes so much memory that this has limited value.

End Remote Session with Server   Disconnects with the server (same function as Alt+F2).

Resume Remote Session with Server   Clears the menu off the screen and returns you to the remote connection (same function as Escape).

Workstation Address   Shows the network and local address of your workstation (same function as Alt+F5).

Configure Keystroke Buffering   Normally, each keystroke is sent immediately to the server. Because of async connections, you may wish to control the delivery of your text. The options are No Keystroke Buffering (send each keystroke immediately), Keystroke Delay (send when the keyboard is idle), Manual Keystroke Send (press Alt+F8 to send), and On-Demand Buffering (press Alt+F9 to enter a buffered command).

Most of the time, you'll use RCONSOLE across the network to connect to a server in your building. You'll connect to the server, check the status of one or more NLMs, check the MONITOR program, and disconnect. If your servers are ten floors up and the elevator is broken, this utility will save you a workout.

When DOS is removed from the server memory, the EXIT command forces a reboot. If your server is configured to boot DOS and go straight into NetWare, this system works great. And there are no stairs to climb.

XCONSOLE via Telnet

Back in the early days of NetWare's support for TCP/IP, some smart Novell programs ported a Telnet server program to the server. It's only good for one thing, but Telnet support makes it possible to connect to a NetWare server via any standard Telnet client program. Really—take a look at Figure 8.59 if you don't believe me.

How hard is this to set up? Type **TELNETD** on the server console, and you're ready. Use the same password when prompted as you set up for RConsoleJ, and you're finished.

NOTE   *I'm not sure if you'll be happy with this Telnet program in contrast to RConsoleJ, but back when many high-end network management systems ran on Unix workstations, this utility allowed any Unix admin to become a NetWare admin, at least for console commands.*

FIGURE 8.59

A vt100 terminal
emulation NetWare
console screen

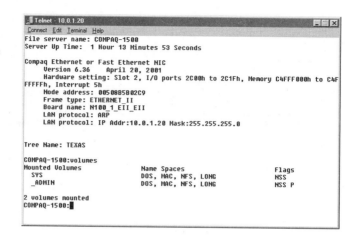

```
Telnet - 10.0.1.20
Connect  Edit  Terminal  Help
File server name: COMPAQ-1500
Server Up Time:  1 Hour 13 Minutes 53 Seconds

Compaq Ethernet or Fast Ethernet NIC
      Version 6.36    April 20, 2001
      Hardware setting: Slot 2, I/O ports 2C00h to 2C1Fh, Memory C4FFF000h to C4F
FFFFFh, Interrupt 5h
      Node address: 00508B5B02C9
      Frame type: ETHERNET_II
      Board name: N100_1_EII_EII
      LAN protocol: ARP
      LAN protocol: IP Addr:10.0.1.20 Mask:255.255.255.0


Tree Name: TEXAS

COMPAQ-1500:volumes
Mounted Volumes                  Name Spaces              Flags
  SYS                            DOS, MAC, NFS, LONG      NSS
  _ADMIN                         DOS, MAC, NFS, LONG      NSS P

2 volumes mounted
COMPAQ-1500:▊
```

ACONSOLE for Modem Connections

IN A HURRY 8.24: CONFIGURE ACONSOLE WITH INETCFG

1. Type **INETCFG** from the console prompt.

2. Choose Manage Configuration, then Configure Remote Access to This Server.

3. Enable Remote Access and provide an appropriate password (if a password hasn't already been defined).

4. Enable ACONSOLE Connection.

5. Set the COM port, baud rate, and any Expert Modem Setup parameters, as necessary.

6. Press Escape twice to return to the main menu.

If you thought XCONSOLE emulating a vt100 terminal was a blast from the past, think about dialing in to a NetWare server at 9.6Kbps for remote management. Makes you want to break out the polyester and hairspray, and turn on the glamour rock from the middle 1980s.

Remote access through a modem directly to the server was a great innovation in the mid-1980s but seems far less important today. For one thing, resetting the COM port when the modem locks up requires a server reboot. Managers try to minimize these reboots, but modems have a mind of their own.

Will anyone really use this method of operation today? Eschew browser-utilities, forego RConsoleJ, and sneer even at XCONSOLE, just so they can blow the dust off their Hayes MicroModem? Yes, they definitely will.

Not every NetWare server hooks to the Internet. Checking a server from home via a slow modem beats driving to the office in the middle of the night, so don't sneer too quickly at ACONSOLE.

If you need a modem connection to the server, INETCFG provides a place to set it up. You use the same screen as you do for RCONSOLE configuration. Figure 8.60 shows the new ACONSOLE information configured.

FIGURE 8.60

Multiple remote-access options to this server

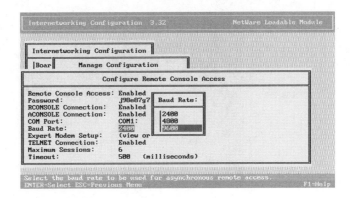

The only options for server COM ports are COM1 and COM2. The Baud Rate options are 2400, 4800, and 9600. (Yes, the default really is 2400; I told you this was an ancient utility.) There are patches available on Novell's Web site to speed up this connection.

The screen painting in ACONSOLE is not at all optimized, and the color palette takes longer than you would think to transmit. If you have particular modem initialization parameters to set, the Expert Modem Setup option will let you type in all you want.

Activating ACONSOLE requires RS232.NLM to be loaded in the AUTOEXEC.NCF file. This NLM controls the COM port for the modem.

Console Screen Support Inside Remote Manager

NetWare Remote Manager includes two versions of console screens. The first version, HTML Based Screen Pages, provides only static screen views. You can see the screen, and you can set the screen to update now and then, but you can't really interact with the screen. Drill down one quick level in NetWare Remote Manager by clicking Console Screens under the Manage Server heading, and bingo, you have some remote-console capabilities.

HTML BASED SCREEN PAGES

Technically, you can send commands to the HTML screen by clicking different command buttons, which squirt commands back to the server and update the screens. Figure 8.61 shows the venerable MONITOR utility being poorly rendered via HTML static pages.

See all the cute little command buttons scattered around the bottom of the screen? You click those rather than actually pressing the key itself. This version improves over the Portal utility that shipped in NetWare 5.1, believe it or not.

The HTML screens do have some value. You can use the Page Refresh Rate setting to update the screen every few seconds to few minutes and see what's happening. Of course, you need to start another screen to do anything about what you've seen, but it's a start.

FIGURE 8.61

Another, lesser, remote-console option

CONSOLE SCREENS

A better option of the two on the Remote Manager Current Screens page is Console Screens, above the HTML Based Screen label. This utility tries to do an RConsoleJ emulation, but doesn't quite make it.

Novell people whispered to me that there wasn't enough time to get all the updates into Remote Manager and fold RConsoleJ directly into the Console Screens page. Too bad, because that's what should happen ... maybe next version.

Figure 8.62 shows Remote Manager's Console Screens page, with the pop-up almost-RConsoleJ application tucked into the white space in the bottom-right portion of the screen from whence it came.

Yes, the screen from inside Remote Manager looks much better than the image in Figure 8.61—no argument there. But does it look as good as the earlier MONITOR images back in Figures 8.44, 8.45, and so on? Doesn't the earlier image look exactly like the screen does on the server console itself (well, except for the fact that I reversed the colors to make the black-and-white reproduction more readable)? I believe it does better echo the MONITOR screen running on a server console.

FIGURE 8.62

Remote Manager's Console Screens option is similar to, but still far behind, RConsoleJ.

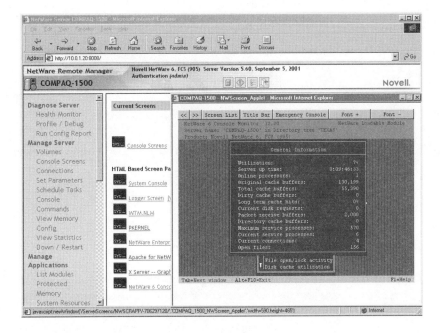

Figure 8.62 shows the best remote console available from within Remote Manager, but it's not quite ready to duke it out in a real-world comparison test. If we didn't have RConsoleJ to spoil us, we'd be happy with the Remote Manager application, even though we couldn't type more than a character every two seconds to avoid dropped characters. We could get used to it if we had to. But we don't, so you probably won't get used to it at all. I haven't.

Protocol Management Tools

NetWare 6 may be the last operating system from NetWare including IPX, so I couldn't in good conscience lump TCP/IP into this chapter as if there were no choices in network protocols. Next time, however, you may see only a footnote for IPX somewhere, and we'll treat TCP/IP as the one and only protocol for NetWare anytime. People have short memories, you know, and quickly forget those who came before, so prepare mentally for the time when you see IPX listed as just "some non-TCP/IP protocol family, now dead." That day will come.

TCP/IP Management

The INETCFG (InterNetworking Configuration) utility is the focal point of all protocols on your server. The LOAD and BIND commands in the `AUTOEXEC.NCF` file, configured when you installed your server, can be moved under control of INETCFG.

You can verify your server's IP address (or addresses) several ways (including typing CONFIG at the console prompt), but changing an IP address or subnet mask calls for INETCFG. It isn't difficult to do those things, and fairly easy to add OSPF (Open Shortest Path First) or check to see that your server calls itself a router or a TCP/IP end node.

Along with INETCFG for configuration, there's TCPCON (I'm sure you knew this was coming; if NetWare had an IPXCON, it should also have a TCPCON). This utility isn't new, but it is suddenly more popular and has overtaken IPXCON by far. If you need to check out the TCP/IP packets zooming through one of your servers, run TCPCON.

For all the details on TCP/IP setup, configuration, monitoring, and heavy lifting, see Chapter 11, "TCP/IP and NetWare 6." That chapter describes how to use INETCFG and TCPCON.

Internetwork Packet eXpired

One would think all the various IPX (Internetwork Packet eXchange) configuration and monitoring tools belong in this section. Alas, IPX now means RIP (Rest In Peace, not Routing Internet Protocol). IPX shuffled off into the great protocol graveyard, two down from the fabled elephant's graveyard.

If you have IPX running on your network, you already have IPX experience and documentation. Take this as a warning to actively wean users and applications off IPX. If you don't have IPX in your network, then a section on IPX will just waste your time.

Hence, we have no IPX details here today. IPX offered many advantages over TCP/IP, especially for local networking, but the market said otherwise. As many technical companies have learned (some not until they hit bankruptcy court), a better product doesn't mean better sales. The world does not beat the path to the door hiding the better mousetrap. The world beats a path to the door with the best directions and advertising.

IPX lasted longer than most non-TCP/IP protocols, but that matters little today. Now, IPX = DEAD.

Bandwidth Management with WAN Traffic Manager

The WAN (Wide Area Network) Traffic Manager utility included with NetWare 6 does a wonderful job that I hope you don't need to worry about: conserving bandwidth. Like money, bandwidth is only precious to those who don't have enough. WAN Traffic Manager (WTM) helps you reserve your bandwidth for data and schedule server-to-server NDS traffic for the time most convenient for you, rather than when it's most convenient for NDS.

Of course, when everyone has T3 lines pumping 45Mbps between every branch office, bandwidth conservation won't be necessary. Just watch out that the flying pigs don't poop on your head.

Seriously, NDS is fairly efficient and won't drag your traffic to a standstill anytime. Okay, if you have 56Kbps links between offices and you start a complete NDS replica reconstruction, traffic will suffer. But normal operations won't overload normal communications channels. Unless you link large and complicated networks through slow connections, you can wait a while before checking your need for WTM.

But you don't always know when something out of the ordinary will happen, do you? Maybe you just like being in control and only want traffic to route through the servers you dictate, rather than building a typical mesh network. Then WTM is for you. But if you run NDS eDirectory on Linux and Solaris, WTM isn't for you yet.

More important, WTM exhibits another area where NDS is far ahead of the pack. Policy control has been a solid foundation of NDS from the beginning, but it was called things like "login time restrictions" and "rights to files and directories." All those things are policies, and now the buzzword police have decreed that *policy* is the name for all these things. With WTM, you manage your WAN through policies.

GETTING STARTED WITH WAN TRAFFIC MANAGER

There may be some type of auxiliary installation program for WTM, but I couldn't find it. If you miss this check box during installation, you can reinstall that portion or try to hack through it, as I did. I started the program the old-fashioned way, by copying files from the server installation CD-ROM to the server hard disk. Take my word for it, it's better to go through Install on the server console and start the program properly, if you didn't load WTM as part of the original installation procedure.

A key component of WTM, the LAN Area object, saves you time and trouble. Policies apply to individual servers unless you group servers in a LAN Area object. If you prefer to craft policies for each and every server separately, that's your choice (but not a smart one).

Create the LAN Area object by choosing the WANMAN:LAN Area object inside the New Object dialog box in ConsoleOne. Provide a name that makes sense, such as a geographical name (Dallas, in my case). Open the property page of your LAN Area object, choose the Members tab, and use the Select Objects dialog box to add servers. Figure 8.63 shows the process, with one server already a member of the group (PROLIANT) and one about to join (COMPAQ-1500).

FIGURE 8.63

Grouping servers for your LAN Area object

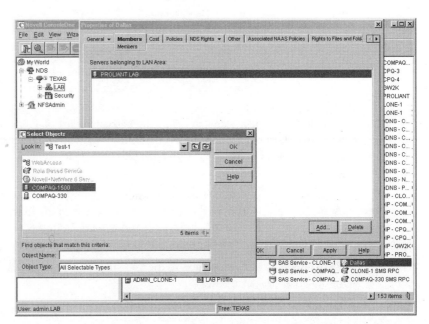

SETTING POLICIES

When you open a WTM-enabled server property page inside ConsoleOne, you'll see a new tab: Wan Traffic Manager. A better way to control WAN traffic, however, is to use the LAN Area object. Atop the property page for the Dallas LAN Area object, along with the normal tabs, are two you haven't seen before: Cost and Policies.

Unlike NetWare 5.1, where the policies appeared in NetWare Administrator, ConsoleOne uses a Load Command button to pull open a search dialog box containing all the policies. Figure 8.64 shows the Load Policy Set dialog box inside the Dallas property page.

FIGURE 8.64

New policy options for NetWare servers

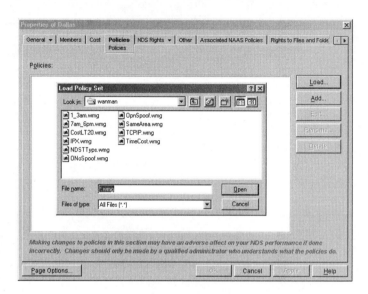

The files (or "policy sets") in Figure 8.64 are a long list of predefined policies that are available. Here, with a short description, are the items in the predefined policy group list. Each is also a file-name, with a .WMG extension, for Wan Man Group (I prefer Blue Man Group, but IBM already hired them).

1–3a.m.   Two policies are used to restrict traffic to those hours. This one requires NA, for No Address, applying to five NDS properties. 1–3a.m. by itself limits the rest of the NDS traffic to those hours. To section off all traffic to those hours, both the 1–3a.m. option and the 7a.m.–6p.m. option must be used.

7a.m.–6p.m.   The companion to the 1–3a.m. option, this one is to keep the hours of 7:00 A.M. to 6:00 P.M. clear of traffic.

CostLT20   Limits traffic-defined links that have a price value set of less than 20.

IPX   This blocks all traffic that's not IPX.

NDSTTyps   A group of variables used to define the properties passed by NDS to the traffic type query.

ONoSpoof   Blocks all traffic to existing WAN connections. How? It stands for, somehow, "Already Open, No Spoofing," blocking all traffic.

OpnSpoof   Turns off all connections to WAN links open more than 15 minutes, figuring that those that are open that long are being spoofed rather than actually being connected.

SameArea   Blocks all traffic that's local only, based on an assumed Class C TCP/IP address.

TCPIP   Blocks all but TCP/IP traffic.

TimeCost   Sets priority links by assigning a cost to connections over time.

If you want to see the predefined policies for a model, just highlight a loaded policy and click the Edit command button. You can also delete or rename policies, and create your own by clicking the Add command button.

Instructions are included in the Help files for those who wish to write their own policies. Not being a programmer, I get lost between IF and THEN, but if you or a friend want to get involved, the instructions are there. More than that, the Policy Editor won't save the new policy until all the syntax is checked, and it oh-so-snidely lists the line number of every mistake. If this sounds good to you, enjoy it.

Just to make sure you understand your limitations (as I do mine about programming), Novell puts a warning in red letters (they really are red) at the bottom of the property page of the LAN Area object. Essentially, the warning says not to mess with these policies because you can screw up NDS big time (point taken?).

Yes, each policy is listed twice inside the Policies text box, the second time with NA afterwards. This stands for No Address and is necessary to make the policy valid in all circumstances. Luckily, you and I don't need to worry about this at all.

After setting a policy, it will take 24 hours for the policy to ripple out to all the servers involved. If that's too long (and I think it is, too), go to the server console and type **WANMAN REFRESH IMMEDI-ATE**. This reloads the policies without waiting.

CHECKING YOUR POLICIES

As I said, there's no real notice that these policies are working. You could put a traffic analyzer on the network and see that your traffic has dropped, but that's a lot of work.

Being rather lazy when possible, my method is to start a directory services trace and see that NDS connections are being refused based on a policy limiting NDS updates until traffic levels have dropped. This says that the policies are working, because the refusal means potential traffic has been stopped. Ergo, less traffic on your WAN links.

Go to the server console (in one form or another) and type **SET DSTRACE = +WANMAN**. This tells DSTRACE to show WANMAN messages. The next step is to start DSTRACE with the SCREEN ON options, so you can see the information echoed to the server console. Figure 8.65 shows the results. This screen is a little hard to read at first, but take a look, and I'll explain what's going on.

The first six lines on the screen don't matter to us. There are five operations, the last of which wraps around to line six. Ah, but lucky line seven tells us our policy is working. What looks like an error ("Sync failed to communicate...") is really a successful policy implementation. I know this because error number 720 means "connection denied" rather than something terrible like "the coffeepot is dry."

This trace screen is nice and colorful, making it easy to pick out these messages. You may also send these lines to a trace file, but then you get just black and white again.

We have successfully limited some of our WAN traffic by setting a policy dictating that to NDS. Let's just see if you can do this with Active Directory, now that it's shipping and people realize the problems dealing with an early version of a "supposedly" enterprise directory.

FIGURE 8.65

DSTRACEing your
new policy setting

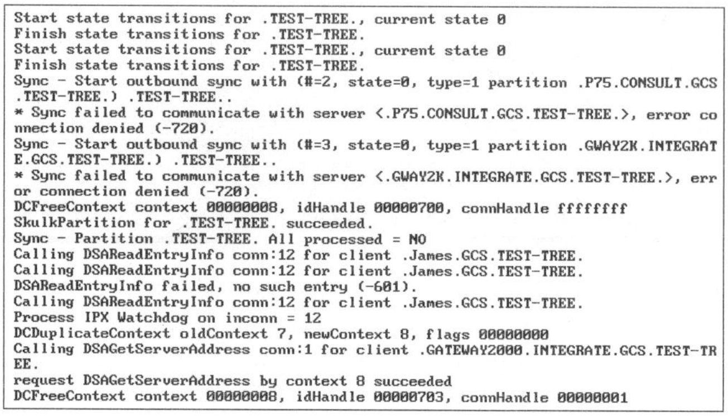

```
Start state transitions for .TEST-TREE., current state 0
Finish state transitions for .TEST-TREE.
Start state transitions for .TEST-TREE., current state 0
Finish state transitions for .TEST-TREE.
Sync - Start outbound sync with (#=2, state=0, type=1 partition .P75.CONSULT.GCS
.TEST-TREE.) .TEST-TREE..
* Sync failed to communicate with server <.P75.CONSULT.GCS.TEST-TREE.>, error co
nnection denied (-720).
Sync - Start outbound sync with (#=3, state=0, type=1 partition .GWAY2K.INTEGRAT
E.GCS.TEST-TREE.) .TEST-TREE..
* Sync failed to communicate with server <.GWAY2K.INTEGRATE.GCS.TEST-TREE.>, err
or connection denied (-720).
DCFreeContext context 00000008, idHandle 00000700, connHandle ffffffff
SkulkPartition for .TEST-TREE. succeeded.
Sync - Partition .TEST-TREE. All processed = NO
Calling DSAReadEntryInfo conn:12 for client .James.GCS.TEST-TREE.
Calling DSAReadEntryInfo conn:12 for client .James.GCS.TEST-TREE.
DSAReadEntryInfo failed, no such entry (-601).
Calling DSAReadEntryInfo conn:12 for client .James.GCS.TEST-TREE.
Process IPX Watchdog on inconn = 12
DCDuplicateContext oldContext 7, newContext 8, flags 00000000
Calling DSAGetServerAddress conn:1 for client .GATEWAY2000.INTEGRATE.GCS.TEST-TR
EE.
request DSAGetServerAddress by context 8 succeeded
DCFreeContext context 00000008, idHandle 00000703, connHandle 00000001
```

Storage Management

NSS (Novell Storage Services) 3.0, the version included with NetWare 6, offers a variety of improvements and new features. Chapter 14 goes into plenty of detail about NSS features.

NetWare 5.1 offered NSS and the "traditional" file services on an equal basis. Partly because NSS couldn't support some of the requirements for the SYS: volume, and partly because NSS didn't handle compression, the traditional volumes remained the safe bet. NetWare 6 says, quite plainly, that NSS provides file services, although legacy support for the traditional file services remain.

Is this a mistake on Novell's part, to push NSS as *the* filesystem with NetWare 6? Not at all. NSS 3.0 meets every challenge the modern network server faces, mashes those challenges into submission, then gets ready for more. Um, perhaps the hype grows a bit thick. Suffice it to say that NSS 3.0 will perform all the tasks you present, and do it while jumping higher and running faster than early Net-Ware file services.

NSS 3.0 introduces the pool concept. A pool is a specific amount of disk space obtained from a partition, including one or more storage devices. While partitions can spread across multiple storage devices, pools are limited to a single partition. Volumes can completely fill pools, or a pool will support as many volumes as you have space to create. With overbooking, you can actually create, for instance, four volumes, each holding 10GB in a 20GB pool. The trick is the limit for space across all four volumes cannot exceed the 20GB pool size, but Volume 2 can be 12GB without a problem if the other volumes don't equal more than 8GB. You'll find more information about pools and NSS architecture in Chapter 14.

The goal of NSS 3.0 is to create another layer of abstraction about disk storage and underlying devices. With the pool format, volumes and underlying disk drives can be stopped and hardware replaced while the rest of the system stays up and running. This is handy, especially when you invest properly by using hardware that can support hot-plug operations. If your managers demand constant uptime, demand adequate hardware.

Viewing Storage Information

Storage management tools have just about fully implemented the NetWare 6 mindset. Both NetWare Remote Manager and ConsoleOne allow you to perform most NSS tasks. The choice of which to use may be personal preference, although both utilities do have different viewpoints at times.

REMOTE MANAGER'S STORAGE DETAILS

See Figure 8.66 for a view of NetWare Remote Manager displaying storage information. Reach this screen by clicking Volumes in the menu in the left frame, then Disk Partitions. Notice the attempt at presenting information in outline form so you can grab the storage lay of the land in one glance.

FIGURE 8.66

A graphical, browser-based disk utility

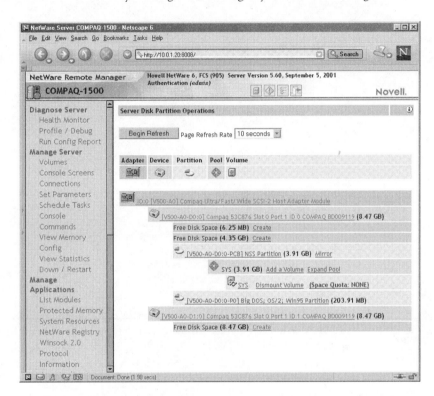

Look at the icons across the top section of the main window, just under the Begin Refresh command button. See Adapter, Device, Partition, Pool, and Volume? Those are the storage components arranged in proper order in terms of building one atop the other. You build devices based on which adapters control them, make partitions from devices, and so on.

Like an outline (remember high school English?), all sections below the icon bar are indented. The indentions are not random.

Notice there is only one line holding an item directly under the Adapter icon on the top icon bar. The first line under the icon bar, the Adapter line, shows an icon of an adapter, and the official name for the adapter (Compaq Ultra/Fast/Wide SCSI-2 Host Adapter) and the appropriate module for the software.

The next icon on the icon bar, Device, lines up with two items below. Immediately below the Adapter listing is the first disk device (Compaq 53C876) and a second disk toward the bottom of the listing. We can tell the bottom one is the second one, because the identifier, Slot 0 Port 1 ID 1 increases the ID tag of the device in Slot 0 Port 1 by one number over the top instance of Slot 0 Port 1 ID 0. (In IBM-influenced hardware, 0 means 1 and 1 means 2.)

ConsoleOne's View of Storage

Compared with ConsoleOne, Remote Manager offers a better overview of storage information, although it provides less depth for operations drilling down into the particulars. To see what I mean, take a look at Figure 8.67, which shows the ConsoleOne Devices view for COMPAQ-1500.

FIGURE 8.67

ConsoleOne device details

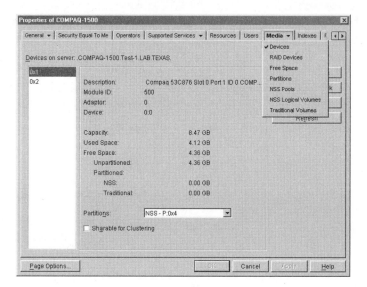

You reach this page by opening the property page for the server, which is COMPAQ-1500 in this case. The Media tab holds seven submenus in proper order of foundation one step to the next, although to illustrate the proper building block image, the list should be inverted so that the NSS Logical Volumes item sits above NSS Pools. The arrangement now means we need to "begat" each item to the next. You know, Devices (including RAID Devices) begat Free Space begat Partitions begat NSS Pools begat NSS Logical Volumes not exactly begat Traditional Volumes. Things get a little confused at the top and bottom, which is why I like Remote Manager better for viewing this information.

The four command buttons hidden behind the tab's menu in Figure 8.67 will play an important part soon. These buttons work as follows:

- Click Scan for Devices to search the server for newly installed hardware.

- Click Initialize Hard Disk to format hardware devices.

- Click Show Partition to drill down one level.

- Click Refresh to update the screen display.

Notice the only way to initialize a disk appears in ConsoleOne, so you'll need to come here for the low-level stuff. Generally, ConsoleOne does the best work, but NetWare Remote Manager provides the best viewing and monitoring options.

NOTE   If you don't see the Media tab inside ConsoleOne, right-click the red N in the system tray, choose Novell Client Properties ➤ Advanced Settings and set File Cache Level=0. If you need to reset it to zero, reboot. While waiting for Windows to crawl back on the screen, go to the server console. Start Monitor, choose Server Parameters, highlight NCP, highlight Client File Caching, and turn it off. Finally, reinitialize your server.

Creating Storage Partitions

Server COMPAQ-1500 includes two of Compaq's rugged 9.1GB SCSI drives tied to a single controller. This offers a perfect chance to use disk mirroring (which is now called Mirror a Partition in NetWare 6).

The first step is to prepare a partition for expansion. I set up only the minimum 4GB volume for SYS: on the first disk of COMPAQ-1500, leaving some open space on that disk and a completely open second disk. Let's initialize the second disk to prepare the space for becoming a second partition.

In ConsoleOne, open the server's property page, click the Media tab, and choose Partitions. You can also reach this area via one of the icons across the middle section of ConsoleOne (like the computer box and the ones with red pie pieces pulled out of disk storage). When you take this route, you'll see the NSS Disk Administration dialog box appear to help you find the server holding the disk devices, just as in Figure 8.68.

FIGURE 8.68

The long way to storage operations

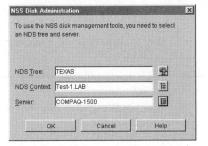

All this extra clicking gets you to the same place as right-clicking the server and picking Properties on the pop-up menu. I prefer going straight to the server holding the drives to configure, but you can take whichever route you please.

Once you find you way to the Partitions property page, you'll notice that the top command button says New. Click that, and something close to Figure 8.69 should appear.

Notice a couple of details here. The Device ID list in the upper-left corner of the Create a New Partition dialog box shows the second device (disk drive) highlighted. Nothing has been put on this drive before (actually I repartitioned it to clear it off, but the effect is the same). Just to the right of the Device ID listing, the Description, well, describes the device in exact terms.

Type, the next section, offers two radio buttons. I chose NSS, as you should almost all the time. If you have storage area network (SAN) components involved, a third option for Remote Storage Device should appear in the Type area.

FIGURE 8.69

Halfway to a new partition

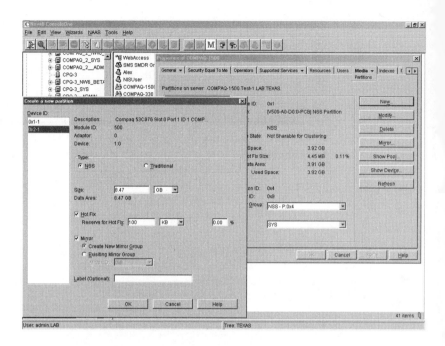

Size, the next block of information, will always show the maximum possible on the device. Accept that listing for the most part, since one partition per device is the easiest way to keep the details organized in your head (or at least it is for me and my head). You can view the size information in GB, MB, KB, and bytes.

Take the default values for Hot Fix. If the system needs more space, it will take more space for Hot Fix. Just hope you get an alert of some kind to know a drive may be failing.

Finally, you can type in a label. It says Optional, and I forgot.

Click the OK command button, and your partition appears back in the property page of the host server. There, you've created a partition.

When you do this through Remote Manager, you have fewer options. You can only Create a New Pool, or Create a New Pool and Volume. You don't get the options for mirroring. You'll get a chance to see how pool creation works in Remote Manager in Chapter 14.

FILLING STORAGE POOLS

You can't create a volume until you create a pool. A partition can be helpful in the state ours is in, but first we'll continue and make this partition into a regular pool and volume before we get fancy.

In ConsoleOne, the next submenu under Partitions on the Media tab of the property page is NSS Pools. SYS, the pool created when I started the server, had to be created to hold the SYS: volume, obviously. Click the New command button to open the Create a New Pool dialog box, shown in Figure 8.70. Notice the rules for pool naming. They're about the same as for servers and most other eDirectory objects. Enter a name and click Next.

FIGURE 8.70

Name your pool

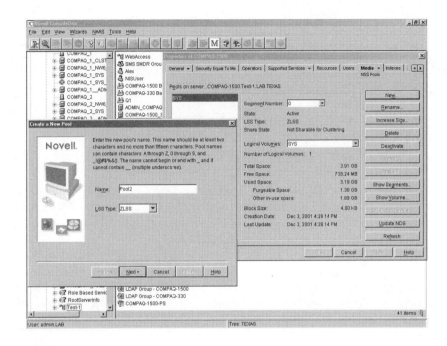

The Storage Information dialog box comes next, as shown in Figure 8.71. It shows how to pick the partition(s) to use for the pool. Yes, you can choose both to make a bigger pool, but that would link two devices into a single partition, and my plan needs them to be separate. So, I'll check only the partition space just created, and then click the Next command button.

FIGURE 8.71

Fill your pool with partitions

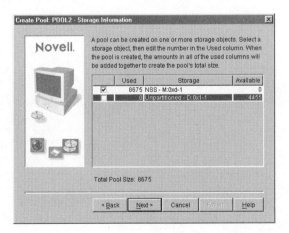

The last screen just provides a bit of information and asks one easy question. As chosen earlier, LSS type is LZSS, and the pool size is 8.47GB. Since the partition was 8.4GB, that makes sense. A check box, selected by default, asks if I want to "Activate on Creation" the new pool. Unless you have something special planned, go ahead and start it up.

If for some odd reason, like an overactive eDirectory, your new pool doesn't appear in eDirectory within a few seconds, check out the Update NDS command button on the Media ➤ NSS Pools page. Go ahead and click it. If the object already exists, you get a warning message and will be able to cancel easily.

EXPANDING STORAGE POOLS

One of the advantages of storage pools, their flexibility, comes in handy when rearranging storage configurations. Although we know volumes can "overbook" and handle more space than was initially configured, sooner or later, the pool will probably need to expand to make up for the increasing volume sizes.

I could show you how to click the Increase Size command button in ConsoleOne to bump up the pool size, but that's not as pretty as the option inside NetWare Remote Manager. Figure 8.72 shows the same server and disks we just reconfigured, but this time we're back in Remote Manager. Look at the difference between Figure 8.72 here and Figure 8.66 back a few pages. Notice the free disk space in Figure 8.66, the last line item in the window, now appears as POOL2 in Figure 8.72.

FIGURE 8.72

More pooling around

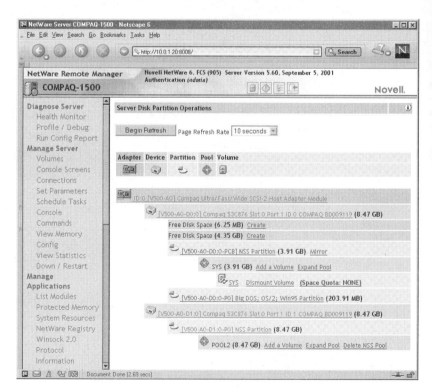

See the other pool in the middle of the items? It has the diamond shape "pool thingee" icon (I have no idea what that's supposed to be—if you find out, drop me an e-mail) and is SYS. The last option on that line, Expand Pool, is our next choice.

Look closely at Figure 8.73, because it can be confusing. For some reason, the display reorganizes the order of disks, and puts the disk we want to expand—the same partitioned space that shares a disk with the SYS: volume—on the bottom of the list. As long as you know which pool you're looking for, and the space to expand to, you won't be tricked.

FIGURE 8.73

Expanding a pool the easy way

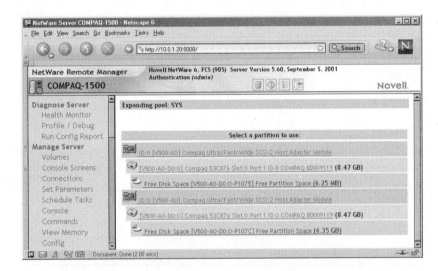

How easy is this? Click the Free Disk Space listing with the 4.35GB of free space, and we're just about done. The next (dull) screen verifies the disk space available is 4.35GB and says I should "Enter the amount of the partition to be used for expanding this pool" with 4465MB in the text box. Since those are equivalent spaces, I'll trust NetWare to handle the math conversion from megabytes to gigabytes and click the Expand hyperlink.

Then the ever-present Confirm message appears, asking "Are you sure you want to add the partition to the NSS Pool?" Since I'm sure, I click the OK button. Disks churn briefly, and the screen refreshes to show me Figure 8.74.

Compare Figure 8.74 to Figure 8.72 to see where our new pool appears. Actually, the new pool just holds the place of the new "pool" created out of the unused partition space. Look at the line next to the top diamond-thingee icon to see that our old friend SYS: now shows a pool size of 8.26GB, which makes sense.

NOTE *If you later decide to delete one of the partitions making up the SYS pool, you must delete all the partitions in the pool. This operation is not graceful yet, but maybe the next version will improve on it. As it stands, if I delete the new partition I just created, I need to reinstall the server, because SYS will also disappear.*

FIGURE 8.74

Another look around the pools

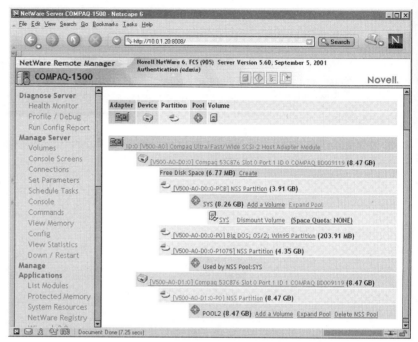

Monitoring Volumes through Remote Manager

Way back in the "Server Management through NetWare Remote Manager" section of this chapter, in Figure 8.27, you saw that Remote Manager opens with the Volume Management screen. Notice that Remote Manager gives you access to the DOS partition on the server. That can be handy at times, especially when you need to add a new management utility for safety's sake.

Figure 8.75 shows the information screen that appears when you click the little *i* icon under the Info heading. Who needs to load NetWare Administrator to check storage statistics when this resource is only one click away?

View Volume Segment Info looks inviting, so feel free to click that button. Then feel free to be disappointed when the information about starting and ending sectors doesn't help you all that much.

Back at the Volume Management screen (Figure 8.27), notice that the items about each volume contain a hyperlink. Clicking the YES entry under the Mounted column pops up a warning message asking if you're really sure you want to dismount the SYS: volume and lose almost all server functionality. Since this YES option is a toggle, just click Cancel to avoid dismounting SYS:.

Clicking the hyperlink under the Name heading opens another screen showing the volume contents along with Size, Attributes, and Date and Time created. Figure 8.76 shows the results of clicking the SYS hyperlink in the Name column.

In this screen's header, the tiny Info button in the upper-right pops up the (actually helpful) Help screen. Let's check out what else the volume details screen has to offer.

FIGURE 8.75
Volume SYS: information via Remote Manager

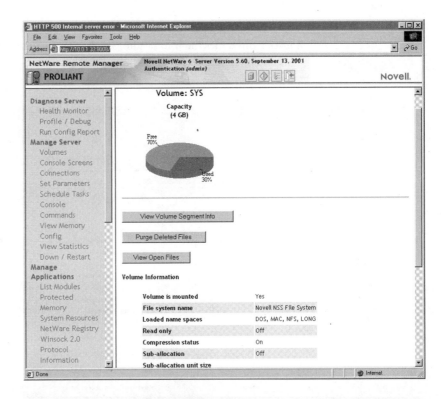

FIGURE 8.76
All /SYS/PUBLIC details on display

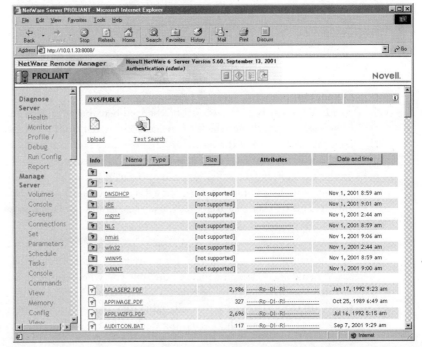

INFORMATION ON FILES AND DIRECTORIES

The question mark icons under the Info heading sit inside folders for a directory, inside of which are pages of paper for a file. Clicking the question mark fetches information about the file (in this case), as shown in Figure 8.77.

FIGURE 8.77

A Remote Manager view of file information

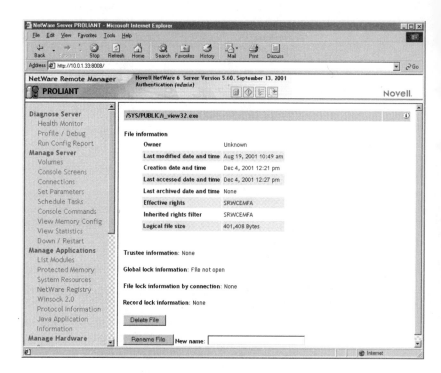

File Options

The File Information details can't be changed here, but you do get a fairly complete look at the file. However, you can change the filename, as you can tell from the Rename File command button and New Name text box at the bottom of the window. But note that the Rename File command button and New Name text box won't appear if the Ri (Rename Inhibit) attribute is set (which you can see on the screen in Figure 8.76). You can also click Delete File to delete the file (go figure). But again, if the attributes listed in Figure 8.76 show Di (Delete Inhibit), the Delete File command button won't appear. This tells me that Remote Manager generates intelligent display pages on the fly.

Directory Options

When you check the information for a directory, a couple of other options appear when appropriate. When you check a directory, a note tells you whether you have any files you can salvage, and you can also rename a directory or create a subdirectory. Handiest when ham-fisted users get carried away with the Delete key is the Salvagable Files entry. (I might more properly say Salvageable Files, in accordance with my dictionary, but perhaps the Novell screen writers used a different dictionary.)

If you have some files that can be salvaged in that directory, a hyperlink saying Select for List will be shown. If you have no files available for salvage operations, there will be no hyperlink under the word None. Since I want to show you this neat function, I copied some HTML files and deleted them, and the result is shown in Figure 8.78.

FIGURE 8.78

Salvage operations underway

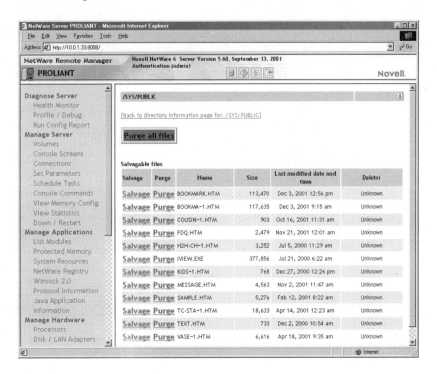

Too bad you don't have a color page in this book. The Purge All Files and Purge words are bright red, and the Salvage words are green. (I hope I don't get salvaged files for Christmas, although sometimes, a recovered file ranks at the top of a user's wish list.)

Novell displays your current location above the giant Purge All Files command button. The hyperlink just above the Purge All Files button goes back one screen, just as if you used the browser's Back button or the Alt+left arrow key combination. A Salvage All Files command button beside the Purge All Files button would be nice, but there isn't one there (yet?).

Next to the Purge buttons, you can see the Name, Size, Last Modified Date and Time, and Deletor (but this information is not available when you delete files through the DOS box, which I did) under the appropriate headings. (Deletor sounds like the name for a WWF wrestler in training, doesn't it?)

While you can delete and rename files on their information pages, directories come with an extra option: Create Subdirectory. Under the Salvagable (sic) Files link, the command buttons are Delete Directory, Rename Directory, and Create Subdirectory. The Rename Directory and Create Subdirectory buttons offer text windows for you to provide the new names. There is also a command button to Delete Directory and Contents, making Remote Manager a good replacement for the FILER

DOS program, which is no longer supported by NetWare 6 (FILER is shipped with NetWare, but not supported).

Is it quicker to create a subdirectory inside a DOS window with the MD (Make Directory) command? Yes, but a DOS box scares many new network managers born with a silver mouse. Acknowledging that fact, Novell makes life easier for the command-line impaired.

FILE EXECUTION AND DOWNLOADS

Clicking the underlined filename in the Name column of the volume details screen triggers your browser into trying to run or download the file. Downloading files is easy: Click the filename, and your browser asks if you want to run the program from the current location or save the program to disk. Make your choice, click OK, and the file-copy process starts immediately.

DETAILS ON ATTRIBUTES

Are you curious about attributes? Figure 8.79 shows the page created by clicking the Attribute listing for a file on the volume details screen.

FIGURE 8.79

Attributes clearly explained and changeable

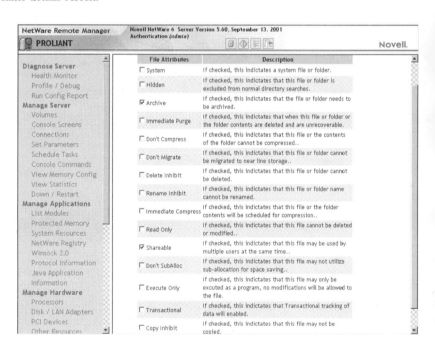

This is a great page. It lists the file's attributes, provides explanations, and offers an easy way to change them.

What you can't see at the bottom of the page are two command buttons: OK and Reset. Check (or uncheck it, as the case may be) a box to change the corresponding attribute. Click the OK command button to make your changes. If you check or uncheck boxes carelessly, use the Reset command button to undo all your changes.

These same attribute changes are possible on the DOS files on your NetWare DOS partition. However, DOS has far fewer attributes than NetWare. Also, there's no question mark icon for file details, because DOS doesn't store those either. Since there is so little information on one screen, Novell went ahead and put a Delete hyperlink for each DOS file on the main page of the Local C:\ listing. Yes, you still have a chance to cancel the file deletion if you hit your mouse button by accident.

TEXT SEARCH OPTIONS

Did you notice the icon at the top of the screen in Figure 8.76—the one with the sheet of paper under a magnifying glass? The hyperlink gives you a good clue: It says Text Search.

New with NetWare 6, Text Search adds a quick, GREP-type search module to the other file and directory tools. Figure 8.80 shows the results of using the Text Search feature. These results mean much more than the rather plain search screen, don't you think?

FIGURE 8.80

Finding the word *iPrint* in a document directory

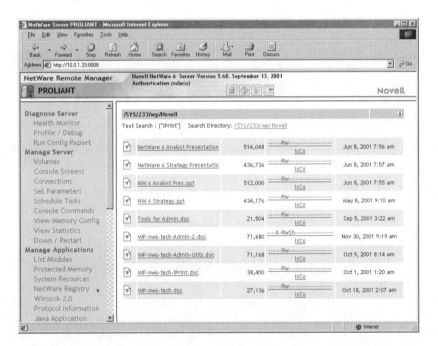

Novell offers ways to make nice forms for Web Search, the big brother of Text Search, in various programmer documentation and utilities (check the Developer sections at www.novell.com for details on creating search forms). Nonetheless, for a search for particular words through a crowded directory, Text Search does fine. Did you notice how it read and retrieved both DOC and PPT (PowerPoint) files, as well as RTF and text files?

UPLOAD

The other icon at the top of the volume details screen has the hyperlink Upload. Click Upload, and a browser screen opens so you can search for your file. Or you can type the name directly into the space provided. After providing the filename one way or the other, click the Upload command line on the second screen, and away goes the file.

NDS eDirectory Management

Welcome to eDirectory management, which now means ConsoleOne and a few pieces available through some of the browser-based utilities. Because NetWare Administrator has not been upgraded to NetWare 6, many of the new directory objects baffle the NetWare Administrator utility and cause it to spread question mark icons about the screen. Since a good network administrator eliminates question marks, Novell has forced us to eliminate NetWare Administrator from this entire section.

If you have earlier versions of NetWare running and prefer NetWare Administrator, then I don't need to tell you how to run that utility. If you have nothing but NetWare 6 software and comparable utilities, then you don't want to know about NetWare Administrator because it will only make ConsoleOne more confusing.

All the last two paragraphs really say is that NetWare Administrator now retires to the rocking chair at the home, grumbling and grousing while that young whippersnapper ConsoleOne wins all the varsity letters and starts dating the homecoming queen.

While ConsoleOne offers most of the management tools you need, several other utilities will figure in your management day. Besides ConsoleOne, eDirectory management functions appear in NetWare Remote Server, Enterprise Web Server Manager, iManage, and particularly iMonitor. This list doesn't even count "legacy" products such as NetWare Administrator and all the various console-bound C-Worthy utilities still hiding inside the management toolbox after nearly two generations.

NOTE   Some tools that had seemed to be gaining strength and popularity no longer appear in the NetWare box. Two of the most prominent ones, NDS Manager and License Manager, suffered from tight ties to NetWare Administrator. Seems as if NetWare Administrator has yet to sink out of sight, probably because it's standing on the heads of part of its own tool family.

Managing eDirectory Partitions and Replicas

The NDS database tracks all the network objects and their rights to use the network. The database is spread around the network for two main reasons: fault-tolerance and speed of execution. The closer the database is to a user requesting services, the sooner those services can be provided. Having more copies of the database running on the network prevents one dead server from locking everyone out of the network.

NetWare 6 divides the eDirectory into *partitions*. Each partition is a distinct unit of data in the eDirectory tree. A partition includes a container object, all objects contained therein, and the data about those objects. No filesystem information is included in a partition. An object can be in only one partition, but copies of the partition allow the object to be accessed from anywhere in the network. Subordinate partitions are labeled *child* partitions; the partition above that is called the *parent* partition.

A *replica* is a copy of one partition. Replicas provide fault-tolerance within each partition by copying the database to multiple file servers. A lost partition can be re-created by using a replica. There are six types of replicas:

Master replica   The primary replica of a given partition. Used to create new eDirectory partitions or to read and update eDirectory information. The Master replica should be near the NetWare manager responsible for maintaining the partition. Only one Master replica of any partition can exist.

Read/Write replica   Reads and updates eDirectory information, such as the addition or deletion of objects. This replica should be near the workgroup serviced by that partition. If a Master replica is lost, a Read/Write replica must become the Master. If the first Master comes back online, the replica currently serving as Master will be deleted automatically in deference to the Master with an earlier timestamp.

Read-Only replica   Primarily a backup that speeds information by allowing users to view the information, without allowing any changes.

Filtered Read/Write replica   One filter per server may be set to allow only certain eDirectory objects, properties, and attributes onto the host server. Changes made to the Filtered Read/Write replica will be propagated to all replicas.

Filtered Read-Only replica   Same as above, but does not allow or propagate changes.

Subordinate Reference replica   Placed automatically by NDS on a server if the parent eDirectory partition has a Master, Read/Write, or Read-Only replica on the server and the child eDirectory partition does not. Subordinate Reference replicas are maintained by NDS.

NOTE   *The filtered replicas are two new options with NetWare 6. Still early in the development, filtered replicas portend the day when so much information not directly related to network authentication fills eDirectory that separating the wheat from the chaff may become necessary.*

During installation, a replica of the partition containing the server's context is added to each new server, unless there are already three replicas. Servers with bindery files will get a replica, regardless of how many replicas are there already.

PARTITION AND REPLICA MANAGEMENT GUIDELINES

Before we get into the details of creating partitions and replicas, let's look at the big picture. Here are some guidelines for managing partitions and replicas:

◆ Make sure you replicate the partition that includes the MyWorld object (which used to be called [Root] in earlier versions). If this partition dies, your NDS eDirectory tree is worthless. Put an extra copy or two on other servers while you're at it.

◆ For NDS fault-tolerance, plan for three replicas of each partition. If your network design allows it, keep replica copies in different physical locations.

◆ Create partitions to group your network users in their natural boundaries. If users from the partition are spread far and wide, move the replicas close to them. The closer the replicas are to the workgroup using them, the better.

◆ Servers that need to run Bindery Services must have either a Master or a Read/Write replica of the partition.

◆ Changes to the replicas, such as adding or deleting objects or redefining a partition, send little traffic across the network. Only the changed information is sent across the network. However, placing or rebuilding a replica requires the system to copy the entire replica across the network. Enough traffic is generated to impact the users slightly. It's better to leave these operations for low-traffic times if possible. Each object in a replica takes about 1KB of disk space.

Follow these guidelines and use your common networking sense, and the management of replicas and partitions will go smoothly. High-speed connections between partitions and replicas, as in a purely local or campus network, will never show a significant performance drop because of replica placement. When you start crossing WANs, however, especially those with slow connections, pay extra attention to replica and boundary placement.

NOTE *During partition operations, you may see some unknown icons as the synchronization between different eDirectory databases settles down and stabilizes. There is no reason to worry unless this continues for a day.*

CREATING A NEW PARTITION

IN A HURRY 8.25: CREATE A PARTITION

1. Log in to the network as the Admin user or equivalent and start ConsoleOne.

2. Highlight the container in which to make a new partition.

3. Choose View ➢ Partition and Replica View.

4. Highlight the container you want to make into a new partition.

5. Select Edit ➢ Create Partition or click the Create a New Partition icon on the toolbar.

6. Click Yes in the information box that appears during the partition operation.

7. Close the information dialog box if you choose, but the screen will reappear with the new partition.

The [Root] is the first partition in your new network. Any new partition from that becomes a child partition. NetWare 6 seems to hide [Root] in preference for MyWorld, but [Root] does a better job of describing the situation (and still appears in the documentation). Any new partition from that becomes another child partition, and the middle partition becomes both a parent and a child partition (sort of what you become when you turn your parents into grandparents).

A new partition must consist of a container and its objects, both leaf objects and other containers. The partition replicas remain on the same servers they were on before you made the new partition, but the information for the partition will be moved to the appropriate replica for the new partition.

Use ConsoleOne or Web Manager to control eDirectory. Here, we'll use ConsoleOne.

NOTE *In NetWare 4.10, you could manage partitions and replicas with Partition Manager, accessed from the Tools menu of NetWare Administrator. In NetWare 4.11, Partition Manager was still available as a DOS utility, but NDS Manager handled the Windows-based work. You could run NDS Manager on its own or add the NDS Manager option to your NetWare Administrator Tools menu. In NetWare 5, the DOS utility disappeared. (See why I say DOS is dead as a management tool?) NetWare 6 moves all eDirectory management away from DOS and now away from NetWare Administrator.*

Figure 8.81 shows partition creation about to begin, so the LAB Organizational Unit will have some directory service fault-tolerance. There is no strain in creating a partition, but large networks may take some time for NDS to become synchronized. Your network traffic will increase slightly, since there will be communication between partitions and replicas across the network.

FIGURE 8.81

Giving the LAB techies and consultants their own partition

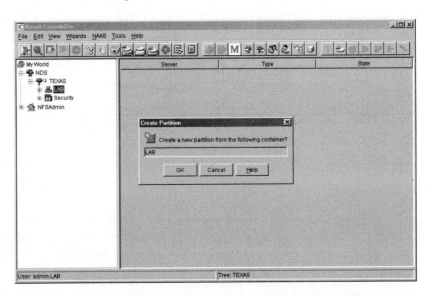

Using the Abort Partition Operation command button that appears after you approve the new partition is usually not a good idea. If you had a sudden attack of conscience and decided that giving LAB-dwellers their own partition was a bad idea, you could click the Abort button quickly. But partition operations are so fast on LANs that you probably wouldn't catch the operation in time to stop it.

I wouldn't even try to stop a partition operation unless I realized a WAN link was down. In a case like that, where a WAN break stopped an operation from completing, you would need to abort the partition operation. Otherwise, on local connections with all servers present and accounted for, wait for the partition operation to finish, and then undo it, as described in the next section.

MERGING PARTITIONS

IN A HURRY 8.26: MERGE PARTITIONS

1. Log in to the network as the Admin user or equivalent and start ConsoleOne.
2. Choose View ➢ Partition and Replica View.
3. Locate the child partition that you want to merge back with its parent partition.
4. Choose Edit ➢ Merge Partition, or highlight the partition and click the Merge Partition icon on the toolbar.
5. Confirm the operation by clicking Yes in the dialog box.

If you change your mind after creating a new partition, you can easily merge it back with its parent partition. This makes sense if the two partitions serve essentially the same eDirectory structure and their information is similar. Your only choice is whether or not to merge a partition back with its parent partition; you're not offered the choice of picking some other partition to merge. Partitions are not deleted; they are just merged. All the information in one partition is absorbed into the parent partition. Here's the dialog box you'll see when you choose to merge partitions:

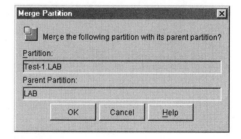

A warning box appears to tell you that this operation may take up to an hour. In large networks with WAN links, merging may take quite a bit of time. Eventually, the warning dialog box will go away, and things will look like they are finished—possibly before they actually are. Wait an extra minute or two between operations, so partitions and replicas don't get confused halfway through the first operation when you start a second one.

ADDING A REPLICA

IN A HURRY 8.27: ADD A REPLICA

1. Log in to the network as the Admin user or equivalent and start ConsoleOne.
2. Choose View ➢ Partition and Replica View.
3. Click the container of the partition you wish to replicate (it will have a little circle icon beside it).
4. Choose Edit ➢ Add Replica or click the Add Replica icon on the toolbar.

Continued on next page

IN A HURRY 8.27: ADD A REPLICA *(continued)*

5. Choose the server and the type of replica you wish to add.

6. Click OK to create the replica.

Replicas, copies of the eDirectory databases, automatically install on the first three servers in each tree. There's no reason to delete replicas; they don't take much space or use much horsepower. Even if they did use one or two percent of your servers' CPU time, the tradeoff for eDirectory fault-tolerance, and the ability to make copies of eDirectory close to users, pays handsome rewards.

NOTE   Don't make a mistake: You get no file or application fault tolerance through replicated eDirectories. You do, however, get a stable, fault-tolerant, world-class directory service for the price of a file server.

If a server didn't get a replica during installation, or you need to add another replica or two across WAN links for fault-tolerance, you can easily create one. We discussed the various types of replicas earlier in this section, so feel free to flip back a few pages if necessary. The "In a Hurry" box will still be here waiting.

The process takes less time to perform than to describe. Find the container to hold the new replica, and then choose Add a Replica from the Edit menu or click the odd little icon toward the far right end of the toolbar. You'll see the dialog box shown below.

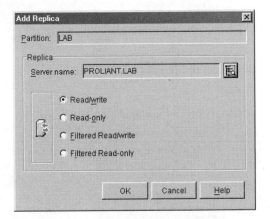

Use the search dialog box to find the server host for the replica. One server can support a variety of replicas, although there is a limit (but a high one). Choose the type of replica to add (Read/Write comes up as the default unless there are plenty of replicas around already), and then click OK. In this example, the PROLIANT server replica will stay in the New state for a few minutes. The time it takes to move a replica from New to On depends on the size of your network.

VIEWING OR MODIFYING REPLICAS

IN A HURRY 8.28: VIEW OR MODIFY A REPLICA

1. Log in to the network as the Admin user or equivalent and start ConsoleOne.

2. Choose View ➢ Partition and Replica View.

3. Highlight the server holding the replica you wish to view or modify.

4. Click the toolbar buttons to Add Replica, Delete Replica, Change Type, or get Information.

5. Verify the server name and the type of replica, if you're changing its type.

6. Click OK to exit the dialog box.

Replica management is generally necessary when you make changes to the NDS design. The improved, cleaner look in NetWare 6 over the old NDS Manager in NetWare 5.1 makes checking replicas a snap. When you choose the Partition and Replica View, you're there.

This dialog box gives you a look at the replicas for the partition that was highlighted. Figure 8.82 shows a good view of the replica information just above the Change Replica Type dialog box.

FIGURE 8.82

Changing the replica type

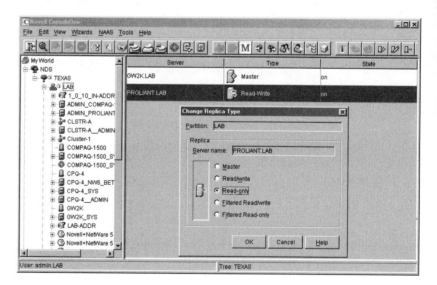

There are six types of replicas that could be installed on PROLIANT; for this example, I opted for the Read-Only type. The copy operation will take a moment, but not much longer with a small network and all LAN connections between the servers. If there are WAN links in the path, it will take more time. The more objects in the partition, the more time it will take to add a partition replica.

What if you want to change the replica type? Let's say that I realized it would be better to make PROLIANT a Read/Write replica rather than a Read-Only replica. All I need to do is right-click the server name and click the Change Type button. This opens the Change Replica Type dialog box in Figure 8.82. When you click OK in the Change Replica Type dialog box, the replica is immediately changed, with little or no network impact.

TIP   Actually, it really is better to have Read/Write replicas. Too many Read-Only replicas are not recommended, because they can't help re-create your NDS structure in case of damage to parts of the database.

When a replica is changed to Master, the current (and replaced) Master replica automatically downgrades to Read/Write. So if you wish to make your Master replica a Read/Write replica, you must set up the new Master replica first.

When you right-click while pointing at a replica, you'll see many choices. If you wish to delete the replica, highlight the Delete menu option, then verify that you know what you're doing. The system won't let you delete the Master replica. (It's certainly embarrassing when you kill the Master replica, but don't ask me how I know this.)

VIEWING PARTITION INFORMATION

IN A HURRY 8.29: VIEW PARTITION INFORMATION

1. Log in to the network as the Admin user or equivalent and start ConsoleOne.

2. Choose View ➤ Partition and Replica View.

3. Highlight the server with the replica of interest.

4. Right-click the server partition listing in the right pane, or click the Information icon on the toolbar. This screen is read-only (nothing in the Replica Information box may be changed here).

5. Click OK when you're finished viewing the information.

Let's say we wish to verify that the PROLIANT server is, in fact, now supporting Read/Write replicas for our partition. Plus, we want to know how the server and its replica are doing. That's where the Information button on the toolbar comes in handy.

Highlighting one of the server replicas in the main window area is the first step. The final step is to either right-click for the menu and choose Replica Information or click the toolbar's Information button. Either way, this step pops open what you see in Figure 8.83.

The information in the Server Information window is read-only, in case you were thinking of making changes here.

If you've been a network manager for any length of time, you may notice something unusual here for NetWare: the Network Address, the last field in the dialog box, shows TCP:10.0.1.33. What kind of joke is this?

FIGURE 8.83

Checking the status of PROLIANT

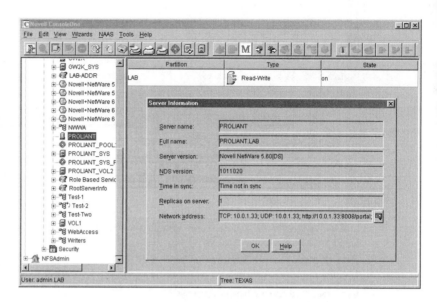

It's no joke. It's just that NetWare servers can now be identified by TCP/IP addresses. In fact, the list also shows a UDP (User Datagram Protocol) address as well, but it's the same as the TCP/IP address. IPX will be the strange sight with NetWare 6, not TCP/IP. However, IPX addresses are still available with a click of the scroll button.

MOVING A PARTITION (AND ITS CONTAINER)

IN A HURRY 8.30: MOVE A PARTITION AND CONTAINER

1. Log in to the network as the Admin user or equivalent and start ConsoleOne.

2. Choose View ➢ Partition and Replica View.

3. Highlight the partition of interest.

4. Click File ➢ Partition Continuity to check that the partition remains in good shape.

5. Click File ➢ Move to open the Move dialog box.

6. Search and choose the proposed new location.

7. Click OK to move, save, and exit.

When a container is moved, all references in the eDirectory database for the container are changed. The common name of the container remains the same, but the full name will obviously change to reflect the container's new location in the NDS eDirectory tree.

The Move Partition button is on the ConsoleOne toolbar according to Novell's documentation, but I can't find it. Use the Move option on the File menu. You must pick and highlight the partition to move, and it must be the root of an NDS partition, without any child partitions. If there are child partitions, you must merge each of them to the parent partition you plan to move before continuing.

Below you see the LAB Organization highlighted in the Move dialog box. One click of the OK button, and the partition moves. Generally, it's a good idea to leave behind an alias, as per the check box, to help users continue to find network resources that you've so carelessly tossed around the network.

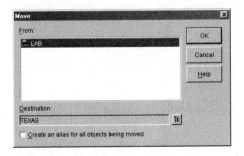

If you have any trouble whatsoever, the first thing to check is Partition Continuity. Although this may sound like some new Hollywood religious cult for those with money left after getting clear, this actually makes sense to check. Highlight a partition and choose File ➤ Partition Continuity. The resulting screen gathers all the replicas together for an easy way to Synchronize Immediately, Send Updates (of eDirectory), or Receive Updates (of eDirectory). This screen forces modified directory updates out to servers, or imports them if the host server has problems. You won't need this often, but when you do, you'll be glad you have it.

When You Mess Up NDS

During research for this section, my lab network (TEXAS-Tree) somehow got quite messed up. Perhaps the fact that I deleted the SYS: volume holding the Master replica of the [Root] (now MyWorld) partition for the network had something to do with the problem. Kids, do not try this at home, or when folks with tender ears are within screaming and cursing distance.

NetWare 3 offered a well-defined process for restoring the server resource information: You retrieved the bindery files from your backup tape. If your backup tape did not copy the bindery files (i.e., was a cheap backup system), you copied the bindery files from the disk you created by telling NetWare to back up the entire server to floppy disks, stopping at the first disk since that one held the three bindery files. Then you hoped you remembered all the network users and printers added since the backup.

The good news with NetWare 6 is that the NDS information is distributed and current. The bad news is that the NDS information is distributed, and it will take a while to recover from major surgery or ham-fisted management. The Read/Write replicas will eventually propagate the information to the newly installed NDS files on the butchered server. During that time, however, you will probably do the following:

♦ Try to make a Read/Write replica a Master replica (using DSREPAIR). The delay will become interminable, and you will try to do the same thing again, then try to force another replica into Master mode.

- Try to reinstall NDS on the afflicted server, getting error messages when you provide the Admin password. Press Alt+F10 to get out of the loop by stopping the installation.

- Try to redo the replica status again.

- Go to the hardware store and decide which sledgehammer will make the best adjustment tool for your servers.

- Notice that the replicas are starting to settle down.

- Try again, without success, to resurrect NDS on the afflicted server.

- Read the employment classifieds.

- Actually get NDS installed once again on the less-afflicted server.

- Be amazed at how much of your network returns in good working order.

The key element in this sequence is the time needed for NDS to heal itself. Of course, a busy network is not a relaxed place. Users want access to their services, and they want it ten minutes ago. Reject the urge to do something, especially something drastic. Help your users find ways to get the resources they need. Check the NDS status and use DSREPAIR a time or two. See Chapter 15 for details on running DSREPAIR.

If possible, make your mistakes on a weekend, so the system has a chance to settle down before the users appear. Just don't make any social plans for that weekend.

Before starting any work on NDS, take a moment to verify that your partitions and replicas are well distributed. Keep Master replicas away from the target of any changes. Make a new Master replica if necessary, and give the network time to settle down before the next step. If you don't, you may need my list of colorful adjectives for describing recalcitrant replicas. E-mail for details, but don't let any children see the list. And before you send that e-mail (I've gotten some from readers of earlier versions of this book), you can get the list by hanging around construction sites or Navy shipyards and listening to sailors.

Using DSMERGE for Tree Management

Companies with large networks often assume that they need multiple NDS eDirectory trees to handle their network design. Part of this feeling is misguided security, and part is a misunderstanding of how well the Organizations and Organizational Unit containers do their jobs.

After the company has multiple trees, the network managers realize that it's difficult for users to see or take advantage of resources outside their own tree. With the first version of NetWare 4, merging two trees into one wasn't possible. This caused some consternation.

Novell engineers developed the DSMERGE (Directory Services Merge) program. Using information gained at customer sites during DSMERGE development, the program was improved in parallel with the client software, so clients can connect to multiple trees at once. But there are reasons to merge trees, and that's exactly what DSMERGE does.

DSMERGE allows you to prune and graft your tree at the highest level imaginable: [Root]. This program is not used to move containers or partitions (use ConsoleOne for those functions).

The program works with only two trees at one time. Your players in this tree drama are the following:

♦ The *local source tree* is the tree that will be folded into another tree. Start the operations from the server holding the Master replica of this tree's [Root] partition.

♦ The *target tree* is the eventual new tree, with your local source tree folded in. The target tree name will be the same as the new tree's name.

TREE MERGING PREREQUISITES

The prerequisites are fairly stiff before a DSMERGE operation. If you think about it, there is nothing more extensive you can do to your NDS network. Every object in your source tree will be changed, and many of your target tree objects will require some adjustment. Here are the prerequisites:

♦ No active network connections are allowed. Close all connections on both trees. If there are users around who may try to log in, disable login on all affected servers.

♦ No leaf or Alias objects are allowed in the [Root] of the local source tree. Delete or move any Alias or leaf objects in the [Root] before starting. Give the eDirectory time to digest those changes.

♦ No similar names are allowed at the top of both trees. You may have identical container objects in both trees if they are not immediate subordinates of [Root]. The immediate container sets their identification. The full distinguished name will let your users tell the difference between ACME.ACCTNG.P1 and ACME.MFG.P1.

♦ NDS must be the same version on both trees. Upgrade all pre-eDirectory or NDS 7 servers that have a replica of the [Root] object, but be prepared to upgrade all servers to the latest eDirectory version. Having all servers running the same version will eliminate some problems and make management less complicated. It's worth the time to get every server on the same version before starting your network redesign.

♦ All servers must be up and running in both trees. If WAN links are involved, verify the servers on the remote side of the link. Technically, only those servers containing a replica of the [Root] must be up, but any down servers will delay the total integration of the two trees. It's best to have every server running.

♦ Schema on both trees must be the same. Any products installed on one tree that modify the schema must be installed on the other tree before merging. Check carefully, since many products are starting to take advantage of NDS features and may change the schema.

♦ The time reference must be the same. Verify that each server in both trees is synchronized within ten seconds of the other. If both trees have either a Reference or Single Reference time server, change one of them to a Secondary or Primary time server. All servers in both trees should then reference the same time source.

♦ The two trees must have different names. If both trees have the same name, one must be renamed before starting DSMERGE.

RUNNING DSMERGE

Here are some details you should know before starting a DSMERGE operation:

◆ DSMERGE does not change container names or contexts within containers. The merged objects are retained. The filesystem is not touched at all, except for changed names of containers holding the volumes.

◆ The [Root] of the target tree becomes the new [Root] for objects in the source tree. Tree names for all servers and other objects in the source tree are changed to reflect their new tree name.

◆ During the merge, all replicas of the [Root] partition are removed from servers in the local tree. After the merge, the local tree replica is replaced by a replica of the combined trees.

You start DSMERGE from a server console or RConsoleJ session. Although you don't log in as the Admin user at the console or through RConsoleJ, you will need the Admin passwords for both trees. At the console colon prompt, type **DSMERGE**.

Figure 8.84 shows the opening screen of the DSMERGE program. You see that there are few options, and the listings are straightforward. These choices are described in the following sections.

FIGURE 8.84

Major tree surgery upcoming

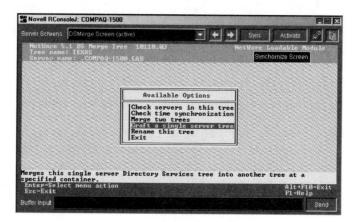

CHECKING THE SERVERS IN THIS TREE

Before you start merging trees here and there, all the servers must be up, running, and current on their software versions. The first option on the DSMERGE menu is Check Servers in This Tree. Press Enter to scan the tree and list all servers. Here are the results of this check on my lab network:

Status Of Servers In The Tree		
Server Name	**Version**	**Status**
.COMPAQ-1500.LAB	5.0 (10110.20)	Up
.GW2K.LAB	5.0 (8.38)	Up
.PROLIANT.LAB	5.0 (10110.20)	Up

What is this telling us? First, the servers are up, and they are in the tree where they belong. If the field shows an error or a status of down, check that before proceeding with the merge operation. The same goes if you see DS Locked, meaning the NDS database is probably still trying to digest some earlier change. The only problem is that one server, GW2K, is still running NetWare 5.1 and an old version of directory services.

The worst news is if a server has an exclamation point in front of the name, as in !FS1. If this is the case, fix that server's problem before attempting the merge.

CHECKING TIME SYNCHRONIZATION

IN A HURRY 8.31: CHECK TIME SYNCHRONIZATION WITH DSMERGE

1. Type **DSMERGE** from the console prompt.

2. Choose Check Time Synchronization.

3. Check the server name, time server type, whether it's synchronized, and the time difference.

4. Press Escape to return to the menu.

"Synchronize your watches!" is a cliché of spy movies and comedies spoofing them, but it makes sense here. NDS eDirectory relies on timestamps to control the database; events in dispute are settled by examining the timestamps. The merge may not continue if time is not properly configured on all involved servers.

When you press Enter on the Check Time Synchronization menu choice, a progress bar displays the query process to all servers. After all servers have responded to the NDS query, the server name and information are displayed. Here is an example of the time synchronization information.

Time Synchronization Information For Tree: TEXAS			
Server name	Type	In Sync	Time Delta
.COMPAQ-1500.LAB	Secondary	NO	0
.GW2K.LAB	Single	YES	6
.PROLIANT.LAB	Secondary	NO	10

The first column shows the names of all servers in the tree. The second column shows the type of time server each is running. In our example, GW2K is a Single Reference server, advertising the time, and PROLIANT and COMPAQ-1500 both listen for time information. They are not in sync, with the time variance between the servers at zero, or less than two seconds difference. The three servers have a larger variance, but nothing so drastic that it can't be fixed by synchronizing the time once or twice (before the tree merge operation).

Just because this screen looks good doesn't mean your time troubles are over. The report here does not check which time servers are referring to which time source. The time arrangement for the new, merged tree must be planned and configured before merging. If the other tree has a Single Reference time server, as does GW2K, one of the two must be downgraded to a Secondary or Primary time server before the merge.

MERGING TWO TREES

IN A HURRY 8.32: MERGE TREES WITH DSMERGE

1. Type **DSMERGE** from the console prompt.

2. Choose Merge Two Trees and press Enter.

3. Provide the Admin name and password for the local tree.

4. Choose the target tree from the list and provide the Admin name and password for that tree.

5. Press F10 to start the merge.

When you select Merge Two Trees, the tree name for your local source tree will be filled in automatically. The full administrator's name, not just Admin, must be placed in the next field. The password is required, obviously. Here is an example of this screen being filled out:

```
                          Merge Trees Information
       Source tree:          TEXAS
       Administrator name:   admin.lab
       Password:             *****

       Target tree:          PINE
       Administrator name:   admin.cone
       Password:             *****
```

If the target tree name you want isn't on the list that appears when you press Enter, press the Insert key and provide the network address of any server in the target tree. To get that address, type **CONFIG** at the server console prompt, and make a note of the IP address or IPX internal network number if you're still supporting IPX. Use that address to latch onto the target tree.

The Admin user password is required for the target tree as well. When all this is filled out, press F10 to perform the merge. The time the merge will take varies depending on the size of the network, but it will be longer than when you organized the partitions earlier.

GRAFTING A SINGLE-SERVER TREE

IN A HURRY 8.33: GRAFT A SERVER INTO A TREE WITH DSMERGE

1. Type **DSMERGE** from the console prompt of the single server about to be grafted.

2. Choose Graft a Single Server Tree.

Continued on next page

IN A HURRY 8.33: GRAFT A SERVER INTO A TREE WITH DSMERGE *(continued)*

3. Provide the Admin name and password for the tree.

4. Type the new name and press Enter.

Grafting a single server running in its own tree into an existing tree takes time and trouble. One could almost make the case that re-installing eDirectory on the new server might save time. Yet some single-server trees can be quite extensive, with many users and objects, requiring more time to re-create than you can afford. So be it, but look at some of your requirements:

◆ Turn off WANMAN on both the source and target trees.

◆ Remove all but the one server to be grafted from the source tree.

◆ Remove all aliases and/or leaf objects from the source tree's Tree object.

◆ Check for similar names on the source and target trees.

◆ Match eDirectory versions.

◆ Make sure that the target graft location partition does not have any replicas (a single-server partition) but that it does have a copy of the [Root] partition.

◆ Match schema versions.

◆ Verify the source tree takes time from a source in the target tree (make the source tree a Secondary server).

These are the major restrictions, but check the Novell Web documentation and support sites for changes and new restrictions.

Once the conditions line up properly, along with the moon and stars, the actual grafting takes little time. Run DSMERGE from the source tree and choose Graft a Single Server Tree. You'll see the information box shown here.

```
                      Graft Trees Information
┌───────────────────────────────────────────────────────────────┐
│  Source tree:            PINE                                   │
│  Administrator name:     admin.con                             │
│  Password:               *****                                 │
│                                                                │
│  Target tree:            TEXAS                                  │
│  Target Tree container:  lab                                   │
│  Administrator name:     admin.lab                             │
│  Password:                                                     │
└───────────────────────────────────────────────────────────────┘
```

Provide administrator names and passwords, and then hit F10.

This is a lot of trouble, right? Next time, plan your network better, so you don't need to start grafting servers onto your tree in some bizarre Frankenstein operation.

RENAMING TREES

IN A HURRY 8.34: RENAME A TREE WITH DSMERGE

1. Type **DSMERGE** from the console prompt.

2. Choose the Rename This Tree option.

3. Provide the Admin name and password for the tree.

4. Type the new name and press Enter.

Although you should give serious thought to naming your tree before you finish the installation, names do change at times. Merging a small tree into a large tree is the most efficient method, but you may prefer the name of the small tree. Your company or division may change names, necessitating a change of your network. You can change the name of a tree here. The physical process of changing the tree name is not difficult.

We covered tree naming in Chapter 1, but here's a refresher of the rules, which are a bit more restrictive than those for a regular object:

- ◆ Tree names must be 32 characters or less.

- ◆ Tree names may only include A–Z and 0–9; the _ and - (underscore and dash) are allowable, but multiple adjacent underscores are not.

- ◆ Tree names cannot start or end with an underscore (_).

After starting DSMERGE on the server console or through an RConsoleJ session, select the Rename This Tree option. You must then type the Admin name and password before you can type the new name. Here is a view of this process in progress:

```
                      Rename Tree Information
  Local tree:           PINE
  Administrator name:   admin.cone
  Password:             *****

  New tree name:        BANANA
```

Okay, the name for the new tree stinks (or is at least turning brown and mushy). This joke belongs to all the NetWare newbies who didn't hear the avalanche of tree jokes when Novell introduced NetWare 4. This joke ranks far above most of those old jokes, believe me.

After you press F10, it will take a few minutes to replicate the new tree name across the network. Don't do any other administrative tasks during that time, since eDirectory will be busy and may behave slightly oddly during the process.

WARNING *Remember, if you change the tree name, you'll need to reset application references on all your user worksta-tions. Make sure you really,* truly, *want to rename a tree before doing so.*

EXITING AND CLEANING UP

After you've finished with DSMERGE (choose Exit on the menu, and say Yes to exit DSMERGE), there are some things that you'll need to do immediately. Whether you merged trees or renamed one or two, a lot of users are suddenly lost in the woods, unable to find their favorite tree.

The bad news: Client details must be changed to find the correct new tree. If you've gone to a single tree, there shouldn't be much problem. If you still have multiple trees on the same physical network segment, users will need to know how to find a particular tree.

One more bit of administrivia: When merging multiple trees, the first tree's Admin user will lose all rights. For example, say you have Tree A merging into Tree B. No problem, both Admin users are fine. Say you now merge Tree B into Tree C. Problem: Admin from the original Tree A finds itself without rights. The Admin from either old Tree B or new Tree C must manually grant rights again to Admin A.

Deleting a NetWare Server Object from NDS

IN A HURRY 8.35: DELETE A SERVER

1. Go to the NetWare server to be deleted and type **DOWN** at the console.

2. Log in to the network as the Admin user or equivalent.

3. Start ConsoleOne.

4. Highlight the server object to be deleted and press the Delete key.

5. Click Yes to delete the server.

Getting rid of a server is serious business. When you press the Delete key, the highlighted server bites the dust, never to rise again. There is no SALVAGE utility to resurrect the server. Gone are all the server's resources, which are now out of reach for all network clients. Still available, thankfully, are all the files and directories on the server volume(s). When (and if) you reinstall NDS on the server, the data will still be there, waiting for your return.

Taking out a server may corrupt your NDS database, so move all partition replicas away from the server before proceeding. If you delete a server holding your only replica, that partition is in deep trouble. There will be a pass/fail test of your tape backup system immediately, which it will most likely fail. If it fails, you must re-create the partition by memory, and by hand.

If you are taking a server out of commission and have removed all replicas from the server, highlight the server and press the Delete key. If the server is still up, you'll see an error message telling you that the server remains operational and you can't delete it. Simply take down the server and try once more to delete it.

eDirectory Management with Tree Walker

Novell people often make a big deal about Tree Walker, although it sounds to me like a slang term for Tarzan. Regardless, this eDirectory Management option inside Remote Manager offers a unique look at your NDS system.

Traversing NDS Tree politely tells you the screen you reach after clicking the Tree Walker hyperlink from the left menu frame. One list, Objects, shows active trees available to the server supporting the Remote Manager application; in this case, the server is PROLIANT.

Click the name of an active tree, and you reach a screen showing the objects in your tree inside ConsoleOne, as seen from the [Root] level. In other words, you don't see much. In my case, I can see .LAB.Texas and .Security.TEXAS.

One more click shows you a list—written ungainly in full, distinguished eDirectory notation, including the leading periods and full context paths—of every object in the container. Containers, such as Test-1.LAB and Writers.LAB, have little plus signs in front of them to tell you that more information is hiding inside. The same plus signs appear before License objects, so you can drill down and see individual certificates. Check out Figure 8.85 for a look at a dull screen.

FIGURE 8.85

Graphical display
wasted on text

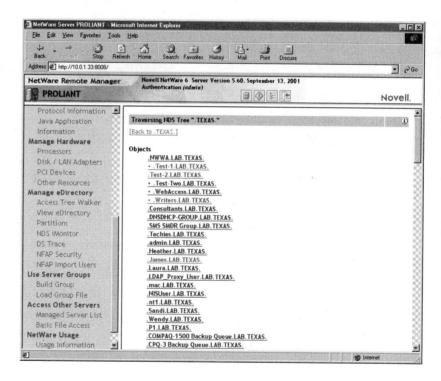

Figure 8.86 shows a wealth of obscure but never before uncovered NDS information for user .James.LAB.TEXAS, including all attributes and values. Nothing can be changed from here, but it's interesting nonetheless.

FIGURE 8.86

NDS info laid out

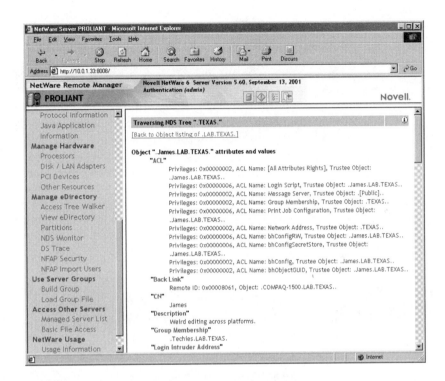

What you can't see below the Login Intruder Address field includes Public Key, Security Equals, Surname, Last Login Time (in unusable format), and Equivalent to Me, which can be helpful. Yes, you can get some of this information through NetWare Administrator pages, but it's much easier to see here. It's also much easier to print; one click of the Print button, and all NDS details for an object slide out of the printer.

One last thing, at the bottom of the page (also not visible in Figure 8.86), is a command button labeled Delete Object. My advice: Don't do it, at least not through this interface. But the fact that you can delete the object here gives me hope that more of the functions from ConsoleOne will find their way into a browser interface sooner rather than later.

The second option from the first screen under NDS Management is eDirectory Partitions. There's nothing of interest here, just a bare listing of each partition/replica name stored on the host server. It isn't really helpful—at least, not yet.

Using UIMPORT to Move Employee Database Records into NDS

UIMPORT (User Import) feeds ASCII data from an existing database into the NDS database. Do you have thousands of students enrolling into your school who need network access? This utility will help you with these tasks:

◆ Create User objects in the NDS database.

- ◆ Update existing User object properties in your NDS database.

- ◆ Delete User objects from the NDS database.

There are some considerations, of course, when creating your ASCII file. Every database can create an ASCII file, but the separators used to tell NDS where one record stops and the next record starts can be a problem. If you have punctuation such as commas in your database, you can't use comma-delimited ASCII files. If you do, NDS won't know which comma is for a new record and which is for, for example, the last-name and first-name separator. To avoid this problem, you can use the caret ($^\wedge$) as a separator rather than a comma or question mark.

Once the ASCII file is clean, you've inserted your record separators consistently, and you have the records selected, you must tell NDS which of the many properties for the new User objects will be filled in and which will be skipped and left empty. You do this by means of the Import Control File. This file can be created by any text editor under DOS or Windows, as long as it will create an ASCII file. There are two types of information in the Import Control File:

- ◆ Control parameters, which define the characters used in the data file and dictate how the data is updated

- ◆ Field definitions, which determine which fields in the NDS database will be given the data

Control parameters go first, followed by the field definitions. A small Import Control File might look like this:

```
Import control
  Name context=.freshman.students
  Separator=^
  User template=y
Fields
  Last name
  Name
  Telephone
```

This file tells the NDS database that the field separator is the caret and that we will apply the template for the container.

NOTE   *The parameters for the Import Control File are not case sensitive, but the format is important. The headings must be flush left, with the entries indented at least one tab or space. (I suggest that you make it at least two spaces so you don't miss one and cause yourself extra problems.)*

Just as when you're creating a new user, two fields are mandatory: the user's login name (Name) and last name (Last Name). If you're updating existing users, only the Name field is mandatory. The fields can be any or all properties of a user. The list includes Account Balance, Account Has Expiration Data, Allow Unlimited Credit, Grace Logins Allowed, Group Membership, Home Directory, and every other user information field.

Some of these fields are single-valued, meaning only one bit of information (for example, a name) can be entered. Other fields are multivalued, meaning multiple entries are allowed (for example,

Group Membership). Check the manual and the readme files for the latest information on the fields and their allowable entries. You can't have data without a corresponding field definition in the Import Control File.

NOTE *If you have used the Import Control File with an earlier version of NetWare 4, be aware that many of the field names have changed. Check the manual and the readme files once again for the latest information.*

The syntax for the DOS command is:

```
UIMPORT [control_file] [data_file] [/C]
```

This assumes that you have both files in the same directory. If they are not, you'll need to use the full pathnames for the files. The /C says to write the screen output continuously (without it, you'll be hitting "any key" forever). If you prefer to route the output to a file, use this syntax:

```
UIMPORT [control_file] [data_file]
>users\james\uimport.log
```

UIMPORT will take hours to run large files and will slow your server performance because of the amount of NDS churning required. Run this at night and come in early to repair any server malfunctions that occur. (Nothing should go wrong, of course, but gremlins bite everyone now and then.)

During the first pass or two, you might have some problems getting the separators and field information correct. No automatic program transfer like this works the first time or every time. Using commas as separators guarantees you extra aggravation, because the exported database will contain spurious characters all over the place. If you have a large database to import, you should definitely begin by bringing in just a few records at first in order to get the bugs worked out.

Novell Licensing Services (NLS) Management

Prior to NetWare 6, Novell sold server licenses (one per server) with a set number of user licenses (one per concurrent user). This worked great with early networks, but as NetWare grew more complicated to support larger networks, inequities appeared. A server with 100 user licenses could be idling along with only 50 concurrent users, while another server one department over owned 50 users licenses but needed 25 more. The two departments couldn't share the user licenses because they didn't fit with the server licenses.

NetWare 6 avoids this mismatch problem by providing user object licenses owned and controlled by the network rather than server licenses with concurrent users. There are no more server licenses as such (except for NetWare Clustering Services server licenses beginning with the third node). All NetWare red boxes ship with unlicensed server software but a set limit of user object licenses.

In the past, one server license and one user license would take care of Wendy, Alex, and Laura if only one of them logged in at any one time. If Wendy grabbed the license, Alex and Laura tapped their feet in frustration until Wendy finished. Think of this as a sort of musical chairs user licenses.

Today, NetWare 6 offers no server license, but a license for each user object. In other words, Wendy, Alex, and Laura will all need a license, even if they aren't using the system. A permanent user licensed attaches itself to each of them, always ready when they log in anywhere in the network.

What's the bad news? You must have a license for every user that gets on the network at any time, not just licenses for users online at the same time. What's the good news? Users licenses work all over the network, so the user/server license mismatch problem never occurs. Novell calls the first method a Server Connection model, and the replacement is known as User Access Licensing.

Installing and Managing User Access Licenses

IN A HURRY 8.36: INSTALL A USER LICENSE

1. Log in to the network as the Admin user or equivalent.

2. Start iManage, log in, then click Install a License.

3. Browse and locate the new license file, then click Next.

4. Choose the license certificate to install, then click Next.

5. Browse the tree for the best location to install the license, then click Install.

6. At the Success screen, click Continue to install more licenses, or click Done.

There's no need to look for any special licensing installation routines, because NLS installs automatically during server installation. You don't think Novell would let licensing be optional, do you? Of course not.

You can do four things with a user license:

◆ Install a license

◆ Move a license

◆ Delete a license

◆ View license configuration

Your initial server and user license files installed during the operating system installation. Remember, you had to find the diskette and plug it into the server? If you bought all the licenses you need, you won't have to read this section. Lucky you.

A specially labeled License/Cryptography diskette delivers user licenses. The files themselves aren't big at all, but they pack a punch for small files.

Figure 8.87 shows the first screen for installing a user license. There's nothing fancy here, or anywhere in this section for that matter. The Browse command button hints that files and directories will be searched, not partitions or organizations and trees.

The other files on your License diskette should match the ones in Figure 8.87, except for the license filename, of course.

Depending on how many licenses await on your diskette, you may face a variety of license "units" as Figure 8.88 shows. Mine appear to be 25 in groups of five. That makes sense, because you may not want to install them all at once, or Novell may build them in blocks of five for ease of assignment. Either way, Figure 8.88 shows that I've checked the top license certificate and am ready to continue.

FIGURE 8.87

Loading from the License diskette

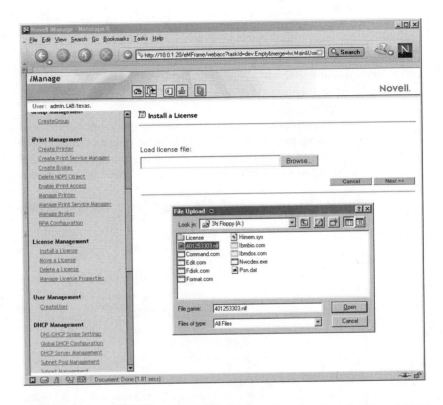

FIGURE 8.88

Pick a certificate, any certificate

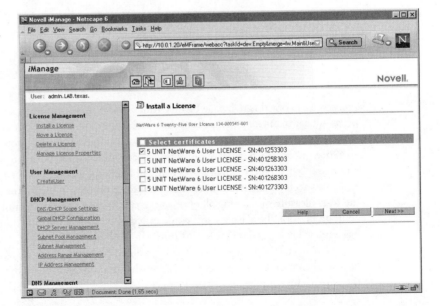

Now, you get to install your license somewhere that makes sense. Put the license certificates in the same Organization with the bulk of your users. If you spread users among Organizational Units, put the certificate in the parent container. That way, each user will look upward for a license and find one the next step up the tree.

Pick a certificate, any certificate, by checking the box. Then click the Next button for more fun and games.

This means you must next place the chosen license certificate somewhere appropriate. Since all my users are in either the LAB Organization or in an Organizational Unit directly under LAB, that Organization makes the best host option for my system. Figure 8.89 shows me just stopping my search because I found LAB quickly. One click on LAB, and the license will light.

FIGURE 8.89

Finding a nice bed for your license

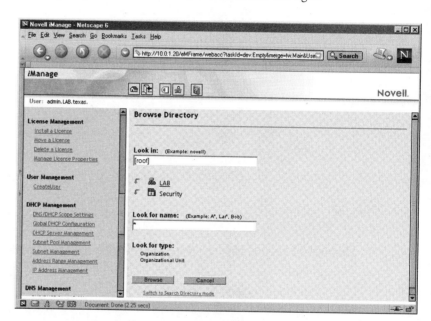

Be wary about this iManage browse function, because confusion awaits. Only a dozen or so search items appear in any one list, so look for the Next >> command button at the bottom of the list. Whenever you don't think you see enough objects in this browser, you're right. Keep looking.

Once the license certificate resting place gets plucked from the browse mode, click the Install command button on the final page. You will likely see a Success screen, but it's okay if you don't.

If you accidentally tried to install a certificate on top of itself, you will be warned and have the dubious pleasure of starting all over once again. Novell should certainly clean up this process a bit in an upgrade soon, because it's still confusing. How can you tell which license certificate on a diskette has already been installed? You can't until you find out the hard way, and must repeat the process.

Delete licenses via the reverse method: Click Delete a License on the iManage menu, find the license, then click the Delete button rather than the Install button. If you need to move a license, use the Move a License iManage menu choice.

The final option under License Management in iManage, Manage License Properties, looks impressive but does little. You're better off setting up a usage-gathering location and reading a report once a week. What a great segue into the next section.

Reporting on License Usage

While one might think NetWare Usage Information would logically hide in the same place as Licensing, that would be too easy. No, Novell hides this back under Remote Manager, tying network-wide usage licenses to a particular piece of server hardware. Hmm, I wonder which vice president we can blame for this one?

Go to Remote Manager for the server you just installed the licenses on (where iManage pointed), and look at the very bottom of the menu in the left frame. See NetWare Usage down at the bottom? See Configuration down there? Click that to get started, and you should see something similar to Figure 8.90.

The defaults provided work well except for the last one: I don't want a year's worth of usage information at one time. Maybe a month would suit me better. You choose the amount you like—I'm not trying to force you into anything (coerce you perhaps, but not force).

Once the network runs for a few weeks, you can click the Usage Information menu and see a truly uninspired listing of usage levels for the time period. This type of report inflexibility explains why third parties do so well providing functionality to Novell eDirectory (as you can tell by my regular Visual Click, `www.visualclick.com`, references).

FIGURE 8.90

Usage collection configuration

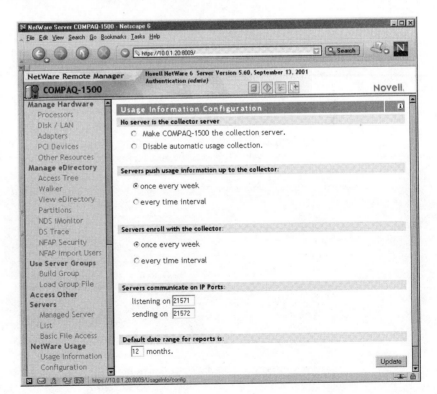

Reporting Tools in ConsoleOne

Finally, Novell includes more reports than those awful ATOTAL DOS reports excreted from Accounting. Good riddance to both of those, and welcome ConsoleOne reports. Even more welcome are some Novell predefined reports. But it's still early in their development, so you must have a NetWare volume to hold them and run ConsoleOne from a Windows workstation of some flavor.

First, go to the ConsoleOne Tools menu and click Install. The dialog box shown below appears, and you can see I want to install the Reporting Services Install Snapin.

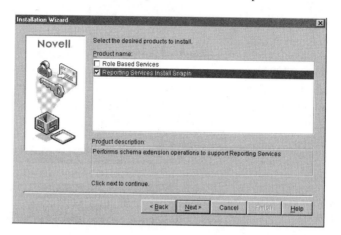

While that appears to be a typo, it really indicates we must install a snap-in to extend the eDirectory schema for the real reporting snap-in. (Don't think about some of these things too hard, or you'll start wandering the halls and mumbling to yourself.)

You will be asked to select the desired tree, if you have more than one active (or maybe even if you have just one). Click the tree, and then click Next. Click Finish at the next summary screen. Then click OK when you see a successful report dialog box.

Next, go back to the ConsoleOne Tools menu, and this time pick Install Novell-Defined Reports. A cute little dialog box appears, asking which of the reports you want to install. Although I highlighted only the middle report, you can hold down the Ctrl key down while selecting to grab them all.

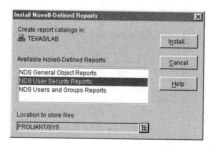

The disks will churn and drive lights will blink for longer than you expect. All that activity, and I would expect a complete installation, but no such luck.

Close ConsoleOne, and go to a deep directory on your workstation or the server, starting at the ConsoleOne directory. It will be under your Novell directory on a workstation, but under SYS:\ PUBLIC\MGMT on a NetWare 6 server. Find there a fat **ODBC.EXE** application, cross your fingers, and run it. Suddenly you feel like a programmer as part of the Novell Development Kit unfolds onto your workstation.

When the Setup Complete dialog box appears, you may want to click Finish, but that would be a big mistake. Check the box for Configure Sample Data Source before clicking Finish.

If you skip this last step in your hurry to see a report (as I did), open Control Panel ➤ ODBC and click the User DSN tab. Look down the Name list to find NDS Reporting, and click the Add button. When asked for your driver in Create New Data Source, once again trust ODBC Driver for NDS. Click Finish, and then put NDS Reporting as the Name in the Data Source Setup dialog box that appears, as shown below. Leave the rest as is.

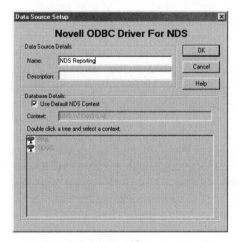

Good luck with this reporting information. My advice? Bang your head against the wall of this complicated mess Novell foisted upon us, or call a SQL programmer for help. Having a few SQL-capable databases to work with wouldn't hurt either.

The real surprise is finding out you need to buy the JReport Designer when you start trying to make some useful forms. I believe the lawyers call this "bait and switch," but perhaps I'm just aggravated because I don't speak SQL, and suddenly that seems important.

Superb Supervision

You don't administer a network; you administer people. Please don't forget that fact. Your users are not computers; they are people. The network is just a tool the people use to do their jobs. I've mentioned this before, but some of you don't believe me. Let me restate: Your job is to help the users.

Does this make you a doormat, subservient to every weird whim of any user? Not at all. The network is there to serve, but certain rules of conduct apply. The users on a network are similar to diners in a fine restaurant: proper dress (decorum) is necessary if the diners (users) wish to be served. Politeness is important. Tips are appreciated (yet so rarely received).

It's easy to get bogged down in the technical details of administering a network, but those details obscure the people on the network. Which do you think your boss would prefer: a network tweaked to the last bit where the users feel left out, or an acceptable network with users who feel like owners of the network?

My friend Stan has a good example of bad network management, and the moral is "keep your opinions to yourself." A user bought a flimsy (though name brand) laptop and had a problem. The tech told the customer the problem came about because the laptop was crap. The customer pointed out that the technical department approved the purchase. In fact, Stan's boss had done so. The problem did turn out to be hardware, because the laptop is the low-priced entry system and the docking station didn't work. Put yourself in that tech's shoes: did mouthing off to the user fix the problem? No. Did it make the tech look stupid, since his department approved the purchase? Yes. Is the user a friend of the network support department today? Not on your life. Imagine the stories of support department stupidity swirling around the water cooler.

When you have a team of technical personnel, make sure that all the members know their place in the team and that their place makes the best use of their abilities. Don't put an irresponsible person in charge of critical backup operations. Bad things will happen sooner rather than later.

Unfortunately, you will never catch up with all that your job requires of you. It's mathematically impossible to cover every possible variable for every possible user, especially when those users want entirely different, contradictory support. Then there is the conflict between your network clients, who want everything possible to make the network faster and more fun, and your boss, who wants to spend less money.

The best chance you have to succeed in a conflict-ridden environment like this is to have your own idea of what the network should be. Your vision, if articulated to your boss and your clients, can bridge the gap between what your boss will pay for and what your clients need. If there is a vacuum, and you have no clear idea of your network, everyone will feel free to force the network into what they want. In that case, I just hope that what they want is something you can (1) provide and (2) live with comfortably.

Before I grew into computers, I worked for a manufacturer. At trade shows, people would come to the booth and ask, "Why don't you have this feature?" It would bother me, because everyone wants their product to make people happy. But we couldn't add every suggestion; the unit price would triple. We were making a low-end, entry product, not the top of the line.

Finally, I came up with a response. After a person asked about a new feature, I said, "That's a good idea. How much would you be willing to pay for that?" Most of the time, the response was the same: "Nothing." Those suggestions I disregarded. I listened to the people with ideas they were willing to pay to use.

When a department begs to have a new network wrinkle, ask the same question: How much are you willing to pay for this? That weeds out most of the suggestions right there.

Chapter 9

Providing Applications for Your Network Clients

As MUCH FUN AS network utilities are, sometimes you must provide applications for your network clients. Your network might need to support a single multiuser application for all the users or many applications for every user. The normal case, fortunately, is for most users to share the core applications. Specific projects will require different software, but most of your users will need access to the same programs.

Some might go so far as to suggest that providing applications is the primary reason for the network. I think that is a bit shortsighted, since I prefer to believe the network is sharing information rather than just programs. But trying to follow the paths of applications begetting information begetting sharing the information begetting using the information in new applications can make you dizzy. Suffice it to say that applications are bound into everything that happens on the network. In this chapter, we'll cover the following topics:

◆ Application categories

◆ Trends in software metering and licensing

◆ Server-based application guidelines

◆ Access rights for application directories

◆ Application and data file protection

◆ Application administration tricks

◆ Application guidelines

Application Categories

Applications have changed over the years, but not enough. Early PC applications were hard-pressed to do a good job supporting a single user on a dual-floppy PC or single hard drive. Each printer was tied directly to the computer. The need for multiple configuration files, remote printer control, dispersed applications, and data directories never arose.

Today, even the smallest freeware program must understand how to install to remote server hard disks and run with separate data and applications directories. If it does not, we throw it away in disgust. Shareware programs routinely support multiple print queues, shared files, and NetWare-controlled record locking. It looks like the application software developers are far ahead of the network.

As if this were not enough, the replacement wave of client/server applications is upon us: Web server systems. Fortunately, Novell and AOL/Netscape teamed up to provide the Netscape-based NetWare Enterprise Web Server for NetWare 5.1. Not only that, NetWare 6 also installs Apache, the most popular server on the Web, for control and administration. Although you may currently have another type of Web server on your network, you should install the Enterprise Web Server and become familiar with its advantages. As users who are shuffled off to Web applications start realizing how slow other Web servers are, they will begin demanding NetWare-level performance.

Network Aware, Enabled, and Integrated Applications

Novell's former application group (now the Corel WordPerfect Suite) divided applications into three categories:

Network-aware   Programs that can run on the network, but do not use any special network features. They cannot use messaging or other communication options.

Network-enabled   Programs that run well on the network, but use proprietary solutions for services such as messaging and user authorization. These application services, such as the user database in an e-mail program, cannot be shared with other applications. This approach adds extra cost to each program, because services aren't shared (often even between applications by the same company) and because the cost of managing all these different systems is high. Do you want to add a new user to the network database, then to the e-mail, scheduling, and database user lists?

Network-integrated   These applications are excellent choices for today's network. They do not have the shortcomings of network-aware or network-enabled applications. They provide good communication and collaboration features. Also, they are well integrated into the advanced services of the network operating system, such as the NDS directory database. This makes them easier to manage, keeping down the cost of ownership.

NOTE   *This is a long way from some applications available in the mid-1980s, which I called* network-hostile. *They hard-coded drive C: into the installation program. Almost as bad were the programs stored on the server hard disk that required a single-license floppy at the workstation to start but were sold as multiuser. Does that make sense? This evolution of applications compares to the leap in medicine from leeches to antibiotics.*

Unfortunately, almost all PC LAN applications are stuck in level two, network-enabled. We can't really blame the software developers, however. The tool they need to share communication channels and the user database is, in fact, a better user database. NDS eDirectory provides a strong global directory with extensions available for developers. Now the smart developers are moving to take advantage of these features with applications that are integrated into the network.

A good example of network-enabled control is the ability for software to store the bulk of the application on a server, requiring minimum disk space on the workstation. Keeping individual configuration files for the software on the workstation is acceptable, but it's better to keep configuration files on the server. Having them under control on the server allows the network administrator to change and update those files quickly and easily. Keeping them on the server also helps protect them from user mistakes. Microsoft, for example, doesn't like this, but does provide this capability with some of its products.

Collaborative Software

Beyond the three levels defined by WordPerfect years ago, we must add a new term: *collaborative software*. Many examples of this type of software abound on the Internet, such as group calendars, scheduling software, and discussion forums. Third-party products appear every day, such as the Linux-based NetWinder from the now-absorbed Rebel.com Inc. (the most successful maker, Cobalt, is now a part of Sun and should stay around). NetWinder is an Internet appliance providing collaboration, Web and e-mail servers, and at least 6GB of storage, wrapped in a cute package the size of a hardback book.

Each of these products runs perfectly well within a local network and local Web server. You can also run collaborative software directly on NetWare servers, as you'll see in later chapters.

Trends in Software Metering and Licensing

Some of you will remember earlier versions of software such as Lotus 1-2-3 that required a "key" disk to activate the software. This disk ensured that you used only a single copy of the software. Many software packages that incorporated key disks were also network-hostile (not to mention user-hostile). Early makers of PC software wanted to ensure that you purchased every copy of software that you actually used. As the PC network grew in popularity, the concept of key disks became more and more impractical due to the complexity of implementing it on a variety of platforms.

Today, off-the-shelf software is more network-friendly; only in specialized software will you find keys, activation codes, or dongles required (a *dongle* is a hardware device that attaches to the PC's parallel port). Friends in the software business during the height of this madness tell me half or more of their support calls concerned problems with dongles or key disks. However, this made tracking software usage more difficult and opened a whole new cottage industry—software metering.

As early as NetWare 2.1, there were third-party tools to track concurrent usage of software. These tools ensured that your network software usage did not exceed the number of copies you actually purchased.

Early versions of these programs had their flaws. Many early software-metering packages did not recognize when a workstation had locked up and had to be rebooted, thus keeping a software license active even when it was no longer being used. These early programs also had problems tracking applications that were installed on the local hard drive of networked workstations.

Software-tracking programs have improved greatly over time, but still lack any sort of standardization rules to focus the product-line offering. More recent products seem to offer fairly similar features.

TIP *Those readers interested in the state of the art when I last reviewed these packages for* Network World *are wel-come to check out* `www.nwfusion.com/reviews/0809rev.html` *for my thoughts on software metering in general and information about particular packages. ZENworks wasn't included because the article is about applications that do meter-ing only. ZENworks pays the price again for crossing so many product boundaries.*

DID YOU PURCHASE EVERY PIECE OF SOFTWARE YOU USE?

Does your organization own every piece of software that it is using? Can you prove it? Do you have the license agreement and invoice records for the purchase of this software? Did you know that you could be fined up to $100,000 for *each* piece of software you do not have licensed legally? You can also be fined up to $250,000 and sentenced to five years in jail for copying software and giving it to a friend!

Software piracy is no joke! I know people who have experienced the penalties firsthand, and I advise you to make sure your network is in compliance now. What can you do?

◆ Collect all your license agreement documents and keep them in a safe place.

◆ Keep copies of all invoices for software purchases.

◆ Periodically audit your software usage to make sure you are not exceeding your authorized usage lev-els or exceeding the number of licenses you can use.

◆ Read and understand the license agreement documents. I have needed to read a few of these documents three times in order to make sense of them, but in the end, I am glad I did, because I have a better under-standing of what the license permits me to do.

◆ Questions? Contact the software vendor and enlist their help to ensure that you purchase the correct number of copies and that you use them correctly.

The best place of find out more about software piracy is the Software Information Industry Association Web page at `www.spa.org`. Here you will find information about software piracy laws, as well as other useful information such as forms and templates to help you set up your own software usage policy and Internet usage policy documents.

Server-Based Application Guidelines

One of the important decisions you will make when deploying your network is where to store the application programs. When I first started installing Novell LANs, in a fit of network enthusiasm, I would install every application I could on the file server's hard disk. This was in the days when I was lucky if a workstation even had a local hard disk. If it did have a local hard disk, it was 10MB or 20MB. Of course, WordPerfect 5 could also be installed in less than 1MB of disk space.

The debate has raged on over the past 10 years. Where do we install the networked applications? Much has changed. Applications have become more network-savvy. The cost of hard disk space for workstations has dropped (and continues to drop) rapidly. Tools have become available to allow you to more easily manage applications installed on a local hard disk.

NOTE *The term* application server *means different things to different people. Many people use the term to designate the NetWare server that stores all their end-user applications such as Microsoft Office, Netscape, GroupWise, and so on. When a server is used to store shared applications, I still call it a file server but refer to the applications as* server-based applications. *Others, myself included, use the term* application server *to indicate a file server or other computer that is providing the server component of a client/server application. For example, if you installed Oracle8i on your NetWare server, that server would become an application server.*

Although I don't really like putting application software on workstation local hard drives, Microsoft Windows gives you little choice in the matter (most of the time). There are still occasions when it's possible to put users' applications on the server hard drives. Questions then arise about where to put programs, data, and system files. There are no hard-and-fast rules about where to put anything, so this is my general rule: Protect your data.

Like everything else about your network, the directory structure for your applications is unique. The setup for your server-based applications will be based on your preferences, the preferences of your users, and, most of all, the dictates of your application. We'll go over some guidelines for your directory structure, but don't get upset when you must bend the rules to fit your situation.

Keeping Your Applications and Your Data on Separate Volumes

The most important guideline is this: Keep your application programs separate from your data. Many network administrators keep their applications on one volume and let users keep their data on another volume. For example, the database application is on volume APPS:, and the data controlled by that database is on DATA:.

This guideline makes good sense in almost every case. If you mingle the applications and the data, something will happen to one or the other. If users have Delete rights for a data directory in the same directory structure as the application programs, something will be erased. I guarantee it.

If your tape backup system is unable to capture everything in one tape, it may be able to back up the data in one tape if it is separate from the application programs. Separating the data and programs also means you need to back up only the data and/or application volumes when something changes.

Although it's possible to choose which directories are copied in a backup operation, it's easier to back up a volume. Your backup parameters take more time to set up and are more prone to errors if you must thread in and around your directories to cover everything.

Take a look at Figure 9.1 for a simple example of separating your data from your programs. This setup uses the RELL server, with one 10GB disk divided into three NetWare volumes:

- The SYS: volume holds all the NetWare operating system files and utilities, the NetWare Java programs, and the working directories for printing. You can see the NetWare system directories on RELL_SYS.

- The APPS: volume in the example holds the Microsoft Office network installation and the GroupWise software.

- On the APPS: volume, under MSOFFICE, are the directories for the Office software, templates, clip art, and more.

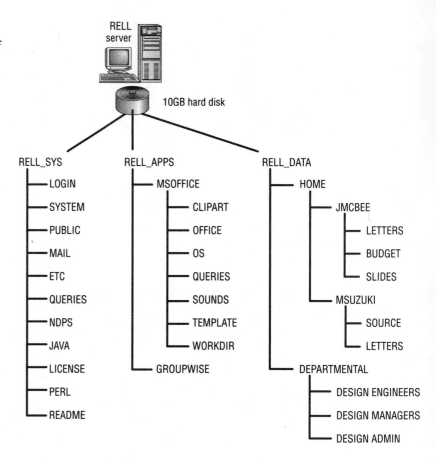

FIGURE 9.1

A simple but effective method for separating your application programs from your data

I like the idea of putting all my applications on a separate volume. Calling a volume APPS:, for instance, makes several things easier. All drive mappings can point to the same volume, so it's easy to remember. It also adds one more level of separation for your tape backup process.

If you don't have a lot of applications, you might put them in the SYS: volume. If you put your application files in SYS:, make sure that you still have plenty of disk space available. I like to have at least 500MB of disk space available on my SYS: volume, or more if I am using that volume to spool print jobs. Low disk space can cause problems for your server, including server crashes. I recommend making a separate APPS: volume to be safe.

In our example, the DATA: volume holds the home directories for users. This is where all the home directories are automatically placed when a new user is created. In Figure 9.1, you can see the directories for JMcBee and for MSuzuki (of course, your network will have more than two users—this is just to give you the idea).

Since these are home directories, users can organize them any way they wish. Your users' home directories will be built around the jobs they must deal with in their workday. User JMcBee may have directories named LETTERS, BUDGET, and SLIDES (for presentations). MSuzuki may have SOURCE, for source code files, and LETTERS.

When the end of the day rolls around and it's time for backup, the most important volume is DATA:. The valuable data is there, where people are creating and using information. If space is tight on the tape for the backup, the APPS: and SYS: volumes could be skipped most of the time. Application files and the NetWare system files change rarely. It may seem like you need a software upgrade every day, but it's not really true.

Keeping the Applications and Data on Separate Servers

It's not unusual to go a step farther down this road and keep the applications and data files on separate servers. Figure 9.2 shows this arrangement. RELL_APPS: is on the left, with the MSOffice and GroupWise subdirectories. You can see the program subdirectories within. The other server, GARCIA, has the HOME and Departmental data directories on GARCIA_DATA:.

FIGURE 9.2

Applications here, data there

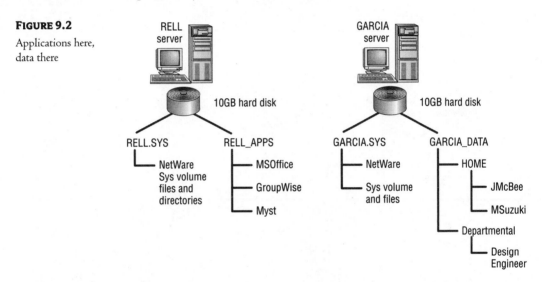

This arrangement also helps balance the load on servers a bit. If your server handles both the applications and the data files, there will be quite a bit of traffic. Multiply this scenario by the number of applications serving the users on your network, and you can imagine the traffic load. The ability of NetWare to support large numbers of concurrent users makes it tempting to load the server with all sorts of application and data directories.

Consolidating Application Licenses

If your workgroups have only a single server and are spread too far apart to use a central server, you have no option for tuning as we just discussed. Worse, you may need to buy many small licenses for network applications rather than one large license. It's more expensive to buy 10 packages, each supporting 10 users, than one package to support 100 users.

However, if your one-server workgroups are all on the same network, the advantages of NetWare may help you in a way you might not have considered. With earlier versions of NetWare, the one-server workgroup made sense because of the high management overhead of mapping each user to several different servers. It was done all the time, of course, but tracking user MSuzuki across six servers meant six times as much work as leaving the user on one server. With NetWare 6 and NDS, however, you can track user MSuzuki across as many servers as you want, with a single login. Even more important for your social life, this can be done with a single administrative step.

Let's go over an example considering three departments: Accounting, Graphics, and Legal. Each has 30 users. Each department has specific software licensed for those 30 users. But what about the general applications that these 90 users need? Why buy three network versions of Paradox, if all 90 users need access to Paradox? We know the Legal department needs access to the legal database, but doesn't everyone need a word processor? Why buy three separate licenses?

Figure 9.3 shows one way to share the load and save some money. The Accounting users must access the Solomon accounting package, but no one else cares about that. So they have a 30-user license for Solomon. The 30 users in the Graphics department need CorelDraw, and the 30 users in the Legal department need access to the Legal database. Nothing unusual here. Then there is the question of buying three licenses each for a word processor, database, and e-mail package (one each for every department).

FIGURE 9.3

Coordinating server
application licenses

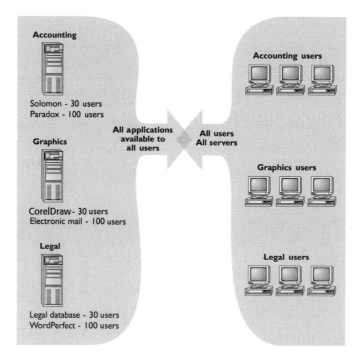

But the horizontal applications can be shared easily. Everyone needs word processing, so the Legal department server holds a 100-user license of WordPerfect. This lets all users in all three departments have access to one network copy of WordPerfect, rather than three separate ones. The same scenario is repeated on the Graphics department server, where the e-mail application is stored. Accounting also helps out by hosting the Paradox database, again with a 100-user license.

With NetWare 3.*x*, you needed to create and manage each user in each department on three different servers. With NetWare 4, NetWare 5, and now NetWare 6, users can connect to the NDS database and be granted access to their job-specific applications and the horizontal applications: one login, three servers, six applications.

As we've seen in earlier chapters, there's no reason each department can't be its own Organizational Unit. The three departments could also be one large Organizational Unit with three separate groups.. Either option, or some other arrangement you may come up with, works for me as long as it works for you. That's until Microsoft changes the rules again, of course, causing everyone to change all their licensing arrangements.

Access Rights for Application Directories

The default rights for all users to new directories are Read and File Scan (for servers in the same container as the user). These allow everyone to see the directories but not take any action in those directories. The primary action we want to avoid is a user accidentally deleting a file or two hundred. And, as you may have already discovered the hard way, the first step in virus control is keeping users (and hence viruses) from modifying executable files.

Managing Access Rights in Application and Data Directories

Keeping our application programs separate from the data generated by those programs forces us to manage the access rights separately. This time, multiple management steps are a good thing. We want all users to have enough rights to read and execute the application programs, but not to be able to make other filesystem changes. Data directories require that appropriate users have full user rights, which I consider Read, Write, Create, Erase, and File Scan. These rights allow the users as much control over the directory on the server as they have on their own hard disks.

The model for these settings is the NetWare system itself. The PUBLIC directory contains all the utility files for users. Every user has access to PUBLIC and must have the ability to find and run each program there. However, since this is a system directory, you don't want anyone to change the files by deleting them or modifying the access rights. As PUBLIC provides Read and File Scan rights to everyone, so should you provide those rights to the application programs.

Applications differ, of course, and the final determination must be made by the application programs. If the installation routine demands more rights, such as the ability to create and delete temporary files in the application directories, you have no choice but to make those changes. But it will be worth a few minutes of testing to see if you can create and delete the temporary files elsewhere. Often, you can satisfy an application's need for a place to work with temporary files with this DOS setting (if Windows didn't put it there):

```
SET TEMP=C:\TEMP
SET TMP=C:\TMP
```

If you make use of the power users in a department as administrative helpers, check their rights to these application directories. They will often need full file access and control rights to administer the applications. This also means they should be made virus-aware, since they have both the ability (file rights) and attitude (let's load this new utility and see if it helps) to introduce a virus to the network.

Setting Rights to an Application Directory

IN A HURRY 9.1: GRANT RIGHTS TO APPLICATION DIRECTORIES

1. As the Admin user or equivalent, start ConsoleOne.

2. Right-click the directory to set user or group rights and choose Properties.

3. Click the Trustees tab.

4. Click Add Trustees to open the Select Object dialog box.

5. Highlight the user, group, or container that needs rights to the application directory, and click Apply.

6. Check the appropriate access rights (Read and File Scan are a minimum).

7. Click OK to save your settings.

Applications do a good job of creating directories and distributing their files (sometimes all over the place), but they don't set rights for your users. You must do this, but because of rights inheritance, you need only adjust the top of the application's directory structure.

The recipient of these rights may be an individual user, several users, a group, a container, several groups or containers, or the entire network. Since the Sun StarOffice directory is our example, and it contains horizontal applications used by everyone, the writers certainly need to be granted access.

Figure 9.4 shows the subdirectory for StarOffice (named StarOfc, because I've done networking a long time and still find directory names over eight characters long somewhat disconcerting) chosen in the SYS: volume of COMPAQ-330. As you can see in the display, the Help, Program, Share, and User subdirectories are directly under the StarOfc directory. Writer Isaac has all necessary rights (including Access Control but not Supervisor), and Alfred will soon match Isaac.

In Figure 9.4, you can also see the Effective Rights dialog box, which I opened to illustrate the exact rights available. The Effective Rights dialog box isn't updated until you save the rights assignment settings and reopen the same view.

Application and Data File Protection

Your application programs must be protected from a variety of disasters. Some of these you have control over; some you don't. Those that you have control over include the following:

◆ Accidental deletion

◆ Intentional deletion

◆ Users allowed access to these files

◆ Concurrent program users as per the license agreement

FIGURE 9.4

Granting Isaac
the right to use
StarOffice

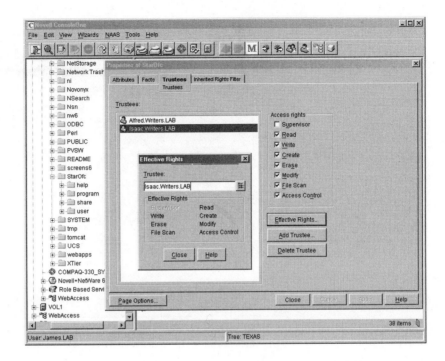

And here are some of the disasters over which you have less control, or no control at all:

◆ Server or disk failure

◆ Catastrophe

◆ Application and data theft

◆ Software updates

We looked at a way to stop authorized users from accidentally (or intentionally) deleting files in the previous section. That method applies to users and their rights to access the files. There is also a way to give the files themselves some self-defense mechanisms. The attributes (often called *flags*) that can be given to directories and files are described in Chapter 7, which covers network security. The file attributes are shown in Figure 9.5.

All these attributes (except Execute Only) can be changed by someone with the Modify right. That is why the NetWare manual strongly cautions you about granting the Modify right to anyone except administrative-level users.

Several of these attributes provide excellent self-defense for your files and directories. The most common flag used to protect files is Read Only. When a file is marked Read Only/Shareable, multiple concurrent users can read and execute the program, but none of them can delete, rename, or write to the file.

FIGURE 9.5

File attributes for
`soffice.exe`

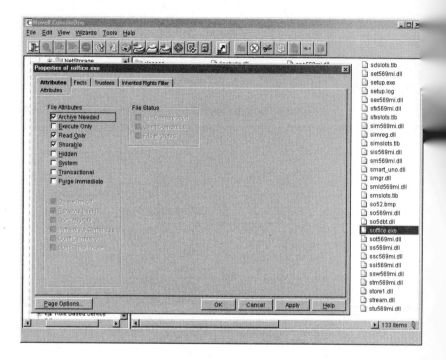

Using File Attributes as a Safety Device

IN A HURRY 9.2: SET FILE ATTRIBUTES WITH CONSOLEONE

1. Log in as the Admin user or equivalent.

2. Using ConsoleOne, browse to the directory where the file attributes need to be changed.

3. Right-click the file you want to change and choose Properties.

4. Click the Attributes tab.

5. Click the Read Only and Sharable attributes.

If you're familiar with the DOS ATTRIB command, just think of ConsoleOne as the ATTRIB command with a few more options. DOS files have a Read Only switch as well. There is more reason to use this type of file protection in a shared environment.

See Figure 9.5, in the previous section, for a list of the file attributes provided by ConsoleOne. Novell still provides a command-line utility, called FLAG, for changing NetWare file attributes. This utility can be useful in many circumstances. You'll read more about FLAG in the next section.

Changing Directory and File Ownership

IN A HURRY 9.3: MODIFY DIRECTORY AND FILE OWNERSHIP

1. Log in as the Admin user or equivalent and start ConsoleOne.

2. Right-click the directory or file to be modified and choose Properties.

3. Click the Facts tab.

4. Click the Browse button at the right end of the Owner field.

5. Choose the owner from the Select Object dialog box and click OK.

6. Click OK to save your settings.

Why would you want to change the owner of a file or a directory? Several reasons come to mind. One is to make tracking the evolution of the network clearer to whoever follows you in your present job. If the owner of a questionable file or directory is Bob, the future administrator will have no idea if Bob is a user or an administrator. If the owner is Admin, there's no question.

The second reason to change file ownership applies to those companies that allocate disk space to users. When Bob creates a directory and copies files there, as in a typical software installation, all that file space counts against his budget. That's not fair to good old Bob, so you should change the file's owner value to Admin.

Another good reason to change ownership is that you may occasionally stumble across an application that requires its program or data files to have an owner. The programs simply stop running if the owner of the file is deleted from NDS. In general, it's a good idea for applications to be owned by the Admin user.

The process for changing file and directory ownership is similar to that for changing file and directory rights. Figure 9.6 shows the screen in ConsoleOne that you use to set the owner of the StarOfc directory from James to Admin. Although you can name the owner of files and directories, one does not influence the other. After changing the directory's owner, you must change the owner for all the files in the directory. You can tag multiple files in ConsoleOne, but each file must be changed individually.

You cannot type the name of the owner in the field. You must click the Browse button at the end of the field to get to the Select Object dialog box. This prevents any typos that could cause confusion and ensures that the entire owner's name, including context, is correct.

CHANGING OWNERSHIP WITH FLAG

Since you can't change the ownership of multiple files at once using ConsoleOne, you might want to use the FLAG command for this chore. Good old FLAG does the trick with a fistful of files (and even files in subdirectories) at once. For example, to change all the files in the current directory and subdirectories to have Admin as the owner, from the command line, type:

```
FLAG *.* /name=Admin /s /c
```

No muss, no fuss.

FIGURE 9.6

Transferring title to the directory

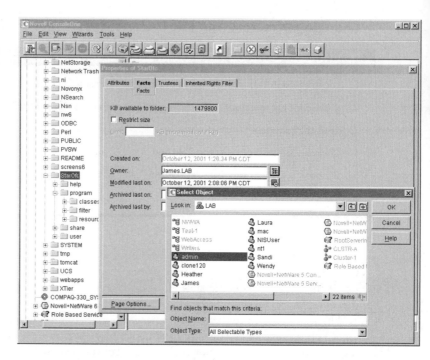

If you're curious as to who owns which files, just typing **FLAG** at the DOS prompt will list the filename, DOS and NetWare attributes, status, and owner. Subdirectories in the current directory will be listed with their owners as well. You can see why I think FLAG is a great utility. For more information about FLAG, check out the doc files or type **FLAG /?** from a DOS command line.

Application Administration Tricks

Perhaps *trick* has the wrong connotation for this section. We aren't pulling rabbits out of hats, but we would like to make life as easy as possible for network clients. Don't think of tricks as in cheating, but tricks as in a clever way to circumvent small irritations.

One customer of mine has a subdirectory named COMMON, to which everyone on the network has full rights. This makes for a low-tech bulletin board, where anyone can put a file for one or more other employees to use. There is no guarantee that the file won't be out-of-date, so it's not the most reliable means of collaboration, but they make it work. Everyone understands the limitations of sharing in this manner, and the people work with one another.

Another customer has become fond of search drives for company budget and word-processing templates. The directories are set up like the PUBLIC directory, with the files set to RoSh (Read Only/Shareable). All files used must be saved in a different directory, of course. But when the wording changes in some contract paragraph, the network administrator places the changed file in the shared CONTRACTS directory in place of the superseded file. Now that all users have been trained to always pull their boilerplate paragraphs from this directory rather than an old contract, changes are available quickly and reliably for everyone.

Drive-Mapping Techniques

There are a couple of nice tricks with the MAP command that you might find useful. If you're a Windows user, you can use its Map Drive dialog box instead of the command line. Another option is to use Directory Map objects. These work like Alias objects, but they should be created only once and placed in a high container for everyone to reference easily.

USING THE MAP COMMAND

If your users have local hard disk directories to be searched before the network drives should be searched, use a command like:

```
MAP INS S16:=COMPAQ-330_SYS:PUBLIC
```

This maps S16 rather than S1 for the first search drive, placing the MAP drives after all the existing search drives set by the PC's PATH statement. Using just MAP without the INS command puts this search-drive reference in the first position of the DOS environment space, overwriting what is there already. When you exit the network, the overwritten PATH commands will not be replaced. Using INSERT (INS) in the MAP command avoids this problem.

Some other interesting uses of the MAP command include providing you with the ability to replace an existing search map with a new one. To do this, use a command like:

```
MAP S1:=COMPAQ-330_SYS:PUBLIC
```

You can also use the MAP command to insert a new search drive mapping at the beginning of the PATH by typing a command like:

```
MAP INS S1:=COMPAQ-330_SYS:PUBLIC
```

If you have placed all the Windows GUI files on the PC, putting network search drives before the Windows directory will create extra, and unnecessary, network traffic. Worse, it will slow response for the user. The exception is the PUBLIC directory; you may want to use MAP INS S1 to place all the NetWare utilities at the forefront of the PATH statement.

If you have several drives to map, use the S16 drive setting for each. The first one will be drive Z:, then drive X:, and so on. The next lowest search number is assigned with each subsequent mapping.

Mapping drives to volumes in other contexts is easy, once you remember the Alias objects for the volumes from different contexts. I always forget to set up an Alias object the first time when mapping a volume from a server in another context. Of course, when I test the login script and see the error messages, I slap my forehead and say, "D'oh!" Then I explain to the customers looking over my shoulder how that was a lesson for them, so they would always remember to use the Alias object. (Most of them fall for it.)

From the command line, erasing a drive mapping is simple. Type something like this:

```
MAP DEL H:
```

And you're finished.

If you prefer to make a new mapping for drive H: without deleting the previous mapping, you'll get a question prompt. When you map a local drive letter (A: through E: are normally set aside for DOS) to a network drive, you'll also get a question prompt. This is just to remind you that if you redirect drive C: to the network, you won't be able to see your own hard disk until you delete the mapping.

USING THE MAP DRIVE DIALOG BOX

Windows clients have made mapping drives even easier using a dialog box accessed through the Network Neighborhood icon (in Windows 95/98) or My Network Places icon (in Windows NT/2000/XP). Simply right-click the icon to display their context menu. Then choose the Novell Map Network Drive option. (Be careful to choose Novell's option; My Computer pulls up the Windows Map Drive dialog box, not Novell's.) You will see the Map Drive dialog box.

The Map Drive dialog box contains check boxes that will specify that the drive you are mapping is reconnected at logon, a root drive, or a search drive. If you click the Browse button, you can browse the network, servers, or NDS tree looking for volumes and directory maps, as shown in Figure 9.7.

FIGURE 9.7

Mapping drives
using the Map Drive
dialog box

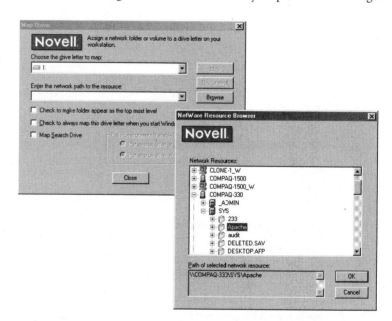

MAPPING A FAKE ROOT

The MAP ROOT command was developed as a response to problems with network-unaware applications in the early days. Many programs expected to be placed on the local hard disk, from the root of the hard disk. They refused to install to a subdirectory. A fake root drive was needed.

Novell added the MAP ROOT option to help fool those applications. For example, to set drive H: to look like the root of my private home directory, I can type this:

```
MAP ROOT H:=COMPAQ-330_SYS:HOME\Jgaskin
```

Any old-fashioned applications will happily install there, thinking they are in fact at the root of the hard disk. You can abbreviate the ROOT to just R in the command if you wish.

Another advantage, especially for home directories like this, is that the volume subdirectory designated as the root becomes the highest directory that drive letter can see. In the example, the DOS

CD .. command to move to the parent directory would not work to move to the USERS directory. This keeps users from accidentally (or on purpose) looking at directories where they have no real reason to look. Some companies use MAP ROOT for this feature alone, even if all their applications understand network directory installation.

Instead of using the MAP utility, Windows users can use the Map Drive dialog box described in the previous section. Just choose the Check to Make Folder Appear as the Top Most Level check box (means the same things as "map root," but no one gets confused by the root concept) and click Map. Figure 9.8 shows an example of mapping the StarOfc directory as the root.

FIGURE 9.8

Mapping a fake root in the Map Drive dialog box

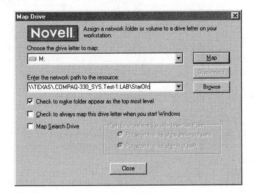

USING DIRECTORY MAPS

A Directory Map object is a leaf object that refers to a directory on a volume, somewhat like an Alias object. Any directory can be used as the object that is referenced by the Directory Map. These may be used in login scripts and from the command line.

A Directory Map is helpful when you have applications that you upgrade regularly or in situations where you want a single point of reference to a directory that changes. When change inevitably comes, you need only change the directory reference in the Directory Map object, not in every login script.

For example, one of my customers (like many other companies) uses Microsoft Word. When Word 2000 came out, superseding Word 97, the administrator didn't want to automatically delete the 97 version at the site. So we installed the 2000 version on a new volume. Was this a disaster, changing all the various references to reflect the new location of Word? Not at all. Changing the Directory Map object, referring to the new Word version in its new location, allowed us to reference Word as always, but have it point to the new location.

See Figure 9.9 for an example of creating a Directory Map object. The browse window on the left shows the location of LAB Organizational container. The window on the right shows the contents of the VOL1 volume. The Directory Map will be created in LAB, since that's where we started by right-clicking.

FIGURE 9.9

Referencing
Microsoft Office

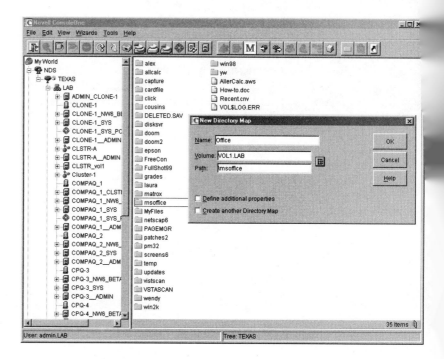

Some Application Guidelines

Fortunately, the understanding of networks among software developers is growing and has been for several years. With more applications available than ever before, custom-fitting each to a network would be impossible. But several trends have pushed software into being more network-friendly.

First, the Windows GUI provides a means for thousands of the products released over the last few years to work on the network by accepting the foundation provided by Microsoft. You might argue that there are better foundations for the software industry (like those used by our friends in the Unix community), but better a well-known foundation than nothing.

Second, Novell has been steadily providing software support for third-party vendors from the beginning. Over the years, application growth for NetWare networks has been tremendous.

The good part of all this is that applications will get more network-aware over the coming years. The bad part is that the new features of applications, including sound and video components, will require more robust networks and increased throughput. Looks like job security for NetWare administrators to me.

Microsoft Windows

Microsoft's Windows has become the standard for Intel-powered desktop computers, just as NetWare has become the standard network to connect those computers. Windows of various flavors and NetWare must work together smoothly.

Unfortunately, the burden of making Windows behave on the network falls to Novell, since Microsoft is busy trying to sell its own networking products. The good part of this has been that it forced Novell to develop client software for Windows that is far better than the software that Microsoft provides.

WINDOWS 95/98

Microsoft has made it nearly impossible to run Windows 95/98 from a server, because many system files demand to be local. To compound the hassle, Windows 95/98 is impossible to install across the network by copying a set configuration to an empty disk. This was tricky but possible with Windows 3.1*x*. (And if you're still running Windows 3.1*x*, see Appendix A for information about using it with NetWare.)

NOTE   Why is downloading a Windows 95/98 installation impossible? We can't blame Microsoft entirely, because some of the problem comes from the Plug and Play technology users have been demanding. Your operating system must be tightly tied to your hardware if Plug and Play has a prayer, and Windows 95 took that to heart. Yes, there may be ways to support Plug and Play yet still support downloaded systems, but then we get to the problem of long filenames. How do you copy directory names like Program Files to a DOS-only hard disk? This can't easily be done. Give up trying to mass-install Windows 95/98, because life is too short to waste banging your head against the Microsoft wall. Even some of the utilities built just to mass-install Windows have problems with Microsoft's unique ID attached to every machine.

You may hear of people devising complicated scripts to copy the Windows 95/98 files into the proper places in the proper ways without going through the official download and installation process. However, none I've heard about save enough time to make up for the retrofits necessary on the machines that don't accept the downloaded files gracefully.

You can, however, use a NetWare CD-ROM drive as the source drive for a workstation Windows 95/98 installation or upgrade. Copying the files across the network will probably be faster than any but the speediest local CD-ROM drives. The only caution is to make sure that the CD-ROM drive is available for application upgrades and Windows modifications after the initial installation. Any time you add something to a Windows 95/98 system, you probably will need the CD-ROM drive once again.

TIP   For more information on automating the installation of Windows 95/98, see the Windows 95 or Windows 98 Resource Kits or the Microsoft Web site at **www.microsoft.com***. Also check out the Windows 95/98 Batch Setup program.*

WINDOWS NT/ 2000/XP

If Windows 95/98 was "almost" impossible to run from the network, Windows NT/2000/XP is beyond impossible. Windows NT cannot be run across the network; you must have a local hard disk. Windows NT/2000/XP also cannot be installed by creating an image of Windows NT on the server and copying it to individual machines.

Windows NT Workstation is a different beast from Windows 95/98 and should be treated as such. I have grown to love Windows 2000 both at home and in the office. It is robust, scalable, stable (at least for Microsoft), and powerful.

There are utilities on the market that will assist you with installing these versions of Windows on your network. Microsoft has come almost to the point of endorsing some of these utilities, but none that are officially supported by Microsoft.

My experience with Microsoft is that if they don't officially support something, I am wary of it. What this means is that when you call Microsoft Technical Support, they are going to say, "Gee, we don't support that option/hardware/software/procedure. Why don't you call us back and let us know how you fixed the problem."

NOTE   *For more information on automating the installation of Windows NT Workstation, see the Windows NT Workstation Resource Kit. Also, there are huge books written on the subject of Windows NT, 2000, and XP. For example, Sybex author Mark Minasi has a series of excellent books on Windows NT networking—including* Windows NT Complete, Mastering Windows NT Server, *and* Mastering TCP/IP for NT Server—*as well as on Windows XP, including* Mastering Windows XP Professional. *For more information on these and other Windows titles, visit the Sybex Web site at* www.sybex.com.

General Application Hints

There's no better advice than to read the manuals for multiuser applications that will be installed on your network. However, you must read the instructions with a level of skepticism and wariness. Many program manuals provide the bare rudiments of network installation details, and it's up to you to fill in the gaps of their network knowledge. Let's go over some quick rules and guidelines. Remember, it may be multiuser software, but it's your network. Don't let some manual rework your network plan without a fight.

Here are some general tips relating to applications on your network:

◆   Install all applications as the Admin user. This keeps the ownership straight, and there are some programs that look for the SUPERVISOR or Admin user, not an equivalent.

◆   Observe the license restrictions on all software. To do otherwise is stealing. If you fudge, bad karma will cause your server to crash the evening before your vacation.

◆   When possible, provide drive mappings for applications. Since most new applications run under Windows, organize your volumes so that each volume is referenced by its own drive letter. This makes the group setups within Windows much easier.

◆   Smart network programs allow the use of UNC (Universal Naming Convention) pathnames.

◆   Feel free to use the MAP ROOT command to fool stupid programs that demand a root directory.

◆   Directory Map objects can help ease installation problems or hard-to-find subdirectories.

◆   Flag application directories Read Only and Shareable (if appropriate).

◆   Make groups for each set of users who need an application. Feel free to have a WP group, a Presentations group, a Spreadsheets group, and all the rest.

◆   Assign Read and File Scan rights to these application groups for their respective applications.

◆   Be sensitive when things look unreasonable; dig deeper. WordPerfect won't let you set the initial font on a network printer, but it will let you set this on the same printer if you say it's a stand-alone printer. Does that make sense? Actually, yes. You don't want each user resetting the printers every which way. What looks stupid at first could be clever programming.

Application Aggravation

I am sensitive to the wails from software developers about how hard it is to keep track of all the different network types and write software to fit. I really am. But I also have some marketing advice for these developers: Grow up, get clever, and grab market share.

NetWare customers want applications to run better with NetWare than they do on a stand-alone computer. Guess what? The good programs do. As a network administrator, you can tell the companies that do a good job with networked applications that you appreciate their hard work. You can also tell those companies that don't do a good job that you aren't interested in buying poorly written software.

How about this slogan: "If you don't network intelligently, I don't buy." Think that will get their attention?

Chapter 10

Teaching Your Clients to Use the Network

FIRST, A REMINDER: YOUR clients don't like the network as much as you do. They don't like computers as much, either. Hardware and software either bore or terrify them. Don't take it personally. You may teach, but you can't make them all learn. Some will learn and do well. Those are your future power users. Others will learn enough to do their job and will even figure out a few things on their own. This group will be the bulk of your user community. A few will regard computerization as a modern version of the biblical plague of locusts and will never learn enough to go beyond basic skills. If your company didn't require employees to use computers before you added the network, expect one or two people to quit their jobs rather than learn how to do something new. As grim as it may sound, this is normal.

To prepare for this situation, you and your management must plan how to handle the user community. Change is stressful, and changing to NetWare 6—even though this network runs better and is easier to use than what you had before—will stress some people. To help you help your users, this chapter covers the following topics:

◆ Preparing the user community

◆ Finding help

◆ Using Windows network user support

Preparing the User Community

Your management has some questions to answer. First of all, what are the top three client issues? These issues will be a major part of the reason for the new network or the network upgrade. What of value to the users will this new system provide? See if you can rank the answers in order of importance. Let's start with the most important reason for the system.

What's in It for the Users?

Is providing the users an easy graphical interface the most important reason? How about increasing disk space? Maybe combining several departments onto one server?

The top user priority for the new system will guide you in presenting the network to your users. If a graphical interface is important, because all your workstations now support Windows 95 or later, show them how easy it is to access resources anywhere with Network Neighborhood (or My Network Places). If disk space is the hook, tell users about the home directories and room for more archived files and online information. If several departments are moving to the same server, or just the same container, show how much easier finding and using network resources are with NetWare 6.

The worst case is learning that your boss had no user benefit in mind when the new network was approved. Be prepared for the users to gripe and complain as you change their system for no tangible benefit. Better yet, quickly figure out a benefit, and show the users how their situation has improved. This isn't cynical; it's making the best of a bad situation.

How Will Users Be Trained?

Now that your boss has weaseled out of the first question, here's another: What's the proposed ratio of user training compared with support staff responsibilities? The more training the users receive, the fewer support headaches for you and your compadres. Less user training, more headaches. No training, order aspirin by the pound.

Remind your boss that there are several kinds of training to be discussed. Network training is obvious, since you're installing a new system. How much network training? Here are some of your options:

- Send everyone on the new system out for training.

- Have a trainer come in and teach everyone.

- Send a few users out for training.

- Have a trainer come and teach a few users.

- Train one person from each department yourself.

- Throw everyone to the network wolves.

Unfortunately, the last choice is often the first choice. I wish I could tell you this has never happened, but users are thrown into new systems all the time. If this happens at your place, you have my condolences.

Remember, we haven't talked about application training yet. Nor have we mentioned desktop operating system training. The more computer training of any kind your network clients have, the better off they (and you) are.

Imagine a pie chart. The complete pie is your goal. The more training for the users, the less staff time filling the rest of the chart. More training, less support staff needed. More training, higher office productivity, and a bonus for your boss. Maybe you should explain things that way.

THE CLIENT'S VIEW OF YOUR NETWORK

There's a famous old map from the Middle Ages, charting what little knowledge people had of the world. The coastline of Europe was not too bad, but after about 100 miles of ocean, no one knew anything. With a dramatic flair, the mapmaker wrote this at the edge: "Beyond here, there be monsters."

Most of your users don't have a good idea what the network is, where it is, or how it works. That's why, when you point out the file server sitting under a table, they're disappointed. Something that causes as much trouble as a network should be big and complicated-looking. Perhaps downsizing companies should buy mainframe facades, with little motors keeping the big tape reels jerking along. That would impress people.

Those users who do claim to know about networking probably mean the Internet. Don't be disappointed if they talk about "logging in" by starting AOL.

Your network clients see only their computer and their printer when they look at the network. The rest of the network is something strange and, as far as some users are concerned, filled with monsters.

Teaching Your Users about the NDS Tree

Object-oriented views of the world have been rare. NetWare 6 is probably one of a few object-oriented programs that will be widely distributed.

I know that network management stations have used objects for years, as have programmers. The trade magazines are full of object-oriented, client/server, user-friendly, fault-tolerant, and browser-to-everything stories, but the typical NetWare user doesn't read those stories. The idea of inheritance never occurred to your users, unless a rich relative started wheezing.

This attitude will require you to present the new network landscape to your users in ways that directly help their daily activities. You should talk about the NDS tree and how it works, but the moment you see symptoms of the MEGO (My Eyes Glaze Over) disease, you should stop. Go straight to hands-on help with the tools they need to do their work. After a bit, you will see that the users are able to stand more explanation before their eyes roll up in their heads, and you will gradually teach them more than you ever thought possible. But don't rush it.

Go over the analogies and illustrations used earlier in this book for examples. Make up your own examples that apply to your business to supplement what's in this book and the manuals.

Use examples of physical items, like describing the NDS tree as a hallway, with Organizations as big rooms off the main hallway, and Organizational Units as smaller rooms off the larger rooms or smaller hallways. [Root] can be the building lobby, with all hallways running from there. Leaf objects such as users and printers and servers are things placed in various rooms. See Figure 10.1 for this example.

FIGURE 10.1

Making the virtual tangible

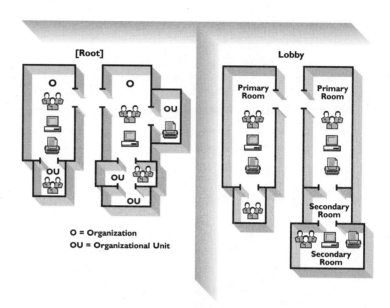

On the left, we have the NDS eDirectory tree. The [Root] object is at the top of everything, with Organizations leading from it. There can be many Organizations, of course, but here we show two. The Organizational Units can be contained only within Organizations or other Organizational Units; they cannot be installed in the [Root] object.

On the right, we have a lobby representing [Root], supporting the primary rooms. Only the primary rooms open from the lobby. Secondary rooms branch off the primary rooms, and often a secondary room supports attached secondary rooms of its own. As with Organizational Units, a secondary room may actually hold more than a primary room. Think of the anteroom leading to a ballroom as an example of this.

Icons for people, groups, computers, and printers are scattered around both drawings. It's easy to imagine real people and other objects in a real room. The same arrangements, with people and their supporting equipment, have the same look when placed in Organizations and Organizational Units. After all, Organizations and Organizational Units are just containers, as are rooms.

Finding Help

Help smoothes the road of life. Sometimes, you need help when you least expect it.

NetWare is complex and powerful. This means your users (and you) will need help on a regular basis. Does asking for help make you appear stupid? No, you appear stupid when you ignore help while struggling with a problem.

Novell Resources

Novell's primary help resource is their Web site, www.novell.com. Here, you'll find a ton of information on Novell, as well as bug fixes, updated software, and so on. Or you can go directly to www.support .novell.com when you need technical help rather than marketing and sales information.

`Comp.sys.novell` leads off a group of nonmoderated, Novell-specific newsgroups on the Internet. The traffic is heavy (100+ messages a day) and comes from all over the world. Since there's no moderator or sub-newsgroups, everything is currently piled into one big heap. You may be assured, however, that the messages you see come from some of the most technically savvy folks in PC networking.

The Electronic Manuals

Remember the problems I listed with paper as a technology-exchange medium back in Chapter 6, when we explored network printing? Novell has taken these comments to heart (okay, they did this independently of me) and now releases all documentation electronically. This started with NetWare 4.11, but the designers have greatly improved the service with NetWare 6.

Manuals are fine, but they are difficult to share. If a person borrows your manual, you can't use that same manual unless you're looking over that person's shoulder—not too practical. Did you ever take a manual home, and then forget to bring it back? Have you ever lost a manual? How about going through six manuals trying to find the notes you made on one page? These problems are eliminated with the new electronic manuals provided with your NetWare operating system.

Novell released documentation in HTML format with NetWare 5.1, and they put their full documentation on their own Web site at `http://www.novell.com/documentation/index.html`.

NetWare 6 arrived with all the documentation done in Adobe PDF format. This makes sense, because Novell can use the same files for a variety of output functions, including to the Web and to paper.

The auto-run function on the CD loads the (included) Adobe Reader version 5.0. I figured out how to copy the files to a NetWare volume, but the only way it would work is if I put the `INDEX.PDF` and `NOVELL.PDX` files in the root of the volume. This same approach works on a workstation hard disk, if you want to create your own personal NetWare documentation library (recommended). After all, if your only documentation sits on the network, you'll have a hard time reading the "Troubleshooting" chapter, won't you?

Novell does a good job with this manual. Unlike many PDF manuals, Novell does it right and turns each table of contents listing into a hyperlink that will jump you to the selected chapter. Figure 10.2 shows the documentation opening pages.

You could peruse through the table of contents and jump to various topics, but when time gets short and patience wears thin, the Search button awaits. I don't know if it will help, but it certainly can't hurt. Figure 10.3 shows the Search function about to launch itself (after I manipulated the screen display a bit to not hide anything behind the pop-up search windows).

To find anything, simply type the word or phrase you are looking for in the text box and set your options. Typically, the defaults will serve you well, but you can modify them as needed and try interesting word combinations just for the fun of it. This is another step Novell took beyond many vendors who supply manuals in PDF file after doing the least amount of work possible.

If you have several indexes to choose from, you can pick the one you prefer. In our case, as shown in Figure 10.3, the default Novell index appears automatically.

FIGURE 10.2

NetWare 6 documentation table of contents

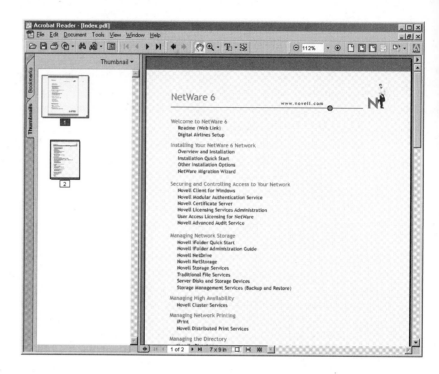

FIGURE 10.3

The Novell 6 documentation Search function

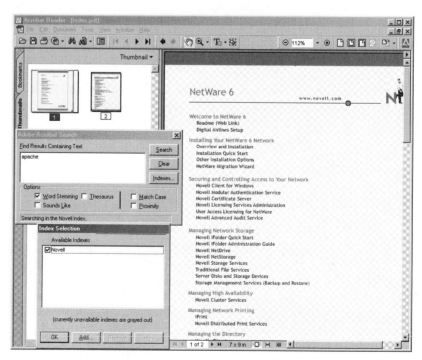

When you get multiple hits on a search, which you should most of the time, you'll have a choice of which to see first, as in Figure 10.4. Highlight the most likely search result as ranked by score (more black in the ball, the higher the score) and click the View command button.

FIGURE 10.4

Search Results, ready for viewing

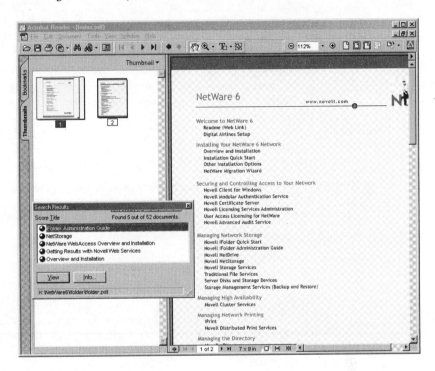

The main thing I want to say here is to play with it. Search for various words and phrases and get used to how the documentation works. The more time you spend getting comfortable with the system, the better off you will be in a pinch when the boss is staring over your shoulder.

Using Windows Network User Support

Starting with Windows 95, Windows changed the rules for your NetWare connection in many ways. Where NetWare client software loaded into DOS before Windows 3.1 started, later clients must integrate with the GUI. Microsoft includes some level of Novell client software as a default, but it's the lowest level of support they can provide. Don't use it.

TIP *I can't begin to explain Windows GUI fully in this section, nor would I want to attempt such a feat. Instead, I'll refer you to* The Expert Guide to Windows 95, The Expert Guide to Windows 98, Mastering Microsoft 2000 Professional, *and* Mastering Windows XP Professional, *all by Mark Minasi (published by Sybex). Also check out Sybex's* The Mark Minasi Windows 2002 Series, *which includes* Windows 2000 Automated Deployment and Remote Administration *and* Windows 2000 Group Policy, Profiles, and IntelliMirror. *There is no shortage of Windows GUI books on the shelves, but I'm assuming you're past the initial learning curve and need some detailed, behind-the-scenes information. Minasi provides that in his books.*

Do not make the mistake of enabling Windows 95/98's NetWare emulation software, File and Print Sharing for NetWare Networks. Microsoft, ever eager to bust Novell's chops, now emulates (but didn't license) the NCP codes necessary in an attempt to look like a NetWare 3.1x server. My objective opinion? It bites like hungry dogs in a butcher shop.

Since many Windows GUI users love their desktop icons and start there for most operations, we'll start there as well. Right-clicking seems to be the first step in computer knowledge anymore, so let's roll.

NOTE   If you're stuck with DOS or Windows 3.1 users, my condolences. Microsoft has turned its back on 3.1, and therefore Novell has done the same with NetWare User Tools, an early compensation for the lack of a Network Neighborhood utility in Windows 3.1. At this writing, the most recent DOS and Windows 3.1 Novell client is over 2.5 years old. Show this to your boss, along with pricing information listing how cheap new computers have become.

Performing Some NetWare Functions from Windows

IN A HURRY 10.1: USE NETWORK NEIGHBORHOOD IN WINDOWS 95/98 (MY NETWORK PLACES IN 2000/XP)

1. Double-click the Network Neighborhood icon (My Network Places).

2. Right-click one of the servers or the NDS tree icon.

3. Click WhoAmI, Change Context, Logout, Authenticate, Login to Server (or NDS Tree, if you clicked the tree icon), or User Administration.

4. If you chose User Administration, click one of the seven submenu choices: Personal Information, Work Information, Mailing Information, Edit NDS Login Script, Login Account Information, Novell Password Administration, or Group Memberships. If you clicked a server, click Send Message; if you clicked a tree, click Set Current Tree.

5. If you right-click a container instead of a server or tree in step 2, you can then click Set Default Context or Edit NDS Container Login Script instead of the options in steps 3 and 4.

By combining the command-line program WhoAmI with the NetWare information feeds threaded into Windows, Client32 provides plenty of information. Look at the details given in Figure 10.5, pulled from the COMPAQ-330 server connection.

FIGURE 10.5

NetWare WhoAmI information via Network Neighborhood

To reach this point, double-click the Network Neighborhood icon on the Desktop to open the Network Neighborhood application. In Windows 2000 and XP, this is called My Network Places. Right-click the NDS tree icon to display a drop-down menu that includes the following:

- ◆ WhoAmI
- ◆ Change Context
- ◆ Logout
- ◆ Authenticate
- ◆ Login to NDS Tree
- ◆ User Administration

The menu changes when you right-click a server, to show these options:

- ◆ WhoAmI
- ◆ Logout
- ◆ Authenticate
- ◆ Login to Server
- ◆ User Administration

After a separator bar, the Tree right-click menu offers a chance to Set Current Tree. The Server right-click menu offers the Send Message option, which works through Novell's long-time Instant Message utility.

If you chose User Administration in any of the above menus, you can then select from the following submenu items:

- ◆ Personal Information
- ◆ Work Information
- ◆ Mailing Information
- ◆ Edit NDS Login Script
- ◆ Login Account Information
- ◆ Novell Password Administration
- ◆ Group Memberships

It's worth noting that the User Administration from Network Neighborhood (or My Network Places) provides the same information that appears when you right-click the red N on the Taskbar and highlight User Administration.

NOTE   *All the features found through either Network Neighborhood or My Network Places can also be uncovered by right-clicking the red N on the Taskbar. Unfortunately for managers with curious users, multiple other operations can be launched from the red N as well, including a chance for users to edit their own login scripts. Since the red N can be eliminated from the Taskbar through the Configure System Tray option, I focused on Network Neighborhood and My Network Places. All users will see, and click, those icons at one time or another.*

If you clicked a server, you can select Send Message; if you chose a tree, you can select Set Current Tree. Figure 10.5 is the result of clicking the WhoAmI menu option on a highlighted server. While you receive the important information about your username and primary server from Network Neighborhood, you also get some quick details that are sometimes useful. I learned that I was NDS-authenticated and connection number 14. The connection information doesn't do a user much good, but it is an easy way for you, the network administrator, to discover a user's connection number. This information is necessary if you must clear a hung connection (assuming that the Windows workstation that you're currently using isn't the one causing the hung connection, of course).

Table 10.1 provides a quick summary of the various options in place, the purpose of each, and where each can be found. Remember that you can reach these choices through either Network Neighborhood (or My Network Places) or the big, red N on the Taskbar. We'll take a closer look at some of these functions in the following sections.

TABLE 10.1: THE SHORTCUT MENUS

MENU CHOICE	WHERE AVAILABLE	PURPOSE
WhoAmI	Tree, Server	Displays logged-in user's distinguished name, connection number, protocol, IP address, and so on
Change Context	Tree	Changes your current context
Logout	Tree, Server	Logs out of specified server or tree
Authenticate	Tree, Server	Authenticates to a tree
Login to NDS Tree or Server	Tree, Server	Logs in to a server or a tree
User Administration, Personal Information	Tree, Server	Allows changes to usernames
User Administration, Work Information	Tree, Server	Allows changes to job title, location, phone number, and so on
User Administration, Mailing Information	Tree, Server	Allows changes to user's address information
User Administration, Edit NDS Login Script	Tree, Server	Allows user to create or edit his or her own login script
User Administration, Login Account Information	Tree, Server	Shows user account and time restrictions; read-only
User Administration, Novell Password Administration	Tree, Server	Displays password restrictions; read-only; and allows password changes

continued on next page

TABLE 10.1: THE SHORTCUT MENUS *(continued)*

MENU CHOICE	WHERE AVAILABLE	PURPOSE
User Administration, Group Memberships	Tree, Server	Displays distinguished names of all groups to which the user belongs
Set Current Tree	Tree	Allows you to select your current tree, if multiple trees exist; for compatibility with some applications
Send Message	Server	Allows you to send a quick message to another user or group
Set Default Context	Container	Sets your current context to the selected container
Edit NDS Container Login Script	Container	Allows (with appropriate rights) the editing of the selected container's login script

SENDING MESSAGES

Since Windows 95 and later offer rudimentary peer-to-peer network functions, you would expect users to be able to send messages to other workstations. Offered as a DOS command-line option since the beginning of NetWare, SEND is reincarnated once again under Client32.

Hiding within the same menu structure as WhoAmI is the Send Message option. Figure 10.6 shows this feature under Windows, with the new logo and all. (One improvement over the Windows 3.*x* version of Send is the ability to select several users and send all of them the same message.)

FIGURE 10.6

Simple communications between users or groups

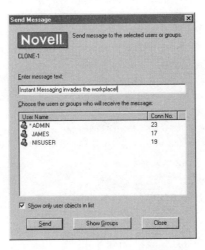

After sending this message to one of the available, logged-in network clients, a results screen appears on the sender's workstation. The screen, lacking in graphical interest, shows the target user's distinguished name, the connection number, and the status of the message. Status is a bit high-falutin' for a column heading, since the message is either "Sent" or "Not Sent," depending on whether the person has elected to block incoming messages. You do get informed, however, if the message made it to the user's screen.

Is this a valuable network feature? I suppose that if you were too lazy to pick up the phone and dial the interoffice number but energetic enough to open Network Neighborhood or My Network Places, type the message, find the person, and click the Send command button, this feature would be helpful. Of course, the phone gives you the option of leaving a voice-mail message. I'm afraid this type of instant messaging still reeks with the smell of AOL, chat rooms, and so much time wasted that many companies block instant messages from outside the firewall.

Messages on the receiver screen must be manually cleared. If your message target is calculating some huge spreadsheet or reformatting a database when the message arrives, he or she will need to stop working and clear the message before continuing. You must then hope that your message carries more importance than the work it interrupted.

LOGGING IN AND OUT

On the surface, the ability to log in from within Network Neighborhood (or My Network Places) makes no sense. If you don't activate all the network connections when you start Windows, how will Network Neighborhood or My Network Places know about your network?

Be that as it may, there are reasons to log in after Windows is up and running. You may have a special login script set up on a particular server, such as for a "backup" user defined to operate the tape backup system for the network. You may have needed to close a DOS box because some program blew up, and now you want to reestablish your original network configuration. You may want to log in as a different person entirely to test some portion of the network configuration.

Regardless of the reason, it's possible to log in from within Windows. Figure 10.7 shows the regular Novell Login dialog box, the same one you see at the beginning of the Windows boot process. The only difference between logging in then versus logging in now is that now the server and tree names are grayed out, since you chose a server explicitly. The login process will proceed the same from here as it does during the initial Windows boot sequence. Universal drive mappings will replace the existing mappings unless you specifically instruct the program otherwise.

If you right-click a server or a tree, you can also choose to log out. If you want to log out of a server but not the tree, you can do so. You will lose access to resources on that server, but you will free a connection for someone else to use. Be forewarned, however, that you no longer get a warning about losing your connections when you click the Logout option. Boom, you're gone.

SETTING YOUR CURRENT TREE

If you have multiple trees floating around (and remember from the discussion in Chapter 2 that neither Novell nor I recommend this practice), you may find from time to time that you need to access resources in another tree. In the old days (NetWare 4.10 and earlier), this was not possible, except through bindery connections. This meant you had all the Bindery Services issues to deal with and couldn't administer more than one tree at a time, and so on.

FIGURE 10.7

Log in here if you want.

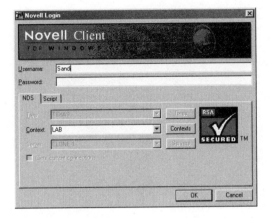

Beginning with version 4.11, and improved in version 5 and thereafter, you can freely use resources in multiple trees. However, a few applications haven't caught up with Novell yet and can be used by only one tree at a time. All you need to do when you meet an application like this is select the tree that you want to make your current tree, right-click it, and select Set Current Tree. You'll see the dialog box shown in Figure 10.8.

FIGURE 10.8

Confirmation of current tree selection

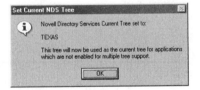

SETTING YOUR CURRENT CONTEXT

You may recall from earlier discussions that context is an object's position in the tree and that it is a permanent location, unless you move the object. Your *current* context, however, can vary at any time, much as you can change your current directory on a hard drive at any time. You may also recall that the way to do this at the command line is with CX. With Windows, however, you can do this graphically through Network Neighborhood (or My Network Places).

To change your context using the GUI, either right-click the container you would like to make your current context and select Set Default Context or right-click the tree the context is in and choose Change Context. If you choose the container, you are finished, as that answers the question of which container you would like to be the current context. NetWare will simply provide a dialog box informing you that your change was successful. If, however, you select a tree and choose Change Context, you will be presented with the dialog box shown in Figure 10.9.

Notice the lack of any kind of Browse button in Figure 10.9. At least NetWare 6 added the small amount of help on the screen. Novell's presumption appears to be that if you want to browse for the context, you'll use Network Neighborhood or My Network Places. If you know where you want to go, however, and just don't want to go to a DOS prompt to use CX, simply select the tree and make the change. It would seem a Select Object box would appear, however, so we lazy users don't need to actually type the context we want. Ah, the overwork in offices today.

FIGURE 10.9

Enter your new default context.

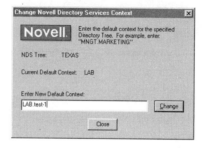

USING USER ADMINISTRATION TOOLS

Along with the new client, NetWare 5 introduced the User Administration choices. In the past, simple user actions, such as editing their own user login script or changing a password that hadn't expired, required either your intervention or the users getting into and using ConsoleOne. Neither choice was good for most people. The new choices are wonderful for most people, although those who love to play, but have little knowledge of what they are doing, may get into more trouble now that they can right-click and edit their user login script. As I discussed in Chapter 8, however, there are ways to deal with this problem. Let's look at the seven actions that users can now take.

Personal Information

Users can now edit the information that describes them. With the dialog box shown in Figure 10.10, they can change their name or any portion thereof. Many users want to have correct information about them as part of their own object. They want their full name spelled correctly; they want their maiden name and so on to be available. Others don't want this information available at all. This information, by default, is in their hands, and they can maintain it. Now you don't need to update names when people get married, divorced, and so on. Let them do so.

FIGURE 10.10

The Personal Information dialog box

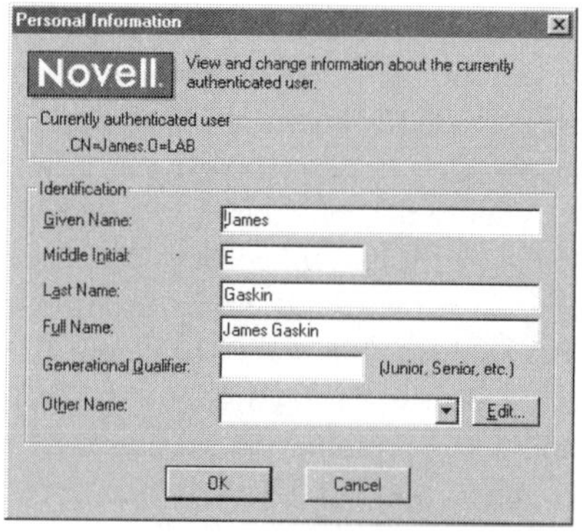

Work Information

In addition to updating their names, users can modify the things that define who they are at work. As Figure 10.11 shows, any user can change his or her title, job description, location, department, telephone number, or fax number. As I mentioned earlier, some users want this information up-to-date; others want greater privacy. Unless you need this information to be accurate and have the time to keep it up-to-date, let your users maintain this for you.

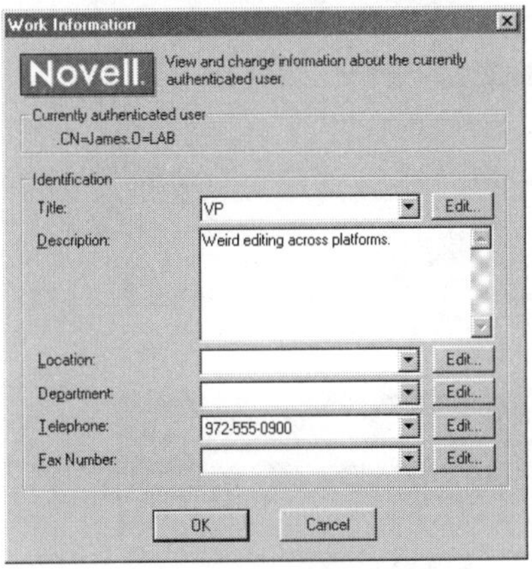

FIGURE 10.11

The Work Information dialog box

Mailing Information

NDS was designed so that most of the HR information for your company could be stored in NDS, with access available to everyone. This includes mailing addresses. In reality, few companies maintained and used the address information stored in NDS to mail things to their employees in the past. Today, however, more third-party products are taking advantage of these features within NDS. With the new Client32 software, any user can maintain this information, just as with the personal or work information. Figure 10.12 shows the dialog box associated with this choice.

If you click the Copy to Label command button, everything gets copied. Well, almost everything—this dialog box didn't pick up my last name, just the login common name. Put your full name in the dialog box if you want to use this for a handy label maker.

Edit NDS Login Script

Users can now edit their own login scripts without going into ConsoleOne (or NetWare Administrator). To do so, a user simply selects a server in the tree or selects the tree itself, right-clicks it, and chooses User Administration ➢ Edit NDS Login Script. Users with the Write right to a container's Login Script property can also edit the container's login script by simply right-clicking the container and choosing Edit NDS Container Login Script. In either case, the Edit Login Script dialog box shown in Figure 10.13 opens, and the user can write or modify a script. (Login scripts are covered in more detail in Chapter 5.) Changes to the script are verified through a dialog box asking whether to save the script: Yes, No, or Cancel.

FIGURE 10.12

The Mailing Information dialog box

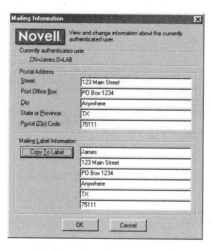

FIGURE 10.13

The Edit Login Script dialog box

If the user clicks the Login Script Commands command button, Client32 makes a Web connection to the Novell help screens. That will allow the users to get creative with their login scripts, causing you no end of future frustration. Don't let them do this if you can avoid it.

Login Account Information

Some of the things that users, particularly power users, may want to know are the specifics of their accounts. The security conscious (some would say paranoid) may want to see when the account was last logged in. A user can get this information easily by selecting the server or tree, right-clicking it, and choosing User Administration ➤ Login Account Information. The biggest "gotcha" here is that you can only view, not change, any of this information, no matter how many rights you have. Figure 10.14 shows the User Login Administration dialog box, which appears when you make this choice.

FIGURE 10.14

The User Login Administration dialog box

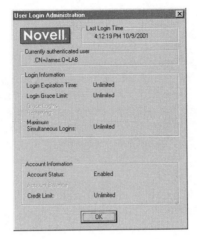

As you can see from Figure 10.14, you can get such details as the following:

◆ Last login time

◆ Grace logins allowed and remaining

◆ Maximum simultaneous logins

◆ Account status

Novell Password Administration

To see password information, users can choose the server or tree, right-click it, and choose User Administration ➤ Novell Password Administration. The User Password Administration dialog box, shown in Figure 10.15, is slightly more useful than the one that displays login account information—not a lot more useful, since most of the data is still read-only, but a little.

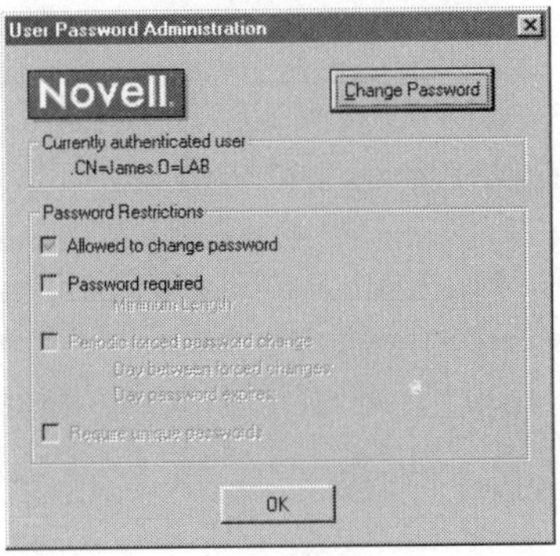

FIGURE 10.15

The User Password Administration dialog box

Users can view their password restrictions, such as if they are allowed to change their own password, if one is required, and if so, what the minimum length is, and so on. This information is not as useless as it seems. When users want to change their passwords or keep them in sync with other systems that have different restrictions, they can view what you have set up for them in NetWare as part of their planning. Or they can just use eDirectory and get a single sign-on to a lot of systems.

The one thing that users can change here is their own password, by clicking the Change Password button. When they do so, a dialog box will prompt the user for his or her old password and new password, and a second line will confirm the new password to make sure the user typed it in correctly. This is a great new feature and ability, in my book.

Group Memberships

How many groups are you affiliated with? Could you name them all quickly? NetWare 6 gives the user easy access to that information. Simply select the server or tree, right-click it, choose User Administration ➤ Group Memberships to open the Group Membership dialog box, shown in Figure 10.16. This dialog box, like the last two in the User Administration category, is read-only. You can quickly locate all the groups to which you belong and see each group's distinguished name. You will not see, however, any Organizational Roles for which you are an occupant. (I'm not sure why the user would want this information, but here it is.)

FIGURE 10.16

The Group Membership dialog box

Performing Filesystem Operations in Windows

One of the major reasons for having a network is to access shared storage on servers. In the past, you had to do some file maintenance in DOS, some in Filer, and still some more in NetWare Administrator, then in ConsoleOne as that grew more mature. This system required you to know not only what had to be done and how to do it, but where to go to find the tool to do the job. You can take care of most, if not all, file-management chores in Network Neighborhood or in My Computer, depending on your particular Windows GUI, as shown in Figure 10.17. You can also reach this point via My Computer and Opening any of the NetWare server connections.

Now let's look at options that are Novell-specific, beginning with a capability in Network Neighborhood added first with NetWare 5, NetWare Copy.

FIGURE 10.17

The Windows 2000 shortcut menu when right-clicking a Net-Ware volume or a directory on a volume

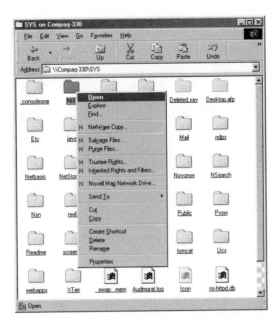

NOTE *The Novell Map Network Drive option opens the Map Drive dialog box, where you can easily map network drives. See Chapter 9 for details on using this option.*

COPYING FILES THE NETWARE WAY

NetWare Copy is a new feature that you can use to copy files, directories, or entire volumes from one place to another. NetWare Copy is essentially a graphical version of XCOPY. You can choose to keep or modify attributes when files are copied.

NOTE *Microsoft has never come up with a graphical version of XCOPY, only COPY with a few extra capabilities (such as copying subfolders) from XCOPY's arsenal. I used to use the switches in XCOPY all the time to control what was going to be copied and how, and I missed a graphical way to do that, often reverting to a DOS prompt. Leave it to Novell to come up with what Microsoft should have had all along.*

Right-click a volume or directory and choose NetWare Copy to open the NetWare File Copy Utility dialog box, as shown in Figure 10.18. As you can see, you can selectively copy certain files, choose file options and set atttributes—all in an easy, graphical way. You can even copy entire volumes if you want to, and to keep the bandwidth requirements down, just copy existing or newer files. I checked the Modify Attributes on Copy radio button so that the list of file attributes would be active (and readable in the figure). Are any left out? I don't think so. This is a great feature that Microsoft will probably be implementing soon. I highly recommend that you learn about it and use it, because it will save you a lot of time and effort later.

FIGURE 10.18

The NetWare
File Copy Utility
dialog box

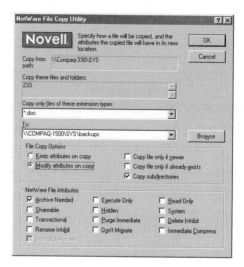

SALVAGING DELETED FILES

Once you delete a file, what happens to it? Is it lost forever? No! NetWare keeps track of it and does not overwrite it with something else until it is out of free space. Even then, it starts overwriting files that have been deleted the longest (unless the files have been purged, as explained in the next section).

How do you get them back, then? In the old days, you had to use a DOS command, SALVAGE, to get them back. This function was then integrated into Filer in DOS and added to NetWare Administrator. What does managing deleted files have to do with NDS? Not much. Nevertheless, that was where you had to go, unless you were a DOS person. Now, however, undeleting files is almost as easy as going to the Recycle Bin on the Desktop.

NOTE *If you don't want deleted files to be salvaged, you can use a SET command to purge them immediately (Immediate Purge of Deleted Files). This is not a smart move, unless you're close to the disk space edge, but it's possible. See Appendix B for a list of SET commands.*

As Figure 10.19 illustrates, you need look no further than the Salvage utility included in the shortcut menus to get back any files from this directory. To access it, simply right-click the directory or volume (remember that deleted files *from deleted directories* will be in each volume's DELETED.SAV directory) and select Salvage Files. NetWare will then show you all the deleted files in that directory.

NetWare tracks a vast amount of information on the file. Figure 10.19 shows that for each file, the following information is maintained: filename, date and time deleted, size, and deletor name (very useful when a user swears that he or she couldn't *possibly* have deleted that file—or to find out who actually did). This is good information, but off the screen to the right is a wealth of additional information: last update date and time, last updater name, creation date and time, owner, last archive date and time, last archiver, and last access date.

To get a file back, simply select it and click Salvage File. To get all the files in this directory back, choose Salvage All. When you've finished, click Close.

FIGURE 10.19

Getting back a
deleted file

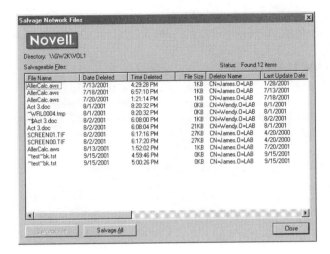

PURGING FILES

If resurrecting files bothers you, you can slam that coffin door shut. Right-click a volume or a directory and choose Purge Files to open the Purge Network Files dialog box, shown in Figure 10.20. Here you can flush all the deleted-but-not-forgotten files.

FIGURE 10.20

Purging deleted files

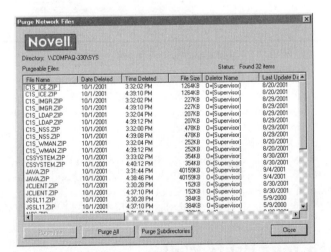

The file list shows the same information that you see in the Salvage Network Files dialog box. The buttons at the bottom provide a few choices. To delete individual files, select them and choose Purge File. You can also purge all the files in this directory by choosing Purge All. To purge all the files in this directory, as well as *all files in all subdirectories* below this one, choose Purge Subdirectories. In either of the last two cases, a dialog box will appear asking you to confirm that this is what you want to do and reminding you that the action can't be undone. When you're finished, click Close. One last reminder: *Purging files affects only already-deleted files.* It does not harm, in any way, any other file.

Printing Is Here, Too

Not only can you map drives here, you can also take care of your printer captures. To do so, browse, if necessary, until you get to the printer or queue in question (for non-NDPS printers), right-click it, and select Novell Capture Printer Port to open the Capture Printer Port dialog box, shown in Figure 10.21.

FIGURE 10.21

Capturing a printer port

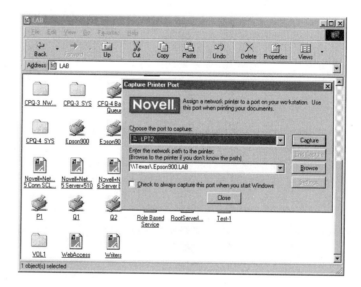

Select the printer port and the path (if another one is desired, click Browse and go find it), and then decide if you want to reconnect at login. If you do, check the box. When you have finished, click the Capture button. (For information on the rest of the printing setup or how to use NDPS printing, see Chapter 6.)

When you do this operation from the big, red N on the Taskbar, you must search for the printer to capture. When you do this from Network Neighborhood, the second line (the printer you want) is filled in automatically. Windows 2000 seems to have a problem finding NetWare objects inside My Network Places, so you may need to use the big, red N with Windows 2000/XP.

Teach Your Users Well

Each user has a job to do. Each job requires information and interaction. Your network is the conduit between the two. This situation does not gain the network, or even you, any respect when things work properly, just the chance to be blamed when things don't work to the user's advantage.

When users are unhappy, it's usually a management failure. Resources must be planned and deployed to support the users. If those resources, particularly your time and any necessary equipment, aren't available, the users become even more unhappy.

The animosity isn't personal, and it isn't deep. While it is aggravating, it's understandable. You get aggravated with your boss because tools you need aren't provided, don't you? When the network tool is not available, it's natural for the users to get mad at you, and it's safer for them than getting mad at their boss.

Track your user complaints. Half or more will be caused by something the users should know. The fact that they don't know usually has more to do with management priorities than user stupidity or apathy. Management's lack of priorities and support for you and your department will cause you more problems indirectly than any user will cause directly.

Part III

NetWare, TCP/IP, and the Internet

In this section:
- Chapter 11: TCP/IP and NetWare 6
- Chapter 12: DHCP and DNS Support

Chapter 11

TCP/IP and NetWare 6

ALTHOUGH NOVELL HAS SUPPORTED TCP/IP in some form or fashion since NetWare 3, TCP/IP never figured prominently in NetWare until version 5. NetWare always used Novell's proprietary network protocol, IPX/SPX, for most network communications. In NetWare 5, however, things changed in a big way. Now, NetWare 6 weaves TCP/IP into NetWare in every conceivable way.

NetWare 5 was a significant milestone for Novell, because it was the first release of NetWare that supported a pure IP environment. In NetWare 5, all NetWare Core Protocols (NCPs) used the TCP/IP transport protocol. NetWare 5 clients and servers did not encapsulate IPX information in TCP/IP packets.

NetWare 6 goes even further into the world of TCP/IP than NetWare 5. No traces of IPX/SPX are left on the network after you choose IP as the default protocol during installation. Want a detail? HTTP (Hypertext Transfer Protocol, the protocol powering the World Wide Web) now functions as a core protocol inside NetWare.

If you want to simplify your network and run a single protocol, you can run TCP/IP exclusively, never introducing IPX/SPX. This can lower wide area network (WAN) bandwidth requirements, simplify supporting routers, and increase client and server interoperability with non-NetWare platforms.

If you have been working on a network that includes non-NetWare servers and/or clients, or if you have needed to connect your network to the Internet, you have worked with TCP/IP. No discussion of TCP/IP goes very far without including some discussion of the Internet, because TCP/IP and the Internet have grown up together. The TCP/IP standards were developed in part because of the specific needs of the Internet and the Internet community.

If you already feel comfortable with terms such as *IP addressing, default gateways, subnet masks,* and *routing,* you can skip the first part of this chapter and head straight to the section called "Planning an IP Network." However, if you feel you need a refresher course on TCP/IP terminology, read on and prepare for TCP/IP enlightenment!

◆ TCP/IP overview

◆ Planning an IP network

◆ Compatibility with existing IPX/SPX networks

◆ Installing TCP/IP on NetWare 6

◆ Using LDAP (Lightweight Directory Access Protocol)

◆ Using the NetWare Enterprise Web Server

◆ Securing your TCP/IP network

◆ Troubleshooting TCP/IP

But First, a Little Background

Way back when the world was young and dinosaurs (IBM mainframes) ruled the computer room, Novell Data Systems was working on the first microcomputer file servers. This was in the late 1970s and early 1980s. Our friends at Novell needed to choose a network protocol for client-to-server communication. They decided to develop their own protocol (based on Xerox XNS) and called it IPX/SPX (for Internetwork Packet eXchange/Sequenced Packet eXchange).

Soon NetWare (and IPX) spread everywhere. NetWare was fast and fairly easy to deploy (those long hours—or days—of waiting for a disk to COMPSURF are now fading from my memory). Better yet, NetWare made network addressing a piece of cake from the network's perspective. Plug in the server, plug in the clients, and it worked!

NetWare originally flourished in small, departmental LANs. Later, it spread through medium-sized businesses, and then eventually spanned the enterprise throughout large companies all over the world. But through it all, the IPX/SPX protocol remained king of LAN protocols (at least from the Novell administrator's perspective and several installed-node reports).

Some have often questioned the wisdom of Novell in developing a proprietary protocol back in the early 1980s when TCP/IP already existed, but not me. TCP/IP was an also-ran to XNS at the time and was far from becoming mandatory in the world of Unix systems. I wince when thinking back to the difficulty I had in deploying my first IP networks. At that time, I certainly appreciated the ease with which an IPX network could be set up.

About early 1994, depending on who is doing the estimates, this thing called the World Wide Web started to take shape, at least from a mainstream perspective. The Internet had already existed in some form for almost 20 years, but it was mainly used by academics, the government, and research institutions.

The protocol used by the Internet then and now is TCP/IP. Internet law officially mandated Internet Flag Day, January 1, 1983, as the day when only TCP/IP-driven systems were allowed on the Internet. If you want to talk to other computers on the Internet and Web, you must use TCP/IP.

It's no secret that the Internet has captured the imagination of the world. Your network users are bugging you about getting faster Internet access on one side, and sales and marketing are hollering for a faster Web server on the other. Luckily for you, NetWare 6 with TCP/IP makes all the Internet connections you need, both as a client of Internet resources and as a provider of those resources.

Today, TCP/IP supports small, medium, and large corporate networks, as well as the Internet. Organizations that must support both TCP/IP and IPX/SPX invest a lot of time and effort to make sure their systems interoperate correctly.

As early as 1990, Novell was including basic TCP/IP support, and later supported interoperability functions such as printing and file sharing with Unix and other TCP/IP hosts. In 1993, Novell released NetWare/IP, which allowed NetWare clients to use TCP/IP instead of IPX/SPX to connect to their NetWare servers; nevertheless, many components of IPX needed to remain in place for years.

TCP/IP Overview

Early NetWare succeeded partly because IPX/SPX handled all network addressing details. Detailed knowledge of the transport protocol was unnecessary. Unlike with IPX/SPX, however, building networks based on TCP/IP requires a good understanding of TCP/IP. Nestled in among all the buzzwords about IP addressing, subnet masking, routing, ports, sockets, and services is an incredibly powerful and versatile network protocol.

Let's first take a look at the history of TCP/IP and at some of the major standards bodies that control TCP/IP, and then let's hash out some of the buzzwords. Actually, there is one term that you need to know before continuing: On a TCP/IP network, all computers (routers, devices, and other gateways) are referred to as *hosts*.

Looking Back at TCP/IP

Would you believe that TCP/IP is a product of the cold war? It is—sort of. In 1969, DARPA (U.S. Department of Defense Advanced Research Projects Agency) funded a research and development project to design a packet-switched network that would allow the DOD's many dissimilar computer systems around the country to communicate reliably. The goal was to allow computer systems to be distributed throughout the country, and thus make the DOD network less vulnerable to a nuclear attack. If a single site were destroyed, the remainder of the computers on this distributed network would continue to operate.

The result of this effort was the Network Control Program, also called NCP. This early predecessor to TCP/IP has been modified, upgraded, and improved continually over the years and gives us today's version of TCP/IP.

The history of TCP/IP also includes information about the Internet. This is because they are so tightly interwoven and because the standards bodies that control TCP/IP standards are the same standards bodies that control the Internet standards. If you know TCP/IP, you understand how the Internet works. Quite simply, the Internet is just a large TCP/IP network.

Over the years, the Internet and networks connected to it have gone by many names, including the following:

- ◆ ARPANET (Advanced Research Projects Agency Network)
- ◆ MILNET (Military Network)
- ◆ NSFNET (National Science Foundation Network)
- ◆ CSNET (Computer Science Network)
- ◆ NIPRNET (Non-Classified IP Routed Network)

SIGNIFICANT EVENTS IN THE TCP/IP AND INTERNET TIMELINE

◆ 1969: The DOD funds research and development for TCP/IP.

◆ 1970: ARPANET starts using NCP.

◆ 1972: The first Telnet specification is introduced.

◆ 1973: File Transfer Protocol (FTP) is introduced.

◆ 1974: TCP is introduced.

◆ 1975: IP addressing and routing standards are published.

◆ 1976: The DOD establishes TCP/IP as a standard.

◆ 1977: ARPANET switches from NCP to TCP/IP.

◆ 1983: TCP/IP is designated as the only protocol for the Internet, and Berkeley Unix implements TCP/IP.

◆ 1984: DNS (Domain Name System) is introduced.

◆ 1985: NSFNET is created, using a 56Kbps backbone.

◆ 1989: 100,000 hosts are connected to the Internet.

◆ 1991: The NSF allows commercial use of the Internet.

◆ 1993: The Mosaic Web browser is released.

◆ 1996: 12,800,000 hosts are connected to the Internet.

Who Controls TCP/IP and Internet Standards?

If you have worked in the networking industry for long, you have already heard about many standards organizations, such as IEEE (Institute of Electrical and Electronics Engineers), ISO (International Organization for Standardization), ANSI (American National Standards Institute), and CCITT (Consultative Committee International Telephone and Telegraph). Each of these organizations coordinates certain standards. I am sure the world would be a much simpler place if we had only one standards body, but we don't (sigh). Now I am about to add some other organizations to this list.

NOTE *The CCITT (Consultative Committee International Telephone and Telegraph) is part of the ITU (International Telecommunications Union), which is a branch of the United Nations. The CCITT produces recommendations rather than compulsory standards. Some of these recommendations include ISDN (Integrated Services Digital Network), X.400 (messaging), and X.500 (directory services).*

The TCP/IP suite of protocols is managed by a group of volunteers from all over the world called the Internet Society (ISOC). The ISOC is a global organization that was created in 1992 to be responsible for internetworking technologies and applications on the Internet. Its principal purpose is to encourage the development and availability of the Internet.

Part of the ISOC is the Internet Activities Board (IAB), a technical advisory group. The IAB is responsible for setting Internet standards, publishing RFCs (Request for Comments—more on them in the next section), and overseeing the Internet standards process. The IAB oversees three task forces:

♦ The Internet Engineering Task Force (IETF) is responsible for developing technical solutions to problems and new challenges as they arise on the Internet and developing Internet standards and protocols.

♦ The Internet Corporation for Assigned Names and Numbers (ICANN), at `www.icann.org`, oversees the assignment of unique protocol identities that are used on the Internet, such as TCP and UDP port numbers, which I will explain shortly. ICANN superseded the Internet Assigned Numbers Authority (IANA).

♦ The Internet Research Task Force (IRTF) is the research and development arm of the ISOC and is responsible for TCP/IP-related research projects.

NOTE *See RFC 1120 for more information about the IAB and its task forces. You'll find a complete listing of RFCs at* `www.isi.edu/rfc-editor/`.

Standards, Meetings, RFCs, and More Meetings

TCP/IP and all Internet functions are standardized in a series of documents called *RFCs*, but not all RFCs actually become standards. TCP/IP standards are not developed by committee, such as the IEEE or the ITU, but rather by consensus.

Throughout this book, you will see references to RFCs that contain more information about a specific feature or function. An RFC describes how a specific function is supposed to work on a TCP/IP network. Not all RFCs are entirely technical in nature, as you can see in Table 11.1.

TABLE 11.1: SOME COMMON RFCs

RFC NUMBER	WHAT IT CONTAINS
768	UDP (User Datagram Protocol)
791	IP (Internet Protocol) and IP addressing
793	TCP (Transmission Control Protocol)
821	SMTP (Simple Mail Transport Protocol)
950	Subnetting
959	FTP (File Transfer Protocol)
1034 / 1035	DNS (Domain Name System)
1118	Hitchhiker's Guide to the Internet
1157	SNMP (Simple Network Management Protocol)
1178	Choosing a name for your computer

continued on next page

TABLE 11.1: SOME COMMON RFCs *(continued)*

RFC NUMBER	WHAT IT CONTAINS
1700	Assigned numbers (TCP and UDP port numbers)
1793	A primer on the Internet and TCP/IP tools
1883	IPv6 (also known as IPng–IP Next Generation)
1918	IP addresses allocated for private networks (networks that will never connect to the Internet)
1939	POP3 (Post Office Protocol version 3)
2026	The Internet standards process
2324	HyperText Coffee Pot Control protocol (I'm not kidding)

Anyone can write an RFC and submit it to the Internet community for consideration to become a standard. If you have an idea about something you would like to see TCP/IP do, write it up as an RFC and submit it to the Internet community. If you are interested in writing an RFC, you can find an RFC that explains the steps for writing an RFC (RFC 2223).

RFC CLASSIFICATION

Documents are usually submitted by members of the ISOC to the IETF, but sometimes they also go directly to the RFC editor. The documents are reviewed by a technical expert, a task force, or the RFC editor and then assigned a classification, which can be one of the following:

Required All TCP/IP gateways, hosts, and devices must implement this RFC. (It is uncommon for newer RFCs to be classified as Required.)

Recommended All TCP/IP gateways and hosts are encouraged but not required to implement this RFC. Recommended RFCs are usually implemented.

Elective Implementation is optional. Application will probably not be widely used.

Limited Use Not intended for general use.

Not Recommended Not recommended for use.

RFC STAGES

Once the RFC is assigned a classification and a number, it goes through development, testing, and acceptance if it is being considered as a standard. During this process, technical experts review the RFC and provide feedback to its author. The Internet Standards Process refers to these stages as *maturity levels*:

Proposed Standard (maturity level 1) The RFC is considered stable and well understood. Enough people have technically reviewed it, and there is enough interest to warrant making it a standard.

Draft Standard (maturity level 2)   The RFC has now been tested and reviewed. It is clear and concise, and implementation details are understood.

Internet Standard (maturity level 3)   The RFC has been thoroughly reviewed by the Internet community. Its implementation is well understood, and it is generally believed that it will provide significant benefit to the Internet community.

Once an RFC is published, it is assigned a number. The number never changes. If updates or new technology need to be incorporated into a particular RFC, a new RFC number is created. The IAB Official Protocol Standard is a document that the IAB publishes quarterly; it indicates the most current RFC numbers for each protocol.

Common Protocols

TCP/IP is not a single protocol but a series of protocols that transport data and provide network services. Table 11.2 lists some of the common protocols and their functions.

TABLE 11.2: COMMON TCP/IP PROTOCOLS

PROTOCOL	WHAT IT DOES
IP (Internet Protocol)	Addresses and delivers packets. Similar to IPX.
TCP (Transmission Control Protocol)	Establishes a connection between two hosts and provides acknowledgments of packets being received. Used when reliable packet delivery is essential. Similar to SPX.
UDP (User Datagram Protocol)	Delivers packets to the host, but does not establish a connection first. Does not acknowledge packet receipt. Used in an environment where 100 percent reliable delivery is not necessary. The choice to use UDP or TCP is the application developer's, not the network administrator's.
ICMP (Internet Control Message Protocol)	Controls errors on IP networks. The PING command also uses ICMP.
ARP (Address Resolution Protocol)	Takes a known host's IP address and learns the host's hardware (MAC) address if the host is on the same network. If the host is remote (on the other side of a router), ARP learns the MAC address of the router instead.
FTP (File Transfer Protocol)	Transfers files between two hosts. To transfer a file, you also need FTP server and client software.
SMTP (Simple Mail Transport Protocol)	Transfers simple, 7-bit character messages between SMTP client software and SMTP server software.
HTTP (Hypertext Transfer Protocol)	Transfers Web pages between a Web server and a Web browser on a client.
DNS (Domain Name System)	Allows a client to look up the IP address of a host based on its name.
TELNET (Terminal Emulation Network)	Allows Telnet client software to connect to a host running Telnet server software, log in, and run programs on the machine running the Telnet server.

The protocols listed in Table 11.2 are by no means the only protocols that TCP/IP supports. Many times, these protocols work together. For example, if you were to take a protocol analyzer such as the Network Associates' Sniffer or Novell's LANalyzer and look at network traffic (such as Web server traffic), you would see an IP datagram carrying a TCP segment that was carrying HTTP data. In the HTTP data portion of the frame would be the actual Web page information. Figure 11.1 shows how this works.

FIGURE 11.1

Protocols encapsulated inside other protocols

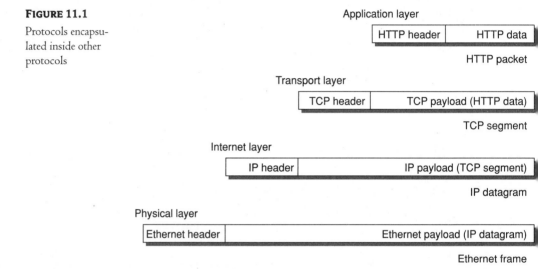

THE TCP/IP NETWORK MODEL

To understand how the protocols in the TCP/IP suite work together, it's helpful to look at the TCP/IP network model. You may be familiar with the ISO seven-layer OSI (Open System Interconnection) model. The OSI model describes, in a perfect networking world, how two hosts communicate and how each layer is handled by a specific networking component. The TCP/IP—or DOD—model is an equivalent four-layer model that describes how two TCP/IP hosts communicate. Table 11.3 lists the four layers and some of the protocols that reside at each layer.

TABLE 11.3: TCP/IP LAYERS AND PROTOCOLS

LAYER	PROTOCOLS THAT WORK AT THIS LAYER
Application	HTTP, TELNET, FTP, DNS, STMP
Transport	TCP, UDP
Internet	IP, ICMP, IGMP, ARP
Network	Ethernet, Token Ring, ATM, Frame Relay, PPP, SLIP

At the Internet layer, IP is responsible for delivering packets. At the Transport layer, TCP can be used for connection-oriented, reliable delivery of data, or UDP can be used for quick, low-overhead delivery of data. The application developer chooses which protocol (UDP or TCP) to use.

How does TCP or UDP know what kind of data it is carrying from one host to another? The simple answer: a database lookup system in Cleveland. But there's a little more technical answer.

PORT NUMBERS

Each Application-layer protocol such as HTTP or TELNET is assigned a specific, unique number. In TCP/IP terms, this is called a *port* number. I like to think of a port as the address of a particular piece of software. When a client application connects to a server application, it needs to know the server's IP address, the transport protocol it uses (TCP or UDP), and the application's assigned port number.

Armed with all this information, the client application can create a socket, or endpoint of communication. The socket identifies a specific program running on a particular computer.

So now when one of your snobby TCP/IP friends says to you <superior attitude>, "I have just changed my Web server's default port to 8080" </superior attitude>, you can respond with <smirk>, "Then how do your Web browsers establish the correct socket?" </smirk>. Okay, I will stop trying to make TCP/IP humor.

Fortunately, we don't normally need to assign port numbers. The developer of your Web browser knew that the standard Web server operates on port 80. RFC 1945 describes how to build a Web server. The IANA assigned the port number for the Web server application before ICANN took over.

These assigned numbers are also referred to as *well-known ports* and are in the range 0 to 1023. Ports can actually range from 0 through 65,535, but only the lower 1024 ports were assigned by the IANA. Private or limited-use applications can use the upper port range. Table 11.4 shows some common TCP and UDP port numbers. For a complete listing of common ports, see RFC 1700.

TABLE 11.4: COMMON TCP AND UDP PORTS

PORT NUMBER	USE
13	Daytime
17	Quote of the Day
21	FTP
23	TELNET
25	SMTP
53	DNS
80	HTTP
110	POP3
119	NNTP (newsgroups)
135	RPC Endpoint Mapper
139	NetBIOS Session Service
389	LDAP (Lightweight Directory Access Protocol)
524	NetWare Control Protocol

Types of Frames on an IP Network

If you use a network analyzer on your network, you will see one of three types of frames: directed, broadcast, or multicast.

A *directed frame* is the network manager's friend. It has the IP address of the host to which it is directed. No other host on the network needs to open the frame and examine the contents to see if the frame is meant for it. In the IPX/SPX world, a frame is considered directed if it has the network address and the MAC address of the destination node.

Most network managers consider *broadcast* a four-letter word. This is because a broadcast frame must be opened by every client on the segment on which the frame originated. In an IPX/SPX world, routers usually forward broadcasts to other subnets. In a larger network, broadcasts can easily consume a large chunk of the network's available bandwidth.

Multicasting is becoming popular as more applications take advantage of it. *Multicast frames* are used with applications such as chat or videoconferencing, in which everyone sees everyone else's pictures or words. Without multicasting, the conference server would need to rebroadcast every frame it sends to every person in the conference. Using multicast, the software that the online participants are using registers itself as part of a specific group address, called a *multicast address* (this address is provided to the client by the server). When the server sends out frames, it sends them out to the multicast group. All routers between the client and the server must support multicasting. The addresses that multicasting uses are Class D addresses, by the way, which range from 224.*x.y.z* through 239.*x.y.z*.

IP Addressing

You might expect to see "TCP/IP Addressing" as the heading here, but "IP Addressing" is more correct. In most circles, TCP/IP addressing and IP addressing mean the same thing, but that's not technically correct. The Internet Protocol (IP) is responsible for addressing and routing frames.

As long as you remember a few basic rules about IP addressing, you will always come out okay. So take a deep breath, and let's dive in.

First, an IP address is a 32-bit binary number. Remember, that is the way your computer sees it. So that we can more easily read and work with this number, we break it into four 8-bit chunks, called *octets*:

```
11001100 10111011 00101110 00001100
```

This is a valid IP address as far as your computer is concerned. Kind of difficult to read, isn't it? But if we break the 32 bits in to four octets and then convert these octets to decimal, suddenly it is not so difficult to read, though still a little difficult to remember. In decimal, the address is:

```
204.187.46.12
```

This notation is also called *dotted-decimal*.

IP addresses are broken into two parts: the network address and the host address. You can tell which part of the address is the network address and which part of the address is the host address based on the class of the address (at least until we get into subnetting).

IP ADDRESS CLASSES

IP addresses are categorized in five classes. Each class's address has certain rules that govern its use and certain characteristics that make it recognizable as part of a specific class.

Class A Addresses

Class A networks are by far the largest of the network classes. With almost 17 million hosts per network, these networks can accommodate the largest organizations in the world, such as the U.S. government, Hewlett Packard, and IBM (and Novell). No more Class A networks are available. Class A addresses have the following characteristics:

- Begin with 1.0.0.0 and go through 127.0.0.0
- 126 possible networks (127.0.0.0 is reserved)
- 16,777,216 hosts per network
- Default subnet mask is 255.0.0.0
- First octet reserved for the network number
- Second, third, and fourth octets indicate the host ID

Class B Addresses

Class B networks are also quite large, with the capacity of more than 16,000 hosts per network. Class B networks are used by large organizations or divisions of giant corporations. All Class B addresses are assigned. Here are the Class B address characteristics:

- Begin with 128.0.0.0 and go through 191.255.0.0
- 16,384 possible networks
- 65,534 hosts per network
- Default subnet mask is 255.255.0.0
- First and second octets represent the network number
- Third and fourth octets indicate the host ID

Class C Addresses

Class C addresses are the only addresses available today, but just barely, and most companies can't even get their own Class C address anymore. These are their characteristics:

- Begin with 192.0.0.0 and go through 223.255.255.0
- 2,097,152 possible networks
- 254 hosts per network
- Default subnet mask is 255.255.255.0
- First, second, and third octets represent the network
- Fourth octet indicates the host ID

Class D Addresses

Class D addresses are not assigned to hosts, but rather are used in multicasting. They begin with 224.0.0.0 and go through 239.255.255.0.

Class E Addresses

Class E addresses are used neither for hosts nor for multicasting. They are reserved and considered experimental. They begin with 240.0.0.0.

OTHER ADDRESS RULES

Now that you know the rules for the address classes, you need to know a few other basic rules about valid and invalid addresses:

◆ No octet is ever larger than 255.

◆ Network address 0.*x.y.z* is invalid.

◆ Network addresses 224.*x.y.z* and above are invalid.

◆ The network address 127.*x.y.z* is reserved and is never used.

◆ A host address cannot end in zeros.

◆ A host address cannot end in 255.

The following are some examples of invalid addresses. The octet that makes the address invalid is in boldface.

```
0.107.210.89
225.47.42.23
213.79.186.0
147.201.34.255
127.0.67.197
```

In addition, you need to remember the following:

◆ An address that ends in zero refers to the network itself.

◆ An address that ends in 255 refers to that network's broadcast address.

◆ The address 127.0.0.1 does not represent a specific host; network 127 is reserved for diagnostic functions and is sometimes called a *loopback address* (the address loops back to the same system).

◆ The address 0.0.0.0 is a special address and is referred to as the *default route*. You will see this address when working on a router or a routing table.

NOTE   *In the good old days, when we just used IPX/SPX on our networks, the only network addresses we needed to worry about were the network addresses on the servers (and maybe third-party routers). IPX/SPX host addressing uses the media access control (MAC) address of the computer's network interface card.*

Okay, so is this all there is to an IP address? Well, basically yes, but things do get a little stickier. Let's say that you need to convert your existing 300-node IPX/SPX network to be part of your corporate TCP/IP. What type of address will work? Can you use a Class C address? No, a Class C address can accommodate only 254 hosts.

Through an amazing stroke of luck, you work for an organization that has the Class B network address 191.180.0.0. Remember, the 0.0 in the host octets refer to "this network." This Class B address will give you a single network with 65,534 hosts. You have some room to grow, for sure.

But wait, you look at your network diagram and realize that you actually have two segments on your network, separated by a router. You really need two networks. What are the chances that you are going to be able to get a second Class B network? None, since all Class B addresses are now allocated. What if you could break that single Class B network into two smaller networks? You can! The key is something called a *subnet mask*.

Subnet Masks

Up until now, IP addressing has not been too hard, right? Remember a few basic rules about which numbers you can use and which numbers you can't use, and you're ready to go. The subnet mask is always the tricky part. If you manage a network of more than a single subnet, you're going to need to work with subnet masks.

Of all the problems in networking, TCP/IP subnet design and numbering are the worst. NetWare folks new to TCP/IP feel stupid when trying to understand subnets and subnet masks for the first time. Don't feel stupid; feel normal. Some of the brightest network gurus I know struggled with TCP/IP addressing and subnet masking.

WHY USE SUBNETS?

Subnetting allows a complex local network to be seen as a single network from the outside. You might want to divide one network into two or more smaller networks for any of the following reasons:

- You need to connect multiple media, for example, Token Ring and Ethernet segments or remote networks.

- You want to reduce congestion. More nodes per network mean more traffic. Segmenting the network keeps local traffic local and reduces overall congestion.

- You want to isolate networks for troubleshooting. Using several smaller networks greatly reduces the chance that a single failure somewhere can take down the entire network.

- You want to optimize your IP address space. Dividing a Class A or B address over smaller subnetworks makes efficient use of your available network addresses.

Each subnetwork behaves as if it were independent. An IP router is used to connect the two subnetworks. Routing between nodes on different subnetworks remains transparent to the users. Routing tables, maintained by each node or router, shield the users from the details.

How Do Subnet Masks Work?

The subnet mask allows hosts on an IP network to determine whether a destination host is on the local network segment or on a remote network. If the destination host is on a remote network, the source host sends the frame to a router to be forwarded. The subnet mask does this by identifying which part of the IP address represents the network and which part identifies the host. Let's look at an address and its default subnet mask:

```
Network Address: 191.180.0.0
Subnet Mask:     255.255.0.0
```

This is a standard Class B network address. The first two octets represent the network, and the second two octets represent the host. As I mentioned, a computer sees an IP address as a 32-bit binary number, not as the dotted-decimal format we see above.

The computer also sees the subnet mask in binary. The subnet mask tells the computer that every 1 in the subnet mask is part of the network address. Here are our network address and subnet mask in binary:

```
Address: 10111111 10110100 00000000 00000000
Mask:    11111111 11111111 00000000 00000000
```

The default subnet mask indicates that all the bits in the last two octets can be used for hosts.

Now let's complicate matters just a little. You actually have two networks of 150 hosts each, rather than one large network of 300 hosts, so you can't use a single network number. You actually need two. Using a subnet mask, you can break your large network into smaller pieces.

Let's use a subnet mask of 255.255.255.0 for this Class B address and see what we come up with. First, here it is again in binary:

```
Address: 10111111 10110100 00000000 00000000
Mask:    11111111 11111111 11111111 00000000
```

This tells us that all bits in the third octet can be used for network numbers (or subnets). This gives us 254 possible combinations of subnet numbers with 254 hosts on each subnet.

So 191.180.1.0 is a subnet, 191.180.2.0 is another subnet, 191.180.3.0 is another subnet—all the way up to 191.180.254.0, which is the last subnet. Some hosts and routers will let you use 191.180.0.0 and 191.180.255.0 as valid subnets, but not all.

NOTE   When we start working with subnets, we need to revise one of the IP host address rules that I gave you earlier. The rule said that an IP host address couldn't be all 0s or all 255s. The real rule is that an IP host address cannot be all 0s or all 1s. Remember to think about it in binary. That is the way that the computer sees it. Host addresses with all zeros refer to the network address, and host addresses with all ones refer to the network's broadcast address.

There, that wasn't too bad, was it? We broke our single large Class B network into 254 smaller networks. But, as with everything, there is always a more complicated side. In the above example, we used the entire third octet to represent the subnet ID. What if we required more than 254 hosts per subnet? Our example gave us a maximum of 254 hosts per network.

CUSTOM SUBNET MASKS

We can use a custom subnet mask to define how much of the IP address is for the network and how much is for the host address. Let's go back to our 191.180.0.0 example. Let's say we need four networks with 500 hosts on each network. We need to select a subnet mask that produces this many networks and this many hosts per network.

Here is a shortcut that I use to calculate the required subnet mask. First, take the number of subnets you require, in our case, four. Convert this number to a binary number. Four would be 100 in binary. How many ones and zeros did that take to represent in binary? Three, correct? Write out three ones. That gives you 111. Fill this number out to eight places with zeros, and you get 11100000. Convert this 1110000 number to decimal, which gives you 224. The subnet mask will be 255.255.224.0. All of the first two octets represent the network number, and the first three bits of the third octet represent the network. The next five bits of the third octet and all eight bits of the fourth octet represent host IDs.

How many possible networks does this give us? Well, if the first three bits of the third octet can form network numbers, it would give us two to the third power minus two, or six possible network numbers. Why subtract the two? Not all hosts and routers support subnet numbers using all zeros or all ones.

How many hosts per network does this give us? Five bits from the third and eight bits from the fourth can be combined to form host addresses. That is 13 bits total. Two to the power of 13 gives us 8192 less two, or 8190 possible hosts. We subtract the two because the host ID still can't be all zeros or all ones.

What complicates custom subnet masking is that, because we humans read IP addresses in decimal, it isn't easy to recognize which portion of the IP address is the host portion and which portion is the network portion. In our example, we got six networks. Table 11.5 shows the binary combinations for subnet numbers in the third octet and the resulting decimal subnet numbers.

TABLE 11.5: IP NETWORK NUMBERS USING AN IP NETWORK NUMBER OF 191.180.0.0 AND A SUBNET MASK OF 255.255.224.0

THIRD OCTET IN BINARY	RESULTING NETWORK NUMBER
000 00000	Possibly invalid (subnet is all zeros)
001 00000	191.180.32.0
010 00000	191.180.64.0
011 00000	191.180.92.0
100 00000	191.180.128.0
101 00000	191.180.160.0
110 00000	191.180.192.0
111 00000	Possibly invalid (subnet is all ones)

Now we have six subnets. If all the hosts and routers on our network support a subnet number with all zeros or all ones, we actually have eight subnets. Most newer TCP/IP software for hosts and routers do support a subnet number with all zeros and all ones, but if you're not sure, consult your software or router vendor.

We now need to determine the valid host addresses for each subnet. Table 11.6 shows one of the subnets and its valid IP host addresses. The subnet is 191.180.32.0, and the subnet mask is 255.255.224.0. We will skip all combinations of the host addresses for the obvious reasons (there are 8190 of them).

TABLE 11.6: IP ADDRESSES WITH A CUSTOM SUBNET MASK

ADDRESS IN BINARY	ADDRESS IN DECIMAL
10111111 10110100 00100000 00000000	191.180.32.0 (Network)
10111111 10110100 00100000 00000001	191.180.32.1
10111111 10110100 00100000 00000010	191.180.32.2
10111111 10110100 00100000 00000011	191.180.32.3
Continue incrementing addresses	
10111111 10110100 00100000 11111111	191.180.32.255
10111111 10110100 00100001 00000000	191.180.33.0
10111111 10110100 00100001 00000001	191.180.33.1
Continue incrementing addresses	
10111111 10110100 00111111 11111101	191.180.63.253
10111111 10110100 00111111 11111110	191.180.63.254
10111111 10110100 00111111 11111111	191.180.63.255 (Broadcast)

TIP   After years of trying to fake subnet addressing, I finally did the research and came up with exactly which subnet masks go with which network addresses. The reason these network numbers work is the subject of an entirely separate book. The best freely available information that I've seen on TCP/IP subnetting is on 3Com's Web site (www.3com.com). Look for the white paper "Understanding IP Addressing: Everything You Ever Wanted to Know." Be warned: It's involved and often complicated, but it's great. If you want more information, here are two books you might want to include in your personal library: TCP/IP Illustrated, Volume I: The Protocols, by W. Richard Stevens (Addison Wesley); and TCP/IP Network Administration, by Craig Hunt (O'Reilly & Associates).

IPv6 (a.k.a. IPng)

When IP addressing was developed in the 1970s, no one ever dreamed that we would come close to running out of IP addresses, nor did anyone estimate the massive growth of the Internet. The Internet has grown exponentially, and we are close to exhausting our supply of available IP addresses. For several years now, the IETF has been working on solutions to this problem.

The current IP addressing scheme is known as *IPv4*, or IP version 4. It uses 32-bit addresses and, if used perfectly, would provide about 3.6 billion hosts. But IP addresses are used nowhere near perfectly. In fact, a tremendous number of IP network addresses have been allocated and never used. Therefore, the IETF has implemented several measures to help prevent waste of IP addresses, including Classless Inter-Domain Routing (CIDR), which I'll discuss later in this chapter.

The IETF is also working on a long-term solution to the IP address shortage. Since the early 1990s, there have been a number of proposals and efforts for addressing limitations and expanding the IP version, including the following:

◆ TCP and UDP with Bigger Addresses (TUBA)

◆ Common Architecture for the Internet (CATNIP)

◆ Simple Internet Protocol Plus (SIPP)

IP Next Generation (IPng), or *IP version 6* (IPv6), is actually a compilation of many proposals, specifications, and efforts to expand IPv4. IPv6 provides several improvements:

◆ Expanded IP addressing and routing

◆ Better options support and a simplified IP header

◆ Support for time-dependent traffic (such as video)

◆ Improved security and privacy features

◆ Support for IP mobility

An IPv6 address is 128 bits! This is 4 billion times 4 billion addresses or, if you just have to know, 340,282,366,920,938,463,463,374,607,431,768,211,456 possible host addresses. IPv6 addresses are broken into 16 octets and written in hexadecimal as eight octet pairs separated by colons (you don't want to see this in binary, trust me). Here's an example of a valid IPv6 address:

```
4A3F:AE67:F240:56C4:3409:AE52:440F:1403
```

Clearly, this is a big change for TCP/IP and Internet users, but the change will be gradual. It will first be implemented on the Internet backbone and then on the larger Internet service providers (ISPs). It will be years before this change affects our own networks. (For more information on IPv6, see RFC 1883.)

IP Routing

Routing is another topic that you could dedicate your life to. Cisco Systems, the world's largest provider of routers, for example, offers weeks of training on internetworking and routing. Simply put, a *router* takes frames that are sent to it and makes a decision about where to forward the frame. Unlike a bridge or a switch, a router understands the protocols that it is routing. All versions of NetWare since version 3 are capable of acting as an IP router.

When an IP host gets ready to send a frame to another host, it examines the destination host's IP address and compares it with its own IP address and subnet mask. If the IP address is on a remote network, the frame is sent to the router, and the router decides how to route the frame.

A routing protocol's job is to allow a router to inform other routers about routes that it is aware of. It does this by either broadcasting or multicasting, depending on the routing protocol. An interior routing protocol is used within an autonomous system. Basically, an interior routing protocol allows routers within your private internetwork to share routing and network information. NetWare 6 supports two major *interior routing protocols*: RIP (Routing Information Protocol) and OSPF (Open Shortest Path First).

RIP

RIP was originally developed at Xerox, as were many common technology gadgets, including Ethernet, the GUI, and the mouse. And you thought all they made was photocopiers. But I digress.

The RIP version implemented for TCP/IP networks is similar to the RIP version used by IPX/SPX on NetWare servers since the beginning of time. RIP is easy to configure and works fine on smaller networks, but has problems on networks of more than 16 hops. The hop count is incremented by one each time an IP datagram crosses a router. RIP starts taking a long time to update routers within the internetwork because it works on the basis of broadcasts. If a new network is added or a route becomes unavailable on the network, the routers farther away may not learn about this change for several minutes. This problem is called *slow convergence*.

In addition, a router using RIP selects routes with the lowest hop count as the ideal route. This is because RIP is a *distance-vector* routing protocol. The number of hops does not always indicate the fastest route. (For more information about RIP, see RFC 1058.)

OSPF

For larger networks, you should consider using the *OSPF* routing protocol, which is a *link-state* routing protocol. It favors faster routes, updates other routers about network topology changes quickly, and reduces the possibility of routing loops.

OSPF is very different from RIP. Routers running RIP broadcast information about the network to all their neighboring routers. An OSPF router shares information with other routers about its adjacent routers only, thereby allowing other routers to build routing tables based on information that is sent to them. You can configure OSPF routers for certain areas of the network or for the entire internetwork.

Naturally, since OSPF is so much faster, more versatile, and more powerful, it is more difficult to configure. My advice: Seek professional help. (For more information about OSPF, see RFC 2178.)

Classless Inter-Domain Routing (CIDR)

To help prevent the total depletion of available IP addresses, the Internet authorities needed to come up with a way to allocate blocks of IP networks. Instead of giving out an entire Class B address to an organization that has only 1500 hosts, an ISP issues a block of addresses that could be used as Class C addresses, but that are actually part of Class B. Since all Class B addresses have been depleted, ISPs can give out a smaller chunk of the Class B that they have been allocated.

For example, instead of giving your organization the entire 186.45.0.0 Class B network, the ISP would give you 186.45.32.0, 186.45.33.0, 186.45.34.0, 186.45.35.0, 186.45.36.0, and 186.45.37.0 (where you would use a subnet mask of 255.255.255.0). These look like six Class C addresses that give you 254 hosts per network, don't they? Well, from your perspective, they are six Class C addresses. ISPs call this *supernetting*.

Here's the problem that then arises: The ISP that gave you those addresses must put four separate entries in its routing table on its routers in order to route network traffic to you. In a short time, these routing tables would become huge. The routers that service the Internet backbone would need hundreds of megabytes of RAM to accommodate all the Class C addresses on the Internet (remember, there are more than 2,000,000 of them!). The amount of work required to maintain these addresses across hundreds of routers would be prohibitive.

To prevent overwhelming the Internet's routers, *Classless Inter-Domain Routing* (CIDR, pronounced "cider") was developed. Before CIDR, we relied exclusively on the IP address to tell us the class of the IP address. Now, we use the subnet mask for this purpose. Essentially, IP networks are no longer bound by the class definitions. The subnet mask can also have fewer bits in it than the default subnet mask.

This technique allows an ISP to collapse all entries for a network into one single router entry. The ISP can put a single entry in its routing tables that would look something like 186.45.32.0, with a subnet mask of 255.255.248.0. If you work in a network operations center supporting hundreds of subnets or if you work for an ISP, you will probably see CIDR in use. Otherwise, people are just going to use the term in your presence and assume you know what they are talking about. (CIDR is defined in RFCs 1518 and 1519; see RFC 1338 for more information on supernetting.)

IP Address Convention

When you get an IP network address from your provider, typically you also receive the subnet mask you are supposed to use, for example, 198.69.176.0/ 255.255.255.0. This has long been standard notation for IP network addresses and subnet masks.

Several years back, I supervised the connection of a small network to the Internet. The ISP wanted to know how many hosts required IP addresses and what growth I expected. I said that I needed 28 hosts on this network. They e-mailed me the IP network address that I was to use. I was expecting something like the example above. What I got was 202.18.193.64 / 27. Does this make sense to you? At the time, it surely did not make sense to me.

This is a newer convention for writing the IP network address and subnet mask. The 27 identifies how many 1 bits are in the subnet mask. A subnet mask with 27 bits looks like this (I have put spaces on each octet boundary):

    11111111 11111111 11111111 11100000

The subnet mask in decimal is 255.255.255.224, which is what I was used to seeing. This mask tells me that only the last five bits of the IP address are available for hosts. This gives me two to the fifth possible IP host addresses, or 32 possible hosts, but I need to subtract two, since I can't use the combination of all zeros and all ones. My first available host was 208.18.193.65, and my last host was 208.18.193.94.

Planning an IP Network

Planning a TCP/IP network is more complicated than planning an IPX/SPX network, because you need to worry about not only unique network numbers but also unique host numbers. In addition, when planning each subnet, you must make sure you have enough IP host addresses to go around.

If you are lucky, someone may hand you a list of addresses to use. As long as you use those addresses, nothing goes wrong. However, it is just as likely that planning your IP internetwork will be delegated to you, the new NetWare 6 internetworking and IP guru. Whether someone is giving you your addresses or you must select your own addresses, you need to know how many hosts you have on each network.

How Many IP Host Addresses Do You Need?

Think about your existing IPX/SPX network for just a minute. How many nodes does it have? Are you sure that is all? I have plugged some rather strange things into IP and IPX/SPX networks. On an IP network, they all require an IP host address in order to communicate with the rest of the network. Here are some examples:

- ◆ File and application servers (NetWare, Windows NT, Unix)

- ◆ Clients (DOS, Windows, Macintosh, OS/2, Unix)

- ◆ Print servers (including devices such as the HP JetDirect)

- ◆ Interfaces on your routers

- ◆ Hubs, bridges, switches, UPS, and other manageable devices

Caltech has a Coke machine on the Web (check it out at rutabaga.caltech.edu/~coke/). I have also seen refrigerators, coffeepots, weather-collection devices, and a hot tub plugged into a network. Armed with this impressive list of devices, be sure you know about all the devices attached to your network. (By the way, if your network has a hot tub attached to it, I want to come work with your company.)

NOTE   *Each host on your IP network must have a unique IP host address. If you accidentally assign a host a duplicate IP address, generally both hosts get an error message, and the second host that tries to use the address does not work. However, some older systems will actually crash or stop working if they detect a duplicate address. Plan carefully, and keep notes.*

How Many Networks Do You Require?

In addition to discovering the maximum number of hosts per network, you need to ascertain how many IP networks you will need. How many IPX/SPX networks do you currently have? One of the most common mistakes people make when planning IP networks is to forget the "network" between two routers on the Internet. As you can see in Figure 11.2, three network numbers are required because of the router network and because each interface on the router must have an IP host address.

Two routers that are separated by a dial-up, an ISDN, or a leased-line circuit will require an IP network between them. This router network will require only two hosts, but it is still a separate network.

FIGURE 11.2

Three networks, two
Ethernet and one
"router"

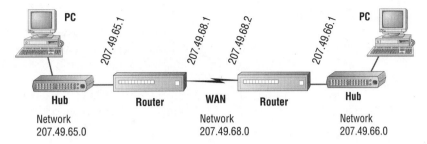

Note that each router interface has an IP address.

The router network rule is no longer hard and fast because many router vendors have proprietary software that eliminates the necessity for a router network. These are sometimes called *network-to-network* connections, but each router vendor has their own name for it.

Who Assigns Your IP Network Addresses?

Where do you go for an official IP network address? If your network is going to connect to the Internet, you must plan your address space carefully. IP network and host addresses that you use cannot be used anywhere else on the Internet. The organization that controls who gets which addresses (and also assigns domain names) is InterNIC (`www.internic.net`).

In years past, if you wanted to put your network on the Internet, you contacted InterNIC and got an allocation of IP addresses. Today, IP network addresses are allocated by ISPs. Your ISP has a block of addresses for customers. When you arrange with your ISP to connect to the Internet, have the following information at hand:

◆ The number of hosts that require an IP address

◆ The number of networks you have

◆ Your estimated growth potential

Don't expect your ISP to give you more IP addresses than you absolutely need. Remember, we are in the middle of an IP address shortage. If you can't justify the number of addresses you are requesting, don't expect to get them.

If your network is part of a larger corporate, government, or academic network, your IP address will come from "upstream." Addresses will be assigned by the head of your network.

If your IP network will connect to a larger network, you must coordinate with the "powers that be," usually the folks who are responsible for connecting your network to the other networks or providing backbone services. They may give you a block of IP addresses and expect you to handle all network and host address assignments yourself. More than likely, though, you will need to coordinate with the upstream support organization. They will assign each network on your LAN a network address, and may possibly require that you assign each specific host (client and server) a specific IP address. This approach certainly limits your flexibility, but it also leaves no room for confusion regarding IP host addresses and subnet masks.

What if you never expect to connect your network to the Internet? Then you have a *private network*.

Private Networks

Some IP networks will never connect to the Internet. These networks are defined as private by RFC 1918. If your network is private, you can assign your networks and hosts anything you want, right? Well, you can. However, RFC 1918 specifies that certain IP network addresses never be assigned to any network on the Internet. These network addresses are set aside for private use. The Internet routers will not route data to these IP addresses. RFC 1918 sets aside a single Class A network, 16 Class B networks, and 255 Class C networks. Here are the addresses:

◆ 10.0.0.0

◆ 172.16.0.0 through 172.31.0.0

◆ 192.168.0.0 through 192.168.255.0

Why should you use one of these addresses? You don't have to, but if you plan to access the Internet in the future through software such as Novell's BorderManager, a proxy server, or a network address translator, you should use network addresses that do not appear anywhere on the Internet. Besides, 10.0.0.1 for your first network device sticks in your memory better than 192.168.212.1.

BorderManager, Proxy Servers, and Network Address Translators

Network managers who would never have dreamed of connecting to the Internet even as recently as two years ago now consider Internet connectivity essential. What is driving this trend? Companies want Internet mail and Web servers. In the future, more business will be conducted over the Internet, including the exchange of orders and inventory information, as well as the buying and selling of goods and services. From the typical business perspective, the Internet is just entering the preadolescent stage of self-discovery and rebellion.

So what is so terrible about the Internet today? How about security? How about the occasional wholesale failure of a particular chunk of the Internet? Okay, the Internet does not often fail completely, but my connection grinds to an intolerably slow pace at times. Let's not ignore the fact that you may not be able to get IP addresses for every host on your network.

Security procedures are getting better. The infrastructure of the Internet continues to be upgraded (both from the reliability perspective as well as speed). Tools to monitor and restrict access to the Internet are improving. The IP address shortage will continue, but hope appears on the horizon. Most company Web sites have upgraded from brochure-ware to singing and dancing e-commerce money-grabbers.

You can use Novell's BorderManager, proxy servers, and network address translators to control what your users are accessing on the Internet and to protect your network from nefarious people on the Internet who might do your system harm.

BorderManager (released in 1997) combines several earlier products, including a DHCP (Dynamic Host Configuration Protocol) server, a DNS server, and a product that had two names: the NIAS (NetWare Internet Access Server) or the IPX/IP Gateway. BorderManager allows you to continue using IPX/SPX as your network protocol, and the BorderManager server connects to the Internet on behalf of your clients. You can restrict usage based on user, time, and the sites to which users can connect. BorderManager is tightly integrated with NDS eDirectory.

A *proxy server* acts in a similar fashion to BorderManager in that it is the only device on your network that actually has a connection to the Internet. Users from your private network connect to the Internet through the proxy server, and it connects to the Internet on their behalf.

A *network address translator* (NAT) is software (and a server) that converts internal (private) IP addresses to official IP addresses and forwards packets to the Internet. You assign a host a private IP address on the private IP network. When the host must communicate with the Internet, the NAT converts the private IP address to a public IP address as the IP datagram passes through the NAT.

Tunneling

Whether you realize it or not, tunneling happens all the time on today's networks. *Tunneling* is the process of encapsulating one protocol inside another and passing it over the network. For example, when you are communicating with a Web server, your computer is speaking IP, but the IP datagram is carrying a TCP segment (sometimes called its *payload*), and the TCP segment is carrying HTTP data.

I set up a WAN several years ago in which the routers' software supported only TCP/IP. Even if the software had supported IPX/SPX, the routers connected two offices through the Internet. The primary purpose was to give employees access to the Internet. After the network was up and running, my client asked, "Oh, by the way" (I always hate that), "how can I map a drive to the server in the other office?"

The options were to convert everyone to the newly released NetWare/IP product or to implement IPX tunneling. The client did not want to move to NetWare/IP.

My client's NetWare servers did support TCP/IP, so I loaded the TCP/IP support and loaded the IPTUNNEL.NLM, which allowed me to specify a virtual IPX network over the Internet. Clients in both offices could now see and map drives to the servers in both offices. When a client mapped a drive, the client sent IPX data to the NetWare server running IPTUNNEL. The NetWare server encapsulated the IPX data in an IP datagram and forwarded it to the NetWare server in the other office running IPTUNNEL, where the IPX data was extracted from the IP datagram and placed back on the network as an IPX frame. This really nifty feature was completely transparent to the end users, and the client thought I was a genius (I kept my mouth shut and didn't ruin the impression).

Many routing vendors, in addition to Novell, support tunneling, and you may find it useful in your bag of network tricks. However, NetWare 6 eliminates tunneling completely if you choose an all-IP network setup. Client-to-server and server-to-server communications all happen over IP, with no IPX involved.

Compatibility with Existing IPX/SPX Networks

Novell used IPX from the early beginnings of NetWare. Though proprietary, it became a de facto standard for networking. Third-party developers have written thousands of applications to work with IPX/SPX networks. Will these applications continue to function if you move to the IP protocol exclusively? Yes, your existing IPX/SPX applications will continue to work as always. Clients that have been updated to use TCP/IP only can still communicate with services that speak only IPX/SPX.

Novell recognized that it would be impossible for many networks to simply switch from one protocol to another overnight, especially given the complexity of many modern networks. These migrations must occur over time.

IPX compatibility mode is a NetWare 6 feature that allows you to gradually migrate from an IPX or a NetWare/IP network to native IP. Most applications should work just fine over IP, but a small percentage of applications may not. In these cases, the developer of the application may have attempted to access IPX/SPX directly rather than following recommended programming conventions. For this reason, the compatibility mode detects that it's necessary to use IPX services, and it encapsulates IPX in an IP frame. As time goes by, the need for compatibility mode will probably diminish because developers will clean up their applications and make them NetWare 6–friendly.

Components of IPX Compatibility Mode

IPX compatibility mode consists of three components: compatibility mode drivers, the Migration Agent, and the Bindery Agent.

COMPATIBILITY MODE DRIVERS

Compatibility mode drivers (CMDs) consist of a client component and a server component. These drivers are loaded by default but are used only if required. On a NetWare 6 server, the CMD is viewed as a network adapter. You can bind both the IP and IPX protocols to the compatibility mode adapter, and it acts like a router when IPX packets need to be sent within the server. If it is not being used, the CMD is idle and uses no resources.

When the CMD is loaded on a NetWare server with the gateway option on, it is linking IP to the IPX world. These compatibility functions are all transparent to the end user.

THE MIGRATION AND BINDERY AGENTS

The *Migration Agent* (or *Migration Gateway*) provides two translations. First, it translates IPX packets to IP (and vice versa), and second, it translates information between the two NetWare 6 naming and discovery services, Service Location Protocol (SLP) and Service Advertising Protocol (SAP). The Migration Agent connects an IPX network and an IP network; however, it is needed only if there are both IPX and IP networks.

NOTE   SLP provides service discovery, thereby replacing the service discovery function of SAP. This can eliminate large amounts of broadcast traffic found in larger NetWare networks. The SLP service provides backward compatibility for applications and services that rely on SAP discovery. SLP registers information in a database that clients can query when looking for a specific service. Services register with SLP when they are brought up, but they do not continue to register themselves, as SAP does. With SAP, the service defaulted to reregistering itself every 60 seconds. For more information about SLP, see RFC 2165.

The Migration Agent is necessary for communication between IP and IPX networks because NetWare 6 supports both natively. NetWare/IP worked differently; it encapsulated IPX frames in IP frames. All the server needed to do was de-encapsulate the frame to get IPX information back. In the NetWare 6 world, the service information must be extracted from the IP frame and retransmitted in an IPX frame in order for IP clients to communicate with IPX services. Figure 11.3 shows the Migration Agent sitting on the network between IPX and IP hosts.

FIGURE 11.3

The Migration Agent handling conversion of data between IP and IPX clients

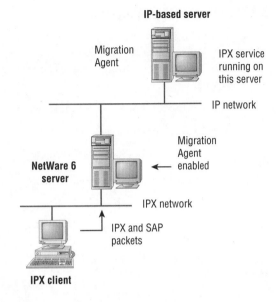

Only one Migration Agent is needed on small networks. Medium to larger networks may require servers running the Migration Agent. When planning a larger network, each LAN should have a server running the Migration Agent.

The *Bindery Agent* allows for compatibility with NetWare 2.*x* and 3.*x* bindery-based clients. This service is necessary if you still have services running on NetWare 2.*x* or 3.*x* servers or if you have applications that require Bindery Services. The Bindery Agent creates static bindery objects in NDS, so that applications that require Bindery Services think there is a bindery.

Setting Up IPX Compatibility Mode

The good news is that CMDs are loaded by default—you do not need to do anything to enable CMD on either the client or the server. However, you need to take a few additional steps to enable the Migration Agent and the Bindery Agent.

To enable the Migration Agent, load the CMD module (SCMD.NLM) with the /G option. Your network requires only a single NetWare 6 server running the Migration Agent. In a multisegment network, load the Migration Agent on any segment that has IPX clients, applications, or services.

To enable the Bindery Agent, create a new NDS Organizational Unit. For example, in the organization called SOMORITA, create a container called BINDERY. At a NetWare 6 server running the Migration Agent, set the bindery context. For the SOMORITA example, type the following:

```
SET BINDERY CONTEXT=.BINDERY.SOMORITA
```

Then load the BINDGATE.NLM. The server that runs the BINDGATE.NLM must also have a read/write replica of the partition where you created the bindery container.

To populate other NetWare 6 servers that don't have the Bindery Agent loaded, put a read/write replica of the partition that contains the bindery container on those servers, and set the bindery context as described above.

Installing TCP/IP on NetWare 6

The most significant new feature in NetWare 5 was the inclusion of "pure" IP support for NetWare clients. The support is *pure* in the sense that clients and servers no longer require an IPX encapsulation (or tunneling) to move IPX information to the server. The advantages of this for many NetWare users include the following:

◆ Consolidation to a single protocol rather than running two or more

◆ More efficient use of network bandwidth

◆ Lower support costs due to supporting only one protocol

◆ Connectivity for remote users over a wide range of systems

◆ Backward compatibility with IPX/SPX-specific applications

Novell accomplished this by modifying NCP to be independent of a specific protocol. NCPs can now use IPX/SPX, TCP, and UDP for delivery. The NetWare 6 operating system was modified to remove any dependencies on IPX. Novell also modified the NDS structure to incorporate DNS for naming of devices (and IP address resolution).

NetWare's TCP/IP Services

At the core of the NetWare TCP/IP services on a NetWare 6 server is the TCPIP.NLM. This NLM is located in the SYS:SYSTEM directory. Other NetWare TCP/IP components include the following:

◆ Native IP support for NetWare (NWIP.NLM)

◆ DNS name server software (NAMED.NLM)

◆ DHCP server software (DHCPSRVR.NLM)

◆ SNMP NLM file (SNMP.NLM)

◆ SNMP Event Logger NLM file (SNMPLOG.NLM)

◆ TCP/IP Console NLM file (TCPCON.NLM)

◆ IP Static Route Configuration NLM file (IPCONFIG.NLM)

◆ ICMP Echo NLM files (PING.NLM and TPING.NLM), for diagnostics

◆ BOOTP Forwarder NLM file (BOOTPFWD.NLM)

◆ IP Filter Support (IPFLT.NLM)

Unix gurus will find familiar files such as HOSTS, NETWORKS, PROTOCOL, and SERVICES in the SYS:ETC directory. Sample IP data files are installed in the SYS:ETC\SAMPLES directory.

NetWare TCP/IP supports both Novell and third-party applications. Third-party products are supported through the TLI (Transport Layer Interface) used by the AT&T-developed STREAMS or the BSD 4.3 Sockets interface. Figure 11.4 shows how the software pieces plug together.

FIGURE 11.4

TCP/IP support in
NetWare

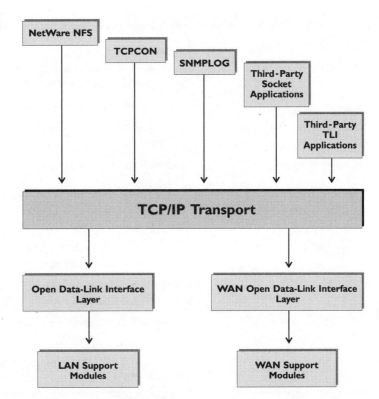

Since the Unix and Internet folks in your organization will want to know the depth of NetWare's TCP/IP support, let's go down the list of services. Table 11.7 summarizes NetWare's TCP/IP support services.

TABLE 11.7: NETWARE'S TCP/IP SUPPORT SERVICES

SERVICE	FUNCTION
TCP/IP application support	Provides a transport interface for higher-level network services, such as NetWare NFS. Both TCP and UDP transport services are provided.
Native IP client support	NetWare clients can now communicate with NetWare 6 servers using the IP protocol exclusively.
DNS	Provides a database of computer names and their IP addresses. Allows a client to look up the IP address of any system on the network.
DHCP	Enables the NetWare server to assign IP addresses, subnet masks, and router addresses to clients automatically when the client boots.
SLP	Provides clients the ability to locate services on an IP network (similar to SAP).

continued on next page

TABLE 11.7: NetWare's TCP/IP Support Services *(continued)*

SERVICE	FUNCTION
FTP Server	Allows the NetWare server to interact with FTP clients for file transfer (now administered through the NetWare Web Manager).
TFTP	Allows TFTP clients to transfer files to and from the NetWare server.
Network Information Services	A distributed database of user and group information that is used specifically by NetWare NFS Services.
Network File System	Allows Unix clients to access NetWare volumes.
Unix to NetWare printing	Provides bidirectional printing support for Unix and NetWare users.
NetWare Enterprise Web Server	Allows a NetWare server to support a full-featured Web server, with all the bells and whistles you need.
IP routing	Forwards IP traffic from one network to another. Novell's TCP/IP software supports link-state, distance-vector, and static routing.
RIP	Uses the distance-vector algorithm for routing operations and decisions. Most TCP/IP networks still use RIP.
OSPF	Uses the link-state algorithm for routing operations and decisions.
Static routing	Manually configures routes, dictating the routers used to reach remote destinations. Static routing may be used exclusively or in addition to dynamic routing protocols.
Router discovery	Used by routers to advertise their presence on a network, similar to the way NetWare servers use SAP to announce themselves.
Variable subnetworks	NetWare 4.1x and up allow different-sized subnetworks through support of variable-length subnet masks.
Directed broadcast	A broadcast sent to all hosts on a particular IP network or subnetwork; often used to find or announce services.
BOOTP forwarding	Used by some systems to discover their IP address and sometimes load other information, such as their operating system. This is similar to the Get Nearest Server packet sent by NetWare clients as they attempt to log in. The questioning host broadcasts a BOOTP request; routers may either block these requests or pass them to the appropriate network if the BOOTP server is on another network. Four BOOTP servers can be referenced.
TCP/IP network management with SNMP	SNMP is the most popular TCP/IP management protocol. All the Unix-based management systems use SNMP as their primary protocol.
Internetworking Configuration Utility (INETCFG)	INETCFG is the menu-driven utility we've seen when setting up AppleTalk. INETCFG replaces the LOAD and BIND commands in the AUTOEXEC.NCF file and provides interactive menus for configuration.

continued on next page

TABLE 11.7: NETWARE'S TCP/IP SUPPORT SERVICES *(continued)*

SERVICE	FUNCTION
XConsole	A way to connect to a server console via Telnet. Quite useful in years past, this has been replaced by newer methods. If you like VT100 terminals, however, load REMOTE.NLM *<password>*, then XCONSOLE.NLM to enable the NetWare Telnet server. Some servers also require the TELNETD.NLM to support XConsole.
Permanent connections	Links to other systems can be configured during initialization to stay up continually. If the line drops, the connection is automatically retried for reconnection.

In the old days (NetWare 3.*x*), you needed to load many of the NLMs yourself. Don't let the list in Table 11.7 make you nervous. Most of your work will be done within INETCFG, and you won't need to worry about loading the right NLM at the right time. The TCP/IP system modules will take care of that themselves.

NOTE   *If you were a NetWare 4.11/IntranetWare user, you will recall that DNS was installed differently. For more information about DNS support in NetWare 6, see Chapter 12.*

While earlier NetWare installations gave you a choice about TCP/IP installation, NetWare 6 pretty much installs TCP/IP no matter what. While we could officially delete the following sections, much of this information helps with troubleshooting and later configuration. So we'll keep all this, but remember that you're stuck with TCP/IP on your NetWare network today. This isn't at all bad, which is a good thing since you're stuck.

Configuring TCP/IP

When configuring TCP/IP on a NetWare server, you must use the INETCFG.NLM rather than doing it the old-fashioned way and putting all your LOAD statements directly in the AUTOEXEC.NCF. The INETCFG.NLM provides you with an easy interface for configuring TCP/IP protocol support and binding IP to the network interfaces.

Before you start, have the following information at hand:

◆   The server's IP address and subnet mask

◆   The IP address of the server's default gateway (router)

◆   The IP address of the nearest DNS name server (optional)

If you have used the INETCFG utility to configure IPX/SPX in the past, the utility has already loaded all your networking LOAD and BIND statements from the AUTOEXEC.NCF file and put them in its own database.

If this is the first time you have run INETCFG, it will prompt you to transfer the LAN driver, protocol, and remote-access commands to the configuration files maintained by INTECFG. You must answer Yes to this question. All networking-related commands in the AUTOEXEC.NCF file will be transferred to INETCFG, and they will be commented out (with a # symbol) in your original AUTOEXEC.NCF.

Figure 11.5 shows the main menu of the INETCFG program, which includes the following options:

Boards   Configures new and existing network interfaces and WAN boards.

Network Interfaces   Configures individual interfaces for WAN boards only. LAN cards do not need to have this choice configured.

WAN Call Directory   Configures WAN connections. This option is not required for LAN boards.

Protocols   Configures protocols such as IPX/SPX, TCP/IP, and AppleTalk.

Bindings   Configures bindings to associate protocols with specific network interfaces.

Manage Configuration   Configures SNMP parameters and allows you to configure Remote Console access and Telnet access.

View Configuration   Displays the console commands that will be executed whenever the server boots or reinitializes.

Reinitialize System   Reloads the LAN and WAN configuration.

FIGURE 11.5

Internetworking
Configuration
(INETCFG)
main menu

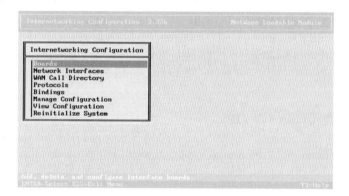

CONFIGURING PROTOCOLS

IN A HURRY 11.1: ENABLING TCP/IP SUPPORT ON NETWARE 6

1.   At the server console, type **LOAD INETCFG**.

2.   Choose Protocols ➢ TCP/IP.

3.   Set the TCP/IP Status selection to Enabled.

4.   Exit and save your changes.

For purposes of configuring TCP/IP support, we will be concerned primarily with two menu choices from the INETCFG main menu: Protocols and Bindings. Choose Protocols ➢ TCP/IP to open the TCP/IP Protocol Configuration screen, as shown in Figure 11.6.

FIGURE 11.6

The TCP/IP Proto-
col Configuration
screen

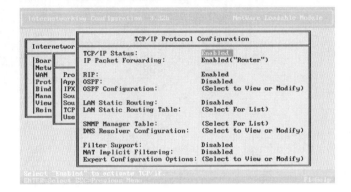

First, enable TCP/IP by changing the TCP/IP Status selection to Enabled. For a standard configuration, you do not need to change the remaining items. If you are using your NetWare server to route
IP packets, see the "Using NetWare 6 for TCP/IP Routing" section, later in this chapter.

BINDING TCP/IP TO NETWORK INTERFACES

IN A HURRY 11.2: BIND TCP/IP TO A NETWORK INTERFACE

1. From the INETCFG menu, choose Bindings.

2. Press Insert to create a new binding, and select TCP/IP.

3. In the Bind To box, select A Network Interface, and then select the Network interface to which you want
to bind TCP/IP.

4. Enter the IP address and subnet mask.

5. Exit and save the configuration.

6. Reinitialize the system or reboot for your bindings to take effect.

Your next task is to bind TCP/IP support to your network interfaces. Choosing Bindings displays
the Protocol to Interface/Group Bindings list. If you are modifying an existing binding, highlight it
and press Enter. Otherwise, press Insert to display a list of supported protocols, and then choose
TCP/IP. In the Bind To box, select A Network Interface, highlight the board to which you want to
bind TCP/IP, and press Enter to open the Binding TCP/IP to a LAN Interface screen, as shown in
Figure 11.7.

FIGURE 11.7

Binding TCP/IP
to a board

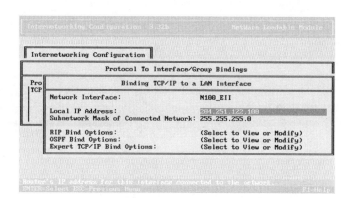

Enter the IP address and the subnet mask for this specific adapter. NetWare will automatically fill in the subnet mask value, but in hex, so it will show FF.FF.FF.0. This will freak out Unix people, so change it to 255.255.255.0 and make it match the rest of the world.

Unless you are using your NetWare servers as routers, you will not need to configure the RIP and OSPF Bind Options. The Expert TCP/IP Bind Options allow you to change your frame type, but unless your network is a really special case, you should leave it at Ethernet_II. Except in very special cases, none of the Expert options should be changed.

CONFIGURING TCP/IP MANUALLY

Okay, so we have just configured TCP/IP using INETCFG, and in my humble opinion, it is much easier to use this utility than to try to remember all of the console commands to be entered in AUTOEXEC.NCF. However, for those of you who are console command people, here is a sample of what we just configured:

```
LOAD TCPIP
LOAD N100 NAME=N100_EII FRAME=ETHERNET_II SLOT=7
BIND IP TO N100_EII ARP=YES, MASK=255.255.255.0 ADDRESS=204.251.122.100
```

Monitoring TCP/IP

To monitor the TCP/IP protocols, Novell provides the TCPCON.NLM, which allows you to view information about protocols, routing, the routing table, and SNMP traps that have been logged. Figure 11.8 shows the TCPCON main menu.

The information on the main screen lets you view how many IP datagrams and TCP segments have been received by this particular NetWare server. If the server is configured as an IP router, you can also view the IP datagrams that have been routed (IP Forwarded).

From the main menu, you have six choices:

SNMP Access Configuration   View and change the current SNMP access configuration.

Protocol Information   View information about the EGP, ICMP, IP, OSPF, TCP, and UDP protocols, including current TCP and UDP connections.

IP Routing Table   View the current IP routing table.

Statistics View protocol statistics for EGP, ICMP, IP, OSPF, TCP, and UDP protocols.

Interfaces View statistics for the LAN, WAN, and logical network interfaces.

Display Local Traps View the local SNMP log if the SNMPLOG.NLM is loaded.

FIGURE 11.8

TCP/IP Console
(TCPCON)

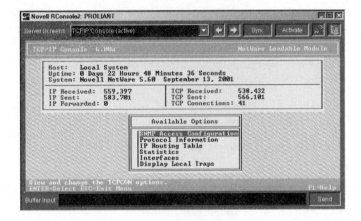

Enabling Remote Console Support via Telnet

XConsole Server allows NetWare administrators to gain access to the NetWare server console from X Window systems or through Telnet clients. The move to browser-based administration tools reduces the need for this, but you may still find it handy.

To enable Telnet and XConsole support, use the UNICON utility. From the UNICON utility, choose Start/Stop Services, press the Insert key, and choose XConsole Server.

TIP *In order for the TELNETD (Telnet Daemon) to work properly, the* REMOTE.NLM *must also be loaded.*

Using NetWare 6 for TCP/IP Routing

If your NetWare server has more than one network interface card, it is possible to enable IP routing between the networks. In addition, you can choose from several routing protocols. The server should have two network interfaces configured, and both should have valid IP addresses and subnet masks configured.

To enable routing, use the INETCFG utility. Choose Protocols ➢ TCP/IP, and set IP Packet Forwarding to Enabled ("Router"). Figure 11.6, earlier in this chapter, shows this menu.

On each network segment, configure the client to use the IP address of the server as the default gateway.

Using NetWare 6 to Build an IP Tunnel

Earlier, I mentioned that you can move IPX/SPX packets through an IP-only network by creating an IP tunnel. Figure 11.9 shows how this works. This is different from the old method of faking a

TCP/IP packet, since NetWare now uses real TCP/IP packets and bundles IPX inside them when necessary.

FIGURE 11.9

IPX/SPX tunneled through an IP-only network

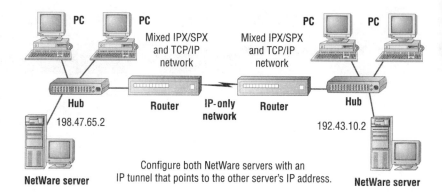

To do this, you must enable IP tunneling on both NetWare servers. In INETCFG, choose Protocols ➤ IPX ➤ Tunnel IPX Through IP ➤ Enabled. Then provide the IP address of the server on the other side of the IP network.

Packets destined for the other IPX network will automatically be encapsulated in an IP packet and forwarded to the other server, where it is de-encapsulated. This is not designed for large throughput scenarios, because it places an additional load on the servers that are handling the tunneling operation.

Configuring TCP/IP Printing Support

NetWare 6 includes bidirectional printing capabilities with Unix and TCP/IP printers. Users on Unix systems, or any system that supports the LPD (Line Printer Daemon) protocol, can print to a NetWare print queue, and NetWare print queues can be redirected to Unix-based printers or IP network printer interfaces such as the HP JetDirect card.

UNIX-TO-NETWARE PRINTING

The Unix-to-NetWare print service takes jobs that were sent to the NetWare server from Unix or other LPD protocol clients and places them in the appropriate NetWare print queue. A NetWare print server then takes over and forwards the job to the appropriate printing device.

Printers that are to be accessible for Unix users should be configured in the UNICON utility. The first step is to make the printer available to accept LPD print jobs. This process is called *exporting*. When you export a printer, you can make it available to all hosts or to only a few hosts.

NETWARE-TO-TCP/IP PRINTING

NetWare-to-TCP/IP printing takes a print job that has been sent to a NetWare print queue and directs it to a TCP/IP printer (essentially and interchangeably, a Unix printer). Before configuring NetWare-to-Unix printing, be sure to complete the items on this checklist:

◆ Create at least one NetWare print server that will serve as the print server for jobs being sent to the Unix side.

♦ Create the NetWare printers that represent Unix printers.

♦ Create the NetWare print queues that you want redirected to the Unix system.

♦ If you are printing to a Unix host, have the Unix administrator create a user account with permissions to print to your desired printing devices. Create this account in the UNICON users list.

♦ In the SYS:ETC\HOSTS file, enter the IP address and hostname of the Unix system to which you are planning to print.

Using LDAP

LDAP provides the rules and commands for accessing information such as usernames, addresses, phone numbers, and e-mail addresses stored in an X.500-compatible directory service such as NDS eDirectory. (X.500, by the way, is a series of *recommendations* from the ITU on building a directory service.)

Today, many larger organizations may have several directories. NDS eDirectory is one of these. Others include the mainframe user accounts database, your e-mail system's directory, the Unix account database, your company's phone directory (which is probably in hard copy), the human resources database, and other sources of information about people and users within your company. The vision of the future is to incorporate all these directories into a single database of information. Computer systems can use this directory when authenticating users, users can use it when looking up a phone number or mailing address, and people from outside your organization can use it to look up your e-mail address.

LDAP moves one step in that direction by providing a standard way to query and update directory databases. LDAP was originally developed as a front-end for accessing X.500 directory services. X.500 defines its own Directory Access Protocol (DAP) for clients to use when contacting directory servers. DAP is a heavyweight protocol that runs over a full OSI stack and requires a significant amount of computing resources. LDAP runs directly over TCP and provides most of the functionality of DAP at a much lower computing cost.

LDAP uses TCP port 389 for normal communications and TCP port 636 for secure communications using SSL (Secure Sockets Layer). (For more information about LDAP, visit `http://developer .novell.com/research/topical/ldap.htm`.)

Configuring LDAP Support

During installation of NetWare 6, you are presented with a list of choices, including LDAP Services and NDS Catalog Services. By default, LDAP Services and NDS Catalog Services are installed.

LDAP is configured and ready to run with the default settings as soon as it is installed. No real customization is necessary; however, you may want to configure some custom options. When LDAP is installed, some additional objects appear in the NDS directory, as shown in Figure 11.10. These objects will be located in the same context as the server on which LDAP is installed:

LDAP Server object Stores configuration for a specific NDS server. This object's configuration includes searching limits, TCP port assignments, log file options, server console screen logging options, and LDAP catalog options.

LDAP Group object   Stores configuration data that can be applied to a single server or to a group of servers. The object's configuration includes defining which portion of the NDS tree can be searched, defining a list of servers this configuration covers, specifying access control, and defining LDAP to NDS attribute and class maps.

LDAP Catalog object   Defines the catalog database that is stored in the directory. The catalog is a flat-file database that contains a snapshot of the NDS database.

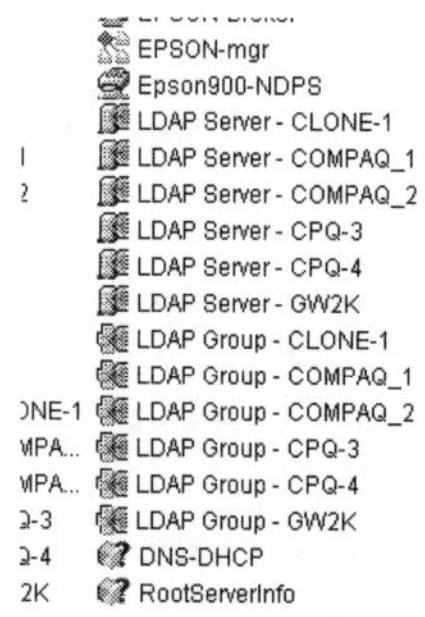

FIGURE 11.10

LDAP objects from
the directory tree

When LDAP is installed, you'll also find the User Mailbox tab on the property page for a User object. This tab allows you to enter e-mail addresses for a user. This address will be displayed when an LDAP client queries information about this user.

Setting Up LDAP Security

By default, all users can connect anonymously and query the directory using the [Public] object. They can see any object to which the [Public] object has access. To tighten security, you can create an LDAP proxy user to be the only one with permissions to the objects, containers, and properties that you want people to view using LDAP.

To create an LDAP proxy user and assign the LDAP Group object using the ConsoleOne utility, follow these steps:

1. In NDS, create a user called, for example, LDAP_Proxy_User.

2. Set this user so that it cannot change its own password and do not assign it a password.

3. Give the LDAP_Proxy_User the Browse object rights to the containers that you want anonymous users to be able to access. Also give this user Read and Compare rights to all properties (or only to the properties you want visible).

4. Select the LDAP Group object, and assign LDAP_Proxy_User to be the proxy user in the Proxy User Name field on the General tab (LDAP Group ➢ General).

Querying the NDS Directory Using an LDAP Client

To query the NetWare 6 NDS database, you need an LDAP client. Both Netscape Communicator and Microsoft Internet Explorer provide an address book utility that allows you to query an LDAP directory service. Here is the procedure for configuring the Microsoft Windows 98 Address Book to query an LDAP directory:

1. Launch Address Book.

2. Choose Tools ➤ Accounts.

3. Click the Add button.

4. Provide the LDAP server name or IP address and click Next.

5. Click the radio button saying Yes to check addresses using the new directory service.

6. Click Finish.

7. Optionally, click the Properties command button to open the Properties page and change the Directory Service Account name.

To perform a directory query, click the Address Book icon, and then click Find People. This displays the Find People dialog box. Click the Advanced tab and choose the directory service you want to search in the Look in pull-down menu, as shown in Figure 11.11. Enter the name you want to search for, click Add, and then click Find Now. Once the names are displayed, pick the one you wish to use.

The Netscape 4.7 Communicator software does a better job of integrating LDAP services, but since just about everyone has Windows of some kind or another, I used the Windows 98 Address Book example. Play with your other address book–type clients (like e-mail programs), and see how easy it is to pull information from your NDS LDAP interface.

FIGURE 11.11

The Microsoft Windows 98 Address Book, which is an LDAP client, querying NDS

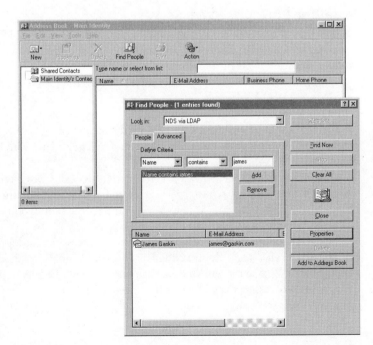

Using the NetWare Enterprise Web Server

Novonyx, a joint venture between Netscape and Novell whose primary goal was to rework Netscape servers to run on NetWare while leveraging NDS, died before moving any real products to market. Luckily, the NetWare 6 design group used what Novonyx created before being folded back into Novell.

The FastTrack Web Server for NetWare showed up first and shipped with NetWare 4.11/IntranetWare. The NetWare Enterprise Web Server, a full-featured Web server that runs as an NLM under NetWare, started shipping with NetWare 5.1 and continues with NetWare 6. Here are some of its features:

- Enterprise Web Server is administered via the Web. You can configure it from any place on the network that has a Web browser.

- Enterprise Web Server supports standard HTML documents as well as standard application-development environments such as Perl, CGI scripting, JavaScript, and NetBasic Scripting.

- Enterprise Web Server supports SSL and allows administrators to restrict which pages users can access. Security is integrated with NDS eDirectory.

Here, we'll go over installing and configuring the NetWare Enterprise Web Server, and then take a quick look at some of the things it can do. The installation and quick setup may make you believe that NetWare Enterprise Web Server is a snap to deploy, but don't be fooled. Setting up and managing Web servers are big topics, covered in many books (some as big as this one).

Installing Enterprise Web Server

The easiest way to install the Enterprise Web Server comes during NetWare installation. But if you skipped it, or forgot the settings of administration port numbers and can't get into your Web server now, reinstallation won't hurt too much.

Adding the Enterprise Web Server is a definite upgrade for NetWare 6 over NetWare 5, which had the FastTrack Web Server. Think of the FastTrack Server as a departmental server, with the Enterprise Web Server able to handle, well, the enterprise. Along with e-commerce, simple Web publishing from any user, and clustering software for the servers themselves, the Enterprise Web Server can become an unstoppable mega-server (see my adventures later with a borrowed Compaq Cluster Server system).

Put the Operating System CD in the server's CD-ROM drive or otherwise make it available somewhere on the network. Switch to the X Server graphical console on the server and run the Install program. The Install program appears when you click the Novell button in about the same place that Microsoft puts the Start button on Windows systems.

The Install program will assume that you want to access the A: floppy drive, as if anything today can be installed via a single floppy. Old habits die hard, I suppose. Click the Resource browse button and highlight NW6 in the left window, assuming you have the CD mounted in the server's CD-ROM drive. If you're accessing the CD across the network, you'll need to search and find it because I can't see it from here; you're on your own.

Once you highlight NW6 on the left side of the Install screen, `PRODUCTS.NI` will pop up on the right side. That's the file holding all the NetWare product details on the CD. Highlight that file, click OK, and wait for a bit (ConsoleOne is slow even on the killer Compaq dual and quad processor servers you'll see later). The Component screen appears to let you check the NetWare Enterprise Web Server box once more, and you're off.

You'll go right to the NDS Authentication Login screen. Security counts, as always, and you must prove that you're authorized to add software to the server. Provide an appropriate username (Admin works best) and the password, and keep going.

You must configure the port settings for client browsers to connect to the Web server. The default port for normal use is 80, as in `www.novell.com:80` (the 80 is assumed, since it's the Web default). The secure port connection offered is 443. Change it if you know what you're doing and why you're changing it, or accept the default.

You may keep your current Web server settings or overwrite them. If you're reinstalling because you forgot something earlier, it's probably safest to overwrite everything and get a clean set of configuration files.

Get out your paper and pencil, because the Web Manager port number (2200 came up every time here) is the port number you must remember in order to configure the Web server later. Change this port if you wish, but write it down before you forget, or you'll need to reinstall all over again. The paranoid among us will change this port every month or so to keep security a bit higher and foil any hackers who guessed the access port number earlier.

Once again, you're offered a summary screen showing the Enterprise Web Server and Server Manager, which gets pulled in automatically. Accept the listing, and choose Customize if you wish some extra masochism and aggravation. Otherwise, click Finish and get some coffee while more than 125MB of files slide from your CD to your server disk.

Here's what you need to know and/or remember for installation:

◆ The server's IP address and Web server name, such as `www.gaskin.com`.

◆ A TCP port number for the Web server. The default is port 80, which you should probably keep.

◆ A TCP port number for the administration server. This number is randomly assigned for you, but you can change it. You will use this port number to connect to the server for administration tasks by typing it at the end of the URL, such as `www.gaskin.com:2200`.

Once you confirm the settings, the software creates new directories under SYS:NOVONYX\ SUITESPOT, which contain the Web server software, scripts, and default content directories.

Configuring the Enterprise Web Server

To configure and fine-tune your NetWare Enterprise Web Server, you must access it through a Web browser using the Admin port that you either chose or accepted as the default during installation. Figure 11.12 shows the main menu for NetWare Enterprise Web Server through NetWare Web Manager. From this menu, you can configure the server. (This menu replaces the default Netscape Administration opening screen shown in NetWare 5.1.) This keeps the theme of Web Manager across all NetWare-based applications, so it's a good change.

FIGURE 11.12

The opening administration screen for an Enterprise Web Server through Web Manager

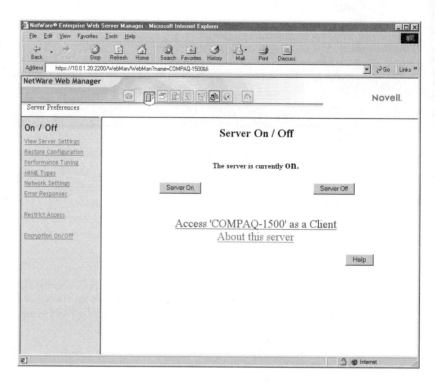

SETTING SERVER PREFERENCES

The Server Preferences section of the NetWare Web Manager page has eight top-level menu choices:

On/Off   Shuts down the server, displays server and NetWare information, and accesses server's Welcome to NetWare 6 page.

View Server Settings   Lets you view or change the Enterprise Web Server's network settings.

Restore Configuration   Rolls back server configuration to earlier settings.

Performance Tuning   Sets DNS and cache parameters for better response.

MIME Types   Sets global MIME types.

Network Settings   Lets you configure the server name, port number, IP address, and names of mail and news servers.

Error Responses   Lets you customize error responses by error number.

Restrict Access   Limits access by server directory.

Encryption On/Off   Sets encryption details, including the Server Certificate object.

ACCESSING WEB MANAGER OPTIONS

Across the top of the Web Manager sit nine new icons. The one to the far left, the house, means Home and will return you to the primary Web Manager pick screen. That one doesn't apply to the Enterprise Web Server, but the rest of them do:

Server Preferences Displays the Server Preferences section, with the options described in the previous section.

Programs Displays the Programs section, with options for defining CGI directories and file types, and activating server-side JavaScript capabilities.

Server Status Displays the Server Status section, with options for viewing the access log and error log, monitoring current activity, changing log preferences, and generating usage reports.

Styles Displays the Styles section with options for creating, editing, and assigning styles.

Content Management Displays the Content Management section, with options for defining the default document directory and additional document directories. It allows you to set up URL forwarding, define virtual hardware and software servers, define document footers, and define proxy server cache values.

Users and Groups Displays the Users and Groups section, where you can choose which directory service to use (defaults to NDS) and control users, groups, and some objects.

WebDAV Turns on or off Web Distributed Authoring and Versioning, an easy, collaborative access for NetWare users to place, access, edit, and manage files on remote Web servers.

Apply Changes Saves and applies your configuration changes.

Starting and Shutting Down the Web Server

The NetWare Enterprise Web Server should automatically load when the NetWare server it is running on is restarted. You should shut down the server from the administrative interface, but you can also execute an `.NCF` file (`NSWEBDN.NCF`) from the server console prompt that will shut down the server.

To restart a server that has been offline, use `NSWEB.NCF`.

Locating Web Documents

The default location for HTML and graphics files on a Netscape/NetWare server is SYS: NOVONYX/SUITESPOT/DOCS. With NetWare 5.1, the DOCS directory sat underneath a directory named for the server, but not with NetWare 6. You may want to put these files in another location, such as SYS:WEBDOCS or something else, depending on which users you want to give access to update the Web content.

To change the default document directory, use the Web Manager. Select the server name, click the Content Management button, and then select Primary Document Directory.

Using Virtual Servers

The virtual server feature allows you to host multiple Web sites on a single server. You configure two options from within the Content Management option of the Web Manager:

Software Virtual Server   Allows you to specify URL names and a document directory associated with that URL. All URLs have the same IP address. The Web server scans the incoming URL request for defined domain names and returns the appropriate content for that Web site.

Hardware Virtual Server   Allows the administrator to assign different Web sites to different IP addresses. Each IP address is then assigned its own document directory. This option is more reliable than the software option, since the browser that is connecting must be able to forward the fully qualified domain name of the site it is requesting, and some older browsers cannot do this.

Using the NetWare FTP Server

NetWare 6 includes an FTP Server from NetWare 4.11 and the (stupidly named) IntranetWare product release. Incredibly, the first NetWare FTP server could accept requests from any FTP client (such as Unix users), convert the request into IPX format, and fetch files from NetWare servers not even running TCP/IP, much less any FTP server software.

But since FTP doesn't come with a fancy graphical interface and support e-commerce by verifying credit cards online, few people care about it anymore. But the ones who do will be pleased to see how Novell has made their FTP life easier with NetWare 6.

Traditionally a command-line product with arcane server configuration details, Novell's new FTP Server now sits happily within the NetWare Enterprise Web Server management utilities. The Net-Ware FTP Server link, the fourth one down on the NetWare Web Manager page, leads to all the FTP controls. You'll find the icons and commands quite similar to what we covered for the Web server.

The FTP Server screen has only two icons across the top: Server Preferences and Server Status. In the Server Preferences section, the User Settings option shows something ill-considered (in my opinion): The default home directory is SYS:\PUBLIC. Change that. Check out Figure 11.13 to see some of the other FTP Server settings and the look of the administration screens.

The Netscape engineers did a good job laying all this out for the Novell/Novonyx engineers to grab, didn't they? It's all clear and straightforward, just like FTP itself.

FTP Server software can help you do some necessary yet unglamorous things, especially when used with automatic file transfers between offices. Short script files can take a report's output, initiate an FTP session back to headquarters, and squirt the file over there, without a single person touching the keyboard—or even being in the building for that matter.

Try some FTP. You might be amazed how nice a clean, unpretentious utility feels after years of browser bloat.

Securing Your TCP/IP Networks

If you're going to access the Internet, security must become a larger concern. I rarely read about hacker attacks on NetWare servers. Without exception, these few attacks required access to the Net-Ware server's console or Admin-level access. In short, it was an inside job; or at the very least, someone got inside to do the hacking.

FIGURE 11.13

FTP Server User
Settings

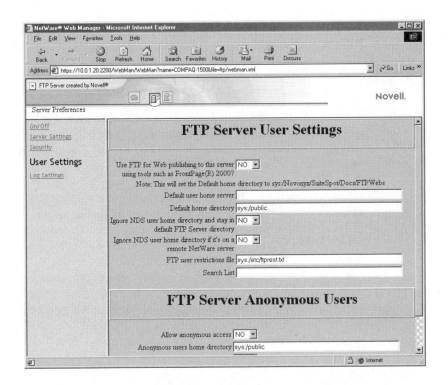

Once you connect your NetWare servers to an IP network that is connected to the Internet, you'll lose peace of mind. Don't get me wrong—NetWare is fairly secure. But no operating system that is connected to the outside world is 100 percent secure. And every system connected to the Internet has multiple server applications running that administrators may not even remember, such as Telnet or TFTP servers.

Even if a hacker cannot gain access to your data, your servers may be subject to *Denial of Service* (DoS) attacks. This type of attack crashes or otherwise renders a specific network service unusable. DoS attacks have plagued the Unix community for years and are becoming prevalent in the Windows world as well. No matter how much forethought Novell's design engineers put into NetWare 6, people are looking for chinks in the armor. Sooner or later, they will find one, or at least that's what you tell your boss in order to get the money you need for protection.

Furthermore, what is preventing your Windows clients from installing their own TCP/IP services, such as Web and FTP servers? Microsoft makes installation of these services the default on some systems, without a decent security warning. When client workstations start offering TCP/IP services, they become vulnerable to attacks as well.

NOTE   *I have read several security studies that state that between 50 and 80 percent of all attacks and data loss come from inside the network. This is something to keep in mind when planning your security infrastructure.*

So how do you protect your network from outside evil? Well, if your network has "official" IP addresses—that is, addresses that were assigned by an Internet authority—the answer is to use a firewall.

Do You Need a Firewall?

If the answer to the following two questions is yes, you need a firewall:

◆ Is your network connected to the Internet and using official IP addresses?

◆ Is your organization the least bit concerned about the security and reliability of your network?

If the answer to the second question is no, you have nothing to worry about (except keeping your resume ready, because your management is obviously bonkers). If you answered yes (and I hope you did), it is time to start planning some type of firewall. One of the functions of Novell's BorderManager product is a firewall, by the way.

Exactly defining a firewall is difficult, since many solutions from many vendors are on the market today. A *firewall* is a system (hardware and software) that allows the administrator to restrict the types of data coming into the network and the types of data going out. It serves as a filter of sorts.

Work with me here for a minute. Let's say a firewall acts like the U.S. Customs Service does at international airports; you are the IP datagram and the United States is the network. You are allowed to bring only certain things into the country, and you can take only certain things out of the country. When you pass through customs, an inspector checks to make sure that what you are carrying is not on the restricted list. There may even be restrictions on which countries you can arrive from. Try coming into the United States carrying Cuban cigars or coming into the United States from Afghanistan and see how much attention you generate.

A simple firewall does this job by examining three parts of the packet (IP datagram):

◆ The source address. Where did this packet come from? Is this source address permitted to talk to my network?

◆ The destination address. Where is the packet going? Is the computer for which this packet is destined allowed to receive data from outside? Is that computer allowed to receive this particular type of data?

◆ The port number. What application type generated this packet? Is this type of application permitted to come into or leave this network?

You might enable all network computers to use the World Wide Web but allow only specific computers to use FTP. Furthermore, you might restrict access to www.amazon-chicks.com or www.dudes-from-baywatch.com. The firewall enforces these restrictions for you.

How Can You Protect Your Network?

Along with installing a firewall, you can take many steps to protect your network. The list is long, but here is a start:

◆ For all operating systems you use, follow a security list or bug-fix list.

◆ Do not install unnecessary services on your servers. If a NetWare server handles only file and print services, do not install Web services or an FTP server on it.

◆ Restrict your users' computers so that users cannot install additional services on their desktops.

◆ Use strong passwords, consisting of uppercase and lowercase letters, numbers, and special characters. Ensure that users do not put their passwords on a sticky note next to their monitor (yes, some users still do that).

◆ Watch for DoS attacks. These manifest themselves as computers mysteriously crashing or not letting people log in or attach.

◆ Beware of the "ping of death" (ping is discussed in more detail in the next section). A malevolent person can use ping functions to send a ping request that is larger than 65,536 bytes (the default size is 64 bytes). This can cause some systems to crash or hang.

Troubleshooting TCP/IP

On networks that are as complicated IP networks, you will occasionally have a problem that requires debugging. The TCP/IP suite includes some excellent tools for diagnosing problems.

What Is My IP Configuration?

First things first. Be sure that your IP host address, subnet mask, default gateway, and DNS addresses are exactly what they are supposed to be. Each platform has a utility that allows you to verify this:

◆ On NetWare servers, use the console CONFIG command.

◆ On Windows 95/98 computers, use the WINIPCFG graphical utility.

◆ On Windows NT/2000 Workstations, use the command-line utility IPCONFIG.

If these utilities do not report a correct IP address, fix this before you continue. Possible problems include incorrect addresses or the software not being installed.

Can I Communicate with Other IP Hosts?

The universal utility for testing whether you can communicate with other IP hosts is PING (Packet Internet Grouper). PING uses the ICMP protocol to send a diagnostics message (an echo) to another host. When the other host receives the echo message, it sends an echo reply to the sending host.

On Windows 95/98 and Windows NT Workstation hosts, PING is a command-line utility. At the console of the NetWare server, it is an NLM with a C-Worthy interface. To properly locate a communications problem, follow these steps:

1. Ping your internal software address (or loopback address). Type **PING 127.0.0.1**.

2. Ping your own IP address. Type **PING 198.67.201.157**.

3. Ping another host on your own network.

4. Ping your default gateway. Type **PING 198.67.201.1**.

5. Ping a host on another network. Type **PING 137.15.225.18**.

If you cannot ping your internal software address or your own IP address, reinstall your software. If you cannot ping another host on your own network, check your IP address and subnet mask. If you cannot ping hosts on other networks, confirm that your default gateway works and the IP address listed on your workstation matches.

Checking Your Default Route

Your client computers have a routing table, even if they have only a single network interface card. Windows 95/98 and Windows NT/2000 Workstation computers have a command utility called ROUTE.EXE that allows you to display and manipulate your computer's routing table. To display the routing table, type **ROUTE PRINT**. Here is sample output for a host whose IP address is 10.1.1.50:

Network Address	Netmask	Gateway Address	Interface	Metric
10.1.1.0	255.255.255.0	10.1.1.50	10.1.1.50	1
10.1.1.50	255.255.255.255	127.0.0.1	127.0.0.1	1
10.255.255.255	255.255.255.255	10.1.1.50	10.1.1.50	1
127.0.0.0	255.0.0.0	127.0.0.1	127.0.0.1	1
224.0.0.0	224.0.0.0	10.1.1.50	10.1.1.50	1
255.255.255.255	255.255.255.255	10.1.1.50	10.1.1.50	1
0.0.0.0	0.0.0.0	10.1.1.1	10.1.1.50	1

How do you read this stuff? Well, starting at the top is the network address 10.1.1.0. This indicates a route to get to this network through interface 10.1.1.50. The address 0.0.0.0 is the route for all addresses that do not have a route in the routing table; if there is no default route, send the packet to 10.1.1.1, which is the default gateway (or router).

Other TCP/IP Diagnostic Utilities

One of my personal favorites for diagnosing problems is the Trace Route utility, or TRACERT.EXE. Here is some sample output:

```
C:\>tracert www.novell.com
Tracing route to www.novell.com [137.65.2.11]
over a maximum of 30 hops:
  1   181 ms   180 ms   160 ms  hnl-nimitz1.inix.com [207.175.193.5]
  2   160 ms   180 ms   180 ms  medusa.inix.com [207.175.193.1]
  3   150 ms   160 ms   181 ms  GW1.HAW2.Alter.Net [137.39.3.138]
  4   200 ms   241 ms   230 ms  ATM2.SFO1.Alter.Net [137.39.74.101]
  5   240 ms   230 ms   251 ms  ATM3.SC1.ALTER.NET [146.188.146.150]
  6   220 ms   241 ms   240 ms  ATM2.PA.ALTER.NET [146.188.146.121]
  7   220 ms   230 ms   221 ms  paix.bbnplanet.net [137.39.250.246]
  8   241 ms   220 ms   240 ms  su-bfr.bbnplanet.net [4.0.1.49]
  9   241 ms   230 ms   240 ms  paloalto.bbnplanet.net [4.0.2.214]
 10   330 ms   241 ms   250 ms  131.119.26.94
 11   260 ms   240 ms   241 ms  Cache.Provo.Novell.COM [137.65.2.11]
Trace complete.
```

Why Novell Moved to TCP/IP

With NetWare 6, NetWare means IP for all intents and purposes today. Let's consider once again the advantages and disadvantages of TCP/IP, and see why Novell chose to migrate to TCP/IP.

Here are the advantages:

◆ TCP/IP has more system support across more systems than any other protocol.

◆ TCP/IP is a great WAN protocol. It's the de facto remote networking protocol suite—the only protocol suite allowed on the Internet.

◆ TCP/IP is small and fast on PCs. Low-overhead Windows protocol stacks are getting faster than ever.

Of course, there are still a couple of disadvantages:

◆ Installation remains painful. Planning and addressing issues and the configuration necessary on every client make TCP/IP much more difficult to administer than IPX/SPX.

◆ Network routing is complicated. Configuration must be done carefully to avoid problems.

If your organization already invested in TCP/IP networking and you were tasked with making the clients communicate with TCP/IP hosts, you have a good argument for using TCP/IP for your servers as well. Reducing the complexity of your network overall is a noteworthy goal. Networks that support both IPX and TCP/IP are inherently more complex to support than a TCP/IP-only network.

Once IPX is eliminated from the network, you will have also eliminated broadcasts associated with RIP and SAP, which can only help your WAN performance.

IPX/SPX didn't lose market share because the protocol couldn't keep up. It lost because the world moved to TCP/IP. If you have any NetWare networks still running on IPX/SPX, make plans to convert. Today, networking means TCP/IP.

Chapter 12

DHCP and DNS Support

THE ADMINISTRATOR OF A TCP/IP network faces two challenges: assigning IP addresses and managing computer names. As you saw in Chapter 11, IP addressing is no trivial matter. It requires adequate planning, both before and after deploying an IP-based network. If an IP address, subnet mask, or default gateway address is entered incorrectly, the host computer does not communicate properly with the rest of the network. Without an accurate database of computer names and their associated IP addresses, network users cannot communicate with hosts throughout the network (meaning no Internet access, either).

IP management tasks for a running network include IP address distribution and management, as well as name resolution management. You need to assign IP addresses and other IP host address parameters, such as the subnet mask, default gateway, and domain name server addresses. You also need to keep track of which computer has which IP host address and make sure none are duplicated. To manage name resolution, you must assign friendly names (sometimes called *hostnames* or *aliases*) to computers on your network, so that their IP addresses can be found easily. Hostname resolution is a critical part of a network's operation.

NetWare 6 includes two features that help network managers with IP addressing and name database issues: Domain Name System (DNS) and Dynamic Host Configuration Protocol (DHCP). DNS and DHCP are actually two completely separate technologies, but they complement each other. DNS is a hierarchical namespace, similar to the NDS database, that allows a network administrator to register computer names. DHCP is a protocol that dynamically assigns IP addresses to hosts. This chapter covers the following topics:

◆ Understanding DNS

◆ Understanding DHCP

◆ NetWare 6 DNS and DHCP support

◆ Setting up and managing NetWare DNS

◆ Setting up and managing NetWare DHCP

◆ Troubleshooting common DNS and DHCP problems

Understanding DNS

IP addresses are not easy to remember. Even in the early days of the Internet, some method had to be devised so that we mere mortals would not need to memorize the IP addresses of all the computers we used. It is much easier for us to remember names.

By 1984, the Internet (then it was still called the ARPANET) had only about 1000 hosts. To make it easier for people to find a specific computer's IP host address, the Stanford Research Institute's Network Information Center (SRI-NIC) in Menlo Park, California, maintained a simple text file called the HOSTS.TXT file. Each line of the file had an IP host address and the host's friendly name, or alias. The file was updated with the newest computers that were connected to the Internet once or twice a week. Other sites on the ARPANET periodically downloaded the latest version of this file. This was a simple solution to a simple problem.

However, it became apparent that the Internet was growing at a rate that would prohibit the use of the HOSTS.TXT file in the future. It had the following problems:

◆ The file was getting large, and the larger it grew, the longer it took to search for a specific computer.

◆ As more and more hosts were added to the Internet, the file needed to be updated several times daily.

◆ SRI-NIC was a single point of failure, since the organization maintained the only master copy of the file.

These and other problems led the governing body of the ARPANET to come up with a better solution for providing hostname-to-IP-host-address resolution (hostname resolution)—a distributed, hierarchical namespace, or DNS. This namespace has a root and branches to different parts of the namespace in a way similar to NDS. Each branch of the DNS tree is similar to an NDS Organizational Unit (OU).

No single DNS name server contains the entire database; rather, the database is distributed to many name servers throughout the Internet to provide better performance as well as fault tolerance. This works in much the same way replicas of an NDS partition work, allowing pieces of the NDS database to reside on many NetWare servers.

Once a host is registered with DNS, other hosts can query DNS, using the host's name, and DNS will return the IP address of the host in question. If you have worked on a TCP/IP network or the Internet, you have used DNS, and you may not even be aware of it. When you launch your Web browser and type www.novell.com in the address box, your client is using DNS to look up the IP host address of Novell's Web server. Without DNS, you would need to remember the IP addresses of every IP-based computer you connect to.

Who should use DNS? In a word, everyone. Connecting to other hosts by entering their IP address rather than a friendly name drives users crazy. Whether you run a private network or you connect to the Internet, DNS remains a critical network service.

Components of DNS

DNS consists of three distinct components: resolvers, name servers, and a domain namespace. Each component has its specific purpose. DNS is not only a service, but also an Application-layer protocol.

RESOLVERS AND NAME SERVERS

Any host on an IP network that may need to look up a domain name is called a *resolver*. The resolver sends queries to the second component of DNS, the *name server.* The resolver first attempts to contact the name server using UDP (User Datagram Protocol). If the network does not reliably deliver the data using UDP, the resolver resorts to TCP for guaranteed packet delivery.

The resolver and the name server are analogous to the telephone company's directory assistance service (411). The resolver sends a request to the name server to look up a phone number (IP address) based on a name. The name server has access to a database of every IP address in the world. The name server searches through these "phone books" and returns to the client the requested number. In the case of DNS, the phone book that the name server uses is the domain namespace itself.

THE DOMAIN NAMESPACE

The third component of DNS is the *domain namespace.* This is the actual database of computer names and their IP addresses. To allow for this database to be broken up and placed in many locations, a hierarchical structure was created. At the top of this structure is the *root.* Off the root are *top-level domains*, which set up the initial distribution of this database. Some of the top-level domains are listed in Table 12.1. There are scores of other top-level domains that I don't mention here, and arguments about more domains (`.biz` and the like) appear in the news regularly.

TABLE 12.1: SOME TOP-LEVEL DOMAIN NAMES

DOMAIN	DOMAIN FUNCTION
`.arpa`	Special reverse lookup domain
`.ca`	Canada
`.com`	Commercial organizations
`.edu`	Educational organizations
`.gb`	Great Britain
`.gov`	U.S. government
`.jp`	Japan
`.mil`	U.S. military
`.net`	Internet service providers
`.org`	Nonprofit organizations
`.us`	United States

The responsibility for each of these top-level domains can be delegated to a separate entity, and, more important, the database can be distributed to many name servers. The database is distributed partly by servers called *root servers*. The InterNIC maintains 13 root servers, distributed around the world, that are the authorities for these top-level domains. Specifically, these root servers know how to contact the name servers for each of the top-level domains. All name servers have a list of the root servers' names and IP addresses.

Each top-level domain has name servers that are the authority for the particular domain. These name servers are also distributed throughout the world and are typically operated by governments. The name servers for the .gov, .com, .edu, .net, .arpa, and .com top-level domains are operated by the InterNIC; the .mil domain is maintained by the U.S. military agency, DISA (Defense Information System Agency).

Registering Your Domain

To become part of the Internet domain namespace, you must register your domain name with the authority that controls your particular top-level domain. Once this is done, you will be given a *second-level domain*, such as novell.com.

The agency or authority that is registering your domain name needs to know a few things. For example, when you register a commercial domain within the United States, you must provide the InterNIC or authorized registrar with the following information:

◆ The domain name you are requesting

◆ Technical, administrative, and billing contact information

◆ The IP host address of at least two name servers that will be the authority for your domain name

The IP addresses of two name servers are important; one serves as a backup in case the other is unavailable. These name servers will contain your host information. For example, if you register somorita.com (a fictitious company) as a domain name, the .com name server only knows the IP address for a name server that will be the authority for your domain somorita.com. Your name server actually contains all the host data for your domain, such as www.somorita.com, ftp.somorita.com, mail.somorita.com, and so on.

If your organization is already registered as a second-level domain, but you want further divisions of your domain, you need to register with whomever maintains the name server for your organization. This person can create subdomains of your second-level domain, such as pipeline.somorita.com or sunset.somorita.com. The name server that is the authority for these subdomains does not need to have the same name server as the second-level domain.

When using DNS, unfortunately, you cannot just use a name such as www or server1, because hundreds of thousands of people would want to use those names. Instead, each layer of the hierarchical name space has a name. To refer to a host, we call it www.somorita.com rather than just www. This is a *fully qualified domain name* (FQDN). Hundreds of thousands or millions of computers may be called www, but there will be only one www.somorita.com.

Domains versus Zones

A *zone of authority* is the portion of the domain namespace for which a particular name server is responsible. Figure 12.1 illustrates a second-level domain (somorita.com) with a name server that is the authority for that particular zone. There are two additional subdomains, design.somorita.com and testing.somorita.com. Both use a different name server as their authority. Server DUKE's zone of authority is for the somorita .com zone; it also has name server records that point to the subdomains. Server RELL's zone of authority is the design.somorita.com zone.

FIGURE 12.1

An example of a second-level domain with two subdomains and name servers in each

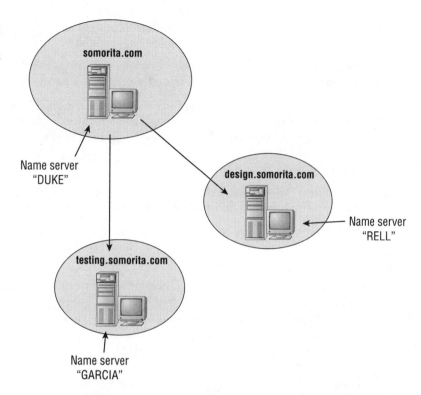

Dividing your domain across multiple subdomains, name servers, and zones of authority can help improve performance, provide better fault tolerance, and distribute management functions. For example, in Figure 12.1, the person assigned to administer the hosts in the `design.somorita.com` domain may be different from the person who administers `somorita.com`.

In a traditional DNS world, the actual domain data, such as the hostnames and their associated IP addresses, are stored in a text file called a *zone file* or a *zone database file.*

DNS zones and objects are represented in the NDS hierarchy as NDS objects, but their position in the NDS hierarchy has no relation to their true DNS hierarchy. You must use the DNS/DHCP Management Console to see the DNS hierarchy correctly, as you'll learn in the "Setting up and managing NetWare DNS" section later in this chapter.

Types of Name Servers

In a traditional DNS environment (Unix), you can install and configure five types of DNS servers:

Primary   Contains the master copy of a particular zone file. When changes are made, they are made to this server.

Secondary   The administrator can configure a server to copy a zone file from another server. This is called a *zone transfer*. The secondary name server keeps a copy of the zone file in case it is needed or for decentralization of the data. A machine can be a secondary name server for one zone file and a primary name server for another.

Master   Any server that has a zone file copied from it can be considered a master server. This can be a primary name server or a secondary name server.

Caching-Only   Contains no zone files, but users still query it for hostnames. When it learns a hostname and address, it caches this information for a set amount of time.

Forwarder   When configuring a name server, you can define other servers as forwarder servers. When your name server cannot resolve a name, it checks with one of the forwarder servers rather than going through a standard name resolution and checking with the root servers.

Name Server Queries

I mentioned that no single name server in DNS contains a copy of the entire domain namespace database. Two types of DNS name resolution make this possible:

Recursive   Resolvers (clients) do recursive queries. When doing a recursive query, the resolver says to the name server, "Give me the IP address of this hostname. If you don't know the answer, go find out. Don't delegate the task to someone else."

Iterative   Name servers typically do iterative queries. As Figure 12.2 shows, if the name server cannot answer the query from its own zone databases or cache, it consults with a root server, which refers the query to a top-level server, which in turn refers it to a second-level domain server. Finally, the name server reaches an authority for the zone in question. That authoritative server returns the answer to the originating name server, and that server returns the answer to the resolver.

FIGURE 12.2

Recursive and iterative queries

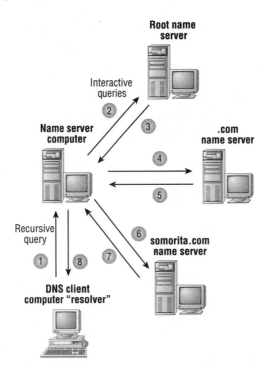

Essentially, all queries are done on the basis of referrals. When the client in Figure 12.2 queries the name server for `www.somorita.com` in step 1, the client's name server goes out to the root in step 2 and asks for a name server to handle queries about the `.com` domain. In step 3, the root name server responds with a referral to a `.com` domain name server, and the client's name server contacts that `.com` server in step 4, getting the response in step 5. In step 6, the client's name server contacts `somorita.com`'s name server and asks for the IP address of `www.somorita.com`. The name server responds in step 7, and the client's name server responds to the client in step 8 with an IP address for the requested host.

NOTE   *Essentially, DNS operates on the basis of referrals. The client asks for a name to be resolved. If the client's name server does not know the answer, it checks with a series of other servers. The client thinks that its name server is a genius and knows everything, but really, the client's name server just knows the right places to look.*

When the client server gets an answer from the name server at Somorita, it puts that information in its own *cache*. The name server at Somorita determines how long that entry can remain in the cache. You don't want to keep entries in the cache too long because the IP address of the host in question could change. The administrator of the server controls how long you can keep an entry in the cache by setting a *time to live* (TTL) for entries on the Somorita name server. When an entry's TTL expires, a name server that holds that entry in the cache must discard it. If that particular entry is requested again, the name server must once again resolve the name.

Inverse Queries/Reverse Lookups

A special-purpose domain has been set aside in the DNS namespace called the `in-addr.arpa` zone. This zone is used for *inverse queries*, which allow a client to look up a FQDN based on a known IP address. It is common for mail servers to deny access to IP addresses that do not have a registered domain name. Some application servers, such as FTP servers, will not allow a client to log in unless it has a registered FQDN, and the application server can do an inverse query using the client's IP address.

Though this looks like smoke and mirrors, it's really simple. The secret is that each IP network address is registered with the InterNIC, as are domain names. Typically, the ISP that supplies your IP addresses will either take care of this or will assist you in creating the proper zones.

Remember, domain names get more specific when reading from right to left, and IP addresses get more specific when reading from left to right. For this reason, the domain names in a *reverse query file* are reversed. For example, if you have IP address 207.188.53.0 for your network, your inverse query zone will be `53.188.207.in-addr.arpa`. Notice that the IP address is reversed and that `in-addr.arpa` is added to the right side of the address.

NOTE   *When you create zones in the NetWare 6 DNS/DHCP Management Console, you must remember that you also need to create reverse lookup zones for any IP addresses you are managing. You'll learn how to do this in the "Creating Reverse Lookup Zones" section later in this chapter.*

Reverse lookup domain names vary, depending on the class of the IP address in use:

- The Class A network 12.0.0.0 will have a reverse lookup zone named `12.in.addr.arpa`.

- The Class B network 178.79.0.0 will have a reverse lookup zone named `79.178.in-addr.arpa`.

- The Class C network 247.187.99.0 will have a reverse lookup zone named `99.187.247.in-addr.arpa`.

DNS Resource Records

A *resource record* (RR) is an entry in a zone file that identifies a certain attribute about a host, a domain, or an IP address. There are many types of resource records, but let's limit the discussion here to the major types:

A   The Address record, which is also called a *host* record, identifies the IP address for a specific hostname.

CNAME   The Canonical Name record, also known as an *alias*, allows you to associate several names with a single host.

PTR   The Pointer record is used in reverse lookup files to point to the name of a host based on its IP address. Its format is the IP host address in reverse, and it also contains the hostname associated with that IP address.

MX   The Mail Exchanger record lets mail servers know which servers in your domain will accept or transfer mail. If you are going to exchange SMTP mail, you must have an MX record.

SOA   The Start of Authority record is usually the first line (and usually spills over onto several lines) of a zone database file. It identifies the name server name and the name server contact, and includes information about caching and zone transfers. This record is required.

NS   The Name Server record lists name servers that service this particular zone file. This list keeps a list of all secondary servers that transfer a copy of this zone file.

NOTE   *The NetWare 6 DNS/DHCP Management Console creates the NS and SOA records for you automatically. You won't always have this luxury on other systems.*

Traditional DNS Files

A traditional DNS runs on Unix systems. The zone data are placed in text files, and these files are usually located in the /etc directory. You will find four types of files on a Unix system that is running a name server:

Zone database   Also called just *zone files*, these files contain the host information as well as other data, such as name servers and mail exchanges for a specific domain.

Reverse lookup   To handle inverse queries successfully, you will need a reverse lookup file for each IP network address whose hosts you manage. These files contain the PTR records that provide IP-address-to-hostname lookups.

Cache   The cache contains a listing of the names and the IP addresses of the root servers. This file is not normally updated often.

Boot   Found on BIND (Berkeley Internet Named Daemon) DNS servers, this file tells the name server software where to find zone database files, reverse lookup files, and the cache file.

This has been a very quick tour through the DNS, but it should get you started. We'll delve into the details of setting up DNS support and servers on your NetWare system after taking a look at another IP addressing tool, DHCP.

NOTE *If your job responsibilities require that you manage a large DNS system or that you integrate with Unix systems, you'll need a more thorough understanding of DNS. A truly great DNS reference is "DNS and BIND" Help for Unix System Administrators by Paul Albitz and Cricket Liu, published by O'Reilly and Associates. Also take a look at RFCs 1034 and 1045. RFCs are all full-text-indexed and searchable on the Web at* `www.rfc-editor.org`.

HOW DOES DNS DIFFER FROM NIS?

DNS provides IP addresses for hostnames. *NIS* (Network Information Services) is another distributed database that provides common information for network use, such as user and group information. Originally developed by Sun, this service was first called "yellow pages," but it turns out that British Telecom owns the rights to that name. Some longtime NIS users still refer to it as "yp."

Similar to NDS eDirectory, NIS uses the database of users and groups to validate access to network resources, especially Sun's NFS (Network File System). The tables of information are called *NIS maps*, which are controlled by the master NIS server.

The NIS domain is controlled by this NIS server. NIS domains consist of local network connections only and generally cover a single network. The domain names are flat, rather than hierarchical as in DNS, and the rules for these names are not as strict. Each domain must have a unique name. NIS and DNS domains may overlap, but it's not necessary.

In an NIS domain, there is only one master server. There are also *replica servers* (just as in NDS) for fault tolerance, but the databases are all read-only. Called *slaves* in NIS, these subordinate systems periodically query the master server for updates.

IntranetWare 4.11, NetWare 5, and NetWare 6 support NIS so that NetWare can interoperate in an NFS environment. Novell has a product called NFS Server that is sold separately. To enable NIS support in NetWare 6, use ConsoleOne. For more information, see the Novell documentation.

Understanding DHCP

One of the major annoyances associated with an IP network is managing the IP host addresses for all the network clients. If client computers never moved from one subnet to another and hard drives were not replaced, managing IP addresses would be simpler. Client computer support gets messier because other IP parameters, such as the IP address of the default gateway and the domain name server, occasionally change.

In a traditional IP network, an administrator or a technician must visit each computer and manually make these changes. Once the changes are made, they must be tracked. You need a way to track which computer has which IP address and where that computer is located. You must do this to ensure that you never allocate the same IP address twice and that you don't end up with IP addresses that are never used.

DHCP is going to be your best friend if your job is managing a pool of IP addresses. As the full name (Dynamic Host Configuration Protocol) implies, it dynamically assigns IP addresses to hosts that need them. To use DHCP, you must have at least the same number of available IP addresses as you have hosts. When a host boots, it broadcasts a message to the local network segment, requesting an IP address. A DHCP server takes an IP address (and the applicable subnet mask) from a pool of available IP addresses and offers it to the client.

The administrator can configure the DHCP server to offer not only an IP address and a subnet mask, but also the default gateway address, the IP address of a DNS server, and other options that the client may require. Further, the administrator can specify that certain IP addresses be given only to certain clients and that other clients be denied IP addresses from the pool of available IP addresses.

The DHCP server stores a database of which computers have which IP addresses, thus making the administrator's job a little easier by relieving him or her of the task of tracking this information. Using DHCP greatly reduces the administrative overhead typically associated with managing IP networks. And since all the information is entered in the DHCP server ahead of time, common configuration errors, typographical errors, and duplicate IP addresses are eliminated.

When to Use DHCP

Since DHCP makes configuration much easier and less prone to mistakes, you should consider using it to assign your IP addresses. Organizations that have managed IP addressing by hand for years may be reluctant to turn over their IP address allocation to an automated process. However, if you were part of this manual management process, you appreciate the difficulty involved in managing IP addresses by hand.

If your computers move from one subnet to another, you want to use DHCP. With the manual method, every time a computer is moved, it must be reconfigured with a new IP address to reflect its new subnet. DHCP automates this process.

If you have problems keeping track of which hosts have which IP addresses or if you have duplicate IP addresses being assigned, consider using DHCP.

NOTE   One possible security concern you may hear from the "by hand" folks is that anyone can plug a computer into any segment on your network and get a valid IP address. Don't you have security? How often does someone have the opportunity to get physical access to your network infrastructure so that they could request an IP address? If your answer suggests that this is truly a major security issue, you can configure DHCP to allocate IP addresses only to previously defined hosts, using a DHCP feature called static allocation of addresses. *Then put locks on the doors and hire security guards.*

The advantages of DHCP include the following:

◆ The management of available IP addresses is centralized.

◆ The DHCP server automatically tracks which clients have which IP addresses.

◆ Configuration errors are less likely.

◆ Clients moved to another subnet automatically get an address on the new subnet.

◆ The possibility of assigning duplicate IP addresses is eliminated.

DHCP works best in an environment in which you have at least as many available IP host addresses as you have clients that require IP addresses. The server can be configured to give the IP address to the client indefinitely or for a specific period of time called the *lease period*. To force DHCP to reuse IP addresses if they are not currently in use, you can configure incredibly short lease periods (20 minutes, for example). If a computer using an IP address is shut down, that IP address can be used by another client within 20 minutes.

WARNING   *If TCP/IP is your only network protocol and a client cannot lease an IP address, it will not be able to communicate with the network. Obviously, this is not a good thing.*

Those suffering from a chronic shortage of IP addresses should check the possibility of using a private internal network addressing scheme. Using 10.0.0.0, an address illegal on the Internet, internally gives you plenty of addresses (millions and millions, actually). Then use Network Address Translation (NAT) to convert the address of outgoing packets to your legal, but too small, network address.

BOOTP (Bootstrap Protocol)

If you have worked on TCP/IP- and Unix-based networks, you'll be interested to know that DHCP is an extension of BOOTP (Bootstrap Protocol). BOOTP was developed so that diskless workstations could start up and automatically get an IP address. Since these workstations are diskless, they also need an operating system when they start up. With BOOTP, a diskless workstation could read an image file of the appropriate operating system. The administrator assigned a specific IP address and a specific boot file to the client.

This is nothing new to Novell gurus who have worked with diskless workstations for years. BOOTP is merely the standard that the Unix community follows.

NOTE   *Do you know why we "boot" a computer? Sometimes you may feel like kicking one, but that is not the reason. Old-timers called starting up a computer "bootstrapping" because of the complexity of starting some older minicomputers and mainframes. It was like pulling the computer up by its bootstraps. Over the years, it got shortened to just "booting."*

How DHCP Works

DHCP uses UDP as a network transport, and it uses UDP ports 67 and 68, which BOOTP also uses. To request an address for the first time, the client and the server send back and forth a series of four broadcasts:

DHCP Discover   The client broadcasts an IP lease request to the network.

DHCP Offer   All DHCP servers that see the DHCP Discover broadcast extend an IP lease offer via another broadcast.

DHCP Request   The client accepts the first IP lease offer it receives and broadcasts back an IP lease selection. Feeling slightly rejected, the other DHCP servers that proposed an IP address withdraw their offer.

DHCP Ack   When the server whose offer was accepted receives the DHCP Request broadcast, it sends the client an IP lease acknowledgment that lets the client know it can have the IP address. The DHCP Ack packet may also contain options such as default gateway and name server addresses. The server records the IP address as being leased to that client.

If a DHCP server does not respond to the initial DHCP Discover broadcast frame, the client rebroadcasts the DHCP Discover three more times at approximately 9, 13, and 16 seconds. If no server responds after these four attempts, the client rebroadcasts DHCP Discover frames every five minutes.

Once a client has a lease for an IP address, it keeps that address until the end of the lease period. By default, at 50 percent of the way through the lease, the DHCP client contacts the DHCP server using a directed frame and asks to renew the lease. If the server does not respond, the client tries again at 87.5 percent of the way through the lease.

LEASE RENEWAL

The lease-renewal process takes two frames and consists of the following:

DHCP Request   In this particular DHCP frame, the client informs the server that it wants to renew its lease.

DHCP Ack   If the client can keep the lease, the server responds and allows the client to renew its lease. The lease period starts over at the full-lease length at this time. Any updated options, such as a new router or name server address, are also refreshed at this time.

If, for some reason, the server cannot renew the lease on the address because it is no longer valid, the DHCP server issues a DHCP Nack (negative acknowledgment) message. This causes the client to issue a DHCP Discover and to attempt to lease a new address.

DHCP clients keep their IP addresses even when they are shut down. However, when a DHCP client restarts, it renews its lease during reboot. If the DHCP server is not available when the client reboots, it keeps its existing address as long as the lease still has time left on it.

IP HOST ADDRESS ALLOCATION

DHCP supports three methods of allocating IP host addresses:

Dynamic DHCP   DHCP clients are assigned IP addresses from a pool, or subnet address range, of available addresses.

Dynamic BOOTP   BOOTP clients are assigned IP addresses from a pool of available addresses, and the DHCP server can provide a boot file with which the client can boot. This is in contrast to traditional BOOTP servers that assign IP addresses statically (each client is given a specific IP address).

Static allocation   DHCP or BOOTP clients are given a specific IP address based on their MAC address. This is sometimes called a *reservation* and should not be confused with manually configuring each client one machine at a time.

NOTE   *DHCP was originally defined in RFCs 1533, 1534, 1541, and 1542. It has been updated in RFCs 2131 and 2132. BOOTP is defined in RFC 1532.*

NetWare 6 DNS and DHCP Support

NetWare 5.1 took a rather revolutionary step forward by incorporating DHCP and DNS database information in the NDS database. This information was managed by a Java-based utility called the

DNS/DHCP Management Console, which ran as a stand-alone or as a snap-in to the NetWare Administrator utility. Now, in NetWare 6, all DNS and DHCP functions start from the iManage browser-based utility.

Traditionally, DNS information is stored in text files (called *zone files*). Previous versions of NetWare DNS support used Btrieve database files, but NetWare 6 incorporates the zone information directly into the NDS database, where it is distributed to all NetWare servers that contain a replica of an NDS partition. This is accomplished by extending the NDS schema. Even though the database is incorporated into the NDS, the NetWare 6 name server can maintain backward compatibility with other DNS systems, such as Unix DNS servers.

DHCP information is typically stored on a single DHCP server in a local database. NetWare 6 stores the DHCP data, such as available IP addresses and which computers have which IP addresses, in the NDS database. Like all other data in the NDS database, DHCP data is distributed throughout servers that contain a replica of the NDS database.

You can configure a NetWare 6 server to be a DNS name server or a DHCP server.

NOTE   *Novell BorderManager includes DNS and DHCP servers. These products use a Btrieve database to store DNS and DHCP information, rather than storing it in NDS. The NetWare 6 DNS and DHCP servers evolved from the BorderManager DNS and DHCP servers.*

Understanding DNS/DHCP Services Licensing

NetWare License Service (NLS) manages the NetWare DNS/DHCP services licenses. You can install licenses through the server-based GUI or the iManage browser-based utility. The DNS/DHCP server software includes a server license certificate and an address license certificate for use with DHCP. This license installs in the same way as other type of licenses are installed (as explained in Chapter 8, "NetWare 6 Administrator Duties and Tools").

Each IP address that DHCP manages must have a license. You can determine the number of DHCP licenses needed by counting the addresses that are managed by DHCP subnet address ranges and the statically configured IP addresses that the server assigns.

How DNS and DHCP Information Is Stored in NDS

DNS and DHCP use the NDS database to store objects relating information such as the following:

- ◆ DNS server information
- ◆ DNS zones
- ◆ DNS resource records
- ◆ DHCP server information
- ◆ DHCP scopes and scope address records
- ◆ DHCP restrictions and other addressing information

NOTE   *Even though the DNS and DHCP objects are stored and are visible in the NDS hierarchy, they can be modified only through the DNS/DHCP Management Console.*

During installation, the NDS schema is modified to support DNS and DHCP object types. The installation process also adds three new NDS objects to the NDS database:

RootServerInfo Zone   Contains the names and IP addresses of all the root servers on the Internet. Your DNS servers will refer to these name servers if they cannot answer a name query. You should never need to edit the root server information; the root server names and IP addresses do not change.

Group   A standard NDS Group object. DNS and DHCP servers get their rights to other DNS/DHCP data within the tree through the Group object.

Locator   A custom object that contains the DNS and DHCP default options for all servers, DHCP and DNS server lists, zone names, and subnet information.

You should place these objects in a container that is accessible from and replicated to all servers on the network that will use DNS and DHCP services. You can create these objects in either an Organization object or an Organizational Unit object. Only one RootServerInfo Zone, Group, and Locator object will exist in an NDS eDirectory tree.

One approach is to create an Organizational Unit that will contain all DNS and DHCP objects, such as the Group and Locator objects, along with the subnets, zones, and resource records.

The DNS and DHCP servers should be geographically close to the clients and users they serve, as shown in Figure 12.3. This can help reduce WAN traffic and improve response time to clients. Ensure that you have an NDS replication strategy in place so that the container that holds the DNS and DHCP objects is replicated to more than one server. Place replicas of DNS and DHCP information so that the servers are adequately load balanced. This is especially important if you have a WAN, since a WAN failure could isolate part of your network.

FIGURE 12.3

DNS and DHCP servers located throughout a WAN

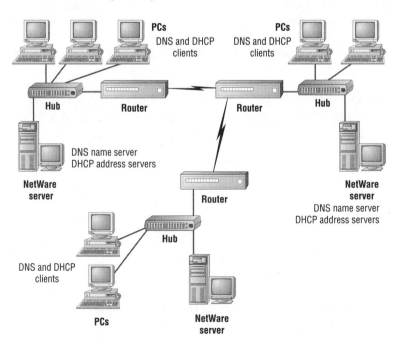

Installing DNS/DHCP Support

During the NetWare 6 server installation, one of the options that the GUI will prompt you for is installing DNS/DHCP support. The files are installed automatically, even if you do not check this option. This option merely extends the NDS schema to support DNS and DHCP. If you choose to install DNS/DHCP support when the server is installed, you will be prompted for the Locator object, Group object, and RootServerInfo Zone object contexts.

If you did not choose to install DNS/DHCP support during the server installation, you can install DNS/DHCP support for the NDS schema by typing **LOAD DNIPINST** at the NetWare server console prompt. When asked to log in to NDS, provide an administrator-level user ID and password.

The procedure to enable the NDS schema needs to be done only once per eDirectory tree. As mentioned earlier, before running the installation utility, you may want to create an Organizational Unit to hold all DNS/DHCP information.

In the example shown here, the NDS Context Query Form (which appears when you run DNIPST, and prompts you to enter an NDS directory context in which to install the DNS/DHCP objects) is filled in with the context OU=DNS-DHCP.O=SOMORITA for each object. This is an Organizational Unit that I created earlier.

NOTE   *Be sure that the container you specify exists. If it does not exist, you will get an error, but the utility will think it has installed the Global and Locator objects. You can remove the schema extensions and start over, as I have needed to do on a few occasions. At the server console prompt, type* **LOAD DNIPINST -R** *to remove the schema extensions.*

After you press Enter, you will receive a message stating that the NDS schema extensions have been added successfully. When completed, the NDS schema will have been extended to include these three new objects in the Organizational Unit that you specified, as in the example shown here.

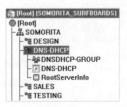

Once you have extended the NDS schema, use the ConsoleOne utility to give users who need DNS/DHCP management privileges Read/Write rights to this object.

And, finally, ensure that the partition that holds the DNS/DHCP objects is replicated to all parts of the network that will use DNS and DHCP services.

TIP   *DHCP and DNS are new technologies to many NetWare administrators. Before inflicting these technologies on users, create a lab and test for the results you expect.*

Setting Up and Managing NetWare 6 DNS

Any NetWare server can be a DNS server. Novell's NetWare 6 DNS name server can interoperate in a traditional DNS environment as a primary, a secondary, or a caching-only name server. However, as explained earlier, Novell's approach is to store all the DNS data in the NDS database and distributed it to all servers that have a replica of the partition that contains the DNS data. Since there is only one copy of the DNS zone information, there is no need to designate a primary or secondary name server. Nor does the DNS administrator need to worry about zone transfers, since NDS synchronization takes care of this automatically.

However, if your NetWare DNS system must be a secondary server or a primary server for another system's DNS, such as Unix, you can designate a server to operate in "compatibility" mode. You'll learn more about this in the "Managing Interoperability with Unix Name Servers" section later in this chapter.

To best explain how to set up a DNS server, zones, and resource records, let's take a fictitious company and set up DNS based on NetWare 6. Our company is Somorita Surfboards, which moved to NetWare 6 and TCP/IP, and plans to connect its private network to the Internet. The private network consists of three subnets in two locations, Haleiwa and Pipeline. One Web server must support the entire company. In addition, each department must be able to build its own internal Web server, and anyone on the Internet should be able to connect to these servers. The company has two locations and three NetWare 6 servers, one for each department—Sales, Testing, and Design. The company's ISP has provided Somorita with three full Class C network addresses and a small chunk of a Class C network address for the router network between the two locations. Figure 12.4 illustrates the layout of Somorita's network, and Table 12.2 shows the network number assignments and server IP addresses.

FIGURE 12.4

The Somorita Surfboards network

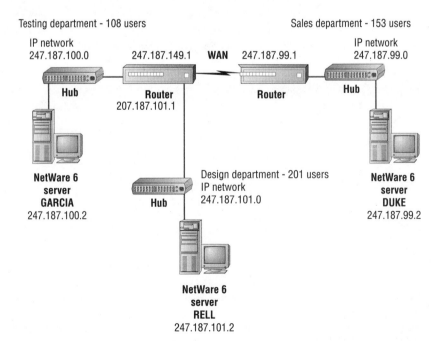

TABLE 12.2: NETWORK NUMBER ASSIGNMENTS FOR EACH DEPARTMENT

DEPARTMENT/SUBNET	LOCATION	NETWORK NUMBER	NETWARE SERVER NAME	IP ADDRESS
Sales	Haleiwa	247.187.99.0	DUKE	247.187.99.2
Testing	Pipeline	247.187.100.0	GARCIA	247.187.100.2
Design	Pipeline	247.187.101.0	RELL	247.187.101.2

The heads of departments and the president of the company have told you they want to access the Web servers for the company using these names:

◆ Company Wide: www.somorita.com

◆ Sales: www.sales.somorita.com

◆ Testing: www.testing.somorita.com

◆ Design: www.design.somorita.com

The company is on a limited budget (is there any other kind of budget?). We can't buy additional hardware, so the NetWare 6 servers that are functioning as file and print servers for each department must also function as Web servers.

Now that we have our requirements, let's get busy setting up our servers.

Registering the Domain

One of our first tasks is to contact one of the licensed registrar companies to register our domain name. For our fictitious company, we are going to request somorita.com. Here is the information we must have when we connect to the registration Web site (www.nsi.com or www.register.com, for example) to register our domain:

◆ Domain name requested

◆ E-mail address

◆ Organization name and mailing address

◆ Administrative, technical, and billing contact information

◆ Primary server hostname (for example, duke.somorita.com)

◆ Primary server IP address (for example, 247.187.99.2)

◆ Secondary server hostname (for example, rell.somorita.com)

◆ Secondary server IP address (for example, 247.187.101.2)

Notice that we assigned one of the Somorita servers to be the primary name server and one of them to be the secondary. It does not matter which one we choose, since all three of our servers will be running naming services.

TIP   *When designating primary and secondary servers, plan to locate secondary servers on a separate network from the primary server. In my environment connected to the Internet, I locate my primary server on my network. I ask my ISP to maintain a secondary server for me. Their name server will then do a zone transfer from my primary server periodically so that it has the latest information for my domain. This does not require additional hardware at the ISP's location; they can use one of their existing DNS servers to host a secondary zone for me. However, don't be surprised if they expect a small fee for their trouble. Your ISP should allow you to point to their name server(s) without a fee, if you don't want to start out managing your own name server.*

Within a few days, your domain name will be functional, and you will receive a bill from the registrar the first two years of service (usually). Companies doing small amounts of business should be prepared to pay for registration via a credit card during initial setup. Subsequent renewals are $35 (full price from NSI), and I recommend paying these bills on time; otherwise, your domain name might be turned off and be up for grabs before you find the buried invoice. (That actually happened to microsoft.com in 2000, but luckily a friend paid their registration before it lapsed.)

NOTE   *In the past, the InterNIC charged $100 for name registrations and $50 for renewals, but this changed April 1, 1998. New registration companies, particularly those offering hosting services as well, often discount the name registration fee. Hooray for competition!*

Creating a DNS Server

IN A HURRY 12.1: CREATE A DNS NAME SERVER

1. Start iManage as Admin or an equivalent user.

2. Select DNS Management ➤ DNS Server Management ➤ Create Server and click OK.

3. Find and select the NetWare server that will host this name server from the NDS eDirectory tree.

4. Enter this server's hostname and a domain name.

5. Click the Create button.

Although you can create a DNS zone prior to creating a DNS server, I highly recommend creating the DNS Server object first. If you create the DNS Server object first, the zones will be easier to create, because you will need to provide less information about each zone object.

NOTE   *Before creating DNS zones or servers, you must install the DNS/DHCP extensions described earlier in this chapter. You can install these during server installation or by running the* DNIPINST.NLM *program at the server console. For more information, see the "Installing DNS and DHCP Support" section earlier in this chapter.*

For our sample company, we have decided to set up each server in our organization as a name server. We must now decide where in the eDirectory tree we will create the DNS Server objects. For our example, we will put the DNS Server objects in each department's Organizational Unit.

To designate NetWare 6 servers as valid name servers, you use the DNS/DHCP Management tools inside iManage. If your organization has more than one eDirectory tree, be sure that you are logged in to the correct tree. Open iManage, the tool of choice for DHCP and DNS operations (actually, the only tool for these functions). As you can see in Figure 12.5, this utility offers two main options DHCP Management and DNS Management.

FIGURE 12.5

The DNS/DHCP
Management Console

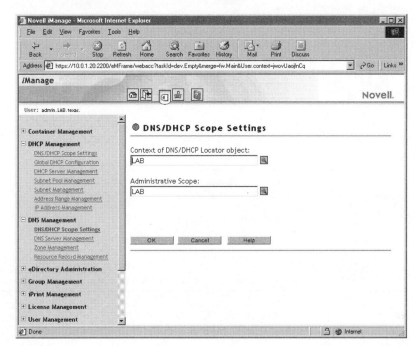

Expand the DNS Management menu item. The first option, DNS/DHCP Scope Settings, should be dealt with unless you enjoy ignoring warning messages (a habit that will cause you grief if you do it automatically). Set the scope to the current context, or the highest context you will use during your DNS/DHCP management session.

The first choice in the pull-down menu when you click DNS Server Management under DNS Management is Create Server. This is exactly what we want. Click OK and continue. You'll see the Create New DNS Server screen, as shown in Figure 12.6.

Next, you must pick the host NetWare server. You'll see a Browse button at the end of the first text field. Click the button and locate the server. Next, provide (that means type) a hostname and domain name in the appropriate boxes. Finally, click Create.

SETTING DNS SERVER OBJECT PROPERTIES

The property page for a DNS Server object has four tabs:

Zones Displays a list of zones that this server has been configured to resolve. Zones are assigned to a server through the Zone object. This tab also has a Comments field, where you can enter a maximum of 256 characters of information about this server.

FIGURE 12.6

Creating a
DNS server

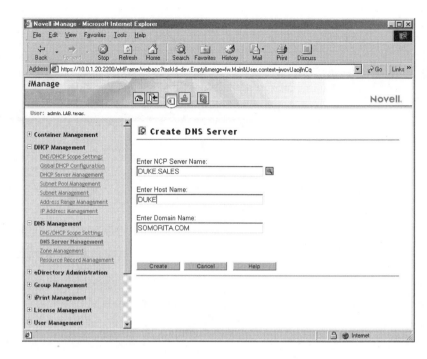

Forwarding List Defines which DNS name server this server will forward name resolution requests to if this server does not have an answer. If you have nothing in these lists, the name server forwards queries to the root servers. To add entries to this list, click the Add button and enter the desired name server's IP address.

No-Forward List Displays a list of domain names for which you do not want to send queries. To add entries to this list, click the Add button and enter the name of the domain for which you do not want to resolve names.

Options Sets Event logging (None, Major Events, or All) and specifies whether to enable an audit trail log.

Creating a Zone

IN A HURRY 12.2: CREATE A DNS ZONE

1. Start iManage as Admin or an equivalent user.

2. Select DNS Management ➢ Zone Management ➢ Create New Zone and click OK.

3. Select the NDS context in which you want the Zone object to appear.

continued on next page

IN A HURRY 12.2: CREATE A DNS ZONE *(continued)*

4. Select the Zone Type, then enter the zone name in the Zone Domain Name field.

5. Assign this zone an authoritative DNS server by picking one from the Assign Authoritative DNS Server drop-down list.

6. Enter the hostname and select the domain in the Select Domain field.

7. Click the Create button.

First, we'll create our main domain name, `somorita.com`. In iManage, expand the DNS Management menu item, select DNS Management, and then choose Zone Management. From the menu, pick Create Zone and click OK.

Unfortunately, Novell changed the screens for DNS zones when they moved DNS/DHCP management to the new iManage utility. That means you can't see the top two entries of the Create DNS Zone process in Figure 12.7. They are Specify eDirectory Context and Enter Zone Domain Name. You've seen those before, or at least something similar.

FIGURE 12.7

Creating your
DNS zone

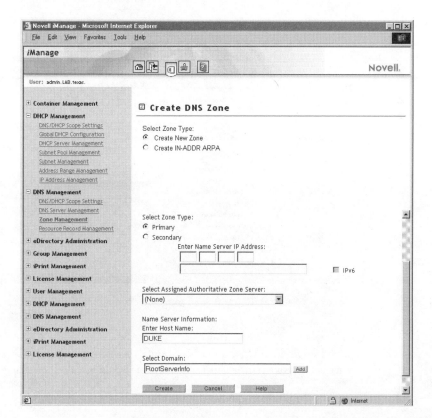

For the first zone, check the Primary radio button for the Select Zone Type option. If you check Secondary, give the primary name server address in the appropriate box in true IP address format (204.187.99.2, for example).

If you've created your first DNS server, as strongly suggested, choose that name in the Select Assigned Authoritative Zone Server drop-down list. Fill in the Host Name and Select Domain (RootServerInfo if one exists) fields, and click Create.

MODIFYING A ZONE

To configure other attributes about this zone, highlight the zone name and choose Modify Zone. The first Modify DNS Zone screen, shown in Figure 12.8, allows you to specify whether the zone is primary or secondary. Servers managed by NetWare NDS will always be primary, which is the default. From this tab, you can assign any of your DNS servers to answer queries for this zone in the Authoritative DNS Servers list. You can also assign a dynamic DNS server. This server is used to manage dynamic DNS data and is used if other non–NetWare 6 name servers will perform zone transfers from this server.

FIGURE 12.8

Starting zone modifications

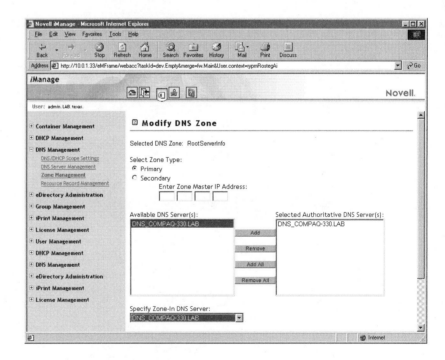

The second screen, shown in Figure 12.9, shows the SOA (Start of Authority) information (even though Novell doesn't call it that) to specify the current version of the zone information and the secondary server zone transfer information. You should not need to change any of the serial number information; the NetWare DNS handles that internally. In the E-mail Address box, enter the e-mail address of the administrator of this zone. The correct form uses periods, even though you are used to seeing an @ sign between the username and the domain name.

WARNING   *Do not change the SOA record's serial number manually if you are managing your DNS through NDS. NDS keeps this record up-to-date and correct. Changing it can cause non-NetWare DNS name servers to fail to perform zone transfers.*

FIGURE 12.9

More zone modifications

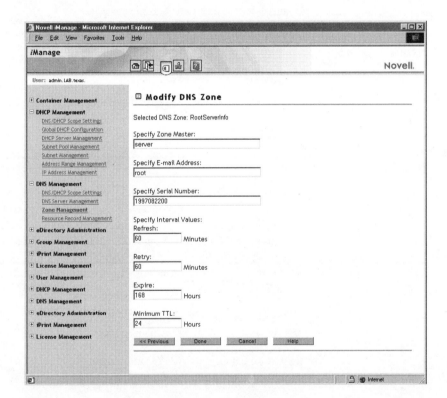

If you configured external name servers to transfer zone information from this zone, the interval values may be important to you. These fields control communication between the secondary and the primary servers.

A value that will prove useful is the Minimum TTL field. It controls how long another name server keeps one of your resource records in its cache before it discards it and needs to query your server again if it needs that information. The default is 24 hours.

CREATING REVERSE LOOKUP ZONES

IN A HURRY 12.3: CREATE A REVERSE LOOKUP ZONE

1. Start iManage as Admin or an equivalent user.

2. Select DNS Management ➢ Zone Management ➢ Create New Zone and click OK.

3. Select the NDS context in which you want the Zone object to appear.

4. Click the Create IN-ADDR-ARPA radio button.

5. Select the Zone Type, then enter the zone name in the Zone Domain Name field.

6. Select the NDS context that will contain this object.

7. Enter the IP address in the proper box.

8. Assign this zone an authoritative DNS server by picking one from the Assign Authoritative DNS Server drop-down list.

9. Click the Create button.

In order for hosts on the Internet or even your private intranet to be able to look up a host's name based on the host's IP address (called an inverse query), your name servers must support reverse lookup zones. I have found this to be much more difficult to set up in Unix than in the NetWare DNS/DHCP Management Console. Though the name looks a little strange, all you are really doing is creating a zone in which the IP addresses and names are reversed.

For example, to create a reverse lookup zone for the hosts on the IP network 204.187.99.0, follow these steps (and see Figure 12.10):

1. Open the DNS Management menu item and choose Zone Management.

2. Choose the Create Zone option and click OK.

3. Click the Create IN-ADDR.ARPA radio button.

4. Select the NDS container that will contain this zone object.

5. Enter the IP address in the IP Address box, such as 204.187.99.0.

6. Assign an authoritative DNS server to resolve queries for this zone.

7. If you have not created your first DNS server yet, enter the hostname of the DNS server in the Enter Host Name field, and choose the DNS server domain from the Select Domain drop-down list.

8. Click Create.

Again, you can't see all of the information in the screenshot. You can't see the Create button at the bottom, but you've seen it before. You can't see the Specify eDirectory Context field with Browse button beside it, but you've seen plenty of those so far. Don't be too literal—expand your thinking and imagine those items are sitting on your page in Figure 12.10.

FIGURE 12.10

Creating your reverse lookup zone

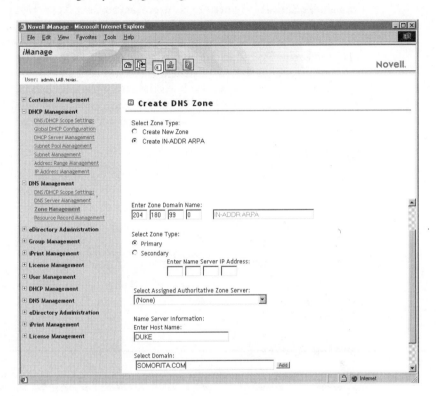

CREATING SECONDARY ZONES

Secondary zones are zones that are actually managed on another server. In the case of the NetWare DNS server, these zones are managed by a system external to NetWare, such as a Unix system. You create a secondary zone if you want your NetWare servers to maintain a copy of the zone and periodically update that copy using a zone transfer.

For example, I need to host a zone name for a domain called northshore.com on my server, but the primary server is on Unix at another site on the Internet. I create a secondary zone and provide the IP address of the server that has the primary zone. The steps reflect almost exactly what we did earlier when we created a new zone, except for one small difference: Check the Secondary radio button for the Select Zone Type option. Then you'll need to put the IP address for the primary name server (which feeds information to the secondary name server) in the IP address field. No big deal.

Your server will transfer the zone from the primary server based on the refresh interval defined in the zone information on the primary server. This refresh interval is stored in the SOA record. The default for NetWare is 180 minutes, but this can vary greatly depending on the person who creates the primary zone.

CREATING SUBDOMAINS

Now we need to create *subdomains* (sometimes called *child domains* or *child zones*) under our `somorita.com` domain. Specifically, we need to create `sales.somorita.com`, `testing.somorita.com`, and `design.somorita.com`. To create a subdomain under a parent domain, in the left pane, highlight the zone for which you want to create a subdomain. Click the Create object, and then choose Zone to open the Create DNS Zone screen. The procedures are the same as those for creating a zone.

Once the zone is created, the parent zone must contain *glue records* or *glue logic*. These are records that point to the name server that hosts the child zone. This means that there must be an NS (Name Server) record and an A (Address) record for the name servers that will resolve queries for the child zone. Without these records, the parent name server cannot refer queries to other name servers.

Creating Resource Records

Now that we have created zones, we must add hosts to them. You will be working with three major types:

◆ Host records (A records)

◆ CNAME records (aliases)

◆ MX records (Mail Exchanger records)

Another type of record that you may need to create is the NS (Name Server) record, which is used to point to a name server for a specific domain. These are used when creating child zones (or subdomains).

CREATING A HOST RECORD

IN A HURRY 12.4: CREATE A HOST (A) RESOURCE RECORD

1. Start iManage as Admin or an equivalent user.

2. Select DNS Management ➢ Resource Record Management ➢ Create Resource Record, then the host-name (optional), and click Create.

3. Confirm that the A radio button is selected.

4. Enter the hostname and its IP address.

5. Click the Create button.

For all hosts, you first create an A record. Open iManage, go to DNS Management, then choose the bottom menu option, Resource Record Management. The pull-down menu offers you a choice of creating, modifying, or deleting a resource record. After choosing Create, click OK.

Choose the domain name (RootServInfo in Figure 12.11) and click Create to start making the new record. The next screen fills in the Specified Domain information, and offers a text field for the Specified Host Name field. (Why no Browse button? I'm not sure— maybe some Novell developer fell behind and didn't get to it.) Make sure the A for Host Record radio button is selected.

Put the IP address information in place (you'll need to type this, too). Then redundantly click Create. Figure 12.11 shows all the excitement.

FIGURE 12.11

Creating a resource record

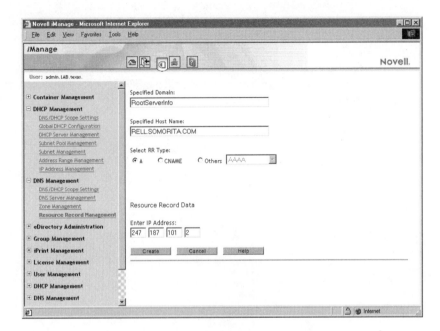

A reassuring screen appears quickly, congratulating you on creating the record. Well, not congratulating, exactly, but at least you get a positive response. When you click OK, the Create Resource Record screen reappears, ready for the next record.

NOTE *All NetWare servers should have an A record created for them, and this record should be associated with that server's NDS object.*

CREATING CNAME AND MX RECORDS

IN A HURRY 12.5: CREATE HOST ALIAS (CNAME) RECORDS

1. Start iManage as Admin or an equivalent user.

2. Select DNS Management ➤ Resource Record Management ➤ Create Resource Record, then the hostname (optional) and click Create.

3. Click the CNAME radio button.

4. Enter the alias for the host in the Specified Host Name field.

5. In the Domain Name of Host Aliases box, enter the FQDN of the host for which this CNAME is an alias.

6. Click the Create button.

Our final step is to create aliases for our servers so that we can use them as Web servers. For example, the DUKE server will host our `www.somorita.com` server. Since we already have an A record for it, we'll need to create an alias.

Much remains the same when creating the CNAME host record rather than the A host record. The biggest difference is that you use hostnames rather than IP addresses.

To make `www.somorita.com` work properly, we need to provide the WWW (for World Wide Web, of course) alias and tie it to the `duke.somorita.com` server. Put **WWW** in the Specified Host Name field, and `duke.somorita.com` in the Domain Name of Host Aliases box. Refer to Figure 12.12 for a graphic representation of this verbiage.

FIGURE 12.12

Host alias on tap

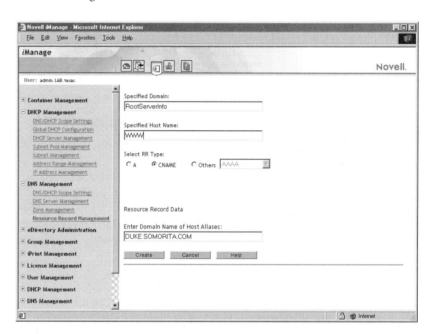

Create any necessary MX records exactly the same way as you've created the last two record types. When you have a chance to Select RR Type, click the Others radio button (beside the pull-down menu) and choose MX from that menu. You've seen the rest of the process twice already.

Enabling the NetWare Server to Support Name Services

Once you define the servers in the DNS/DHCP Management Console and assign the zones, you can enable NetWare 6 to support Name Services. To do so, at the server, type **NAMED.NLM** and press Enter.

You can use various startup options with NAMED.NLM. Some particularly useful ones are listed in Table 12.3. To display all of the options, load the NAMED.NLM with the -? or -h option, as in:

```
NAMED.NLM -?
```

TABLE 12.3: SOME *NAMED.NLM* OPTIONS

OPTION	FUNCTION
−h and −?	Display help.
−v	Allows the NLM to load in verbose mode and provides a troubleshooting screen.
−s	Displays the current status of the NAMED.NLM program after it is loaded.
−i	Reinitializes a currently running NAMED.NLM.
−l	Allows the NAMED.NLM to bypass its own login and log in to NDS as an administrator. If you use this option, you provide a login name and password. Use this option only if the name server will not start any other way. Run DSREPAIR to repair the NDS Name Server object.
−m *<zonefile.dat>*	Specifies that NAMED.NLM should import the specified zone file and create a new zone.
−u *<zonefile.dat>*	Specifies that the NAMED.NLM should update information about a previously created zone with the information in *<zonefile.dat>*.
−r *<zone.com>*	Tells NAMED.NLM to remove all information in the database for *zone.com* and delete the zone.

Managing Interoperability with Unix Name Servers

The NetWare 6 DNS name server NLM can interoperate with other name servers as either a primary or a secondary name server. NetWare 6 Name Services can act as a secondary name server and load data into NDS via a zone transfer with a Unix primary server. It can also act as a primary server for Unix systems that need to be secondary servers (if your IT Unix/Linux people will allow this). The Unix systems that need to be secondary servers are configured to do a zone transfer with a NetWare 6 name server that you define as the dynamic DNS server. The *dynamic DNS server* is a server that the administrator has defined for a specific zone. It maintains the information needed if a zone transfer is requested.

If the dynamic DNS server is on a system that will act as a primary server for other name servers, its job is to make sure that the DNS data from the NDS database is available and up-to-date when a secondary server requests a zone transfer. If the dynamic DNS server is on a NetWare system that is acting as a secondary server, it is responsible for connecting to a primary server and transferring data into NDS.

There can be only one NetWare server defined as a dynamic DNS server for each zone.

CONFIGURING A PRIMARY SERVER

To define a NetWare server as a primary server from which other systems can transfer zones, you must configure one zone at a time. Drill down through iManage ➤ DNS Management ➤ Zone Management ➤ Modify DNS Zone until you reach the screen that appears in Figure 12.13.

FIGURE 12.13

In the left pane, select the server.

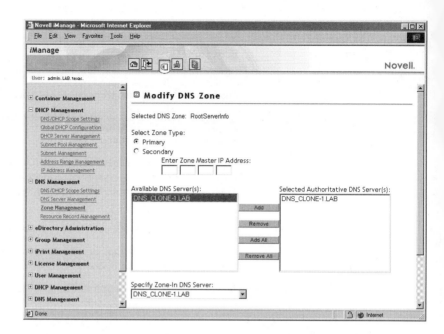

Highlight a server in the Available DNS Server(s) list on the right, and then pick an option cleverly linking the two boxes. In Figure 12.13, I picked the only available server and clicked the Add link between the two boxes. Since this was the first server so configured, the utility automatically filled in the Specify Zone-In DNS Server listing.

What you can't see are the Enter Comments box and the command buttons for Previous, Next, Cancel, and Help. The next two screens offer a chance to modify Zone Out Filter and Zone In Filter settings. When you're finished, click Done to set all into stone (or at least a configuration file on the server in question).

You do not need to do this for other NetWare 6 DNS servers to resolve queries for this zone. Instead, select the server name and add it to the Authoritative DNS Servers list so that other NetWare DNS servers can service queries for this zone.

CONFIGURING A SECONDARY SERVER

A time may come when you merely want to transfer data from a Unix name server to your NDS. If your DNS server is a secondary server, any zone data that NDS contains is read-only. (If you want the ability to modify the data yourself, your NetWare server must be the primary server.)

You use NetWare name servers as secondary servers if your DNS servers are already running under Unix and you don't want the hassle of moving them to NetWare 6 DNS (or you are not given that responsibility). For purposes of redundancy and better performance, you can transfer these zones to your NetWare name servers.

To change a primary server to a secondary server, drill down through iManage ➤ DNS Management ➤ Zone Management ➤ Modify DNS Zone. There you'll see the Select Zone Type details, with Primary and Secondary radio buttons. When you click Secondary, you must provide the IP address for the primary server holding the zone file.

The server you define as the dynamic DNS server will transfer data from the other server into NDS based on an interval that the other server administrator defined in the SOA record.

Migrating from a Unix System

If you are migrating from a Unix DNS name server to a NetWare name server and you don't want to reenter all the zone file information, you can use the DNS/DHCP Management Console to import files that are in the BIND format.

To import a file into your NetWare 6 DNS data, follow these steps:

1. Drill down through iManage ➤ Zone Management ➤ Import Zone.

2. Specify the eDirectory Context, the DNS Server Distinguished Name, and whether it's primary or secondary.

3. Type the DNS Bind File location, or use the Browse button to locate the files. Then click OK to start (and quickly finish) the file-import process.

Configuring Clients to Use DNS

Once DNS services are configured and running, you will need to configure your client computers to use a DNS server. This is really quite simple in comparison to getting the DNS server up and running. You must enter the IP address (or addresses) of the DNS servers that you want the client to query. For Windows 95/98 clients, this is done from the DNS Configuration tab of the TCP/IP Properties dialog box, shown in Figure 12.14.

FIGURE 12.14

The Windows 95/98 TCP/IP Properties dialog box

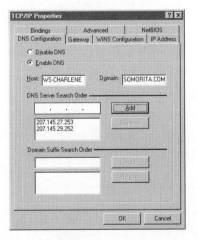

To view the TCP/IP Properties dialog box, choose Control Panel ➤ Network ➤ TCP/IP <*for your network adapter*> ➤ Properties ➤ DNS Configuration. Note that you can enter several IP addresses in the DNS Server Search Order field. The client will use only one of these, generally the first one in the list. It will resort to a second DNS server only if the first one is not available.

The hostname is the computer name. Though it can be different, to keep things simple, I leave them as the same names. You should also enter a domain name in the Domain box.

The domain name is used in hostname resolution if you attempt to contact a host without providing an FQDN. The TCP/IP software adds the domain name from the Domain box to the hostname. For example, if I go to the command prompt and type PING RELL, but do not put a domain name after RELL, my TCP/IP software will contact my DNS and ask for the IP address of RELL.somorita.com. This is, of course, provided I have somorita.com entered in the Domain box.

TIP   You can automatically assign the domain name server IP addresses and the domain name using the DHCP Scope option. Keep reading for more information!

For Windows NT/2000/XP clients, assign the IP address of a DNS server by choosing Control Panel ➢ Network ➢ Protocols ➢ TCP/IP ➢ Properties and selecting the DNS tab. For Unix or Linux systems, the information is generally entered in a file in the /etc directory called RESOLV.CONF or something similar.

Setting Up and Managing NetWare DHCP

The steps for setting up a DHCP server are similar to those for setting up a DNS server. Before setting up your first DHCP server, plan your IP address allocation carefully.

Preparing for DHCP

Before deploying DHCP, you need to gather some information about your network. Here is a sampling of questions that you need to answer:

◆ What are the IP network addresses for each subnet?

◆ How many hosts are on each subnet?

◆ Where are the NetWare servers and what are their IP addresses?

◆ What are the IP addresses for routers and the DNS name servers?

◆ What are the IP addresses, MAC addresses, and names of any computers that must have the same IP host address all the time?

◆ Should any hosts be denied IP addresses?

◆ Do you have sufficient IP host addresses for all clients?

◆ Will each segment have its own DHCP server?

This information affects the scopes of addresses, the scope options, and the number of servers that you deploy. Additional considerations include whether DHCP servers exist on the opposite side of routers from the clients they serve and whether any redundancy is required.

SETTING UP IP ROUTING

If you put your DHCP server on one segment and the clients that it serves on another segment, how do the DHCP client broadcasts reach the DHCP server? Since DHCP lease requests occur via broadcasts and routers do not forward broadcasts, network designers face a problem, which also existed for the designers of the original BOOTP protocol.

This problem is solved by using a special software program that you can find on most routers called a *BOOTP relay agent* (or sometimes called a *forwarder*). The BOOTP relay agent is configured with the IP address of nearby DHCP servers. It listens for DHCP broadcasts and forwards them to the DHCP on behalf of the client. From the perspective of the DHCP client, the relay agent looks like a DHCP server.

If you are using your NetWare server for IP routing, you may need to use BOOTP relay on your server. NetWare supports DHCP relay as an NLM. To enable BOOTP relay on your NetWare server, use the BOOTPFWD.NLM. It has three startup options:

SERVER=   Specifies the IP address of the nearest DHCP server

LOG=   Specifies whether the BOOTPFWD.NLM creates a log to the console or a file

FILE=   Specifies a log filename

Here is a sample statement that loads BOOTP relay support on your NetWare 6 server:

```
LOAD BOOTPFWD SERVER=204.187.99.2 LOG=YES FILE=SYS:ETC\BOOTPFWD.LOG
```

If your NetWare 6 server is going to support BOOTP relay, this statement should be included in your server's AUTOEXEC.NCF file after the protocol BIND and LOAD statements.

WARNING   *Do not load* BOOTPFWD.NLM *and the DHCP server on the same NetWare server. Both applications require UDP port 67. Only one application at a time can occupy that port.*

How Many DHCP Servers Are Required?

An easy question to ask, but not an easy one to answer. No hard-and-fast rule says that you must have a DHCP server for *x* number of clients. You should ensure that DHCP servers are near the client computers they serve. Since DHCP is administered centrally through the NDS database, administration is not a problem. Any NetWare 6 server can run the DHCP server NLM, but you must assign it a subnet address range; only one server can service a specific subnet address range.

Though you could configure a single DHCP server for thousands of users throughout your corporate intranet, this would probably generate a lot of unnecessary network traffic, and IP address distribution would have a single point of failure. On the other hand, you could configure a DHCP server for every little ten-node segment on your LAN. Though managing DHCP is easy, this is probably taking distribution of the DHCP servers to the other extreme.

An ideal distribution is a single DHCP server for each larger geographic area, such as a regional office. When I have more than about 300 users per office, I designate a second server in that office as a DHCP server to provide some backup and redundancy.

TIP   *Each DHCP server will need to read and write from the NDS schema whenever addresses are leased or leases are renewed. To maximize performance, these servers should have a Read/Write replica of the partition of the NDS database on which the Subnet Address Range object is created.*

PLAN FOR SOME REDUNDANCY

For fault-tolerance purposes, you may want to assign addresses for a specific subnet to two different servers. A good rule of thumb is to assign 75 percent of the available addresses to the closest DHCP server and to assign the remaining 25 percent to the second-closest server. The scopes should not overlap; if they do, you risk assigning duplicate IP addresses.

In Figure 12.15, we have two DHCP servers: one on subnet 1, and the other on subnet 2. The IP network address for subnet 1 is 198.55.201.0, so we assign the DHCP server on subnet one the range of 198.55.201.10 through 198.55.201.193. We assign the subnet address range 198.55.201.194 through 198.55.201.254 to the DHCP server on subnet 2. The DHCP server on subnet 2 can assign IP addresses for subnet 1 if the DHCP server on subnet 1 is not available. Notice that the first subnet address range starts with address .10, rather than address .1. This is so that we can manually assign IP host addresses for the router and servers.

FIGURE 12.15

Two segments with a router and two servers, using the 75/25 rule

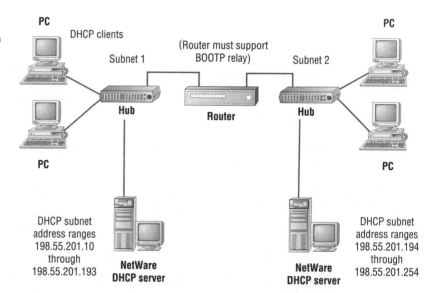

LEASE CONSIDERATIONS

When planning scope options, one of your choices is the lease period. The lease period controls how long a client can keep a lease before it must contact the server and extend the lease. The default lease period is three days. The client contacts the server halfway through the lease in order to renew the lease. If the DHCP server is not available at halfway through the lease, the client tries again at seven-eighths (⅞ or 87.5 percent) of the way through the lease.

You can use only the maximum number of available IP addresses. For example, if you have 254 available IP host addresses and 500 computers that require IP addresses, only 254 hosts can be using IP addresses at a single time. Make absolutely sure that you have enough IP addresses for all concurrent computers active on the network.

If your organization has a night shift and a day shift and each person has his or her own computer, you could find yourself with a shortage of IP addresses. In such a case, set short lease periods. Then, when a client is not active, the server makes its IP address available again at the end of the lease.

Novell recommends a lease period of 15 minutes in an environment that is extremely low on IP addresses. However, if the DHCP server is down for more than 15 minutes, clients will give up their IP addresses. In addition, 15-minute lease periods result in additional traffic since the client will be issuing a request to keep the address every seven and a half minutes (50 percent of the way through the lease).

TIP *Your life will be much simpler if you have enough IP addresses for every computer. Inevitably, if you do not have enough IP addresses for everyone, some users will not be able to connect to the network because they cannot lease an IP address.*

If you have sufficient IP addresses, consider lease periods longer than the default of three days. A lease period of ten days ensures that even if the DHCP server becomes unavailable for several days, clients will still have IP addresses.

DHCP SCOPE OPTIONS

When DHCP servers lease an IP address to a client, DHCP automatically provides a subnet mask. The administrator can also specify additional client options, providing the client supports them. Some of the more useful options include those listed in Table 12.4.

TABLE 12.4: SOME DHCP SCOPE OPTIONS

NUMBER	NAME	DESCRIPTION
3	Router	Sets the client's default gateway (router) IP address
6	Domain Name Server	Sets the IP address for the client's DNS name server
15	Domain Name	Sets the client's DNS domain name
44	NetBIOS over TCP/IP Name Server	Used typically in a Microsoft environment to look up NetBIOS computer names
46	NetBIOS over TCP/IP Node Type	Used typically in a Microsoft environment to set the order in which a client attempts to resolve a NetBIOS name
62	NWIP Domain Name	Used only by NetWare/IP to set the NWIP domain name
63	NWIP Options	Used only by NetWare/IP to set options such as the NWIP primary DSS, preferred DSS, and nearest servers
85	NDS Server	Sets the default server IP address for the NetWare client
86	NDS Tree	Sets the default NDS tree name for the NetWare client
87	NDS Context	Sets the default NDS context for the NetWare client

TIP *A partial list of all DHCP options is available in the NetWare 6 documentation. You can also view these with the DNS/DHCP Management Console inside iManage by clicking the Global Preferences button. For a complete list of DHCP options, see RFC 2132.*

There are dozens of other DHCP options, although most of them are not used by NetWare clients. Developers can add their own options, as Novell has done with options 62, 63, 85, 86, and 87. By taking advantage of these options, you can avoid additional visits to configure each client manually.

Setting Global Preferences

Global preferences are settings that affect all DHCP servers throughout your NDS eDirectory tree. To view your global preferences, in iManage, expand the DHCP Management option and select the Global DHCP Configuration option. Then click OK to choose Set Global Preferences.

You can use the Global DHCP Options screen to set DHCP options that will be sent to all clients that lease IP addresses from any DHCP server. Note that DHCP options for a specific scope or IP address will override any global options you set.

One of our requirements for the sample DHCP setup we'll be working through (details in the next section) is that all clients that get an IP address from this DHCP server should also be assigned the NDS default tree name. Since this will be universal for all clients, we will set this as a global DHCP option.

From the Global DHCP Preferences screen, click the Modify button to open the Modify DHCP Options dialog box. Scroll down (way down) the list to find NDS Tree Name, and click Add. This moves the entry, 00086 NDS Tree Name, to the Selected DHCP Option(s) box, and opens a text field begging for the NDS tree name value to add. You don't actually add the Tree object, you just fill in the tree name to each workstation that pulls an IP address from this DHCP server. Figure 12.16 shows the details, and you can see all of this screen.

FIGURE 12.16

Save time—
add your tree

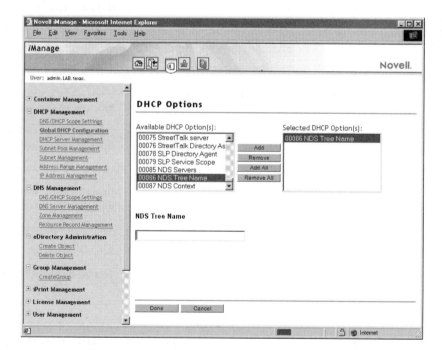

The second page shows that we have chosen this option, and offers us a chance to modify, delete, or cancel the choice, as well as the Help button and, most important, the Next command button. Try Next for some excitement.

Okay, excitement may not be the right word. Any hardware addresses to exclude? If so, this screen offers you that chance, but you need to type in the hardware address yourself. Then you have a chance to list specifically added hardware addresses. When you add MAC addresses to this list, be sure you enter them in the following format (colons included): 00:60:97:23:D4:C6:28. Click Next again, please.

The final Global Preferences page is the DHCP Options Table, which lists the available DHCP options and lets you define your own DHCP options. Don't do this unless specifically instructed by someone (perhaps even yourself) who really knows DHCP and the problems incorrect options can create.

Page down the long list several times, then click the Done command button. You will be rewarded with a liver treat (sorry, that's for dog training)—I mean a success screen. Congrats!

Creating a DHCP Server

IN A HURRY 12.6: CREATE A DHCP SERVER

1. Start iManage as Admin or an equivalent user.

2. Select DHCP Management ➤ DHCP Server Management ➤ Create Server and click Create.

3. Browse NDS, select the NetWare 6 server that will run DHCP server services, and then click Create.

You are the network administrator for Somorita Surfboards and you have decided that DHCP will be the best way to allocate the IP addresses your ISP provided. You collect information about each subnet in your organization and the assigned IP address for that subnet and format this information in a table similar to Table 12.5. For a detailed look at Somorita's intranet, refer to the network diagram in Figure 12.4, earlier in this chapter.

TABLE 12.5: SOMORITA SURFBOARD'S IP NETWORK INFORMATION

LOCATION	FUNCTION	NUMBER OF HOSTS	NETWORK ADDRESS	DEFAULT GATEWAY	NEAREST DNS
Haleiwa	Sales	153	247.187.99.0	247.187.99.1	247.187.99.2
Pipeline	Testing	108	247.187.100.0	247.187.100.1	247.187.100.2
Pipeline	Design	201	247.187.101.0	247.187.101.1	247.187.101.1

The DHCP server automatically assigns the following IP options:

◆ IP address and subnet mask

◆ Default gateway address

◆ Nearest domain name server

- Default NDS tree name

- Default NDS tree context

- Nearest NetWare server's IP address

Since we have plenty of IP host addresses available for all hosts, we will use the default lease period for IP addresses (three days). If we had a shortage of IP host addresses, we would reduce the lease time to possibly even a few hours, so that unused IP addresses would quickly return to the pool of available IP addresses.

The first task is to define which of our NetWare 6 servers will support DHCP servers. Since each department will use a subnet and have its own NetWare server, we will define each of those servers as a DHCP server and define a range of available addresses for that subnet.

Once again, start drilling down from iManage through DHCP Management to DHCP Server Management. The first menu option is Create (although Modify, Delete, Start/Stop Server and log settings are hiding in the menu), so choose it and click OK. Then choose the server from the Select Object dialog box. Then click Create. That's it, and you've earned another liver treat ... I mean, success screen.

IP address ranges and the like are not set when you create the DHCP server. That comes when you start creating and managing some subnets.

Creating a Subnet Pool

IN A HURRY 12.7: CREATE A SUBNET POOL

1. Start iManage as Admin or an equivalent user.

2. Select DHCP Management ➤ Subnet Pool Management ➤ Create Subnet Pool and click Create.

3. Enter a name for the Subnet Pool object.

4. Select an NDS context in which the Subnet Pool object will appear.

5. Click Create.

Subnet pools contain subnet address ranges and static IP addresses reserved for specific hosts. Before creating static IP addresses or subnet address ranges, we need to create subnets pools. This is not a hard thing to do. Novell leans toward ease-of-use in this area, rather than quick. After all, you don't do this often, so you want hints along the way.

Start iManage (same old instructions) and go to Subnet Pool Management. One subnet pool can contain multiple smaller subnets, making life a bit simpler. Think of this as the NSS "pool holding volume" philosophy applied to IP addresses.

After drilling down through iManage, through DHCP Management, and into Subnet Pool Management, click Create Subnet Pool. As might be expected, the other options here are Modify and Delete a Subnet Pool.

Figure 12.17 shows the rather simple screen used to create a pool. Name the pool, and select the context, and you're pretty much finished. If something goes wrong, just delete the pool and try again.

FIGURE 12.17

DHCP first step

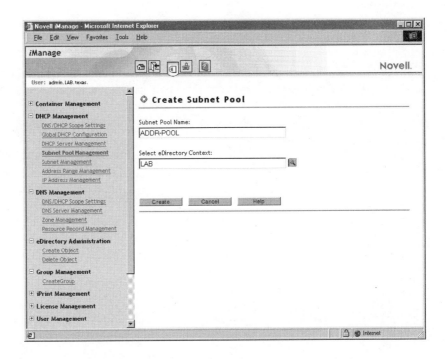

Again, you receive a success screen, letting you know that you've been successful.

Creating a Subnet

IN A HURRY 12.8: CREATE A SUBNET

1. Start iManage as Admin or an equivalent user.

2. Select DHCP Management ➢ Subnet Management ➢ Create Subnet and click Create.

3. Enter a name for the subnet.

4. Select an NDS context for the Subnet object.

5. Provide the subnet IP address.

6. Enter the subnet mask (255.255.255.0 for most situations).

7. Select the DHCP server to license addresses from this subnet.

8. Click the Create button.

Now that we have a subnet pool, we're ready to create the subnet. In iManage, drill down to Subnet Management and choose to create a subnet. Provide a name for the Subnet object, different from the name of the Subnet Pool object. As always, select the NDS eDirectory context for the new object. These are NetWare items.

The IP addressing DHCP details come next. Provide the IP address of the actual subnet for the IP addresses; in other words, enter the IP network. In our case, this is a Class C address carved out of the private net 10 (10.0.0.0) network address range.

Subnet masks limit broadcasts. Providing the subnet mask keeps broadcast queries within the small subnet, rather than letting them propagate throughout the network.

Then pick the DHCP server, and you're finished. Figure 12.18 shows the Create Subnet screen. This is not hard, but it requires a bit more information than some of the earlier screens.

FIGURE 12.18

Creating a
Subnet object

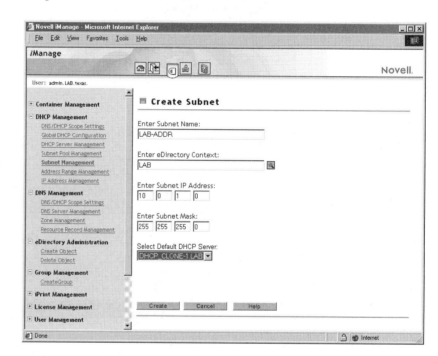

Next comes the real, IP address portion of the process.

Creating Subnet Address Ranges

IN A HURRY 12.9: CREATE A SUBNET ADDRESS RANGE

1. Start iManage as Admin or an equivalent user.

2. Select DHCP Management ➤ Address Range Management ➤ Create Address Range and click Create.

3. Enter a name in the Address Range field.

4. Enter the IP address range start and end IP addresses.

5. Click Create.

The *subnet address range* is the actual pool of addresses from which the DHCP server assigns an IP address. Because a subnet address range is contained under a subnet, you must first create the subnet.

One subnet pool can hold several address ranges. Our goal here—setting a range of IP addresses to license—defines which IP addresses will be provided to clients requesting an IP address.

Go through the startup drill, then choose Address Range Management. If you've only defined a single subnet address range, it will automatically be loaded for you (see Figure 12.19). Provide a name (every object needs some identification, after all) and the starting and ending IP addresses for this range.

FIGURE 12.19

Setting the range of IP leased addresses

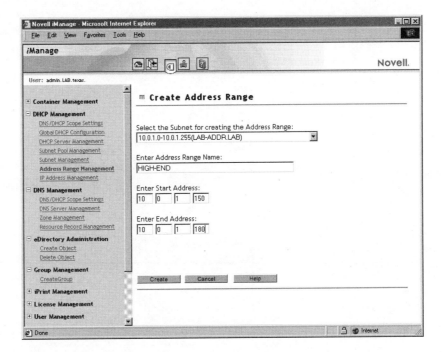

These IP addresses are inclusive, so don't put an address in here that you don't want used. IP addresses will be licensed from the low numbers to the high numbers, as available.

Go back to the beginning of this section and choose Modify Address Range, because there's more to this than just one screen. As you might expect, this choice leads to the Modify Subnet Address Range screen, shown in Figure 12.20. Address management offers a variety of options. In the Enter Range Type drop-down list, you can select from the following choices:

Dynamic BOOTP   Indicates that IP addresses in this range are dynamically assigned to BOOTP clients.

Dynamic DHCP with Automatic Host Name Generation   Indicates that IP addresses in this subnet address range will be allocated to DHCP clients and that a name will be automatically generated for those clients in the DNS zone chosen for the subnet.

Dynamic DHCP   Indicates that IP addresses will be leased to DHCP clients.

Dynamic BOOTP and DHCP   Indicates that IP addresses will be leased dynamically to both BOOTP and DHCP clients.

Excluded   Indicates that all IP addresses in this range are not to be leased.

NOTE   *Excluded subnet address ranges and IP addresses will not be leased to any computer. This is useful if you have manually configured a computer and its address exists right in the middle of a range of addresses that you want to use.*

FIGURE 12.20

Options for IP address assignments

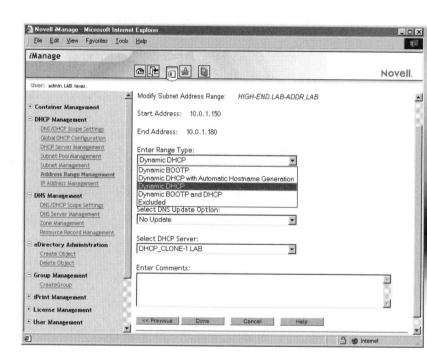

Depending on the option (the expanded menu shows them all), you can choose what the automatically generated hostname starts with and whether to automatically register computer names with the DNS when the client gets an IP address. Finally, you can specify which DHCP server handles this particular scope. The default is the server that was chosen for the subnet.

Sometimes, you must provide a DNS update option or DHCP server name. If necessary, the fields will become interactive. Check them out before clicking the Done command button.

NOTE   *A subnet can contain multiple subnet address ranges. You might want to use this option if you are going to assign 75 percent of your addresses to one DHCP server and 25 percent of them to a second DHCP server.*

NETWARE DHCP VERSUS LINUX OR UNIX DHCP

How well does the NetWare 6 DHCP match up with other "official" DHCP servers running on Unix or Linux? Take a look at the graphic from a cool departmental Linux-based server from Rebel.com, the NetWinder OfficeServer.

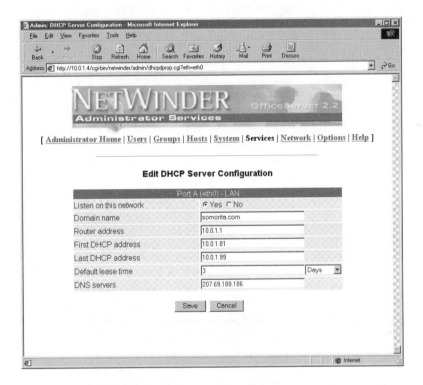

Notice the similarities? DHCP servers must do the same things, whether on NetWare or Linux or Unix: set the subnet address and subnet mask, set the IP address pool range, and set the lease time. This is another example of the value of standards. When you have standards, the same jobs on different server platforms work pretty much the same way.

Creating IP Address Records

IN A HURRY 12.9: CREATE AN IP ADDRESS RECORD

1. Start iManage as Admin or an equivalent user.

2. Select DHCP Management ➢ IP Address Management ➢ Create IP Address and click OK.

3. Select the IP address to create and click OK.

continued on next page

IN A HURRY 12.9: CREATE AN IP ADDRESS RECORD *(continued)*

4. Select the subnet containing the about-to-be-created IP address record.

5. Enter the IP address.

6. Specify whether the IP address is an exclusion or a manually configured address.

7. If it is a manual address, enter the MAC address for the client in the MAC Address field.

8. Click Create.

IP address records are contained in either a subnet or a subnet address range. These record types allow you to assign the same IP address to a specific computer each time it leases an address. Novell refers to this as *IP address management*, though some systems call this a *reservation*. To get to this management area, in iManage, work your way through Address Range Management to IP Address Management, and choose Create IP Address.

You must know the client's MAC address in order to assign it a dedicated IP address. You can also use IP addresses to exclude individual IP addresses that should not be leased.

Let's say that, in the past, someone gave your e-mail server an IP address of 10.0.1.175. Why? Who knows. Blame it on your predecessor.

Since you've just created a block of IP addresses for DHCP to give out that includes that IP address, you must make an exception of that IP address. It would cause no end of trouble if your e-mail server crashed, some other client received that IP address, and the e-mail server rebooted and got a different IP address. Your e-mail couldn't be found, because it would have moved, and the new client at 10.0.1.175 would be getting all sorts of strange messages it didn't know what to do with.

Your solution? Exclude the 10.0.1.175 IP address from those addresses under control of the DHCP server. This happens regularly, or at least much more often than assigning a particular manual address to a specific machine. In that case, I just hard-code that particular machine with the correct address. Then again, I don't need to manage 1500 IP clients, either. Large companies may need to use the manual option.

Back to our exclusion. First, create the IP address you want excluded, and exclude it from the address block. Figure 12.21 shows the simple procedure.

The MAC addresses and identifiers are for the manual assignments. Fill those in if you wish, but look at what we have for the exclusion IP address first. This IP address record will stop the DHCP server from giving out this particular address.

NOTE   *If the Enter IP Address option does not appear, you have not selected a Subnet object in the pull-down menu (or have not created one).*

Importing DHCP Information

Upgrading DHCP servers can be a pain, but not if you import the DHCP configuration file. Whether from an earlier NetWare DHCP server or a third-party server that provides the proper configuration file, you can import the configuration and save yourself some trouble. Avoiding extra work? That's always a good thing.

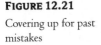

FIGURE 12.21

Covering up for past mistakes

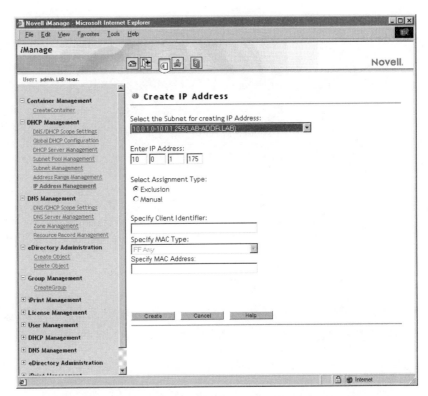

You can use the DNS/DHCP Management utility to import information from another DHCP server. To do so, follow these steps:

1. In iManage, expand the DHCP Management option and select the Global DHCP Configuration option.

2. Select Import DHCP Configuration from the drop-down menu, then click OK

3. Specify the eDirectory context, the DHCP server name, and the DHCP configuration file (with the Browse button, if you wish).

4. When you are prompted for the location of the DHCP database file, choose the file and click OK.

Configuring Dynamic DNS

Dynamic DNS is the result of integrating the DHCP server and the DNS data stored in the DNS database. In a traditional DNS environment, the DNS zone files need to be updated every time a client's IP address changes. If all clients are assigned static IP addresses, this is not a problem. However, if client IP addresses change often, such as when you are using DHCP, updating zone files manually is not an option.

You can configure NetWare DHCP servers to automatically update the DNS data in NDS whenever a client is given an IP address. This includes creating a host (A) record and a reverse lookup (PTR) record. Both records are needed so that DNS clients can do name-to-IP-address resolution as well as IP-address-to-name resolution (reverse lookups).

To configure this support, you must enable it at the subnet address range level. Follow these steps:

1. In the DNS/DHCP Management utility within iManage, select Address Range Management.

2. Select the subnet address range and click OK.

3. Under Select DNS Update Option, choose Always Update.

4. Click Done.

Let's say that you created a DHCP subnet address range and turned on dynamic DNS for this zone. You assigned all leased IP addresses to the somorita.com zone. Since a name is assigned to computers running Windows, a computer whose name is KAHUNA2 would automatically have a FQDN of kahuna2.somorita.com.

For clients that do not have assigned names, such as DOS clients, you can configure the DHCP server to automatically assign the client a name. This feature is also enabled at the subnet address range level.

When an IP address is assigned, the DHCP server updates the resource records for the appropriate zone. It also stores the lease time in the DNS information. If the IP address lease is not renewed or if the client releases its IP address, the DNS server automatically deletes the A and PTR records associated with that client from the DNS zone files at the end of the lease.

Enabling the *DHCPSRVR.NLM*

After you create your DHCP servers, subnets, and subnet address ranges, you need to load the DHCPSRVR.NLM. To do so, at the NetWare console, type **DHCPSRVR** and press Enter. Naturally, you will want to put this line in the AUTOEXEC.NCF file so that it loads each time the NetWare server starts.

The DHCPSRVR.NLM has some load options that you can use for diagnostics and testing. The -d option turns on a console background screen of diagnostic information. It has three flags:

◆ -d1 turns on a background screen to display DHCP activity.

◆ -d2 turns on the background screen to display DHCP activity as well as debugging statements.

◆ -d3 turns on the background screen, displays debugging information, and writes a log of activity to the SYS:ETC\DHCPAGNT.LOG text file.

The -p option sets the interval in minutes that the DHCPSRVR.NLM uses to poll NDS for changes. The -s option forces the server to read from and write to the master replica.

Here is a sample command that will load DHCPSRVR.NLM with a background activity screen and check for changes every five minutes:

```
DHCPSRVR -d2 -p5
```

Configuring Clients to Use DHCP

The final step in configuring a client to use the DHCP server to get IP addresses is to enable it in Control Panel on the same tab that you would have entered a TCP/IP address and subnet mask.

In Windows 95/98, choose Control Panel ➤ Network ➤ TCP/IP *<for your network adapter>* ➤ Properties to open the TCP/IP Properties dialog box, and select the IP Address tab, as shown in Figure 12.22. To use DHCP, click the Obtain an IP Address Automatically button.

FIGURE 12.22

The IP Address tab of the Windows TCP/IP Properties dialog box

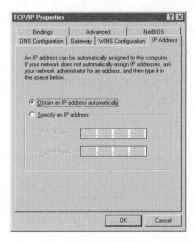

For Windows NT/2000/XP clients, the procedure is similar. Choose Control Panel ➤ Network ➤ Protocols ➤ TCP/IP ➤ Properties. From this screen, click the Obtain an IP Address from a DHCP Server button. Procedures vary for other clients that support DHCP.

Troubleshooting Common DNS and DHCP Problems

Although DNS and DHCP can help reduce your administrative load, there may be times when something just doesn't work right. You need to have a bag of troubleshooting tricks. Since DNS and DHCP are separate systems, there are separate troubleshooting tools for each.

Troubleshooting DNS Problems

DNS-related problems will manifest themselves quite clearly. Clients will not be able to resolve IP addresses from hostnames. This may include not only your internal clients, but also clients connecting from the Internet that may need to resolve your hostnames.

COMMON PROBLEMS

Let's look at a few possible problems and the steps you can take to resolve them.

A client cannot resolve hostnames.

- Verify connectivity to the network.

♦ Use the PING utility and ping another host's IP address.

♦ Check to see if the client can ping other hostnames.

♦ Verify that the client computer has the correct IP address of a valid name server.

♦ Confirm that the name server in question is indeed active.

♦ Ping the IP address of the name server.

♦ Try changing to a different name server's IP address.

Clients cannot access a specific host.

♦ Confirm that the host has been added as a host in your DNS tables.

♦ If you are using secondary name servers, verify that the secondary server has done a zone transfer from the primary (designated) server.

Clients or mail servers can't connect to certain hosts on the Internet.

♦ Check to make sure that they can access other hosts on the Internet.

♦ Verify that the client or mail server has a reverse query (PTR) record in the `in-addr.arpa` zone. Many FTP servers and mail servers will not allow clients to connect to them unless the host can do a reverse lookup of the client's IP address.

Client computers can do name resolution for hosts within your network, but not for hosts on the Internet.

♦ Verify that the name servers are communicating outside your own LAN.

♦ Ensure that your name servers are forwarding queries to one another only and not to the Internet root servers.

♦ Be sure that you have a list of the Internet root name servers in your NDS eDirectory tree.

Client computers on the Internet cannot resolve your hostnames.

♦ Verify with the InterNIC that they are pointing to the correct DNS server's IP addresses. You can verify your InterNIC registration information on the Web at `rs.internic.net`.

Client computers can resolve computer names in your main domain, but they cannot resolve computer names in the subdomains.

♦ Be sure that the A and NS records at the parent domain match the A and NS records at the subdomains.

♦ Be sure that the IP addresses are correct for the name servers.

The name server program (NAMED.NLM) will not load.

◆ Ensure that TCP/IP is loaded and bound to an adapter. The NetWare Console command CONFIG can help you verify this.

◆ Be sure that you have sufficient memory on the server.

◆ Verify that the particular NetWare server has been configured as a name server in the DNS/DHCP Management Console.

OTHER PROBLEMS

A good rule of thumb for strange problems related to DNS is "reload and DSREPAIR." If you have problems relating to DNS, such as error messages that the name server generates to the console or messages indicating that it is not reading a particular zone object, try these two things:

◆ Unload and reload the NAMED.NLM.

◆ Run DSREPAIR.

In addition, turn on the console debug screen for the NAMED.NLM by loading it with the –v option (type **LOAD NAMED –v** and press Enter). This displays information such as DNS queries that the server is handling and automatic maintenance.

NSLOOKUP QUERIES

Your number-one troubleshooting tool for DNS-related problems is NSLOOKUP, a utility that can perform a number of queries for you.

NOTE   *Windows NT/2000/XP includes a command-line NSLOOKUP utility, but Windows 95/98 does not. You can find many other shareware utilities on the Internet.*

Under Windows NT, NSLOOKUP has two modes of operation: interactive, which allows you to type commands that NSLOOKUP interprets, and batch, which you use from the command line. Both modes use the same command-line options.

Using NSLOOKUP, you can do the following types of searches:

◆ Host (A) records

◆ CNAMES (aliases)

◆ Mail Exchanger (MX) records

◆ Name server (NS records)

For example, to look up an address record for the host DUKE.somorita.com, use the following command:

```
NSLOOKUP –Q=A DUKE.SOMORITA.COM

Server:   rell.somorita.com
Address:   204.187.101.2
Name:   duke.somorita.com
Address:   204.187.99.2
```

Notice that the name server that resolved the request was 1RELL.somorita.com. Get to know the NSLOOKUP utility; it's a great timesaving tool when debugging DNS problems.

Troubleshooting DHCP Problems

When a client does not lease an IP address, this problem is also quickly and painfully obvious, especially if TCP/IP is the only network protocol. Without an IP address, the client cannot communicate with the IP network.

COMMON PROBLEMS

Windows workstations are quite helpful when this problem occurs. The user receives a message indicating that a DHCP server could not be found and that an IP address could not be leased. The following are some sample problems and resolutions.

A client cannot lease an address.

- ◆ Verify physical connectivity to the LAN.

- ◆ Be sure that an IP address is available on the client's subnet.

- ◆ Confirm that there is not an exclusion for this particular client.

A client gets a duplicate IP address, indicating that another client has probably had that address manually configured.

Using the DNS/DHCP Management Console, select the DHCP server that has the particular scope from which the address came, and then select the Options property page. At the bottom of the right pane, select the Ping Enabled check box. This causes the DHCP server to check to see if the address is already being used before leasing it. This will increase the time it takes to lease an address by a few seconds.

IPCONFIG AND WINIPCFG OPTIONS

Windows NT/2000/XP includes a command-line utility called IPCONFIG that will prove especially useful when troubleshooting DHCP problems. Windows 95/98 also provides the same utility in a graphical form called WINIPCFG. Using this utility, you can view your current IP configuration, release an IP address, or force your client to renew its lease on an IP address.

IPCONFIG has four command-line options:

- ◆ /ALL displays all the available IP configuration information.

- ◆ /RENEW forces renewal of a DHCP lease.

- ◆ /RELEASE forces the client to release an IP address that it had leased.

- ◆ /HELP or /? displays online help, in case you forget these options.

Figure 12.23 shows the WINIPCFG utility from Windows 98. You can renew or release IP addresses with this graphical utility.

FIGURE 12.23

The Windows 98 WINIPCFG IP utility for reporting your TCP/IP configuration

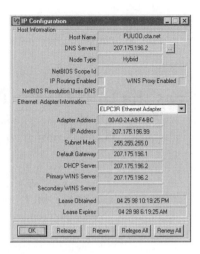

LOG FILES

The DHCPSRVR.NLM creates a text log file, SYS:ETC\DHCPSRVR.LOG, if the −d3 option is used when the server NLM is loaded. You can use this log file to track possible problems. Console alerts are logged to the SYS:SYSTEM\SYS$LOG file.

CONSOLE MESSAGES

We all know that it is difficult to see every message that appears on the server console screen, especially if the messages are passing by quickly. You can use CONLOG.NLM to capture information and messages that appear on the NetWare server console.

AUDITING

You can also use the DNS/DHCP Management utility to view events and details. To view events and alerts from a specific name server, choose DHCP Server Management from DHCP Management within iManage. Choose Events Log or Audit Trail Log to see when IP addresses were leased, to which clients, and other lease details.

SNMP EVENTS

If you are using an SNMP management system, you can configure the DHCP server to generate SNMP traps. By default, the DHCP server generates traps for major events. A major event represents critical events that should not be ignored, such as server startup or shutdown errors.

The other options are No Traps and All Events. Choosing All Events generates traps for warnings and minor events and should not be turned on unless your server is experiencing problems and you need to diagnose them using the SNMP management system. Warning events include server faults that were recovered automatically and IP addresses not being available for clients. Minor events include something such as a client "declining" an IP address.

To change the types of SNMP events that are generated, in the DNS/DHCP Management Console, choose the server for which you want to change the event status, and then select the Options property page.

NetWare 6 Really Goes the Unix/Linux Road

Any questions from NetWare detractors and Unix/Linux fans (a common group of people, in many cases) about how well NetWare 6 plays in a Unix/Linux environment can be answered by this chapter. More DNS and DHCP support comes with NetWare 6 than with any other non-Unix/Linux operating system available today. And although Unix/Linux systems may have as many (or even more) DNS and DHCP options, they don't have the ease of use provided by the NetWare utilities.

NetWare 6 (and 5.*x* for that matter) can do any DNS/DHCP operations a large network requires. Technically, they can do it all. Realistically, don't go crazy and run yelling at your IT services co-workers to scrap all their Unix/Linux servers and services.

NetWare 6, using NDS eDirectory as the DNS engine for replication and fault tolerance, performs faster and more reliably than most DNS primary and secondary server pairs. That's a fact. It's also a fact that all these new DNS features evolved several generations since they were pulled from Unix systems into NetWare.

New equals scary to many people, including IT personnel who love Unix/Linux. We won't get into any NetWare versus Unix/Linux fights in this book, but be aware that your network personnel have been supporting Internet access and IP networking for years (if you're in a medium to large company, and in many small companies as well). Your IT co-workers over in Internet Services (or whatever) do not care that NetWare 6 offers all sorts of DNS improvements. If your company's DNS infrastructure works, they will almost certainly leave it on Unix/Linux and not accept your offer of NetWare support. Don't get mad, because they aren't insulting you personally, or even NetWare. They just don't want to change.

DHCP may be a bit different, however, especially if you're adding new PCs or adding new IP addresses to existing PCs. DHCP failures do not affect the company network, just the individual systems that can't get connected.

What's the bottom line? Big company NetWare 6 servers will rarely, if ever, get into the DNS loop because of IP and IT inertia. DHCP services are a different story. Start with DHCP, and offer NetWare 6 servers as secondary DNS servers. Then relax.

The new iManage utility makes DNS and DHCP easier to manage than ever before. You may not have much opportunity to let the NetWare DNS tools shine in an existing network environment, but the DHCP tools offer plenty of timesaving features, and are a good first step in showing your Unix/Linux fanatical co-workers other operating systems (NetWare) can play in a multivendor environment. In fact, NetWare can certainly "play well with others" if you remember your grade school report cards.

Part IV

Taking Advantage of Special Network Features

Chapter 13

Remote File Access with iFolder and NetDrive

TODAY, REMOTE PROBLEMS FOR many customers break down into two critical areas: secure remote file access and file synchronization across multiple client platforms. NetWare 6 handles these problems in new and innovative ways that lead the network operating system market in simplicity and security.

NetWare 6 includes two ways to make remote file access simple, secure, and speedy: iFolder and NetDrive.

iFolder automatically synchronizes users' files in a private server subdirectory with any and all remote PCs for those users. Desktops in the office, PCs at home, and laptops on the road synchronize as if by magic. Additionally, any user with an Internet browser and the proper eDirectory authentication can download, upload, and modify files on a remote NetWare 6 server. Any browser, such as a kiosk PC in an airport or coffee shop, can provide the link to a user's NetWare 6 files.

NetDrive is a utility that puts a remote file server drive mapping on a personal computer across the Internet. No file synchronizing comes with NetDrive, but easy drag-and-drop file controls do the trick for many users.

This chapter covers the following topics:

◆ An overview of remote-access solutions

◆ Using iFolder for remote file synchronization

◆ Using NetDrive for remote file access

◆ A look at NetStorage

An Overview of Remote-Access Solutions

Since the early days of the mainframe, the ability to access a computer remotely has been important. Traditional remote access solutions for LANs have typically been remote-control solutions. Software such as Carbon Copy or pcANYWHERE allow users to access a network by taking control of a host computer connected directly to the network. The applications execute at the host computer, and the host computer processes all data. The only data that actually come across the phone line are keystrokes and screen updates. (Microsoft actually bundled this technology into Windows XP, threatening yet another third-party product line by bundling this technology into the operating system.)

On the other side of the coin are remote-node solutions. A remote-node solution allows a remote PC to function as if it were directly attached to the LAN. File and application data are transferred over the remote-node link to the remote PC, just as if it were connected directly to the network. The applications execute at the remote computer, and the remote computer processes the data.

WARNING   *An important consideration when implementing remote-node solutions is that applications stored on a remote server must be downloaded across the remote-node link. This can be excruciatingly slow, even with a 56Kbps modem. Remote-node users should have the applications installed on their local hard drives for better performance.*

Many of the advantages of remote-node systems disappeared, through no fault of their own. Web-based applications that communicate over an encrypted SSL link to a thin client through the Internet offer much more convenience than building a remote-node architecture. Will companies still need remote-node options? Yes, at least for the next two or three years. But look for new applications to rely on Web servers rather than client/server applications as in the past.

NetWare 6 ships without the asynchronous connection tools Novell included with NetWare 5.1 and earlier. Why are these tools gone? They're gone because the Internet has made much of this technology obsolete. When every traveler can reach the Internet and reach home from there, why dial directly into home and pay the long-distance charges?

Discussion within Novell, and customer-response surveys, may push Novell to repackage some of the earlier access methods into a NetWare 6 update or service pack. The Small Business Suite may include some of these features, since small companies are less likely to use hardware routers for remote access or have enough in-house Web expertise to rework applications through a Web interface. Time will tell, but I can't yet.

Using iFolder for Remote-File Synchronization

Let's be right up front about this: iFolder alone should push you to upgrade to NetWare 6 from any earlier version. Sure, you can add iFolder to NetWare 5.1, but why? iFolder, developed with NetWare 6 and tied to the Apache Web Server included with NetWare 6, will save your users hours and hours of frustration. When users are less frustrated, you get bothered less, which is another good reason to quickly embrace iFolder.

One critical problem comes packed inside every laptop: How do you back up laptop files? Can you trust users to do any type of backup, such as copying files to some server directory whenever they come back to the office and dock their laptop? Not if you want to keep your job. Users with laptops will rarely (let me be more emphatic: NEVER) take proper care of their laptop files. Even though you may be 2000 miles away when they realize that they forgot their critical PowerPoint files an hour before their presentation, you will still get the blame.

Install iFolder on every laptop in your company, and suddenly you gain several layers of insulation between laptop user incompetence and your frustration level. If our PowerPoint friend in the previous paragraph used iFolder, the only necessary step for file recovery would be to connect to the Internet and let iFolder synchronize the files. The PowerPoint file, even if it were created at home, would be synchronized to the server. When the laptop user connects, the PowerPoint file is replicated to the laptop. Bingo, your laptop user has the day saved, even if you won't get the credit.

Think of the server iFolder directory as the main file repository, and the clients (whether local office desktops or remote home PCs) as the access points to the centralized storage point. Whatever happens to the central storage set of files is reflected in the remote systems the next time they log in. Work at home, save a file, and it's waiting on the server when you get to work.

A quick note on the hidden technology of iFolder: Only 1KB chunks of file are synchronized. Change a 4MB PowerPoint file over a competing product, and you wait forever at hotel phone rates for the file to synchronize between server and client. Change one slide in a 4MB PowerPoint presentation and synchronize with iFolder, and only the portion of the presentation that changed is transferred. Can you say *timesaving*?

Do you work at home? Do you create files at home, or wish you had some of your office files on your home system? Are you sick of trying to e-mail files back and forth to yourself? Then iFolder will help you as much as it helps your users.

Installing iFolder on a NetWare 6 Server

What's the easiest way to install iFolder on your NetWare 6 server? Install this software along with all the other NetWare components during initial installation. If you didn't, find your NetWare 6 Operating System CD and head toward your server.

Whether running the installation routine during NetWare 6 setup or from ConsoleOne on the physical server, the trick comes with the configuration screens. Check the manual for installation (the online manual at `http://www.novell.com/documentation/lg/nw6p/index.html` for needed updates) or the PDF format manual on the Documentation CD. Here are some installation hints to make life easier:

◆ Put your LDAP server and iFolder server on the same physical server.

◆ Remember usernames and passwords inside the Apache Web Server are case-sensitive, in contrast to the rest of NetWare.

◆ Check the box allowing Clear Text Passwords.

◆ Write down all the URLs and port numbers.

Novell recommends one sure way to improve iFolder performance: Increase server RAM. Yes, you've heard that solution for any number of problems, but it's still good advice. If you set your clients to communicate too often with the iFolder server, the load can become heavy and drag down server performance in other areas.

Yes, you can put iFolder on Windows NT/2000 running Internet Information Services (IIS) 4.0 or later, if you really, really want to for some odd reason. Perhaps Novell salespeople believe iFolder can get their foot through the door of some Windows-only companies. Good for them, if it works.

Administering iFolder

I suggest you spend time configuring the iFolder environment on your server before starting to roll out this cool, new tool to users. Install one client, just to get the feel of how the client works, and then do your administration. You'll be happy you did, because once you turn the iFolder hordes loose, you won't be able to corral them again.

Start the iFolder administration screen from NetWare Remote Manager, or directly by using a URL of `http://iFolderServerIP/iFolderServer/Admin`. Put this URL in one of your Favorite slots, whether you use Internet Explorer from Microsoft or Netscape Navigator. Both work, supposedly, but I have better luck with Internet Explorer (not my favorite, so maybe Novell will fix things for Netscape, Opera, and other browsers).

A login to iFolder masks a login to the Apache Web Server, so case sensitivity matters (a pain). If you have troubles, try the username and password in all capitals, and then one in initial capitals, and then one in lowercase, until it works. Restarting Apache a time or two seems to be a normal occurrence as well.

GENERAL IFOLDER SETTINGS

Not wanting to waste paper by showing you a screen with a login and password (and occasional rejections), let's skip right to the General Information page in iFolder Server Admin. Figure 13.1 shows the details. The main screen required a little adjusting to show all the information in the framed page.

FIGURE 13.1

Administering iFolder, step one

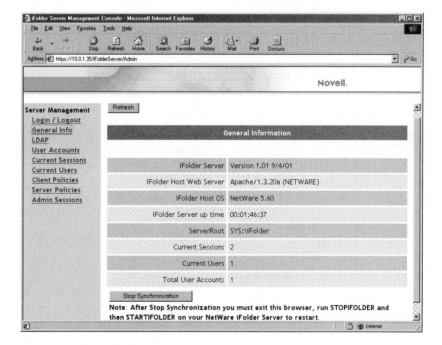

Notice that the iFolder Server version says 1.01, even though this screen comes from the first batch of NetWare 6 shipped from Novell. Notice also that the iFolder Host OS listing says NetWare 5.60 for some reason. I guess that's the secret name for NetWare 6.

WARNING   *If you leave the utility open too long, your login will timeout, and you'll need to log in once again. I haven't found anything that says "Admin timeout," but the Session Timeout (default to 60 minutes) option in the Server Policies seems to control this.*

Also notice the ServerRoot listing: SYS:\iFolder. This is not the best storage place if, like me, you're paranoid about filling up the SYS: volume. During installation, you can decide where to put the iFolder directory structure, but the Apache Web Server must be loaded onto the SYS: volume.

LDAP SETTINGS

LDAP (Lightweight Directory Access Protocol) has its own menu option in the left frame. Most NetWare managers use NDS rather than trusting LDAP for anything. However, remote clients can use LDAP, as can partners who may be allowed access to some NetWare services but not given a full NetWare Client32 software package.

Primary LDAP Host, `proliant.gaskin.com`, is the same physical system running the iFolder server software. As I mentioned, it's a good idea, to keep both on the same system. See the details in Figure 13.2.

FIGURE 13.2

LDAP Settings for your iFolder server

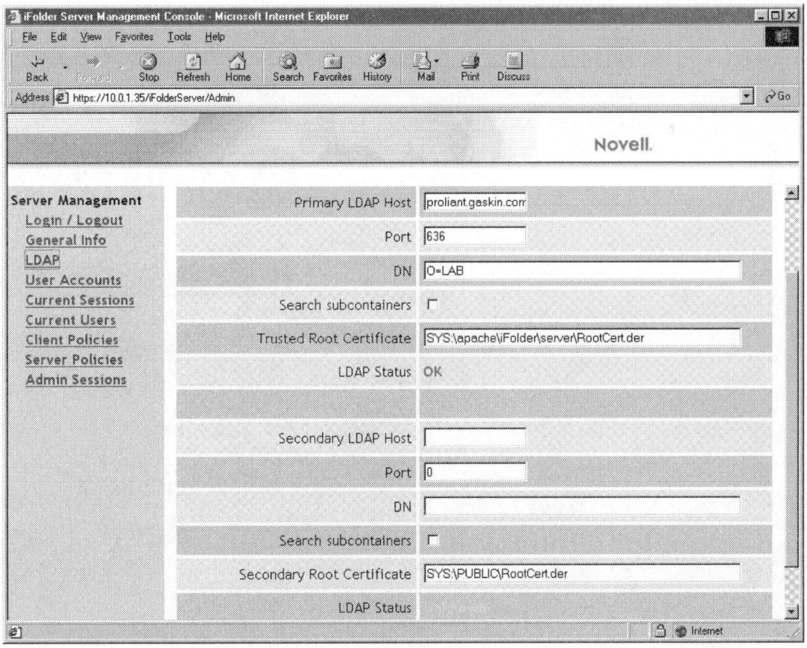

Everything shown here echoes what you put in the installation screens. DN (Domain Name) is LDAP speak for Organization, or vice versa, and the Trusted Root Certificate field shows the default location for the Apache Web Server.

If you change anything, such as checking the box for Search Subcontainers (a good idea or I wouldn't bring it up), click the Update button at the bottom of the screen. iFolder will verify you really want to update your LDAP settings, and you do.

NOTE *What does "LDAP Status: Unknown," sitting at the very bottom of the main window, mean? I have no clue, and nowhere does the documentation (public and private) mention this. Perhaps it's another future feature. Since I'm using the NetWare LDAP, one would think the iFolder Admin tool could make sense of the LDAP server, but maybe not.*

CHECKING IFOLDER USERS

As you'll soon see, the majority of server-side client details are set by the clients when they log in, along with the short list of options available for iFolder in this first iteration. Yet, there are several user-monitoring features.

User Account Information

First off, iFolder shows you just how many user accounts you have active and total. As per my earlier instructions, I've set up a single user to test the system and massage the configuration details. Figure 13.3 shows the one user and some details on the User Accounts page.

FIGURE 13.3

Checking user account information

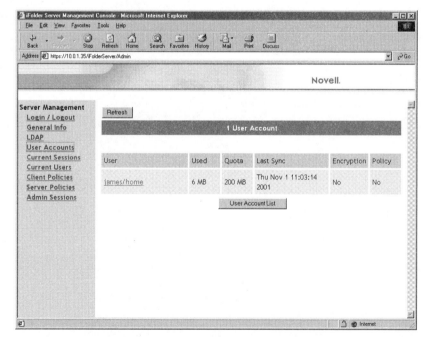

One quick glance, and you can tell who is now connected to the system. Notice the Used heading. This shows how much server disk space this user filled. The Quota column shows the total amount of server disk space this user can fill. Last Sync is self-explanatory. The Encryption column shows whether this user encrypts files stored on the server—a bad idea we'll cover soon. Finally, the Policy column shows whether this user must follow policy guidelines set by the administrator (you).

The User Account List command button looks impressive, but does little. Click there, and you'll just see a list of usernames by their NDS names, with no more details. It's a somewhat useless screen, but it must have been easy to program.

Individual User Information

The individual user screen that appears when you click the *user/folder* name in the left column, such as james/home in Figure 13.3, is more helpful. It provides more information than the Current Sessions screen. Notice the extras you get in Figure 13.4.

Most useful, and therefore well placed at the top, the Disk Quota master setting can be changed per user. Change the number in the text field, then click the Change command button to save that change. Of course, making a change for just one user means you haven't followed my advice to the contrary. Let this be a trap for administrators who will pull their hair out in a few months trying to track down what changes they've made for individual users. Perhaps soon this and other iFolder settings will get folded into ConsoleOne, so iFolder storage space settings can apply to a group called Remote Users or something equally clever.

FIGURE 13.4

Checking individual user information

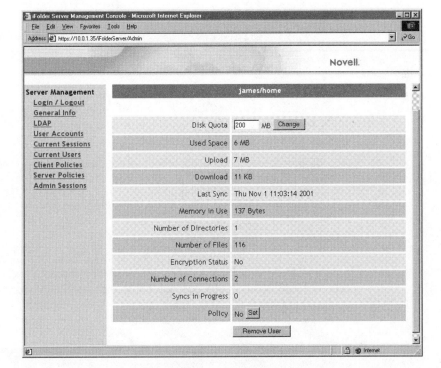

Let's delve into an iFolder secret. Run your cursor over the *user/folder* name (james/home in the case of Figure 13.3) and notice what appears on the status line at the bottom of your browser. See that huge, long number? That's the "secret" key used to identify each iFolder user.

On the server hosting iFolder, go to the \iFolder and list the directory. You will see a directory starting with the first two numbers of this unique ID. Drill down into that directory, and you'll see more directories. One of them, probably 0, will hold all the iFolder files transferred from different clients, but list them with hexadecimal names. You'll see how this works for backup and restore operations in just a bit.

The rest of the page doesn't allow any changes, except for the bottom-line item of Policy. Click the Set command button, and an individual Policy page opens so you can administer one user at a time (a bad idea last paragraph and still a bad idea in this one).

"Remove User" ominously states the command button at the very bottom of the page. Don't want a user to have access any longer? Click here, verify, and that user disappears as quickly as if you sprayed a can of User Be Gone in her cubicle.

One more quick detail: See the Encryption Status line item, fourth from the bottom? It reads No in Figure 13.4. Make sure that yours always says No as well. You can't set this option here, but I'm warning you: Don't let users encrypt the files on the server. If they forget their password or leave the company, you'll never recover a copy of those files. It's bad karma to let users encrypt their own files on your server, so don't let it happen.

Other iFolder Administration Options

Several other options along the left side of the iFolder Server Admin window relate to user information:

- Clicking Current Sessions opens a dull screen showing just the *user/folder* names (james/home in my example) and the machine information. Since users can connect from as many machines as they wish, this information could be helpful in the future.

- Clicking Current Users opens a screen that bores us even more than the previous Current Sessions screen, while presenting the same info. (Personally, I would have called the User Accounts screen the Current Users screen instead, since it shows more information than the Current Users screen, but they didn't ask me.)

- Clicking Admin Sessions shows current browser sessions being run by a person with administrator privileges.

All of these are rather dull, so we'll skip the screen shots. Feel free to peruse them on your own.

SETTING IFOLDER CLIENT POLICIES

When you click the Client Policies option on the left side of the iFolder Admin window, you see the screen shown in Figure 13.5. This screen offers you the chance to configure all your iFolder clients at once. Use this to make any changes, rather than the previous screen, where you can adjust a single individual's configuration.

Let's take a look at each setting in turn, and I'll give my recommendation.

TIP   *If you make a mess of the settings, and forget to write down the defaults (as if real managers need to write down such petty details), click the Restore Defaults command button at the bottom.*

FIGURE 13.5

Controlling all
iFolder clients

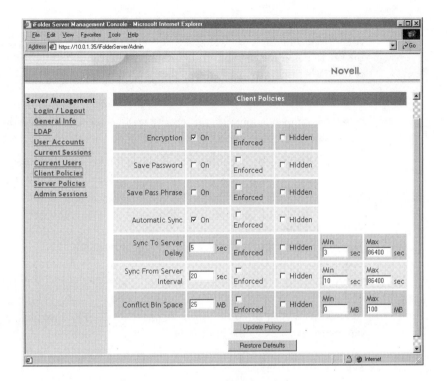

Encryption

Encryption sets whether the user can encrypt files on their portion of the iFolder server storage space.

◆ Default: On

◆ Recommendation: Off, because you can't break the encryption on the server

Save Password

Save Password offers users the chance to store the password rather than type it each time they start iFolder.

◆ Default: Off

◆ Recommendation: Off

The password, same as their NDS eDirectory password, must be typed each time for any semblance of security, especially for laptops. Maybe you should even hide this option by checking the Hidden box.

Save Pass Phrase

A *pass phrase*, a multiple-word slogan that is easy to remember (such as Pointy Haired Boss), provides the key to power the encryption algorithm. This setting offers users the chance to store the pass phrase rather than type it when they start iFolder.

- Default: Off
- Recommendation: Off, for security reasons—again, *if* you let them use this option, which you shouldn't

Users should always type their passphrase and never even have the option of saving the phrase on their system. When they save passwords or passphrases, anyone gaining access to that computer has full access to all the user's information.

Automatic Sync

Automatic Sync tells the client to initiate synchronization.

- Default: On
- Recommendation: On

Don't trust clients to synchronize iFolder, because they won't do it regularly. Perhaps even hide this choice by checking the Hidden box.

Sync to Server Delay

Sync to Server Delay tells the client how long after file activity stops to wait until synchronizing with the server.

- Default: 5 seconds
- Recommendation: 5 is okay, but you should consider making it slightly longer if the majority of your iFolder users work remotely and file activity may be delayed by slow links

Sync from Server Interval

Sync From Server Interval sets how long between pings from the server to each client, to verify they're still connected and to transfer any files added to the server side not yet on the client.

- Default: 20 seconds
- Recommendation: 300 or 600 seconds

Forcing the server to ping a large number of iFolder clients every 20 seconds will slow server performance. Every 5 or 10 minutes should be enough.

Conflict Bin Space

The *conflict bin* holds local files overwritten or deleted from the server storage space. This allows users to reclaim files accidentally deleted from one client, and therefore to the server, by restoring them from the conflict bin. I would rather see this on the server, but the client side is better than nothing.

- Default: 25MB

- Recommendation: More, because disk space costs far less than re-creating deleted files

You might set this to 50MB for moderately active users, and 100MB for active file deleters.

SETTING IFOLDER SERVER POLICIES

Compared to configuring Client Policies, setting up Server Policies is a snooze alarm. You have two real settings, both of which you might consider changing.

Initial Client Quota

Initial Client Quota sets how much disk space each iFolder client can claim on the server.

Default: 200MB

- Recommendation: More, unless you're positive you have no PowerPoint gurus filling long presentations with fancy animated slides, complete with music

The limit doesn't preallocate space, so allowing more won't use up server storage unless needed.

Session Timeout

Session Timeout sets how long the server will keep checking the client if there is no file activity.

- Default: 60 minutes

- Recommendation: 30 minutes

Keep the load on your server down. If a client saves a file 45 minutes after saving the last file, the client synchronization process will wake up the server.

Debug Output

The final option, Debug Output, provides server logs to help track problems. Do this if you're curious, but it's really only useful for troubleshooting.

IFOLDER BACKUP AND RESTORE

Novell doesn't say anything about iFolder backup and restore in the documentation or help screens, but sure as the world, some user will come crying to you about a lost file. The Conflict Resolution screen on the user's system helps, but server-based backup and restore remains the savior of users everywhere.

Backup works fine, even if the files are (stupidly) encrypted. The iFolder files get sucked out to tape (or whatever backup media) without a problem.

Restoring the entire volume works with no problem. All the iFolder directory structure, re-created during the restore, awaits iFolder clients as always.

Restoring becomes a problem when you're trying to target just one user. Why? iFolder disguises the client name as a long, apparently random, alphanumeric string (the one that appears when you roll your cursor over the *user/folder* name). You must track down that number, and then restore the directories under that numbered directory from the backup. It's a pain, but doable.

Using the iFolder Client

The cleverly named IFOLDERCLIENT.EXE file, just over 2MB in size, runs all the iFolder installation routine automatically. Clients can download this file from the iFolder Web page the first time they connect. In fact, anyone can download this file, because the client relies on NDS eDirectory for authentication. Having the client software without eDirectory does hackers no good at all.

An automated installation routine takes off, and users don't have a thing to do until they get to the login screen. The first time they log in, they will create the subdirectory structure for themselves in the iFolder server storage area. Figure 13.6 shows the login screen, with a little extra.

FIGURE 13.6

iFolder login screen

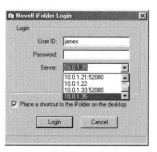

Users must provide their own name and password. This password, the same as their NDS eDirectory password, is case sensitive. Beware of this, and the fact that early iFolder users report problems with certain password characters, such as the exclamation point.

A drop-down server list appears, but the first time there may not be anything in that list to pick. Notice that two of the IP addresses use port number 52080 after the address. This directs the iFolder client to the Apache Web Server on NetWare servers running with a single IP address. The highlighted IP address, 10.0.1.35, is really the same physical server as 10.0.1.33, but reworked to have multiple IP addresses available on a single network interface card.

The "Place a shortcut to the iFolder on the desktop" check box always appears checked. Don't worry—the user's desktop won't be littered with iFolders. If a shortcut is there, a new one does not appear. Users need only click the iFolder icon to pop open an Explorer window.

VIEWING IFOLDER CLIENT ACCOUNT INFORMATION

Unless it is opened by using the iFolder icon on the Taskbar (and opening Account Information), the iFolder client stays hidden. Figure 13.7 shows the opening iFolder client screen in the middle of a synchronization operation.

Notice the login details in the top third of the information area. You can see the username, local iFolder placement, and server. You can change the local iFolder placement by editing the Windows Registry for each user. Certainly, Novell will add a way to specify a different local drive letter for the \MyDocuments folder in an update.

FIGURE 13.7

The iFolder client screen

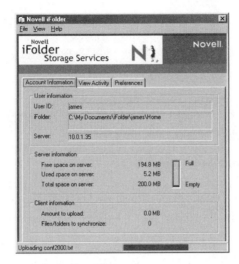

The middle third of the screen shows the server information. Well, it shows how much total space the user has and how much remains available. A thermometer graph exists to help managers check their available space (manager's credo: never read when you can look at a picture).

There is not much of interest on the bottom, because the short delay between when new files appear on the client and when they get sent to the server has a default of five seconds. I actually caught a file upload in progress in Figure 13.7, as you can see from the progress bar and the status information on the bottom of the window.

VIEWING IFOLDER CLIENT ACTIVITY

Although the tab in the iFolder client window says View Activity, it really means View Log. I guess that would confuse regular users, so Novell hid that nomenclature under the pseudonym of View Activity. See what I mean in Figure 13.8.

FIGURE 13.8

Client activity, or the log file

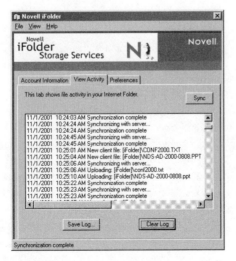

Notice the log file information presented. In the middle of the log file list, you can see I added two new client files. Two seconds later, the client synchronized with the iFolder server, and uploaded the two files. I hope the users don't get paranoid and think the files physically moved, because they didn't. In any case, the files zoom upward, and the activity is logged.

See the Sync command button on the top right? Users can manually activate the synchronization process (as if they would remember such a thing).

You, or rather the user, can save the log to a text file. Since there isn't a setting to limit the size of the client log file, clearing it out now and then wouldn't hurt.

SETTING IFOLDER CLIENT PREFERENCES

All the settings we made at the iFolder Server Admin screens can be undone by the client, simply by clicking the Preferences tab in the iFolder client window. Let's just hope the client understands the implications of the changes. See Figure 13.9 for all the trouble you may face.

FIGURE 13.9

iFolder client preference settings

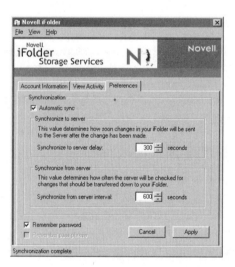

Yes, the Automatic Sync check box must remain checked. The time delay I have set for the client to synchronize to the server after file activity is, in retrospect, too long. You don't want to give the user time to save a file, then turn off the machine before iFolder can perform the synchronization. Three hundred seconds, or five minutes, gives the user time to make a mistake, so set that back to ten seconds or so in the Server Admin pages shown in the previous section.

Remember password? Sure, and open the door to all the client files for any miscreant who steals or finds the laptop. On the iFolder settings back in Figure 13.5 you can mark the Save Passphrase as hidden, so the user can't change that setting. You can do the same with Save Password. Force the users to type their password each and every time. After all, it's the same password they use with eDirectory.

The Restore Defaults and Update Policy command buttons at the bottom hold no mystery. Make a change, then cancel or apply that change.

VIEWING THE IFOLDER CONFLICT BIN

I'm not thrilled with the name, but I can't think of a better one besides something like "pending changes" which could easily be misunderstood. At least the *conflict* part of the name intimates there's a problem somewhere.

The idea behind the conflict bin is to keep local files from being overwritten or deleted by the server during a synchronization operation. Most of the time, the files are changed based on what another client system for the same user did earlier, and those changes are replicated to each client via the server. So most of the time, the user won't need to visit the Conflict Bin Viewer screen.

You can't reach this screen through the iFolder client screen shown in the previous section. To open it, right-click the iFolder icon on the Taskbar and choose View Conflict Bin. The Conflict Bin Help menu item, alas, doesn't help, but maybe it will with the next iteration.

The two files in Figure 13.10 were deleted on the server via the browser client (see the next section). When the iFolder client synchronized, these files were set aside to verify they should really be deleted. Think of this like the SALVAGE NetWare setting, where deleted files can be rescued.

FIGURE 13.10

Resolving iFolder file conflicts

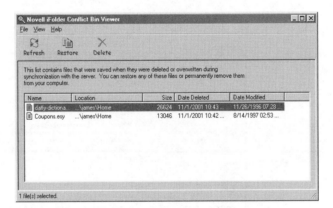

Click Refresh to update the file display. Highlight one or more files, as shown in Figure 13.10, then click either the Restore or Delete icons. If you click Delete, you will be asked to verify your choice, so click a second time to be rid of the file.

See how neatly the iFolder client works? Even the lack of good online documentation shouldn't hold your users back from utilizing the iFolder client software. Once you implement this feature of NetWare 6, your users will never let you take it away and go back to the "e-mail files to yourself" method of synchronization.

Using the iFolder Non-Client (Browser Mode)

What if you don't want to run the iFolder remote-client software and have NetWare provide synchronization services for you? You can still use iFolder by connecting via any recent browser (officially, anyway, but Internet Explorer 5 and above seems to work the best).

Something that you're more likely to want to do is use the browser version of iFolder to upload or download files from your iFolder server stash to any Internet-connected computer. Suppose that you have an hour at an airport kiosk and want to update your expense account. You can download your spreadsheet, work (assuming the kiosk system has the proper application, of course), and upload the file with all your changes.

All this happens securely and simply, using NDS eDirectory just like the iFolder client version. You didn't think you could bypass NDS, did you?

The first screen you find is the welcome screen, such as the one in Figure 13.11. A little sales pitch, a little help information, and the critical Login link.

FIGURE 13.11

The iFolder
non-client

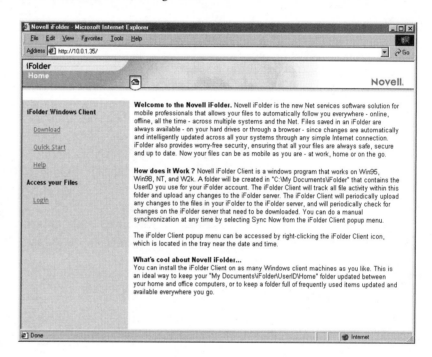

Is there anything unusual here? Not really. Click the Login link, and a slightly different login screen from the PC-based client appears, as you can see in Figure 13.12.

FIGURE 13.12

Browser-based
iFolder login

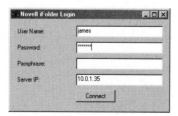

The login screen grabs the server IP address from the browser, as one would expect. The Passphrase option unlocks the file encryption you were warned not to implement. With this, if you do, for some crazy reason, have encryption enabled, the user will be able to download and use the files that drop encryption when they get to the client. Encryption only concerns files on the server side. If you want encryption on your personal PC or laptop, you'll need to get a third-party utility.

When you reach your iFolder server stash via browser, you'll see a more crude directory structure than with Windows, but still functional. In fact, these screens follow the open-source guidelines fairly well, so if you're used to non-Windows software you'll feel right at home. Actually, you'll feel at home either way, as you can tell in Figure 13.13.

FIGURE 13.13

Ready to control iFolder files

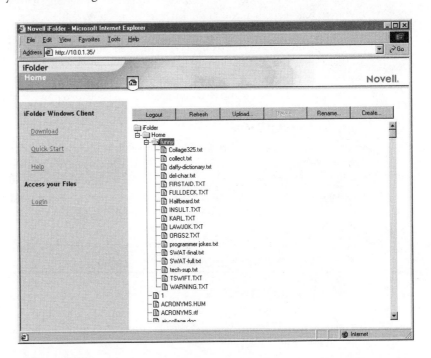

You can see the directory structure from the local client (under the \My Documents\iFolder\UserID\Home directory) is faithfully re-created. It isn't graphically enhanced, perhaps, but all the structure you need is there.

Notice the command buttons across the top. You can read all the ones except Delete, the one near the middle that's inactive and therefore gray. If you highlight a file, the Create button disappears, since the idea is to create a new folder, not a new file. The Refresh button connects back to the iFolder server and reads the directory structure there to display any changes on either side.

When a file is highlighted, the Upload command buttons morphs into a Download button. This makes sense, when you think about it.

If you click the Upload command button, iFolder opens the Windows Search dialog box. You may need to drill down to find the file you want, but users are comfortable with the Windows utility and should be successful without needing any training.

Using NetDrive for Remote File Access

Early Novell operating systems introduced the concept of file redirection. While drive A: connected to your floppy disk and drive C: connected to your hard disk, suddenly drive F: connected to the NetWare file server somewhere in the building. Clients gasped in amazement, and Novell's market share led the network operating system business.

NetDrive makes the same file redirection possible across the Internet rather than just across your local network. Anywhere clients have an Internet connection, they can use the NetDrive client software to link securely through the Internet to a NetWare file server.

Do you notice something missing in this description? The client system (some version of Windows 95 through XP) needs the NetDrive client software but not the Novell Client32 software. In other words, the remote client does not need to load the full Novell client to gain access to NetWare servers via the Internet. NetDrive relies primarily on FTP (File Transfer Protocol) or WebDAV (Web Distributed Authoring and Versioning) for the client-to-remote-server link.

Installing NetDrive

This takes no brains: Insert the NetWare 6 Client CD and click NetDrive. If you prefer, or if you want to save yourself the trouble of going to every client workstation with CD in hand, load the `NETDRIVE.EXE` program somewhere on a server volume and let people run the software themselves. Since the file is only about 2.3MB, clients can download the file and install the software remotely. Sure, 2.3MB takes a bit to download over a dial-up link, but no longer than it takes some people to download their fantasy football team roster.

You have nothing to do during the actual software installation. All the configuration happens after you're finished, so relax. It won't take too long.

Adding a NetDrive Site

Launching NetDrive opens a dialog box unlike anything Novell presented in the past. However, if you've used graphical FTP programs and the like, you should feel at home. Take a gander at Figure 13.14 and see what I mean.

FIGURE 13.14

The NetDrive dialog box

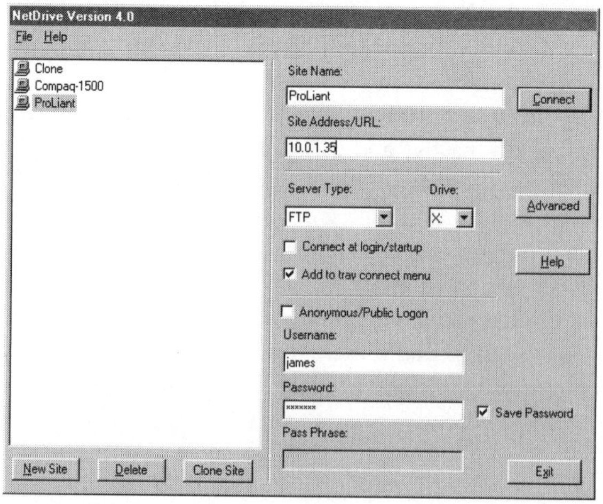

Notice the "NetDrive Version 4.0" in the upper-left corner? This could be a clue that Novell made a deal with a small company to add this to NetWare 6, if I was guessing (not that you should check out `www.webdrive.com`).

Notice the FTP look and feel of NetDrive. Addresses for sites use URLs rather than NetWare server names. You may specify a port number (10.0.1.33:8998) to make arranged connections through a firewall or to increase security. The two server types, FTP and WebDAV, never mention NetWare anywhere.

The Anonymous/Public Logon check box, located in about the middle of the dialog box in Figure 13.14, strongly says FTP, since anonymous logins to FTP servers happen regularly. Most FTP servers tend to connect to any client, since FTP became the public file storage location of choice across the Internet.

TIP   Do you want to give everyone easy access to support files for your hardware? An FTP server, running on any Unix or Linux box (and NetWare for the last several versions), allows anyone who knows the address to log in, see the file contents, and download those files. Controls on the FTP server stop clients from renaming, modifying, or deleting files on the server.

Obviously, you as network manager, must decide whether to allow anonymous connections to your FTP or WebDAV server. These controls are set at the NetWare Enterprise FTP Server configuration screens inside NetWare Remote Manager.

Filling out the new site information takes little time or trouble. Click the New Site command button at the bottom left of the NetDrive dialog box, and fill in two blanks, as shown in Figure 13.15.

FIGURE 13.15

Adding a
NetDrive site

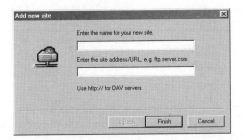

As you can see, configuring NetDrive for your clients is easy. If no designator (`ftp:` or `http://`) shows at the beginning of the address, NetDrive assumes FTP (historically more popular than the newcomer WebDAV). The name for the new site appears in the Site Manager (connection window) for reference.

Mapping a NetDrive

Once NetDrive site information is saved in the NetDrive Site Manager, one click makes the connection to the host. Well, one click after the name and password information has been saved.

Back up in Figure 13.14 (the main NetDrive dialog box), notice the check box asking about Anonymous/Public login and the text fields underneath asking for a username and password. A check box offers to Save Password, is convenient, but as I've stressed earlier in this chapter—saving a password pretty much ruins your remote-security controls. A stolen laptop with Save Password checked suddenly provides more access to your network than a million dollar campaign contribution to your congressperson. I wish they left out the Save Password check box, but they didn't.

Users connecting with the iFolder protocol should use the Passphrase option to encrypt traffic back and forth between client and server. Only FTP and WebDAV show in the Server Type drop-down menu currently, but perhaps an iFolder connection option will appear soon.

Once the name, drive letter, server type, and authentication method are set, click the Connect command button. Suddenly, Windows Explorer pops open with a new drive listing. Is this your typical NetWare Client32 listing? Not at all, as you can see in Figure 13.16.

FIGURE 13.16

Exploring a NetDrive

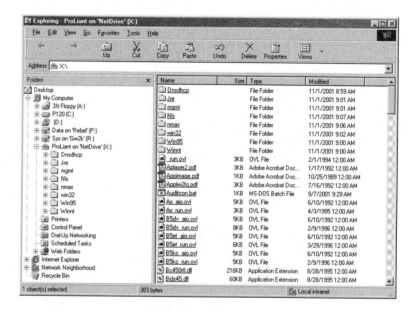

Notice what you don't see—there's no evidence of NetWare client software. Drive X:, normally reserved by NetWare for search drives, appears as the first option for NetDrive on most PCs. Hmm ... not NetWare-ish at all.

Other connections in Figure 13.16 show Windows networking links connected by SAMBA from a Linux-based NetWinder all-in-one Web, file, and e-mail servers from Rebel.com (now owned by Zentra Solutions Inc.). These use the standard SAMBA software employed by most Linux distributions to support Windows clients.

NOTE *If you go to a DOS command box and type NET USE, the crude Windows NET utility will display current connections. Don't be surprised if your NetDrive appears as DISCONNECTED. Since Microsoft didn't create or usurp it, they don't quite know how to handle it (at least not in Windows 98 during my last test), unless you're sitting on that drive letter at the time you run NET USE.*

If you click the Show Monitor menu item on the Taskbar's NetDrive icon, a Monitor window will appear, as shown in Figure 13.17. It's quite interesting, especially if you're curious to see how FTP sessions start, progress, and stop. The NetDrive Monitor also offers Disconnect and other command buttons.

FIGURE 13.17

NetDrive's Monitor shows FTP session guts

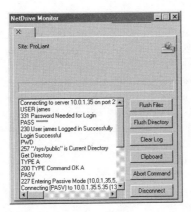

Your users probably don't care about these details. But the next section covers some areas here in the Monitor and other places you should care about.

Managing NetDrive

Every user utility, no matter how benign, must be managed. One configuration quirk (stupidity) of the NetWare FTP Server, and hence NetDrive, concerns the initial connection point: SYS:\PUBLIC. Is that dumb? Yes, at least in my book (and technically, this is my book, so there).

There are two places to fix that particular mistake. When you click the Advanced command button in the main NetDrive dialog box, a set of seven tabbed pages appears, as shown in Figure 13.18. We won't delve into much of this, because the defaults here work pretty well, and you shouldn't change them unless you feel confident of your FTP management capabilities.

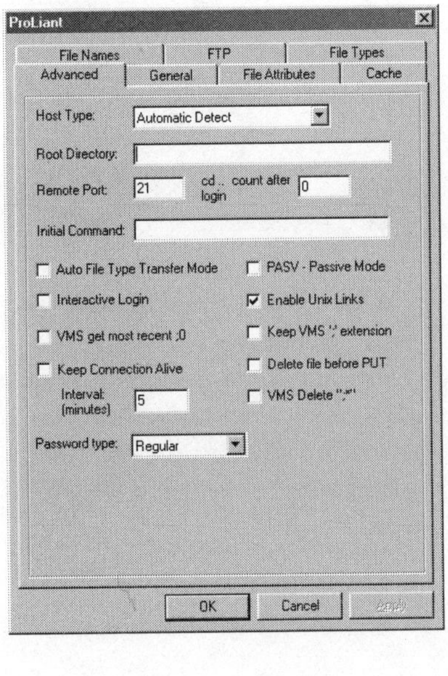

FIGURE 13.18

Advanced NetDrive settings

Leave Host Type to Automatic Detect, unless you're positive only one of the 14 listed host type options, including IBM MVS and VMS/VAX/Multinet, will be the only host system contacted. Novell host type appears, as does OS/2 Warp and Tandem, which should help you understand the huge reach and support of FTP servers in IT over the past decades.

Notice you can change the root directory for each user. An excellent idea, but changing anything for single users leads straight downhill to Administrator Inferno Level 7, a black hole of time-sucking demons. Don't go there.

Instead, fix this problem at the source: the FTP server. For NetWare FTP Server, the source is the FTP Server configuration screen reached through NetWare Web Manager. Figure 13.19 shows this screen for our lab server ProLiant.

FIGURE 13.19

Fix these FTP user settings before unleashing NetDrive

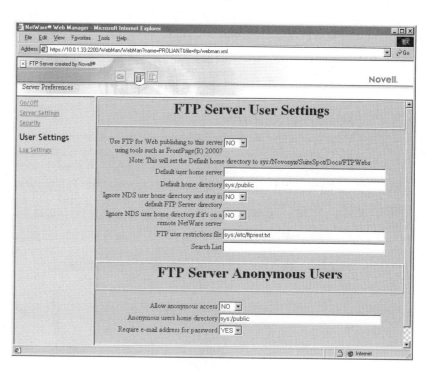

The caption for Figure 13.19 is not a joke. Notice the third entry shows the default home directory listed as SYS:/PUBLIC. This, I repeat, makes no sense.

Replace the SYS:\PUBLIC setting for the default home directory with something intelligent and safer, such as VOL1:\USERS. Then, place each user's NetWare home directory under that heading. Automatically, they all get rights to their own directory, but not anyone else's. NDS handles authentication, and you don't need to worry about someone trashing the SYS:\PUBLIC directory.

As you can see, there's not too much management involved. Of course, non-NetWare FTP servers don't have the advantages of simple-yet-secure user authentication and home directories to corral everyone. So dump the FTP server on your Linux box that requires too much user management time, and move FTP functions to NetWare. If you're the more cautious sort, at least try it for your NetDrive users as a pilot project, then see what happens.

A Look at NetStorage

My idea is that Novell included NetStorage before they got iFolder working correctly. Take a look at Figure 13.20, and tell me that NetStorage is anything except a copy of the iFolder utility using browser access.

FIGURE 13.20

The unnecessary NetStorage

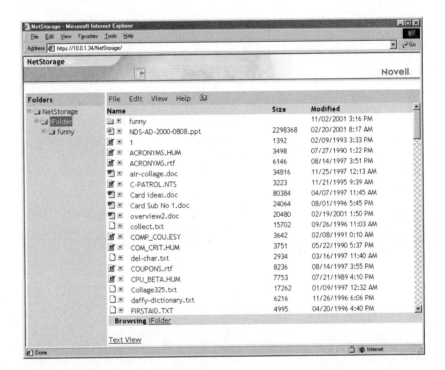

Use the same NDS eDirectory login name and password with NetStorage as with iFolder. Notice that you connect to the iFolder directory structure. Why have two of these? Maybe Novell will make that clear sometime in the future. Until then, use iFolder and ignore NetStorage. I like iFolder better, and it has more panache and flair. And NetStorage sounds like a product from a specialized network storage capacity manufacturer, so Novell may need to give up the name in the future, anyway.

Again, here's my suggestion: Use iFolder and forget NetStorage.

All's Well That Remote's Well

Remote access may not complicate your life, because all your users may stay trapped in their cubicles. If so, count yourself as far luckier than you imagine. Hassles with remote access are legendary and ongoing.

Novell can't solve all the remote-access problems in the world, but iFolder and NetDrive go a long way. What do remote users need? They need easy-yet-secure file access. What does iFolder and Net-Drive give them? These utilities provide easy-yet-secure file access from anywhere.

Play with iFolder, if only to help you keep files straight between home and office. You'll have fun and discover a way to help most of your remote clients replace pain with happiness, all synchronized in the background.

Chapter 14

Clusters of Enhancements and Special Features (Including Clusters)

NETWARE 4 AND 5 introduced many new features and benefits that changed the way people look at and use NetWare. With this newest NetWare version, Novell continues its tradition of improving server performance and reliability. NDS eDirectory has been fortified with new administrative features. Also significant is Novell's attempt to transform NetWare 6 into a major application platform. A number of new APIs have been made available to encourage alliances with hardware and software developers. This effort focuses on several areas, including Java, Internet applications, printing devices, storage, backup, and security.

This chapter highlights some previously existing NetWare features and introduces some features that are new to NetWare 6, such as virtual memory support and enhanced clustering support. Some of these are features, and some are benefits. These are my definitions: a *feature* is something the system does; a *benefit* is something positive you get from that feature.

I organized the topics in this chapter roughly in order of how valuable I feel these features are to the greatest number of users. However, each network is unique. What turns you on may leave the network manager in the next building cold. Hot features—the ones that provide real benefits—tend to change over time. What you care little about today may become very important when it solves a problem for you tomorrow. The following topics are covered in this chapter:

- ◆ NetWare memory management
- ◆ Symmetric multiprocessing
- ◆ Novell Storage Services (NSS)
- ◆ File compression
- ◆ Storage Management Services (SMS) and SBACKUP

- Server-based Java support

- Security-related features

- Simple Network Management Protocol (SNMP)

- Hot Plug PCI and Configuration Manager

- NetWare 6 Web enhancements

- NetWare Cluster Services

A Review of NetWare 6 Enhancements

Before I start talking in depth about some of NetWare 6's features, I want to take a moment to introduce you to some features that are covered elsewhere in this book. For many of you, these features won't provide any additional benefits, but I am betting that an equal number of you will be just as excited about these features as I am.

iFolder Why have a file server? To make file access more convenient. While NetWare leads the market in network operating system technology, keeping files organized from one place (the server) to an increasing number of other places (desktop at work, computer at home, laptop on the road, and so on) challenges everyone. iFolder solves this problem in a way so clever, so unique, and so painless, other people in the business should hang their head in shame and embarrassment. Without requiring the Client32 NetWare software, iFolder automatically synchronizes the user's files on every system to the central file server. When the user dials in from home, the home computer synchronizes automatically with the server. Laptops do the same. See Chapter 13, "Remote File Access with iFolder and NetDrive," for implementation details.

iPrint Nothing in the printing world matches the user benefits Novell provides with iPrint. Built upon NDPS (see next blurb), iPrint turns one of the largest user hassles and tech support headaches into a dream. OK, it may not revolutionize networking and regrow hair on bald heads, but iPrint makes printing easier by automatically downloading printer drivers and showing users where printers are on graphical map pages. Since users love to print already, and iPrint makes printing easier, you may need to order more paper than usual. See Chapter 6, "Network and Internet Printing" for details on iPrint.

Novell Distributed Print Services (NDPS) Years ago, one of the main reasons that small and medium-sized offices installed networks was to share printers. Network printing—print drivers, queues, printers, print servers, and the general hassle of troubleshooting network printers—has traditionally been a major pain in the neck for network administrators. Novell, along with companies such as Xerox and Hewlett-Packard, has moved network printing forward once again with NDPS. The goal of NDPS is to make network printers easier to install and manage while increasing their performance. Smart network managers now recognize that NDPS should be hidden underneath iPrint. I discuss NDPS in depth in Chapter 6.

NetDrive   While iFolder synchronizes files automatically between different systems, sometimes you need a different option, such as mapping a local drive letter to a NetWare 6 server anywhere on the Internet. Would you like to drag a file across a desktop and drop it into a server a thousand miles away? Check out NetDrive, which is covered in Chapter 13.

NetStorage   NetStorage allows clients using any Java-friendly browser to perform NetWare file access across a public (Internet) or private network. Clients? We don't need no stinkin' clients! But I think you'll find NetStorage less satisfying than iFolder, which also allows access without a client, through a browser.

Native TCP/IP support   Over the years, Novell has been increasing NetWare's support for TCP/IP technologies. NetWare 5 introduced native IP support, and NetWare 6 finishes that trip by making HTTP (HyperText Transfer Protocol, used for Web server-to-client communications) a core service. NetWare Core Protocol (NCP) data is transported natively via IP. This is a significant enhancement if you support both TCP/IP and IPX/SPX networks, and an even bigger deal if your company wants to be all TCP/IP. See Chapter 11, "NetWare 6 TCP/IP Support," for more information.

Domain Name Service (DNS) and Dynamic Host Configuration Protocol (DHCP)   When managing a TCP/IP network, network administrators are faced with two significant challenges: tracking IP addresses and resolving computer names to their current IP addresses. NetWare 6 provides support for both a DHCP server to automatically allocate IP host addresses to IP clients and DNS to manage the database of computer names and their IP host addresses. I discuss these in Chapter 12, "DHCP and DNS Support."

NetWare Memory Management

NetWare 6 requires that the file server have a minimum of 256MB of RAM. Application services based on Java can increase the RAM requirements, and the Apache Web Server software loads automatically for utility support, making 512MB of RAM a realistic minimum memory configuration for a NetWare 6 server.

The server works with its available resources to respond to clients' file and print requests, NLM applications, Java applications, and NetWare's own demands. Do not allow your server to become short on memory!

Novell developed a logical memory-addressing scheme that minimizes memory fragmentation during its daily routines. This memory-addressing scheme allows NetWare to allocate more memory than is physically present. This is called *virtual memory*.

Low-memory conditions can abend the server or result in sluggish performance. The administrator can isolate problem applications with the MONITOR utility and optimize memory usage on the server with SET parameters and console commands.

Figure 14.1 shows a partial list of NLMs that are loaded on NetWare 6 server COMPAQ-330. Shown here inside NetWare Remote Manager, the list of loaded NLMs are sorted by allocated memory. Clicking any of the NLM names opens a new screen, showing version, code, and memory details. Command buttons on the inside screen allow you to quickly see the amount of resources used by the NLM and to unload it with a single click, if necessary.

FIGURE 14.1

NLM information

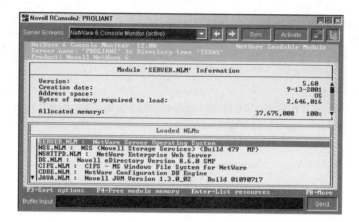

MEMORY MANAGEMENT RULES OF THUMB

When dealing with NetWare servers, more RAM almost always equals better performance. This is especially true if the server acts as a file and print server. When people ask me if a server needs more RAM, I answer yes without even looking first. I am half joking, but I am a big fan of making sure servers have plenty of RAM. There is also a point of diminishing returns that occurs when your server has sufficient memory and just can't effectively use any more, but that point remains far away now that NetWare uses virtual memory. Your boss is probably not going to share my enthusiasm for adding RAM indiscriminately and will ask you for hard-core numbers.

Here are a few rules of thumb that I follow with respect to server memory:

◆ Don't keep the Java-based GUI loaded on the server console if it is not in use.

◆ Don't load the Java components if they are not going to be used.

◆ Don't load unnecessary namespace modules or add namespace support to volumes that do not require that particular namespace.

◆ Avoid loading unnecessary NLMs.

◆ If the server's Long Term Cache Hits value drops below 90 percent, add RAM. To display this value, use the MONITOR utility at the server. From the main MONITOR screen, press Tab to display the General Information statistics, as shown here.

```
              General Information
    Utilization:                         2%
    Server up time:                1:20:35:23
    Online processors:                    1
    Original cache buffers:          15,822
    Total cache buffers:              5,145
    Dirty cache buffers:                  0
    Long term cache hits:                97%
    Current disk requests:                1
    Packet receive buffers:             128
    Directory cache buffers:             31
    Maximum service processes:          570
    Current service processes:           19
    Current connections:                  5
    Open files:                         152
```

Virtual Memory

Virtual memory appeared as one of the new features in NetWare 5, designed to support application services. In the past, NetWare has not used virtual memory, but rather only the physical memory found in the machine.

Virtual memory allows applications and programmers to access very large blocks of memory, even beyond the amount of memory that is physically installed in the machine. The operating system assigns the application a range of virtual memory and maps the application's virtual memory addresses to blocks (or pages) of memory that are physically in RAM.

When the amount of physical memory that an application requires exceeds the amount of memory in the machine, the operating system creates temporary files that extend actual RAM in the server. When a user sends a request to the server to open a file or runs a query or a report on a database, data is placed in active RAM, using some of the available pool of resources on the system. The file server saves recent requests to RAM to speed response time.

How NetWare Uses Virtual Memory

To increase RAM efficiency, NetWare transfers data that is in low demand to temporary files, or *swap files*, which will be accessed when needed. NetWare maintains a translation table that tracks usage of RAM data, helping it to make decisions about swapping files to disk. The amount of swapping that NetWare does could possibly decrease the system's performance, since CPU and disk resources are required to manage the swapping operation. However, it can also help overall system performance by making more memory available to applications that need it. If you ascertain that your server is swapping too often, it may be time to add more memory to the server.

NOTE   *The NetWare server operating system and the server's modules do not use virtual memory because they cannot be swapped out to disk.*

Modules that are loaded into protected memory spaces and programs that run as part of the Java Virtual Machine (JVM) use virtual memory. These programs and the data they access are subject to being swapped out to disk.

Tuning Virtual Memory

By default, NetWare creates a swap file in the SYS: volume. You can create one swap file on each volume. Type **HELP SWAP** at the server console to display the options for the SWAP command. Actually, it doesn't matter which volume you use for swap files, since any RAM data can be stored in any swap file found on any volume. Use the fastest and largest hard drives for your swap files for the best results.

To add a swap file on volume 1, type **SWAP ADD VOL1** at the server console prompt. To delete a swap file on volume 1, type **SWAP DEL VOL1**.

To control the minimum and maximum sizes of a swap file, you use options with the SWAP command, as in the following example:

```
SWAP ADD VOL1 MIN=5 MAX=100 MIN FREE=100
```

The default minimum size (MIN) is 2MB, and the maximum (MAX) swap file can use all available disk space on the volume. The MIN FREE parameter specifies the amount of space to be left on the volume; if you don't specify a value for this parameter, the default is 5MB. The MIN and MAX parameters are in megabytes (millions of bytes).

To modify an existing swap file, use the PARAMETER option, as in this example:

```
SWAP PARAMETER SYS MIN=5 MAX=100 MIN FREE=100
```

When a volume is dismounted, the swap file is deleted. Add swap commands to your AUTOEXEC.NCF file if you want them to be available whenever the server is reset.

To display statistics about a server's virtual memory information, use the MONITOR utility. Choose MONITOR ➤ Virtual Memory, and then press the Tab key to display the full Virtual Memory Information statistics, as shown below.

```
           Virtual Memory Information
 Page-in requests, total:              7,691
 Page-in requests per second:              0
 Page-out requests, total:            12,160
 Page-out requests per second:             0

 Swap pages, total:                    7,680
 Swap pages, free:                        12
 Swap pages, reserved:                 7,677

 Page faults, total:                  34,322
 Page faults per second:                   0
```

See how few free swap pages you have? Get more memory for your server.

Server Self-Tuning

NetWare's flat-memory model allows processes that need more memory to be assigned more memory. This happens automatically, without any intervention on your part.

Each time the server is restarted, the settings that were adjusted during operation are set back to the defaults. You can change the defaults to more accurately reflect the performance profile of your server after it has had time to tune itself. The tuning happens fairly quickly, but not as quickly as it would have if the right values were in place when the server started. Many administrators don't need to adjust their systems. In certain situations, though, a certain amount of fine-tuning is helpful.

You might want to fine-tune some parameters for Directory Cache Buffers and File Caches. *Caches* work under the assumption that users make multiple requests of active files, such as saving and resaving a document or searching for data in a database. So, a file server saves recent requests in RAM to speed response time.

NetWare allocates a minimum of 20 directory cache buffers of 4KB each, which saves the names of requested files in server memory. Each cache buffer contains 32 entries linked to 32 files. This is appropriate for small workgroups. The default maximum value for cache buffers is 500, or about 2MB. The maximum value is 200,000. To increase the level of directory cache buffers, type the following SET commands at the console prompt, and add them to STARTUP.NCF so that your system uses them every time the server boots:

```
SET MINIMUM DIRECTORY CACHE BUFFERS=2000
SET MAXIMUM DIRECTORY CACHE BUFFERS=4000
```

Optionally, you can use the MONITOR utility at the server console to set server parameters (or my preference, NetWare Remote Manager, as described in Chapter 8, "NetWare 6 Administrator Duties and Tools"). To set these parameters from the MONITOR utility, choose MONITOR ➤ Server Parameters ➤ Directory Caching. Then locate the parameter you want to set and make the change.

The Help file pops open in the middle of the screen, offering a few words about the highlighted parameter. Figure 14.2 shows what happens when you highlight a parameter value.

FIGURE 14.2

Tuning server parameters

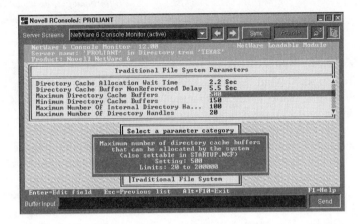

Each NetWare volume maintains a directory entry table (DET) of files stored there. Each type of namespace used on the system adds a directory entry for each file, so DOS, NFS, and LONG namespaces require three names for each file. Therefore, a directory cache buffer that contains 32 entries would account for only 10 files.

NetWare will try to accommodate multiple DET entries by self-adjusting the directory cache buffers. After a few weeks, look at the Directory Cache Buffers value on MONITOR's General Information screen to view the highest number of buffers allocated. Use that value to set the minimum, and add 100 for the maximum setting. If you need to add a namespace type, use the formulas below, and then use the SET commands I described earlier:

*# of namespaces * high value in MONITOR = minimum cache buffers*

minimum + 100 = maximum

Check the MONITOR screen regularly to get an idea of your performance profile during heavy network traffic sessions. Make a note of those settings. Then use NetWare Remote Manager or MONITOR to adjust the SET parameters as necessary.

NOTE *In earlier versions of NetWare, the server-based program SERVMAN allowed you to set parameters on the NetWare server. This functionality has now been incorporated into the MONITOR and NetWare Remote Manager utilities.*

Memory and Old Network and Disk Adapters

Older ISA and microchannel network and disk adapters cannot access memory above 16MB. To make sure that these devices have enough memory below 16MB, allocate sufficient buffers below 16MB with a SET command. Add the following line to your `STARTUP.NCF` file:

```
SET RESERVED BUFFERS BELOW 16 MEG = 200
```

Then reboot the server so this option takes effect.

TIP   *My personal feeling about older, slower adapters is that you should not be using them. Servers that support the newer, faster PCI bus are inexpensive these days, as are PCI network and disk adapters. Dump those old boards today. Better yet, keep an eye out for the first servers using the high-speed InfiniBand bus, the planned upgrade to PCI. Servers get faster every week.*

Memory Protection

Starting in NetWare 4.1, it was possible to load certain NetWare server-based applications into a protected memory space, which was called a *domain*. The advantage of this is that applications running in protected memory space do not interfere with the server operating system. I cannot tell you how glad I was when this feature was announced. I have caused a server to abend more than a few times while running tape-backup software or database utilities at the server console.

In NetWare 6, the memory-protection feature is called a *protected address space*. Some operating systems call this memory space the *user address space* or *Ring 3*. Any application operating in a protected address space cannot interfere with applications running in other protected address spaces, nor can these protected applications interfere with the NetWare operating system. You can use this address space to load NLMs that are problematic or that have not been thoroughly tested.

The NetWare operating system, device drivers, and core services run in an address space that is sometimes called the *OS address space*, the *kernel address space*, or *Ring 0*. The applications that must run in the OS address space include the following:

◆ SERVER.NLM

◆ LAN and disk device drivers

◆ NSS filesystem (NSS.NLM)

◆ MONITOR.NLM

◆ Applications or modules that were not designed to run in a protected address space

FEATURES OF PROTECTED ADDRESS SPACE

NetWare 6's protected address spaces have these characteristics:

◆ Modules loaded into protected address spaces are part of the server's virtual memory system and are subject to being swapped out to disk if the code the module is using is not currently in use.

◆ If you use the RESTART option when creating protected address spaces, the system will automatically close up an address space, clean up the address space's resources, restart the address space, and reload the modules if the address space abends.

◆ If you load a module into a protected address space that requires other supporting modules, such as C-library (CLIB) functions, those supporting modules are loaded into the same protected address space.

◆ NLMs can be loaded multiple times, even if they were designed to be loaded only once, as long as they are loaded into separate protected address spaces.

MANAGING PROTECTED ADDRESS SPACES

You create protected memory spaces at the server console, and you load modules into these spaces from either the server console prompt or through the AUTOEXEC.NCF. When you create a new address space, it is automatically assigned a name that starts with ADDRESS_SPACE and ends with a unique number. For example, the first address space created would be ADDRESS_SPACE1, the second address space would be ADDRESS_SPACE2, and so on.

When you load modules into a protected address space, NetWare assigns whatever memory the module may require. As other modules are loaded into this space, it can grow as necessary. However, the maximum size of any NetWare 6 protected address space is 512MB.

There are a number of console commands for creating, manipulating, and unloading modules in protected address spaces; these are described in Table 14.1.

TABLE 14.1: PROTECTED ADDRESS SPACE COMMAND OPTIONS

COMMAND	DESCRIPTION
LOAD PROTECTED module_name	Loads module_name into a new protected address space called ADDRESS_SPACEx.
LOAD RESTART module_name	Loads module_name into a new protected address space with restart functionality.
LOAD ADDRESS SPACE = space_name module_name	Loads module_name into an address space called space_name. You can use this command if you want to create your own address space names or if you want to load additional modules into the same address space.
PROTECT filename.ncf	Runs the filename.ncf file and loads all NLMs that are loaded in that NCF file into a protected memory space called filename.ncf.
PROTECTION RESTART space_name	Adds the restart functionality to the memory space called space_name.
PROTECTION NO RESTART space_name	Removes the restart functionality from the memory space called space_name.
UNLOAD ADDRESS SPACE = space_name module_name	Unloads the module module_name from the protected memory space space_name.
UNLOAD ADDRESS SPACE = space_name	Unloads all modules from the protected address space space_name.
UNLOAD KILL ADDRESS SPACE = space_name	Removes the address space without unloading the modules first. Use this only if you cannot unload the modules in the space first.

VIEWING ADDRESS SPACE AND VIRTUAL MEMORY

To view information about which modules are loaded and which virtual memory spaces these modules are loaded into, use the server console command MODULES. This displays the module name, the version, the date, and the address space into which the module is loaded.

To display a list of all protected address spaces, at the server console prompt, use the PROTECTION command. This generates a list of all address spaces that have been created, along with the module names loaded into those address spaces.

Additional information about virtual memory is available through the server's MONITOR utility. To display virtual memory from the MONITOR utility, choose Monitor ➢ Virtual Memory ➢ Address Space. This displays a list of address spaces and information about them, as shown in Figure 14.3. Highlight any address space and press Enter to display a list of NLMs that are loaded into that particular address space.

FIGURE 14.3

Address space information shown by the MONITOR utility

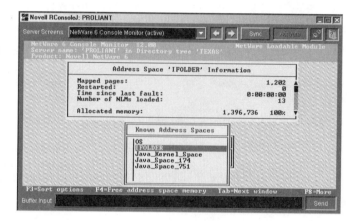

Symmetric Multiprocessing

NetWare 6, like NetWare 4.x, supports SMP (Symmetric Multi-Processor). This means that a computer with multiple processors will provide increased performance for servers that have a busy CPU. In years past, I have maintained that SMP capabilities were not terribly important in a NetWare environment. Even on servers with many hundreds of users, the server CPU was rarely the system bottleneck. Generally, the system bottleneck on a file and print server turns out to be memory, the network interface card, or the disk channel.

However, in today's NetWare network, the NetWare server is doing much more than acting as a simple file and print server. NetWare 6 servers now host application services such as Web servers and database servers, as well as run Java applications. These services running on the NetWare server will contribute to the need for faster (or more) processors.

SMP allows the server to run multithreaded processes simultaneously on different processors. Since many of NetWare 6's core processes, such as RSA encryption, routing ODI (Open Data-Link

Interface), and CLIB functions, are multithreaded applications, the performance of multiprocessor servers will be enhanced. A NetWare server with multiple CPUs will have more capacity to handle single-threaded programs, since processing power is shared in parallel.

NetWare 6 automatically detects multiprocessor systems. Unlike NetWare 4.x, the new version of SMP now shares the same kernel for single and multiprocessor systems, and servers can employ as many as 32 processors, as compared with the previous four-CPU limit. In NetWare 6, Novell has SMP-enabled almost every server process. That's a great improvement over NetWare 5.1, especially since the TCP/IP protocol stack and utilities now support multiprocessing. This allows different processors to handle communications and server applications.

To inspect multiprocessor settings on your server, open the MONITOR utility at the server in question, and then choose Available Options ➤ Server Parameters ➤ Multiprocessor. You'll see that the default value for the Auto Start Processors setting is On.

The console command CPUCHECK shows information about your processor. Figure 14.4 shows the CPUCHECK results for a dual-processor Compaq system. Notice that both processors are online, as one would hope.

FIGURE 14.4

Two processors
ready to work

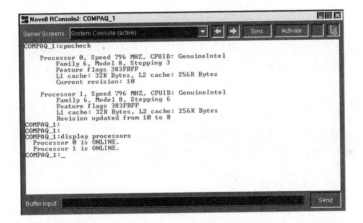

Using NetWare Remote Manager, as shown in Figure 14.5, curious network administrators can discover exactly which application runs on which processor. Notice the last two lines of Figure 14.5: The TCP NLM and the LAN driver for the Ethernet card run on two different processors. Need any more convincing that NetWare engineers truly split the load equitably with NetWare 6's SMP support?

Novell Storage Services (NSS version 3.0)

Novell Storage Services (NSS) was a new feature of NetWare 5. The first volume on the server, SYS:, needed to be a traditional NetWare filesystem (NWFS) volume in NetWare 5.1. In NetWare 6, the first volume can be an NSS volume. See Chapter 1, "Installing NetWare 6," for a comparison of the traditional NWFS volumes with NSS volumes.

FIGURE 14.5

Splitting the processor load

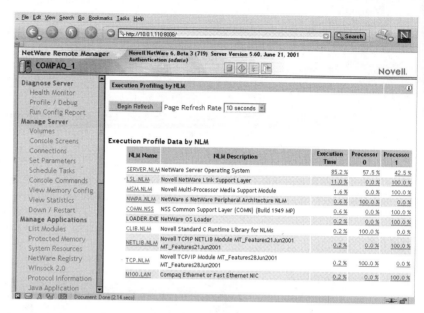

During the NSS beta-testing period, when I first started reading about NSS and tinkering with it, I experienced two distinctly separate emotions: excitement and dread. I was excited about this great new feature, and I dreaded figuring out a way to explain it to others. Here's the simple explanation I came up with: NSS allows an administrator to combine areas of free space from empty partitions, NetWare volumes, and even CD-ROMs together into one large, logical volume. We'll get into the more complicated descriptions in a moment.

Features of NSS

When designing NSS, Novell had specific goals in mind:

♦ To create volumes that could hold millions of files

♦ To eliminate the current file and volume size restrictions

♦ To ensure that servers running NSS would be backward-compatible with NWFS

♦ To ensure that even large volumes could be quickly repaired and mounted

♦ To optimize the use of server memory

♦ To be modular and versatile, and to support new generations of storage

I don't think that saying NSS is a revolutionary step forward in storage systems is an exaggeration. NSS employs logical rather than physical partitions to better manage storage by pooling free space on all storage devices. It handles large volumes with files up to 8 terabytes (TB) and billions of files, much more than traditional NetWare volumes. It takes less time to mount and rebuild NSS volumes—less than a minute in most cases—than it does to manage NWFS volumes. Multiple namespaces share the same storage space under NSS.

NOTE *To support additional namespaces on a server volume, you used to need to load the appropriate supporting module (these files are NLMs, but they end with* `.NAM` *instead of* `.NLM`*). NetWare 6, however, handles all types of files automatically, if you pick the full NetWare package during installation. NSS volumes automatically support all namespaces.*

Novell engineers love to demonstrate the worst possible file server crash to show how NSS eliminates post-crash pain. After a billion (yes, billion) files are copied to a server running NSS 3.0, an engineer pulls the plug for that server right out of the wall. After such a sudden death, the traditional filesystem must be read, recovered, read, and recovered for hours. Within literally seconds, the file server running NSS 3.0 boots up and mounts the volumes, ready for business.

A "journaling" filesystem, NSS uses 64-bit addressing to control huge amounts of storage space and files. Recovering after system crashes takes seconds rather than minutes or hours, since NSS 3.0 doesn't read the entire disk contents to boot. Only the journal, or file about the files on the disk, is read and loaded into memory, and only a portion of all file handles are loaded at once. As more file information requests come in, appropriate file metadata (data about data) is loaded into the server operating system.

NSS PUSHES YOU INTO THE STORAGE POOL

NetWare 6 adds a step between creating your disk partitions and creating your volume. Normally, adding administrative steps causes unnecessary pain and aggravation. This extra step, however, adds a new concept for storage: the *storage pool*. The benefits gained from adding storage pools more than repays you for the extra step required.

A storage pool, created from open disk space found on one or all of your storage devices, contains all logical volumes. One volume can fill the entire storage pool if you want, or you can create any number of volumes in a storage pool (really, thousands or more if you want). Volumes can be as small as you want or up to 8TB in size.

No longer must you take a server down to add more disk space. Storage pools can expand as needed by adding space. You may deactivate pools and their contained volumes, add or subtract disk devices, and reactivate the pool to use the new space. This assumes you have storage devices housed separately from your server, of course.

The airlines overbook, and now so can NetWare 6 with NSS 3.0. Storage pools hold logical volumes, meaning an individual volume cannot be larger than the storage pool holding said volume. However, the total size of multiple logical volumes can add up to larger than the storage pool containing them.

Here's what happens: Take a storage pool of 36GB, and create three volumes, each with a volume limit of 20GB. The total storage space of the three volumes adds to a greater total than the storage pool containing the volume. That's a neat trick, right?

Just like the airlines, however, you can't put 243 people into 200 airplane seats, and you can't put 60GB into a 36GB storage pool. NSS 3.0 allows you to create more logical volume size limits than the storage pool can hold, but the total space within the volumes must stay under the space limit for the pool. Volume 1 may fill up to 20GB, but only if Volume 2 and Volume 3 don't total more than 16GB together. Volumes within a storage pool can "borrow" space from other volumes.

You really no longer work on individual volumes; you work on the pool, which holds those volumes. This gives volumes more flexibility than ever.

NSS PROVIDES RAID 0 WITH MIRRORED PARTITIONS

RAID (Redundant Array of Independent Disks) provides multiple levels of hardware fault tolerance. NSS 3.0 provides the lowest level, RAID 0, by mirroring partitions. You can mirror NSS logical volumes to other logical volumes and traditional volumes to traditional volumes, but not NSS volumes to traditional volumes. Make sure you mirror partitions between storage pools using single partitions, even though a storage pool can cover multiple partitions. If you mirror partitions in pools containing multiple partitions, you can lose data.

You can configure RAID striping across multiple disks when your partition contains multiple devices. Up to eight elements on a device are accommodated. RAID 0, much like disk mirroring in earlier NetWare versions, improves performance by spreading the reading and writing disk operations across multiple disks at the same time.

SEND DELETED FILES TO A VIRTUAL SHREDDER

NS 3.0 adds a new data-shredding feature that overwrites deleted and purged files with random characters. Up to seven layers of new random patterns may overlay deleted files. Performance takes a hit with data shredding, and performance gets hit harder with every overlaid layer of bits. Government concerns, however, prompted Novell to add data shredding, which obviously boosts security in certain situations. Hackers or malicious insiders can't recover purged files once they've been shredded.

There are probably some important-sounding government standards that dictate this shredding, but I didn't take the time to look them up. Feel free to research this topic if you're curious (and let me know what they are and why you use them).

NSS Architecture

NSS has a modular architecture, consisting of six main layers. Figure 14.6 illustrates the NSS modular architecture and shows where some of these components fit.

Here's what the various layers, interfaces, and modules do:

Physical Storage Layer   Provides the only physical part of this chain. NetWare supports RAM, magnetic drives (or silicon-based drives that mimic hard drives), CD-ROMs, and DVDs. As new storage media appear (laser-driven optical storage cubes sound pretty cool), NSS will handle them.

Media Access layer (MAL)   Provides access to the actual storage media. It manages an *object bank*, which is responsible for the storage manager and storage object registration. The storage managers access the actual media. There are three types of storage managers: consumers, providers, and modifiers. The Consumer Storage Manager takes ownership of storage space types such as free space, DOS partitions, and CD-ROM space. The Provider Storage Manager manages storage objects such as the NWFS and DOS partitions. NSS has two types of providers: NWPRV for NetWare volumes and files and MMPRV for IBM partitions and files. The Modifier Storage Manager manages the storage information by changing the input and output data paths.

Loadable Storage Subsystem (LSS) layer   Provides the files that define the various filesystems that NSS uses, such as DOS, NetWare, and ISO 9660 (CD-ROMs). Future LSS modules could include the Windows NT filesystem, Macintosh filesystem, optical jukeboxes, DVD, NFS Gateway, and other filesystems.

Object Engine layer Manages the actual storage resources. It provides a high degree of reliability, optimal memory usage, and performance.

Common Interface layer Defines the interfaces that the semantic agents use to access the object engine. It provides naming services, object services, and management services.

Semantic Agent layer Contains the loadable modules that provide access to NSS services. One module, for example, provides access for NetWare clients. Other modules might provide access to storage services for clients such as Web clients, Microsoft SMB (Server Message Block) network clients, NFS (Network File System), or others.

Confused? Don't worry if you are; I sure was. These are a lot of layers, modules, and interfaces to absorb. The bright side is that you don't need to understand the architecture to create an NSS volume.

FIGURE 14.6

Novell Storage Services components

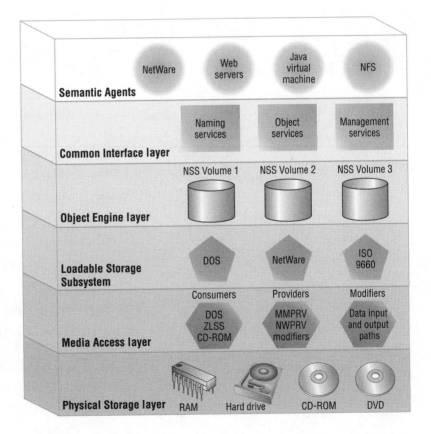

Managing NSS

NSS is automatically installed when you install NetWare 6. If for some reason you don't install NSS with NetWare, type **LOAD NSS** (or just **NSS**) at the server console. This starts the necessary NLMs.

TIP *You will find that Novell has eliminated the need to type LOAD for many operations that used to require it. Now, if you just type the name of the NLM you want to load, NetWare 6 will automatically load it. It's hard to teach an old dog new tricks, so you will catch me using the LOAD command quite often. Also, this way I don't get spoiled when I need to work with earlier versions of NetWare.*

The NSS module has a number of command-line options. The most commonly sued options are shown in Table 14.2. Some of these require the slash key; others do not. You can use the slash key for all commands, and this is what I tend to do. This way, I am always consistent and don't need to think about which options require the slash and which ones do not.

TABLE 14.2: SOME NSS COMMAND-LINE OPTIONS

OPTION	DESCRIPTION
/Help	Displays a list of options
/Exit	Dismounts all NSS volumes and unloads NSS and all NSS supporting modules
/Version	Displays the current version of NSS
/Modules	Displays all NSS support modules loaded and their current version
/Menu	Enters the NSS configuration menu
/Status	Displays all NSS configuration information
/Volumes	Displays a list of all currently available NSS volumes
/Activate=NSS_volume_name	Switches *NSS_volume_name* to the active state
/Deactivate=NSS_volume_name	Switches *NSS_volume_name* to the deactivate state
/Maintenance= NSS_volume_name	Switches *NSS_volume_name* to the maintenance state
/VerifyVolume=NSS_volume_name	Checks *NSS_volume_name* physical integrity
/RebuildVolume=NSS_volume_name	Repairs *NSS_volume_name*
/AutoVerifyVolume=NSS_volume_name	Sets *NSS_volume_name* to be automatically verified during each startup
/StorageAlarmThreshold=	Sets the value in megabytes that will trigger a storage warning if the disk space drops below that value
/StorageAlarmReset=	Sets the value in megabytes that will reset a low storage warning

Continued on next page

TABLE 14.2: Some NSS Command-Line Options *(Continued)*

OPTION	DESCRIPTION
/(No)StorageAlertMessages	Turns on or off storage alert warnings to all users
/(No)CacheBalance	Turns on or off the cache balancing
/CacheBalance	Sets the percentage of free memory that is used for the NSS buffer cache
/Salvage=*NSS_volume_name*	Enables salvage of deleted files for *NSS_volume_name*
/NoSalvage=*NSS_volume_name*	Disables salvage of deleted files for *NSS_volume_name*

You can also use several NetWare console commands to see volume and NSS information:

◆ The VOLUMES command displays information about currently mounted NSS volumes.

◆ The NSS VOLUMES command shows specific NSS information.

◆ The NSS VERSION command displays the current version of NSS and whether it is enabled.

Figure 14.7 shows examples of using these commands on a NetWare 6 server with NSS and CD-ROM support loaded.

FIGURE 14.7

Volume information from the server console

The NETWARE_6_DOC volume is actually a CD-ROM. If you load NetWare CD-ROM support, NSS provides it and automatically makes the CD-ROM a read-only volume.

NOTE   All of the NSS-supported volumes include all namespace modules. The traditional NFS volume includes only DOS and LONG namespaces.

Creating an NSS Volume

To create an NSS volume, you can use either ConsoleOne or NetWare Remote Manager. (You no longer use the NWCONFIG program or the NSS menu from the server console, as with previous versions.) Chapter 8 described how to create NSS volumes and pools using ConsoleOne. Here, we'll go over the same tasks in NetWare Remote Manager.

After starting and authenticating to NetWare Remote Manager, drill down through Volume Management to Partition Management by clicking the Disk Partitions link. Click on the pool or free space you wish to use for the new volume. In the case of the example shown in Figure 14.8, I chose to click the Create link beside Free Disk Space (4.35GB).

FIGURE 14.8

Creating a
new volume

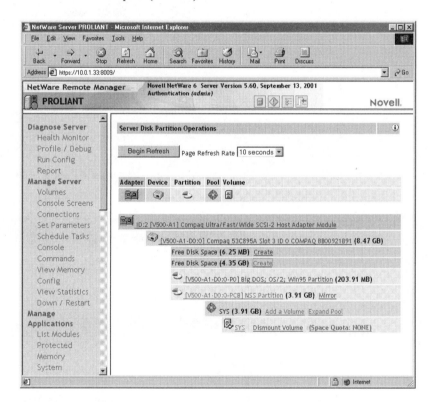

Next, you must make more choices, as shown in Figure 14.9. You may create a new partition or a new partition and volume for the NetWare Traditional File System, or you may create a new pool or a new pool and volume for NSS.

Of the four choices, NSS always wins the prize for me. So many enhancements make NSS an improvement over the traditional filesystem I could write most of a chapter about them (oops, I did). Of the two NSS choices, I chose to create a new pool to hold the new volume. I could have expanded the pool if I preferred (you can see that choice back in Figure 14.8 at the end of the pool sign, or the lumpy blue doughnut).

FIGURE 14.9

Quick choices on the road to a new volume

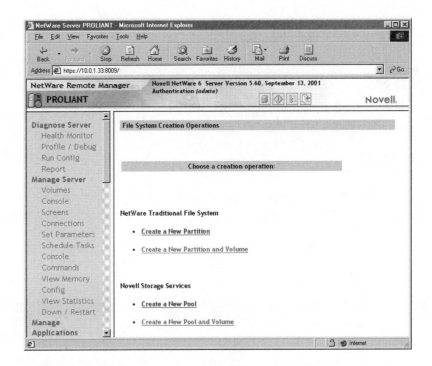

Next, you'll see the NSS Volume Create screen, as shown in Figure 14.10. If you click the Change Volume Type link at the top right of this screen, the screen switches to the NetWare traditional volume type creation screen. You see fewer volume attributes under the traditional model; only Compression, Sub-Allocation, and Migration appear. The first two are enabled by default. For NSS volumes, compression is not turned on by default.

Once you click the Create link, you will be asked to verify that you do, in fact, wish to create your new pool and volume. Click OK to assert your creative intentions. If you're near the server, you'll hear two beeps as the console screen echoes the "Created directory DESKTOP.AFP on volume PROLIANT.VOL2" message, followed by the note that "Desktop Rebuild started on volume PROLIANT.VOL2." (Well, your screen probably won't say PROLIANT, but you get the idea.)

Your server console will probably show the new volume as mounted, but feel free to move back to the Server Disk Partition Operations screen (Figure 14.8) and click the Mount Volume link on your new volume listing.

NSS and Fault Tolerance

If you create large NSS volumes and store critical information on them, you should make sure you have two things on your side:

Reliable, consistent tape backups Although any type of tape backup system can back up the NSS volume, Novell highly recommends that you use a backup that is compatible with the

NetWare Target Service Agent (TSA500). Backups using older versions of the TSA are not efficient when backing up large files. NetWare 6 ships with an enhanced SBACKUP utility, which works well with NSS. Personally, however, I prefer third-party backup tools that provide more administrative control, but suit yourself. SBACKUP is covered later in this chapter, in the "Storage Management Services (SMS) and SBACKUP" section.

Disk fault tolerance   RAID 5 arrays, as well as duplexed or mirrored partitions, can be incorporated into an NSS volume. Either make sure that you have a consistent way to restore your data or include disk fault tolerance in your server designs. Remember that an NSS volume may reside across many disks. If any one of these disks fails, you risk losing all your data.

NOTE   If you have a new network, your dealer should have provided a backup solution for your servers when the system was installed. Not having a reliable file backup system is beyond imprudent; it is sheer folly. If you are setting up your system yourself without the help of a dealer or consultant, go directly (do not pass GO, do not collect $200) to a reseller or dealer and buy a tape backup system before another sunset. Shop for a tape backup system, both hardware and software, that protects your network data well enough to make you (and your management) comfortable.

FIGURE 14.10

Creating your new pool and volume

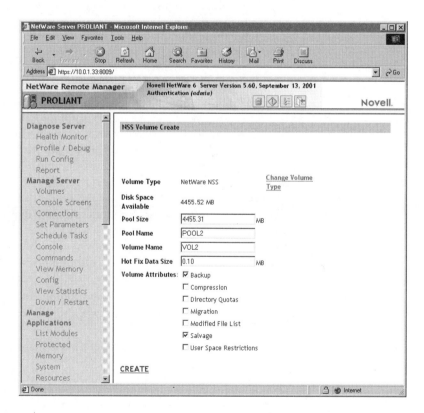

Repairing an NSS Volume

NSS includes a command-line option specifically for repairing corrupt or damaged NSS volumes. To repair a damaged volume, type the following command from the console prompt:

```
NSS /POOLREBUILD=NSS_Volume_Name
```

The *NSS_Volume_Name* argument is the NSS volume that needs to be repaired.

WARNING   *The old NetWare utility* VREPAIR.NLM *does not work with NSS volumes.*

Once the rebuild process finishes, take a look at the errors and transactions listed in the error file called *volume_name*.rlf. This file will await your perusal on the root of the DOS drive on the host server. If you want to keep this file, move it or rename it, because each rebuild overlays existing RLF files.

Verify the rebuild process by using, interestingly enough, this command:

```
NSS /POOLVERIFY
```

This command provides a list of pool names, allowing you to highlight the pool to verify.

NOTE   *The POOLVERIFY utility appears to be a holdover from NetWare 5.1's comprehensive NSS /MENU command, which doesn't appear in NetWare 6 for some reason. I'm guessing these utilities will wind up inside ConsoleOne, but didn't make it in time for the NetWare 6 release date. Keep an eye on the* support.novell.com *Web pages.*

File Compression: Buy One Disk, Get Two Disks' Worth of Space

My friends at Novell report that *file compression* is the most exciting feature to small enterprises that have limited financial resources. Larger enterprises, with limited administrator resources, tend to be more excited about eDirectory, NSS, and clustering. I guess that covers the spectrum—everyone has either too little money or too little time (or both).

File compression has these characteristics:

◆ Automatically enabled on all NetWare volumes

◆ Activated by volume, directory, or file

◆ Able to get better than 2:1 compression on some files

◆ Can be set to compress files after any amount of time you wish (including immediately after being written to disk)

◆ Can be archived (but the files must be restored to a volume that supports compression)

On volumes that have been upgraded from earlier NetWare versions, file compression is set to On by default. Earlier NetWare versions left compression off, and that's still the case with NSS volumes in NetWare 6. You must specifically turn on compression. Some companies prefer to leave compression off and provide fault tolerance through disk mirroring and the like, opting for safety over disk space. Since disk pricing dropped more than the Internet dot-com stock market, this approach entices as well.

The File Compression Process

Files are compressed in the background, and an internal NetWare 6 operating system process handles the compression. The file compression process goes this way:

- The system verifies that compression is enabled on the volume.

- The system verifies that compression is enabled in the directory and for the file to be compressed.

- The file to be compressed is examined.

- If more than 2 percent of the disk space will be saved (the setting for the amount of disk space is configurable) by compressing the file, the compression process begins by creating a temporary file describing the original file.

- The compressed file is checked for errors.

- If the file verifies correctly, the original and compressed files are swapped (the original becomes the temporary file and is purged as needed for space).

If an error occurs or if there is a power failure, the file compression process is stopped, and the compressed file won't replace the original file. In other words, the original file is kept, and no compression is performed until the next pass.

Compressing a File Immediately

To compress a file immediately or to check on the status of a compressed file using the ConsoleOne program, choose the file you want to compress by highlighting the volume in the NDS eDirectory tree. Navigate down through the NetWare volume and subdirectories to find the file, right-click it, choose Properties, and select the Attributes tab to see the page shown in Figure 14.11.

FIGURE 14.11

Checking individual files details

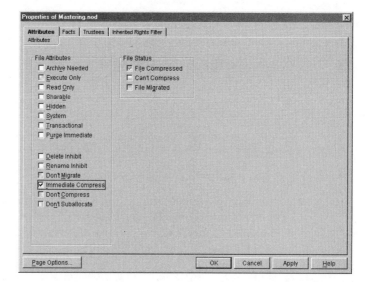

The Attributes tab lets you change all the file's attributes, including the Compression attribute. The File Status box will also let you know if the file is currently compressed, is migrated, or can't be compressed.

WARNING *NetWare 6 and NSS 3.0 change the rules for compression. Once you turn compression on for a volume, you can't turn it off. With NetWare 5.1, you could disable file compression if you were ready for many files to decompress all at once, but you could schedule this procedure carefully to avoid affecting your server performance.*

Checking File Compression Status

IN A HURRY 14.1: CHECK FILE COMPRESSION STATISTICS

1. Open ConsoleOne and highlight the volume to check.

2. Right-click the volume and choose Properties.

3. Click the Statistics tab on the top of the page, and choose Statistics, NSS Quota Usage, or NSS Statistics.

ConsoleOne provides an easy way to check the status of compressed files. You can see these charts from ConsoleOne in the example in Figure 14.12. To view this information, open ConsoleOne, highlight the volume name you want to check on, right-click the volume name, choose Properties, and then select the Statistics tab choice you prefer (Statistics, NSS Quota Usage, or NSS Statistics).

FIGURE 14.12

Statistics for volume PROLIANT_SYS

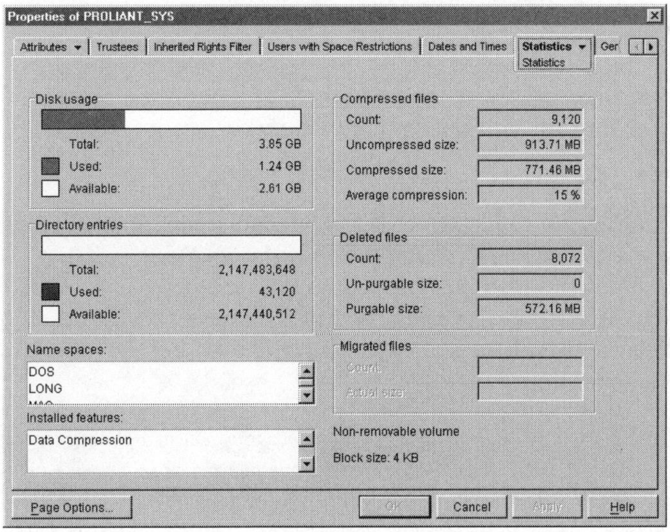

Is compression worthwhile? Take a look at the numbers on the screen in Figure 14.12. On the Statistics display of the Statistics tab, a text breakdown says the subdirectories compressed were originally 913.71MB in size and are now mashed down to 771.46MB. The average compression, according to the screen, rang up to 15 percent. I look at the number as nearly 140MB of free disk space. Your actual mileage may vary, depending on the type of data that is stored on the disk. Word-processing files and spreadsheets tend to compress really well, but files such as executables and some images do not compress as much.

Managing File Compression

These are the only reasons to disable compression for a volume:

◆ There's too little memory in the server to support the compression overhead.

◆ All files are active data files, and production speeds demand the best possible performance.

If these reasons don't apply to your situation, you should use compression on each volume. Compression management involves two steps:

1. Enable a volume to support compression. This is automatically set to On during the creation of the volume.

2. Activate compression per volume, directory, or file.

Generally, compression is enabled and activated per volume, but you can turn compression off without reworking your volume. When you do so, no more compression will take place on that volume until you turn compression back on.

You have these choices about how file compression is handled:

◆ Files can be decompressed the first time they are read.

◆ Files can be decompressed the second time they are read within a set time limit (read the file twice in a week, leave it uncompressed).

◆ Files can stay compressed.

The options allow you to keep active files from being compressed, eliminating the extra overhead to read a compressed file and maximizing throughput.

The default setting is to compress a file after seven days of inactivity. If that doesn't work for you, adjust it to any interval you wish. Check Chapter 1 for the details on setting compression options during initial volume setup, and Chapter 8 for using NetWare Remote Manager to modify compression settings per volume.

TIP   Compression is much more intensive than decompression, so schedule the compression at a time when there is no network activity, such as midnight. You can enable file compression on a volume any time. You can suspend (disable) compression with a SET command or by using the MONITOR utility's Server Parameters menu. Novell engineers recommend that you leave compression on at the volume level and then selectively turn off compression at the file or directory level using ConsoleOne.

Improved Performance of Peripheral Devices

Ever alert for more TLAs (three-letter acronyms), in NetWare 4.11 Novell introduced *NPA (NetWare Peripheral Architecture)*. Although this is not a new feature, if you are moving to NetWare 6 from a version of NetWare prior to NetWare 4.11, you should be aware of NPA. NPA makes it easier for developers to add and support different storage devices and their associated controllers. There are two levels to NPA: one for the controller board in the system and the other for the device attached. The `NPA.NLM` file, which is loaded during the initial server boot sequence, handles all this.

The Media Manager is a database built into NetWare that tracks all peripheral storage devices and media attached to the server. In earlier NetWare versions, the single interface between the NetWare operating system and the hardware was a `.DSK` file (a device driver file with the `.DSK` extension). No matter how many devices were connected to one host adapter board in the server, only one `.DSK` file could be used to connect the systems.

As you might guess, today's modular world demands more layers in between the operating system and the hardware. More is better in this case, because several layers make it easier to upgrade the driver for one storage device without messing up another storage device. The NPA layers are as follows:

Platform Support Module (PSM)   Hardware-specific software module supplied by vendors of multiprocessor systems. The NetWare installation routine will search for a PSM during installation in areas used by vendors to store configuration files. If a PSM is loaded on a system without multiple processors, no performance penalty will occur, so you can leave the module loaded.

PCI Hot Plug Module   Again, the hardware vendor providing hot plug support (the ability to insert or remove adapter and network boards while the server remains up and powered) will put the PCI Hot Plug modules on the system.

Host Adapter Module (HAM)   The driver controlling the host adapter hardware. Each HAM is adapter-specific and may be supplied by either Novell or the third-party manufacturer of the adapter. HAM drivers route requests across the bus to the specific adapter required.

Host Adapter Interface (HAI)   Programming hooks (APIs) within the NPA that provide a means of communication between the HAM and the Media Manager.

Custom Device Module (CDM)   The storage-device component software that handles details with the HAM. CDMs are normally supplied by the device manufacturer, although common ones are supported directly by NetWare. One CDM must be loaded for each physical device; for example, you'll need four CDMs for four devices attached to one HAM. To set this up during installation, you will need to use the Custom installation routine.

Custom Device Interface (CDI)   APIs within the NPA that provide a means of communication between the CDMs and the Media Manager.

Are these modules worthwhile? Yes, especially as more vendors get with the NetWare development program. If everyone making storage devices follows the rules laid out in the NetWare development guidelines, storage devices of all kinds will be less trouble to install and they will provide higher performance. Even if the third-party vendors don't do their part, this modular technique allows Novell engineers to make improvements more easily than ever before.

Storage Management Services (SMS) and SBACKUP

In NetWare 4, Novell introduced new storage management capabilities called Storage Management Services (SMS). The SMS system is independent of the backup and restore hardware and the filesystems (DOS, OS/2, Macintosh, Windows, or Unix) being backed up. SMS describes the architecture provided by NetWare to support reliable, cross-platform backup and restore procedures. It's up to the product manufacturers to implement SMS (and many of them do).

In NetWare 6, Novell improves on SMS by enhancing the backup server abilities. Here are some of the new features of NetWare 6's SMS:

◆ Protocol independence—you can use either TCP/IP or IPX/SPX to back up remote servers

◆ NDS for name resolution rather than SAP (Service Advertising Protocol)

◆ Support for backing up files larger than 4GB

◆ Ability to back up a server's local DOS partition

◆ Support for backing up remote Windows workstations

◆ Windows GUI for managing backups

◆ A NetWare server console backup utility for managing backups from the server console

◆ Concurrent job support if you have multiple backup devices

SMS now offers scheduling capabilities, workstation backup, and customization options. Enhanced SBACKUP copies data files to tape and generates log and error files that are saved to a specified directory on the host server.

The Novell documentation lists vendors of SMS-compliant hardware; check with your NetWare resellers for their recommendations. You should always use certified backup hardware.

SMS standards are almost a requirement now for backup product vendors. They must meet these standards in order to properly back up and restore NetWare 6 information. However, there is a difference between backing up NetWare 6 data and backing up NDS.

The additions in NetWare 6 that affect backup systems include extra attributes and flags on the files. The backup system must understand and handle compressed and noncompressed files without a hiccup.

NDS is a different story altogether (at least it is when speaking of multiple servers on a network). There are no database files with special attributes to back up. The NDS database is replicated across multiple network servers. If there is a problem with NDS on a server, the last thing you should do is restore some NDS files from a backup tape.

The active replicas on other servers in your network will copy their NDS information to your problem server over time. Several management tools available in ConsoleOne allow you to move or copy replica information (see Chapter 8 for details on managing replicas). From the server console, DSREPAIR offers several ways to rebuild or copy a damaged NDS database on one server (see Chapter 15, "Troubleshooting Your Network," for information about DSREPAIR). When a server suffers a catastrophic failure, rebuild NDS through these methods if at all possible.

TIP   If you want confirmation that you're not as prone to stupidity as I am under stress, look back in Chapter 8 and read about when I deleted the SYS: volume holding the master replica of [Root] for my network. Believe it or not, I recovered the network without restoring a tape backup of NDS. If I can resurrect NDS after deleting the main replica, you can resurrect NDS as well.

If none of the above methods works, reinstall NDS. Then go back through the previous suggestions to force other servers to update your problem server with the latest NDS changes. DSREPAIR is probably the best place to start resynchronizing the NDS database information. Although it may not be your first choice, it is important to have NDS on tape as an additional safety net for your network.

WHAT'S SIDF?

System Independent Data Format (SIDF) describes a common way for data to be read and written from media. Normally, a backup tape made with Seagate software is worthless when loaded into a server running Cheyenne backup software, for example. However, companies that follow the SIDF guidelines can read and write any other SIDF-compliant tape or optical disk.

The SIDF Association is working with other standards organizations, such as ANSI (American National Standards Institute), ECMA (European Computer Manufacturers Association), and ISO (International Organization for Standardization), to ratify SIDF as a true industry standard. Although SIDF began as part of Novell's SMS strategy, the idea of cross-platform backup media is too valuable for one company alone, and Novell has turned over SIDF to the SIDF Association.

Components of NetWare 6 SMS

NetWare 6 SMS is not a single program, but a collection of NLMs that provide various services. Like the other NetWare features we've looked at in this chapter, SMS has a modular architecture, which allows vendors to incorporate their own components. Figure 14.13 shows some of the components that are part of a NetWare 6 SMS system. Some of these are located on the server that is actually running the Storage Management Engine (this is where the backup media are located), and other components are located on other machines on the network.

This collection of components and software includes the following:

- ◆ SME.NLM (Storage Management Engine), which includes the enhanced SBACKUP software utility that provides backup and restore functions.

- ◆ SMDR.NLM (Storage Management Data Requester), which manages communications between SME and TSAs (Target Service Agents).

- ◆ SMSDI (SMS Storage Device Interface), which manages communications between SBACKUP and storage devices and media.

- ◆ Device drivers (IDE.DSK, TAPEDAI.DSK, and AHA2940.DSK), which handle the physical and mechanical operations of storage devices. They act on commands passed through SMSDI from SBACKUP.

- ◆ NetWare server TSAs (such as TSA500.NLM, TSA410.NLM, and TSA312.NLM), which manage communications asking for data from SME to the NetWare server holding the data. They then return the data through SMDR to SME, which passes it to the physical device.

- ◆ NetWare server DOS partition TSADOSP.NLM, which allows the backup software to back up the local server's DOS partition.

◆ Database TSAs (such as TSANDS), which manage communications between the server hosting SBACKUP and the database on the server hosting the data, then back through the SMDR to SBACKUP.

◆ Workstation TSAPROXYs (such as TSADOS, Win95 TSA, and Windows NT TSA), which manage communications between the SME host server and the workstation holding the data to be backed up. You can install the Windows TSAs when you install the client software.

NOTE   *The TSAPROXY manages a list of workstations available to be backed up. The workstations regularly send "I'm alive" packets. You must load the* TSAPROXY.NLM *in order to support remote workstations.*

◆ Windows Novell Storage Management Service program (SYS:PUBLIC\NWBACK32.EXE).

◆ NetWare server utility SBCON.NLM, which allows you to manage and schedule jobs from the NetWare server console.

NOTE   *In earlier versions of NetWare, the SMS backup engine was contained in the* SBACKUP.NLM *program. NetWare 6 does not have an* SBACKUP.NLM. *Novell often refers to the enhanced SBACKUP capabilities, but these features are actually in the* SME.NLM, SMDR.NLM, *and* SMSDI.NLM *programs.*

FIGURE 14.13

The components of
NetWare 6 SMS

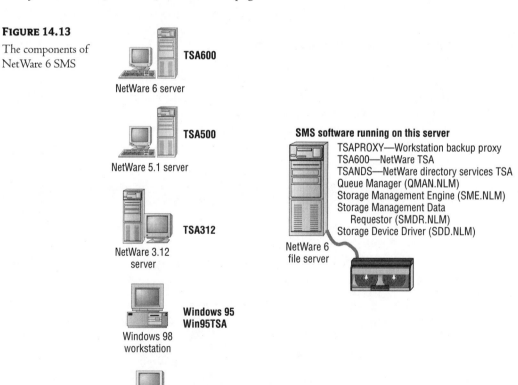

TSA600

NetWare 6 server

TSA500

NetWare 5.1 server

TSA312

NetWare 3.12
server

Windows 95
Win95TSA

Windows 98
workstation

Windows NTTSA

Windows NT
workstation

SMS software running on this server

TSAPROXY—Workstation backup proxy
TSA600—NetWare TSA
TSANDS—NetWare directory services TSA
Queue Manager (QMAN.NLM)
Storage Management Engine (SME.NLM)
Storage Management Data
     Requestor (SMDR.NLM)
Storage Device Driver (SDD.NLM)

NetWare 6
file server

Understanding the Role of the TSA

The TSA is a software program that runs on any computer on the network, acting as an agent that communicates with SME on the host server. TSAs are loaded on the host server, target servers, and clients. The TSA advertises the presence of a target to the server so it can be backed up. TSAs are designed specifically for the server and client operating systems:

TSA600   NetWare 6 host server

TSA500   NetWare 5.x host server

TSA410   NetWare 4.11 and 4.10 target server

TSA312   NetWare 3.12 target server

TSANDS   NDS database

W95TSA   Windows 95/98 client

NTTSA   Windows NT workstation

MACTSA   Macintosh client

GWTSA   GroupWise data

Installing SMS on the Backup Server

During installation of the NetWare server, you should choose to install SMS as one of the optional components. All this installation does, however, is copy files from the NetWare 6 CD-ROM to the NetWare server's SYS: volume. The files on the CD-ROM are in the \PRODUCTS\SMS directory.

NOTE   The NetWare server that is going to host the backup device or devices should have at least an extra 128MB of RAM available (you always need more server RAM).

When you load the `SMDR.NLM` the first time, you will be asked for two pieces of information:

◆ The SMDR context, which is the NDS context where the SMDR object will be created

◆ The SMDR group context, which holds the SMDR Group object that is used when searching for multiple SMDR servers

You will then be asked to provide an Admin-level user ID and password. The default for both of these is the container in which the NetWare Server object resides.

This procedure will create a configuration file called `SYS:ETC\SMS\SMDR.CFG`. This file has the two pieces of data you provided above. If you need to change the SMDR object or SMDR Group object context, I recommend deleting the file. You can also re-create the `SMDR.CFG` file by typing **LOAD SMDR NEW** at the server console prompt. When the `SMDR.NLM` is reloaded, you will be asked to re-create it.

Next, you need to configure the Queue Manager module, `QMAN.NLM`. When you configure QMAN for the first time, you will be asked some QMAN configuration questions. First, you must identify the SMS job queue context. This is the NDS context in which the queue object will be created. The default is the NDS context in which the NetWare Server object resides.

The second request is for the name of the backup queue. For example, if the backup server's name is DUKE and the backup server's context is OU=SALES.O=SOMORITA, the default backup queue name is CN=DUKE Backup Job Queue.OU=SALES. O=SOMORITA. You will also be prompted to enter an Admin-level user and password.

This process creates a file called SYS:ETC\SMS\SBACKUP.CFG that the QMAN.NLM program uses. If you need to re-create the backup queue or change the parameters, you can delete this file and reload the QMAN.NLM; you will be prompted for the information again. You can also type **LOAD QMAN NEW** at the server console to re-create the file.

The final step is to add all the correct statements to your STARTUP.NCF file and AUTOEXEC.NCF file. Here are some lines that were added to the STARTUP.NCF file for a NetWare 6 server that has the tape drive on an Adaptec 2940 SCSI host adapter:

```
LOAD AHA2940.HAM SLOT=4
LOAD SCSIHD.CDM
```

And here are some lines that were added to the AUTOEXEC.NCF file, to back up the NDS database, the NetWare 6 filesystem, remote workstations, and the local DOS partition:

```
LOAD TSANDS
LOAD TSA600
LOAD TSAPROXY
LOAD TSADOSP
LOAD QMAN
```

The QMAN.NLM manages the job scheduling; it will automatically load the SMDR.NLM and supporting NLM files.

Configuring SMS on Windows Workstations

Don't forget to load any required TSAs on workstations or other NetWare servers. The Windows workstation clients give you the option of installing the SMS software. You can do this during the NetWare client installation by checking the Novell Target Service Agent choice during a custom installation, as shown in Figure 14.14.

FIGURE 14.14

Loading the TSA software on a Windows client

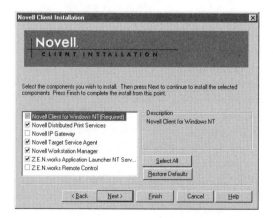

After you install the SMS software, you can configure and customize properties. For example, to configure the Windows NT/2000 TSA software, choose Control Panel ➢ Network ➢ Services, highlight Novell Target Service Agent, and click the Properties button to open the TSA Preferences dialog box, shown in Figure 14.15.

FIGURE 14.15

Configuring the TSA software on a client

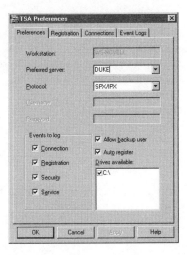

Here, you can configure the preferred server, the default protocol, and event logging; specify which drives are available to be backed up; and more. The Windows 95/98 TSA software configuration is similar.

Tape "Restore" System Procedures

Years ago, I had a boss who used to say, "Customers don't buy tape backup systems; they buy tape restore systems. They just don't realize it." This quote has stuck with me over the years because it is really profound. To this day, this quote affects my planning and implementation of any backup system. The bottom line is that you need to make sure the data you expect to be on your backup media is really there and that you can get it off. I could fill a chapter with tape backup horror stories.

So you have your tape drive installed and tested. Now you are ready to start backing up your data. You face these questions:

◆ What should I back up each day?

◆ How many tapes should I use?

◆ Is just doing backups enough?

◆ Am I ready to face my boss if I need to restore important data but can't?

These are all important questions—especially the last one. It is time to start planning your "restore." Even if you never end up restoring a single byte of data thanks to duplexed disks or RAID 5 drive arrays, you need to be prepared.

BACKUP TAPE HINTS

Here are some tape "restore" system hints:

◆ When installing a new tape system, test all options. Run large backups and restores.

◆ Rotate your backup media. Don't use the same tape night after night.

◆ Retire tapes when they reach a certain age. I don't trust 4mm or 8mm tapes for very long. I retire 8mm tapes after 25–40 uses and 4mm tapes after 50–75 uses. DLT and other 1/4-inch technologies can typically be used longer. If you are not sure, check with the manufacturer of your tape drive. Don't push the usage limits too far; better to retire tapes early rather than late.

◆ Purchase data-grade tapes.

◆ Check your backup logs daily.

◆ Do a bimonthly test restore.

◆ Always do a verification pass when data is backed up.

◆ If you can, do a full backup of your servers every night. I recognize that this is not possible on many systems, but it is usually my goal when setting up a system.

A SAMPLE TAPE ROTATION

I could spend the next 20 or 30 pages discussing possible tape-rotation strategies. It is also quite possible that you already have an adequate tape-rotation strategy. Table 14.3 shows the tape rotation that I use and recommend to clients. This rotation strategy will not work for all systems, but I have found it to be sufficient for most systems.

TABLE 14.3: TAPES REQUIRED FOR THE SAMPLE ROTATION

DAILY TAPES	WEEKLY TAPES	MONTHLY TAPES
Monday–Even	Friday–First	January
Monday–Odd	Friday–Second	February
Tuesday–Even	Friday–Third	March
Tuesday–Odd	Friday–Fourth	April
Wednesday–Even	Friday–Fifth	May
Wednesday–Odd		June
Thursday–Even		July
Thursday–Odd		August
		September
		October
		November
		December

The daily tapes are used over a two-week period. On Monday the 7th, I use the Monday–Odd tape, but on Monday the 14th, I use the Monday–Even tape. On the first Friday of the month, I use the Friday–First tape, on the second Friday of the month, I use the Friday–Second tape, and so on.

I select a day during the month that I do the monthly backup—usually the first day of the month. However, if you support a system that has an accounting, order-entry, or some other type of system that does a month-end close, you might want to select either the day before or the day after that close occurs. I also allocate a few backup tapes in my library just for "special" occasions, such as accounting systems and database repair.

TIP   The whole reason we back this data up is in the event of a disaster. The disaster may be a failed hard disk, or it could be something as dramatic as a flood or a computer room fire. It's a good idea to store at least some backup tapes in another location. I try to keep my Friday tapes stored in an alternate location, whether this is at a special off-site storage company or just in my briefcase.

SCHEDULING BACKUPS

To schedule backups, you need to have Read and File Scan rights for those files and directories you want to back up. There are three backup methods:

- A *full backup* copies all files in selected volumes and directories, clearing the archive bit for each file.

- A *differential backup* copies all files changed since the last backup and does not clear the archive bits.

- An *incremental backup* copies all files changed or added since the last full or incremental backup, clearing the archive bit for each.

You can create and save data sets that list specific directories and/or files to be backed up. Use the Exclude option to choose most of the files or NDS eDirectory tree and omit a small portion. Use the Include option to add particular files and directories. You can actually combine the two options to create your data set. Name the set for reuse.

You can mix and match backup methods on successive days. Differential and incremental sessions have the advantage of speed, since they do not work on all files and may be suitable on a daily basis. But the most complete method is, of course, a full backup. Since enhanced SBACKUP will not copy active files, it's best to schedule backup sessions at times of no or low activity.

NOTE   Remember that your backup will help you to restore your system to its prior state when you make major changes, as well as restore your users' data and applications.

FILE SNAPSHOT FOR OPEN FILES

The last paragraph said "…SBACKUP will not copy active files …." This used to be a serious problem. Some third-party products solved this problem, and now Novell includes a "file snapshot" feature to keep an original copy of all data files.

A file snapshot captures the most recently closed copy of all files. This copy, not actively open, can be backed up without problem. Data changed between the snapshot and the backup may be lost, but at least you'll have a recent copy of the file.

NSS commands for a file snapshot must be given at the server console. Start a the file snapshot feature for a particular volume, say PROLIANT_VOL2, with this command:

```
nss /FileCopyOnWrite=PROLIANT_VOL2
```

Obviously, substitute your volume name for mine (or name your volume PROLIANT_VOL2, if you prefer).

To set the file snapshot parameter for all server volumes, use this command:

```
nss /FileCopyOnWrite=all
```

This is actually easier than naming the volume, isn't it?

Turn off the file snapshot feature by typing this command at the server console:

```
nss /NoFileCopyOnWrite
```

This solves the open file problem.

NOTE *Other tape vendors actually freeze open files, copy them, and then unfreeze the file, which offers more protection than SBACKUP. That's why I recommend checking out third-party backup options.*

Managing SBACKUP

The SBCON.NLM program allows you to manage backup operations from the console of the NetWare server or from a Windows workstation with a GUI.

RUNNING SBCON FROM THE SERVER

After activating SBACKUP, you can use the options on the SBCON main menu, shown in Figure 14.16. These options work as follows:

Job Administration   Displays a submenu that allows you to do backups, restores, and verification passes.

Storage Device Administration   Configures tape drive properties.

Log File Administration   Allows you to view session activity and errors from the log files and to configure the default location for the log files.

Change Target to Backup From or Restore To   Specifies the target drive for backup and restore sessions.

Administering Jobs

Choosing Job Administration from the main menu displays the Select Job menu:

FIGURE 14.16

The SBCON main menu

From here, you have the following options:

Backup   Selects files and directories to be copied from a hard disk drive to tape.

Restore   Selects files that had been backed up to tape to restore to a hard drive, if files have been damaged or lost.

Verify   Checks backed-up files on tape with originals on a hard disk to make sure they were backed up correctly.

Create Session Files   Creates session files from data on a selected device.

Current Job List   Displays a list of all pending and active jobs in the backup queue.

Managing SMS Log Files

SMS creates two types of files: log and error files. By default, these files are in the SYS:SYSTEM\TSA\LOG directory.

From SBCON, you can view the log and error files, as well as change their storage location. From the SBCON main menu, choose Log File Administration to open the Error/Log File Administration menu, shown below.

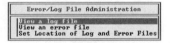

Choose the appropriate View option to see the logs. To change the file location, select Set Location of Log and Error Files, and then enter a valid path for the log files.

USING THE WINDOWS GUI

You can also activate SBACKUP at a Windows workstation with a GUI. Locate and run NWBACK32.EXE in the Public directory on the SYS: volume. Figure 14.17 shows the Quick Access dialog box, displayed when you choose File ➤ Quick Access.

FIGURE 14.17

The Novell SMS
(NWBACK32.EXE)
GUI

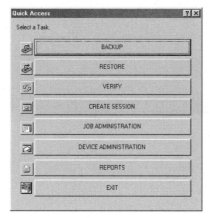

The Quick Access dialog box offers the following options:

Backup   Selects files and directories to be copied from a hard disk drive to tape.

Restore   Selects files that had been backed up to tape to restore to a hard drive, if files have been damaged or lost.

Verify   Checks backed-up file sizes on tape with originals on a hard disk.

Create Session   Records session activity and errors in a log file for later reference by the backup operator.

Job Administration   Lists scheduled jobs, which can be viewed or modified.

Device Administration   Configures tape drive properties.

Reports   Prints sessions and log files.

Server-Based Java Support

NetWare 6 continues Novell's commitment to making NetWare a Java development platform and to Java-based administration. You'll notice this the first time you install NetWare 6, since the server installation tool is a Java GUI (this trend started with NetWare 5). The NetWare installation "experience" has been transformed to a wizard-driven procedure that collects information about protocols, configurations, and NDS, and generates a customized network environment.

ConsoleOne is a Java application that loads at the server or at Windows workstations. With its mouse-enabled, Windows-style graphical look, ConsoleOne makes much of NetWare Administrator's functionality available at the server. Novell plans to offer snap-in modules to incorporate all its management tools into ConsoleOne's unified interface, including NetWare Administrator, ManageWise, ZENworks, GroupWise, BorderManager, and NDS for NT.

The Novell Upgrade Wizard is another example of the Java influence in NetWare 6. This utility upgrades the NetWare 3 bindery, printers, and data to NetWare 6. It also verifies system options and identifies potential problems for the upgrade process.

Security-Related Features

NetWare 6 provides security APIs and services that allow developers to use cryptographic services and authentication systems rather than providing their own cryptographic services. NetWare includes the following security-related features:

Cryptographic services   The Novell International Cryptographic Infrastructure (NICI) is a modular framework that can use various cryptography mechanisms. The Controlled Cryptography Service (CCS) API is an important aspect of NICI, providing developers with the capability to integrate cryptographic algorithms with their applications. The United States currently limits the length of cryptographic keys to 40 bits, although European countries allow 128-bit keys. NICI can recognize both 128- and 40-bit cryptographic keys within an application, so that applications can be used anywhere in the world, regardless of local ordinances.

Secure Authentication Services (SAS)   NetWare 6 extends version 4.11's C2-certified capabilities with SAS. The SAS API will support new authentication techniques as they are developed. NetWare's SAS supports the Internet standard, Secure Socket Layer (SSL) version 3.

Public Key Infrastructure Services (PKIS)   NetWare 6's PKIS supports public key cryptography and digital certificates, which can be stored and managed by new objects in the NDS eDirectory tree. The Certificate Authority Object (CAO) contains the public key, private key, certificate, and other information. The Key Material Object (KMO) represents a private key in encrypted form. The Security container is created when SAS is installed. It holds security-related objects.

NOTE   *For more information about NetWare cryptographic and security services, check out Novell's developer Web site at* `developer.novell.com`.

SNMP: A Management Solution

SNMP (Simple Network Management Protocol) is widely used for TCP/IP networks and Unix hosts. Because of this, many people mistakenly believe SNMP is a TCP/IP-only management solution. This is not true.

The developers made sure that SNMP was transport-protocol neutral. As management becomes more critical to PC networks, SNMP systems will become available for IPX-only networks. The only restriction today is marketing, not technology.

WARNING   *If you are going to activate SNMP, you should go directly to your Unix system administrator and work out the details. There are no NetWare-only SNMP packages, so this isn't something you get into just as a lark. If you start SNMP, you must have a large network with active network management.*

Although NetWare Management Systems (NMS) can use SNMP clients, check the installation of NMS before you add SNMP to the server. With a NetWare-only network, there is no need for the SNMP overhead.

A BIT OF SNMP HISTORY

SNMP was developed by four gentlemen over dinner in Monterey, California, in March 1987. Two of the gentlemen were working in universities, and the other two worked for a leading Internet service provider. Being engineers, the group developed the SGMP (Simple Gateway Monitoring Protocol) in two months.

By August 1988, SNMP (the spiffed-up subsequent protocol that improved upon SGMP) was a reality. The protocol details were officially declared an Internet draft standard, meaning they were completed, implemented, and under production at several companies.

In April 1989, SNMP became recommended, making it the de facto operational standard for managing TCP/IP networks and internetworks. More than 30 vendors displayed products at the InterOp trade show in San Jose, California, in October 1989. SNMP had officially become "The Protocol" when speaking of network management.

In enterprise networks, SNMP is still The Protocol and shows no signs of slowing down. Although SNMP was developed to be small enough to run in an IBM XT (at least, the Agent part), it isn't used on many PC-only networks. This probably won't change any time soon. Most of the serious management consoles for SNMP are Unix systems, and they are designed and priced for large networks, not for small and medium LANs.

Now waiting in the wings is SNMP version 2, adding some capabilities and security to SNMP. Unfortunately, the two SNMP camps are fighting about security details, so the IETF has yet to release an official SNMP version 2. NetWare server and client software will be compatible with any updated SNMP management consoles that support SNMP version 2; management is too important for companies to drop the ball at the start of a new version.

How SNMP Works on the NetWare 6 Server

Network and object details for SNMP are kept in an `.MIB` (Management Information Base) file. Since NetWare 6 is object-oriented, the idea of SNMP managing objects rather than computers and printers should not cause you any mental strain.

Each device to be managed runs a small bit of software called the SNMP Agent. The agents monitor certain functions depending on the device hosting them. When some event happens, the agent sends a message to a predetermined address. The SNMP management console software collects these traps and uses them to monitor the health of the network.

The NetWare server can easily run the SNMP Agent software, and that capability is included in the TCP/IP software. You can add TCP/IP support without SNMP, but if you're in an enterprise network with SNMP management consoles, your servers deserve to be monitored.

Management consoles are most often Unix workstations with special software. The most popular management software is produced by Sun and HP. These systems may cost close to $100,000 when fully configured—overkill for a NetWare-only network. However, if you have a graphical management package for your wiring concentrators, you have a subset of an SNMP management console.

`SNMP.NLM` handles the agent chores for SNMP management consoles and also helps control the TCP/IP module for the `TCPCON.NLM` utility. The community name used during SNMP message authentication must be provided before SNMP starts. The default community name is *public*, used for read-only SNMP activities. Therefore, no SNMP management console can change any parameter on the NetWare server.

Configuring SNMP

The INETCFG.NLM allows you to configure the SNMP parameters from the SNMP Parameters menu, shown in Figure 14.18. To change these parameters, from the main INETCFG menu, choose Manage Configuration ➢ Configure SNMP Parameters.

FIGURE 14.18

The SNMP Parameters menu in INETCFG

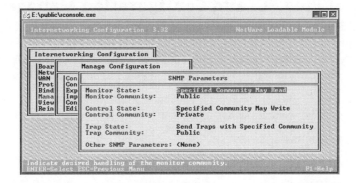

You can configure three community name options from the SNMP parameters screen:

Monitor Community   Determines which SNMP management consoles can read this information.

Control Community   Determines which SNMP management consoles can write (change) this information.

Trap Community   Designates where traps will be sent (management consoles to inform of changes).

Each option in INETCFG has three choices:

◆ Any community can access the server (read or write).

◆ No community can access the server.

◆ Only specified communities can have access.

The default option leaves read authority for the public community.

Setting SNMP Information

Also from the INETCFG Manage Configuration menu, you can choose Configure SNMP Information to open the General SNMP Information for This Node menu:

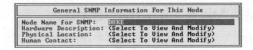

Here, you can enter information that an SNMP management console would see when it queries this particular agent. This includes the server's name, contact information, location, and a description of the system hardware.

Hot Plug PCI and Configuration Manager

The first time that I saw Hot Plug PCI, I said to myself, "This will make life easier!" And it does! Hot Plug PCI gives you the ability to replace or upgrade PCI cards such as network boards while the server is running. You can start yanking PCI cards out of your server while it is online.

The hardware must support Hot Plug PCI, and you must make sure that three elements properly support it:

- The operating system
- The device drivers
- The server hardware

NetWare 6 does support Hot Plug PCI, but you must have the supporting software from your server vendor. For an example of Compaq's Hot Plug PCI support in action, check out Figure 14.19.

FIGURE 14.19

Hot Plug details on the first and last two entries in the log file

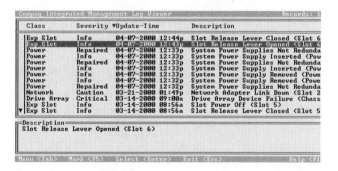

TIP   *You'll find a lot of good information about Hot Plug PCI on Compaq's Web site at* www.compaq.com, *or contact your server vendor.*

One new feature of NetWare 6 helps track the current server configuration. The Configuration Manager detects the hardware configuration of devices that support auto-detection on the following hardware buses: PCI, EISA, MCA, and PnP ISA. If a hardware change is detected, NetWare automatically loads the appropriate configuration NLM.

NetWare 6 Web Enhancements

Some have called NetWare 6 the version when Novell finally filled in all the gaps and added a premier Web server to go along with its award-winning file and print services. Microsoft's Windows NT with Internet Information Server has claimed, with at least a little bit of justification, the file/print/Web server triple crown. The days of Microsoft Windows NT/2000 being a better Web server platform than NetWare are now, officially (I just said so), over.

Several upgraded Web server applications are included with NetWare 6, along with a few applications that are brand new. Let's take a look at them and see where they will help your company the most.

NetWare FTP Server

Enough detail about the NetWare FTP Server appeared in Chapter 11 for you to get the idea so that you could set up the server if you're familiar with FTP. If you're not familiar with FTP and skipped the information in Chapter 11 because you don't see why you would want an FTP server running on your NetWare server, keep reading—I'll try to show you why.

First of all, as mentioned in Chapter 11, if one NetWare server has an FTP server running, you can "reach through" that server and get files from any other NetWare server on your network. This unusual feature comes courtesy of Novell's server-to-server communications capabilities and the use of NDS for authentication.

FETCHING A FILE

Have you ever been at home and desperately needed a file from work? This trick offers savvy network administrators a way to retrieve a file (I wouldn't trust too many users to handle the details). If you want to fetch a file from an office server that's not on the Internet and runs only IPX, and your only connection is through the Internet, let me show you how to do it.

You can navigate to a remote server, or fetch or put a file directly on the remote server. Let's navigate to one and show a directory.

Connect to your FTP server via the command line with the FTP client program included with Windows (limited though it is), and authenticate to NDS by giving a NetWare username and password. Then, use the CD (Change Directory) command to connect to the remote, non-FTP server through NDS. Why does CD work? In the Unix and NFS world, remote filesystems are treated like local filesystems. This is very handy. (It's too bad that Microsoft's view of the world is so limited that they didn't know how to "emulate" this technology.) Look at Figure 14.20 for an example of a session reaching through an FTP server to another NetWare server.

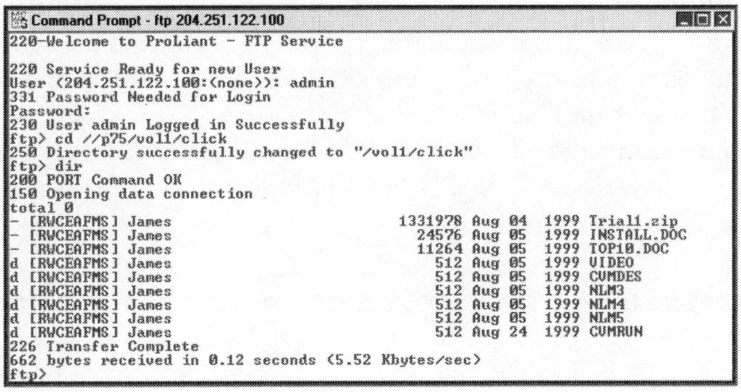

FIGURE 14.20

Connect to PROLIANT, reach through to P75

See the list of commands and responses? You can't see the command opening the connection within the screen, but Windows NT shows the command in the top status line of Figure 14.20. I put the Welcome message in the system by creating a WELCOME.TXT file in the SYS:\ETC directory.

Notice one other interesting thing about this FTP server pass-through: P75 is a NetWare 5 server, not a NetWare 6 server. It's not connected to the Internet. It does happen to use TCP/IP to communicate, but FTP pass-through works over IPX (I know because I've done it before).

USING GRAPHICAL FTP CLIENTS

Of course, command-line applications like FTP are passé, and no user will ever willingly use one. Luckily, a variety of graphical FTP clients are available.

Let's look at one of the best FTP client programs, WS_FTP Pro from Ipswitch, Inc. (www.ipswitch.com). Figure 14.21 shows the opening screen of a client FTP connection to the Net-Ware FTP Server on the Compaq ProLiant here in the lab.

FIGURE 14.21

One of several view-ing options for WS_FTP Pro

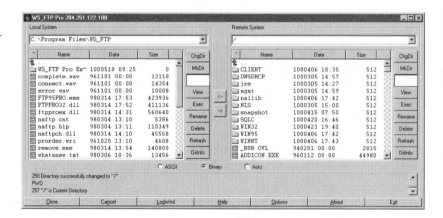

Is PUBLIC a dumb location for a default directory for FTP service? You bet. Change that loca-tion immediately, if you really plan to use FTP, to something where critical client and system files aren't hanging out for all to see. The easiest way to change this setting is to use the Netscape-derived NetWare Server Administration utility. Let's change the directory setting.

Once the Server Administration screen appears in your browser, click the NetWare FTP Server command button. The settings in Figure 14.22 are on the User Settings page, so click that link on the left side of the first FTP Server screen.

Can you think of any directories that would be better for anonymous FTP clients than PUBLIC? I sure can. Create a SYS:\FTP directory for users, and you won't be wondering what happened to some of your PUBLIC files.

NetWare 6 Web Developer Services and the Apache Web Server

NetWare 6 includes the NetWare Enterprise Web Server. This is actually Netscape's server, one of the most powerful and scalable Web engines available today, which Novell licensed and renamed. But since Web developers also love the Apache Web Server to the point of making it the most popular

Web server on the Internet, NetWare 6 also includes Apache (`www.apache.org`). Apache, one of the major triumphs of the open-source software movement, jumped to an early lead as the dominant Web server on the Internet and still (according to most research) remains as the leading server.

FIGURE 14.22

Change both of the two default directory settings.

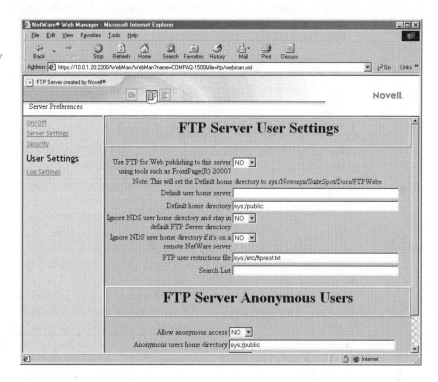

Actually, Novell does much more than just "include" the Apache server. Many of the new Net-Ware 6 services we've discussed so far in this book run on the Apache Web Server included with Net-Ware. These NetWare Web Services components include the following:

- iFolder
- iManage
- NetWare Web Manager
- NetWare Web Search Manager
- NetWare Web Search Print and Search Services
- NetWare Web Access

The NetWare Enterprise Server is a full-featured Web server that runs as a NetWare 6 NLM. This Web server provides Web publishing services, Web-based administration, and secure Web services.

Yes, you can run both the NetWare Enterprise Server and the Apache Web Server at the same time on the same server. Yes, you can host multiple Web servers, using either the virtual hardware or virtual software approach. Yes, you have full control over the Apache server applications and also run normal Web services, just like the Apache server you know and love on the Linux platform. Who says NetWare doesn't make an application server?

NetWare 6 replaces IBM's WebSphere servlet engine with the Tomcat servlet engine developed by the Apache.org group (see `http://jakarta.apache.org` for the latest Tomcat news). Complete instructions for migrating WebSphere applications to Tomcat come in the red box. The Migration Utility creates Tomcat 3.3 Web applications from WebSphere Web applications.

Adventures in Cluster Land

Before going on this adventure, we need to define what a NetWare cluster is. A *cluster* of servers sits between the network clients and data storage devices, each ready to ensure access in case of a server hardware or software failure. Resources, such as applications (Web servers are a great example) or data devices (shared storage, like a storage area network), run on a primary server with one or more other servers designated as fail-over sites. If the primary server fails, the resources migrate to one or more other servers.

Novell introduced clustering add-on software with NetWare 5.1 in a big way (what came before doesn't count for much). NetWare Cluster Services costs extra ($4,995 per server), which makes it the only real optional product I'll describe in much detail. I don't normally spend much time on optional products, because there's so much to cover with normal NetWare features. But I had the chance to play with a mega-server from Compaq and write two articles for *Network World* comparing building your own cluster of servers against buying a preconfigured cluster.

One huge advantage comes with NetWare 6: the first two clusters are free. *Free* trips happily off the tongue, right? You bet. NetWare 6 provides everything you need to build a two-node cluster for free. Well, you need to buy the operating systems, of course, and the hardware, but the $5,000 for another server cluster license doesn't kick in until server number three.

Am I being pushy putting this clustering story in here? Maybe, but I think you can learn some interesting things from the article. Besides, it was too much fun to see it run once and disappear into landfills. At least this way, people will need to throw two things into landfills to get rid of this article.

The following is more than just the article; it includes some extra information, extra comments, and no editing by *Network World*. I made a few adjustments to include NetWare 6 experiences. Therefore, I claim this as my copyright (no one else seems to be rushing to claim it), and I can run it here if I want. So there!

Two Options for NetWare Cluster Services

"Mission-critical" today means Web server uptime at many companies, especially since Web site outages now make national news headlines. But even if your company doesn't make headlines during every Web site hiccup, you still lose revenue and customer goodwill during every minute of downtime.

Once management agrees to spend the time and money necessary to increase server uptime, the modern network manager faces multiple options. Put all your eggs in one basket with a new mega-server? Distribute applications across multiple servers, each with standby capability? Set up server clusters? If clustering appeals to you, do you use your existing servers, buy new servers and cluster them together yourself, or buy preconfigured clusters?

Then come the software choices. Should you stick with something you know? Follow the hot fad and hope it works for you? Bet your company's Web site on newly released server software? (Any ideas which products I'm referring to with the last two sentences? Linux and Windows 2000 would be good guesses.)

For this test, we narrowed down the questions by using NetWare 6 as the server operating system, supporting the included NetWare Enterprise Server. NetWare servers have a strong track record of reliability earned by measuring uptime in years, not days. The NetWare Enterprise Server shipping with NetWare 6 is the third generation of NetWare/Netscape server application, and it has been tweaked to use NDS for easier management and security.

NetWare 6 SMP support handles up to 32 processors under the basic NetWare license. Novell just upgraded its NetWare Cluster Services software to version 1.01 to support NetWare 6 (actually they renamed it to Cluster Services 1.6). This new combination caps nearly a decade of fail-proofing started by Novell with their SFT (System Fault Tolerant) software in NetWare 3.

The remaining questions are simple. First, how hard is NetWare Cluster Services to install and use? We tested by installing the software on existing lab servers. Second, should you roll your own cluster or buy a preconfigured system, such as the one provided for us by Compaq?

For the cluster comparison described here, Compaq provided us a complete ProLiant Cluster for NetWare, including all hardware and software. We took four existing servers (Compaq ProLiant 3000, Pentium 120 clone of undetermined origin, and two Gateway2000 Pentium 120 systems, all with 128MB of RAM) running NetWare 5.1 and added the NetWare Cluster Services software. Performance wasn't the issue; we tested installation, configuration, and management. Novell provided all network software. Infrastructure components came from 3Com (EtherLink III network adapters) running through a LinkSys 24 port SNMP-managed hub.

CLUSTER INSTALLATION AND CONFIGURATION

NetWare generally installs easily, albeit more slowly recently with Novell's new insistence on the Java-based GUI. However, mashing four existing NetWare servers into a cluster required more work than anticipated. Note that clustering demands that TCP/IP be installed on each NetWare server to handle IP addressing used for fail-over support, but that isn't a problem since TCP/IP has become the default protocol choice. Installing new management utilities and extra configurations, along with assigning the new clustering licenses, took more time than expected.

Novell now includes a Certificate Authority with Secure Authentication Services (SAS), primarily for Enterprise Web Server users. Yet a known error with older SAS files and the Enterprise Web Server required several Web server deletions and reinstallations. Perhaps it's my fault, but user licensing errors come and go on a seemingly random basis. (Could it be all the strange stuff I do to these servers during testing?)

These errors helped me reach the conclusion that combining existing servers takes more time and is more trouble than starting from scratch. Adding a storage area network (SAN) to an existing network involves plenty of other technical considerations and requires software modifications and new hardware for all cluster servers.

NOTE *A storage area network, or SAN, is a special-purpose subnetwork connecting data storage devices through one or more (usually more) servers to the main network for storage access. Typically, multiple servers link both to the main network through Ethernet and the back-end storage network through SCSI or Fibre Channel network components. NetWare 6 makes setting up SANs easier than ever before.*

Actually installing the NetWare Cluster Services software went fairly easily, until the Web server/SAS problem. A Windows client handles the installation honors, after the Novell-recommended upgrade of the network client software and adding a new version of ConsoleOne. After rebooting the servers (a rare occurrence for NetWare server installations but one required to update the 5.1 kernel), each server searched for, and found, the others ready to cluster. From CD insertion to clustering took about an hour.

The ProLiant Cluster for NetWare 5.1 from Compaq avoided all those problems. Although *Network World* lab policy blocks vendor technician involvement unless the tech does every installation for every customer, Compaq does send a tech out to set up each ProLiant Cluster of this size.

Nothing is left out of the Compaq system when delivered. NetWare is installed (Compaq has long been tightly connected to Novell), the SAN runs as various NetWare volumes, and extra Compaq utilities add to the ease of management. The stand-alone ProLiant 3000 server also used in the lab for testing was easier to install than a regular NetWare server because the Compaq SmartStart utility handles many hardware details during installation.

Once the existing servers reboot and start up as cluster-enabled, the Novell CMON (Cluster MONitor) screen appears, showing each server in the cluster and a few other details. Check out Figure 14.23 for an update. This screen loads automatically on clustered servers.

FIGURE 14.23

Quick display of clustered servers

The updated ConsoleOne utility includes a Cluster object (added automatically) and a new screen showing cluster-specific information. Figure 14.24 shows the new cluster logo made from the balls laid off from the old Novell *N* logo.

ConsoleOne's Cluster Policies page is plain but important. Start Mode (the default is Automatic) groups the cluster resources (applications) from each server into the assigned cluster upon booting. Failover Mode (the default is Automatic) tells the resource to automatically move to the next assigned server in case of failure. Fallback Mode (again, Automatic is the default) tells the resource whether to migrate back to the original server when it reappears or just stay put.

FIGURE 14.24

ConsoleOne shows
the Compaq cluster.

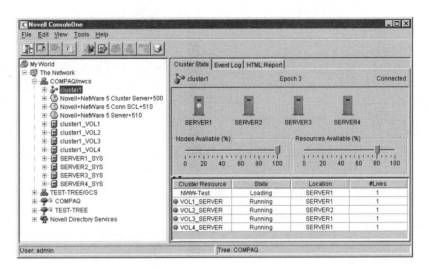

You can set a Quorum number so cluster resources don't start loading until just some or all (your choice) of the cluster servers are online. A check box on the Cluster Policies page allows you to bypass the Quorum rule and load the resources on the first server available. This option makes sense when a stout server with plenty of horsepower handles the majority of the load and spreads critical applications to other, smaller servers in case of a failure.

Shared volumes must be up and running—and accessible to each NetWare server—before starting the cluster installation. Novell has strict rules about placing cluster information on certain disks, but the installation notes cover the needed details well.

Novell includes templates for cluster resources such as Enterprise Web Server, GroupWise, Oracle8i, and NDPS. The templates are a good start, but installation still requires you to edit several text files, including load and unload scripts for resource startup and shutdown. Cluster-enabled applications must use the shared volume to allow other servers to pick up in case of fail-over or migration. The exceptions are certain applications like GroupWise, which can't use shared volumes. Again, read the installation notes carefully.

USING NETWARE CLUSTERS

Most important, does NetWare Cluster Services work? Yes, and quite well. Once configured properly, both the lab servers and the Compaq cluster servers send keep-alive and watchdog packets across the network to verify that all servers and cluster resources are operating properly. If hardware or cluster-enabled software goes down, the next assigned server in the cluster takes over the stranded applications within a few seconds. Web clients will never know that the delay isn't a typical Internet traffic jam.

Load balancing now implies automatic sharing of the application load, and Novell misuses the term slightly. Rather than true load balancing, NetWare Cluster Services makes it easier than ever before to migrate applications from one server to another without client interruption. Do you want to add a new server to the cluster with more horsepower? You can migrate cluster applications to the new server with three mouse clicks rather than an afternoon of work. The Cluster Resource Manager dialog box shifts applications between servers in much less than a minute. Do you need hardware maintenance? You can migrate the applications, do the maintenance, and then migrate the applications back to their original server. This results in less hassle for you and zero downtime for your clients.

Internal NetWare clients using file and print services do require some client software adjustment, mainly to support swapping from one server to another in case of failure or migration. The modifications are nothing serious, but you should record these configuration file changes as another reason to get an automatic software rollout utility.

It's hard to tell where the NetWare services stop and the Compaq value-added services start on the ProLiant Cluster. Each rack-mounted server pulls out on rails to provide access to the PCI connectors. Novell supports hot-plugged PCI slots, and so does the Compaq hardware, so who gets credit for the easy replacement of a network interface card while the server is running?

Compaq gets the credit for quickly restructuring data when we pulled a 9.1GB drive from the SAN during operation. Early RAID systems taxed the server tremendously when rebuilding data from a failed drive, but the ProLiant Cluster barely bumped up the NetWare utilization level.

Web-based Compaq Management Agents cover every server hardware detail from any client with a browser and a password. On the server console, added utilities include the Compaq Integration Maintenance Utility, Compaq Software Support Utility, Compaq Online Configuration for the Fibre Array, and the Compaq Power Subsystem Utility, all indistinguishable from the NetWare utilities. Figure 14.25 shows just one of the many online screens available from Compaq.

FIGURE 14.25

Software version information with great detail

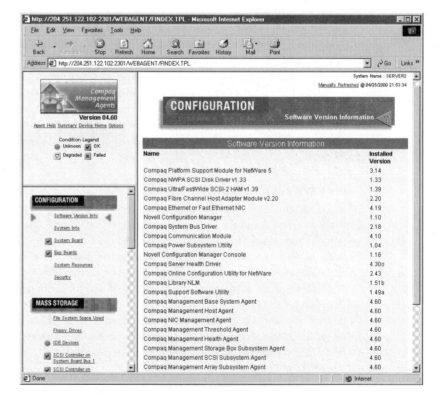

NetWare Cluster Services offers a variety of options to parcel out the applications during a failure. Applications on one server can go to a second server or be spread to multiple servers. The same holds true for control over shared NetWare volumes. Each cluster resource can be configured differently from any other resource, if you want to take the time and effort. One server can fail over to one server, one can fail to many, many can fail to one, or many can fail to many. This flexibility comes from NetWare, not the hardware. However, the faster you can resolve hardware problems, the better. By comparison, your car's spare tire works fine, but you want to use it as little as possible.

CLUSTER QUIBBLES

Perhaps it's just early in the NetWare Cluster Services product cycle, but the lack of utility support and lack of templates for non-Novell applications are troublesome. NetWare installation and management, even for a relatively small addition like the 1MB of Cluster Services files on the various NetWare servers, still bounced around between ConsoleOne (Java based), NetWare Administrator (Windows based), and NWCONFIG (DOS based).

These three utilities offer competing and overlapping features on one hand, with painful restrictions on the other. ConsoleOne looks great, but the Java utility crawls around like Windows NT on a 486, even running on a quad-processor Pentium III at 550MHz with a gigabyte of RAM and no other load.

NetWare 5 and 6 make an outstanding application platform, and Novell wisely tries to spread that word. But couldn't some other, non-Novell applications have templates for load balancing? You would think that Novell's push to become a Web application server company would encourage development of these templates.

PRICING

Our Compaq support team frankly worried about price comparisons between their preconfigured cluster and the cost of adding NetWare Cluster Services to existing servers. "Our solution is not inexpensive," they said honestly. They were worried that the apparent high price for one ticket for everything would stick in our minds, rather than accurately totaling up the price of a comparable system assembled piece by piece.

Here's what Compaq included:

- Four PL6400R/550MHz-w/4 2MB processors each
- One RA41000 storage enclosure
- Twenty 9.1GB Ultra2 drives (two drives per server and one populated array)
- Four 64-bit/66MHz StorageWorks Fibre Channel Host Bus Adapter Kits (Persian)
- One 7-port FC hub and mounting kit
- One 22U rack (9122)
- One 6-port KMM switch box
- Six KMM cables (2M)

The exact price: $167,110. Yes, that seems like a lot, but we must avoid comparing apples to oranges.

NOTE *As an update, the pricing for all cluster components have dropped since early 2000 when I first started gathering details. In a bit, you'll see NetWare 6 Cluster Services on a two-node cluster from Compaq, really a "ready-to-roll" SAN.*

An apples-to-apples comparison of the Compaq 6400R cluster we tested requires four servers capable of supporting four Intel Pentium III XEON processors and up to 4GB of RAM. Each tested 6400R server has dual-power supplies (pull one out and the server never blinks). Hot Plug PCI support allows you to add or remove network cards without taking the server down. Hot-swappable redundant hard disks allow you to add or remove storage any time. You can't find these systems at Joe's Computer Shack.

NetWare's reliability lulls some people into believing that any clone desktop PC can become a server. Yet the first step up on either the horsepower or reliability scale illustrates the limits of cheap PC servers. Dual- or quad-processor-capable systems are not found on the bargain table, and high-quality storage costs more than the use-three-years-and-replace IDE drives in many new computers today.

Speaking of storage, the Compaq 4100 SAN pushes hot-swappable storage capacity into the terabyte range. Fibre Channel SANs with high-throughput Ultra/Fast/Wide SCSI-2 drives and controllers stand at the top end of performance, reliability, and price charts from every manufacturer.

ROLL YOUR OWN OR BUY A CLUSTER?

The Intel-based, multiprocessor server market gets more crowded each day. Compaq made some of the earliest heavy-duty NetWare servers, but history counts for little in today's market. Every one of Compaq's major competitors has similar hardware products in their catalog, all claiming to be "the best."

While every hardware vendor claims high availability on their marketing brochures, detailed examination of the technical specifications can show a different story. The Compaq ProLiant 3000 performs quite well in the stand-alone tower case, although the size and shape are more those of a small, metal hope chest than a tower. The Compaq ProLiant Cluster for NetWare performs even better in the heavy rack enclosure that tucks four powerful servers, an SAN, and the attendant controllers and cables for all of the above in a sturdy package two feet wide, three feet deep, and almost four feet tall (and very, very, heavy). Every support module comes in pairs, pulls out while the system stays running, slides smoothly back into place, and locks down into a single block of solid server.

Another apparent pricing disadvantage for clusters concerns the bundled-in software expense. Hardware catalogs highlight software prices, but the software needed to power any cluster for NetWare adds up quickly. NetWare 6 uses per-user pricing (about $184 each user). NetWare Cluster Services software runs $4,995 per cluster node after the first two. You must purchase software for your own cluster, and you must include that software total in your comparison figures to be fair to the preconfigured cluster. The tested Compaq cluster came with $19,980 of cluster software.

Companies realizing the value of a never-fail server system should also recognize the value of setting up new servers from scratch rather than mashing together existing servers, as we did. Clean server installations are less trouble, and new servers more often match the horsepower needs at hand rather than taking the servers that are available.

Adding up the convenience of a complete, ready-to-go cluster with highly available hardware in a single convenient package pushes our vote toward the ProLiant Cluster for NetWare. Adding in the Compaq utilities such as SmartStart and Compaq Management Agents makes the vote even more strongly in favor of a ProLiant Cluster.

So ends the cluster experiment with NetWare 5.1, with a few additional NetWare 6 comments thrown in for clarification now and then. Now let's look at the new and improved clustering support in NetWare 6.

Clustering Improvements in NetWare 6

Since NetWare 6 includes two-node clustering support as part of the NetWare operating system, more people than ever should be getting involved in clustering. Let's catch up on some of the clustering details, especially as they pertain to an SAN.

STORAGE AREA NETWORKS (SANs)

Three components make an SAN:

- Controlling server (or servers)

- High-bandwidth channel interface(s)

- Storage unit(s)

One huge advantage of an SAN over network attached storage (NAS) appliances appears when looking at data traffic. NAS appliances plug into the same corporate network as other servers and their clients. Backups between NAS devices travel across the corporate network. All data copying or large file transfers bump the network traffic levels up for all users.

An SAN's back-end network keeps all data traffic between data devices off the corporate network. Files transferred between storage devices occur within the channel-attached network only. Backups happen across the channel-interface links, not on the corporate network.

Speed between the disk storage units and SAN controllers remains the key criteria for most customers. A second consideration for many users is the distances allowed between the SAN controllers and disk storage units. There are four types of channel interfaces used for SANs: SCSI, ESCON (Enterprise System CONnections), Fibre Channel, and Gigabit Ethernet.

SCSI Interface

SCSI (Small Computer Systems Interface) works fine between a server and a disk drive or three. While Ultra-3 SCSI (sometimes called Ultra160/m) supports burst speeds up to 160Mbps, maximum distance tops out at a terribly short less than 40 feet (12 meters). That distance may be fine for linking one server to a disk drive subsystem, but it doesn't allow for any location flexibility. Ultra-3 SCSI tops out at 16 drives as well.

ESCON Interface

ESCON fixes the distance and speed problems limiting SCSI, but at a price. ESCON, using fiber-optic cables and dynamically modifiable switches called ESCON Directors, reaches up to 37.3 miles (a neat 60 kilometers) at speeds up to 2Gbps. But unless you also have IBM S/390 mainframes in your network, ESCON will be a new, and expensive, neighborhood.

Fibre Channel Interface

Fibre Channel has taken the lead for most SAN vendors, by offering an accepted standard, data speeds up to 1Gbps (with plans underway to reach 10Gbps), and a reach of 6 miles (10 kilometers). Using either coax cable or even twisted-pair wiring for short distances drops the investment level for the Fibre Channel switches and hubs.

Much like 10/100 Base-T Ethernet, Fibre Channel offers two types of controllers to link the SAN server(s) and disk subsystems. A Fibre Channel hub uses an arbitrated loop technology that shares bandwidth among up to 127 devices. Think of this hub as just like a 10Base-T hub that shares the Ethernet channel with all attached nodes, although the loop arbitration allows nodes to bid for access by sending a signal around the loop. If the originating node receives the signal back, that node can transmit data until it finishes with that I/O cycle (beware bandwidth hogs).

The Fibre Channel switch acts more like an Ethernet switch, providing full bandwidth between each node and the switch itself. If two or more servers ask for data from the same storage device, like the same RAID controller, the switch interleaves the traffic and shares the bandwidth equally. Multiple servers can access multiple storage devices at full speed. A series of switches organized in a mesh network can interconnect up to 64,000 devices.

Gigabit Ethernet Interface

Although Fibre Channel is in the lead, coming up fast on the outside is Gigabit Ethernet. As Gigabit Ethernet products hit the market, the standards groups are already pushing 10 Gigabit Ethernet. Based on the typical Ethernet frame format and LAN protocols, Gigabit Ethernet already powers many corporate backbone networks, and 10 Gigabit Ethernet products will appear soon. Infiltrating the SAN market won't take an enormous technical leap, just applications and hardware development time. Since companies already trust Gigabit Ethernet for network backbones, making use of the technology for SANs will be an easy step.

NETDEVICE

What's missing in this information? I haven't mentioned Novell's new NetDevice product, a software NAS. Load the modified NetWare 6 software onto any PC with hard disks, and the automated installation procedures turn the PC into an eDirectory-enabled NAS box.

Why does this new product matter? If Novell marketing is smart (little hope there) or listens to me (probably less hope), the NetDevice will automatically support dual Ethernet network adapters (it already does, according to pre-release specifications). How does this help?

Let's make an SAN on the cheap (if all the parts from Novell get there as they should). Take two NetWare 6 servers. Take a NetDevice. Put two NICs in each box (total of six). Two NICs on the NetWare 6 servers will connect to the company network, and two will connect to the SAN. The NetDevice's two connections will link to the SAN hub, offering redundancy or even (dare we hope) load balancing.

What do we have? The result is a NetWare 6 cluster using a NetDevice as the shared storage box. What's the price for the clustering improvements? We have just the cost of the NetDevice software and supporting hardware. Gigabit Ethernet NICs and hubs running over Category 5 wiring, dropping in price daily, keep high performance affordable. Even 100Base-T will provide acceptable performance for a small SAN and certainly help you stay within your budget.

Compaq Dual-Node Cluster Screens

For my review of NetWare 6 beta software for *Network World*, Compaq sent me another cluster. This time, four dual-processor ProLiant 360 servers shared a smaller set of disks in the 4100 Storage Array. The servers were grouped into two separate clusters, even though they were in the same enclosure. Compaq's Storage Array was smart enough to support multiple clusters accessing the shared disks, and the six disks were split into two groups of three disks for the review.

NetWare Remote Manager adds new functionality when connecting to clustered servers. Figure 14.26 shows cluster configuration details for two of the Compaq servers, including many of the software resources running on the cluster.

FIGURE 14.26

Two servers are better than one

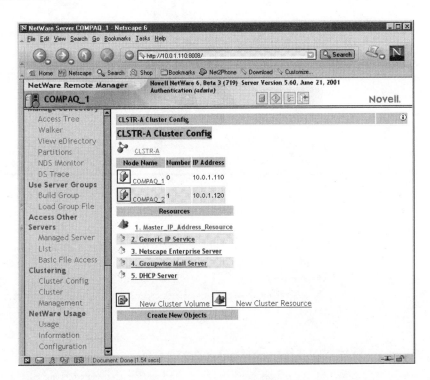

No matter what other applications run on the clustered servers, storage availability tends to transform the cluster from hope to hardware and software. No company wants to lose access to their data, even if they don't have multiple e-commerce Web servers loading revenue-producing transactions every minute. Once you start rolling revenue through your Web server, however, the need for reliable storage loosens purse strings on the stingiest boss.

Will you need to learn anything new to manage a cluster? I don't think so. Figure 14.27 shows NetWare Remote Manager looking at the same storage array shown in the previous figure, yet this time through the second server in the cluster.

FIGURE 14.27

Cluster volumes look like regular volumes

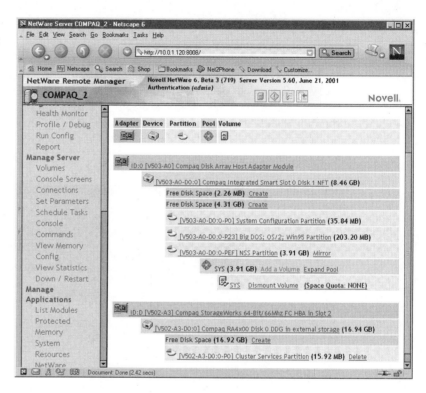

Clustering adds a new dimension to NetWare services—one many users will happily exploit. You should be one of those exploiters (it's a good thing in this case), and try out clustering. If you skipped Chapter 8 to get here, you'll be glad to know a few of the configuration screens show clustering details rather than single-server screens. That's how close clustering is to "regular" NetWare with version 6.

Using the Enhancements

Some of the enhancements I discussed in this chapter are part of the core NetWare 6 product, and some are highly specialized and of interest to only a few customers. File compression is the most popular of all enhancements, since you get something (more space for files) for almost nothing (some server RAM).

If you don't use any of the extra enhancements, such as cryptographic services or SNMP, don't feel bad. Most NetWare users don't take advantage of all these technologies.

But don't you feel smart using an operating system with more horsepower than you'll ever need? Too many NetWare competitors offer the opposite—horsepower is promised, but the release date of these features keeps fading into the distant mists of the future.

It's a common statement that most users leave 80 percent of their application programs unexplored. In other words, users are happy using only 20 percent of the product's power. NetWare doesn't use that ratio; more like 70 percent of the power is used by everyone, with 30 percent reserved for those with special needs. Few, if any, customers ever need more PC LAN features and horsepower than NetWare delivers.

The third-party additions, particularly from Netscape and Apache, make a huge difference in the functionality of your NetWare server. Critics who rated Windows NT/2000 higher than NetWare because of Internet applications must rethink their position. Of course, if they had an open mind, they wouldn't be so thrilled with Microsoft to start with, but that's another personal diatribe we don't have time for now.

If you see features here that you like and think you want to incorporate into your own network, experiment with them on a pilot system. Always test things before putting them to work on your production network. If you don't, pay close attention to the next chapter on troubleshooting.

Chapter 15

Troubleshooting Your Network

NO MATTER HOW CAREFULLY you plan, how carefully you build your network, and how carefully you train your users, things will go wrong. In fact, having things go wrong is a normal part of your network operations. When things don't go wrong, you should worry.

When something on the network is not working properly, you must change hats from strategic thinker to ambulance driver. Even if the problem is not much of a problem to the network as a whole, the affected user needs to be reassured. Psychology is important. When users have a problem, they don't want to hear that it isn't a big problem, because it is big to them. They want to hear that you understand their problem and are working to fix that problem. They will be reasonable (probably) if you acknowledge their distress ("I feel your pain") and inform them of your actions to resolve the problem.

The following topics are covered in this chapter:

◆ General troubleshooting tips

◆ Learning your network's normal operation

◆ Component failure profiles

◆ Common workstation, server, and cabling problems and solutions

◆ iFolder troubleshooting

◆ NDS problems and solutions

General Troubleshooting Tips

What changed? This question must spring immediately into your mind when a problem appears. Something almost always changes. Computer hardware has gotten so reliable that it's rare to find outright physical failures. Disk drives still wear out and power supplies still die, but hardware failure will not be a problem at the top of your list of aggravations.

I contend that you don't manage a network; you manage network changes. If nothing is changing, there's no troubleshooting to do. When nothing changes, you can focus on the future and try to keep up with your computer trade magazines. When you're adding users, software, and hardware, there will always be something to fix.

There are, however, occasions when a hardware component does cause your problem, even if it isn't a component failure. How about someone moving a wiring concentrator plug from a UPS to a wall plug? When the power blips and takes your concentrator offline, is that a component failure? Yes, and no. Something changed, and you can't blame that on component failure.

Many network managers have developed a "top-ten" list of troubleshooting or prevention tips. Rather than stopping at ten, here's everything I could find, think of, or steal. Let's start with preventive measures.

A TROUBLESHOOTING SCENE

Let's look at a troubleshooting situation as a scene from a movie, or, more appropriately, a sitcom.

(SCENE: Irate user who can't boot his computer to the network.)

YOU: "What's the problem?"

USER: "Your stupid network is broken." (User registers disgust and waves an arm toward the defunct computer.)

YOU (sitting at the computer): "Your hard disk seems to be dead."

This is the time many network managers try to defend their network, pointing out that the user's problem is caused by and limited to the user. Your "stupid" network had nothing to do with this problem. However, resist this urge. The user is angry, and he will now be embarrassed. Anything you say in defense of the network will be seen by the user as "rubbing my nose in it."

YOU: "Let me configure a spare computer, so you can get logged in to the network. We'll order a new hard disk for you, and I'll bring your system back as soon as possible."

USER: "Thanks for your prompt attention to this matter. I apologize for disparaging the network, but I was upset by this disk failure. Please forgive me. Allow me to buy you lunch today in apology."

(ACTION: Glowing sunshine warmly colors the scene. Birds sing. Flowers bloom. Theme music swells.)

Perhaps this scenario is a bit far out, even for Hollywood. But the idea of not defending your network against an angry user is a good one. Angry people often need to blow off steam, and you're a good target. You aren't the boss, so you can't fire them. You aren't an immediate co-worker, so the user won't be embarrassed every morning afterward. You are a fairly safe target for the user's anger. Anything you say in defense of your network, or that insinuates that the problem is self-caused, will only make the user angrier. This is a "no-win" situation for you, at least in the short term.

Letting the user win doesn't make you a doormat. The network administrator's favorite fable is "The User Who Cried Wolf" for good reason. You will soon learn which users howl the loudest with the smallest problems. When several problems arrive at once, as they often do, you may safely put these users at the bottom of the help list. After all, you have already documented your multiple quick responses, right? How can they complain if they were served quickly many times and only served slowly when a larger network crisis appeared? Well, they will complain, but no one will listen to them, because you have documentation. That's the beauty of CYAWP (Cover Your A** With Paper).

Prevention Tips

The following are some prevention strategies you can try.

Ask your management to decide on a downtime "comfort level."   The faster you want to resurrect the network, the more money you must spend in preparation. A maximum of a few minutes of downtime can be guaranteed by using the two-node Cluster Services license included with NetWare 6 and by having backup hardware for every system wiring component. Downtime will stretch to several hours if you have some, but not all, of your replacement equipment available. Downtime will stretch to a day or more if you rely completely on outside resources.

Have your management decide which users must get back to work first.   In case of a serious network problem, you may be able to support only a few users. Which users will those be?

Know what you have.   Inventory all your network hardware and software. How else will you buy spare parts and get updated replacement drivers?

Expect everything and everyone to let you down.   If you expect the worst, you're prepared for anything. You're also pleasantly surprised almost all the time, since the worst rarely happens.

Anything that *can* fail *will* fail.   Be prepared for any LAN component to fail, be stolen, or be tampered with.

Know your component failure profiles.   On a server, failures are likely to be (in order): disks, RAM, the power supply, or network adapters. The same applies to a workstation, but only one user is inconvenienced.

Balance your network to eliminate as many single points of failure as possible.   Many network administrators spread every workgroup across two wiring concentrators, so one failure won't disable an entire department. You can also spread a group's applications across multiple servers, which is easy to do with NetWare 6.

Spend the money necessary to back up your system every night.   The quickest way to recover from corrupt or lost data files is by using a complete backup made the night before. Most restores will be user files deleted by accident. The previous night's tape will solve that problem if the NetWare SALVAGE command doesn't do the job.

Test your backup and restore software and hardware.   How long does it take to completely restore a volume with your backup hardware and software? You can't bring a replacement hard disk online until the restored files are in place.

Duplicate system knowledge among the administrative staff.   If a person, even you, is the single point of failure, take precautions. I know you feel you're always there, but do you want to come back from your honeymoon to replace a disk drive? Start some cross-training.

Your suppliers will let you down sometime, somehow.   Support organizations have problems, too. Don't bet the ranch on your dealer stocking a replacement drive that they "always" have. If you must have one without fail, have it on your shelf.

Find sources of information before you need them. Check out Novell's Web site, and participate in NetWare-oriented bulletin board services and Internet newsgroups. The more you know, and the more places you can go for quick information, the better off you are.

Document everything far more than you think necessary. Write down everything about your network, then fill in the blanks. Assume that your manager must recover the network while you're on your honeymoon (definitely without your beeper or cell phone). Will your documentation provide the manager with enough information? If some or all of your documentation is stored electronically, reprint the information after every substantial change and store the paper in a safe location. It's hard to read electronic documentation from a dead server disk.

Keep valuable network information in a safe. Your password, some backup tapes, boot disks, software licenses, proof of purchase forms, and a copy of your network documentation should be in a safe—literally. Only network administrators and your manager should have access to this safe.

Make your network as standardized as possible. Hardware and software consistency is not the hobgoblin of small minds; it's the savior of the harried administrator. Standardized configuration and policy files make life easier. It may be impossible to keep them consistent, but try. Find a good network adapter card and stick with it. Make as few different Windows Desktop arrangements as you can.

Make a detailed recovery plan in case of a partial or complete network disaster and test your recovery plan. Companies with workable recovery plans stay in business after a disaster. Those with no recovery plans are rarely in business two years after the disaster. But you'll never be sure that the plan works until the plan is tried. Do you want to try the plan after office hours in a test or while the CEO is looking over your shoulder? Test the plan as well as the people involved.

Put step-by-step instructions on the wall above every piece of configurable equipment. Every server, gateway, or communications box should have a complete operational outline on the wall above the equipment. It should cover all steps necessary for a computer novice to take the system down and/or bring the system back up. Large companies with a night support staff will find this particularly useful.

Tips for Solving Problems

Network problems can be both physical (cable) and virtual (protocols). This makes troubleshooting more fun than normal.

No matter how prepared you are, something will go wrong. It's nothing personal—it's just life. When faced with a problem, the following hints may be of some help.

What changed? I said this at the beginning, but it's worth repeating. When there's a problem, 99 percent of the time, somebody changed something somewhere. Scientists have disproved the idea of "bit rot," where software that did work goes sour and mutates into software that doesn't. However, it's common for workstation software to be pushed beyond its capabilities or to be modified by new applications. But that is a change, isn't it?

When you hear hoofbeats, look for horses before you look for zebras. Check the simple things first; hoofbeats are more likely to come from horses than from zebras (at least in Texas, where I'm writing this). Is the plug in the wall? Is the power on? Is the monitor brightness turned up? (I once drove across town in a snowstorm to turn up the brightness on a Unix system monitor.) Is this the right cable? Is the cable plugged in on both ends? Is a connection loose? You get the idea—nothing is too simple to verify before going on to the next step.

Isolate the problem. Does this problem happen with other machines? Does it happen with this same username? Will this system work on another network segment? Will the server talk to another workstation? Can you ping the system having trouble?

Don't change something that works. If you change a configuration parameter and that doesn't fix the problem, change the parameter back to what it was. The same goes for hardware. No use introducing new variables from new hardware or software while you're still trying to find the problem. Let me say this again: If you change something and it doesn't fix your original problem, change it back. It may look okay now, but you will more often than not mess up more than you fix if you change things all over the place.

Check your typing. Typos in the configuration files will cause as much of a problem as the wrong command. Your software won't work well if your path includes \WINCOWS rather than \WINDOWS.

Read the documentation. Equipment documentation may not be good enough, but it's better than nothing. Print out the readme files from the installation disks and keep the printout with the manuals. It's much easier for manufacturers to put crucial manual modifications in the readme file than in the manual.

Look for patches. Check Novell's Web site for files to update your troublesome hardware. Call the vendor of third-party products for new drivers for network adapters and drive controllers.

Refer to previous trouble logs. Keep a log of problems and solutions for your network. Even a new problem may be related to an old problem you've solved before.

Trust, but verify, everything a user tells you. People interpret the same events different ways. What is unnoticed by a user may be a crucial bit of information for you. If a user tells you a screen looks a certain way, take a look for yourself.

Call your NetWare dealer early in the process. Buying your NetWare hardware and software from a local dealer gives you the right to call and ask for help. This is especially true during and just after installation. If you have a good relationship with your dealer, the support people should answer specific questions (such as, "Does this network adapter have a different driver when used in the server?") without charge. Be prepared to pay for support if your questions are open-ended ("Why doesn't this server talk to the workstation?") or you request a technician to come and look at your system.

Check out a Novell Support Connection subscription. Tons of information are on every update. Patches, white papers, compatibility reports, and tips of all kinds are there if you look.

Call Novell technical support. It's better to spend the money on 1-800-858-4000 than to leave your network down for a second day. But don't call until you've gone through the documentation, the Novell Web site, and all local support resources. It's embarrassing to find out during a paid support call that the solution is in the manual.

Do things methodically, one by one.   Don't make a "brilliant" leap of deductive reasoning; that's a high-risk/high-reward procedure. Las Vegas casinos are rich because suckers play long odds. Keep following the plan, and don't try to be a hero.

Learning Your Network's Normal Operation

Do you know what your car sounds like when it's working properly? Do you know the beeps and buzzes your computer makes as it boots? Do you know how your body feels as you struggle out of bed?

Of course you do. You know these things from regular repetition. More important, you know that when one of those sounds or feelings is not right, something needs to be checked out.

Your network is the same way. You must learn how it is when it's normal so you can quickly tell when it isn't normal.

Tracking Aids

Several obvious things help you track the details of your network's normal operation.

Paper, in this case network documentation, is more necessary than you may imagine. You have about 2000 items to remember for every user. If you have a lot of users, learn to write down everything, or every day will be a rough day.

An activity log is vital to managing large networks. This log doesn't need to be fancy, just consistent. If you keep the log on paper, you should regularly put it in a database to organize and comment on the results of each action. Having it available on the system makes it easier for other administrators to share, but having a backup copy on paper (current copy, of course) keeps it useful when the system dies.

Help desk software is becoming inexpensive enough for small- and medium-sized companies. By tracking every support call from users, you maintain a single database with all trouble calls listed, cataloged, and indexed. Most important, this type of software tracks and shares the little, but aggravating, configuration details for many software packages that cause your network problems. If you have more than two network managers, you can benefit from help desk software.

Tracking Downtime

Networks are often judged harshly by old mainframers, since one or more stations or printers may be unavailable at any one time. To some, especially those who wish to cast aspersions on your network, this will count as downtime and be held against you. Don't let them define downtime to fit their terms. In fact, let's define downtime and another type of network time:

◆   *Downtime* is the time when a network service or resource is unavailable to any user.

◆   *Crosstime* is the time when a service object, such as a printer, is down, but the user has easy options to use comparable services.

If a server is down, but all users can log in through eDirectory, they are not down. The few users who need access to volumes on the down server do suffer downtime; everyone else suffers crosstime. Routing to another printer in place of your normal printer is not downtime; it's crosstime.

You should track the times that resources are down, but you must put this information into context. If you have ten servers, and one server is down for one day, your servers are 90 percent available that day. If that is the only down day in a 30-day month, the monthly total for server availability is 99.67 percent available (299 available server days divided by 300 possible server days). This is very acceptable, even to mainframe bigots.

TIP *If the mainframe people give you too much trouble, ask for their remote-access uptime. It's usually lousy. They'll blame it on the phone lines. Just laugh and walk away.*

Of the 2000 details you must track for users, about 1950 of them are tied to their workstations, especially if they run a Windows operating system. Don't feel bad if you never feel in control of Windows workstations on your network. With the added complexity that comes with the Registry, it is often difficult to get a handle on exactly what is happening on a particular computer. Thank you, Microsoft, for foisting on us a system where every new application can (and regularly does) overwrite critical system files for other applications.

Regardless of the hassle factor, you must make some baseline of your workstations, servers, and network in general. You might want to check some of the third-party server management software available, but you can also monitor your network fairly well with the tools NetWare provides.

Tracking Normal Server Performance

It's easy to ignore the server when it's running as it should. You have so many other little problems, such as printers that act strangely and users who behave even more strangely, that you leave the server alone.

Although it's easy not to pay attention to the server, it isn't advisable. You must spend a few minutes now and then checking on the server when it's running well so you'll have some idea of what it should look like under normal circumstances. Believe me, when it's down and you can't figure out why, you'll wish you had a few screen shots and configuration files saved in a notebook on your desk (hint, hint).

MONITORING PROGRAMS

MONITOR was your best bet for tracking server performance during the day (now the NetWare Remote Manager's Health Monitor screens work better). Many network managers leave MONITOR on-screen all the time. Even the snake-like screen saver (SCRSAVER.NLM) indicates server activity. The longer and faster the snake gets, the more server activity going on.

When the MONITOR program is running, four important performance indicators are evident from the General Information screen:

◆ The Utilization field shows how much CPU time is being spent servicing the network. This is half of the network load, with disk activity being the other half. If this number regularly stays over 50 percent for more than a minute or two at a time, you need more horsepower. It's possible for this number to run over 100 percent, so don't overreact if you see 103 percent utilization sometime.

◆ The Total Cache Buffers field is an indicator of file performance. The lower this number, the slower file performance will be. If less than half of your cache buffers are in the Total category, you need to get more RAM.

◆ The Current Service Processes number indicates outstanding read requests. When a read request comes in but there is no way to handle it immediately, a service process is created to perform the read as quickly as possible. Having too few cache buffers will run up this number. If you have plenty of RAM but increasing service processes, you need disk channel help. Upgrade the controller or disk, or move high-load applications to another server.

◆ Packet Receive Buffers hold packets from workstations until they can be handled by the server. They will be allocated as needed, but a gradually increasing number indicates that the server isn't keeping up with the load. Two thousand buffers are allocated automatically to support the Enterprise Web Server.

Figure 15.1 shows the MONITOR main screen, with the General Information window open to show all statistics. You can press Tab to shrink or expand this window. Shrink it to use the Available Options menu.

FIGURE 15.1

The standard server performance check

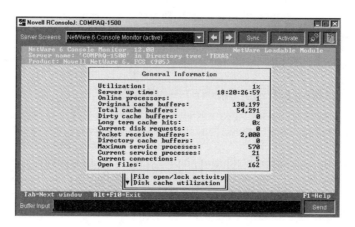

The other screen you may leave open in MONITOR is the Disk Cache Utilization Statistics view. You can see the Disk Cache Utilization menu choice at the bottom of Figure 15.1. If the Long Term Cache Hits figure stays above 90 percent, you have a server that's well configured for file service.

You should take a few screen shots of your server's MONITOR screen now and then. Using RConsoleJ makes this easy (old-timers used to scratch the numbers in stone tablets, since there was no way to capture a server console screen to a printer before RCONSOLE, the IPX-based predecessor to RConsoleJ). Make a few of these screen shots for each server now and then, with a notation of the date and time. Connections and open files are shown at the bottom of the window. Both of these are good load indicators for referencing the server activity.

If you prefer, you can use NetWare Remote Manager's Health Monitor and Multiple Server Monitor screens to monitor your servers. In this utility, you can see all of the important parameters at a glance, with links to click for more information. A traffic light indicates the status of each parameter, glowing green for good, yellow for suspect, or red for bad.

See Chapter 8, "NetWare 6 Administrator Duties and Tools," for more information about using MONITOR, RConsoleJ, and NetWare Remote Manager.

SERVER LOG FILES

NetWare automatically creates three server log files: SYS$LOG.ERR, VOL$LOG.ERR, and TTS$LOG.ERR. One more server log file, CONSOLE.LOG, is optional.

NOTE   *The* BOOT$LOG.ERR *file in the SYS:\SYSTEM directory holds comparatively little information. The* ABEND.LOG *is one error file I hope you never see.* ABEND.LOG *is moved to the SYS:\SYSTEM directory when the server is restarted after an abend (ABnormal ENDing). This term is an old mainframe term, believe it or not. How it got loaded into NetWare in the early versions is anyone's guess.*

SYS$LOG.ERR

SYS$LOG.ERR contains file server errors and general status information. This log file is stored in the \SYSTEM directory and can be viewed with ConsoleOne or any file viewer.

The SYS$LOG.ERR file is normally checked using the ConsoleOne program, but this viewer can't show a long log file. The beginning of the log file will not be shown, on the assumption that you are more interested in immediate history. If you wish to see the entire log file, you must use a text viewer.

Figure 15.2 shows the error log file for GW2K displayed in ConsoleOne. Vertical scroll bars are available to allow you to see more of the file. The text viewer always complains the log length makes it impossible to show, so some must be truncated.

FIGURE 15.2

Errors and server information

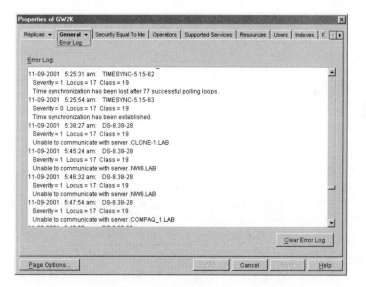

Notice that items that are not normally considered errors are tracked in this file. The first two messages complain that Time Synchronization dropped, then time became synchronized again. The other complaints concern servers revised or moved out of the LAB network but not yet out of eDirectory.

VOL$LOG.ERR

The volume log, VOL$LOG.ERR, shows volume errors and status information. It is created automatically and stored in the root of each traditional NetWare volume. There are no special viewers or ways to reach this log except to read it as a text file, but you won't need to read it often.

Figure 15.3 shows an example of a volume log in the life of a lab server. It's up, it's down, it's up, it's down, it's up—but mostly it's up. Most of your volume log will indicate this yo-yo type of activity. It may stretch over several years, since many volumes stay mounted for months at a time.

FIGURE 15.3

Volume log

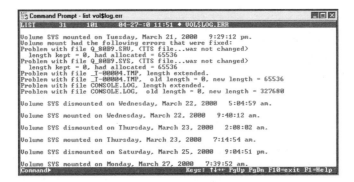

Notice the errors listed in the volume log at the top of the screen. There were no real problems, but files were enlarged to hold more information. The term "errors" may be a bit harsh, but you can see that everything got cleaned up and all is well.

TTS$LOG.ERR

The last automatic log file, TTS$LOG.ERR, is activated only on those servers where TTS (Transaction Tracking System) is enabled, meaning only on traditional NetWare filesystem volumes (not on NSS volumes). If TTS is started, the log is started. Those servers without TTS enabled will not have the log file.

This file is stored in the root of each traditional NetWare volume with TTS active and can be viewed with a file viewer.

TTS guarantees that transactions are completely finished or completely undone back to the pre-transaction state, the precursor to the journaling filesystem used in NSS. The log file lists times and data file names rolled back because of an incomplete transaction. This file won't have much inside it, except a time and date stamp of when TTS was started or shut down. These times will match those in the volume log.

CONSOLE.LOG

CONSOLE.LOG is a bit different. It keeps a copy of all console messages that normally scroll by quickly as the server boots. This is an optional log file, which is started by the line LOAD CONLOG in the AUTOEXEC.NCF file. This log file is stored in the \SYS:ETC directory and can be viewed using INETCFG or with a file viewer. Figure 15.4 shows a part of the CONSOLE.LOG file.

FIGURE 15.4

Console comments
in a file

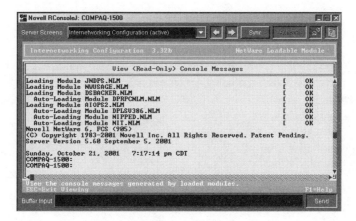

This viewer is in the INETCFG utility, loaded at the server console. To see the file, type **LOAD INETCFG** at the console or go through RConsoleJ (choose View Configuration ➤ Console Messages). All the messages sent to the console are tracked here.

As the screen in Figure 15.4 says, the log is shown read-only. You can open the log in the \SYS:ETC directory with a file viewer if you wish. You can also use a text editor to make notes about the log process before you print the log for safekeeping.

SERVER CONFIGURATION FILE COPIES

Printing logs for safekeeping is a good idea. Having a clean server boot record may come in handy someday when you're trying to re-create a load sequence for a long list of NLMs.

The log files just mentioned are easy to find and print. There are a couple of other quick options, as well. Figure 15.5 shows the option to copy all SET parameters to a file.

The MONITOR utility offers a chance to copy all parameters to a file every time you leave the Select a Parameter Category menu of the Server Parameters option. When you choose to copy all parameters to a file, the SETCMDS.CP file is copied to the SYS:\SYSTEM directory. That location is the default, but you can change that path. Once the file location is chosen, every SET command is listed with the current setting.

FIGURE 15.5

Take advantage of
this option.

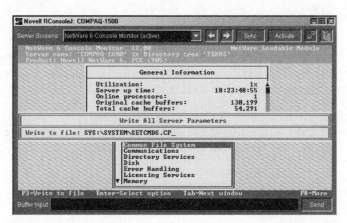

There isn't any help information in this file, and the file is nearly 9KB of ASCII text (on my server), but it's good to have. Some of the SET parameters can be a real problem if they are incorrect. Having a clean copy of the parameters for each of your servers is handy if a problem should arise.

You can also do this from NetWare Remote Manager. Select Set Parameters from the menu on the left, and the 14 configuration screens will appear under the heading of Category Name. At the end of the 14 screens, the Save Settings to a File on Volume SYS: option awaits, just below a bar labeled Set Parameter Control.

The AUTOEXEC.NCF file is kept in the \SYS:SYSTEM directory. It's easy to find, so make a quick printout of it every time it changes. Put it in the server notebook. Keep the old ones, so you can return to a former configuration if necessary.

The easiest way to get a copy of STARTUP.NCF is while the server is down. This file is kept in the \NWSERVER directory of the DOS partition by default. You may have placed it in a different directory during installation, but I asked you not to at the time. So look in \NWSERVER first. If it is there, copy it to floppy disk and print it later. Your alternative is to look at it in the Install program (choose NCF File Options ➤ Edit STARTUP.NCF File). From there, you can print the screen.

If you have used the INETCFG utility to manage your protocols, the AUTOEXEC.NCF file will have all the protocol statements commented out with the number sign (#). There is a message telling you to check the INITSYS.NCF and NETINFO.CFG files in the \SYS:ETC directory. There is also a warning in the message not to edit those files directly, but to use the INETCFG utility. However, you can certainly print these files and put the printouts in your server notebook.

Tracking Normal Workstation Details

An easy place to check the performance of a workstation is through the MONITOR screen on a server. When you choose Connections and press Enter on the user connection name, you'll see the connection details.

Alternatively, you can use NetWare Remote Manager to view server connections. Start the Net-Ware Remote Manager program either directly or through Web Manager, and click the Connections menu item in the left frame under Manage Server. You'll see an information screen similar to the one shown in Figure 15.6.

What does this tell us? Well, first, if you see the user's name on the connection list, the network connection must be in fairly good shape. The connection time is listed, as is the connection type from workstation to server. The resulting kilobytes read and written aren't shown in Remote Manager, but they do appear in MONITOR, where these numbers update in real time.

The bottom of the window shows open files, and again, this display is updated in real time in MONITOR but a bit more slowly in Remote Manager. If you click a filename, the Record Lock Information window will pop up. If the user stops an application or otherwise closes files, those changes will appear in the window after a Remote Manager update.

NOTE *Notice the identifying address for the workstation: 10.00.01.57. It's odd for an old NetWare dog like me to see an IP address there, but I can still learn a new trick now and then.*

FIGURE 15.6

A healthy, active workstation connection

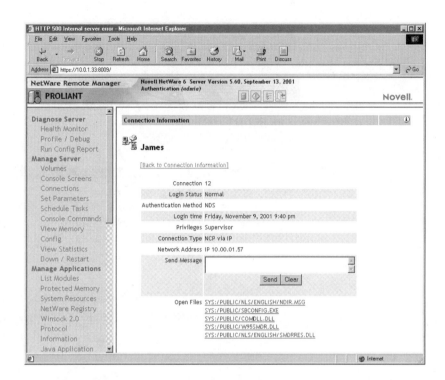

WORKSTATION CONFIGURATION FILE COPIES

During installation of each workstation or shortly thereafter, it's a good idea to make a backup copy of the important configuration files. For Windows 95/98 computers, this means creating an Emergency Boot/System Disk, either during the installation of the operating system or through the Add/Remove Programs applet in the Control Panel. This principle is continued for Windows NT Workstation computers, except that the disk is called the Emergency Repair Disk (ERD). That's also the name for the Windows 2000/XP version of this disk, but you make it through the Backup utility. Each of these is a disk that contains the configuration information for the computer and can be used during the repair processes in the event that you experience the dreaded catastrophic failure.

Yes, these workstation disks are just one more thing to keep track of, but they will come in handy. As these disks start piling up, your urge to develop and enforce a standard workstation configuration will grow.

WINDOWS NT/2000 UTILITIES

If you have Windows NT Workstation computers in your network, you have some extra tools for determining how those workstations are operating: Performance Monitor and Windows NT Diagnostics. Windows 2000 offers corresponding System Monitor and Performance Logs and Alerts utilities.

NOTE *Since this is a book about NetWare, not Windows NT or 2000, this is not the place to find full coverage of the Windows NT/2000 utilities. For details, refer to the NT/2000 online documentation or perhaps some books cleverly titled* Mastering Windows NT *and* Mastering Windows 2000, *both from Sybex.*

Performance Monitor is used to track NT counters that monitor all aspects of the computer, from the percentage of CPU time being used by applications to the number of packets being sent through a network interface. It displays the information retrieved from these counters in a real-time chart, as shown in Figure 15.7.

FIGURE 15.7

The Windows NT Performance Monitor

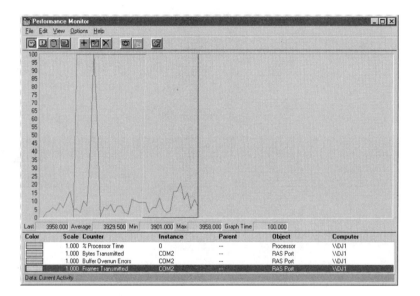

To start Performance Monitor, select Start ➤ Programs ➤ Administrative Tools (Common) ➤ Performance Monitor. In Windows 2000, choose Control Panel ➤ Administrative Tools ➤ Performance utility.

You can add counters to the chart by clicking the plus sign on the menu bar and selecting the appropriate object and counter. An *object* is a system component, such as the network interface or processor. A *counter* is a particular function of that object that is tracked, such as the number of bytes transmitted per second.

NOTE *Some objects in Performance Monitor allow you to track more than one instance of the object. These occur when there is more than one of a particular object installed in a system, such as multiple hard disks, network interfaces, or processors.*

Here are some of the more useful counter and object pairs to track with Performance Monitor:

Memory–Page Faults/sec   The average number of page faults per second for the current processor instance. If this number is more than double what you see during normal operation, it's time to put more RAM in your computer.

Network–Bytes Total/sec The total amount of traffic through the computer's network adapter, both inbound and outbound. When this counter begins to approach the theoretical maximum for your network medium, it's time to consider increasing the speed of your network or dividing it into separate segments.

Network–Output Queue Length The number of packets awaiting transmission across the network. If there are more than two packets queued at any particular time, network delays are likely and a network bottleneck should be investigated.

Processor–%Processor Time The percentage of time since Performance Monitor started that the CPU has been busy handling non-idle threads. If this counter is continuously greater than 80 percent, the machine is heavily taxed and steps should be taken to alleviate the load.

As you can imagine, there are many, many more counters than the ones listed here. The best way to make the most of Performance Monitor is to take the time to familiarize yourself with all the available objects and counters.

*TIP There are two objects that relate to the operation of the hard disks in your system: Physical Disk and Logical Disk. Because of their tax on system performance, these counters must be enabled manually and should be disabled immediately after the measurements are taken. To enable the disk counters, run **DISKPERF -Y** from a command prompt and reboot the computer. To disable the counters, run **DISKPERF -N**.*

Tracking Normal Network Performance

When Network General released their Sniffer products in the late 1980s, I worked for a company that sold them. Every customer I visited had the same question: "How busy is my network?" At the time (1988), Sniffers cost between $15,000 and $32,000 and came in a Compaq 286 luggable that weighed more than 20 pounds (and did a major number on your shins if you didn't carry it carefully).

People still want to know how busy their network is, but they don't need to spend thousands of dollars unless they want special protocol decoders and intelligent network analyses. If you just want to see how many packets are whizzing through your network and which stations are generating those packets, software-only traffic monitors are readily available.

Many companies make competitive software-only analyzers. Some other products I'm familiar with are Intel's LANDesk, Triticom's LANdecoder32, and even Microsoft's Network Monitor, which is included with Windows NT. EtherPeek, TokenPeek, and LocalPeek from the AG Group do the same job from both Macintosh and Windows platforms. The Sniffer, now part of Network Associates, still carries the high-end lead banner (a personal feeling, not based on exhaustive testing), but there is plenty of competition in all price ranges.

Component Failure Profiles

That's an ugly phrase, "component failure," but it does happen. Your job as network administrator includes figuring out what will fail when and how to fix it quickly.

Guide to Managing PC Networks by Steve Steinke, with Marianne Goldsmith, Michael Hurwicz, and Charles Koontz (published by Prentice-Hall PTR), is a book about managing PC networks of all kinds. This book includes one section that has details of expected faults in a mythical network, based on research in the late 1990s. The graphs don't list exact percentages, but I can guess fairly well. What are the causes of network downtime? In order, these are the reasons for downtime and the percentage each item is responsible for:

47 percent	Cabling or physical infrastructure
20 percent	Servers
13 percent	Drivers, network operating system
13 percent	Improper configuration
3 percent	Routers
2 percent	Hubs
2 percent	Wide area links

Do you believe these numbers? I would like to see the data behind these statistics because I would bet that cable problems cause more than half of the network downtime. Some studies rate cabling as the cause of 90 percent of network downtime, but those studies are paid for by people who are selling either high-grade cable or physical plant management products. See the section about cabling problems later in this chapter for some tips.

One area this list doesn't address is users, since they aren't a component that will fail. However, they will cause plenty of downtime, one way or the other.

Part of the relatively low failure rate for cabling may be explained by another chart in the book, named "Causes of Cabling Fault Events on a Mythical Network." Once again, here are my estimates of the percentages:

88 percent	Coax Ethernet
8 percent	Token Ring
4 percent	10BaseT Ethernet

These numbers I do believe without question. Anyone who has ever crawled under desk after desk looking for the loose BNC Thin Ethernet connector that is causing the network problems is a strong advocate for 10BaseT Ethernet. Fortunately, none of the popular cabling schemes being promoted today are a shared-bus system like coax Ethernet. Is it any wonder twisted-pair Ethernet swamped coax and Token Ring in the marketplace?

On the server itself, the breakdown of breakdowns goes this way:

69 percent	Disk drives
18 percent	RAM
11 percent	Network interface boards
2 percent	Power supply

This list makes sense. The two highest failure rates belong to the only moving part (disk drive) and the part most sensitive to overheating (RAM). However, it isn't only heat that will cause RAM to stop a server. The cause can be voltage fluctuations, components running beyond their specifications, or just plain component failure.

Common Workstation Problems and Solutions

You will have more problems from users running Windows than from Macintosh, Unix, or Linux users. But you knew that already, didn't you? Primarily, Windows presents the most problems because it's the most popular platform and because it must track the most variable hardware and software resources.

NOTE *Novell actually had a disproportionate amount of tech support people dedicated to OS/2 during the rollout of NetWare 4.10. But IBM's fading desktop fortunes changed that statistic for NetWare 5 and forever more.*

Some problems and solutions are common to all PC workstations. Again, we're assuming a workstation was working, then developed a problem. Questions about installation are covered in the appropriate chapters about that workstation type.

The following sections cover the most common workstation problems and provide some suggestions for solving them.

Workstation Can't Connect to the Server

The following are typical workstation connection problems and some solutions to try.

Check the workstation cable to the wall. Many patch cables that run between the workstation and the wall plug have been kicked out of their sockets. Others have been rolled over by a desk chair one too many times. Check that the plug for the patch cable is plugged into the wall. My friend Greg Hubbard says all 10BaseT Ethernet cards should have a speaker. That way, when you plug the Ethernet card into a phone plug, you'll hear the dial tone and realize your mistake. (Of course, if your phone still uses RJ-11 jacks—the ones that are smaller than 10BaseT RJ-45 connectors—this won't be a problem.)

Check the link between the wall plug and the wiring closet. Has anyone added cabling anywhere in that part of the building? It's common for new cabling installation to bump and loosen old cabling.

Verify that the port on your wiring concentrator working. Switch the problem connection with a known good connection into a known good port.

Check the frame type. Have the protocol details under the Networking program in Windows been changed? Is this workstation now trying to reach a new server? The default frame type for early versions of NetWare 4 was not Ethernet 802.3. Since NetWare has used that frame type since the beginning of time, many managers forget to check frame types when upgrading from NetWare 3. The same may be happening with the move to TCP/IP in many companies.

Verify the login name and password.   Wrong login names or passwords will obviously prevent a user from connecting to the server. If the user can't remember his or her password, change it immediately.

Check for a locked account.   With intruder detection, stations may be locked out of the network after a configurable number of unsuccessful login attempts. When a user comes to you with a password problem, check to see if the account is locked.

Verify that all the workstation files were loaded properly.   Error messages go by fast, and sometimes they are missed by users. Changes in the workstation may use some network memory.

Make sure the network adapter is seated properly.   Adding a card to one slot often loosens cards in other slots. Remember that a card can look well seated from outside the case but actually be disconnected. Patch cables, when tugged on, can loosen network adapters.

Check timeout values for WAN links.   WAN links are much less reliable than LAN links. If you're trying to reach a remote network service, always assume the WAN link is at fault before changing anything at the workstation. WAN links take longer, and some workstations may time out before reaching the remote server and getting authenticated properly. Increase the SPX timeout value.

Check routers.   Routers, both local and remote versions, sometimes get flaky on one port or another. Test other connections running through the same router in the same manner. You may need to check the router and reset a port.

Check hubs.   Wiring hubs rarely fail, but they sometimes become unplugged. Check to see if other computers connected to the same hub are able to communicate. Hubs are also liable to run out of space, and the wiring plan gets reworked on the fly to add another station or two. When this happens, your station may be left out of a concentrator altogether.

Verify that the server sees the workstation's request.   Use the TRACK ON command on the server to monitor requests from clients. If you know the client's MAC address, you can watch the server monitor to ensure that connection requests are received and the server responds.

Reboot the workstation.   This can't hurt, and you'll be amazed at what a reboot can fix.

Workstation Can't Use an Application

The following are workstation application problems and some solutions to try.

Find out what changed at the workstation.   Some new utility may have changed a few critical DLLs. A new Windows application may have modified the Registry. All applications have the potential for wreaking disaster.

Check the user's rights.   Does the user have the trustee rights to run the application? If you assign trustee rights to the directory and not the file, this shouldn't be much of a problem. This problem usually occurs with new applications, because few applications properly handle setting the rights for the users. Make sure to check all the application directories created by the installation. It is becoming common to place some directories for the same application on the same level of the eDirectory tree, rather than placing all the directories under one main directory. You may need to grant rights to another directory or two so that the user has rights to use some of the application files in the oddly placed directory.

Be careful after upgrading an application.   The rights will probably be the same in the existing directories, but a new directory or two is often added during an upgrade. You'll need to grant trustee rights to those directories as well.

Check the flags.   Most applications should have flags set to Read-Only and Shareable. Data files will be marked Shareable and Write, but the application must support multiple-user file access. In particular, check upgraded applications, since new files in the new version will probably not have the proper flags set. Verify your tape-restore procedure, since some vendors don't copy the extended file attributes NetWare uses to set the flags. An application that was Read-Only when backed up may become Normal (Read, Write, Erase, and so on) after being restored by tape. If someone then accidentally erases some files, the application won't work.

Check the user's current directory.   Many users never understand the drive redirection used by NetWare. When you ask where a problem is for them, they'll say, "drive K:." Make sure drive K: still points to the same subdirectory. New users are especially vulnerable to changing directories within a drive mapping without realizing what they've done.

Check the application's need for installing at the volume root.   Some applications demand to be placed in the root directory. Others don't but have a limit of how deep they can be installed in a directory structure. Some say they can be installed anywhere, but references to other directories are based on indexing from the root of the directory. You will need to use fake root mapping if any of these problems occur.

Does the application need NetBIOS?   Some applications, even on NetWare, still require Net-BIOS (thank goodness these are almost completely gone). Check that out, and load NetBIOS on a test workstation. If NetBIOS is used and has worked before, verify that the workstation is loading NetBIOS properly. Workstation changes may have ruined some necessary client files. If NetBIOS is needed, set up batch files so NetBIOS can be loaded and then unloaded after the application is exited. There is no use wasting more RAM than you need to for NetBIOS.

Verify that the application files are not mangled and that the application isn't missing some files.   If an application is corrupted, you must reinstall it. In a Windows application, the DLL files may be missing or some users may be picking up old versions of them through poor search mapping.

Check for file handles and SPX connections.   Database programs in particular often eat a lot of file handles. Check the application's documentation in the off chance that the writers have done their job and listed this information.

See if the application directory looks empty.   This means that the user doesn't have rights to the directory. Check the rights of the container or group for the user before making a change for one user alone.

Workstation Shows "Not Enough Memory" Errors

The following are typical memory problems and some solutions to try.

Check to see what has changed.   If a working network client suddenly has too little memory, something has changed. Check drivers and other TSR (terminate-and-stay-resident) programs in the workstation. Many of these hide on the Taskbar today.

Unload sneaky resident programs.   Some applications, such as fax and e-mail programs, sometimes leave little notification programs or utilities to fax from within your application on workstations. These can take up memory without explaining their presence to the user.

Beware of the network client software upgrade.   New driver and client files often require more room than the previous versions. You may wish to postpone an upgrade for some workstations that are critically short of memory. Make a note of those workstations in your network logs.

Beware of new video boards.   Video boards and network interface cards often fight over particular memory locations in PCs.

Beware of new monitors.   High-resolution monitors can force a video board to a higher resolution requiring more memory. Then the upper memory for a network driver won't be available, forcing the driver to load low. The result is "RAM cram." It doesn't matter whether you have a gigabyte of RAM in the workstation if the monitor and network adapter both want the same few bytes.

Windows Doesn't Work Right

Everything in Windows affects everything else. Users are constantly adding utilities, screen savers, and wallpaper, all of which can mess up something else.

Sometimes, the user is not at fault. Demo software programs under Windows now often add DLL files, modify the Registry, and load more fonts into the local Windows system. Did anyone ask for this? No. Do you need to fix it? Yes.

Believe me, something is always changing in Windows. As much as you're tempted, you can't always blame Microsoft for this. Every application vendor has its problems, and some problems aggravate Windows more than others.

The following are some common problems and solutions to try.

Restart Windows daily.   Microsoft has not yet stopped the memory leaks within Windows. Applications regularly leave fewer resources available after they unload. Windows doesn't need to leak, but careless programming is everywhere. Windows 95/98 systems require a daily reboot, but Windows 2000/XP systems don't. Windows NT sits in the middle, and needs a reboot every few days.

Check System Resources or Task Manager before and after loading an application.   This will give you an idea of the application's resource needs. Then check again after the application is unloaded. It's likely that you'll have fewer resources than when you started.

Check to see if the user has logged in from the wrong workstation.   Shared Windows files on the server make great sense and save time for administration, but they are dependent on the correct workstation configuration. If a user logs in from a different workstation, details such as the permanent swap file will be different on that machine.

Check for new fonts.   Many applications add special fonts to Windows. Each font loaded takes memory and slows performance. If your workstations have little RAM, pare down the fonts. One font family can take enough resources for an application to have trouble where it didn't have trouble before.

Don't use wallpaper if memory is critical.   Wallpaper may take just enough memory to cause trouble in RAM-deficient systems. Until you can add more memory or upgrade the workstation, strip out all nonfunctional pieces of Windows.

Get a good uninstall program for Windows.   Many applications, even when they uninstall themselves, don't clean up behind themselves very well. Cleanup has improved with later versions of Windows, as application guidelines now require an uninstall program. Programmers don't always follow that advice, of course, being programmers.

Printing Problems

The following are typical printing problems and some solutions to try.

Verify that the proper printer or print queue is captured properly.   With Windows printing choices, it's easy for users to pick the wrong printer by accident. Verify that the chosen printer is the correct printer. It's best to use a login script to assign the default printers for your network and discourage too much printer experimentation among users.

Verify that the job is in the print queue and that a print server is connected.   Use ConsoleOne to check the status of the print queue. See if the job has actually arrived and whether the correct print server is attached to the queue. In most cases, the job will arrive in the queue, but the print server is not processing the job. Upgrade to iPrint and NDPS to help the users struggle less.

Check the print job configuration.   If you have multiple print job configurations, verify that the proper one is still used by the user. This is something else that is easy to change by accident. Under Windows, verify these settings through the Printers Control Panel (Properties).

Check the printer hardware.   Is the printer plugged into the print server? Can other users print to this printer? Are the proper paper and font cartridge (if used) in place?

Check which page description language was used in the print job.   Sending PostScript output to a non-PostScript printer guarantees problems and the need to reset the printer. Do the users understand the different types of printers they have available and how to send print jobs to those printers?

Common Server Problems and Solutions

Let me summarize the NetWare manuals' advice on server problems: Add more RAM. The manuals provide quite a bit more help than that, of course, but more RAM is a constant mantra for NetWare servers. I have regularly suggested that you add RAM whenever possible, so take this as another polite request. Save yourself the headache— *get more RAM.*

As servers support more users, more RAM is necessary. As more NLMs are loaded, more RAM is necessary. More disk space means more RAM for traditional NetWare volumes even if not for NSS volumes.

Some applications, such as the NetWare NFS Services, demand a ton of RAM on their own (20 to 24MB of RAM just for NFS Services). Want to tune your NetWare Enterprise Web Server? RAM demands jump from 128MB to 256MB just for the Web server. More insidious is the RAM-creep of little programs and utilities that gradually eat your available cache buffers until you reach rock bottom.

Your servers are the core of the network. Server hardware is not a place to save a few pennies. When your boss complains about the cost of quality components in the server, amortize the cost across all potential server users. The more users you expect to support, the less investment per user a quality server will require. And this isn't just sales talk. Your server is an investment in the knowledge-sharing infrastructure necessary to propel your company into the future.

NetWare is a resilient operating system, and server hardware is more reliable today than ever before. Even before you start considering mirrored or duplexed disk drives or a clustered system, off-the-shelf computer components work faster and longer today than ever before. However, this is of little comfort as you stand before a dead server, with the howling mob at your back. Problems do happen. You must learn to manage these problems before and after they occur.

ADD MORE RAM

I hate to sound like a broken record (or a CD with a tracking error, for you kids), but more RAM cures many server ills. More applications running on the server take more RAM, since the program must have a segment of RAM in which to run.

The move that replaced two or three NetWare 3 servers with one NetWare 4 server meant that one server must have the RAM of the earlier three, plus some to support NDS. Now, some companies are consolidating three NetWare 5 servers onto two NetWare 6 servers (mostly because NetWare 6's NDS now has a cache and responds much more quickly). This is why I advise you to put RAM on every budget request for everything else.

RAM needs go up over time, but not because the software changes. Every server adds disk space and NLMs now and then. Each time you add something, you check the RAM and it doesn't look too bad. Then you add another NLM and another few users, and it doesn't look much worse than it did last time. Unfortunately, your available RAM for file cache is now about half what you had when you started the server the first time. Your server gets gradually slower and flakier until you fix things. And how do you fix things? Add more RAM.

Server Availability: A Management Decision

Your management decides how available your servers will be. Your job is to maintain service to the agreed-upon level. How available is that?

The quick answer is 24-7, meaning every hour of the day, seven days a week. Do you need this? Think about the answer. When will you do maintenance? Must you keep the system available during tape backup? How will you add a new disk drive to a server?

Guarantee that your network will be available during normal business hours. If you have no one in the office at 3:00 A.M., why does the network need to be available? Would it be reasonable for your network to be generally available, but with no guarantees, after 7:00 P.M. and before 7:00 A.M. (excluding certain Web servers and services, of course)? They must remain up forever (hello, NetWare 6 Cluster Services).

Every system needs maintenance. If your entire network must be up overnight, pick one window of time on the weekends or during an evening for maintenance. Network management demands accessibility to the servers, including taking them down now and then.

WARNING *If you work in a large company, network-hostile mainframe bigots will track every minute a server is down. They will point to the fact that your network is unavailable more than the mainframe. Remember, mainframes don't need to shut down to add new disks. I hope your situation isn't this bad, but such hostility happens in some companies. Mainframers are feeling a bit unloved lately (with good reason, perhaps) and will spend a lot of energy to discredit the networks that are replacing mainframes. Be prepared.*

The Hardware Scale and the Costs

Even if your network consists of one server and 15 users, management personnel must decide how much availability they are willing to pay for. Nothing is certain with computers, but more guaranteed uptime translates into more cost.

Any chart showing dollars in the computer business is suspect, since prices generally fall. Those prices that don't fall reliably, such as the cost of memory chips, tend to gradually fall with occasional spikes to weaken the hearts of purchasing managers everywhere. Hard drives today are amazingly inexpensive, and the prices continue to drop. Today, you are able to get large (80GB or 120GB) IDE drives for about the same price as a 500MB drive only a few years ago.

The ascending hardware listing is explained this way:

Peer-to-peer networks Low cost, low numbers of users supported comfortably. This is the wrong book for you if you want information about peer-to-peer networks, but they are inexpensive.

Desktop PCs as dedicated servers Common choice for low-end servers. Desktop PCs don't have as much space for hard disks or RAM. Power supplies are sometimes inadequate for multiple disk drives.

Mirrored or duplexed drives Disk mirroring (two drives, one controller) and disk duplexing (two drives, two controllers) improve performance and provide protection against a single disk failure stopping your server. With the dropping cost of hard drives, it's hard to justify trusting your network to a disk drive as a single point of failure.

PC server models Extra space for drives, more RAM, and beefier power supplies help these systems look and act more like servers. Always in a tower case, these systems look more expensive and rugged, making management happier with the investment.

RAID storage systems RAID (redundant array of inexpensive disks) systems go further to eliminate the disk as a point of failure and add performance. These systems are often able to swap hard drives while the server is running, eliminating downtime due to a bad disk.

Servers on steroids   Companies such as Compaq, HP, Acer, Dell, and AST (among others) are placing their servers at the top of the food chain. Diagnostic software and hardware offer a level of control and management unattainable with regular PC servers. Many of these systems now offer multiple processors, boosting horsepower even higher if your software is able to use the extra CPUs.

Clustered servers   The new replacement for SFT III (System Fault Tolerance, level III), clusters primarily aim at keeping critical applications, such as Web servers, available. I've had the fun of playing with a killer Compaq ProLiant cluster, and I must say proper use of such equipment will eliminate downtime completely. The first two-node cluster license comes free with NetWare 6, but after that, Novell charges $5,000 per clustered-server license, so only the critical applications will pass budget muster.

The further up the scale you go, the more money you must invest in your network. This extra investment buys peace of mind and better performance. Management must make the decision on the proper amount of investment for your network. See if you can find a subtle way to remind the people making the decisions that you can't get a Rolls Royce for a go-cart price.

Operating System and RAM Problems

The following are typical operating system and RAM problems and some solutions to try.

Abend messages occur.   An abend (abnormal end) is a system shutdown due to an internal error of some sort. The best course of action after an abend is to write down the abend error message number and look it up in the "System Messages" section of the online documentation. Reboot the server, then check for sufficient RAM. Verify current versions of NLMs and drivers. If new hardware or software has been added, restart the server without the new component as a test. If all else fails, you may need to reload the operating system, but that doesn't happen often.

Users can't see server.   Check the frame type in use. Multiple frame types are easily supported, but both clients and servers must use a common frame type in order to communicate. Check the LOAD and BIND statements to make sure nothing has changed. Some third-party utilities may un-BIND or un-LOAD drivers during installation or by accident. Driver errors may also cause a network interface card to disconnect.

Server can't see users or other servers.   Again, check the frame type in use. Also check the LOAD and BIND statements. Check that SAP (Service Advertising Protocol) is active and not disabled. Verify network numbering of internal and external network numbers for the server. Driver errors may also cause a network interface card to disconnect.

Server goes up and down for no reason.   Check the power supply. This fails more often in a server than you might think. If your server UPS isn't doing the job, low voltage may cause the power supply to reset the computer motherboard. You should have a dedicated circuit for all your server equipment. Also, keep the cleaning crew from using AC plugs in the server area. I once saw a cleaning crew unplug servers to power their vacuum cleaners.

Server Memory

As I've said many times before, the main thing to do when you're low on RAM is to buy more RAM quickly. Here are some suggestions for freeing some server memory temporarily (until you can add more memory to the server):

◆ Type **REMOVE DOS** or **SECURE CONSOLE** to release the DOS memory in the server for the file cache.

◆ Forcibly purge files on traditional NetWare volumes to free the directory entry table space. (This is not necessary on NSS volumes.)

◆ Unload NLM programs that are not needed, such as MONITOR (often left up). The X Server Graphical Console eats a ton of memory and may be the only reason you need the Java Virtual Machine loaded, which requires another ton of memory.

◆ Dismount volumes that are not being used (this suggestion is straight from the manual, as if you have extra disks hanging off your server that no one needs).

◆ Turn off block suballocation and specify a 64KB block size on traditional NetWare volumes. This requires the volume to be reinitialized, meaning all data on the volume must be backed up and restored. This measure saves RAM but is a lot of trouble, takes the server offline for quite a while, and runs a slight risk of losing data. However, you might try it if you need to add a new volume with the smallest RAM impact possible. This method does use quite a bit more disk space, especially if you turn off file compression to save that RAM as well.

◆ Move volumes from this server to a different server with more RAM.

◆ Migrate all your traditional NetWare filesystem volumes to NSS storage pools.

Disk Errors

For volume dismounts and other disk problems, try the following:

◆ If you have an external disk subsystem, verify that the power is on and the cables are still connected.

◆ Check for error messages on the console. Ordinary disk errors will force a volume to dismount.

◆ Verify settings for the controller and driver combination.

◆ Check for increased numbers of Hot Fix redirection areas used. Increasing Hot Fix numbers generally indicate your disk is dying and should be replaced. The manual offers instructions on increasing the Hot Fix redirection area; I say dump the drive or at least reformat it and start all over.

◆ Run VREPAIR on the traditional volume (not on an NSS volume). This loads from the console, and if your SYS: volume is having a problem, you will need to reference the file on the DOS partition or the floppy. Run VREPAIR at least twice each time you use it.

Running out of disk space is a problem you don't want to have. Don't let this sneak up on you. If it happens to your SYS: volume, the server usually shuts down. Even if it isn't your SYS: volume, it still causes extra work and other hassles.

Check your volume space regularly. To produce a quick report on your current volume, use this command:

```
NDIR /VOL
```

This replaces the VOLINFO command from NetWare 3.x. Figure 15.8 shows the command and result for the ProLiant SYS: volume.

FIGURE 15.8

Good space left, and good compression

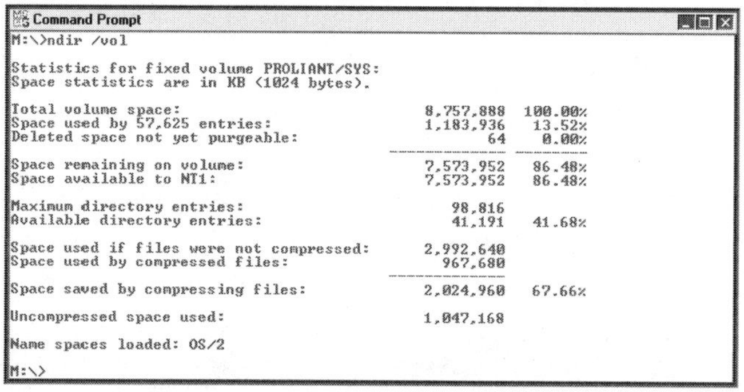

```
Command Prompt                                                    _ □ ×
M:\>ndir /vol

Statistics for fixed volume PROLIANT/SYS:
Space statistics are in KB (1024 bytes).
Total volume space:                            8,757,888  100.00%
Space used by 57,625 entries:                  1,183,936   13.52%
Deleted space not yet purgeable:                      64    0.00%

Space remaining on volume:                     7,573,952   86.48%
Space available to NT1:                        7,573,952   86.48%

Maximum directory entries:                        98,816
Available directory entries:                      41,191   41.68%

Space used if files were not compressed:       2,992,640
Space used by compressed files:                  967,680

Space saved by compressing files:              2,024,960   67.66%

Uncompressed space used:                       1,047,168

Name spaces loaded: OS/2

M:\>
```

When space becomes a serious concern, type **PURGE /ALL** for each volume. If the command-line PURGE doesn't clear enough space, delete unnecessary files still taking up directory entry table space. Change the Minimum File Delete Wait Time SET parameter to 0 so that files can be purged immediately. This stops them from being kept whole and salvageable on the volume.

Cabling Problems

As mentioned in this chapter, cabling causes lots of network problems. Vendors of new cable will tell real horror stories of old cable and the problems it caused. Introduce those vendors to your boss. Make it your goal to eliminate any coax or low-grade twisted pair left in the network.

As was also mentioned earlier in this chapter, coax Ethernet causes more than 20 times the number of network outages than are caused by 10BaseT Ethernet. Log your time spent chasing cable problems for two weeks, and then figure out the cost of those problems in your time alone. This is especially effective if your company is faced with a need to hire more network technicians. Replacing the cable will probably keep down your head count.

The first step when your network is having problems is to check all cables to make sure that they are plugged in. Don't laugh. Cables that aren't plugged in never work. Here are some other suggestions for avoiding cable problems:

◆ Find a cable contractor you like and stick with that contractor. Cabling consistency counts for a lot. If you find a cabling contractor who does good work, tests the cables with digital equipment, and offers a good warranty, you're lucky. Don't switch contractors for a few cents per foot.

◆ Buy quality cable. Cheap cable is good for telephones but not for data networks. High-speed systems in development now will push quality cable and will quickly overload cable not up to par. Buy the best cable (Level 5 and above) now, and you're covered for the foreseeable future.

◆ Declare a truce with any hostile telecom folks in your company. Some companies have telecom and datacom departments that are openly hostile. If your company is that way, I'm sorry. Go to management and request a meeting with all parties involved. If you can get over your differences, you will find that the telecom folks can be a great help.

◆ Verify cable distances, especially on new runs. All UTP (unshielded-twisted pair) cable networks have a length limit, usually 100 meters (300 feet plus a little). Going slightly beyond that limit will cause random problems. Going far beyond that limit will stop the connection entirely. There are third-party products that extend the cabling distance over UTP. Buy one of those, or just add a powered wiring concentrator to help cover the extra distance.

◆ Take care to avoid interference for your cable runs. Strong interference will blitz your cable and disrupt your network. Did you ever hear stories about networks that always went down at dusk? The cable was routed by a light switch. When that light was turned on, the cable interference overloaded the network and blocked all the packets.

◆ Provide UPS systems for all powered wiring components. In a blackout, your server and your desktop machine will likely continue on battery power. But if the wiring concentrator is powerless, how will you connect to the server from your workstation?

FOR COAX ETHERNET OR ARCNET USERS

If you have coax Ethernet, or worse, ARCnet, you no doubt turned to this troubleshooting chapter quickly. Let me tell you what you may or may not want to hear: *upgrade*.

You have been told this several times before. You know this is necessary every time you crawl under a desk to check a BNC connector. You know coax ages, gets brittle, and breaks time after time. You just need to convince your management.

Put the boss's secretary on the worst coax leg of your network. This isn't dishonest, but it is in your self-interest. Every time you go up to the executive area to fix the network (again and again), be sure you know how much it will cost to replace the coax Ethernet with 10BaseT or 100BaseT Ethernet. Basically pennies, nowadays. Remember that number when you're crawling under the secretary's desk, and repeat it to the boss when you emerge.

Monitoring Network Cable Performance

The best way to stop network downtime remains preparation, and knowing what your network does regularly may be the most critical part of your preparation. Let's look at another method of cable-related preparation you may not have considered.

Wiring hubs have gotten far smarter while getting far cheaper. One of the hubs used in my lab is from LinkSys (www.linksys.com), and they included an SNMP module to manage the 24-port hub. Check out the details in Figure 15.9, and we'll discuss some of them.

The top frame of the browser reflects the front of the hub. Yes, the active lights on the left and the colored port plugs on the right mean something and change in real time. Plugs with 10BaseT connections are green; the 100BaseT links are blue.

FIGURE 15.9

Physical network details unfolding every five seconds

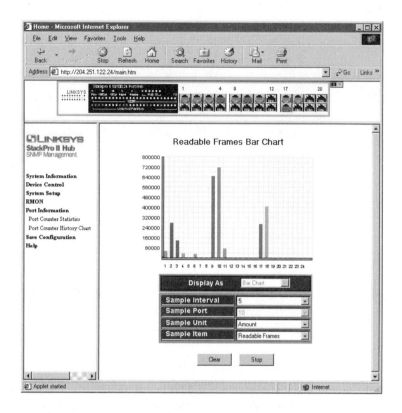

Most of the informative details opened by the menu choices in the left frame are text oriented, with tables of packet details and the like. These are interesting on a fine-grained level but are not too graphically pleasing.

The screen shot in Figure 15.9, however, colors port summary information with five-second updates (configurable). The tallest (those with the most packets) ports are the servers in this picture, and they should be in your network as well. If one of those server bar lines drops down to nothing, your phone will magically start ringing. It happens every time.

SNMP modules add a couple hundred dollars to the cost of the 24-port hub, but they are worth it for at least your servers. LinkSys engineers allow you to control up to six 24-port hubs with one SNMP module, spreading the couple hundred dollars across 144 connections. That's getting too cheap to pass up. Show this page to your tightwad boss—I mean, aggressive fiscal management member—and see if that helps loosen the budget strings at least a little.

iFolder Fun and Games

Without a doubt, iFolder will amaze current NetWare users and intrigue those not using NetWare. Many companies may justify upgrading to NetWare 6 on iFolder's advantages alone, forgetting iPrint and clustering and performance. iFolder is that good.

Unfortunately, iFolder—as shipped with NetWare 6 First Customer Ship, and the late beta copies I examined—sometimes requires more effort than necessary to get going. One odd fix to many weird problems, based on reports on Novell Support forums and my own experience, is to delete any proxy settings for the copy of Microsoft Internet Explorer on the iFolder client system.

Novell support folks guess there is a 5000-user limit per server of iFolder clients, but they aren't sure. One thing that is sure is that Novell support folks will have plenty of iFolder calls during the first few months of the NetWare 6 rollout.

Understanding the Dreadful Error 107

Error message "Check user error - 107" became far too familiar during my iFolder testing and configuration. What does "user error 107" mean in English? It means that something is messed up between eDirectory and your LDAP server, even when the LDAP server runs on the same NetWare server as the iFolder server.

TIP   *Newsreader to the rescue: iFolder managers, set your newsreader to keep up with* `novell.support.internet` `.ifolder` *inside the* `support-forums.novell.com` *newsgroup hosted by Novell. You will need the help you find there.*

The "something" that's messed up bounces around, depending on which Novell person gets involved, between eDirectory versions, LDAP implementation, and even whether the presented username is case sensitive or not. You may even need to edit one of the Apache configuration files, using a text editor such as Notepad, to ensure you get connected. If you wanted to feel like a Unix manager, start looking for the context settings for your NetWare login context inside the `httpd_additions_nw.conf` file.

Those of you hesitant to upgrade your current version of NDS to eDirectory 8.6 will lose this battle. Only the most recent eDirectory version will correctly (at least most of the time) start iFolder on the server when requested.

Sometimes, the advice from Novell for iFolder server problems is to unload and reload the `LDAP.NLM` utility. Sometimes things work better for me after rebooting the entire server, rather than just trying STOPIFOLDER and STARTIFOLDER to reload new changes (and some good luck helps, too).

More realistically, check for updates for all the LDAP services, and verify that the Allow Clear Text Passwords check box is checked in the LDAP Group for your server name. Find this setting in ConsoleOne, on the LDAP Group General page. Try turning off your proxy server settings for the client as well (some people say this helps). Obviously, keep an eye out for updates.

Waiting for Better iFolder Management Tools

When you see advice from Novell support to start editing the client Registry files, some product shipped too soon. I believe iFolder shipped a month or three too soon, if only for the lack of management tools available.

Sure, there are tools, and we covered them in the appropriate places earlier in the book. But NetWare always had a management tool interface, no matter how clunky, from the days of the S/Net server (late 1980s for you youngsters). Asking users now to modify client Registry files and check the Context settings for server configuration files doesn't push Novell closer to the "ease of management" award at next year's Golden Globe ceremonies, does it?

Keep playing with iFolder, but keep watching Novell's help, download, and support sites for more help. The help will arrive, and iFolder will be an outstanding product by the time the second patch to all the systems has been downloaded and applied. But Novell usually cooks products all the way until they're ready to ship. This time, they seemed to pull iFolder out of the oven just before the oven timer rang.

NDS Problems and Solutions

NetWare 6 provides two utilities that are handy for catching and repairing NDS problems. The DSTRACE (Directory Services Trace) utility traces server communications concerning NDS. DSRE-PAIR repairs database-related problems. You'll also find graphical versions of these utilities in iMonitor.

DSTRACE Tracks NDS Synchronization Processes

NetWare's TRACK ON console command has always been helpful. Watching server communications as clients connect to servers and servers exchange network routing information gives a nice, warm feeling that things are working as they should be.

That same warm feeling is now extended to the NDS communications between servers. The DSTRACE utility, run from the server console, will display server chat concerning NDS. Figure 15.10 is a screen full of (luckily) boring (and almost incomprehensible) NDS communications.

FIGURE 15.10

Replica repair

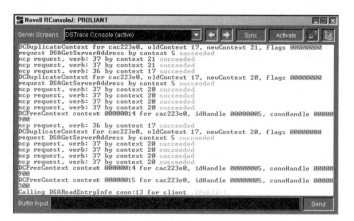

Look for a nice ending to all the processes: succeeded. This will be the hoped-for tail end of a DSREPAIR automatic repair session. All the directory services details, including all the schema operations, were listed by the DSREPAIR utility, discussed in the next section.

You can't see it here, but he word *succeeded* is in bright purple. Computer and partition names are all in blue. Purger operations are in hot pink. This isn't exactly graphical, but it certainly is colorful.

Here are some reasons you may wish to watch such a boring but colorful display:

◆ To check whether the NDS replicas are finished with a process

◆ To watch for NDS errors, especially during and/or soon after adjusting or moving NDS objects

NDS-related system messages are numbered −601 through −699 and F966 through F9FE. Not all NDS system messages are bad news, just like regular NetWare system messages. However, you know the old story: No news is good news. If you see system messages that don't clear up as NDS settles down after changes, they are usually error messages. The System Messages section of the documentation describes all the system messages in mind-numbing detail.

TURNING ON DSTRACE

To see the NDS synchronization information using DSTRACE, go to the server console or start an RConsoleJ session. At the console prompt, type:

```
SET DSTRACE TO SCREEN = ON
```

To stop the trace, replace the ON with OFF. (Use the up arrow on the console to repeat the command, then just backspace over the ON to type **OFF**.)

If you wish to save this information for your server archives, or send the file to a support person, use this command at the server console:

```
SET DSTRACE TO FILE = ON
```

The file will be sent to DSTRACE.LOG in the SYS:SYSTEM directory. To write the file elsewhere, use this command:

```
SET DSTRACE FILENAME = path\filename
```

When you feel there is enough information in your file, repeat the DSTRACE TO FILE command, adding OFF. If you don't stop it, the file will wrap at about 500KB. Old information will be overwritten with new information as long as the log file is open.

NOTE   *As with most log files, not everything is written faithfully to the log. If your log and screen information look good but things are still strange, trust your feelings rather than the log file.*

USING A GRAPHICAL DSTRACE

IN A HURRY 15.1: USE DS TRACE FROM iMONITOR

1. Log in as Admin or equivalent and open iMonitor.
2. Click the Trace Configuration button (the icon with arrows and a check mark) on the toolbar.
3. Provide the administrator name and password (if asked again).
4. Choose the DS Trace options switches with the check boxes.
5. Click the Submit command button to set the configuration.
6. Click the Trace On command button to start the trace.
7. Click the Trace Off command button to stop the trace.

The new iMonitor utility also includes a graphically configured DS Trace. Clicking the squiggly arrows with the check mark icon, next to the wrench on the toolbar, opens the Trace Configuration screen.

I'm still not sure what to call this. Novell calls it DS Trace most of the time, but it's just Track On and Track Off from the server console, albeit easier to customize. Look at Figure 15.11 and see if a better name springs to your mind.

FIGURE 15.11

Configuring DS Trace via check boxes

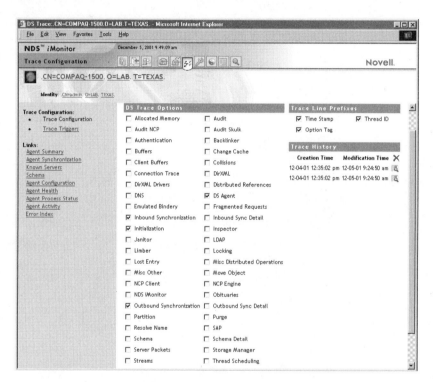

Just above the DS Trace Options bar sit two command buttons (I rolled them out of sight to show more options). Submit tells the Trace Configuration program to accept any changes in the check boxes for the next trace session. The second button says Trace On until you start the trace. Then it changes to Trace Off.

Resulting log files wind up under the Trace History heading, and stack up until you hit the red X for Delete All. One real advantage of the graphical DS Trace is that servers, other NDS objects, and error codes all have hyperlinks. Do you want to see details of a server? Click the hyperlinked name. Do you want an explanation for an NDS error message? Click the hyperlink.

Although the graphical utility is a welcome innovation, I do hesitate to rely solely on iMonitor for NDS repair functions. Clobbered servers may not have their Web services up, making these graphical NDS control pages unavailable. Also, quick repairs on NDS should load and run faster under DSTRACE (or DSREPAIR) NLMs than under a browser window.

However, the new features, especially in DS Trace, make me happy. Many eDirectory hiccups can easily be handled without rebooting the server (most can, actually), so staying at my desk with iMonitor saves time, trouble, and shoe leather.

DSREPAIR Means Directory Services Repair

If you read the computer magazines, you know that distributed database technology is fraught with peril for database vendors. Trying to manage database pieces spread across multiple computers is beyond the ability of most commercial database vendors today. Part of the problem is the learning curve for database designers just starting to investigate using the network as a constant, reliable communications platform to tie all the database pieces together.

Novell has a considerable head start over database vendors in the network communications area. Servers have been negotiating with each other across the network since 1986. And as we saw with the DSTRACE utility, the NDS database must keep things synchronized through regular cross-network communication.

But things can still go wrong. Some customers (and network administrators as well) can tear up a ball bearing with a powder puff. When the unlucky object of these attentions is the NDS database, DSREPAIR will put things right once again.

DSREPAIR works on one single-server database at a time. There is no option to repair all the databases from remote servers in one operation from one server console. However, you can easily run DSREPAIR on multiple servers sequentially using RConsoleJ.

Here's what DSREPAIR can do for you:

◆ Repair the local database. The DS.NLM file on a server will be addressed by the DSREPAIR utility.

◆ Repair the local replicas. Examine and repair replicas, replica rings, and server objects. You can also verify that each replica has the same data as the others.

◆ Repair a single object to fix inconsistencies in the object's references.

◆ Search for local database objects. A browser function helps you locate and synchronize objects in the local database.

◆ Analyze the servers in each local partition for synchronization problems. View errors and list the partition name, server name, synchronization time, and errors with error codes.

◆ Write replica details to a log file. Detailed information about local partitions and servers is made available to check for database damage. If the local server has a wrong address for a remote server, you can check that here.

◆ Create a dump file of a damaged database. A compressed file is dumped, so you must use DSREPAIR to work with the file.

◆ Check the remote server ID list. Verify identification numbers for all remote servers and change those numbers as necessary.

Some NDS problems are less serious than others, and your eDirectory may continue to function. However, if you see a message saying that the server can't open the local database, go directly to

DSREPAIR and start to work. Reinstalling the NDS database from a tape backup is more trouble, and that backup is probably slightly out of date. Try DSREPAIR before trying anything else.

Now that you know what DSREPAIR can do, here's what it can't do:

◆ Repair a remote NDS database

◆ Recover Unknown objects that do not have the mandatory object properties

DSREPAIR looks a lot like all the other NetWare C-Worthy utilities. Its opening screen shows the current version in the upper-left corner above the name of the tree and server being examined. The bottom of the screen shows helpful keystroke information and a brief description of the highlighted menu choice. Figure 15.12 shows the opening menu of DSREPAIR.

FIGURE 15.12

Preparing to repair
the NDS database
with DSREPAIR

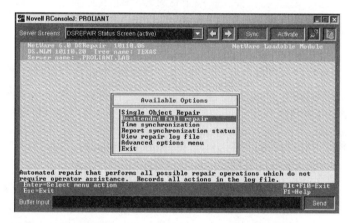

Following are the DSREPAIR Available Options menu items:

Single Object Repair   Every eDirectory object has an Object ID. If details about a single Object ID get mangled for some reason, use this setting to straighten out and rework that Object ID.

Unattended Full Repair   Most of your work in DSREPAIR will be quick and simple, accomplished with this menu choice. In fact, if you start DSREPAIR and press Enter, your eDirectory will probably be back in shape in just a few seconds. Then you can press Enter again after reading the results of the operation and press Escape to exit DSREPAIR altogether.

Time Synchronization   Contacts every server in the local database and checks NDS and time synchronization details. If this server holds a replica of the [Root] partition, every server in the tree will be polled. Each server will be listed with its DS.NLM version, type of replica code, time source, whether time is synchronized, and the difference in time to the remote server. This process starts immediately when this option is selected, and the results are written to the DSREPAIR.LOG file.

Report Synchronization Status   Determines whether the NDS eDirectory tree is healthy by checking the synchronization status of each replica on each server. You must provide the Admin name and password to start this function. A log entry is added to the DSREPAIR.LOG file.

View Repair Log File   Shows the entire DSREPAIR.LOG file, allowing you to view all entries. The log file is controlled with the Log File Configuration option in the Advanced Options menu.

Advanced Options Menu   Opens another menu allowing you to manually perform each of the automatic repairs done by the first menu option. The advanced options give you more power and flexibility, as well as more potential for disaster. Use them carefully.

Exit   Exits DSREPAIR; you can cancel by entering No or pressing the Escape key.

RUNNING THE UNATTENDED FULL REPAIR

IN A HURRY 15.2: REPAIR THE NDS DATABASE AUTOMATICALLY WITH DSREPAIR

1. Type **DSREPAIR** from the console prompt.

2. Choose Unattended Full Repair (the default) and press Enter to start the repair operation.

3. Press Enter after reading the automatic repair results to view the log.

4. Press Escape to return to the main DSREPAIR menu.

When you press Enter on this first option, you won't be asked to verify your choice or to provide any information. The option is labeled Unattended and means just that. Press Enter, and the repair starts immediately.

During the repair process, the NDS database must be closed for obvious reasons. Just like any database record, if the file can be written to while it's being overhauled, dangerous things can happen.

Because the locking of the directory database will inconvenience users, it stays locked the shortest time possible. Repair of the GATEWAY2000 server took seven (yes, 7) seconds. Obviously, a small network with no real problems will take less time than a large network with a reason to use DSREPAIR.

Figure 15.13 shows the DSREPAIR process under way. The lines whiz by so quickly you can't read any of them during the process. The whizzing stops a time or two, but not long enough to consider the pause as a breakdown in the process. Although the display in the upper-right corner shows no errors, seven minor errors of no consequence to anything except the database were found and listed in the log file.

FIGURE 15.13

Repair work in progress

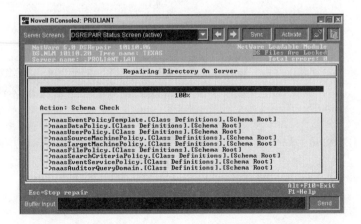

The bottom of the screen, depending on the operation running at that second, shows several interesting options:

F2=Options menu	Shows the DSREPAIR Options menu.
F3=Pause the screen	Stops the screen and the repair so you can examine the process.
Alt+F10	Exits DSREPAIR.
Esc=Stop repair	Abandons the repair and returns to the menu.

NOTE *Little of what zooms by is helpful to a network administrator. But what great technical names: External synchronizer and attribute definitions are some of the functions that scroll by. I can almost hear Scotty now, yelling over the warp engines, "Cap'n, I canna keep the External Synchronizer up much longer! Our Attribute Definitions are blown!"*

USING THE ADVANCED OPTIONS MENU AND SUBMENUS

If the automatic full repair procedure doesn't fix your eDirectory problem, the Advanced Options menu is the next choice. You have little to lose at this point. Alternatively, your next step after the unattended repair is to restore from tape (not generally a good idea for directory services) or to delete the local database and copy it from another server. You might as well try a few advanced options before searching through the tape library.

Figure 15.14 shows the Advanced Options menu that appears as a submenu to the opening DSREPAIR program. The look is consistent with what you've seen before, including the identification information on the top and the help information at the bottom of the screen.

FIGURE 15.14

Serious DSPREPAIR tools

WARNING *Remember that each of the DSREPAIR options locks the eDirectory database. No one can be authenticated by NDS on this server during that time, since the database will be unavailable.*

Before you choose any of the advanced options, you should definitely know what it does. The following sections describe the effects of each Advanced Options menu item.

Log File and Login Configuration

The default DSREPAIR log file, which will be created automatically for you, is SYS:SYSTEM\DSRE-PAIR.LOG. If you wish to delete the log file, the first menu choice is one place to do so. Figure 15.15 shows the screen that appears when you choose Log File and Login Configuration from the Advanced Options menu.

FIGURE 15.15

Combo screen: log file configuration and directory login

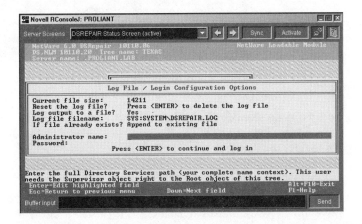

The first field, Current File Size, cannot be changed here. The Reset The Log File? option, to delete the current log file, is the first choice you have. Pressing Enter by accident as you go into this submenu may teach you the value of the Salvage option in FILER.

The option to log output to a file (coincidentally named Log Output to a File?) of your own choosing is the same as is available in DSTRACE, but it provides a more complete capture of information. This file will be helpful if your eDirectory gets so messed up that you need help from Novell support technicians. You can send a copy of this file for their perusal. In the Log File Filename option, you may rename the log anything you wish or leave the default name. In the next option, if the named log file already exists, you can append or overwrite the file. If you don't want to specify the log file, a temporary one will be created during repair operations. This will be shown to you after the repairs are finished.

To continue, you must provide the Admin user's name and password. The name and password will be authenticated by the NDS database before you can save your log file changes.

Repair Local DS Database

This option does much of the same work as the Unattended Full Repair option on the main menu, with a few extra choices. One important distinction is that this option performs the repairs on a temporary file set, and you have the opportunity to back out before the temporary files become permanent. Figure 15.16 shows the choices you'll be able to make.

FIGURE 15.16

NDS database repair
options

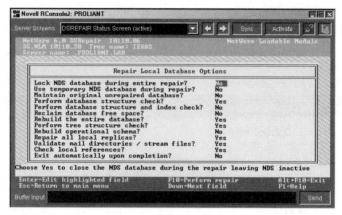

Here are the questions and what your answers mean:

Lock NDS database during entire repair? You used to have no choice, but now you have some. Keep it locked (choose Yes) if you're doing this when traffic should be light; keep it unlocked otherwise (choose No).

Use temporary NDS database during repair? Saying Yes locks the database so a copy can be worked on and then can replace the original.

Maintain original unrepaired database? If the old database has problems, why keep it? It eats a lot of disk space. Your answer here should be No.

Perform database structure and index check? Yes, these are two areas that must be checked.

Reclaim database free space? This should really say "Delete unused database records?" because that's what it does.

Rebuild the entire database? Repairs, cleans, and rebuilds the database, but this can take a while on a large network.

Perform tree structure check? Verifies connectivity for all tree points to the appropriate database entries.

Rebuild operational schema? The operational schema is the schema required for basic operation of NDS, making things very messy if rebuilt unnecessarily. Do this only under orders by Novell technical support; it's rarely needed.

Repair all local replicas? Fixes all replicas stored on this physical server. Saying Yes is a good idea.

Validate mail directories/stream files? Mail directories are not required by NDS; those were necessary in NetWare 3 for storing login scripts. If you have mail directories for an e-mail program built like the old bindery mail system, make sure this is set to Yes. If you have users who access the server through Bindery Services, they will need their login directories for login scripts as well.

Stream syntax files, like login scripts, are a type of object property. These are stored in a special reserved area of the SYS: volume, along with the NDS database. If you choose Yes, orphaned stream syntax files are tagged and deleted.

Check local references?   This option takes more time, because it verifies the information within the local database. In large networks, it will extend the repair time, but this option should be set to Yes whenever time permits.

Exit automatically upon completion?   If you know enough or are so incurious as to not care what happens with the rebuild, change this to Yes. Otherwise, leave it alone. Even if you don't know a lot about how NDS works, you will be able to understand some of the log files and explanations given at the end.

After you've answered these questions, press F10 to perform the repair.

Servers Known to This Database

Here, you can fine-tune the local NDS database per server and see what the local server knows about the remote servers. Each of the known servers is listed, with its status and its local ID. See Figure 15.17 for a look at the server display as seen from PROLIANT.

FIGURE 15.17

Know thyself and thy fellow servers in the NDS database.

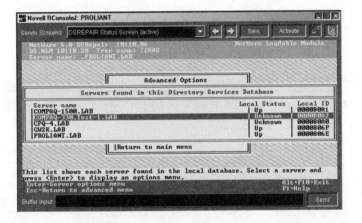

The information imparted in this screen is easy to understand. The servers listed are those in the NDS database of PROLIANT. Three of the servers, according to the local database, are up. The local ID for each server is listed. Two other servers, in the process of being deleted, appear as Unknown. Those would bear investigating if I didn't know why they show up as Unknown.

It's possible for a server to be listed as up on this screen but really be down. It's possible to go the other way, with a server really active though shown as down here. Once the servers exchange some information, the display will match reality.

Pressing Enter while highlighting any of the listed servers opens up a new menu, named Server Options. The action occurs immediately after you press Enter, so if you're unsure, check the Help screens first by pressing F1.

The Server Options menu has these choices:

Time Synchronization and Server Status Contacts every server in the local database and requests time and NDS information. If this server contains a replica of [Root], it will poll every server in the tree. The information presented here is the same as that shown from the main DSREPAIR menu choice of Time Synchronization.

Repair All Network Addresses There needs to be an entry for each remote server in the local SAP tables. These tables match the remote server object's IPX network address and the address in the replica (when IPX protocols are used). If the addresses don't match, the RNA (Repair Network Address) function updates the local tables. If there is no name for an SAP address entry for a remote server, there is little else to be done.

Repair Selected Server's Network Address Same as above, but for the highlighted server only.

View Entire Server's Name Shows the full distinguished server name for the highlighted server; for example, PROLIANT.GCS.

Return to Server List Backs out of this menu, or you can use the Escape key.

Replica and Partition Operations

This innocent-looking entry hides multiple submenus and powerful processes. Figure 15.18 shows the first of the submenus. After you choose this option, the Replicas Stored on This Server box opens, showing all the replicas on our local server.

FIGURE 15.18

Specific replica options for PROLIANT

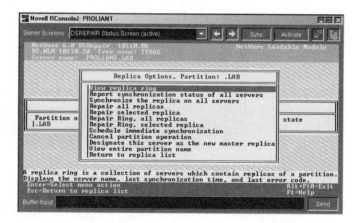

The first menu option, View Replica Ring, brings up a new term: *replica ring*. As you can read on the lower part of the screen, a replica ring is basically a group of replicas within a partition. Remember all the copies of replicas you can spread everywhere? These functions help keep them coordinated and functional.

You're not missing anything interesting in the background box, which explains that the LAB partition on this server holds a Read/Write replica and that it is On.

The main Replica Options menu has these choices:

View Replica Ring   Brings up a box labeled Servers That Have Replicas of This Partition. Choose a server to see another submenu of choices, described in the following section.

Report Synchronization Status of All Servers   Runs a quick report and details time synchronization status of partitions.

Synchronize the Replica on All Servers   Reads the table of remote servers and replicas on the local server and forces all servers to synchronize with all other servers.

Repair All Replicas   Checks the replica information on each remote server defined in the local eDirectory database tables and makes any modifications necessary. If the local database hasn't been repaired in the last 30 minutes, repair it before trying this option.

Repair Selected Replica   Same as above, but for one highlighted replica rather than all replicas.

Repair Ring, All Replicas   Repairs all the replicas on the ring, validating remote ID information. Run the Repair Local Database option before doing this.

Repair Ring, Selected Replica   Repairs the selected replica on the ring. Again, make sure you run Repair Local Database first.

Schedule Immediate Synchronization   Provides a good way to force synchronization, especially if you're watching the DSTRACE screen and are tired of waiting.

Cancel Partition Operation   Stops the partition operation on the selected replica, if the process hasn't gone too far.

Designate This Server As the New Master Replica   If the original Master replica is damaged or lost, this option makes this replica the Master replica. If the old Master replica comes back from a hardware failure, there will be two Master replicas, causing some confusion until the synchronization checks and forces the issue by deleting the original Master replica.

View Entire Partition Name   Shows the entire partition name, regardless of its length.

Return to Replica List   Backs up one menu (same as pressing Escape).

These operations force repairs and synchronizations while writing full details to the log file. They provide a rifle approach, as opposed to the shotgun approach of the Unattended Full Repair option.

As with VREPAIR in past NetWare versions, you may need to perform some operations several times. While the replica and partition information is updated throughout the network, small errors here and there may be magnified, or they may not appear until later in the process. So don't expect any of these options to be able to work magic and quickly fix your problem. Things take longer when working across a distributed network, and this is no exception.

Viewing a Replica Ring   Choosing the View Replica Ring choice, the first option on the Replica Options menu, brings up a list of servers. In our case, two servers have replicas of this partition.

Highlight the server and replica type of your choice, and still another new menu appears: Replica Options, Server (and the name of the current chosen server). Here we have nothing but actions, with no pause for reflection. If you've come down this many levels in your server operating system, you might as well go for it. These are your choices:

Report Synchronization Status on the Selected Server   Gathers partition details on a specific server and replica.

Synchronize the Replica on The Selected Server   Same as above for a single, highlighted replica.

Send All Objects to Every Replica in the Ring   This may create high network traffic. All other replicas are relabeled as new replicas, and the old replicas are destroyed. The host server sends a new copy of the replica to the remote servers that had their old replicas deleted. Modifications made to the now-deleted replicas that didn't have time to get back to the host replica are gone.

Receive All Objects for This Replica   Again, this may create high network traffic. This option is the reverse of the above. The old replica is marked deleted, and any objects are deleted. The Master remote replica replaces the host server replica.

View Entire Server Name   Another look at the server name, for those servers with names that can't fit in the small box of text in the earlier menu.

Return to Servers with Replicas List   Backs up one menu (same as pressing Escape).

Check Volume Objects and Trustees

This Advanced Options menu choice tests and verifies that everything on the server's volumes is correctly listed in NDS, as illustrated in Figure 15.19. If a volume object can't be found, an attempt will be made to create one. All mounted volumes are checked for compliance. You must log into NDS to perform these checks.

FIGURE 15.19

Volumes verified

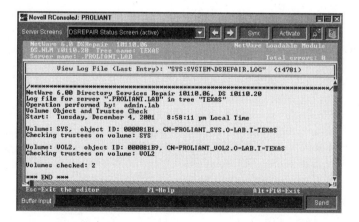

The problem with new and faster servers and faster hard disks is that these volume checks whiz by too quickly to catch. Take a look at the log file to see the types of information checked for and verified. If there were any errors, they will appear in the log file.

Check External References

When you choose Check External References from the Advanced Options menu, each external item referenced is checked to see if a replica containing the object can be located. If there is no joy, a warning will be given, but nothing dire happens immediately. Just keep working on your NDS repair until everything matches.

Global Schema Operations

The *schema* consists of the rules governing objects and their relationships to NDS. It's important to have all servers on the same schema. Think of the schema as somewhat like the NDS program that tracks and controls all the objects. Having all servers on the same version of the program is smart, and it's also necessary. The submenu shown here appears when you choose Global Schema Options from the Advanced Options menu.

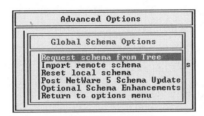

The first step in the upgrade looks at known servers in the tree and checks their schema version. If it's current, nothing happens, and the next server is checked.

Why would Novell engineers put a choice here, when the Help screen for the choice admits there will be network errors if all servers aren't up to the same level? The answer is that this is placed here for servers that were down or having an NDS problem when the updates were done. If at all possible, don't do any NDS maintenance unless all of your servers are up and running.

View Repair Log File

The DSREPAIR.LOG file keeps track of every result from every procedure run against the NDS on this server. Figure 15.20 shows results from looking for now-departed servers.

FIGURE 15.20

Viewing the DSREPAIR log file

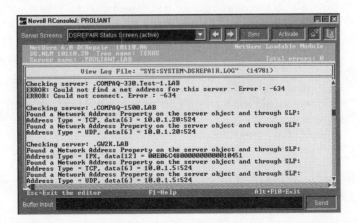

COMPAQ-330, the same physical server as PROLIANT, was merely an earlier installation of Net-Ware 6. I didn't delete the server officially after I reloaded the latest shipping version of NetWare 6, because I wanted to show some errors in DSREPAIR. That's my story, and I'm sticking with it.

The first three lines of the repair log show that COMPAQ-330 couldn't be found. No surprise there—it's hard to find something that no longer exists.

COMPAQ-1500 does exist, and the second block of repair log information shows the server seems fine and up to date.

The last and longest block of repair log information shows GW2K, an old Gateway 2000 Pentium 120 with 128MB of RAM. If you remember, NetWare 6 requires a minimum of 256MB of RAM. That's why GW2K remains a NetWare 5.1 server. Notice GW2K still runs both IPX and TCP/IP.

When you've finished viewing this file, press Escape and select to save the log file under the same name, or just exit.

Return to Main Menu

Believe it or not, we are finished wandering in the world of partitions, replicas, schemas, and eDirectory databases. Once you choose the Return to Main Menu option or press Escape, you're out of the Advanced Options section. Back at the main menu, you'll see that we're out of DSREPAIR altogether.

USING A GRAPHICAL DSREPAIR

IN A HURRY 15.3: USE DSREPAIR FROM iMONITOR

1. Log in as Admin or equivalent and open iMonitor.

2. Click the DSREPAIR icon (wrench) on the toolbar.

3. Provide the administrator name and password (if asked again).

4. Choose the NDS Repair Switches with the check boxes.

5. Click the Start Repair command button.

Hidden within iMonitor is a fully graphical, almost complete copy of DSREPAIR. Novell marketing managers haven't made much noise about this utility, but they should, because it's pretty cool. (I guess there probably is not much publicity yet because iMonitor itself needs more awareness among administrators.)

Figure 15.21 shows the DSREPAIR window you can get to from iMonitor. See the little wrench on the toolbar in iMonitor? That's DSREPAIR, although iMonitor just calls it Repair.

Why would you use the console DSREPAIR if this version is here? Because the console version is more complete (all those advanced options, remember?) and may work on systems too crippled to support users. Besides, the more you use the console version, the more you appreciate the graphical option.

Running DSREPAIR functions from iMonitor provides the same log file as the console version. Unfortunately, you must go to the server console to view the log file, drilling through DSREPAIR.

One new and handy option for DSREPAIR in iMonitor is the Periodic Information capability, which is essentially a scheduling system for DSREPAIR. Click the Advanced Options command button to see the expanded screen display, as shown in Figure 15.22.

FIGURE 15.21

DSREPAIR goes
Hollywood

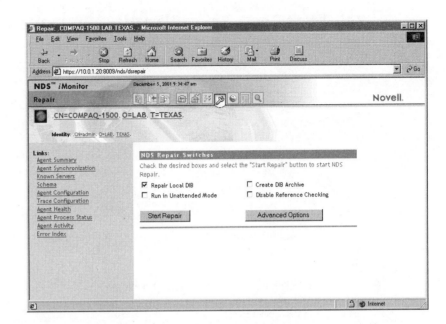

FIGURE 15.22

DSREPAIR
Advanced Options
within iMonitor

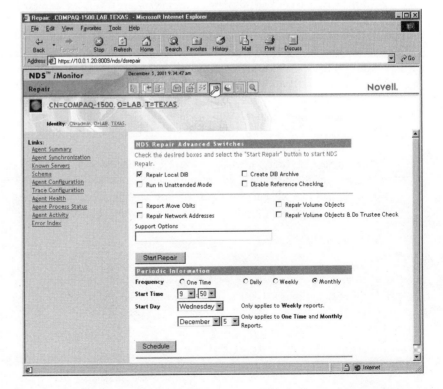

Tell Your Boss: Prior Planning Prevents Poor Performance

Every decision made during the design and implementation of your network impacts the performance and reliability of that network. Some of these choices are easy to evaluate: a fast multiprocessor server will perform better than a lower-end single-processor system. Other design choice ramifications don't appear until something has blown up, taking your network and peace of mind with it.

Keep in mind crosstime (as opposed to downtime) and explain the idea to your management. The option to support network clients through alternative servers and other resources is a sign of network flexibility, not fallibility.

Building fault-tolerance for your network means more work and more money. It's also the only way to guard against downtime. Mirrored or duplexed disk drives are a quick, easy example. If one drive dies, the other one keeps going without missing a beat. Try that in a server with a single disk. NetWare 6 and NSS 3.0 extend mirroring to partitions, adding fault tolerance to larger volumes across multiple disks. External disk arrays, especially with removable disks, mean you can now swap hard disks in and out without taking down the server. A volume may go offline for a moment, but not the server itself.

Including free, two-node clustering support into NetWare 6 jumps reliability way up the scale. Even without shared disk storage, some processes, such as DHCP and DNS servers, provide fail-over fault tolerance right out of the box. Well, actually two boxes, since two-node clustering requires two licensed NetWare servers.

Your network, when you add Web server software, turns from a local network to a global network. Running e-commerce software on your NetWare 6 Web server means downtime costs you hard dollars, not "lost productivity" and inconvenience. Remote options such as iFolder and iPrint mean employees or offices anywhere in the world depend on your network services every minute of the day. Uptime changed from a nice statistic to a management demand when the Web kicked into gear.

What can your boss do to help the troubleshooting process? Provide money for training (you and your users). Provide network analysis and management tools. Provide spare parts.

The best your boss can provide is a reasonable atmosphere. High expectations are met with high resources. Low resources lead to low results. Your management must make the decision on how important the network is and then provide resources accordingly.

In a typical company, management will try to force high expectations from low resources. That's possible for a time, especially if you're smart and work hard. However, one day the lack of spare parts and support tools will catch up to you. Your network will be down for at least one day. Your boss will try to blame you. Don't let that happen; point to the empty shelf labeled spare parts. Keeping a copy of your rejected proposals for network upgrades won't hurt, either.

Part V

Appendices

In this section:
- ◆ Appendix A: NetWare Web Services
- ◆ Appendix B: Upgrades, Migration, and Windows Client and Server Installation Support
- ◆ Appendix C: NetWare 6 SET Commands
- ◆ Glossary

Appendix A

NetWare Web Services

YES, VIRGINIA, THERE IS A Web server sitting on top of the best file server in the business. In fact, there are now two Web servers. Since Web service consists of serving lots of files to many users as quickly as possible, NetWare has a tremendous performance edge. Novell Marketing remains adept at hiding its light under a bushel basket: Tests by Novell and by other firms show that performance with NetWare and its Enterprise Web Server far outstrips anything from Microsoft. I haven't seen any tests with Apache on NetWare, but I bet they're pretty fast as well.

Netscape Enterprise Server provides a stout Web server and an equally stout FTP server. Net-Ware 6 dropped the NetWare Multimedia Server and NNTP News Server, although you can check the NetWare support Web site to see what they say about running the NetWare 5.1 versions of those applications with the Netscape server included in NetWare 6.

NOTE *Netscape Enterprise Server and NetWare Enterprise Web Server are the same product. It's Netscape's server, licensed (and renamed) by Novell.*

The open-source Apache Web Server debuts with NetWare 6, providing the infrastructure for several new features. A great many NetWare applications run under Apache. Because Apache runs the majority of Web sites in the world (over 60 percent in many tabulations), teaming Apache with NetWare makes a great deal of sense. Putting the two best Web servers on the world's fastest file-service engine helps you in a variety of ways. Have you read any reports of Web servers hosted by NetWare becoming virus targets? Successful hacks into NetWare services, including Web services? Didn't think so.

NOTE *Including competing Web servers indicates a bit of Novell developer schizophrenia that may not last into the next NetWare revision. Since all the new management products appear in Apache, you should point your development team in that direction.*

No room remains in this NetWare 6 book to tell you all the ins and outs of building and running Web servers. However, there are one or two (thousand) other books available offering plenty of information, especially about general Web site development and about Apache Web Server. My goal here is simply to get your Web servers and services up and running on NetWare 6 so you and your Webmaster can go from there.

TIP   Many of the browser-based utilities work in both Netscape Navigator and Internet Explorer, but not all. If you have a problem starting a utility, try a different browser.

In this appendix, I'll introduce you to:

♦   NetWare Web Manager

♦   Netscape Enterprise Server

♦   Apache Web Server

♦   Tomcat Servlet Engine for NetWare

♦   NetWare Web Search Server

♦   WebAccess for Clients

NetWare Web Manager

New with NetWare 6, Web Manager provides a variety of browser-based tools in one convenient location. Think of this as a front door to managing your Web services.

Almost all Web-based management tools, including Web Manager, run on the new Apache Web Server installed within NetWare 6. When you modify or reboot Web Manager, you affect Apache, not NetWare Enterprise Web Server.

That said, let's take a quick look at Web Manager. Simple, barely-graphical, and modifiable, Web Manager provides views inside the particular hardware server hosting the Web Manager server-side components. Take a look at Figure A.1 to see your Web management entry point.

Novell Marketing won't let us call this a Portal anymore; that name now belongs to a separate program. I understand the reasoning, but it would be nice if Novell Marketing acted on such things rather than reacted to them. Changing names causes more confusion and other problems than picking a new name for the other product would, but perhaps I underestimate the problems. (I doubt it.)

Web Manager really offers a handy way to reach local management tools across the Internet. Obviously, the tools work quite well locally, but the Web-based hook offers many advantages. Just remember this next time your beeper drags you from sweet dreams at 2:00 A.M. and you have to get dressed and go to the office because you haven't configured the browser-based utilities.

As you can see in Figure A.1, you have direct links from Web Manager to Enterprise Web Server maintenance, eDirectory (minimal operations through Netscape's NDS interface), the server hardware and software (Remote Manager), the FTP server, Web Search Server configuration, and the tools in iManage. Can you go directly to these other utilities? Sure, but then you'd have to remember all the details or bookmark each of them. Web Manager saves you some time and trouble.

Of all the tools, the eDirectory piece leaves the most to be desired. One may question how much of one's heart and soul to allow access to from remote sites; some managers may be upset at any access. By focusing on users and groups, Web Manager walks a fine line, I believe, between too much access and too little.

No extra installation routines need be mentioned, because Web Manager comes as part of the Apache Web Server package. The NSWEB.NCF file in the SYS:\SYSTEM directory gets listed in AUTOEXEC.NCF when any Web services are installed.

FIGURE A.1

The new NetWare
Web Manager

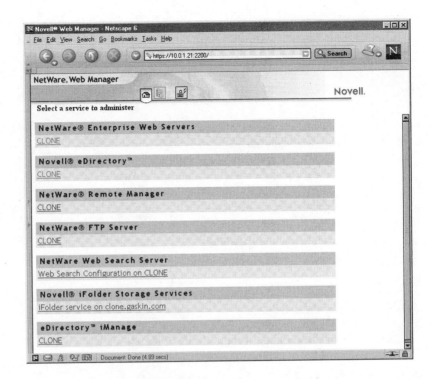

To take Web Manager down, type **NSWEBDN** at the server console colon prompt. Type **NSWEB** to restart the services, again at the colon prompt.

Setting Web Manager Preferences

Click the icon at the top of Web Manager that appears to be a desk with check marks next to it. This opens the Admin Preferences page, shown in Figure A.2.

You can't change too many items about Web Manager, but for security and control's sake, you can change the port number assignment. Although the default number of 2200 should work for most networks (according to the decent list of port number assignments in the online documentation section "Getting Results with Web Services"), you can change the number from the screen in Figure A.2.

Notice that you may change Encryption from the default setting of On to Off. Don't do that. This tool controls a large segment of your operating system components, and any security breach could severely damage your network. Remote administration without a fully secure connection should make you nervous.

The final setting on this page shows the source of your SSL certificate for this server. You may choose others if you wish, but if your host server issues certificates, take the easy road here and save your energy for another fight later.

Other menu items on the left frame of this page link you to:

Log Settings, where you choose the file locations for the access log and error log.

FIGURE A.2

Web Manager
Admin preferences

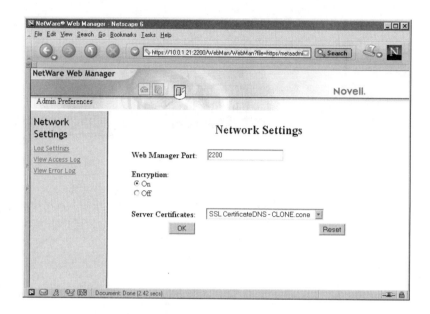

View Access Log, where you view the access log. You can set the number of entries that appear per screen and can search for text strings.

View Error Log, where you have the same options as for the access log.

NetWare Web Manager offers a clean look, easy access to important utilities, and security. When it works, it works great. When you can't get a browser to connect, restart the Web server or unload and reload Apache a time or two. There's still a conflict or two about which service gets loaded on which server and which port number, so if a connection proves difficult to find, try servers with and without a partition, with or without iFolder, and similar types of troubleshooting.

Firewall configuration, for allowing outside users into Web Manager on a server inside the protected network, includes opening TCP port 443, the common port for HTTPS (Hypertext Transfer Protocol Secure). If you already allow this opening, you will have to come up with another port for use by Web Manager, such as 5051, which must be set inside both your firewall and the Web Manager configuration screen.

Netscape Enterprise Server

NetWare 5 included Netscape FastTrack Server, the smaller version of Netscape's two Web servers. NetWare 5.1 included Enterprise Server, as does NetWare 6. In case you thought nothing new came with NetWare 6 on the Web server front, remember that Apache Web Server installs automatically when you add any Web services at all during NetWare installation.

Netscape Enterprise Server (now called NetWare Enterprise Web Server) and Apache Web Server can, and do, run well together. The Netscape server takes the default port number 80, but (if you remember the installation step) you can provide secondary IP addresses for Apache or use different port addresses.

NetWare 5.1 included the IBM WebSphere Application Server engine, but NetWare 6 replaces that with the Tomcat Servlet Engine. Any WebSphere applications written for 5.1 must be converted to Tomcat for NetWare 6, but only a few steps provide the conversion for you. If you upgrade the 5.1 server to version 6, read the migration information before starting the upgrade or you may ruin your day.

Enterprise Web Server supports multiple Web servers on a single physical host. You can configure either hardware virtual servers or software virtual servers. Either way, one NetWare server can host a large number of virtual Web servers.

Installing Enterprise Web Server

Web services components, including Netscape and Apache servers, automatically install whenever you ask for any Web components or use the Express installation process.

If Enterprise Web Server wasn't installed with the rest of the NetWare server, use the GUI Console Install routine to add the server. Follow these steps:

1. Put the CD-ROM holding NetWare into the server drive.

2. Mount the disk (type **CDROM** at the colon prompt if it doesn't mount automatically), and use the file browser to select the PRODUCT.INI file that holds the details about installable products. Files will churn and copy.

3. Select NetWare Enterprise Web Server from the list of products. Don't worry if the system automatically selects other products to install along with the Web server.

You're set. Files will copy, messages will come and go, and then your Web server will be ready for use.

All management goes through the NetWare Enterprise Web Server interface at the URL https://server-IP_or_DNS-name:2200 (as opposed to port 8008 for NetWare Remote Manager). Notice the https: in the URL. The s designates a secure connection over SSL (Secure Sockets Layer).

Administering Enterprise Web Server with Web Manager

Novell—or, technically, Novonyx, a joint venture between Novell and Netscape before AOL swallowed Netscape—ported the standard and comprehensive General Administration utility to NetWare. More than just running the utility on top of NetWare, Novonyx infused Netscape with NDS, making a powerful server for intranet use. No other Web server offers NetWare customers so much control over access, authentication, and content. The version shipping with NetWare 5.1 barely framed the Netscape utilities under a NetWare header, but NetWare 6 includes a reworked interface in keeping with the rest of the NetWare browser-based utilities.

The default opening screen when you click from Web Manager's opening screen to Enterprise Web Server could hardly be more dull: Server On / Off. Let's skip this screen and show you Figure A.3, the Server Settings menu option under Server Preferences.

FIGURE A.3

Server settings for
Enterprise Web
Server on CLONE

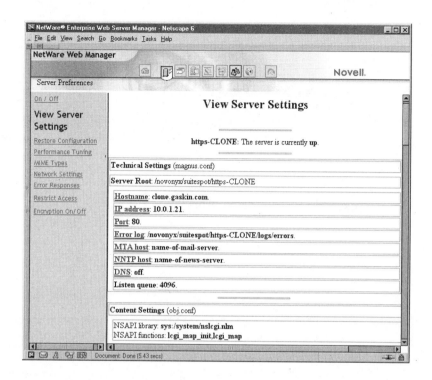

Web Manager replaced NetWare 5.1's Enterprise Server General Administration screen, which led to the FTP Server, Enterprise Server details, and even the Management Portal (now Remote Manager). The new Web Manager utility now offers access to many non-Netscape server functions, making the new arrangement more practical and more Novell-flavored.

NDS management features delve far too shallowly for real administration, but do offer enough depth to handle many simple problems. You wouldn't choose this option in place of ConsoleOne, but the ability to handle any NDS functions across the Internet may save you a midnight trip to your office.

Managing Enterprise Web Server from the Console

Interestingly enough, Novell/Novonyx also includes console controls, or at least Web server status information, on the NetWare console. The screens look just like the MONITOR screen, and they work the same way.

Figure A.4 shows the main screen from the Web Manager on the server console. Unlike MONITOR, the top screen doesn't expand when you make it active by pressing the Tab key.

Since the Netscape General Administration page doesn't show any throughput figures for the Web server itself, this screen on the NetWare server console comes in handy. Even the information in Portal doesn't break down the Web server parts of throughput and file activity.

FIGURE A.4

Old-fashioned management of a newfangled Web server

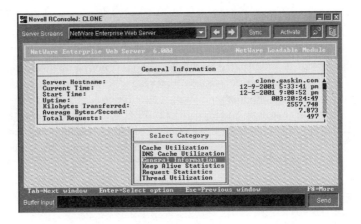

Handy breakdowns include the Request Statistics screen, shown in Figure A.5. The different numbers (2xx, 3xx, etc.) are status report numbers, defined by the World Wide Web Consortium (www.w3.org). You're no doubt as familiar with the 404: File Not Found message as I am and just as tired of cursing it when it appears; the 4xx statistic is a quick-and-easy flag if your server is generating these headaches for your visitors.

FIGURE A.5

Quick HTTP status information

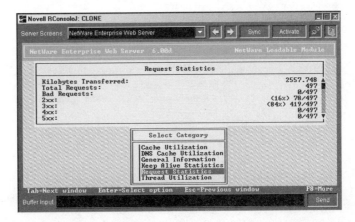

Do these screens provide as much information as a good Web site–monitoring package? Not at all. Do they help? Yes. Are they free? Yes, making them good, usable tools to carry you to the point where Web server success requires better tools to keep up with the marvelous traffic your site generates. Until then, C-Worthy yourself some status information.

Apache Web Server

Could Novell be suffering from bipolar Web disorder? Why add a second Web server when it already has the Netscape-built NetWare Enterprise Web Server under the hood?

Because customers want choices, and Apache Web Server remains the first choice for a huge number of Web services companies. Your ISP's "free Web pages" for every customer likely use Apache server software to keep the cost down.

Cost down? Yep. Apache Web Server comes from the open-source community; the not-for-profit Apache Software Foundation (`www.apache.org`) organized Apache development and helps focus and guide continuing development. Want the source code? You can get it.

Why use Apache as an alternate Web server (and probable replacement, although Novell won't tell me that outright)? Apache is free. Apache is stable. Apache is popular. Did I mention Apache is free?

Novell developers embraced Apache Web Server during NetWare 6 development. The following NetWare 6 functions depend on Apache:

- iFolder
- iManage
- iPrint
- NetWare Web Access
- NetWare NetStorage
- NetWare Web Manager
- NetWare Web Search Manager
- NetWare Web Search and Search Print Services

See a trend here? New Web-based tools or browser-based utilities all wound up written with Apache. Will Apache be the only Web server shipping in NetWare 6.1? I wouldn't bet against that idea.

NOTE *PC-speak warning: The name "Apache" reflects neither Indian (Native American) involvement, support, nor admiration. During development, someone realized the source code became "a patch-y" system because of all the updates. From there to Apache took little time.*

Using Apache Web Server

There's no installation extra steps necessary for Apache. If you add any Web services to your NetWare 6 server, Apache will get installed automatically.

It's a good thing this is so, because Novell didn't have time to integrate much information about Apache Web Server into its own documentation. In fact, you can hardly find any direct reference to Apache. You'll see the name in passing when discussing iFolder or Web Search Manager or the like, but I can't find any section heading offering "Apache Configuration."

Good thing Novell included the Apache manual, somewhat sparse though it may be. Figure A.6 shows the manual's index page.

If you can't read the URL in the screenshot, don't waste your time trying to find the manual via the front door to your Web server. The only way I can get the manual onscreen is via the File ➤ Open option on the Apache files on the file server.

In this case, ProLiant's SYS: volume holds the file. Browsing through File ➤ Open on the Netscape toolbar, I drilled down through APACHE ➤ HTDOCS ➤ MANUAL, then opened the INDEX.HTML.EN file. According to the Table of Contents, Apache became available for NetWare back as far as NetWare 5.0, but nobody told me.

The primary directory for Web files in Apache on NetWare 6 is the APACHE ➤ NWDOCS directory. Put your INDEX.HTML in this file and Apache Web Server becomes yours.

Unfortunately, Novell hasn't yet gotten around to wrapping the Apache CONF files in an HTML blanket. Web administration in Netscape offers more help files, more easily, than does the Apache method of studying the included configuration files. Maybe with NetWare 6.1 we'll get all the Apache configuration operations customized for NetWare users.

Supporting User Web Pages

Users can create and maintain private pages on the Apache server, just as with NetWare Enterprise Web Server. There's one small warning posted by Novell for servers used this way, however.

Make sure the server hosting the Apache Web Server software includes an NDS replica. For some reason, if the host server does not include a replica, users can't see their private pages. The users authenticate through NDS, but the page access request returns one of those ugly 404 errors.

This will likely be fixed in the first support pack, but until then, keep a replica on the Apache server. Not hard, but you do have to remember.

Tomcat Servlet Engine for NetWare

Network administrators may not spend much time reading this section, but your Webmasters and development team might. If your company uses server-side applications, you want to know about Tomcat. This open-source application server, from the same group that developed Apache Web Server, replaces the WebSphere Application Server included with NetWare 5.1.

The Novell documentation includes the quick few commands required to prepare WebSphere applications for use by Tomcat when upgrading a NetWare 5.1 server to NetWare 6. Check out the "Getting Results with Novell Web Services" listing on the online documentation so you'll get all the updates. You'll also find instructions to undo the migration, if that becomes important.

Novell also put the Tomcat documentation on the NetWare 6 file server. Check Figure A.7 for the opening screen.

Just as with Apache, the Tomcat applications (both versions 3.3 and 3.2 are included) have their own directory starting at the root of the SYS: volume. Drill down to the DOC directory of whichever version you prefer.

FIGURE A.7

Tomcat documenta-
tion for Web
developers

NetWare Web Search Server

Ever noticed Novell's Web site search engine seems faster and more accurate than many others on the Web? Now you can put the same search technology to work in your own network. Whether you use NetWare Web Search Server internally only or put it on your outward-facing Web site for the world to use, all the search horsepower you need comes in the red box with the rest of NetWare 6.

The NetWare Web Search Server reads common HTML and XML files as you would expect, but it doesn't stop there. Most of the "office productivity" files used today also get indexed, including Word, PowerPoint, Quattro Pro, RTF, and regular TXT files. Indexed sites supported by a single Search Server are limited only by the hosting server horsepower.

If, for some reason, NetWare Web Search managed to avoid the clutches of the installation routine, load it directly like any other program. But adding almost any Web service during NetWare installation tends to pull the Web Search application into the mix, so check the SYS: volume for the \NSEARCH directory. That's where the automated installation process puts Web Search by default.

Using NetWare Web Search

You may believe building a search site will take hours and hours and cost you handfuls of hair tugged in frustration. Let me put your mind (and hair) at ease. Take a look at the opening search screen in Figure A.8.

FIGURE A.8

Play digital hide and seek.

Want to know how much time and trouble it took to write this screen? Zero. This is the default screen. For internal use, your search screen can roll out tomorrow with no problems.

Notice I put a search phrase in the text entry box, "NetWare 6." The results, again by default without having to code a single HTML tag, appear in Figure A.9.

Not hard, and it doesn't take long.

Building a Search Site

The NetWare Web Search Server administration screens most easily come off the Web Manager page. By default, the Web Search Manager displays Global Settings focusing on the Site List. The opening site list, as configured by default, appears in Figure A.10.

How did the user find this? Just use the Web Search Server host's Web server URL with a /novel-1search after the domain name or IP address. See the command button at the bottom of the page asking you to Add New Site? It's not hard. Click the button, then supply the following information:

Site Name	This can be any name to identify the site, but it's best to use the domain name to be indexed.
Site Alias	The IP address
Store Files At	The disk location to keep the index files (*.IDX) generated by the search process

Those who wish to dive deeper may build templates to transform the search interface, the material transmitted, and the results page provided to the users. If your Webmaster has been complaining about upkeep on search engines, show them Novell Web Search Server and see how they like it.

FIGURE A.10

Management tool
opening screen

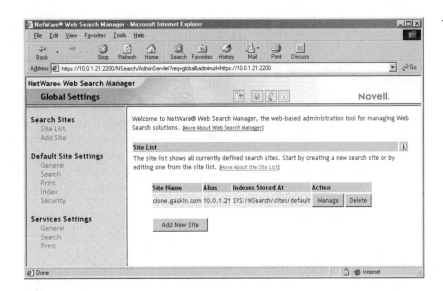

WebAccess for Clients

NetWare WebAccess will grow into a cool product, but it isn't quite there yet. The promise, however, makes it worth the time to take a quick look.

The best way to describe WebAccess? It provides access to Web services for users. Any wonder how they stumbled on that name?

Think of WebAccess as sort of a Web Manager for users—a gateway to several tools they can use. Figure A.11 shows the best formed of the tools not already covered.

FIGURE A.11

Michael is a
popular name.

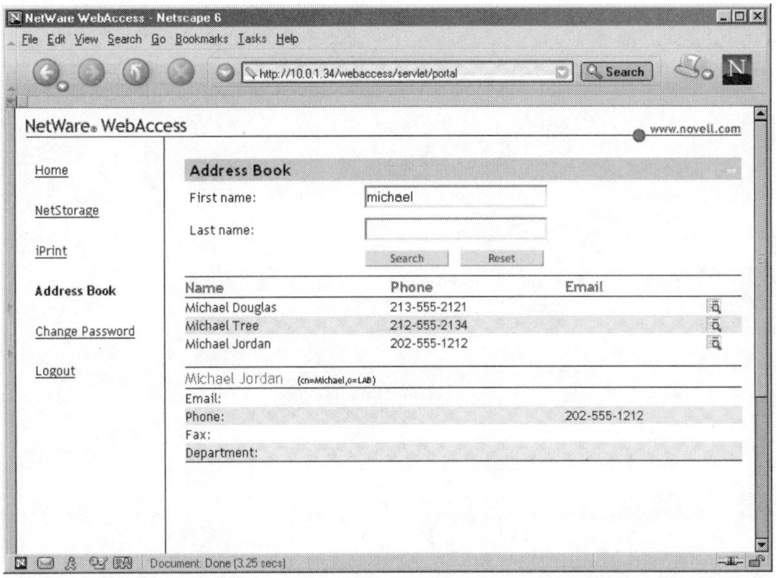

Notice the five functions in the left frame (six if you count Logout as a function). Home pops you back to the Login screen. NetStorage opens the NetStorage utility, tied to the username and password given for WebAccess authentication. We talked about iPrint all through Chapter 6, and I'm tired of it now, so don't ask me again. Change Password provides an easy way for users to change their own passwords, if you allow them to do so.

The last utility, Address Book, works as a demonstration tool in two ways. One, it shows how the WebAccess utility gathers useful tools in one place. Two, it shows that Novell engineers still believe all customers should use NDS eDirectory as the corporate name and address file.

The top half of the Address Book screen stays blank awaiting a user request. When you first see this screen, the two name text fields remain empty and everything below the Search and Reset buttons is white space. Type in either a first or last name, click Search, and the results appear in the bottom of the Address Book screen.

When you click the magnifying glass to the far right of the name listings, the full name and other information appear. Since I clicked Michael Jordan (not that one—this is a one-legged bookkeeper for a trucking firm), more information appears.

With a bit of work, your programmers, Webmasters, and other clever folks can tie in GroupWise, Exchange, Lotus Notes, NIMS (Novell Internet Messaging Service), or any IMAP e-mail service. These are called "gadgets," and more can be added through ConsoleOne. Look inside the WebAccess organizational unit created during the installation of WebAccess, and pay special attention to the WebAccess_Configuration_All_Users object. When you click the Configure button, a wizard starts to lead you through WebAccess configuration.

Appendix B

Upgrades, Migration, and Windows Client and Server Installation Support

MANY BUYERS OF NETWARE 6 will be current NetWare customers. That has been the case with previous NetWare upgrades, and it will be the case in the future. Once you're a NetWare customer, you tend to remain a NetWare customer (much to Microsoft's chagrin).

Being a NetWare customer doesn't mean that you automatically upgrade with every NetWare release. This causes Novell engineers some problems, because they must support users back on NetWare 3 as well as those running NetWare 6. This wide range of supported NetWare versions has created several upgrade options, which are the subject of the second half of this appendix.

First, however, I want to discuss Client32 for Windows 95/98. I'll describe how to install it and how to configure the client once it is installed.

Upgrading Windows 95/98 Clients to Client32 Version 3.00

Novell's new NetWare 6 Client32 family of products, available for Windows 95, 98, NT, 2000, and XP, are the clients of choice for connection to NetWare networks. They offer many more features and capabilities than Microsoft's clients. You may ask, "Why bother installing Novell's client when Microsoft's client is on the operating system CD for 95, 98, NT, and 2000?" The answer is simple: Microsoft has nothing to gain by giving you a powerful, full-featured client. Microsoft needs to provide connectivity with Novell servers for marketing reasons, but it would much rather you use NT/2000 Server instead of NetWare. Novell, on the other hand, has a vested interest in providing you the best possible client to keep you as a customer.

In this section, I'll discuss installing and configuring Client32 and discuss the Windows 95/98 version of the client. Other installations are similar. For complete information and for other versions of the client or other operating systems, see the online documentation.

NOTE *Don't bother looking for clients for DOS and Windows 3.1 systems, however. They aren't included. If you still have those systems in place, I feel for you, but you'll have to go to Novell's Web site to download those clients.*

Installing Client32

Installation is about as simple as it can get. You have several options, all discussed in the online documentation, to automate rolling out the client to many users. They include the Automatic Client Upgrade (ACU) and several options for installing Client32 while Windows 95/98 is being installed. I will focus on running the setup program and understanding how it works.

Inserting the NetWare Client CD into a CD-ROM drive in a Windows 95/98/NT/2000 system with auto-run enabled pops open a new Novell client splash screen, as shown in Figure B.1. Only the options that can be installed on the target computer will be highlighted when running the cursor over the text, as the Windows 95/98 pop-up text shows in the figure.

FIGURE B.1

An intelligent splash screen for Novell client installation

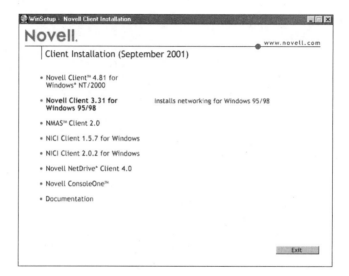

Another option, if you don't have the auto-run toggle set to start each new CD automatically, is to run WINSETUP.EXE on the Client CD. When ready, click the client installation routine of your choice, such as the one highlighted in Figure B.1 for Windows 95/98 (this client only works for Windows 95 with Service Pack 1 installed).

You'll see a fairly typical license agreement (does anyone read those things?). Click Yes to display the Welcome screen, shown in Figure B.2.

As you can see, you have two choices here:

◆ Typical

◆ Custom

When you select Typical, the default button in the bottom of the screen is Install. If you are installing the client for the first time, you can choose the directory in which to install (take the default). If you are upgrading, the client is installed in the directory where it was installed previously (which should be the default).

Click the View README button at least once. You won't learn interesting stuff there, but you should check it out.

FIGURE B.2

Typical won't hurt, but Custom offers more control.

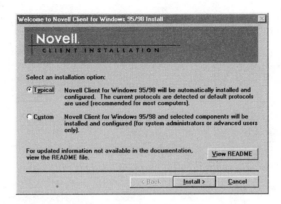

There are no more choices for you when you choose Typical: The installation takes off, using IPX and IP for the protocols and using all the IP configuration information within Windows. Your next move is to reboot to activate the new client.

I suggest you try the Custom option, at least until you feel comfortable with the client choices NetWare provides. For one thing, I feel helpless when the dialog box pops up saying "removing existing client software" and I can't stop the process, when I haven't even been told exactly what the process includes. I don't want you to feel helpless, so learn what's happening, then choose Typical if it works for your network.

Protocol choices come in the next screen after choosing the Custom installation (Figure B.3). As you can see, you can choose to communicate with NetWare servers over the following:

◆ IP Only (and optionally remove IPX if it is installed)

◆ IP with IPX Compatibility

◆ IP and IPX

◆ IPX

FIGURE B.3

Protocol choices aren't forever, but they are most conveniently made here.

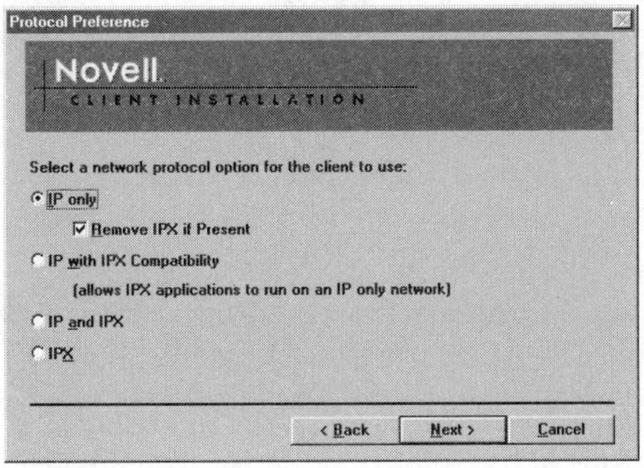

Unless you are sure that you have a pure IP or IPX environment and it's certain to stay that way, I would choose IP and IPX (the default) to ensure access to all servers. The memory used by adding IPX to your client mix won't ruin anything, and this option may eliminate a problem or two with some legacy software. Figure B.3 shows the IP Only box checked to better show the Remove IPX If Present option.

Click Next, and you are asked if you want to default to an NDS or a bindery connection when logging in (NDS is the default). Unless you have only NetWare 3 servers (in which case you probably aren't reading this book), leave the default NDS selected.

Once your eDirectory client needs are finished, click Next to display the Optional Components screen. This appears in Figure B.4.

FIGURE B.4

Custom choices for clients

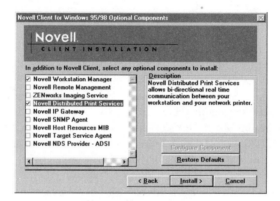

Selecting Custom in the Welcome screen installs the core client and the following options:

- ◆ Novell Workstation Manager
- ◆ Novell Distributed Print Services (NDPS) client

The documentation describes these options in detail, so I will give you only a brief overview. Before I do that, though, I want to point out that you can modify these settings later. Here are the steps:

1. In Control Panel, choose Network.

2. Choose Add ➢ Service ➢ Novell, and select the component you want to modify.

3. To add a component, enter its location.

4. To delete a component, select it and choose Remove.

WARNING *You are not prompted before removing anything, so be sure to select the correct component before clicking Remove.*

You can add or remove all components, except for the Novell NDS provider, ADSI, in this manner. You can install the ADSI provider only during setup. To configure an optional component (if possible; some are not), simply select it, click Properties, and modify the settings in the dialog box.

NOTE   *I won't discuss the configuration options here, but you'll find some of them in the body of this book, and you'll find all of them in the online documentation.*

Click the Install button, and watch files load and semi-informative dialog boxes tell you what's happening. Then cross your fingers and reboot. Well, that's not fair. Installation improvements by Novell almost always guarantee success. (Almost always.)

NOTE   *XP Upgrade Note: If you're upgrading a computer from Windows 2000 to XP, you must uninstall the Net-Ware client, upgrade the computer, then reinstall Client32.*

Understanding the Options

From the Optional Components screen, you can choose from among several components. When you select one, you'll see a description of it in a box on the right. Let's briefly look at each of these options.

Novell Workstation Manager   Allows user and desktop settings to be centrally stored and managed. Users can access their personal settings anywhere on the network, but at the cost of downloading (possibly across WAN links) profile information. This is a great option for central control and, therefore, is selected by default.

Novell Remote Management   Relies on the Workstation Manager software components to allow remote control over workstations, especially with ZENworks management software.

ZENworks Imaging Service   More ZENworks help (and push to manage with ZENworks). Allows ZENworks to take a snapshot of the computer's configuration details and reset them if necessary.

Novell Distributed Print Services (NDPS)   The client portion of the NDPS system that allows you to browse for printing resources and automatically download and install drivers for printers as they are used. Unless you are not installing NDPS and have no plans to do so, select this option. For more information, see Chapter 6.

Novell IP Gateway   This was a big deal before Microsoft loaded TCP/IP onto every client (without proper security settings or help information, may I kvetch), and Novell and other vendors made special gateway servers that translated IPX packets into TCP/IP for Internet connections. This component is rarely used now, even though using IPX internally with an IP gateway provides the highest internal security possible. Don't know why they kept this in NetWare 6, but here it is.

Novell SNMP Agent   As you may recall from earlier discussions, the Simple Network Management Protocol (SNMP) allows you to request information from a workstation from a central network monitoring station (called a *management console*). In addition, it allows a workstation to notify a management console about an unusual event. If you have SNMP and a management console (such as ZENworks) installed, select this option.

Host Resources MIB for the Novell Client   Allows the management console to request inventory information (such as CPU, amount of RAM, and so on) and have the client reply. If you have SNMP and a management console installed, select this option.

Network Target Service Agent   Allows you to back up a workstation's hard drive during the normal backup process for your servers. You will not normally advertise this fact to your clients, as one of the benefits of using a network is central storage and backup. If your clients know they can store anything on their local drives and still have them backed up, they will, and then they will bother you whenever something gets deleted, damaged, and so on. With rare exceptions, I would not make this capability known, nor would I want to do it if possible.

Novell NDS Provider—ADSI   Microsoft has come up with a new method of doing what NDS has done for years and is calling it ADSI (Active Directory Services Interface). It appeared in Windows 2000, but since Microsoft hasn't released version 1.1 as of this writing, the marketing hype remains unfulfilled. Oh, yeah, there are lots of security problems, too. This client allows ADSI client applications to access data stored in NDS, such that the client application doesn't have to be aware of whether the server being accessed is based on ADSI or NDS. I would install this choice for compatibility with future ADSI-aware applications. Remember, this is the only option that you cannot add or remove after setup.

Once you make all your selections, click Install to install them. When you have finished, click Reboot to restart your computer so that all the changes can take effect. You don't have to cross your fingers anymore, since this process works almost all the time, but you may bite your lip with apprehension if you wish.

Configuring the Client

Once the client is installed and operating, you may want to modify some of the options you installed or change some of the parameters for an installed option. To do so, follow these steps:

1. Choose Control Panel ➢ Network.

2. Select the component you want to modify.

3. Choose Properties.

NOTE   Help is available by clicking the ? in the upper-right corner of the dialog box or by clicking the Help button. It is also available, in great detail, in the online documentation.

The component that you will be modifying most often is the core component of the client. You do so by choosing Novell NetWare Client ➢ Properties to open the Novell Client Configuration dialog box, which you can see in Figure B.5. You can also find this same dialog box by right-clicking the big red *N* on the taskbar and choosing Novell Client Properties.

As you can see, this dialog box has nine tabs:

Client   This tab is the most used. Here you can specify the preferred server and/or tree, the default name context, and the first network drive.

FIGURE B.5

More client proper-
ties than a landlord

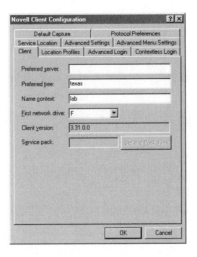

Location Profiles   Here you can specify locations that are useful if a user travels or if multiple users share a computer. Each profile tracks items such as user name and context to make it easier for users to log in.

Advanced Login   If you want to give users more control over the login process, this is the place to do so. The four check boxes here give the user some additional options:

♦   Show Location List on Login

♦   Show Advanced Button on Login

♦   Show Variables Button on Login

♦   Show Clear Connections on Login

Contextless Login   Here you can enable login to the network without a context within eDirectory.

Service Location   This tab allows you to configure how the client will get information from the Service Location Protocol (if you are using TCP/IP).

Advanced Settings   The only one of these 11 settings that you may need to modify is to change the File Cache Level from 3 (lots of cache) to 1 (not so much cache) for RAM-limited stations.

Advanced Menu Settings   This is the place where all the old NET.CFG options are set, as well as many new ones. You'll rarely need this tab, but it is very handy when you are directed to change a parameter to fix some problem. There are 63 parameters here.

Default Capture   Here you can specify the default capture settings, such as banners, form feeds, and so on, so that when a login script simply has Capture P=Printer, your preferred settings are used. I like to set defaults here as well as in every login script, explicitly specifying any options that I want (even those that I set as defaults). You'll find more information on printing in Chapter 6; login scripts are covered in Chapter 5.

Protocol Preferences   Here you can specify your primary (or first choice) protocol as IP or IPX. To resolve server names to IP or IPX addresses, you can specify which methods should be used and in what order.

As I mentioned, this is only a brief overview of what is available. Many of the options in this section and the previous one are discussed elsewhere in the book, and references have been made to them. The Novell Web site online documentation is the source of the latest, as well as the most detailed, information.

Other Client Installations

Back in Figure B.1, we took off and installed the appropriate NetWare Client32 software (version 4.81 for Windows NT/2000/XP or version 3.31 for Windows 95/98/ME) before looking at other installation options. Let's fix that oversight right now.

NMAS Client 2.0   Novell Modular Authentication Service (NMAS) offers extra ways to protect information on the network and coordinate NDS eDirectory across multiple platforms. Available optionally, a limited version of NMAS ships with NetWare 6. Some security and administration functions require NMAS support, explaining the presence of the NMAS client on the CD-ROM.

NICI Client 1.5.7 for Windows   Novell International Cryptographic Infrastructure provides the client underpinnings for security modules. This version, 1.5.7, supports NMAS and Novell Single Sign-on.

NICI Client 2.0.2 for Windows   This version of NICI supports the Certificate Server.

Novell NetDrive Client 4.0   Chapter 13 describes using a smaller NetWare client (not the full Client32 software) to link to NetWare servers. Any Windows 95/98/NT/2000/XP system with this small client software can use NetDrive to map a single drive letter to a NetWare server.

Novell ConsoleOne   Administration workstations should definitely install the ConsoleOne software locally. Not only does the administration application load and run faster, extra software snap-ins get loaded that aren't reachable when running the utility from the NetWare server.

Documentation   A cheat: the documentation doesn't transfer from the CD-ROM to your local hard drive as in some earlier NetWare versions. This menu item merely kick-starts your Web browser and connects to www.novell.com/documentation.

Options for Upgrading Your Server

Depending on your current system, you can use one of the following methods to upgrade to NetWare 6:

The NetWare 6 installation program   The INSTALL.BAT program offers an easy way to upgrade your NetWare 3.1x, 4x, or 5.x server to NetWare 6. With this option, there is little difference between upgrading and installing a new server.

Novell Upgrade Wizard   The Novell Upgrade Wizard, running on a Windows 98/NT/2000/XP client workstation, copies bindery information and server data between a Net-

Ware 2, 3, 4, or 5 server to the new NetWare 6 server. The data on the older NetWare server is only copied, not changed. Bindery entries are migrated to NDS objects. This option used to be called an Across-the-Wire Migration.

If you upgrade a NetWare 6 server with NSS volumes enabled, you must run the following procedure from the server console to upgrade those NSS volumes to NSS 3.0:

```
NSS /XLSSVOLUMEUPGRADE=ALL
```

Let me say this for the first of many times: no matter how you upgrade your server, make at least two (2) copies of all data that will be migrated. Any information of value on the earlier version of NetWare that you want to use under NetWare 6 should be backed up to tape or rewriteable optical disks. Doing both would be an excellent safety measure.

Am I paranoid? Yes, always, especially about server disk operations. Make a backup before doing any operation that affects a server disk. Converting to a new version of NetWare is no different: back up or be sorry. That's such a good line, let's say it again: back up or be sorry.

Okay, back to your options for upgrading. Which of these routes makes the most sense for your situation? Here's a matrix that should give you some guidance.

FROM NETWARE VERSION	HARDWARE (SAME OR DIFFERENT)	RECOMMENDATION
NetWare 2.x	Different	Novell Upgrade Wizard
NetWare 3.x	Same (are you sure?)*	INSTALL.BAT
	Different	Novell Upgrade Wizard
NetWare 4	Same	INSTALL.BAT
	Different	Novell Upgrade Wizard
NetWare 5	Same	INSTALL.BAT
	Different	Novell Upgrade Wizard

Are you sure that you want to use the same hardware? See the next section, "Before You Upgrade Your Server, Think Again," for cautions.

Remember, there are two pieces to your upgrade: the bindery information (in the case of NetWare 2 and 3) and NDS information (in the case of NetWare 4 and 5), and the data on the server.

Before You Upgrade Your Server, Think Again

I want to distinguish between upgrading your network operating system to NetWare 6 and upgrading your existing physical server to NetWare 6. The first is usually a good idea; the second is often not.

When you bought your old server—say, the server now running NetWare 4.1—you bought the best hardware you could afford. If you're lucky, and price wasn't an option, you got a serious server with lots of RAM, a big hard disk, and as fast a processor as possible (Pentium 120 was a popular model at the time). The serious server likely had an EISA (Extended Industry Standard Architecture) bus, or perhaps it was an IBM model using a Microchannel bus. Today, unfortunately, this setup doesn't even make a good workstation.

Look what has happened to each of your server's features:

RAM   16MB used to be plenty for a server (believe it or not); now that amount is barely adequate for a PDA. Retail PCs often come with 128MB or more of RAM; your server should start at 512MB and increase RAM quickly.

Hard disk   1GB was a big disk for early NetWare 3.x. Today, PCs bought at office supply stores and Wal-Mart have 20GB (and larger) hard disks.

Hard disk controller   SCSI (Small Computer Systems Interface) controllers were the rage as NetWare 3.x became popular. Today, SCSI-2 and Fast and Wide SCSI multiply the throughput of your SCSI adapter. EIDE (Enhanced IDE) drives and controllers have broken the 512MB disk-size barrier and offer great speed and throughput, although SCSI is still preferable.

486 or Pentium I or II processor   NetWare 3.x ran well on a 486, even on a processor slower than 50MHz. However, the number of NLMs has grown, and the addition of Java and a GUI at the server places more pressure on the server processor than ever before. Your average user would be insulted to get a PC with "only" a Pentium III processor. A fast Pentium 4 (or Pentium III) processor is necessary for any server supporting more than a workgroup.

EISA or Microchannel bus   Microchannel has been officially stopped by IBM; no other vendors seriously supported it. EISA unofficially died. PCI (Peripheral Component Interconnect) bus slots and corresponding adapters are winners in the server bus race. PCI slots provide the throughput necessary for the 100Mb Ethernet adapters now standard, and they support the Gigabit Ethernet cards becoming cheaper each week.

CD-ROM drive   Does your old server have a bootable CD-ROM drive? Make sure your new one does.

What does all this mean? Your old server is way underpowered today, even if you bought the box last year. Upgrading the server would probably take too much money, especially if your motherboard doesn't support high-capacity RAM modules. Your old disk controller is outdated, so just getting a bigger disk won't help enough. Besides, new servers are becoming more affordable as disk prices plummet and the cost of Pentium processors is forced lower by their new processor competitors.

Face it, your old server needs to be retired.

Of course, you must read this with your particular situation in mind. If you have a P/60 with 64MB RAM, 2GB hard disk, and an ISA network adapter supporting 20 non-power users, your server has some life left—as an underpowered e-mail client. That configuration is not even adequate for a workgroup server today.

What can you do with it? If your server is the same configuration (or close) as the example, it will work as a low-end workstation or spare computer.

How Data Migrates

The first thing to do before migrating your data from an old server to a nice, new NetWare 6 server is to back up your data. Then back up that same data again, preferably with a different type of device so any errors in your hardware or software won't mess up two backups. If you do two backups with the same hardware and software, you might reproduce in the second backup any error made during the first backup.

Of course, if you are migrating to new server hardware, you'll have less fear and paranoia about your backup. If both the old and the new replacement server are up and running, any migration glitch is merely inconvenient rather than catastrophic. But even in the two-server scenario, you aren't absolved from the need to back up the original server. (Remember, back up or be sorry.)

Before any data-file migration, there are some things you must do in preparation for the big move:

◆ Delete unneeded files. No sense in taking old, worthless files to your nice, new server. If you want to consolidate some directories, the time to do so is before the migration.

◆ If you are upgrading from NetWare 2 or 3, run BINDFIX before migrating. BINDFIX will clean up the trustee rights and mail subdirectories of deleted users.

The Novell Upgrade Wizard is a new utility that helps organize NetWare 2 and 3 bindery information into NDS format before migration. It allows you to choose which volumes to migrate. You can migrate all volumes or different volumes to different NetWare 6 servers. You might want to move files on one NetWare 2.x or 3.x server to several NetWare 6 servers. Any upgrade or other change is a good time to reorganize your network. Use the wizard or INSTALL.BAT to move from NetWare 2, 3, 4, or 5 servers.

A Windows 98/NT/2000/XP management station is required when using the Novell Upgrade Wizard. The same tool facilitates file migration.

How File Attributes Migrate

The advantage of using the Novell Upgrade Wizard is the retention of all NetWare file attributes. If a file on a NetWare 3.x server is marked as Read Only and Shareable, it will transfer to the new system as Read Only and Shareable.

There are some new file attributes to consider: migration attributes and compression. The migration attributes do not concern the migration from one NetWare version to another, but the migration from the server hard disk to a near-line data storage facility.

After you run the Novell Upgrade Wizard, you must manually go through the files and directories on the NetWare 6 system and set any compression attributes. Don't trust the migration utility to read your mind when setting the compression attributes on the new files. Manually check each volume and directory after migration to ensure that attributes are set the way you want them. If you want the defaults, the migration utility is fine, but if you want to force immediate compression or to never allow a file to be compressed, you will need to set the attributes manually.

Upgrading Bindery Information

NetWare 3.x servers became the workhorses for most corporate networks, so migrating the bindery information became critical. It's one thing to re-create the security profile for a dozen users after a migration, but quite another to re-create thousands of security profiles. If you still have NetWare 3 servers around, this will matter.

The largest area of concern is trustee rights. The Novell Upgrade Wizard will do much of the work for you, but you will (again) be forced to verify that the rights have been transferred properly.

System login scripts are not migrated. These have been replaced in NetWare 6 by Container login scripts. Since there may be several Container login scripts on every NetWare 6 server, the earlier System login script has no direct correlation in NetWare 6.

User login scripts are transferred, but no corrections are made. The new names of servers and the changed directory structure will not be reflected in the transferred login scripts. You must manually make these changes in all login scripts or, better yet, disable local login scripts completely.

Take special care with the directory paths in the new system. The volume names are probably the same in the NetWare 6 server as the older NetWare server in a one-to-one server upgrade. However, many companies use the upgrade as a chance to combine several older servers onto one new server or change the location of files and directories to reflect their new network design. In these cases, volumes will have new names and/or servers. These changes must be made in the login scripts.

With NetWare 3.x, multiple servers were available through the ATTACH command. NetWare 6 doesn't use the ATTACH command; NDS makes it easy to connect one user to many NetWare servers. All NetWare 3.x–specific login commands must be updated. Refer to the online documentation for details and issues when upgrading.

Where to Go from Here

The first place you should go from here is to telephone your NetWare reseller and buy a new server rather than upgrade your old server. The only possible exceptions are when upgrading from a later version of NetWare 5 to NetWare 6 or when you are placing the upgraded server into a light-duty situation. If you're coming from NetWare 3.x, your server is far too old, slow, and limited in memory and hard drive even to probably even install NetWare 6.

But since your budget or your boss (or both) may restrict your ability to buy the hardware you know you need, we must push onward. Right or wrong, you've got to get a system up and running.

Be sure to read the online documentation for the hardware requirements for a good NetWare 6 server. All the detailed information on installation and upgrading existing NetWare servers is in there. After you read Chapter 1 of this book, review my instructions before beginning.

Upgrades Always Have a Hang-Up

There are lots of problems the manuals don't warn you about, of course. Whatever you think is adequate for your data backup procedures probably isn't. Go back and add one more backup or file copy of critical files.

Whatever time you have budgeted for the upgrade and changeover, increase the time. Double it if possible; more time will be needed than you imagine.

It isn't your fault (or mine) if it takes you longer to upgrade your existing system than you thought it would. You upgraders may have some information to "unlearn." Administrators new to NetWare 6 start without the baggage of remembering how things used to be and getting confused when NetWare 6 is different from the NetWare version in use now.

Life is tough enough; don't make it harder by rushing into NetWare 6 before you check out the terrain. Every hour spent planning your upgrade or new installation will repay you tenfold in making your network a positive experience for your users.

Appendix C

NetWare 6 SET Commands

THIS APPENDIX DESCRIBES A few of the SET commands and parameters, which are grouped in 14 categories. The parameters not described here are those that are infrequently used or otherwise not generally modified. See the online documentation for more information about these parameters. The values shown are defaults.

Here are the categories of SET commands. I don't talk about every one, but the ones I do discuss are in this order—except that I start off with the miscellaneous commands, for a specific reason you'll see in a minute:

◆ Common File System

◆ Communications

◆ Directory Services

◆ Disk

◆ Error Handling

◆ Licensing Services

◆ Memory

◆ Miscellaneous

◆ Multiprocessor

◆ NCP (NetWare Core Protocol)

◆ Novell Storage Services

◆ Service Location Protocol (SLP)

◆ Time

◆ Traditional File System

Introduction to SET Commands

You will rarely need to change any SET parameters during normal use. NetWare has come a long way, and many of these settings are dynamic in NetWare 6. Change a setting only in response to a specific problem or when directed by support personnel.

Here's the list of parameters dynamically adjusted by the NetWare operating systems as needed during regular operations:

- Directory cache buffers

- File cache buffers

- File locks

- Kernel processes

- Kernel semaphores

- Load balancing for multiple processors

- Maximum number of open files

- Memory for NLM programs

- Packet receive buffers

- Router/server advertising

- Service processes

- TTS transactions

- Turbo FAT index tables

Early on, there was one way to change SET parameters: the console command line. Now we have three ways, at least officially: the console command line, MONITOR, and NetWare Remote Manager.

Realistically, we now have only one way to deal with SET parameters. Take a look at Figure C.1, showing the new way to view and change SET commands.

Set Parameters, the third menu option under the second heading (Manage Server) in the left frame, provides more information inside Remote Manager than ever before

Contrast the new management tool with the old, shown in Figure C.2. The old C-Worthy interface still lives, and probably will for another version or two.

You should recognize this interface as the MONITOR program. This screen hides beneath the Server Parameters menu item on the MONITOR opening screen. MONITOR took a giant step forward over the console command line option, and Remote Manager takes just as big a step over MONITOR. Big improvement, I promise.

The help screens in MONITOR ➢ Server Parameters gave a bit more information with NetWare 5.1, but that advantage no longer rings true. Help screens, or more technically "information" screens (the little *i* icon stand for Information, not I Need Help), inside NetWare Remote Manager offer all the MONITOR information plus a bit extra. There's no reason now to go back to the command console or MONITOR if you have NetWare Remote Manager available.

FIGURE C.1

Web browsers are now the best SET command interface.

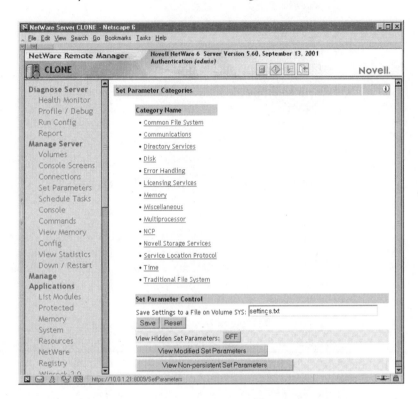

FIGURE C.2

The old SET command interface

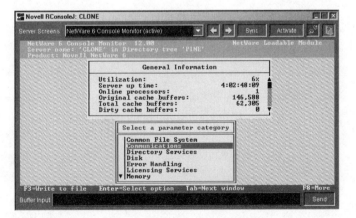

Miscellaneous SET Commands

```
Sound Bell for Alerts = On
```

This parameter sets the console to beep or not when an alert appears. My first change on every new server is to set this parameter to Off.

```
Replace Console Prompt with Server Name = On
```

This parameter places the server name to the left of the console prompt (a colon, :).

Sorry to start out of alphabetical order, but the Sound Bell for Alerts default setting makes my teeth grind with all the "alerts" banging the little beep button. If your servers sit within earshot of any other employees, you owe it to them to stop the beeping before it even starts.

Common File System SET Commands

```
Minimum File Delete Wait Time = 1 Min 5.9 Sec
```

Files deleted are not gone until purged. This is a wonderful feature, especially when you immediately realize that you have deleted drive F: when you meant drive A:. This parameter says that a file must be salvageable at least this long, even when the volume is full and users have no new space. If there is plenty of room on the volume, a file may be salvageable for weeks. The range for this setting is 0 seconds to 7 days.

```
File Delete Wait Time = 5 Min 29.6 Sec
```

The Minimum File Delete Wait Time setting defines the minimum wait time; this setting is for the wait time, and the same situation applies. If the file is deleted but there is plenty of room on the volume, it will not be purged for quite a while. When the volume finally fills with regular and purgeable files, the oldest purgeable files are erased first. The range for this setting is 0 seconds to 7 days.

Directory Services SET Commands

```
NDS Trace to Screen = Off
```

When set to On, this parameter displays NDS events on the server console screen.

```
NDS Trace to File = Off
```

When set to On, this parameter sends NDS events to a trace file. The default file is SYSTEM\DSTRACE.DBG, but that can be changed when starting the NDS log file (see the following setting, NDS Trace Filename). The maximum size of the trace file is about 500KB, after which new information overwrites the oldest.

```
NDS Trace Filename = SYSTEM\DSTRACE.DBG
```

This parameter is the default value for the NDS trace file mentioned previously. The maximum path length for the complete filename, including the path, is 254 characters. It is always stored on the SYS: volume.

Disk SET Commands

```
Enable Disk Read After Write Verify = Off
```

Enable this portion of Hot Fix if you have a single disk or multiple disks that are not mirrored. If your disks are mirrored and reliable, you can gain extra speed by setting this parameter to Off. Disable this parameter for disks and drivers that perform their own read-after-write verification to avoid doing this verification twice. This setting affects disks loaded after the parameter is changed; put it in your STARTUP.NCF file for regular use.

```
Ignore Disk Geometry = Off
```

This setting allows creation or modification of nonstandard and otherwise unsupported partitions. The default is Off.

WARNING   *Setting Ignore Disk Geometry to On may have drastic, negative consequences for any other file system (such as FAT or NTFS).*

Error Handling SET Commands

```
Server Log File Overflow Size = 4194304
```

This parameter sets the maximum file size for the SYS$LOG.ERR file. The range for this setting is 65,536 to 4,294,967,295 bytes. When this value is reached, the action specified in Server Log File State occurs.

```
Server Log File State = 1
```

This parameter specifies what happens when the SYS$LOG.ERR file grows larger than the set limit. The settings are:

0   Do nothing

1   Delete the log file

2   Rename the log file

Memory SET Commands

```
Average Page In Alert Threshold = 2000
```
A "page in" occurs when the virtual memory (VM) system needs data returned to memory that has been paged out to disk. An alert will be issued at the console when the average over the last five seconds exceeds this value. If this is a frequent problem, it means either that your server needs to offload a process that is consuming RAM or that more RAM is needed. The range is 1 (which is far too low—you will get a lot of alerts) to 4,294,967,295.

```
Memory Protection No Restart Interval = 1
```

When an address space crashes (or faults), NetWare may automatically try to reclaim its resources and restart the server software if Memory Protection Fault Cleanup is set to On. If this process occurs more than once in the specified number of minutes, you should stop this process because server resources and time are being wasted. Setting this value disables this feature, potentially wasting valuable time.

Multiprocessor SET Commands

```
Auto Start Processors = On
```

If this parameter is set to On, all secondary CPUs will be started (and therefore used) when the PSM (Platform Support Module) is loaded. If it is set to Off, you must enter the command **START PROCESSORS** to activate them. Unless you suspect a problem with a CPU, leave it On.

NCP SET Commands

```
NCP File Commit = On
```

Some NetWare-aware programs prefer to force files to write to disk before receiving confirmation of the success of the write. Normal files are placed in the cache, and the cache responds to the application with verification, even though the file hasn't actually been placed on the disk. The default setting of On allows this forced writing.

```
Display NCP Bad Component Warnings = Off
```

Poorly written programs may not handle NetWare system calls properly. This setting allows (On) or prevents (Off) alert messages from going to the console.

```
NCP Packet Signature Option = 1
```

NCP packet signatures are a security feature that uses embedded identification in the packets to guarantee identity. The values and their definitions for the server are as follows:

0   No packet signatures ever

1   Packet signatures at the request of the client

2   Packet signatures if the client can and wants to (but don't force them)

3   Force packet signatures

If either the client or the server is set to 3 and the other is set to 0 (or is unable to do packet signatures), a connection between them will not be possible. Packet signatures use CPU resources and slow performance on both ends of the network transactions. Few situations require this level of security.

Novell Storage Services SET Commands

```
NSS Low Volume Space Warning Threshold = 10
```

The number sets the number of megabytes when a warning alert propagates to alert network administrators that volume space requires some quick attention.

Service Location Protocol SET Commands

`SLP SA Default Lifetime = 3600`

This parameter controls how long a service will remain registered (without an update) with the SLP. In an unstable environment, you should reduce the number; in a highly stable one, you could increase it. The range is 0 to 65,535 seconds.

Time SET Commands

`TIMESYNC Configuration File = SYS:SYSTEM\TIMESYNC.CFG`

This parameter sets the location of the `TIMESYNC.CFG` file. You can have a maximum of 255 characters in the full path name.

`TIMESYNC Configured Sources = Off`

This parameter specifies the time sources for this server to listen to. When this is set to On, the server ignores SAP time sources and listens only to those sources listed in the `TIMESYNC.CFG` file.

Reset Environment

It may happen that you change a SET parameter you shouldn't, or hit the wrong key by mistake and your typo causes a server problem. There are two ways to handle this problem.

First, find the large command button at the bottom of Figure C.1 that says View Modified Set Parameter. When you click this button, all the parameters you've changed appear on one screen, listing the current value and default. Figure C.3 shows this screen inside Remote Manager.

FIGURE C.3

Change SET parameters to unchange if necessary.

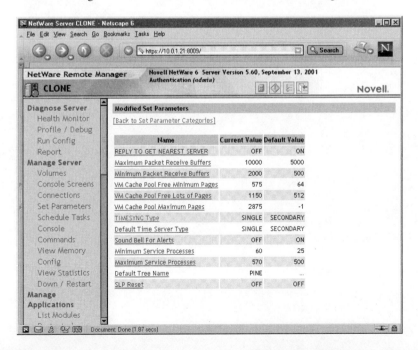

Click any of the highlighted SET parameters to go back and change the values to the default, or at least to something that causes less hassle. Changes are quick and easy to find with NetWare Remote Manager.

The second option would be worth a headline on its own if it weren't for the superiority of the Remote Manager SET parameters system. At the console colon prompt, type **RESET ENVIRON-MENT**. This console command prompts you with every changed SET parameter, allowing you to reset the parameter to default, or to some setting other than that currently in force. Use NetWare Remote Manager, because it's really quicker, more targeted, and much more fun.

SET Little

A repeat of the earlier warning: you won't need to mess with these SET parameters very often. Earlier NetWare versions required more fiddling with these settings, but NetWare has matured, and developers are better at following NetWare application guidelines.

You'll rarely need these parameters, but check them all out at least once. You never know what the future will hold, and you may have to SET yourself a parameter one day.

Glossary

List of Acronyms

ACL	Access Control List
ACU	Automatic Client Upgrade
ANSI	American National Standards Institute
API	application programming interface
ARP	Address Resolution Protocol
BDC	backup domain controller
BOOTP	Bootstrap Protocol
C	Country object
CCITT	Consultative Committee for International Telegraph and Telephone
CDI	Custom Device Interface
CDM	Custom Device Module
CGI	Common Gateway Interface
CHAP	Challenge Handshake Authentication Protocol
CIDR	Classless Inter-Domain Routing
CIFS	Common Internet File System
CMOS	complementary metal oxide semiconductor
DDP	Datagram Delivery Protocol
DET	directory-entry table
DHCP	Dynamic Host Configuration Protocol
DMA	dynamic memory access
DNS	Domain Name System
DoS	Denial of Service
FTP	File Transfer Protocol
HA	high availability
HAI	Host Adapter Interface
HAM	Host Adapter Module
HBA	host bus adapter
HCSS	High-Capacity Storage System

HSM	Hierarchical Storage Management
HTML	Hypertext Markup Language
HTTP	Hypertext Transfer Protocol
ICP	Internet Cache Protocol
ICS	Internet Caching Service
IDE	Integrated Drive Electronics
IEEE	Institute of Electrical and Electronic Engineers
IMAP	Internet Mail Access Protocol
InterNIC	Internet Network Information Center
IP	Internet Protocol
IPP	Internet Printing Protocol
IPX	Internetwork Packet eXchange
IRF	Inherited Rights Filter
IRQ	interrupt request
ISDN	Integrated Services Digital Network
ISO	International Standards Organization
ISP	Internet service provider
ITU	International Telecommunications Union
LAN	local area network
LAP	Link Access Protocol
LDAP	Lightweight Directory Access Protocol
LIP	Large Internet Packet
NAAS	Novell Advanced Audit Service
NAS	network attached storage
NCP	NetWare Core Protocol
NCS	NetWare Cluster Services
NDIS	Network Driver Interface Specification
NDPS	Novell Distributed Print Services
NDS	Novell Directory Services

NFS	Network File System
NIC	network interface card
NIS	Network Information Services
NLM	NetWare Loadable Module
NLS	Novell Licensing Services
NLSP	NetWare Link Services Protocol
NMAS	Novell Modular Authentication Services
NSE	Network Support Encyclopedia
NSS	Novell Storage Services
NTFS	NT File System
NTP	Network Time Protocol
NWFS	NetWare File System
NWPA	NetWare Peripheral Architecture
O	Organization object
ODI	Open Data-Link Interface
ODINSUP	Open Data-Link Interface/Network Driver Interface Specification Support
OSI	Open Systems Interconnection
OSPF	Open Shortest Path First
OU	Organizational Unit object
PAP	Password Authentication Protocol
PBP	Packet Burst Protocol
PKIS	Public Key Infrastructure Services
POP3	Post Office Protocol v3
PPP	Point-to-Point Protocol
PPTP	Point-to-Point Tunneling Protocol
RAID	redundant array of inexpensive disks
RAM	random access memory
RBS	Role Based Services
RCONSOLE	Remote Console
RFC	Request for Comment

RIP	Router Information Protocol
SAN	storage area network
SCSI	Small Computer Systems Interface
SDI	Storage Device Interface
SIDF	System Independent Data Format
SLIP	Serial Line Internet Protocol
SLP	Service Location Protocol
SMB	Server Message Block
SMS	Storage Management Services
SMP	Symmetric Multi-Processor
SMTP	Simple Mail Transfer Protocol
SNMP	Simple Network Management Protocol
SPX	Sequenced Packet eXchange
SQL	Structured Query Language
SSL	Secure Sockets Layer
TCP	Transmission Control Protocol
TCP/IP	Transmission Control Protocol/Internet Protocol
TFTP	Trivial File Transfer Protocol
TSA	Target Service Agent
TSM	Topology-Specific Module
TTS	Transaction Tracking System
UART	Universal Asynchronous Receiver/Transmitter
UDP	User Datagram Protocol
UNC	Universal Naming Convention
UPS	uninterruptible power supply
UTP	unshielded twisted-pair
VPN	virtual private network
WAN	wide area network
WTM	WAN Traffic Manager

10BaseT, 100BaseT, 1000BaseT

Wiring standards to support Ethernet over twisted-pair wiring in increasing speeds from 10Mbps, 100Mbps, and now 1Gbps for 1000BaseT.

A

abnormal ending (abend)

An unexpected halting of a file server.

Access Control List (ACL)

AN NDS object property that allows other objects to access the object, including object and property rights. The ACL also includes the Inherited Rights Filter (IRF).

Access Control right

The right to change trustee assignments and/or the Inherited Rights Filter (IRF) of a file or directory.

accounting

When engaged, a process that tracks network resources used by clients.

ACONSOLE

The nearly obsolete utility that allows connection to NetWare servers via dial-up modems connected to the server.

Add or Delete Self right

The property right that specifies whether a trustee can add or remove itself as a value of that property.

address

A unique identifier on the network, most often the number assigned to the network card by the manufacturer. It may also refer to memory location in an operating system.

IP addresses (such as 204.251.122.48) are identifiers for systems on the Internet or other TCP/IP (Transmission Control Protocol/Internet Protocol) networks. E-mail addresses use the *domain name* after the @ sign, such as info@novell.com.

Address Resolution Protocol (ARP)

The Internet protocol that provides the physical address when only the logical (IP) address is known.

addressing, disk channel

A system used by SCSI systems as hardware identification numbers, 0 to 7.

addressing space

Supported RAM under the NetWare 6 operating system. The limit of 4GB is theoretical, not practical, since no server hardware supports 4GB of RAM today.

Admin object

The practical equivalent to SUPERVISOR in earlier versions of NetWare. The only User object defined during installation, Admin has the rights to create and manage objects.

AFP Server object

A specialized server leaf object that represents an AppleTalk Filing Protocol (AFP) server.

Alias object

A leaf object that represents an object in a different location in the NDS eDirectory tree. Using Alias objects, one object (such as a NetWare volume) can appear to be in several containers at one time, thus enabling users in each container to easily locate and use the original object.

American National Standards Institute (ANSI)

The United States-based organization for the development of technology standards. It is a member of the International Organization for Standardization (ISO).

Apache Web Server

The leading open-source Web server on the Internet (many believe it's the leading server of any kind) developed originally by the not-for-profit Apache Group. Apache supports all the new NetWare browser-based utilities, including iFolder and iPrint.

AppleTalk Filing Protocol (AFP)

The Macintosh version of file-sharing services.

AppleTalk protocols

Specifications for the AppleTalk network, such as LAP (Link Access Protocol), LLAP (LocalTalk LAP), and ELAP (Ethernet LAP). Other AppleTalk protocols include ASP (AppleTalk Session Protocol), DDP (Datagram Delivery Protocol), NBP (Name Binding Protocol), PAP (Printer Access Protocol), RTMP (Routing Table Maintenance Protocol), and ZIP (Zone Information Protocol).

application

A software program, which may or may not use the available network resources. Also referred to as a *program.*

application server

A server that runs the server portion of a client/server-based application, such as SQL (Structured Query Language) database servers.

archive

To save files to a longer-term, but slower-access, media than the hard disk. Archive normally refers to optical disks or magnetic tape.

Archive Needed attribute

A NetWare/DOS file attribute indicating that the file has changed since the last backup.

attach

To make a connection between the workstation and a NetWare server. (The ATTACH command used in earlier NetWare versions is not valid in NetWare 4.1x and higher.)

attributes

Extended bits after the filename describing file-specific operating system characteristics. Attributes are often called *flags.* Attributes include Read-Only, Write, and Compressed.

NetWare's extended file attributes can be set to aid in security. Listing a file as Read-Only, for instance, makes it less possible for a user to accidentally delete the file or for a virus to change that file.

audit

The ability of a user, defined as an auditor, to monitor, but not change, network events and records. This is done through the Novell Advanced Audit Service (NAAS) utility.

authentication

A security procedure that verifies that an NDS user has permission to use the network service requested. NetWare's authentication is based on the public key encryption system, and it is extremely reliable and safe.

AUTOEXEC.NCF

The script of commands used by the SERVER.EXE program when booting and setting up the NetWare environment. This file is similar in purpose and organization to the AUTOEXEC.BAT file of a personal computer.

Automatic Client Upgrade (ACU)

A method to upgrade Novell client software during the login process, powered by four different executable programs called during the login script. This method is handy for mass upgrades when the client population uses standardized workstation configurations.

automatic rollback

A security feature of the Transaction Tracking System (TTS) for traditional volumes that, when engaged, guarantees a database transaction is completed. If the network, client, or server fails during a TTS transaction, the database is returned to the state existing before the transaction started. Novell Storage Services (NSS) volumes use the journaling software to perform the same function.

B

backup

A copy of hard disk information made to a tape system, optical disk, or another hard disk. A backup is used more often to recover from accidents than from catastrophes.

backup domain controller (BDC)
A Windows NT server that stores a copy of the domain directory database to provide fault tolerance and authentication services.

backup host
A NetWare server with attached storage devices such as tape, hard disk, or optical disk equipment.

backup target
Any workstation, server, service, or third-party device with the Target Service Agent (TSA) utility loaded.

bind
To initiate protocol-support software for a network board.

bindery
A security database controlling user privileges in earlier NetWare versions (2.x and 3.x). NetWare 4.x and higher use NDS.

Bindery object
A leaf object that represents an object unidentified by NDS, placed in the NDS eDirectory tree by an upgrade or a migration process.

Bindery Queue object
A leaf object that represents a bindery print queue in the NDS eDirectory tree.

Bindery Services
A feature that mimics bindery databases for software that requires the bindery of earlier NetWare versions. Many existing third-party print servers, for example, require Bindery Services.

block
The smallest unit of disk space controlled by the NetWare operating system. Size ranges from 4KB to 64KB. Smaller blocks require more server memory. The best utilization is achieved by using the 64KB block size with block suballocation for traditional volumes.

block suballocation
A traditional NetWare filesystem feature that allows partially used blocks to contain blocks of data from other files, thereby improving overall disk space usage. Novell Storage Services (NSS) volumes do not support block suballocation.

boot files
Files that control the operating system parameters and configuration when the system starts. For example, AUTOEXEC.NCF for NetWare servers is a boot file.

BOOTCONF.SYS
A remote boot image file for diskless workstations. Avoid using this file if at all possible.

BOOTP (Bootstrap Protocol)
Early configuration protocols used by TCP/IP systems to provide IP address and other configuration details to diskless workstations. Enough code was placed in a chip on the system motherboard to find the BOOTP server and request information. BOOTP has been superseded by DHCP (Dynamic Host Configuration Protocol).

BorderManager
Comprehensive network protection and Internet access software from Novell that provides firewall, circuit-level gateways, and proxy services.

bridge
A powered network device that connects two or more network segments and passes packets based on physical addresses only. Bridges operate at the second layer of the OSI model. In contrast, routers use protocol-supplied addresses and operate at the third layer of the OSI model.

broker
A Novell Distributed Print Services (NDPS) service that provides management services for printers. For example, brokers provide event notification and storage of printer resources, such as device drivers.

Browse right

The object right that allows users to see NDS eDirectory tree objects.

Btrieve

Software using key-indexed records for high performance. Novell owned the company that developed Btrieve for many years (but no longer), so many applications expect to find the Btrieve utility running on NetWare servers. The new name for Btrieve is the Pervasive SQL database.

buffer

Memory area set aside to hold temporary data until the data can be accepted by either the workstation or network.

C

cabling system

Physical wires connecting your network.

cache buffer

A server memory buffer that improves performance by keeping recently used files in server memory.

cache buffer pool

The total amount of memory available for server cache operations. The cache buffer pool is used to cache volume file allocation tables (FATs), volume directory tables, recently used files, directory names, and FAT indexes for large files.

cache memory

Another name for a *cache buffer* or *cache buffer pool.*

Can't Compress attribute

A flag indicating that a file can't be compressed.

channel

A logical memory connection point between workstation memory and hard disk controllers. Also refers to a pathway through a communications medium, such as a channel on a multiplexer, or the bearer (B) and data (D) channels on an ISDN (Integrated Services Digital Network) line.

CHAP (Challenge Handshake Authentication Protocol)

A more secure authentication mechanism for validating users than PAP (Password Authentication Protocol). Passwords are passed over the network in an encrypted form. Computer systems that can use both PAP and CHAP will try CHAP first since it is more secure.

CIFS (Common Internet File System)

The open-source version of Microsoft's SMB (Server Message Block) protocol for file access. CIFS is supported automatically by NetWare 6 File Access Packs.

Classless Inter-Domain Routing (CIDR)

A method that provides an efficient way to allocate blocks for IP addresses so that only the numbers required are actually allocated.

client

A machine that uses any of the network services provided by a network server. In NetWare, clients may be DOS, Windows, OS/2, Macintosh, or Unix systems.

Client32

A Novell client software upgrade that takes advantage of 32-bit technology and expanded memory, developed for Windows 95 Service Pack 1 and above.

cluster

Two or more independent computers, often tied to a storage area network (SAN) for access to shared data, with software that continues to perform even if one system in the cluster stops. NetWare 6 includes Novell Cluster Services for two systems, but it's an extra-cost option for three to thirty-two clustered systems.

Common Gateway Interface (CGI) scripting

A programming method that provides a standard way for a Web server to pass control to an application program and receive data back from the program.

communication protocol

Rules governing the sending and receiving of data between two machines.

Compare right

The property right granting the ability to compare values to those of another property.

complementary metal oxide semiconductor (CMOS)

A device used for storing system configuration information. CMOS is supported by a battery to retain information when the system is turned off or unplugged.

Compressed attribute

A file attribute declaring the file's compression status.

Computer object

An optional leaf object that represents a computer on the network in the NDS eDirectory tree.

configuration

Details concerning the physical or software components of a system and how each is instructed to work with the other pieces of the system.

connection number

A NetWare server-assigned number for each workstation, print server, process, or application that requires a server connection. The connection numbers are assigned on a first-come, first-served basis.

ConsoleOne

A Java-based NetWare control utility with versions for the server and the workstation. Unfortunately, the two versions do not perform all the same functions.

Consultative Committee for International Telegraph and Telephone (CCITT)

A committee that is part of the United Nations and is devoted to developing international standards for communications.

container login script

A login script that affects all users in the container. This replaces the System login script in NetWare 3.x. Container login scripts are optional. When they are used, they execute before profile and user login scripts.

container object

An object that can contain other objects within the NDS eDirectory tree.

context

Shorthand to represent the specific container of an object within the NDS eDirectory tree.

controlled-access printer

A Novell Distributed Print Services (NDPS) Printer Agent that has been created in the NDS database. Users can be granted or denied access to this printer.

controller address

A unique number for each controller board in a disk channel.

controller board

Hardware that connects the computer to other devices, such as hard disks, tape systems, or optical jukeboxes.

Copy Inhibit attribute

A Macintosh-specific file attribute that prevents a file from being copied.

Country (C) object

A container object that must be located directly under the [Root] object in the NDS eDirectory tree. It defines the country for a specific part of your network. The Country object is not mandatory, but it is necessary for connecting to external networks that rely on X.500 directory services.

Create right

A filesystem right that allows new files and subdirectories to be created. The Create right is necessary for file salvage. Create is also used in NDS as an object right.

cryptography services

Security functions provided by the Novell Certificate Server to allow NetWare administrators to create, issue, and manage public key and private key secure communications.

cylinder

A concentric, distinct area on a hard disk for storage. The more cylinders in a disk, the greater its storage capacity.

D

daemon

In mythology, a daemon was an attendant of power or spirit. In Unix, a daemon is a program that runs continuously in the background providing some type of service. NetWare calls these NetWare Loadable Modules (NLMs).

data migration

The movement of inactive files from migration-enabled NetWare volumes to another near-online or offline storage format.

data protection

In NetWare systems, duplicate file directories and the process of moving data from bad blocks to known good blocks.

To protect data location information, duplicate directory-entry tables (DETs) and file allocation tables (FATs) are used to provide fault-tolerance on the hard disk. Having copies of each of these tables reduces the risk of loss due to a bad block or two. To protect data against surface defects, NetWare uses the following methods:

- *Read-after-write verification* verifies that every bit written to the disk before the copy is erased from server RAM (NetWare default).

- The *Hot Fix* method uses a separate area of the hard disk to copy data from bad blocks on the disk. The bad block is then marked as bad so no other data will be written there.

- The *disk mirroring* method places data on two disks connected to the same controller.

- The *disk duplexing* method places data on two identical disks connected to two separate controllers.

data set

NetWare's SBACKUP software utility information.

default drive

The current disk drive in use, as indicated by the drive prompt.

default server

The server that responds to a workstation's Get Nearest Server request when the user first starts the login process. In earlier NetWare versions, the default server name was often specified in the NET.CFG file on the workstation. NDS has replaced the need for the default server destination with the default context.

Delete Inhibit attribute

A file attribute that prevents file deletion.

Delete right

AN NDS object right that allows users to delete files or NDS eDirectory tree objects.

delimiter

A symbol or character that differentiates between commands, parameters inside commands, or records. Common delimiters are comma (,), period (.), forward slash (/), backslash (\ ), hyphen (-), and colon (:).

demigration

A High-Capacity Storage System (HCSS) method of moving a file back from the jukebox to the server (after migration) when requested.

Denial of Service (DoS) attack

A hacker attack on a system that does not necessarily crash the system but renders it unable to perform some tasks, such as allowing new users to connect or log in.

destination server

The target server in NetWare server migration.

device driver

Software that connects a system's operating system to the system's hardware, such as a disk or network controller.

device numbering

A unique identification number or address used to identify network devices. The number may be a physical address, device code, or logical number determined by the operating system.

device sharing

Allowing more than one person to use a device, and a great excuse for a network. Shared devices include hard disks, printers, modems, fax servers, tape backup units, and communication gateways.

DHCP (Dynamic Host Configuration Protocol)

A protocol used to provide IP address and other configuration details from available IP addresses. DHCP is an update of BOOTP. Novell ships a DHCP server as part of NetWare 6's TCP/IP support.

Dial-Up Networking (DUN)

Client software provided with Windows systems that allows these clients to dial out and make PPP (Point-to-Point Protocol) connections.

Directory/directory

With an uppercase D (Directory), the database supporting the hierarchical structure of NDS, the upgrade from the bindery. With a lowercase d (directory), a filesystem organization method. A directory may contain both files and other directories.

directory caching

A NetWare technique of keeping directory names in server memory for quicker access, rather than reading the directory from the disk.

directory entry

A basic unit of filesystem control, including the file or directory name, owner, date and time of last update (files), and physical location of the first data block on the hard disk.

directory-entry table (DET)

A system that tracks basic information concerning files, directories, directory trustees, and other entities per volume. The maximum number of entries per directory table is 2,097,152, since each of the 65,536 maximum directory blocks per volume can each hold 32 entries. A directory entry is 32 bytes long.

Directory management request

AN NDS database modification method, including new eDirectory partitions and replica management.

Directory Map object

A leaf object similar to an Alias object, in that it represents another object in another context in the NDS eDirectory tree. This object is used mostly with login script MAP commands to represent the locations for common applications.

directory path

A complete filesystem specification, including the server name, volume name, and the name of each directory, ending in the filename.

directory rights

Attributes that allow access to directories.

directory services

A system that controls access and use of network resources through some manner of authentication. At minimum, an encrypted password file verifies a username and password match before allowing a user to log in. At the high end of the directory service spectrum is Novell Directory Services (NDS).

Directory Services request

A user or administrator request to the eDirectory database to read or modify the database contents. There are three types of requests:

♦ *Directory-access requests* are user requests to create, modify, or retrieve objects.

♦ *Directory-access control requests* are administrator requests to allow access rights to the eDirectory database for users.

♦ *Directory-management requests* are administrator requests to manage the physical eDirectory database, such as to perform partitioning operations.

directory structure

The filing system of volumes, directories, and files that the NetWare server uses to organize data on its hard disks. A directory structure is the hierarchical structure that represents how partitions are related to each other in the eDirectory database.

Directory tree

Container objects and all the leaf objects that make up the hierarchical structure of the NDS database. Also known as *NDS eDirectory tree*, *NDS tree*, or *eDirectory tree*.

disk controller

A hardware device (interface card) that connects the computer with the disk drive. The disk controller translates signals for file manipulation from the operating system into physical movement of the disk drive heads to find the requested file location.

disk coprocessor board (DCB)

An early hardware disk controller with a microprocessor to off-load storage operations from the main server microprocessor to improve disk performance. This method has been replaced by speedier disk-storage options.

disk driver

Software that connects the NetWare operating system to the disk controller. The four Novell-supplied disk drivers are ISADISK.DSK (ISA disks), IDE.DSK (IDE disks), PS2ESDI.DSK (ESDI controllers in an IBM MicroChannel Architecture system), and PS2SCSI.DSK (SCSI controllers in an IBM MicroChannel Architecture system). Third-party vendors often supply their own disk drivers.

Components of the NetWare Peripheral Architecture (NWPA) include the Host Adapter Module (HAM), which is adapter-specific; the Host Adapter Interface (HAI), providing software programming interfaces; the Custom Device Module (CDM), device-specific for the storage device; and the Custom Device Interface (CDI), the programming interface for the storage device.

disk duplexing

Two controllers supporting two hard drives, each written with the same information. If either disk or controller fails, the system continues without interruption.

disk format

Hard disk preparation to allow the disk to receive information. The disk format depends on the operating system.

disk interface board

See *disk controller*.

disk mirroring

Two drives, supported by one controller, each written with the same information. If either disk fails, the system continues without interruption.

disk partition

A hard disk section treated by the operating system as if it were a separate drive. With NetWare, each disk can have more than one partition, and volumes can span multiple partitions.

disk subsystem

An external hardware housing holding one or more disks, tapes, or optical drives. The disk subsystem is connected to the NetWare server via cable to the controller board.

domain

In a Windows NT system, an arrangement of client and server computers referenced by a specific name that share a single security permissions database. On the Internet, a domain is a named collection of hosts and subdomains registered with a unique name by the InterNIC.

Domain Name System (DNS)

A service developed in the early 1980s to automate the previously manual editing of host files on Internet-connected systems. DNS allowed the number of hosts to double each year, and it is still the directory service in use on the Internet and the World Wide Web.

Don't Compress attribute

A file attribute that prevents the operating system from compressing the file.

Don't Migrate attribute

A file attribute that prevents the operating system from migrating the file.

DOS client

A NetWare client running DOS.

DOS device

A mass storage unit supporting the DOS disk format. It is used by UPGRADE and SBACKUP (NetWare's backup software utility).

drive

A *physical drive* is a physical mass storage device that supports the reading and writing of data. A *logical drive* is a network disk directory addressed as a separate drive with a drive-letter prompt.

drive mapping

The process of assigning various network disk directories as separate drives, each with a unique drive letter.

driver

Software that connects the NetWare operating system to physical devices, such as drive controllers and network interface boards.

DSL

Digital Subscriber Line, a technology providing high-bandwidth over ordinary copper telephone lines. Aimed primarily at residential and small-business customers, DSL offers a wide range of speeds (144Kbps to 6.1Mbps), depending on distance and line quality.

DSREPAIR

A server-run NetWare Loadable Module (NLM) program that repairs and corrects problems with the eDirectory database. With DSREPAIR, records, schema, bindery objects, and external references can be repaired, modified, or deleted.

DSTRACE

A utility that echoes eDirectory messages to the server console screen or a log file for troubleshooting.

dynamic configuration

The ability of NetWare to allocate resources from available server processes first, and to allocate new processes if an available process fails to answer the request in a timely manner.

dynamic memory

Memory chips that require constant electrical current to hold the information written to them. Dynamic memory is used for RAM.

dynamic memory access (DMA)

A method of transferring information from a device such as a hard disk or network adapter directory into memory without passing through the CPU. Because the CPU is not involved in the information transfer, the process is faster than other types of memory transfers. The DMA channel must be unique for each device.

E

eDirectory
Novell Directory Services (NDS) version 8.6. This version is named *eDirectory* to differentiate cross-platform NDS from NetWare-specific directory services.

effective policies
In a NetWare system, the sum of all policies that have been assigned to a user through containers, groups, and directly to the User object. When two policies that perform the same action are applied, the user policy overrides a group policy and a group policy overrides a container policy.

effective rights
A user's access rights to a file, a directory, or an object based on the combination of trustee assignments, inherited rights, Group object rights, and any security equivalence. NetWare calculates a user's rights before every action. Effective rights are based on a combination of the following:

- The object's direct trustee assignments to the directory or file in question

- Any inherited rights from parent directories

- Rights to the object gained from being a member of a group with trustee rights to the object or file/directory

- Rights from a listing in a User object's security equivalence list

Embedded SCSI
A hard disk drive with a SCSI controller built into the hard disk logic.

Erase right
The authority to delete files or directories.

Ethernet configuration
The Ethernet standard followed by network connections. NetWare supports four Ethernet configurations:

- Ethernet 802.3 (raw Ethernet frame)

- Ethernet 802.2 (NetWare 3, 4, and 5 default frame type)

- Ethernet II (frame type for TCP/IP, AppleTalk Phase I, and DECnet)

- Ethernet SNAP (frame type for AppleTalk Phase II)

Execute Only attribute
A file attribute that prevents the file from being copied. Use this sparingly; it's difficult to change.

F

fake root
A NetWare function that lets applications accept a subdirectory as the root of the drive. Network-aware applications don't require tricks such as the fake root.

FastCache
Novell's implementation of the ICS (Internet Caching Service). ICS builds a second-generation cache server on top of NetWare to provide faster access to Web content by holding already requested data at the server for future requests. FastCache can be purchased as part of BorderManager or separately.

fault tolerance
A means of protecting data by providing data duplication on multiple storage devices. Fault tolerance distributes the NetWare eDirectory database among several servers to provide continued authentication and access to object information, even if one server goes down.

Fibre Channel
A fiber-based system often used for linking servers with storage devices. The fiber foundation allows data connections between components up to six miles away (ten kilometers). Variations include Fibre Channel over IP and Fibre Channel over TCP/IP. Short-distance links allow coaxial or twisted-pair wiring, making the Fibre Channel name somewhat silly.

file allocation table (FAT)

The DOS index that tracks disk locations of all files and file fragments on the disk partition. NetWare uses the DOS FAT, accessed from the directory-entry table (DET). Files that exceed 64 blocks are listed as a *turbo FAT* and are indexed with all FAT entries for that particular file. This speeds access to the complete file.

file caching

A technique for caching recently used files in server RAM to speed file reading and operations.

file compression

A method of replacing repeating characters in a file with shortened characters, thus reducing the file length. NetWare supports file compression, enabled by volume, directory, or file.

file indexing

NetWare's means of indexing FAT entries for better performance while accessing large files. Any file larger than 64 blocks is indexed automatically.

file locking

The process of limiting access to a file so the first user or application can modify the file before a second user or application makes changes.

FILER

A DOS workstation utility that allows both users and supervisors to manage the filesystem on NetWare servers.

file rights

The authority to modify files.

File Scan right

The authority to see files and directories with the DIR and NDIR commands.

file server

A machine used to run the network operating system. Referred to as the NetWare server when speaking of a machine running the NetWare operating system.

file sharing

An operating system feature that allows multiple users concurrent access to a file.

filename extension

The three characters after the period in a filename.

filename space

A feature of the NetWare filesystem that allows it to support more than just the DOS 8.3 character file types. NetWare 6 automatically supports long filenames for Windows clients. NetWare 6 can also be configured to supported NFS (Network File System, for Unix systems) and Macintosh filenames.

filesystem

The overall data organization on the hard disk, tracking each file in its specific hierarchical location. NetWare supports filesystems across volumes, directories, subdirectories, and files.

firewall

A combination of hardware and software that protects private networks from public networks by limiting the types of packets and data that can come in to the private network.

flag

Another name for file or directory attributes in NetWare.

FLAG

A utility program that allows you to view or modify the extended NetWare attributes of files on NetWare volumes.

frame

A packet-format specification. NetWare supports Ethernet 802.3, Ethernet 802.2, Ethernet II, Ethernet SNAP, Token Ring, and Token Ring SNAP frames.

FTP (File Transfer Protocol)

An Internet protocol that permits transfer of files between dissimilar clients.

FTP server

Server software included with NetWare 6 that allows remote clients to place and retrieve files from the server, generally over the Internet.

G

gateway

A link between two or more networks allowing dissimilar protocols to communicate.

global group

In Windows NT systems, an organization of user accounts that can be used within the domain and in other trusted domains. A global group can contain only user accounts from its own domain.

Group object

A leaf (not container) object listing one or more User objects in the NDS eDirectory tree. Whatever access is granted to the Group object is passed to all User objects within the group.

H

handle

A computer system pointer that specifies a resource or feature. For example, a system may use file handles, device handles, and directory handles.

hard disk

A magnetic storage device that uses rigid platters turning at high speeds.

Hardware-Specific Module (HSM)

See *Open Data-Link Interface (ODI)*.

hashing

An index file in server memory calculating each file's physical address on the hard disk. By skipping the sequential disk directory reads, file operations can be serviced much more quickly.

hexadecimal

An alphanumeric numbering system that uses 0 to 9 and A through F to represent 10 through 15: A=10, B=11, C=12, D=13, E=14, F=15.

Hidden attribute

A file attribute that prevents a file from being seen with the DOS or OS/2 DIR command. It also prevents the file from being copied or deleted.

high-availability (HA) solution

A system or component continuously operational over a long period of time, aiming for the magical 99.999 percent uptime (five nines). HA systems, such as Web sites, rely on redundant hardware, server clustering, and storage area networks (SANs) to maintain operation.

High-Capacity Storage System (HCSS)

A file-manipulation system that moves files from the server hard disk to optical disks in a jukebox.

Migration is the method of moving a file from the server to the jukebox. *Demigration* means that the migrated file is moved back to the server hard disk when it is requested. The file pathname remains the same as far as the user is concerned, no matter where the file is physically located.

HCSS uses a directory table on the server hard disk to track the directory contents on different jukebox optical disks. Each jukebox can have more than one HCSS directory, and all optical disks can be assigned to one HCSS directory or grouped within several directories.

home directory

A user's private area on the server hard disk. The user has full control over his or her home directory.

hop count

The number of network routers a packet passes through. NetWare allows only 16 hops between the IPX packet source and destination. NSLP (NetWare Link Service Protocol) supports up to 127 hops. IP packets are limited to 15 hops unless specifically increased.

host

A mainframe, traditionally, but the Internet designers called every connected system a *host*, causing confusion from that day forward. *Host* is also used to indicate an SBACKUP (NetWare's backup utility) server.

host bus adapter (HBA)
A disk controller with enough intelligence to speed disk access. NetWare handles up to five host adapter channels, each supporting four controllers per channel and eight drives per controller.

Hot Fix
A NetWare data-protection method that moves data from disk blocks that appear to be defective to a safe, reserved area. The suspect disk area is marked and not used again. The default redirection area is two percent of the disk partition's space.

Hot Plug PCI
A NetWare 6 feature that provides the ability to remove PCI adapter cards while the server is online and operating. The server hardware and device driver must also support this feature.

HTML (Hypertext Markup Language)
A standard set of "markup" symbols or codes inserted in a file so that when it is displayed by a Web browser, it appears formatted properly.

HTTP (Hypertext Transfer Protocol)
An Internet protocol designed to allow the exchange of text, graphics, and multimedia information between an HTTP Web server and a Web browser client.

hub
A physical wiring component that splits or amplifies the signal. The word *hub* is generally used with ARCnet cabling.

I

identifier variable
A login script variable. For example, the identifier variable LOGIN_NAME is replaced with the login name supplied by the user when logging in.

iFolder
A new service with NetWare 6 that provides automatic, secure, and transparent synchronization between a user's files on a NetWare server and any client machines used by that individual. When using a system without the iFolder client, users can use a browser to upload, download, rename, or delete files on their server storage area.

iManage
A new NetWare 6 browser-based utility for controlling iPrint, NetWare Licensing, and DNS/DHCP configurations.

IMAP (Internet Mail Access Protocol)
An Internet protocol used to access e-mail stored on a mail server in a user's mailbox. This protocol will eventually replace POP3 (Post Office Protocol version 3), which is currently the most popular protocol used to access e-mail.

Immediate Compress attribute
The filesystem attribute that specifies that files are to be compressed as soon as possible.

Indexed attribute
The status flag indicating that the file is indexed as a file allocation table (FAT) for quicker access.

INETCFG.NLM
The Internetworking Configuration utility, which used to enable TCP/IP on the server and configure the IPX/IP Gateway. Now, this utility is limited to setting IPX remote-connection details and providing a method for editing the AUTOEXEC.NCF file.

Inherited Rights Filter (IRF)
The list of changes in a user's inherited file access rights, as the user moves down the file directory tree. The IRF only revokes rights. You must have Write and Access Control rights to a file or directory to change the IRF.

To allow flexibility in filesystems and NDS design, there must be a way to lock users out of areas below those in which they have access. The IRF blocks rights by revoking rights at directories or containers. This allows the network supervisor to freely grant access to higher levels, thereby saving time by granting rights to many people at once while retaining the ability to lock users out of sensitive areas. An example is allowing everyone rights to the \ACCOUNTING directory but using the IRF to limit access to \ACCOUNTING\PAYROLL.

Institute of Electrical and Electronic Engineers (IEEE)

A professional society of engineers and scientists. This society has numerous standards committees that control and promote network standards such as 10BaseT, Ethernet, and Token Ring.

Integrated Services Digital Network (ISDN)

A set of standards for providing digital data service over ordinary telephone copper wiring. A Basic Rate ISDN line provides data rates from 64 to 138Kbps. The ISDN channels can be used for data, voice, video, or link management.

International Organization for Standardization (ISO)

An international standards organization that has developed standards such as the Open Systems Interconnection (OSI) model for networks, which is widely used in Europe but not as commonly used in the United States.

International Telecommunications Union (ITU)

A telecommunications standards branch of the United Nations, formerly known as the Consultative Committee for International Telegraph and Telephone (CCITT).

Internet Assigned Numbers Authority (IANA)

A task force of the Internet Society responsible for coordinating the assignment of IP addresses and protocol port numbers for the Internet. Most of the IANA functions have now been assumed by ICANN (Internet Corporation for Assigned Names and Numbers).

Internet Engineering Task Force (IETF)

A task force of the Internet Society responsible for the development of new TCP/IP protocols and updating current TCP/IP protocols.

Internet Network Information Center (InterNIC)

An organization responsible for providing information about Internet domains under the .com, .edu, .gov, .net, and .org top-level domains.

Internet Research Task Force (IRTF)

A task force of the Internet Society that researches network technology.

Internet service provider (ISP)

An organization that provides connectivity to the Internet as well as other Internet services, such as e-mail and Web server hosting.

Internet Society (ISOC)

An international nonprofit organization, consisting mostly of volunteers, which oversees various task forces to improve the Internet, including the Internet Research Task Force and the Internet Engineering Task Force.

internetwork

Two or more smaller networks that communicate with each other through a bridge, router, or gateway. Also called an *internet*.

interoperability

Support for one user to use resources from two or more dissimilar networks. Advances such as ODI (Open Data-Link Interface) and TCP/IP support in the server make interoperability easier, but interoperability is not automatic.

intranet

A local network infused with Internet technology. For most companies, this means Web servers and clients used for connections within the company network, rather than outside to the Internet. NetWare supports this function well.

IntranetWare/intraNetWare

Novell's name-mistake bundle that included the operating system, the Web Server, NetWare/IP, the Multi-Protocol Router (MPR), and the IPX/IP Gateway (Novell Internet Access Server) with

NetWare 4.11. The name emphasized the value of an existing NetWare network, now infused with Web and Internet technologies. Thankfully, the intraNetWare name was dumped after a single release, and every box of NetWare now includes Internet technology.

IP (Internet Protocol)

Part of the TCP/IP protocol suite. IP is similar to IPX (Internetwork Packet eXchange) in that it makes a best-effort attempt to deliver packets but does not guarantee delivery. TCP is required for that step, as SPX (Sequenced Packet eXchange) is required in the IPX/SPX suite.

IP address

The four-byte address, which must be unique in the entire Internet if connected, that identifies host network connections. IP addresses are normally seen in the dotted-decimal format, such as 204.251.122.12. Internet committees oversee IP address coordination and distribution.

IPP (Internet Printing Protocol)

The official way, based on RFC 2911, for users to address and use printers across the Internet.

iPrint

Expansion of Novell Distributed Print Services (NDPS) to include IPP (Internet Printing Protocol) support, enabling anyone to print to properly configured NetWare printers from anywhere with Internet access.

IPX (Internetwork Packet eXchange)

The Novell-developed and Xerox Network Services (XNS)-derived protocol used by NetWare. Addressing and routing for IPX is handled by NetWare, unlike the corresponding functions in TCP/IP.

IPX external network number

The unique network number that identifies a single network cable segment. The IPX (Internetwork Packet eXchange) network is defined by a hexadecimal number of from one to eight digits (1 to FFFFFFFE). A random number is assigned during installation, or the installer can specify the external network number.

IPX internal network number

The unique network number that identifies a NetWare server. Each server on a network must have a unique IPX (Internetwork Packet eXchange) internal network number. A random number is assigned during installation, or the installer can specify the internal network number for each server.

IPX internetwork address

A 12-byte number (24 hexadecimal characters) made up of three parts: a four-byte IPX (Internetwork Packet eXchange) external network number, a six-byte node number (derived from the interface card's unique address), and a two-byte socket number.

IPX/IP Gateway

Generically, any software that converts datagrams from IPX (Internetwork Packet eXchange) to IP (Internet Protocol). There are at least a dozen vendors that sell IP translation gateways, most of which are focused on the NetWare market. Specifically, IPX/IP Gateway is the name of Novell's IP translation software running under NetWare 4.*x* and higher versions and was included as part of intraNetWare.

IPXODI (Internetwork Packet eXchange Open Data-Link Interface)

The client software module that accepts data from the DOS requester, attaches a header to each data packet, and transmits the data packet as a datagram.

J

JavaBeans

An object-oriented programming interface from Sun Microsystems that lets programmers develop reusable applications or program building blocks, called *components*.

JavaScript

An interpreted programming or scripting language from Netscape now used by many Web sites to add functionality to Web browser clients.

journaling filesystem

An advanced, efficient, and reliable filesystem pioneered by the Unix world. Journaling filesystems support huge numbers of files and directories, load quickly, and maintain an accurate activity log to roll back mistakes in case of a rare crash.

jukebox

A clever updated meaning for the old musical device. A jukebox for NetWare is a device holding multiple optical disks, which plays one or more at a time as requested by the operating system. Capacity for jukeboxes ranges from two disks and one reader to hundreds of disks and a dozen readers.

L

LAN driver

Software in the server and workstation that interfaces the physical network board to the machine's operating system.

Large Internet Packet (LIP)

A feature that allows packets going through routers to have more than 576 bytes. The small packet size was a limitation of ARCnet packets, and NetWare defaulted to the small size in case ARCnet was on the other side of the router. Because the use of ARCnet is dwindling, this restriction has been lifted.

LDAP (Lightweight Directory Access Protocol)

An emerging Internet protocol that allows client software to query a directory database in a standard fashion, regardless of the type of directory database or the platform on which it is stored.

leaf object

AN NDS object that cannot contain other objects. Examples are users, volumes, printers, and servers.

license certificate

A piece of paper entitling you to use software you have purchased (or obtained legally) under the conditions outlined. Novell Licensing Services (NLS) also creates License Certificate objects in the NDS directory to represent NLS-enabled applications.

License Services API

An application programming interface (API) that allows application developers to use Novell's Licensing Services (NLS) to control usage and metering of applications that are used on the network or on workstations where the application is installed locally but the workstation is connected to the network.

Link Support Layer (LSL)

The client and server software between the LAN drivers and the communications protocols. The LSL allows more than one protocol to share a network board.

loadable module

An executable file with the extension .NLM (for NetWare Loadable Module) that runs on the server. NLMs can be loaded and unloaded without taking the server down.

local area network (LAN)

A network connected by physical cables, such as within a floor or building.

local groups

In a Windows NT system, an organization of user accounts and/or global groups used to assign permissions to resources on local computers. They can contain user accounts and global groups from one or more domains that have trust relationships established with the domain.

Locality object

A rarely used eDirectory object, which functions as a subcontainer to Country. Locality objects are used most often as state or province containers.

log in

The process by which a user requests and receives authentication from the operating system and then is able to use network resources. Login scripts configure details such as printer setup and drive assignments.

LOGIN directory

A default NetWare directory, created during installation. The SYS:LOGIN directory contains LOGIN and NLIST utilities to support users who are not yet authenticated.

login restrictions

User restrictions that control certain network security parameters. Login restrictions include the workstation a user is allowed to log in from, the time of day, and whether the user is allowed to have more than one active connection to the network.

login script

An ASCII text file that performs designated commands to configure a user's workstation environment. The login scripts are activated when the user executes the LOGIN command.

Container login scripts set general parameters for all users in a container and execute first. *Profile login scripts* also set parameters for multiple users, but only for those users who specify the profile script. This script executes after the container script. *User login scripts* set parameters for individual users and are the least efficient for administrators to use.

login security

An aspect of NetWare security. The NetWare supervisor establishes login security by using the LOGIN command to control who can access the network. Users must be authenticated by NDS by use of the login name and the correct password (although they are optional, passwords are strongly recommended). Passwords travel between the client and server in an encrypted mode, so network protocol analyzers cannot capture any passwords.

log out

To disconnect from the network. The LOGOUT command does not remove the Novell client software from workstation memory.

M

Macintosh client

A NetWare desktop client using a Macintosh computer.

MAIL directory

SYS:MAIL, a default NetWare directory created by the system during installation. Earlier NetWare versions stored each user's login script in his or her personal mail directory; now login scripts are a property of the User object.

MAP

A command-line utility that checks drive assignments and allows users to modify those assignments. If MAP commands are placed in a login script, they can assign drive letters to directory paths during the login process.

Media Access Control (MAC) address

A unique address assigned to the network adapter hardware.

Media Manager

NetWare functions that abstract backup storage device control, allowing applications to address different storage devices without using device-specific drivers.

Media Support Module (MSM)

See *Open Data-Link Interface (ODI)*.

member server

A Windows NT server that is part of a domain but does not contain the directory database for the domain. It provides resources for use by the domain.

memory

A computer's internal storage under control of the operating system, generally called random access memory (RAM) in desktop computers. The storage and retrieval speed of RAM is more closely matched to that of the CPU than any other system storage.

memory allocation

Segmenting random access memory (RAM) for specific purposes such as disk caches, extended memory, and application execution space. NetWare has replaced the five memory allocation pools with a single, more efficient memory pool.

Message Handling Services (MHS)

Early (NetWare 2.x through 4.10) e-mail integration and coordination software. MHS provided a standard means of connecting disparate e-mail systems. The focus on Internet technologies has moved the LAN e-mail world to Internet standards, leaving MHS behind.

message packet

A basic unit of transmitted network information.

message system

The set of application program interfaces (APIs) running on top of IPX (Internetwork Packet eXchange), which facilitate messages between nodes on the network.

Metered Certificate

A Novell Licensing Services (NLS) directory object that helps track usage and provide metering for applications.

Migrated attribute

A NetWare file indicator showing whether a file has migrated through Hierarchical Storage Management (HSM) off the server hard disk.

migration

The process of moving bindery and other data from earlier NetWare servers or a different network operating system to NetWare 6. Part of a High-Capacity Storage System (HCSS) method of moving a file from the server to the jukebox (*migration*) and, when requested, back to the server hard disk (*demigration*).

Migration Agent

NetWare 6 software that converts packets from IPX (Internetwork Packet eXchange) clients into IP (Internet Protocol) packets that are destined for IP servers.

Modify bit

A status file attribute that indicates whether the file has been changed since the last backup. This bit is used by backup systems such as SBACKUP to know which files to protect when a partial backup is used. Commonly known as the *Archive bit*.

Modify right

The authority to change file or directory names or attributes.

MONITOR

The utility that displays a NetWare server information screen. MONITOR tracks the state of the server and, to a lesser extent, the state of the network. As a NetWare Loadable Module (NLM), it executes only at the server.

Multiple Layer Interface Driver (MLID)

See *Open Data-Link Interface (ODI)*.

multiport serial adapter

A serial adapter port that provides one, two, four, eight, or more high-speed asynchronous ports. Some of these adapters include built-in modems.

Multi-Protocol Router (MPR)

An expansion of Novell's long-time ability to route multiple protocols through the NetWare server operating system. Starting with the intraNetWare/4.11 product, MPR is included with NetWare. Any currently available WAN connection, up through T1 lines, may be controlled by WAN boards in a NetWare server running the MPR software.

multiserver network

A physical network with more than one server. Internetworks have more than one network connected by a router or gateway.

N

name context

The location of an object in the NDS eDirectory tree.

namespace

The ability of a NetWare volume to support files from non-DOS clients, including Macintosh, OS/2, FTAM (Open Systems Interconnect), and Unix (Network File System, or NFS) systems. Each client sees files on the file server in its own file format. A

Macintosh client will see a file as a Macintosh file, while an OS/2 user (are there any left?) will see that same file as an OS/2 file.

Namespace support is enabled per volume. Net-Ware Loadable Modules (NLMs) with an extension of .NAM are loaded to provide the filename translations. The ADD NAME SPACE command is necessary for each volume, after the appropriate namespace NLM is loaded (for example, LOAD NFS, then ADD NAME SPACE). This process creates multiple entries for each file in the namespace of the volume's filesystem.

Namespaces cannot be removed without using the VREPAIR utility or by deleting the volume and creating a replacement volume without the namespace.

National Science Foundation (NSF)

A United States government agency that has funded the development of a cross-country backbone network, as well as regional networks designed to connect scientists to the Internet. It operates the National Science Foundation Network (NSFNET).

NCP (NetWare Core Protocol)

The NetWare Presentation-layer protocol and procedures used by a server to fulfill workstation requests. NCP actions include manipulating files and directories, changing the eDirectory, printing, and opening programming connections (*semaphores*) between client and server processes. The process of starting and stopping a connection between the workstation and server is indelicately called creating and destroying a service connection.

NCP Packet Signature

The NetWare security feature that allows each workstation to add a special "signature" to each packet going to the server. This signature changes with every packet, and this process makes it nearly impossible for another station to pretend to be a station with more security privileges.

NDS for NT

An add-on product from Novell that allows the integration and management of Windows NT domains from within NetWare Administrator. Now often called NDS Corporate Edition.

NDS eDirectory tree

Container objects and all the leaf objects that make up the hierarchical structure of the NDS database. Also known as a *Directory tree* or *eDirectory tree*.

NetBIOS

A peer-to-peer networking application interface used by IBM and Microsoft. Also a naming standard for computer names on Microsoft networks.

NETBIOS.EXE

The client networking file that emulates NetBIOS, the peer-to-peer network application interface used in IBM or IBM-inspired networks. The INT2F.COM file is necessary when the NETBIOS.EXE file is used.

NET.CFG

The client workstation boot file that contains configuration and setup parameters for the client's connection to the network. This file functions like the DOS CONFIG.SYS file and is read by the machine only during the startup of the network files.

NetDrive

A new feature in NetWare 6 that allows Windows computers to map a drive to a remote NetWare server without loading the typical Client32 and fighting with remote-access software. Standard Internet protocols, primarily FTP and WebDAV, are used to link to the NetWare server.

NetStorage

A remote file access method. NetStorage differs from NetDrive in that NetStorage lacks any client software. File access, through a standard browser, includes uploading, downloading, renaming, and deleting files on the server side.

NETSYNCx

Two utility programs for NetWare 3 and NetWare 4 servers (NETSYNC3 and NETSYNC4, respectively) that allow NetWare 3 servers to be managed by NDS.

NetWare Administrator

The once-primary program for performing NetWare 4.1x and higher supervisory tasks. This application is fully graphical and runs within Windows supporting a 32-bit NetWare client. Now, however, the torch passes to the ConsoleOne and NetWare Remote Manager utilities.

NetWare Cluster Services (NCS)

An enhanced version of NetWare 6 enabling two or more servers (up to 32) to link together and provide automatic fail-over support to provide high availability to the applications or services running on those servers. Clustering, especially the free two-node clustering included in NetWare 6, supports many Web site designs.

NetWare DOS Requester

Client software for DOS and Windows computers. The DOS Requester replaces the earlier NetWare shell software. Modules of the DOS Requester provide shell compatibility for applications.

NetWare/IP

Server modules and client software that replace IPX (Internetwork Packet eXchange) as the transport protocol between NetWare clients and NetWare servers by encapsulating the IPX information inside an IP (Internet Protocol) datagram. NetWare 5.1 and higher support NCP (NetWare Core Protocol) natively over IP, so this functionality is no longer necessary in a pure NetWare 5.1 or later network.

NetWare File System (NWFS)

Once the name for all server-based storage methods, the increased stability and expandability of Novell Storage Services (NSS) has supplanted the NWFS (now called the traditional filesystem) as the default on NetWare 6 servers. By another version or two, we will only reference NSS.

NetWare Loadable Module (NLM)

A program that executes at the NetWare server. NLM programs are loaded at the command line, by one of the configuration programs, such as AUTOEXEC.NCF, or

by another NLM. Types of NLMs include disk drivers (.DSK extension), LAN drivers (.LAN extension), namespace (.NAM extension), and utilities/applications (.NLM extension).

NetWare NFS Services

A collection of NetWare Loadable Modules (NLMs) that allows a NetWare server to participate in Unix networks as both a Network File System (NFS) client and server.

NetWare operating system

The operating system developed by Novell in the early 1980s to share centralized server resources with multiple clients. The seven important features of the NetWare operating system are directory, file, print, security, messaging, management, and routing services.

NetWare partition

A disk partition on a server hard disk under control of NetWare.

NetWare Remote Manager

The NetWare 6 replacement for the NetWare Management Portal from NetWare 5.1. This utility provides more functionality and boasts added features over its predecessor. The name change, however, comes as a result of marketing, not technical, upgrades.

NetWare Requester for OS/2

NetWare Requester software for OS/2 clients provides the same NetWare client functions as those provided by the NetWare DOS Requester.

NetWare Runtime

A specialized version of the NetWare operating system that allows only a single concurrent client. This is used most often as a platform for communication or application servers that provide their own user authentication. NetWare Runtime servers support all NetWare Loadable Modules (NLMs), both from Novell and third-party vendors.

NetWare server

An Intel (or equivalent processor) based PC running the NetWare operating system.

NetWare server console operator

A user authorized by the Admin or equivalent supervisory personnel to run server and print server software. Standard management tasks, such as print server loading and unloading or checking a file server using MONITOR, can be done by console operators.

NetWare Server object

A leaf object representing a NetWare server in the NDS eDirectory tree.

network attached storage (NAS)

A specialized server providing access to storage separate from any file server. NAS includes a pared-down operating system that just controls file access through common protocols such as TCP/IP, SMB, and AppleTalk.

network backbone

A special network generally connecting only specialized devices such as servers, routers, and gateways. The backbone is a separate cabling system between these devices, isolating the backbone from regular client/server traffic.

network board

See *network interface card*.

network communication

Data exchanged in packet format over a defined network.

Network Driver Interface Specification (NDIS)

A process similar to Open Data-Link Interface (ODI) that allows a workstation to support multiple protocols over one network interface card. This was developed by 3Com, Microsoft, and Hewlett-Packard and released before Novell released the ODI drivers. ODINSUP (ODI NDIS Supplement) supports NDIS drivers under ODI when necessary.

Network File System (NFS)

File-sharing software developed by Sun Microsystems and considered to be the standard file-sharing protocol for Unix networks.

Network Information Services (NIS)

A naming and administration system developed by Sun Microsystems that is similar to the Domain Name System (DNS). NIS is most commonly used in the Unix community.

network interface card (NIC)

A network board, card, or adapter (choose your term) that connects a device with the network cabling system. More recent Novell documentation favors network board rather than NIC or adapter; other companies and references are less restrictive.

network node

An intelligent device attached to the network. Traditionally, nodes are servers, workstations, printers, routers, gateways, or communication servers. However, other devices such as fax machines, copiers, security systems, and telephone equipment may be considered network nodes.

network numbering

A unique numbering scheme to identify network nodes and separate network cable systems. IPX (Internetwork Packet eXchange) automatically adds the node number for the client, while the server installation process sets the network cable segment number (IPX external network number) and the address of the server (IPX internal network number). TCP/IP networks require the installer to set and maintain all network addresses.

network printer

A printer that is attached to either the network cabling, file server, or workstation and is available for use by any network client.

network supervisor

A traditional term for the person responsible for the network, or a portion thereof (subadministrator).

Also called the network administrator. Truly, a hero for the modern age.

Network Support Encyclopedia (NSE)

The CD-ROM–based information resource including Novell patches, fixes, drivers, bulletins, manuals, technical bulletins, compatibility testing results, press releases, and product information.

NETX

The Virtual Loadable Module (VLM) under the client DOS Requester that provides backward-compatibility with the older versions of the NetWare shell.

NLSP (NetWare Link Services Protocol)

A routing protocol designed by Novell that exchanges information about the status of the links between routers to build a map of the internetwork. Once the network map is built, information is transferred between routers only when the network changes. RIP (Router Information Protocol), the previous method for routers to exchange information, requires regular broadcasts that add network traffic. Using NLSP reduces routing traffic across WAN links. NLSP uses RIP to communicate with NetWare clients.

node number

Similar to a network number, a node number generally refers to a client machine only. Under NetWare, node numbers are based on the unique, factory-assigned address (Ethernet and Token Ring) or the card's configurable address (ARCnet and Token Ring cards supporting Locally Administered Addresses, or LAA).

Normal attribute

The default setting for NetWare files, indicated by a specific filesystem attribute.

Novell Administrator for Windows NT

Software that allows the synchronization of Windows NT and NetWare accounts.

Novell Advanced Audit Service (NAAS)

An upgraded audit service new for NetWare 6, NAAS uses four components: an Audit utility, Audit Agent, Audit server, and Audit database. Control, granularity, and report options now rank as usable rather than putrid (the rank for the replaced AUDITCON).

Novell Client32

See *Client32*.

Novell Client Install Manager

A new file (`NCIMAN.EXE`) that helps set the installation options for client stations when using the Automatic Client Upgrade (ACU) software.

Novell Directory Database (NDD)

The database that stores and organizes all objects in the NDS tree. The objects are stored in a hierarchical structure, mimicking the hierarchical arrangement of NDS itself.

Novell Directory Services (NDS)

The distributed security and network resource-locating database released with NetWare 4.*x* and higher versions to replace and upgrade the bindery. The database in NDS is distributed and replicated among multiple servers for fault tolerance and high performance. Network resources controlled by NDS include users, groups, printers, volumes, and servers.

This database works on the network level, not per server. NDS allows access to network resources independent of the server holding those resources. With the bindery, each user was required to know the server responsible for each network service. NDS allows users to access resources without knowing the server responsible for those resources.

Users no longer establish a link to a single server in order to log in. Users are authenticated (logged in and verified) by the network itself through NDS. The authentication process provides the means for the client to communicate with NDS, as well as to check the security profile of each user.

Novell Distributed Print Services (NDPS)

Novell's next-generation printing architecture that centralizes and standardizes usage, service, and management of the printer. The NDPS architecture consists of Printer Agents, Brokers, NDPS Managers, and gateways.

Novell Internet Access Server (NIAS)

The server software module that translates data requests from a client running on IPX (Internetwork Packet eXchange) to TCP/IP for connection to the Internet or TCP/IP host. NIAS is not included with the first release of NetWare 6.

There are two pieces to this technology, one at the client and one at the server. The client software includes a special version of Winsock that "spoofs" the TCP/IP client software, such as Netscape, into believing the client is running the TCP/IP protocol stack. In reality, only IPX is running at the client.

The server portion of the Winsock software converts the data transport protocol from IPX to IP for connection to the TCP/IP systems. Outgoing packets are assigned port numbers in addition to the IP address of the NIAS, which is shared by all systems. Incoming packets, identified by their port numbers, are routed back across IPX to their original stations.

Novell Licensing Services (NLS)

AN NDS management feature that tracks application use to ensure that you have enough valid licenses for the number of concurrent users for each application.

Novell Modular Authentication Services (NMAS)

A feature that offers new ways to increase the security and usefulness of eDirectory, including support for biometric devices such as fingerprint scanners, smart cards, and tokens. Graded authentication, another advantage, allows different access levels based on the login method.

Novell Storage Management Services (SMS)

See *Storage Management Services.*

Novell Storage Services (NSS)

Now the default NetWare filesystem. NSS 3.0 creates larger storage spaces with better performance and improved stability over the traditional file services still available.

NT File System (NTFS)

The native filesystem for Windows NT, which provides the ability to place file-level security on a Windows NT Server or NT Workstation machine.

O

object

In NetWare 6, an NDS database entry that holds information about a network client or another resource. The categories of information are called properties. For example, a User object's mandatory properties are login name and last name. The data in each property is called its value.

NetWare objects include users, printers, servers, volumes, and print queues. Some of these are physical; some are virtual, like the print queue and groups of users. Container objects help manage other objects. Leaf objects—such as users, printers, volumes, and servers—are the end nodes of the NDS eDirectory tree.

Containers (called *branches* in some other systems) are Country (C), Organization (O), and Organizational Unit (OU) objects. A container object can be empty. Leaf objects cannot contain any other objects.

Object names consist of the path from the root of the NDS eDirectory tree down to the name of the object. The syntax is *object.container.container.root.* There may be one or more containers in the middle section. Typeless names list just the names (LPRATT.CONSULT.MLD). Typeful names list the designators (CN=LPRATT.OU=CONSULT.O=MLD). An advantage of NetWare 6 over earlier versions of NetWare is that it allows the constant use of typeless names.

object rights

Rights granted to a trustee over an object. An example is the Create object right for a container object, which allows the trustee to create new objects in that container.

Open Data-Link Interface (ODI)

Novell's specification, released in 1989, that details how multiple protocols and device drivers can coexist on a single network interface card without conflict. The ODI specification separates device drivers from protocol stacks. The biggest advantages of ODI over the Network Driver Interface Specification (NDIS) are speed and size. ODI routes packets only to the appropriate frame type, rather than to all frame types as in NDIS. The major components of the ODI architecture are as follows:

◆ Multiple Layer Interface Driver (MLID) is a device driver that manages the sending and receiving of packets to and from a physical (or logical) network. Each MLID is matched to the hardware or media and is therefore unique.

◆ Link Support Layer (LSL) is the interface layer between the protocol stacks and the device driver. Any driver may communicate with any ODI-compliant protocol stack through the LSL.

◆ Media Support Module (MSM) is the interface of the MLIDs to the LSL and the operating system. This module handles initialization and runtime issues for all drivers.

◆ Topology-Specific Module (TSM) is the software layer that handles a specific media type, such as Ethernet or Token Ring. All frame types are supported in the TSM for any media type supported.

◆ Hardware-Specific Module (HSM) is the software layer that handles adapter startup, reset, shutdown, packet reception, timeouts, and multicast addressing for a particular interface card.

Open Data-Link Interface/Network Driver Interface Specification Support (ODINSUP)

Refers to the interface that allows both ODI and NDIS protocol stacks to exist on a single network interface card.

Open Shortest Path First (OSPF)

A routing protocol developed for large, complex TCP/IP networks.

open systems

Technically, a goal of guaranteed interoperability between disparate operating systems. Marketing has recast this term to mean any system that can be coerced to communicate with TCP/IP. Realistically, open systems utilize Internet and Web technologies to support any client connecting to any server.

Open Systems Interconnection (OSI) model

A reference model for the layering of common functions in a telecommunications system. This model consists of seven layers that define how an ideal network operates. These layers include Application, Presentation, Session, Transport, Network, Data Link, and Physical.

optical disk

A high-capacity disk storage device that writes or reads information based on reflecting laser light for bits, rather than reading magnetic fluctuations as on a standard hard or floppy disk. Disks may be read-only (a CD-ROM), read-once (a WORM, for Write Once Read Many), or fully rewritable.

optical disk library

A jukebox, which is an optical disk reader with an auto-changer that mounts and dismounts optical disks as requested.

Organization (O) object

The container object below the Country (C) object and above the Organizational Unit (OU) object in an NDS eDirectory tree. Organization objects can contain Organizational Unit objects and leaf objects.

Organizational Role object

In an NDS eDirectory tree, a leaf object that specifies a role within an organization, such as Purchasing Manager or Workgroup Leader. The Organizational Role object usually has special rights, and these rights tend to rotate among different users as job responsibilities change.

Organizational Unit (OU) object

The container object below the Organization object in an NDS eDirectory tree. The Organizational Unit object can contain other Organizational Unit objects or leaf objects.

OS/2 client

A computer running NetWare client software for the OS/2 operating system (remember that?). OS/2 clients can perform almost all the same user and administrative operations that DOS or Windows workstations can perform.

P

packet

A block of data sent across the network; the basic unit of information used in network communications. Service requests, service responses, and data are all formed into packets by the network interface card driver software before the information is transmitted. Packets may be fixed or variable length. Large blocks of information will automatically be broken into appropriate packets for the network and reassembled by the receiving system.

Packet Burst Protocol (PBP)

The NetWare IPX version of the TCP/IP *sliding windows* feature. Rather than send one packet to acknowledge the receipt of one packet, PBP acknowledges multiple packets at one time. This improves the performance of NCP (NetWare Core Protocol) file read and writes, especially across WAN connections. These IPX changes were not enough to hold of TCP/IP, and such details as PBP remain niche technologies.

packet receive buffer

The memory area in the NetWare server that temporarily holds arriving data packets. These packets are held until the server can process the packets and send them to their proper destination. The packet receive buffer ensures that the server does not drop arriving packets, even when the server is heavily loaded with other operations.

paging

A NetWare performance feature that takes advantage of the Intel 80386 and above architecture to group memory into 4KB blocks of RAM. The NetWare operating system assigns memory locations in available 4KB pages, then uses a table to allow the noncontiguous pages to appear as a logical contiguous address space.

PAP (Password Authentication Protocol)

Used by PPP (Point-to-Point Protocol) dial-in systems to authenticate users. The user ID and password are sent over the telephone line in unencrypted format.

parent directory

In a filesystem, the directory immediately above any subdirectory.

parent object

An object that holds other objects. In NDS, an Organization is a parent object for all included Organizational Unit and leaf objects.

parity

A simple form of error checking in communications.

partition

In a hard disk, a section treated by the operating system as an independent drive. For example, there are DOS and NetWare partitions on a server hard disk.

In NDS, a partition is a division of the NDS eDirectory database. A partition consists of at least one container object, all the objects therein, and all the data about those objects. A partition is contained in a replica. Partitions contain only NDS information; no filesystem information is kept in a partition.

Partitions are useful for separating the eDirectory to support parts of the network on different sides of a WAN link. Multiple partitions are also advised when the network grows to include many servers and thousands of NDS objects. More partitions keep the NDS database closer to the users and speed up lookups and authentication.

The [Root] object at the top of the NDS eDirectory tree is the first partition created during installation. New partitions are created with the ConsoleOne or NetWare Remote Manager utility. Each partition must contain contiguous containers. The partition immediately toward the [Root] of another is called that partition's *parent*. The included partition is referred to as the *child partition*.

password

The most common security measure used in networks to identify a specific, authorized user of the system. Each user should have a unique password. NetWare encrypts the login passwords at the workstation and transmits them in a format only the NetWare server can decode.

path

The location of a file or directory. An *absolute* path is the complete location of a file or directory, listed from the root of the drive through each directory and subdirectory and ending with the filenames. A *relative* path is from the current location.

Perl

A scripting language similar to C, but with many Unix functions such as sed and awk.

permissions

Used for access control in Windows NT systems, similar to filesystem rights in NetWare.

Pervasive SQL database

See *Btrieve*.

physical memory

The random access memory (RAM) in a computer or server.

pool

New with NetWare 6, a specified amount of physical space obtained from some or all of a server's storage devices. Pools hold logical volumes.

POP3 (Post Office Protocol v3)

An Internet protocol for retrieving e-mail from a mailbox located on a server.

port

A *hardware port* is the termination point of a communication circuit, as in parallel port. A *software port* is the memory address that specifies the transfer point between the microprocessor and a peripheral device.

power conditioning

The method used to protect electronic equipment from power fluctuations. Power conditioning can work by suppressing, isolating, or regulating the electric current provided to that equipment.

PPP (Point-to-Point Protocol)

A protocol for communication between two computers using a serial interface, typically a personal computer connected by telephone line to a server. PPP is commonly used to connect to the Internet via modem.

PPTP (Point-to-Point Tunneling Protocol)

A protocol that allows corporations to extend their own corporate network through private "tunnels" over the public Internet. Effectively, a corporation uses a WAN as a single, large LAN. A company no longer needs to lease its own lines for wide-area communication but can securely use the public networks.

primary domain controller (PDC)

A Windows NT Server machine that contains the master directory database. The PDC serves as the administration point for the domain. There is only one PDC for each domain.

Primary time server

The NetWare server that provides time information to Secondary time servers and workstations. Primary time servers must synchronize time with at least one other Primary or Reference time server.

print device

Any device that puts marks on paper or plastic, such as a laser, dot-matrix, or inkjet printer or a plotter. NetWare's defined print device files have a .PDF extension and can be configured by using the Net-Ware Administrator or iManage utility.

print device mode

The sequence of printer commands (or print functions, control sequences, or escape sequences) that control the appearance of the printed file. Print device modes can define the style, size, boldness, and orientation of the typeface. Modes are set by using the NetWare Administrator or iManage utility.

print job

Any file in a print queue waiting to be printed. Once the print server forwards the print job to the printer, the print job is deleted from the queue.

print job configuration

Characteristics that define how a job is physically printed, rather than how the printed output looks on the page. For example, a print job configuration may specify the printer the job will print on, the print queue the job is sent through, the number of copies to print, or the use of a banner page.

print queue

The directory on a volume that stores print jobs waiting for printer assignment. In NetWare 5.1 and later, the print queue directory may be stored on any volume. Earlier NetWare versions (including Net-Ware 4 servers in bindery mode) limited the print queue to the SYS: volume. Print queue capacity is limited only by disk space. Print queues can be created by using the NetWare Administrator utility.

print queue operator

A user with additional authority to manage the print queue. Print queue operators can edit the status of print jobs, delete print jobs, change the service mode, or modify the print queue operational status. This is an excellent job for subadministrators.

print queue polling time

The interval between print server status checks of the print queue for jobs. Users can modify the time period.

print server

In a NetWare 6 server, the NDPSM.NLM software moves print jobs from the print queue to the appropriate network printer. NetWare print servers can service up to 256 printers and associated print queues.

Third-party print servers are small hardware devices that connect directly to the network cabling and support one or more printers remotely from the file server. Printing performance is increased by using remote print servers rather than printers attached to the file server itself.

Print Server object

The leaf object that represents a network queue-based print server in the NDS tree.

print server operator

A user granted extra authority to manage a print server. Rights include the ability to control notification lists, supported printers, and queue assignments.

printer

Any device that puts marks on paper or plastic, such as a laser, dot-matrix, or inkjet printer or a plotter. A network printer can be attached to the file server or an external print server. In NDS, Printer objects are independent of the Print Queue and Print Server objects. Novell Distributed Print Services (NDPS) treats each printer as a network object controlled by an NDPS Printer Manager.

Printer Agent

Represents a Novell Distributed Print Services (NDPS) Printer object. It replaces the Print Queue, Printer, and Print Server objects found in traditional NetWare printing models.

printer definition

The control characters, specific to the printer model, that interpret the commands to modify printed text.

printer form

A print system option that allows users to specify which type of paper (letter, legal, memo, and so on) to use for any print job. Each defined printer form is given a unique name and number between 0 and 255. Printer forms may be specified in the print job configuration or with the workstation printer utility CAPTURE. The mounted form must match the requested form or the print job won't print.

Printer object

The leaf object representing a physical printer on the network in the NDS eDirectory tree.

private key security

See *public key/private key security*.

privilege level

The rights granted to users or groups by the ConsoleOne program. These rights set the level of network access for that user or group.

Privilege level also refers to the microprocessor access level determined by the Intel architecture for 80386 and higher microprocessors. Four levels are defined: 0 through 3. NetWare uses the 0 and 3 levels. These levels, also known as *protection rings*, are controlled by the NetWare memory domains.

Profile login script

A special type of login script that can be applied to several users with identical login script needs. Profile login scripts are not mandatory. They execute after the container login script but before the user login script.

Profile object

The special leaf object that represents the profile login script in the NDS eDirectory tree.

program

A software program, which may or may not use the available network resources. Also referred to as an *application*.

prompt

An on-screen character(s) that awaits your input. Examples are the DOS prompt, the OS/2 prompt, and the colon prompt of the NetWare server console.

property

A piece of information, or characteristic, of any NDS object. For example, User object properties include login name, last name, password restrictions, and similar information.

property rights

Rights to read, create, modify, or delete properties of an NDS object.

protected address space

An area of memory that is protected from programs that are not part of that memory space. Programs in a specific memory space cannot interfere with programs in other memory spaces. This prevents one NetWare Loadable Module (NLM) from crashing another (or the entire operating system).

protected mode

The mode in 80286 and higher Intel processors that supports multitasking and virtual memory management. This mode is the default used by processors. They switch to real mode only when forced to emulate the earlier 8086 processor functions. In protected mode, 80286 processors can address up to 16MB of memory. 80386 and higher processors can address up to 4GB of memory.

protection ring

See *privilege level*.

proxy server

A server that acts as an intermediary between a workstation user and the Internet so that the enterprise can ensure security, administrative control, and caching service. A proxy server is associated with or part of a gateway server that separates the enterprise network from the outside network and a firewall server that protects the enterprise network from outside intrusion.

public-access printer

A Novell Distributed Print Services (NDPS)-compatible printer that has been installed on the network but not yet created as an object in NDS and is therefore available to everyone on the network.

PUBLIC directory

One of the NetWare system directories created during installation. PUBLIC stores NetWare utilities and files for use by all clients. The default login script for users maps a search drive to SYS:PUBLIC, with Read and File Scan rights granted automatically.

public files

Files kept in the SYS:PUBLIC directory, placed there during NetWare installation. These include all command-line utilities, Help files, and printer definition files.

Public Key Infrastructure Services (PKIS)

A service supported by Novell that allows developers to take advantage of a public/private key infrastructure, rather than writing their own public/private key systems.

public key/private key security

An encryption mechanism that employs two unique keys for encrypting data. The publicly available key is used to encrypt the data, and the private key is used to decrypt the data. The public key cannot be used to decrypt data that it has previously encrypted.

Public Switched Telephone Network (PSTN)

The public telephone network, sometimes called POTS (for Plain Old Telephone Service). The

telephone network in the United States is limited to a maximum transmission speed of 53Kbps by the FCC.

Public trustee

A special NetWare trustee, used only for trustee assignments. It allows objects in NDS that do not have any other rights to have the effective rights granted to the [Public] trustee. This works similarly to the user GUEST or group EVERYONE in earlier NetWare versions. [Public] can be created and deleted, just like any other trustee. The Inherited Rights Filter (IRF) will block inherited rights for the [Public] trustee.

Rather than use the [Public] trustee to grant rights to large groups of objects, it's more secure to grant those rights only to a container object. The difference between the two options is that rights granted to a container object are only passed to those objects in the container, while [Public] rights go to all objects.

Purge attribute

The filesystem attribute that allows the NetWare operating system to completely erase a directory or file that has been deleted.

R

random access memory (RAM)

The main system memory in a computer addressed by the operating system. RAM is used for the operating system, applications, and data. The memory is dynamic, and the information contained in RAM is cleared when power is discontinued.

RCONSOLE

The NetWare utility (Remote Console) that echoes the server console to a workstation. This ability is also included in the NetWare Administrator program under the Tools drop-down menu. Any function that can be done at the server console can be done via RCONSOLE. RCONSOLE is based on IPX. NetWare 6 includes the Java-based RConsoleJ remote-management utility running over TCP/IP.

RConsoleJ

The NetWare utility that allows a Java-based session on a network client to echo the server screen and redirect keyboard input across the network. RConsoleJ runs over TCP/IP and is the replacement for IPX-based RCONSOLE (Remote Console). The new utility offers unsecured connections (like RCONSOLE) and secured (SSL-encrypted) connections between the workstation and server.

read-after-write verification

The method used by NetWare to guarantee the integrity of data written to the hard disk. After data is written to the disk, it is compared to the data still held in memory. If it matches, the memory is cleared. If the data does not match, the hard disk block is marked as "bad" and the Hot Fix feature redirects the data to a known good block in the Hot Fix Redirection area.

Read-Only attribute

The filesystem attribute indicating that the file can be read, but not modified, written to, or deleted.

Read right

The filesystem right that allows a user to open and read files.

real mode

The 8086 emulation mode in 80286, 80386, and 80486 Intel processors. Real mode is limited to 1MB of RAM address, as the 8086 itself is limited, and no multitasking is possible.

record locking

The operating system feature that prevents more than one user from modifying a record or file at the same time.

recursive copying

Copying the complete contents of a directory or directory structure, using the recursion property that enables a subroutine to call itself. For example, XCOPY and NCOPY use recursive copying to copy all files in a directory structure.

Reference time server

A NetWare server that provides the network time to Primary and Secondary time servers and workstations.

remote boot

The process of booting a workstation from the files on a NetWare server rather than from a local drive.

remote workstation

A personal computer linked to the LAN by a router or through a remote asynchronous connection. Remote workstations can be either stand-alone or part of another network.

Rename Inhibit attribute

The filesystem attribute that prevents a file or directory from being renamed.

Rename right

The authority for an object to change the name of an object. This technically changes the Name property.

replica

A copy of an NDS partition, used to eliminate a single point of failure, as well as to place the NDS database closer to users in more distant parts of the network. There are six types of replicas, five of which can be managed:

- The Master replica is the primary replica, created during installation. A Master replica of the [Root] partition is stored in a hidden directory on the SYS: volume of the first file server installed.

- The *Read/Write replica* is used to read or update the database. Actions such as adding or deleting objects or authenticating users are handled by the Read/Write replicas. There should be at least two Read/Write replicas for each partition, to ensure that the eDirectory will function if one or two of the servers that hold replicas are unavailable.

- The *Read-Only replica* is the least powerful replica, used to access or display NDS database information, but unable to support changes. (Read-Only replicas are generally not very useful.)

◆ The *Filtered Read/Write replica* limits the types of eDirectory attributes copied to the filtered replica.

◆ The *Filtered Read-Only replica* limits the types of eDirectory attributes copied to the filtered replica.

◆ The *Subordinate Reference replica* is maintained by the system. This type of replica cannot be modified by a user (even the supervisor).

Replica synchronization is the process of a partition's replicas exchanging information to stay up-to-date. When a change is made to one replica, the synchronization process guarantees that all other replicas obtain the same information as soon as it is practical.

Request for Comment (RFC)

An Internet or other technical standard or formal document that is the result of committee drafting and subsequent review by interested parties. As an Internet standard, the final version of an RFC becomes an established document that cannot be changed. (However, subsequent RFCs may supersede or elaborate on all or parts of previous RFCs.)

resolver

Name given to a Domain Name System (DNS) name server client.

resource tag

An operating system function call that tracks Net-Ware server resources. Screens and memory allocated for various tasks, as well as the memory resources used by NetWare Loadable Modules (NLMs), must be tracked so that the resources can be made available to the operating system once the NLMs are stopped or no longer require the resource.

resources

Technically, any part of the network, including cabling, concentrators, servers, gateways, and the like.

Practically, resources are the components on a network that are desired by the network clients. Under this definition, resources tend to be server volumes, gateways, printers, print queues, users, processes, and the security options of a network.

restore

To replace a file or files from the backup media onto the server hard disk. This is done when the file or files on the server hard disk have been erased or corrupted by accident (most commonly) or when an entire disk's worth of files needs to be replaced after a disk failure.

ribbon cable

Flat cable with each conductor glued to the side of the other conductors rather than twisted around each other. This type of cable is used most often for internal disk and tape drive connections.

rights

Privileges granted to NetWare users or groups of users by the Admin user (or equivalent). These rights determine all functions the user can perform on the system, including reading, writing, creating, deleting, and modifying files and directories.

Trustee assignments grant rights to specific directories, files, or objects. An object with a trustee assignment to a directory, file, or another object is called a *trustee* of that directory, file, or object.

Each object maintains a list of which other objects have rights to the object in the Access Control List (ACL).

Directory rights apply to the directory in the Net-Ware filesystem in which they were assigned, as well as to all files and subdirectories in that directory. Rights flow downhill. By granting trustee rights to the top level of a directory, the trustee has the same rights to all files and subdirectories.

Rights can be reassigned or modified by the Inherited Rights Filter (IRF) in lower levels of the eDirectory tree. These rights are part of the filesystem only and have no relevance to NDS objects.

The following types of rights apply to a NetWare network:

- *File rights* apply to only the file to which they are assigned. Trustees may inherit file rights from the directory containing the file.

- *Object rights* apply to only NDS objects. These rights do not affect the properties of the object, just the object itself.

- *Property rights* apply to only the properties of NDS objects. These rights may be assigned to each property, or a default set of rights may be assigned to all properties.

A trustee must have the Access Control right to a directory or file before granting directory or file rights to other objects. A trustee must have the Write, Add or Delete Self, or Supervisor right to the ACL property of the object before granting other objects property or object rights to the object.

RIP (Router Information Protocol)

A widely used protocol that allows routers to communicate with one another to share routing information. RIP is most effective for smaller, private networks.

Role Based Services (RBS)

A new NetWare 6 feature that defines specific tasks for authorized users to perform. Authority for limited functionality allows the users attached to RBS to modify only enough eDirectory properties to perform their role.

root container

The highest container in an NDS eDirectory tree partition. The partition and replicas are named after the applicable root container.

root directory

The highest directory level in a directory structure. The root directory is the volume in NetWare, and all directories are subdirectories of their volume.

[Root] object

The highest object in an NDS eDirectory tree. The purpose of the [Root] object is to provide an access point to different Country and Organization objects. Rights granted to the [Root] object are granted to the entire NDS eDirectory tree. The [Root] object holds no information; it merely acts as a reference point.

router

A combination of hardware and software that examines the internet or network layer of a datagram in order to make a decision about the best route that datagram should take to get to its destination. The router maintains tables of available routes and forwards the datagram on based on the optimal route. Routers function at the third layer of the OSI model.

S

salvageable files

Files that have been deleted by a user or application but are still tracked by NetWare. The Remote Manager utility shows the list of salvageable files and can recover files if they have not been overwritten on the server disk.

If the directory that contained a deleted file was also deleted, the file is saved in a system directory labeled DELETED.SAV in the volume's root directory.

Deleted files can be purged, eliminating any chance of salvage. If the NetWare server runs out of available allocation blocks on the volume, it will start purging files to make room for new files. The files are deleted on a first-deleted, first-purged basis.

SAP (Service Advertising Protocol)

The NetWare IPX-based protocol that allows servers of all types to broadcast their available services across the network. Routers and other NetWare servers receive and track these broadcasts to keep their router information tables up-to-date.

SBACKUP

A software utility that provides the means for NetWare backup and restore operations.

scheduled tasks

A new, time-based function to execute console commands based on the time of day, week, or month. Copied from the Unix cron utility.

schema

NDS database design components, hidden from direct manipulation. Applications that use NDS may modify and expand the schema; for example, the schema is extended when the IPX/IP Gateway adds new objects to the NDS database.

SCSI (Small Computer Systems Interface)

The industry standard that sets guidelines for connecting peripheral storage devices and controllers to a microprocessor. SCSI (pronounced "scuzzy") defines both the hardware and software requirements for the connections. The wide acceptance of the SCSI standard makes it easy to connect any disk or tape drive to any computer.

SCSI bus

Another name for the SCSI interface and communications protocol.

SCSI disconnect

A feature in NetWare that allows communications with SCSI disks to be more efficient by informing the disk of upcoming input/output (I/O) requests.

search drive

A designated drive used by the operating system to look for a requested file that is not found in the current directory. Search drives allow users working in one directory to access application and data files in other directories. NetWare allows up to 16 search drives per user.

search mode

A specification that tells programs how to use search drives when looking for a data file. When an .EXE or .COM file requires support files, the file-open request is made through the operating system. This request may or may not specify a path to the support files. When a path is specified, that path is searched. If no path is specified, the default directory is searched first. If the files are not found, the Novell client software uses the search mode of the executable file to determine whether or not to continue looking in the search drives.

Secondary time server

A NetWare server that requests and receives time information from another server, then provides that time information to requesting workstations.

secret key encryption

An encryption mechanism that employs a single key (or password) to encrypt data. The same key is used to decrypt the encrypted information.

Secure Sockets Layer (SSL)

Program extensions created by Netscape that manage the security of data crossing a network by encrypting the data. SSL can be implemented between many different types of clients and servers, including Web browser and mail clients.

security

The operating system controls used by the network administrator to limit user access to network resources. The six categories of NetWare security are login security, trustees, rights, inheritance, attributes, and effective rights.

security equivalence

The assignment of one set of rights to an object that has the same needs as another object. Security equivalence is a quick way to give the same access privileges to two or more objects, but it should be used with extreme caution.

Being a member of a group list gives a user the same trustee rights as those granted to the Group object. The same security equivalence is granted to all users listed in the occupant list of an Organizational Role object.

Each object also receives an "implied" security equivalence to its own container. If the container is granted the Supervisor right to a volume, all users in that container will also have the Supervisor right to that volume.

semaphore

A file-locking and control mechanism to facilitate control over the sharing of files. Semaphores with byte value 0 allow file sharing; byte value 1 locks the file while in use. Semaphores are also used to limit the concurrent number of users for applications. When the user count is reached, the semaphore blocks any more users from gaining access until a current user closes the file.

serial port

A hardware port. IBM PCs and compatible computers generally come with COM1 and COM2, which transmit data one bit at a time. Serial ports are primarily used for a modem or a mouse on the workstation. In the past, these ports were used on file servers for serial printers. Today, most printers are parallel printers, so it is rare to see a serial printer attached to a file server.

serialization

The process of branding each NetWare operating system with a unique serial number to prevent software piracy. If two NetWare servers discover (through non-filterable broadcasts) that both are using software with the same serial number, copyright violation warnings are shown at the server console and at each connected workstation.

server

A *NetWare server* is a PC providing network resources through the use of the NetWare operating system.

A *print server* is a device that routes print jobs from a print queue and sends them to a printer. The print server may be software in a file server or workstation, or a stand-alone unit attached to the network cabling. The NDS object that represents this device is referred to as a Print Server object.

A *time server* is a NetWare server that provides time to network clients and is capable of providing time for other servers. All NetWare servers are time servers of some type (Primary, Secondary, Single Reference, or Reference).

A *Web server* is a software system based on HTTP communications to send HTML-enabled documents to Web client systems. Both the NetWare Enterprise Web Server and Apache Web Server come standard with NetWare 6.

server console

The information screen for the NetWare server operating system. Monitoring traffic levels, setting configuration parameters, loading additional software NetWare Loadable Modules (NLMs), and shutting down the server must be done at the server console.

The physical keyboard and monitor on the file server are the primary server console. The RConsoleJ utility allows a Java-based session on a network client to echo the server screen and redirect keyboard input across the network.

server protocol

An inaccurate shorthand method of referring to NCP (NetWare Core Protocol). NCP is used on more devices than just the server.

SERVMAN

The server-based utility that provides an interactive front end to NetWare's SET commands. SERVMAN configures the `AUTOEXEC.NCF`, `CONFIG.SYS`, and `TIME-SYNC.CFG` files through the traditional NetWare menu interface. Starting with NetWare 5.0, SERVMAN folded into MONITOR under the Server Parameters setting. All of the SERVMAN functions can now be done through the NetWare Remote Manager browser interface.

Shareable attribute

The filesystem extended attribute for NetWare that allows more than one user to access a file concurrently.

short machine type

A short (four letters or fewer) identifier specified in the `NET.CFG` file. The default is IBM. The short machine type is used specifically with overlay files, such as `IBM$RUN.OVL` for the DOS windowing utilities.

Single Reference time server

A NetWare server that provides time to workstations and Secondary time servers. The Single Reference name comes from the fact that a server so designated is the single source of time for the network. This is the default for the first server in an NDS eDirectory tree.

SLIP (Serial Line Internet Protocol)

An Internet protocol used for dial-up connections. It is used to transfer IP (Internet Protocol) datagrams across a dial-up link.

SLP (Service Location Protocol)

An Internet protocol used for automatic discovery of resources on IP (Internet Protocol) networks. The equivalent of this protocol on IPX/SPX (Internetwork Packet eXchange/Sequenced Packet Exchange) networks is the SAP (Service Advertising Protocol). NetWare 6 uses SLP filtered through the advantages of eDirectory to eliminate broadcasts and extra traffic.

SMB (Server Message Block)

A client/server protocol linking file-access requests from the client to a server operating system over a network. SMB can be run over TCP/IP and powers Microsoft's peer-to-peer and Windows NT-based networking. SMB is now offered to the open-source communities by Microsoft as CIFS (Common Internet File System).

SMTP (Simple Mail Transfer Protocol)

An Internet protocol standard used for transporting e-mail messages across the Internet from SMTP clients to SMTP servers.

SNMP (Simple Network Management Protocol)

An Internet protocol that defines functions for monitoring and managing devices on an IP (Internet Protocol) network.

socket

The destination point within an IPX (Internetwork Packet eXchange) packet on a network node. The socket number is part of an IPX internetwork address. Many sockets, such as those used by NCP (NetWare Core Protocol), are reserved by Novell. Third-party developers may also reserve socket numbers by registering their intentions with Novell.

source routing

The IBM method of routing data across multiple networks by specifying the route in each frame. The end stations determine the route through a discovery process supported by source-routing bridges or routers.

There are two types of source routing:

◆ In *single-route broadcasting*, designated bridges pass the packet between source and destination, meaning only one copy of each packet arrives in the remote network.

◆ In *all-routes broadcasting*, the packet is sent through all bridges or routers on the network. This results in many copies of the same frame arriving at the remote network—as many frames as there are bridges or routers.

sparse file

A file with at least one empty block, often created by databases. Some operating systems will write any file to disk in its entirety, even if only 12 bytes were written. NetWare copies only the last block to disk, tracking the application's request and saving time and disk space. The NCOPY utility will not copy sparse files unless forced to with the /f option.

SPX (Sequenced Packet eXchange)

The part of NetWare's transport protocol suite that guarantees packet delivery at the protocol level. If an SPX packet is not acknowledged within a specific amount of time, SPX retransmits the packet. In applications that use only IPX (Internetwork Packet eXchange), the application program is responsible for ensuring that packets are received intact. Because of the guaranteed nature of SPX, this protocol is often used for backup systems based in workstations.

STARTUP.NCF

The first of two boot configuration files on a NetWare server. The STARTUP.NCF file primarily loads and configures the disk driver and namespace support. Some SET parameters may also be set through this file. It is located on the DOS partition and in the directory where SERVER is executed.

station

Usually, short for *workstation*, but can refer to any intelligent node connected to the network.

storage area network (SAN)

A special-purpose subnetwork connecting data-storage devices through one or more (usually more) servers to the main network for storage access. Typically, multiple servers link both to the main network through Ethernet and the back-end storage network through SCSI or Fibre Channel network components.

Storage Device Interface (SDI)

SBACKUP (NetWare's backup software utility) routines that are used to access various storage devices. If more than one storage device is attached to the host server, SDI supplies a list of all devices.

Storage Management Services (SMS)

NetWare services that support the storage and retrieval of data. SMS is independent of filesystems (such as DOS, OS/2, Unix, or Macintosh) and the backup and restore hardware.

SMS NetWare Loadable Modules (NLMs) and other software modules that run on NetWare servers include the following:

- *Storage Management Engine* (SME) provides backup and restore capabilities through the SBCON utility.

- *Storage Management Data Requester* (SMDR) sends commands and information between SBACKUP and Target Service Agents (TSAs).

- *Storage Device Interface* (SDI) sends commands and information between SBACKUP and the storage devices.

- *Device drivers* control the mechanical operation of storage devices and media under orders of SBACKUP.

- *NetWare server TSAs* send requests for SBACKUP-generated data to the NetWare server where the data resides, then return requested data through the SMDR to SBACKUP.

- *Database TSAs* send commands and data between the SBACKUP host server and the database where the data to be backed up resides, then return the requested data through the SMDR to SBACKUP.

- *Workstation TSAs* send commands and data between the SBACKUP host server and the station where the data to be backed up resides, then return the requested data through the SMDR to SBACKUP.

- Workstation Manager accepts "I am here" messages from stations available for backup. It keeps the names of these stations in an internal list.

STREAMS

The common interface between NetWare and transport protocols that need to deliver data and requests for services to NetWare. STREAMS makes protocols (such as IPX/SPX, TCP/IP, SNA, and OSI transport protocols) transparent, allowing services to be provided across internetworks.

NetWare can install the protocols of your choice (if your applications support these protocols), and the service to the user will be unchanged.

The following are NetWare STREAMS and related NetWare Loadable Modules (NLMs):

- STREAMS.NLM contains the STREAMS application interface routines, the utility routines for STREAMS modules, the log device, and a driver for ODI.

- SPXS.NLM provides access to the SPX protocol from STREAMS.

- IPXS.NLM provides access to the IPX protocol from STREAMS.

- `TCPIP.NLM` provides access to the TCP and UDP protocols from STREAMS.

- `CLIB.NLM` contains the function library required by some NLMs.

- `TLI.NLM` provides the application program interface (API) that sits between STREAMS and applications.

strong password

A password that has a combination of letters, numbers, and special characters. Strong passwords are more difficult to guess and are less susceptible to "dictionary" type password-guessing programs.

subdirectory

A directory contained within another directory in a filesystem.

subnet mask

An IP address technique used to differentiate between different TCP/IP networks. Each client must have a subnet mask, so it will know the exact network address range. The format is in dotted decimal. The most common subnet mask is 255.255.255.0 (often shown by NetWare in hexadecimal as ff.ff.ff.00).

subnetwork

A network that is part of a larger network and connected by a router. From the outside, the subnetwork's identity is hidden and only the main network is visible, making addressing simpler.

Supervisor right

The filesystem trustee right that conveys all rights to directories and files. The Supervisor object right grants all access privileges to all objects and all rights to the property when speaking of property rights.

Misuse of the Supervisor right may be the single largest security hole in many networks. Grant Supervisor privileges with extreme caution.

surface test

A hard disk test that scans for bad blocks. The NetWare INSTALL program offers two surface tests:

destructive and nondestructive. These may be run in the background on a dismounted hard disk so you can keep the server up, but the server performance will be impacted. Although the nondestructive test works the vast majority of the time, it is best to not perform hard disk operations until the disk has two fresh backups.

Symmetric Multi-Processor (SMP)

A computer system (and the operating system) that can take advantage of more than one CPU. It is "symmetric" because the work is automatically divided evenly among all the CPUs, rather than certain types of work being assigned to individual CPUs.

synchronization

Replica synchronization is the process of ensuring that eDirectory partition replicas contain the same information as that of the other replicas in the partition.

Time synchronization is the process of ensuring that all servers in an NDS eDirectory tree agree on the time.

System attribute

The filesystem attribute that specifies that files or directories are to be used only by the operating system.

SYSTEM directory

The directory created during installation on each server that contains the NetWare operating system files. Also included are NetWare Loadable Modules (NLMs), the `AUTOEXEC.NCF` file, and many of the NetWare utilities used by the Admin user to manage the network. The name of this directory is SYS:SYSTEM and should not be changed.

System Independent Data Format (SIDF)

A tape format designed to allow interoperability among different vendors' tape backup products.

System login script

In NetWare 3, the login script that affected all users on the server. In NetWare 4.*x* and higher, the System login script has been replaced by the container login script.

T

tape backup unit
A tape drive that copies information from hard disks to tape.

target
Any local storage device on the network that should be backed up and is running the Target Service Agent (TSA) software. The target may be the same server that holds the backup system, another server, or a workstation.

During the merger of two NDS eDirectory trees, the tree that retains its tree name and [Root] partition is called the *target tree*.

Target Service Agent (TSA)
Software running on a workstation or server that allows Novell Storage Management Services (SMS) compatible tape backup software to see and back up these workstations, servers, and databases. TSA resources are categories of data created by each TSA. These may be major resources or minor resources, depending on the TSA.

TCP (Transmission Control Protocol)
The Internet protocol that provides reliable, connection-oriented delivery of data between a client and a server. TCP requires that a connection be negotiated with the client and the server first; then it requires acknowledgments of data transmitted.

TCP/IP (Transmission Control Protocol/ Internet Protocol)
The primary, industry-standard suite of networking protocols, and the only protocol allowed on the Internet since 1983.

TCP/IP is built upon four layers that roughly correspond to the seven-layer OSI model. The TCP/IP layers are process/application, host-to-host, internet, and network access.

NetWare TCP/IP refers to the collection of NetWare Loadable Modules (NLMs) that add support for TCP/IP onto the NetWare server. Routing can be enabled, as can RIP (Router Information Protocol) to support that routing. One advantage of

TCP/IP support in the NetWare server is the ability for IPX packets to travel across a TCP/IP-only network by using IP tunneling.

The NetWare TCP/IP suite of protocols is a necessary foundation for all Network File System (NFS) products from Novell. The NetWare TCP/IP suite provides both the 4.3 BDS Unix socket interface and the AT&T Streams Transport Layer Interface (TLI).

TCP/IP support at the NetWare server is particularly important for the new Internet-enabled NetWare. The Web server relies on TCP/IP to communicate with the Internet and intranet clients. Older NetWare IPX clients can use the IPX/IP Gateway to provide the TCP/IP protocol stack necessary for connection to TCP/IP hosts, either locally or on the Internet. More recent Windows and NetWare clients include TCP/IP support automatically.

Telnet
An Internet protocol providing terminal emulation to remote systems using TCP/IP. All TCP/IP applications today use fancier emulation, but basic Telnet functionality provides the foundation for all of them.

termination
The process of placing a specific resistor at the end of a bus, line, chain, or cable to prevent signals from being reflected or echoed, causing transmission problems. Typical devices that need terminating resistors include hard disk drives and SCSI devices.

TFTP (Trivial File Transfer Protocol)
A subset of the FTP (File Transfer Protocol) suite, used without any security measures such as passwords. TFTP is rarely used today, but it was a mainstay of automated file-transfer functions, such as e-mail transfer.

time synchronization
The method of guaranteeing that all servers in an NDS eDirectory tree report the same time. Any NDS function, such as a password change or renaming of an object, requires an NDS timestamp.

The *timestamp* is the unique code that includes the time and specifies an event. The NDS event is assigned a timestamp so the order of events may be recounted.

NDS uses timestamps to do the following:

♦ Establish the order of events (such as object creation and partition replication)

♦ Record "real-world" time values

♦ Set expiration dates on accounts, passwords, and other items

The time server software specifies each NetWare server as either a Single Reference, Primary, Reference, or Secondary time server.

Time source servers must find each other. The two ways to do so are NTP (Network Time Protocol) and custom configuration. Primary, Reference, and Single Reference servers use SAP to announce their presence on the network by default. Primary and Reference time servers also use SAP packets to determine which other servers to poll in order to determine the network time. Secondary time servers use SAP information to pick a time server to reference. SAP is easy to install and works without regard to the network layout. It does create a small amount of network traffic.

Alternatively, you can set up a custom configuration. Specific time servers that a particular server should contact may be listed. You can also specify that a server should ignore SAP information from other time sources and that it shouldn't advertise its presence using SAP.

The network supervisor retains complete control of the network time environment using this method. However, the custom configuration method does require extra planning and installation time.

topology

The physical layout design of network components, such as cables, workstations, servers, and concentrators. There are three design options when planning your network topology:

♦ *Star networks* have end nodes that are connected directly to a central concentrator but not to

each other (used for ARCnet and 10BaseT Ethernet).

♦ *Ring networks* have all nodes cabled in a ring; a workstation's messages may need to pass through several other workstations before reaching the target station or server (used by IBM's Token Ring network and followers).

♦ *Bus networks* have all nodes connected to a central cable (called a *trunk* or *bus*). The electrical path of a 10BaseT Ethernet network is really a bus.

Topology-Specific Module (TSM)

See *Open Data-Link Interface (ODI)*.

Transaction Tracking System (TTS)

A standard, configurable feature on NetWare servers that protects database applications. By "backing out" of any incomplete transactions resulting from a network failure, the system guarantees to return the database to the state it was in before the interrupted transaction. For the most part, the journaling filesystem in NSS 3.0 replaces TTS, but TTS can be enabled on NSS volumes via special instructions. However, a server can support TTS on only one type of volume at a time.

Transactional attribute

The filesystem attribute that indicates Transaction Tracking System (TTS) is protecting this file.

trusted domain

In a Windows NT system, the domain that has permissions to use resources in another domain.

trustee

A User or Group object that has been granted access to an object, a file, or directory. A *trustee assignment* determines how a user can access an object, directory, or file.

A *trustee list* is kept by each directory, file, and object. This list includes those objects that can access the object, file, or directory. The trustee list is kept in the object's ACL property.

Rather than granting trustee rights to multiple objects one at a time, you can grant them to a group of users. Trustee assignments granting access for the group enable each individual user to have the same trustee rights as the group.

A *[Public] trustee* is a special case that grants the trustee rights of [Public] to all users. Users who try to access an object, directory, or file without explicit rights still have the rights granted to the [Public] trustee.

Rights are the access levels assigned to an object to a directory, file, or object. Trustee assignments grant to an object the rights to other objects. Assign the right to the trusted object, not the trustee. For example, to grant LYNNE the right to delete a Print Queue object, make LYNNE a trustee of the Print Queue object, not the Print Queue object a trustee of LYNNE.

trusting domain

In a Windows NT system, a domain that lets remote users and global groups in the trusted domain use its resources.

turbo FAT index table

The special file allocation table (FAT) index created when a file exceeds 64 blocks and the corresponding number of FAT entries. NetWare creates the turbo FAT index to group all FAT entries for the file in question. This turbo FAT index allows a large file to be accessed quickly.

typeful name

The complete NDS pathname for an object, including the container specifiers. An example is CN=Terry.OU=Consult.O=Pratt. This was the default in earlier versions of NetWare 4.

typeless name

The complete NDS pathname for an object, excluding the container specifiers. An example is Terry .Consult.Pratt.

U

UDP (User Datagram Protocol)

The Internet protocol that provides best-effort delivery of data on an IP (Internet Protocol) network. Unlike TCP (Transmission Control Protocol), UDP does not require acknowledgments or an initial connection prior to transmitting data.

UIMPORT

A DOS utility (User Import) for adding user names and details into NDS from an external database. The information must be placed in ASCII format.

unbind

To remove protocol-support software from a network board.

Unicode

A 16-bit character code, defined by the Unicode Consortium, that supports and displays up to 65,536 different unique characters. With Unicode, multiple language characters can be displayed with a single code. Different Unicode translation tables are needed when you change code pages.

All objects and their attributes in the NDS database are stored as Unicode representations. Clients use only a 256-character code page comprised of eight-bit characters. The Unicode pages and translations are one of the reasons you must define a country code for different locales. These Unicode files are necessary for each language and translation table:

- `437_UNI.033` translates the specific code page to Unicode.

- `UNI_850.033` translates Unicode to the specific code page (page 437, supporting English, French, and German, among others).

- `UNI_MON.033` handles the proper display of upper and lowercase letters.

uninterruptible power supply (UPS)

A power backup system that every server should have. The UPS maintains power to an attached device when source AC power is disrupted. There are two types of UPS:

- An online UPS monitors the power going through the unit. The power goes through the internal battery that feeds power to the protected device. These systems are more expensive but do an excellent job of smoothing out rough power before providing power to the end device.

- An offline UPS monitors the power line and becomes activated when the power drops. There is a tiny lag before the UPS can kick in completely.

NetWare includes UPS serial port support, which allows you to connect your UPS directly into the server's serial port.

Universal Asynchronous Receiver/Transmitter (UART)

Serial port controller chips that control the flow of data between the CPU and the serial port. Older PC UARTs could not transfer data to the serial ports of a PC any faster than 9600 baud. Newer PCs should have at least a 16,550 UART chip.

Unix client

A NetWare client running the Unix operating system.

Unknown object

The leaf object that represents an object that NDS cannot identify. This object is either corrupted or is an object that has become unstable after a partitioning operation. Sometimes, the Unknown object will become known as the partitioning settles down. If the Unknown object remains, delete it.

unloading

To stop NetWare Loadable Modules (NLMs) and remove them from NetWare's operating system memory. This is done with the UNLOAD command.

unshielded twisted-pair (UTP)

Cable with two or more pair of wires twisted together and wrapped with a plastic sheath. Each individual wire is twisted around its mate; the more twists, the less interference. Originally used for telephone wiring, UTP is now the LAN wire of choice. Various grades of cable run from the low end (level 3 is telephone wire) to the high end (level 5), supporting high-speed data transmissions.

upgrade

The process of converting your network operating system from an earlier version of the operating system to a more current version. Many customers will upgrade from NetWare 3.x to NetWare 4.x, or NetWare 4.x to 5 or 6.

Migration refers to the process of upgrading to NetWare 6 using one of the following methods:

- The Across-the-Wire upgrade transfers the network information from an existing server to an existing server on the same network.

- The Same-Server method upgrades the network information on the same server hardware (but upgrade your hardware when you get the chance).

NetWare 6 includes the Novell NetWare Migration Wizard to support upgrades across the wire.

UPS monitoring

The connection between a NetWare server and an attached uninterruptible power supply (UPS) that allows the NetWare server to know when the UPS becomes active after power has been lost. When the UPS becomes active, the system sends a signal to the NetWare server, and the server notifies users of the backup power situation. A timeout may be specified, giving the users time to close their files and log out. When the time expires (and the power has not returned), the NetWare server closes all open files and shuts itself down properly.

User login script

The login script specific to the user and the environment set up for that user. A user login script might include specific drive mappings or an extra printer connection for a special job. User login scripts execute after the container and profile login scripts.

Adding the NO DEFAULT option in a container script bypasses the user login scripts.

User object

The leaf object in NDS that signifies a person on the network. The following facts are important when dealing with User objects:

- The login name is the name the user logs in with, and it is mandatory.

- You may assign a user to Group objects, which means that the user inherits the rights assigned to that group.

- Home directories are the user's personal space on the server hard drive. It is easiest to group all the home directories into one directory or one volume, if there are many to support.

- Trustee rights are the user's rights to access specific directories and files (other than those assigned by the system).

- Security equivalence is a quick way to give one user the same rights as another user.

- User login scripts are the configurable script for individuals. Login scripts for individual users will take a great deal of your management time; avoid them if possible.

- Account management options are available for workgroup administrators to perform some network supervisory jobs without being granted full Supervisor status. You may grant the Supervisor object right to one user to manage other User objects and fulfill specific functions, such as checking and updating user addresses and telephone numbers.

- User account restrictions are the quickest security control for all users. Restrictions can be placed on everything from the time of day users have access to the system to the number of bytes they may use on the server hard disk.

user template

A feature that allows a new User object to inherit default property values based on predefined information. This speeds the creation of many users at one time, especially if those users share details such as account restrictions, locations, fax numbers, and so on.

utilities

Programs that have a specific purpose and add specific functionality to an operating system. NetWare utilities are included for DOS, Windows, and OS/2 clients. Utilities that execute on the server and are listed as NetWare Loadable Modules (NLMs) are run from the console prompt. Examples of NLMs are MONITOR, INETCFG, and NWCONFIG. The server NLMs add LAN drivers, disk drivers, namespace support, and other low-level network utilities to the NetWare operating system. Workstation utilities execute on a client workstation and are .COM or .EXE files.

V

Value Added Process (VAP)

First-generation NetWare Loadable Modules (NLMs) that ran on NetWare 2.x.

Virtual Loadable Module (VLM)

The modular, executable client program that connects each DOS workstation with the NetWare server. There are many VLMs called by the VLM.EXE program; some add new NetWare client features and others ensure backward-compatibility.

There are two types of VLMs: *child VLMs* and *multiplexor VLMs*. Child VLMs support particular implementations of a logical grouping. For instance, there is a child VLM for each NetWare server type:

- NDS.VLM is for NDS (NetWare 4.x and higher) servers.

- BIND.VLM is for bindery-based servers (prior to NetWare 4.x).

- PNW.VLM is for NetWare desktop-based servers (Personal NetWare).

Multiplexor VLMs are the multiplexing modules that route network calls to the proper child VLM.

virtual memory

Temporary storage on the local hard disk. Operating systems that support virtual memory can swap data out of real memory (RAM) to the local hard disk. This allows the operating systems to appear to have more RAM available than just the physical RAM installed. Virtual memory is important for application servers, but using the virtual memory too much can affect performance.

virtual private network (VPN)

A data network that makes use of public data networks such as the Internet. VPN software typically encrypts data while it is crossing public networks.

volume

A logical grouping of physical hard disk storage space. A NetWare volume is fixed in size and is the highest level in the NetWare directory structure, similar to the DOS root directory. Each volume is represented by a Volume object in the eDirectory.

A NetWare server can support as many as 64 volumes. These volumes may be divided logically on a single hard disk, as a single volume per hard disk or as a single volume spanning multiple hard disks. The first and only mandatory volume is labeled SYS: and includes the NetWare system and client support files. Other volumes can have names between two and 15 characters in length.

A volume must be "mounted" by NetWare in the following sequence:

- The volume becomes visible to the operating system.
- The volume's file allocation table (FAT) is loaded into memory. Each file block of data takes up one entry in the FAT. Because of this, volumes with a smaller block size require more server memory to mount and manage.
- The volume's directory-entry table (DET) is loaded into memory.

volume definition table

The table that tracks volume-segment information, including volume name, volume size, and volume segments on various server hard disks. The volume definition table is required for each NetWare volume and is created by the system during volume initialization.

Volume object

The leaf object that represents a volume on the network in the NDS eDirectory tree. The Volume object's properties store information concerning the NetWare server holding the physical volume and the volume name.

volume segments

The physical division of a volume. A volume may be composed of up to 32 volume segments; the maximum number of segments on a single NetWare disk partition is 8.

Volumes can have multiple physical segments spanning multiple hard disks. This allows you to create larger volumes, with NetWare maintaining the volume definition table to track all the segments. Be aware that if one drive of a volume fails, the entire volume must be re-created. For this reason, some networks prefer to stick with a one-disk, one-volume setup.

W

wait state

The period of time a microprocessor does nothing but wait for other processes. For instance, slow memory forces many wait states on a fast CPU.

wait time

The number of seconds the uninterruptible power supply (UPS) will wait before signaling to the attached NetWare server that normal power is lost. The NetWare server then sends a message to all workstations warning their users to log out.

WAN Traffic Manager (WTM)

A utility that helps control server-to-server eDirectory information going over a WAN link. The three parts to WTM are the WTM software residing on each server, the traffic policies, and the ConsoleOne snap-ins to control WTM.

watchdog

Packets sent from the server to make sure a workstation is still connected. Watchdog packets are sent until the workstation responds or the server clears that connection.

WebAccess

A Java application running on the server with "gadgets" for users to click and use easily. The software portal gadgets include NetStorage for file access, iPrint for printing, e-mail, an address book, and a change-password routine.

Web Manager

A Web utility based on NetWare Enterprise Web Server functioning as a management portal to a variety of Web-based server management tools. Functions include iFolder, Remote Manager, eDirectory, Web Search Server, and iManage.

Web Search and Search Print Services

A customizable Web search server running under Apache on NetWare 6 that provides a fast search engine, along with templates to print files from a wide variety of sources.

Web server

A software system based on HTTP (Hypertext Transfer Protocol) communications to send HTML (Hypertext Markup Language)-enabled documents to Web client systems. Novell and Netscape ported the NetWare Enterprise Web Server to NetWare via their joint venture, Novonyx.

wide area network (WAN)

A network that communicates long distance across nonphysical media, such as public or private telephone lines, satellites, or microwaves. Traditionally, a WAN includes modems connecting different LANs (local area networks) across leased telephone lines.

Winsock

Software that resulted from a vendor group meeting in 1991 to provide a single, standard application platform separate from the underlying network transport protocol. The top part of the Winsock software residing on a client machine interfaces with a TCP/IP application, such as Netscape. The bottom part of Winsock interfaces with the TCP/IP protocol stack on the machine, regardless of the TCP/IP developer.

workstation

A personal computer connected to a NetWare network. The term *workstation* may also refer to a Unix or OS/2 machine. Synonyms are client, station, user, and end node.

workstation import

The step that an administrator goes through to take workstations that have been registered with an NDS container and import them into NDS as Workstation objects.

workstation registration

An automatic process when a user logs in from a network workstation. The workstation is automatically registered with the container object in which the user that logged in exists. The workstation remains in a list of registered workstations until the administrator imports them into NDS.

Write right

The filesystem right that allows a user to open and write to files. Also, the property right that allows a user to add, change, or remove any values of the property.

X

XCONSOLE

A utility included with server TCP/IP support that allows a remote VT100 (or equivalent) terminal or terminal emulation program to run a vt100 version of the DOS RCONSOLE.

XON/XOFF

The handshaking protocol that negotiates the sending and receiving speeds of transmitted data to ensure that no data is lost.

X/Open

A group formed by competing and cooperating vendors in 1984 to ensure that standards were fair to all companies, not dictated by market share. As Unix has waned in public consciousness, so has X/Open. Novell granted the UnixWare name and reference code technology to X/Open in 1994 for continued sharing of Unix standards.

Z

ZENworks

A collection of tools and NDS objects that allow administrators to manage workstations, distribute software, control network workstation configurations, and enforce restrictions on users.

Index

Note to the reader: Throughout this index **boldfaced** page numbers indicate primary discussions of a topic. *Italicized* page numbers indicate illustrations.

The Craig Hunt Linux Library

- ◆ Written under the direction of Craig Hunt, renowned Linux and TCP/IP guru

- ◆ Developed specifically for networking professionals working in Linux environments

- ◆ Offers the most advanced and focused coverage of key topics for Linux Administrators

by Craig Hunt
0-7821-2736-3
$39.99

by Charles Aulds
0-7821-2734-7
$39.99

by Rámon J. Hontañón
0-7821-2741-X
$39.99

by Vicki Stanfield and Roderick W. Smith
0-7821-2735-5
$39.99

by Craig Hunt
0-7821-2737-1
$39.99

by Erez Zadok
0-7821-2739-8
$39.99

by Roderick W. Smith
0-7821-2740-1
$39.99

Craig Hunt is a noted TCP/IP and Linux expert who lectures regularly on the topics at the NetWorld+Interop, ComNet, and other networking trade shows. His other books include the best-selling *Linux Network Servers 24seven* from Sybex®.

SYBEX®

25 YEARS
OF PUBLISHING
EXCELLENCE

WWW.SYBEX.COM

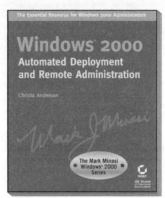
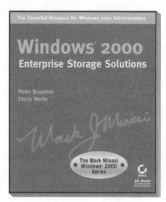

TELL US WHAT YOU THINK!

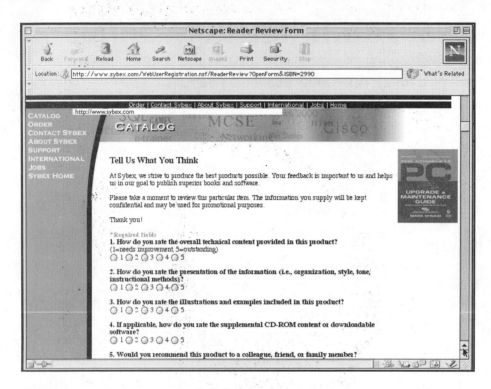

Your feedback is critical to our efforts to provide you with the best books and software on the market. Tell us what you think about the products you've purchased. It's simple:

1. Visit the Sybex website
2. Go to the product page
3. Click on **Submit a Review**
4. Fill out the questionnaire and comments
5. Click **Submit**

With your feedback, we can continue to publish the highest quality computer books and software products that today's busy IT professionals deserve.

ww.sybex.com

Inc. • 1151 Marina Village Parkway, Alameda, CA 94501 • 510-523-8233